THE NEW INTERNATIONAL COMMENTARY ON
THE NEW TESTAMENT — F. F. Bruce, *General Editor*

THE BOOK OF THE ACTS

COMMENTARY ON THE
BOOK OF THE ACTS

THE ENGLISH TEXT WITH INTRODUCTION,
EXPOSITION AND NOTES

by

F. F. BRUCE

Professor of Biblical Criticism and Exegesis,
University of Manchester

WM. B. EERDMANS PUBLISHING CO.
GRAND RAPIDS, MICHIGAN

COMMENTARY ON THE BOOK OF THE ACTS
BY F. F. BRUCE

WM. B. EERDMANS PUBLISHING COMPANY
GRAND RAPIDS, MICHIGAN, U.S.A.

Reprinted, July 1986

ISBN 0-8028-2182-0

PHOTOLITHOPRINTED BY EERDMANS PRINTING COMPANY
GRAND RAPIDS, MICHIGAN, UNITED STATES OF AMERICA

To
Cecil and Robina Howley

PREFACE

The first edition of this work contained a foreword from the General Editor of the series, the late Ned Bernard Stonehouse, in which he introduced the commentator to the readers, using characteristically generous terms in which to do so. Many years have elapsed since then, and since Dr. Stonehouse's lamented death in 1962 the commentator himself has been General Editor. Now that a new edition of the commentary is called for, it has seemed appropriate to replace the original Editor's Foreword and Author's Preface by a single new preface.

When Dr. Stonehouse first invited me to contribute the volume on Acts to this series, I was engaged on a commentary on the Greek text of that book, which was published by the Tyndale Press in 1951. I accepted his invitation the more readily because the preparation of the work on the Greek text had suggested various trains of thought which could not be brought within its scope, and it seemed that an exposition of the English text would give an opportunity to develop them. (The English text prescribed for this commentary, as for the whole series, is the American Standard Version of 1901.)

Some notable contributions to the study of the Lukan history as a whole, and of Acts in particular, have been made since this volume was written. Shortly before its publication there appeared Hans Conzelmann's influential work *Die Mitte der Zeit* (Tübingen, 1954), later translated into English under the less precise title *The Theology of St. Luke* (London, 1960), in which it was argued that, moved by the deferment of the once imminently expected *parousia*, Luke replaced the primitive Christian perspective by a new one in which the ministry of Jesus was recognized no longer as the *eschaton* but as the middle age of history, followed by the age of the church, a period of indefinite duration, as it was preceded by the age of the law and the prophets (cf. Luke 16:16). Professor Conzelmann has also contributed the new commentary on Acts to Lietzmann's *Handbuch zum Neuen Testament* (Tübingen, 1963). Ernst Käsemann, in a number of papers, has maintained that Luke is the first representative of "primitive catholicism" (*Frühkatholizismus*), with a perspective in which not the ministry of Jesus but the age of the church is the centre of time and the original and Pauline *theologia crucis* has been replaced by a *theologia gloriae*. (It could, I believe, be argued that the deferment of the *parousia* played a much more modest role in early Christian thinking than writers of this school think, and that "primitive catholicism" is even more primitive than they allow.)

The noblest work on Acts thus far produced by this school is Ernst Haenchen's commentary, first contributed to the Meyer series (Göttingen, 1956), and now available in a fine English translation: *The Acts of the Apostles* (Oxford: Blackwell, 1971). While his affinities are recognizably with Dibelius, Conzelmann and Käsemann, Professor Haenchen does not follow them uncritically; his concern is to expound Luke's composition—a composition marked by a sovereign freedom which makes the historical narrative the vehicle of Luke's theology. This theology is not a declension from true Paulinism; it is one of the variant forms of Gentile theology which grew up alongside and after the theology of Paul, and in virtual independence of him.

But these writers have not monopolized recent literature on the subject: Luke-Acts remains, as W.C. van Unnik has put it, "a storm center in contemporary scholarship." These words form the title of his essay (the first of nineteen) in the *Festschrift* for Paul Schubert, *Studies in Luke-Acts*, edited by L.E. Keck and J.L. Martyn (Nashville-New York, 1966). The variety of perspectives which find expression within this symposium demonstrates the aptness of Professor van Unnik's designation. By way of illustrating this variety from outside the Schubert symposium one may mention Johannes Munck's works, notably *Paulus und die Heilsgeschichte* (Aarhus-Copenhagen, 1954), E.T. *Paul and the Salvation of Mankind* (London, 1959), and also his posthumously published commentary on Acts in the Anchor Bible (Garden City, N.Y., 1967), in which he waged a courageous battle against the prevalent trends and insisted that justice could be done to the history and literature of the apostolic age only when the last vestige of the influence of F.C. Baur and his associates was removed; and, in another genre, the judicious studies of Jacques Dupont (editor of Acts in the *Bible de Jérusalem*): *Les Sources du Livre des Actes* (Bruges-Paris, 1960), E.T. *The Sources of Acts* (London, 1964), and *Études sur les Actes des Apôtres* (Paris, 1967). Were I commenting afresh on Acts today, there would be ample occasion to grapple with issues which had scarcely surfaced twenty years ago.

In the preface to the second edition of his *Römerbrief*, Karl Barth complained of the tendency of many biblical commentators to confine themselves to a form of textual interpretation which in his eyes was "no commentary at all, but merely the first step towards a commentary." As an example of a real commentary he adduced Calvin on Romans: "how energetically Calvin, having first established what stands in the text, sets himself to re-think the whole material and to

8

wrestle with it, till the walls which separate the sixteenth century from the first become transparent! Paul speaks, and the man of the sixteenth century hears."

No doubt, by Barth's criterion, my volume on the Greek text was but "the first step towards a commentary," devoted as it was to the critical study of the linguistic, textual and historical aspects of Acts. Be it so: a man who does not take the first step will never take a second. It cannot be claimed, indeed, that even the present volume has made the wall between the first and twentieth centuries transparent. I may, however, be permitted still to indulge the hope, first expressed in 1954, that whatever I have heard in the course of this study, not only of the voice of Luke but of the word of God, may be caught by some of my readers also in the second half of the twentieth century.

F.F. Bruce

ABBREVIATIONS

AJTh   – *American Journal of Theology*

ARV   – American Revised Version (American Standard Version, 1901)

AV   – Authorized Version (King James Version, 1611)

Beginnings – *The Beginnings of Christianity,* edited by Foakes Jackson and Kirsopp Lake, Vols. I-V (London, 1922-33)

Cod., Codd. – Codex, Codices

DB   – *Dictionary of the Bible*
(unless otherwise indicated, ed. J. Hastings, 5 vols., Edinburgh, 1898-1904)

Eng. tr. – English translation

EQ   – *The Evangelical Quarterly*

ERE   – *Encyclopaedia of Religion and Ethics,* ed. J. Hastings (13 vols., Edinburgh, 1908-26)

ERV   – English Revised Version (1881-5)

EVV   – English Versions

Exp.   – *The Expositor*

ExT   – *Expository Times*

Gk.   – Greek

HThR   – *Harvard Theological Review*

INT   – *Introduction to the New Testament*

JBL   – *Journal of Biblical Literature*

JThS   – *Journal of Theological Studies*

LXX   – Septuagint (earliest Greek version of OT)

MNT   – Moffatt New Testament Commentary

MT   – Massoretic Text

NS   – New Series

NT   – New Testament

OS   – Old Series

OT   – Old Testament

RSV — Revised Standard Version (1946-52)

TB — Babylonian Talmud

TJ — Jerusalem (or Palestinian) Talmud

TWNT — *Theologisches Wörterbuch zum Neuen Testament*, edited by G. Kittel and G. Friedrich (Vols. I ff., Stuttgart, 1933–).

WThJ — *Westminster Theological Journal*

ZAW — *Zeitschrift für die Alttestamentliche Wissenschaft*

ZNW — *Zeitschrift für die Neutestamentliche Wissenschaft*

The Scripture text used in this commentary is that of the American Standard Version of 1901. This text is printed in full for the sake of readers who do not read Greek; the expositions are, however, based upon the Greek text.

CONTENTS

13

INTRODUCTION

(a) Acts in the New Testament

The Acts of the Apostles is the name given since about the middle of the second century A.D. to the second volume of a *History of Christian Origins* composed by a first-century Christian and dedicated to a certain Theophilus. The first volume of this *History* is also extant as one of the twenty-seven documents included in the New Testament canon; it is the work ordinarily known as *The Gospel according to St. Luke*.[1]

Originally, no doubt, these two volumes circulated together as one complete and independent work, but not for long. For about the end of the first century or the beginning of the second—quite soon, in fact, after the publication of St. John's Gospel—the four canonical Gospels were gathered together into one collection and began to circulate as the fourfold Gospel. This meant that the first volume of our twofold *History* was detached from the second and attached to three works by other writers which covered more or less the same ground, relating the story of Jesus and ending with an account of His resurrection. The second volume, therefore, was left to pursue a career of its own, but an important and influential career, as it proved.

About the same time as the four Gospels were gathered together to form one collection, another collection of Christian documents was also taking shape—the collection of the Pauline Epistles. These two collections—*The Gospel* and *The Apostle,* as they were called—make up the greater part of the New Testament. But there would be a hiatus between these two collections were it not for the second volume of the *History of Christian Origins*, the document which we shall refer to briefly as Acts. Acts played an indispensable part in relating the two collections to each other. As regards the first collection, Acts forms its general sequel, as it was from the first the proper sequel to one of the four documents in that collection,

---

[1] That these two documents were written by the same author is almost universally acknowledged; the only serious denial of identity of authorship in recent years came from A. C. Clark, *The Acts of the Apostles* (Oxford, 1933), pp. 393 ff.; his arguments are scrutinized and effectively answered by W. L. Knox, *The Acts of the Apostles* (Cambridge, 1948), pp. 2 ff., 100 ff.

15

the third Gospel. As regards the second collection, Acts provides the narrative background against which the writings of Paul can more readily be understood, and—more important still—Acts provides clear and convincing evidence for the validity of the apostolic claim which Paul makes for himself in his letters.

The importance of Acts was further underlined about the middle of the second century as a result of the dispute to which Marcion and his teaching gave rise.[2] Marcion, about A.D. 144, promulgated at Rome a revolutionary doctrine which maintained that Christ was the revealer of an entirely new religion, completely unrelated to anything that had preceded His coming (such as the revelation to Israel in the Old Testament), and that Paul was the only apostle of Christ who faithfully preserved this new religion in its purity (uncontaminated by Old Testament or Jewish influence). Marcion drew up what he believed to be the true canon of divine scripture for the new age. This canon comprised two parts—one called *The Gospel* (a suitably expurgated recension of the third Gospel) and the other called *The Apostle* (a similarly edited recension of Paul's nine letters to churches and his letter to Philemon). The publication of Marcion's canon was a challenge and stimulus to the Roman church and the other churches which adhered to the catholic faith. It did not compel them to *create* the canon of holy scripture which has ever since, with minor variations, been accepted by the Church Catholic, but it did compel them to define that canon with greater precision. For them, the New Testament canon did not supersede that of the Old Testament, but stood alongside it as its divinely ordained complement.[3] For them, *The Gospel* comprised not one document only but four, and these four included the true text of the one which Marcion had published in a garbled form. For them, *The Apostle* included not ten but thirteen Pauline epistles, and not only epistles of Paul but epistles of other apostolic men as well. And, linking *The Gospel* and *The Apostle* together, Acts was now seen to have greater importance than ever, for not only did it present irrefragable proof of Paul's apostleship but it provided

[2] Cf. E. C. Blackman, *Marcion and his Influence* (London, 1948).

[3] These matters are treated in detail in the standard histories of the Canon of Scripture. It should be pointed out that, in the first instance, the Biblical writings are not divinely authoritative because they are included in the canon; on the contrary, they were included in the canon because they were recognized as divinely authoritative. See N. B. Stonehouse's essay, "The Authority of the NT," in *The Infallible Word* (edd. N. B. Stonehouse and P. Woolley, Philadelphia, 1946), pp. 88 ff.

16

evidence of the apostleship of the other apostles too—those whom Marcion had repudiated as false apostles and corruptors of the truth as it is in Jesus. The pivotal position of Acts in the Christian canon[4] was now appreciated as it could not have been before.

One token of this appreciation is the place occupied by Acts between *The Gospel* and *The Apostle*, from that day to this. Another is the title by which it has ever since been known, *The Acts of the Apostles*.[5] So far as extant evidence goes, it first receives this title in the Anti-Marcionite Prologue to the Third Gospel,[6] a document to be dated perhaps between A.D. 150 and 180, which is also probably the earliest extant document ascribing the authorship of the two volumes to Luke the physician of Antioch. The title *The Acts of the Apostles* may have been intended to point out that Paul was not the only faithful apostle of Christ (even if much more is said about him than about the others in Acts). This point is emphasized to an exaggerated degree in another document emanating from orthodox circles in Rome late in the second century, the Muratorian list of sacred books,[7] where the volume is called *The Acts of All the Apostles*.

(b) Origin and Purpose of Acts

The important part played by Acts in the middle of the second

---

[4] See A. Harnack, *The Origin of the NT* (Eng. tr., London, 1925), pp. 44 ff., 63 ff.

[5] M. Dibelius (*Aufsätze zur Apostelgeschichte* [Göttingen, 1951], p. 92) thinks that the title may be earlier than this. "In the book-market, where these writings [Luke and Acts] were publicly sold, by contrast with other early Christian documents, they were probably called 'Luke's *Acts of Jesus*' and 'Luke's *Acts of the Apostles*'."

[6] The anti-Marcionite prologues to the Gospels were drawn up in order to exclude the Marcionite interpretation of the gospel story and have been preserved in some Latin Gospel manuscripts; that to Luke's Gospel is extant both in Greek (in a single Greek MS.) and in the Latin translation, those to Mark and John in the Latin translation only, while that to Matthew is lost. They were identified by D. de Bruyne in *Revue Bénédictine* xl (1928), pp. 193 ff. ("Les plus anciens Prologues latins aux Évangiles"); his identification was accepted by Harnack, *Sitzungsberichte der preussischen Akademie*, phil.-hist. Klasse, 1928, pp. 322 ff. *Cf.* also W. F. Howard in ExT xlvii (1935–6), pp. 534 ff., and Huck–Lietzmann, *Synopsis* (Tübingen, 1936), pp. vii f. All these scholars take the view that the Prologues depend on Papias but precede Irenaeus. The view that they are dependent on Irenaeus, and possibly even on Tertullian, is upheld by B. W. Bacon, JThS xxiii (1921–2), pp. 134 ff., JBL xlix (1930), pp. 43 ff., *Studies in Matthew* (London, 1931), pp. 452 ff.; *cf.* A. H. McNeile and C. S. C. Williams, INT (Oxford, 1953), pp. 285 ff.

[7] So called because it was discovered by Cardinal L. A. Muratori in 1740. I have given a translation of it in *The Growing Day* (London, 1951), pp. 106 f.

17

century has suggested to a number of scholars that (in its final form at any rate) it was composed about that time in order to play that part.[8] Against this view two considerations tell with special weight. In the first place, the historical, geographical and political atmosphere of Luke-Acts as a whole, and of Acts in particular, is unmistakably that of the first century and not of the second.[9] In the second place, the internal evidence of the work does not suggest that its primary purpose was to vindicate the apostleship of Paul, or to show that the other apostles were as faithful as he was, or to represent Paul and the other apostles as being on terms of complete mutual respect and harmony. It did, to be sure, serve these purposes in due course, but these are not the main emphases of Acts.

The primary purpose of Acts cannot be considered in isolation from the purpose of the "former treatise" of which it is the continuation. The two parts are parts of one integral whole, with a coherent purpose running throughout. And we are not left to speculate what that purpose might be; it is stated for us explicitly at the very outset of the twofold work. Here it is, in the words of the author himself:

> Inasmuch as many have undertaken to compile a narrative of the things which have been accomplished among us, just as they were delivered to us by those who from the beginning were eyewitnesses and ministers of the word, it seemed good to me also, having followed all things closely for some time past, to write an orderly account for you, most excellent Theophilus, that you may know the truth concerning the things of which you have been informed. (Luke 1:1–4, RSV.)

In these words he sets out the purpose not only of the third

[8] This was the view of the Tübingen school of last century, according to which Acts reconciled the sharply opposed viewpoints of Petrine and Pauline Christianity in the comprehensive viewpoint of the Catholic Church—the synthesis of the Petrine thesis and the Pauline antithesis. More recently J. Knox (*Marcion and the NT* [Chicago, 1942], pp. 119 ff.) has argued that Luke-Acts made its first appearance about the year 150, being a "Gospel-plus-Apostle" compilation in answer to the "Gospel-plus-Apostle" canon of Marcion and preceding the "Gospel-plus-Apostle" canon of the Catholic Church. See the critique of Knox by N. B. Stonehouse in WThJ vi (1943–4), pp. 95 ff.

[9] This has been demonstrated in particular by Sir William Ramsay's archaeological research in Asia Minor; *cf.* his *St. Paul the Traveller and the Roman Citizen* (14th edn., London, 1920), and *The Bearing of Recent Discovery on the Trustworthiness of the NT* (London, 1915).

Gospel but of the whole work of which that Gospel was the first volume.

He himself, it appears, could not claim to be an eyewitness of the earlier events recorded in his history, but he had access to the information which such eyewitnesses could supply. He was not the first to draw up an account based on information of this kind, but he claims for his account that it rests upon thorough and accurate research and that it is arranged in a proper sequence.

Let it be said briefly here that throughout this commentary the Lukan authorship of the twofold work is accepted.[10] The external evidence for Lukan authorship goes back to the early decades of the second century, beyond the Muratorian list and the anti-Marcionite prologues; while the original text of Luke-Acts does not reveal the author's name, the belief in Lukan authorship found its way at an early date into one or two recensions of the text of Acts, as the exposition and notes on Chs. 11:28 and 20:13 will show (see pp. 243, 409). The evidence of the NT writings in general, and of Luke-Acts in particular, does not conflict with the external evidence, and in fact the work itself shows signs of having been composed by someone who was from time to time a companion of Paul and who travelled with him to Rome, where we know Luke to have been in his company.[11] When some parts of the narrative of Acts, dealing with journeys made by Paul and a few of his friends, are cast in the first person plural (whence they are known as the "we" sections),[12] the most reasonable inference is that the author of the whole work was present with Paul on these particular journeys.[13]

Luke, then, announces that his purpose in writing his *History* was to give a certain Theophilus an accurate and orderly account of the origins of Christianity, about which Theophilus had some information already. For the later part of his narrative he could draw largely on his own experiences; for the earlier part he could depend on reliable first-hand informants.

[10] I have set out the reasons for this belief more fully in my commentary on the Greek text, *The Acts of the Apostles* (London, 1951), pp. 1 ff. For a survey of recent opinions on authorship, etc., see J. Dupont, *Les Problèmes du Livre des Actes d'après les Travaux récents* (Louvain, 1950), pp. 17 ff.

[11] See Col. 4:14; Philem. 24.

[12] These are Chs. 16:10—17; 20:5—21:18; 27:1—28:16.

[13] See pp. 328 (n. 22), 406. On the relation of the "we" sections to the main body of Acts see McNeile and Williams, *op. cit.*, pp. 106 ff., and for a general discussion see their whole chapter on "The Acts" (pp. 92 ff.).

His first volume is in essence a record of the apostolic witness to Jesus' ministry of word, deed, suffering and triumph.[14] His second volume takes up the tale after the resurrection of Jesus and carries it on for some thirty years; he traces the progress of Christianity from Judaea to Rome, and ends with the chief herald of the gospel proclaiming it at the heart of the empire with the full acquiescence of the imperial authorities.

When we examine the way in which Luke develops his narrative, we can hardly fail to be struck by his apologetic emphasis, especially in the second volume. He is concerned to defend Christianity against the charges which were popularly brought against it in the second half of the first century. We must recognize that in the eyes of those who set some store by law and order in the Roman Empire Christianity started off with a serious handicap. Its Founder had admittedly been condemned to death by a Roman governor on a charge of sedition.[15] And the movement which He inaugurated seemed to be attended by tumult and disorder wherever it spread, both in the Roman provinces and in Rome itself. Luke sets himself to reduce this handicap, or rather to remove it altogether.

The crucifixion of Christ is presented as a gross miscarriage of justice. True, He was accused of sedition before Pontius Pilate, but Pilate pronounced Him not guilty of the charges, and Herod Antipas, the tetrarch of Galilee, agreed that there was no substance in them (Luke 23:13 ff.). It was the influence of the chief priests of Jerusalem, and the clamour of the city mob incited by them, that compelled Pilate against his own judgment to pass the death-sentence which they demanded.

Similarly in Acts a variety of officials, Gentile and Jewish, show good will towards Paul and other Christian missionaries, or at least admit that there is no basis for the accusations brought against them by their opponents. In Cyprus the distinguished proconsul of the island is favourably impressed by the apostles and their message (Ch. 13:7, 12). At Philippi the chief collegiate magistrates of the colony apologize to Paul and Silas for their illegal beating and

[14] See the commentary on Luke in this series, by Norval Geldenhuys (London and Grand Rapids, 1950).

[15] Thus Tacitus's estimate of the criminal character of Christianity in general is partly based on the fact that its founder, "Christ, was executed by sentence of the procurator Pontius Pilate when Tiberius was emperor" (*Annals* xv. 44).

imprisonment (Ch. 16:37 ff.). At Corinth Gallio, the proconsul of Achaia, decrees that the charges brought by the local Jewish community against Paul and his colleagues relate to internal matters of Jewish religion and pronounces them guiltless of any offence against Roman law (Ch. 18:12 ff.). At Ephesus the Asiarchs, leading citizens of the province of Asia, are Paul's friends, and the chief executive officer of the city administration absolves him of the charge of public sacrilege (Ch. 19:31, 35 ff.). In Palestine the procurators Felix and Festus successively find him innocent of the serious crimes of which the Sanhedrin accuse him, and the Jewish client king Herod Agrippa II and his sister Bernice agree that he has done nothing deserving death or even imprisonment (Chs. 24:1-26:32). And when he appeals, as a Roman citizen, to have his case heard by the emperor in Rome, he carries on his missionary activity for two years in that city, under constant surveillance, without anyone trying to hinder him (Ch. 28:30 f.). If Christianity were such a lawless movement as was widely believed, Paul would certainly not have been allowed to propagate it by the imperial guards in whose charge he was!

How then, it might be asked, was the advance of Christianity attended by so much strife and disorder? Luke arraigns the Jewish authorities as responsible for this. It was the Jerusalem Sanhedrin who prosecuted Jesus before Pilate and Paul before Felix and Festus; and most of the disturbances which broke out when the gospel was proclaimed in the Roman provinces were fomented by the local Jewish communities, who refused to accept the gospel themselves and were annoyed when their Gentile neighbours believed it.[16]

We have, then, to look for an appropriate life-setting for a work which strikes the apologetic note in just this way. One attractive suggestion recently made[17] points to the period A.D. 66-70, when the chief accusers of Christianity, the Jewish authorities in Palestine, so completely discredited themselves in Roman eyes by the rebellion against the empire. In those years it would have been

---

[16] There are two occasions recorded in Acts when the Christian missionaries were attacked by Gentiles, and on both the reason was a real or imagined threat to vested property interests—at Philippi (Ch. 16:16 ff.) and Ephesus (Ch. 19:23 ff.).

[17] By T. W. Manson, "The Work of St. Luke," BJRL xxviii (1944), pp. 382 ff. C. S. C. Williams in JThS xlix (1948), pp. 204, adds a few other pointers to a date between 66 and 70.

specially effective to emphasize that, unlike the rebellious Jews, Christians were not disloyal to the empire—that, in fact, the Jewish authorities themselves had always done their best to disown Christianity.

Certainly there is nothing in Acts—or even in Luke[18]—that presupposes the destruction of the city and temple of Jerusalem (A.D. 70) as having taken place before the time of writing. But there was another event which took place a few years previously which we should have expected to be reflected fairly clearly in an apologetic document written not long afterwards. That was the persecution of the Christians of Rome which followed the great fire of A.D. 64. This marked the end of the official policy which Paul had found so helpful in the fifties. For Luke to relate decisions of imperial officials favourable to Christianity in the years preceding A.D. 60 might well appear irrelevant when everybody knew the complete reversal of those decisions which Nero's action in the sixties involved. To be sure, at the end of Nero's reign (A.D. 68), the relation of these favourable verdicts might have been intended to suggest that Nero's anti-Christian policy was an irresponsible and criminal attack by that discredited monarch in person upon a movement whose innocence had been amply attested by many worthier representatives of the Roman authority. But there is really no hint in Acts that Nero's anti-Christian policy had yet manifested itself as it did in the year 64.

The fact that the death of Paul—which traditionally was an incident of the Neronian persecution—is not mentioned in Acts is not decisive for the dating of the book, for Luke's purpose is accomplished when he has brought Paul to Rome. But if in fact Paul had been condemned and executed before Acts was written, we might have expected a rather different atmosphere and emphasis in the book (especially at the end) from that which we actually find. It is better to suppose that when Acts was written Christianity was suspect, but not yet proscribed.

If we can date Luke's *History* a little earlier than the persecution of 64,[19] we find a reasonable life-setting for the work. Paul's

[18] Certainly not in the eschatological discourse of Luke 21; cf. C. H. Dodd, "The Fall of Jerusalem and the 'Abomination of Desolation'," *Journal of Roman Studies* xxxvii (1947), pp. 47 ff.

[19] If it be thought impossible to date Luke's Gospel so early, consideration may be given to a suggestion of C. S. C. Williams, that Acts was written as a sequel to "Proto-Luke" (Q + L), about the time when Luke became

arrival in Rome, his apostolic witness there for two years, the legal procedure occasioned by his appeal to Caesar, must have brought Christianity to the notice of the Roman middle classes. Previously, if they knew of it at all, they thought of it as one more of those despicable eastern cults which infected the lower orders of the city as the sewers of the Orontes discharged themselves into the Tiber.[20] But Paul's case may have moved some to take a little more interest in Christianity. If Theophilus was a representative of the intelligent reading public (or rather listening public)[21] of Rome, here was Luke's opportunity to provide such people with a more accurate account of the rise and progress of Christianity than they were likely to get elsewhere, and also to vindicate the innocence of Paul and other Christians in relation to Roman law.[22] Luke's narrative as such cannot have been directly intended to serve as the evidence for the defence when Paul's appeal came up for hearing in the imperial court; some of the material included in it would have been useful for that purpose, but there is much in Luke-Acts that would be forensically quite irrelevant—we may think, for example, of the details of the voyage and shipwreck in Ch. 27, or of the emphasis throughout on the dominant rôle of the Holy Spirit.

Would this emphasis on the Holy Spirit have been equally irrelevant for the intelligent Roman public whom Luke had in view? To most of them it would have meant little, but Theophilus himself may well have been a convert to the new faith.[23] In any case, Luke wishes to make it clear that the progress of this faith was no

acquainted with Mark's Gospel. This would explain why some features of Mark appear in Acts and not in Luke. (JThS xlix [1948], p. 204; *Church Quarterly Review* cliii [1952], p. 254; "The Date of Luke-Acts," ExT lxiv [1952–3], pp. 283 f.; McNeile and Williams, INT, p. 34.) But this hypothesis seems unnecessary, especially if we agree with T. W. Manson that "a date before 60 would be quite possible" for Mark (BJRL xxviii [1944], p. 131 n.). However, the exact date of Luke-Acts must remain uncertain, and it is an unimportant question by comparison with the authorship and historical character of the work.

20 *Cf.* Juvenal, *Satire* iii. 62.

21 See p. 31, cn Ch. 1:1. It was customary at Rome for a company to gather to listen to a new work being read aloud by its author or someone else.

22 Paul was being prosecuted by the Jewish authorities of Palestine; it would blunt the edge of their charge if it were shown that it was but the latest of a long series of vexatious accusations and attacks which Paul had had to endure throughout his apostolic career.

23 This probability has been thought to indicate a date in the reign of Domitian (A.D. 81–96), when Christianity had penetrated not only into the middle classes of Rome but into the highest ranks of all. See p. 31.

mere question of human planning; it was controlled by a divine agency. In one way, this may have contributed to Luke's apologetic purpose, although it would not have been of much use as a plea in a Roman law-court.[24]

Luke is, in fact, one of the first Christian apologists. In that particular type of apologetic which is addressed to the secular authorities to establish the law-abiding character of Christianity he is absolutely the pioneer. But other forms of apologetic appear in the course of his work, especially in some of the speeches of Acts. Thus, Stephen's speech in Ch. 7 is the prototype of Christian apologetic against the Jews, designed to demonstrate that Christianity and not Judaism is the true fulfilment of the revelation given through Moses and the prophets. Similarly, Paul's speech at Athens in Ch. 17 is one of the earliest examples of Christian apologetic against the pagans, designed to show that the true knowledge of God is given in the gospel and not in the idolatrous vanities of paganism. And Paul's speech before Agrippa in Ch. 26 is, of course, the crowning *apologia* for his own missionary career.

(c) Paul in Acts

Paul, in a number of his epistles, found it necessary to defend his apostolic status against those who denied it, and appealed in support of his claim to the "signs of an apostle" which attended his ministry. It was, of course, unnecessary for him to describe these signs in detail to people who had first-hand experience of them. But other readers of his epistles might be uncertain of the validity of this appeal were it not for the record of Paul's apostolic labours preserved by Luke.[25] No one could read Acts and doubt the reality of Paul's call to be an apostle!

This was plain enough as early as the second century. Tertullian points out the inconsistency of those heretics (the Marcionites in particular) who rejected the authority of Acts but appealed so confidently and exclusively to the apostolic authority of Paul. "You must show us first of all who this Paul was," he says to them. "What was he before he became an apostle? How did he

---

[24] Of course the doctrine of the Spirit is not presented simply for apologetic reasons in Acts; it is emphasized throughout the book for its own sake. The Christian community is Spirit-filled and Spirit-led (*cf.*, *e.g.*, Chs. 5:3; 15:28), and the whole evangelistic enterprise, from Jerusalem to Rome, is directed by the Spirit (*cf.*, *e.g.*, Ch. 16:6 ff.). See p. 33.

[25] Although, as has been said above, the validation of Paul's apostolicity was not Luke's primary purpose in writing.

become an apostle?" (*Prescription against Heretics*, 23).[26] It was, of course, difficult to give an adequate answer to these questions without appealing to Acts.

Those who date Acts in the middle of the second century and regard it as a product of the anti-Marcionite reaction may consider that one of its aims is to show that Peter and the rest of the twelve were as much apostles as Paul (which Marcion denied).[27] But it shows even more conclusively, if incidentally, that Paul was as much an apostle as Peter and the rest of the twelve—that, in fact, he laboured more abundantly than they all (*cf.* I Cor. 15:10).

And in showing this Acts may well have achieved a success considerably beyond Luke's immediate intention. There is something to be said for the view that Paul's influence declined in his Aegean mission-field (especially in the province of Asia) soon after he left it, and that his Judaizing adversaries won a temporary victory.[28] But if so, it was a very temporary victory; before long, Paul's name and renown were firmly re-established and venerated in the areas which he had evangelized. Two reasons may be assigned for this vindication of Paul's memory. Firstly, the fall of Jerusalem and the dispersal of the church there dealt a heavy blow to the prestige of the Judaizing party.[29] And secondly, the circulation of Acts among the Aegean churches—a more extended public than that to which Luke first addressed his *History*—must have brought about a revival of interest in Paul; it may even, as E. J. Goodspeed suggests, have stimulated the collection of his letters into a literary *corpus* and their circulation among the churches.[30]

[26] We may compare what Tertullian says of Acts in the preceding section (22) of the same work: "Those who do not accept this volume of scripture can have nothing to do with the Holy Spirit, for they cannot know whether the Holy Spirit has yet been sent to the disciples; neither can they claim to be the Church, since they cannot prove when this body was established or where it was cradled."

[27] See p. 387, n. 13 for some parallels drawn in Acts between Peter's ministry and Paul's.

[28] This is a reasonable inference from 2 Tim. 1:15, and is in keeping with Paul's foreboding in Acts 20:29 f.

[29] The major work on this subject is S. G. F. Brandon, *The Fall of Jerusalem and the Christian Church* (London, 1951). I am, however, far from sharing many of Dr. Brandon's most distinctive conclusions, especially those which involve a rehabilitation of the essence of the Tübingen doctrine.

[30] *Cf.* E. J. Goodspeed, INT (Chicago, 1937), pp. 210 ff. It is a point of considerable importance in considering the date and authorship of Acts that the author betrays no knowledge of the canonical epistles of Paul. A writer who tried to write an account of Paul's career any time after A.D. 90, when

For Paul no doubt is Luke's hero. What an ineffaceable picture he gives us of the apostle! And in giving us this picture, what a contribution he has made to the record of Christian expansion! His narrative, in fact, is a source-book of the highest value for the history of civilization.

It may, or it may not, be a good thing that over so much of the world to-day Christianity is looked upon as a European religion. But how does it come about that a faith which arose in Asia should have come to be so integrally associated with European rather than with Asian civilization? The answer surely is that, in the providence of God, its leading herald and missionary in the three decades following its inception was a Roman citizen, who saw how the strategic centres and communications of the Roman Empire could be turned to the service of Christ's kingdom, and planted the Christian faith in those centres and along those lines of communication. "In little more than ten years St. Paul established the Church in four provinces of the Empire, Galatia, Macedonia, Achaia and Asia. Before A.D. 47 there were no Churches in these provinces; in A.D. 57 St. Paul could speak as if his work there was done, and could plan extensive tours into the far West without anxiety lest the Churches which he had founded might perish in his absence for want of his guidance and support" (Roland Allen, *Missionary Methods: St. Paul's or Ours?* [London, 1927], p. 3).

And Luke is the historian of this enterprise—one of the most far-reaching in world history. He shows plainly how it was done. "Generally speaking, Paul's activity was based on certain centres, from which he undertook his longer and shorter journeys, and which in the course of years were transferred from one province to another" (M. Dibelius, *Paul* [Eng.tr., London, 1953], p. 69). The first of these centres was Damascus, from which Paul penetrated Nabataean Arabia. He would have made his next centre Jerusalem, had he not been warned in a vision not to settle there (Acts 22:17-21). He went back therefore to his native Tarsus, and from that centre he preached the gospel in Cilicia and Syria for the best part of ten unchronicled years. Then, for shorter or longer

these epistles began to be more generally accessible, could hardly have avoided making use of their first-hand evidence. On the other hand, a man who belonged to the circle of Paul's close friends might well have dispensed with the use of his letters, even if they had been at his disposal—which they probably were not.

periods, his successive centres were Antioch, Corinth, Ephesus, Rome.[31] Something of his achievements as he worked in one after another of these centres, and preached the gospel as he journeyed on the roads from one to the other, may be gathered from allusions in his epistles. But it is Luke that we have to thank for the coherent record of Paul's apostolic activity. Without it, we should be incalculably poorer. Even with it, there is much in Paul's letters that we have difficulty in understanding; how much more there would be if we had no book of Acts!

"O God, who, through the preaching of the blessed apostle Saint Paul, hast caused the light of the Gospel to shine throughout the world; Grant, we beseech thee, that we, having his wonderful conversion in remembrance, may shew forth our thankfulness unto thee for the same, by following the holy doctrine which he taught; through Jesus Christ our Lord. *Amen.*"

"Almighty God, who calledst Luke the Physician, whose praise is in the Gospel, to be an Evangelist and Physician of the soul; May it please thee, that, by the wholesome medicines of the doctrines delivered by him, all the diseases of our souls may be healed; through the merits of thy Son Jesus Christ our Lord. *Amen.*"

[31] See D. T. Rowlingson, "The Geographical Orientation of Paul's Missionary Interests", JBL lxix (1950), pp. 341 ff.

I. THE BIRTH OF THE CHURCH
(Chs. 1:1–5:42)

The first five chapters of Acts present us with a series of pictures of the primitive Jerusalem community of believers in Jesus, from the period of His resurrection appearances to them during the six weeks that followed His passion to the descent of the Holy Spirit upon them at the end of the seventh week and the profound stirring of the whole life of the city in consequence of the immense expansion of their numbers on that occasion.

Much of the material in these chapters shows signs of having been drawn, immediately or indirectly, from Aramaic sources.[1] There is no clear evidence, however, that these were written sources. Nor can we be sure who Luke's informants for this introductory section of his second volume were. It has been suggested that some of the information was obtained from Mark, who may indeed have compiled some notes towards a sequel to his Gospel.[2] We may be very sure that Luke made full use of the opportunities afforded him when he visited Jerusalem with Paul in A.D. 57 (Ch. 21:15 ff.). He stayed on that occasion with one Mnason, who had been a member of the believing community from the beginning, and made the acquaintance of James, the brother of Jesus, and his fellow-elders. In any case, the primitive Jerusalem church was largely Aramaic-speaking, and so Aramaisms in these chapters are what we should expect.

Attempts have been made to distinguish sources in these five

---

[1] C. C. Torrey, *The Composition and Date of Acts* (Cambridge, Mass., 1916), argued that the Greek text of Chs. 1:1b–15:35 is the straightforward translation of an Aramaic document. This is the kind of exaggeration that discredits a serious thesis. A more reasonable case is that put forward by J. de Zwaan, "The Use of the Greek Language in Acts", *Beginnings* ii (London, 1922), pp. 44 ff.; he argues that the strongest evidence for Aramaic substrata is present in Chs. 1:1–5:16; 9:31–11:18; and possibly parts of Chs. 12 and 15. *Cf.* also M. Black, *An Aramaic Approach to the Gospels and Acts* (Oxford, 1946), for a sober assessment of the position.

[2] *Cf.* Th. Zahn, *Geschichte des NT Kanons* ii (Erlangen, 1892), p. 931; F. Blass, *Philology of the Gospels* (London, 1898), pp. 141 f.; F. C. Burkitt, *Christian Beginnings* (London, 1924), p. 83; W. K. L. Clarke, "The Ending of St. Mark," *Theology* xxix (1934), pp. 106 f.; F. F. Bruce, "The End of the Second Gospel", EQ xvii (1943), pp. 169 ff.

chapters. The best known of these is Harnack's attempt to isolate two parallel sources, a "Jerusalem A source" and a "Jerusalem B source" (*The Acts of the Apostles* [Eng.tr., London, 1909], pp. 162 ff.).[3] He pointed out that these chapters contain two speeches by Peter (Chs. 2:14 ff.; 3:12 ff.), two arrests of apostles (Chs. 4:3; 5:18), two defences before the Sanhedrin (Chs. 4:8 ff.; 5:29 ff.), two fillings with the Spirit (Chs. 2:1 ff.; 4:31); two estimates of the number of converts (Chs. 2:41; 4:4), and two accounts of the pooling of property (Chs. 2:44 ff.; 4:32 ff.). Accordingly, he distinguished a markedly superior source "A" for the continuous narrative of Chs. 3:1–5:16, and a source "B", of inferior quality, represented by Chs. 2:1–47 and 5:17–42. But this piece of source-criticism, while plausible at first sight, appears less convincing on closer study. The healing of the lame man in Ch. 3 follows naturally on Ch. 2 as an example of the "many wonders and signs" of Ch. 2:43. The arrest and examination of the twelve in Ch. 5:18 ff. is a natural sequel to the previous dismissal of Peter and John with a caution in Ch. 4:21 (indeed Ch. 5:28 seems to point back directly to Ch. 4:18). The five thousand of Ch. 4:4 represents an increase of the earlier estimate of three thousand in Ch. 2:41—an increase such as one would expect in a mass movement of the kind. The second summary of the pooling of property is introduced in Ch. 4:32 ff. as a preface to the contrasted narratives of Barnabas and Ananias. This does not mean, of course, that Harnack's analysis is to be rejected out of hand; it means that, on examination, it can be accorded no more favourable verdict than "Not proven." As one distinguished commentator on Acts has emphasized, "we should constantly remember that source-criticism in the New Testament is largely guess-work" (F. J. Foakes Jackson, *The Acts of the Apostles* [MNT London, 1931], p. xv).

---

3 Harnack's arguments are carried farther by Jackson and Lake, "The Internal Evidence of Acts," *Beginnings* ii, pp. 121 ff. But see the critique by W. L. Knox, *The Acts of the Apostles* (Cambridge, 1948), pp. 19 ff.

CHAPTER I

1. THE FORTY DAYS AND AFTER

(Ch. 1 : 1–26)

The first chapter of Acts provides a brief introduction to the narrative of the Day of Pentecost and its sequel: it deals with two topics—our Lord's conversations with His disciples on the eve of His ascension, and the co-option of Matthias to fill the vacancy in the apostolate occasioned by the treachery and death of Judas Iscariot.

(a) Prologue (Ch. 1:1–5)

1 The former treatise I made, O Theophilus, concerning all that Jesus began both to do and to teach,

2 until the day in which he was received up, after that he had given commandment through the Holy Spirit unto the apostles whom he had chosen:[4]

3 to whom he also showed himself alive after his passion by many proofs, appearing unto them by the space of forty days, and speaking the things concerning the kingdom of God :

4 and, being assembled together[5] with them, he charged them not to depart from Jerusalem, but to wait for the promise of the Father, which, *said he,* ye heard from me :

5 for John indeed baptized with water; but ye shall be baptized in the Holy Spirit not many days hence.

1–2 Theophilus, to whom the second volume of Luke's history is here dedicated, is similarly addressed at the beginning of the

---

4 The original Western text of v. 2 probably ran: "until the day in which he by the Holy Spirit commissioned the apostles whom he had chosen, and commanded them to preach the gospel." The omission of "he was received up" (Gk. ἀνελήμφθη) is noteworthy, because the corresponding words in Luke 24:51, "and was carried up into heaven" (Gk. καὶ ἀνεφέρετο εἰς τὸν οὐρανόν) are missing from the Western text (they are among a number of passages at the end of Luke which Westcott and Hort bracket as "Western non-interpolations").

5 Gk. συναλιζόμενος. The rendering "being assembled together" is unlikely, in view of the singular number and the present tense. Two more probable alternatives are (1) that the word is cognate with Gk. ἅλς ("salt") and means literally "eating salt with" and then, more generally, "eating with"; (2) that it is a spelling variant of συναυλιζόμενος and means "dwelling with."

30

first volume, where he receives the title "most excellent" (Lk. 1:3). There has been much indecisive speculation about him. Some have even suggested that he was no particular individual, but that the name Theophilus—which means "dear to God"— is used here to designate the "Christian reader." The use of the honorific title "most excellent" makes this improbable. We cannot be sure, however, whether the title "most excellent" is bestowed on Theophilus in a technical sense, indicating his rank, or is given him by way of courtesy.[6] Nor is much to be gained by pondering the reason for the omission of the title in this place, or by advancing such suggestions as that Theophilus had become a Christian since the "former treatise" was written and therefore would no longer expect or receive wordly titles of honour from a fellow-Christian.

Another suggestion is that Theophilus masks the identity of some well-known person, such as Titus Flavius Clemens, cousin of the Emperor Domitian.[7]   Even this is unlikely; the name Theophilus was a perfectly ordinary personal name, being used from the third century B.C. onwards. The seventh letter of the philosopher Seneca was addressed to a man of this name, who must have been roughly contemporary with our Theophilus; but there is no ground for identifying the two.[8] Despite the evident apologetic motive in Luke's history, it is equally outstripping the evidence to regard Theophilus as the advocate briefed for Paul's defence at the hearing of his appeal to Caesar.[9] It is quite probable that Theophilus was a representative member of the intelligent middle-class public at Rome whom Luke wished to win over to a less prejudiced and more favourable opinion of Christianity than that which was current among them. This much is certain from the prologue to Luke's first volume (which serves as a prologue to the twofold work), that

[6] Gk. $\varkappa\rho\acute{\alpha}\tau\iota\sigma\tau\sigma\varsigma$ might be used to designate a member of the Roman equestrian order (representing Lat. *egregius*), or as a courtesy title (like Lat. *optimus*). *Cf.* the later occurrences of the word as a title in Acts, where it denotes one who holds an official position—Felix (Chs. 23:26; 24:3) and Festus (Ch. 26:25).

[7] This suggestion is made by B. H. Streeter, *The Four Gospels* (London, 1924), pp. 534 ff.

[8] Still less ground exists for identifying our Theophilus with the Theophilus who was high priest of the Jews from A.D. 37 to 41 (*cf.* R. Eisler, *The Enigma of the Fourth Gospel* [London, 1938], p. 208). *Cf.* also p. 98, n. 14 (on Ch. 4:6).

[9] *Cf.* J. I. Still, *St. Paul on Trial* (London, 1923), pp. 84 ff. More generally, G. S. Duncan suggests that Luke's narrative was "designed to supply information which it was hoped might reach those who would decide the apostle's fate at Rome" (*St. Paul's Ephesian Ministry* [London, 1929], p. 97). *Cf.* M. Aberle in *Theologische Quartalschrift*, 1855, pp. 173 ff.; 1863, pp. 84 ff.; D. Plooij in *Expositor* VIII. viii (1914), pp. 511 ff.; VIII. xiii (1917), pp. 108 ff.

Theophilus had already learned something about the rise and progress of Christianity, and Luke's aim was to put him in possession of more accurate information than he already had.[10]

Such dedications were common form in contemporary literary circles throughout the Roman Empire. For example, Josephus dedicated his *Autobiography,* his *Jewish Antiquities* and his treatise *Against Apion* to a patron of the name of Epaphroditus. At the beginning of his first volume *Against Apion,* he addresses him as "Epaphroditus, most excellent[11] of men"; and he introduces the second volume of the work with the words, "By means of the former volume, my most honoured Epaphroditus, I have demonstrated our antiquity." These opening words are remarkably parallel to those of Luke's second volume.

Luke begins with a brief reference to his former[12] volume, as an account of "all that Jesus began both to do and to teach, until the day in which he was received up"—or, if we follow the Western reading, ". . . until the day when he by the Holy Spirit commissioned the apostles whom he had chosen, and commanded them to proclaim the gospel." This, of course, exactly summarizes the scope of Luke's Gospel; the commissioning of the apostles is recorded in Luke 24:44 ff. The implication of Luke's words is that his second volume will be an account of the things which Jesus *continued*[13] to do and teach after His ascension—by His Spirit in His followers. The expression "to do and to teach" well sums up the twofold subject-matter of the canonical gospels: it consists of *The Work and Words of Jesus* (to quote the title of a recent presentation of this subject-matter).[14]

---

[10] On the significance of Luke 1:1–4 *cf.* H. J. Cadbury, "Commentary on the Preface of Luke", *Beginnings* ii, pp. 489 ff.; N. B. Stonehouse, *The Witness of Luke to Christ* (London, 1951), pp. 24 ff.; Norval Geldenhuys, *Commentary on the Gospel of Luke* (London and Grand Rapids, 1950), pp. 51 ff.

[11] Gk. κράτιστε (vocative) as in Luke 1:3.

[12] The word "former" in v. 1 represents Gk. πρῶτος, which literally means "first." W. M. Ramsay presses the classical force of πρῶτος here and concludes that Luke envisaged a work of three volumes (*St. Paul the Traveller and Roman Citizen* [14th edn., London, 1920], pp. 27 f., 309). *Cf.* Th. Zahn, *Die Apostelgeschichte des Lucas* (Erlangen, 1922), pp. 16 ff. But in Hellenistic Greek πρότερος, the word which strictly means the "former" of two, was largely displaced by πρῶτος. Luke never uses πρότερος, and it occurs very rarely in the papyri.

[13] This implies that the verb "began" (Gk. ἤρξατο) in v. 1 carries a certain emphasis and is not to be regarded merely as a Semitizing auxiliary.

[14] By A. M. Hunter (London, 1950).

It was "through the Holy Spirit" that Jesus gave His parting charge to His apostles, commanding them to be the heralds of the good news which He had brought. This strikes the chief theological keynote of Acts. At His baptism Jesus had been anointed "with the Holy Spirit and with power" (Ch. 10:38), and more recently He had been "declared to be the Son of God with power, according to the spirit of holiness, by the resurrection from the dead" (Rom. 1:4). In the Johannine account of the commission which the risen Christ gave to His disciples, He indicated the power by which they were to carry out the commission when He "breathed on them,[15] and saith unto them, Receive ye the Holy Spirit" (John 20:22). And Luke makes it plain that it is by the power of that same Spirit that all the apostolic acts which he goes on to narrate are performed, so much so that some have suggested, as a theologically more accurate title for his second volume, *The Acts of the Holy Spirit*.[16]

3 Over a period of forty days between His passion and ascension (beginning, of course, on the third day after the former event), Jesus appeared at intervals to His apostles in a manner which could leave no doubt in their minds that He really was alive again, risen from the dead. The most comprehensive list of these resurrection appearances is that given by Paul in 1 Cor. 15:5 ff., although the Gospel narratives make it plain that even Paul's list is not exhaustive.

What did He teach them during these forty days? The Gnostic schools which flourished in the second century claimed that He gave them certain esoteric teaching, not recorded in the canonical literature of the catholic church, of which they themselves were the custodians and interpreters.[17] Within the frontiers of Christian

---

[15] Gk. ἐνεφύσησεν, which might be rendered more literally "he breathed into them", with an allusion to Gen. 2:7, where LXX uses the same verb of the Creator's "breathing into" Adam's nostrils the breath of life. *Cf.* also Ezek. 37:9. The relation of the insufflation (as the act of Christ in John 20:22 is commonly called) to the outpouring of the Spirit on the day of Pentecost (Acts 2) is an interesting critical and theological question. It is a relevant point that Luke appears generally to think of the Spirit as coming with power —with external manifestation—whereas the incident recorded by John is marked by none of the visible and audible phenomena of Acts 2, and may be regarded as an inward anticipation of the outward manifestation of Pentecost.

[16] This is the title of a study of Acts by A. T. Pierson (2nd edn., London, 1913).

[17] The Coptic work called *Pistis Sophia*, a product of Valentinian Gnosticism,

orthodoxy there was one line of tradition which represented Him as giving His apostles instructions about church order.[18] But Luke declares that He continued to instruct them on the same subjects as had formed the burden of His teaching before His passion—"the things concerning the kingdom of God."

From the earliest times in Israel, God was acknowledged as King (*cf.* Ex. 15:18). His kingship is universal (Ps. 103:19), but is manifested most clearly where His creatures recognize it in practice by doing His will. Therefore in OT times His kingship was specially manifested on earth in the nation of Israel, to whom He made known His will and whom He called into covenant-relationship with Himself. When human kings arose over Israel, they were looked upon as vicegerents of the Divine King, representing His sovereignty on earth. With the fall of the monarchy and the end of Israelite independence, there arose a new conception of the Kingdom of God as something to be revealed on earth in its fullness at a later date (*cf.* Dan. 2:44; 7:13 f.). It is in the light of this later conception that we should understand the NT teaching of the kingdom of God. Jesus brings the kingdom in; it "drew near" with the inception of His public ministry (*cf.* Mark 1:14 f.); His death and exaltation released it in power upon the earth. "The things concerning the kingdom of God" at the beginning of Acts are identical with "the things concerning the Lord Jesus Christ" at the end of the book (Ch. 28:31; *cf.* also Chs. 8:12; 20:24 f.; 28:23). When they related the story of Jesus, the apostles proclaimed the good news of the kingdom of God—the same good news as Jesus Himself had announced earlier, but now given effective fulfilment by the saving events of His passion and triumph. We may reasonably conclude that the teaching which He gave the apostles about the kingdom of God during these forty days was calculated to make plain to them the bearing of these saving events on the message of the kingdom. Luke supplies a sample of this teaching towards the end of his Gospel, where he describes the risen Lord as opening His disciples' minds to understand the Scriptures and as telling

claims to record revelations made by Jesus to His disciples eleven years after His resurrection, not over a period of merely forty days.

[18] The full title of the second-century manual called the *Didaché*—"The Teaching of the Lord through the Twelve Apostles to the Gentiles"—bears some such implication. The fourth-century Syriac manual, *The Testament of our Lord,* claims explicitly to be Jesus' own directions on church government given to the apostles before His ascension.

them: "Thus it is written, that the Christ should suffer, and rise again from the dead the third day; and that repentance and remission of sins should be preached in his name unto all the nations, beginning from Jerusalem" (Luke 24:45–47). "The kingdom of God is conceived as coming in the events of the life, death, and resurrection of Jesus, and to proclaim these facts, in their proper setting, is to preach the Gospel of the Kingdom of God." These are the words of Professor C. H. Dodd in *The Apostolic Preaching and its Developments* (London, 1936), pp. 46 f.; and we may adopt them with one qualification.[19] When the apostles proclaimed the good news of the divine kingdom, they did not stop short at the resurrection and exaltation of Christ, but went on to speak of another event which would consummate the series of soteriological and eschatological events. Peter told the household of Cornelius how Christ had charged His apostles "to preach unto the people, and to testify that this is he who is ordained of God to be the Judge of the living and the dead" (Ch. 10:42). Paul told the Areopagus at Athens that God "hath appointed a day in which he will judge the world in righteousness by the man whom he hath ordained; whereof he hath given assurance unto all men, in that he hath raised him from the dead" (Ch. 17:31). The Second Advent of Christ will coincide with the final and complete manifestation of the kingdom, when every knee will bow in His name and every tongue confess Him as Lord (Phil. 2:10 f.), when God's will is to be done on earth as it is done in heaven (Matt. 6:10).[20] At Christ's first coming the age to come invaded this present age; at His second coming the age to come will have altogether superseded this present age. Between the two comings the two ages overlap; Christians live temporally in this present age while spiritually they belong to the heavenly kingdom and enjoy the life of the age to come. Biblical eschatology is largely, but not completely, "realized"; there still remains a future element, to become actual at the Second Advent, the *parousia*. A balanced account of the NT pre-

[19] Professor Dodd believes that the teaching of Jesus and the primitive apostolic preaching presented a completely "realized" eschatology; cf. also his *Parables of the Kingdom* (London, 1935) and *The Coming of Christ* (Cambridge, 1952).

[20] O. Cullmann suggests that the Second Advent bears a relation to "the Christ-event at the mid-point" of history analogous to that which the Victory Day celebrations bear to the decisive battle in a war (*Christ and Time* [Eng. tr., London, 1951], pp. 139 ff.). Cf. also J. Baillie, *The Belief in Progress* (Oxford, 1950), pp. 203 ff.

sentation of the kingdom of God requires that due regard be paid to both these aspects.[21]

4 The rendering of ARV margin,"eating with them," is probably to be preferred to that of the text, "being assembled together with them."[22] That the risen Christ ate in the presence of His disciples when He appeared to them is stated explicitly in Luke 24:42 f. (*cf.* also Acts 10:41). But many Christians find it difficult to accept such statements as literally true. Plainly the resurrection body of our Lord had no need of material food and drink for its sustenance. But why may He not have taken food in the company of His disciples, not for any personal need of His own, but in order to convince them that He was really present with them and that they were seeing no phantom?

In the course of these resurrection appearances, Jesus instructed His disciples not to leave Jerusalem until the Father fulfilled His promise to them and they were "clothed with power from on high"—to quote from the parallel narrative of Luke 24:49. He had already told them, He reminded them, of this promised gift. But when and where? Surely on the night of His betrayal, in the upper room in Jerusalem, after they had celebrated the Last Supper together, before they left the house to cross the Kidron valley and spend the remaining hours on the slope of Olivet. Certainly we have no account of a previous reference by Jesus to the promised Spirit which fits the present allusion so well as the five well-known passages in John 14–16. And it is particularly noteworthy "that the emphasis of these five passages is precisely that which underlies the conception of the Spirit in Acts 1–15."[23]

5 This promise, moreover, was foreshadowed by the ministry

[21] On this subject see, in addition to literature mentioned above, R. Otto, *The Kingdom of God and the Son of Man* (Eng. tr., London, 1943); H. B. Sharman, *Son of Man and Kingdom of God* (New York, 1943); G. H. Lang, *The Gospel of the Kingdom* (London, 1944); S. H. Hooke, *The Kingdom of God in the Experience of Jesus* (London, 1949); H. N. Ridderbos, *De Komst van het Koninkrijk* (Kampen, 1950); G. Vos, *The Kingdom and the Church* (new edn., Grand Rapids, 1951), and *The Pauline Eschatology* (new edn., Grand Rapids, 1952); G. E. Ladd, *Crucial Questions about the Kingdom of God* (Grand Rapids, 1952); J. Bright, *The Kingdom of God* (New York, 1953).

[22] See n. 5 above.

[23] W. F. Lofthouse, "The Holy Spirit in the Acts and The Fourth Gospel", ExT lii (1940–1), pp. 334 ff. (The words quoted above appear on p. 336.) *Cf.* also W. F. Howard, *The Fourth Gospel in Recent Criticism and Interpretation* (3rd edn., London, 1945), pp. 228 f., *Christianity according to St. John* (London, 1943), pp. 71 ff.

of John the Baptist. John had said to those who came to receive the baptism of repentance at his hands, "I baptized you in water; but he [the one who is coming after me] shall baptize you in the Holy Spirit" (Mark 1:8).[24] And the time was drawing very near, said Jesus, when these last words of John would be fulfilled: "ye shall be baptized in the Holy Spirit not many days hence." According to OT prophecy, the days of fulfilment would be marked by a widespread outpouring of the Spirit of God,[25] and John's baptism in water not only prepared his repentant hearers for the coming judgment but also pointed them on to that spiritual baptism of which the prophets had spoken.

(b) The Ascension (Ch. 1:6–11)

6 They therefore, when they were come together, asked him, saying, Lord, dost thou at this time restore the kingdom to Israel?

7 And he said unto them, It is not for you to know[26] times or seasons, which the Father hath set within his own authority.[27]

8 But ye shall receive power, when the Holy Spirit is come upon you: and ye shall be my witnesses both in Jerusalem, and in all Judaea and Samaria, and unto the uttermost part of the earth.

9 And when he had said these things, as they were looking, he was taken up; and a cloud received him out of their sight.

10 And while they were looking stedfastly into heaven as he went, behold two men stood by them in white apparel;

11 who also said, Ye men of Galilee, why stand ye looking into heaven? this Jesus, who was received up from you into heaven, shall so come in like manner as ye beheld him going into heaven.

---

[24] Matt. 3:11 and Luke 3:16 say "in the Holy Spirit and in fire"—a reading which is commonly regarded as a conflation of the Markan "in the Holy Spirit" with the Q reading "in fire." For the idea of fire *cf.* Ch. 2:3. Justin Martyr records a tradition that when Jesus was baptized by John, "a fire was kindled in Jordan" (*Dialogue* 88); the collocation of this with the descent of the dove is suggestive.

[25] *Cf.* Joel 2:28 ff., quoted in Ch. 2:17 ff.

[26] The original Western reading may have been "no one can know" (so Zahn, *Urausgabe der Apostelgeschichte* [Leipzig, 1916], p. 241).

[27] Or, "which the Father has fixed by his own authority." See Ch. 17:26 for a similar idea; *cf.* also Mark 13:32.

6–7 The apostles maintained their interest in the hope of seeing the kingdom of God realized in the restoration of Israel's national independence. They had in earlier days been captivated by the idea that in such a restored order they themselves would have positions of authority (*cf.* Mark 10:35 ff.; Luke 22:24 ff.). So now, hearing their Master speak of the coming gift of the Spirit, the mark of the new age, they asked if this was to be the occasion for restoring the kingdom to Israel.

Jesus' answer did not take the form of a direct "No." He told them that the epochs of the fulfilment of the divine purpose[28] were matters which lay within the Father's sole authority. So, earlier, He had assured them that He Himself did not know the day or hour of His *parousia*; this knowledge was reserved to the Father alone (Mark 13:32). Even for the nation of Israel according to the flesh, God may have purposes of His own; but these were not the concern of the messengers of Christ. The kingdom of God which they were commissioned to proclaim was the good news of God's grace in Christ. The question in v. 6 appears to have been the last flicker of their former burning expectation of an imminent political theocracy with themselves as its chief executives. From this time forth they devoted themselves to the proclamation and service of God's spiritual kingdom, which men enter by repentance and faith, and in which chief honour belongs to those who most faithfully follow the King Himself in the path of obedience and suffering.

8 Instead of the political power which had formerly been the object of their ambitions, a power far greater and nobler would be theirs. When the Holy Spirit came upon them, Jesus assured them, they would be clothed with heavenly power—that power by which, in the event, their mighty works were accomplished and their preaching made effective. As Jesus Himself had been anointed at His baptism with the Holy Spirit and power, so His followers

---

[28] For "times" (Gk. χρόνοι) and "seasons" (Gk. καιροί) *cf.* I Thess. 5:1. In his comment on that passage G. Milligan says: "The two words . . . are often distinguished as if they referred to longer and shorter periods of time respectively . . ., but χρόνος rather expresses simply duration, time viewed in its extension, and καιρός a definite space of time, time with reference both to its extent and character: *cf.* Tit. 1:2 f. where this distinction comes out very clearly. . . In the present instance therefore χρόνων may be taken as a general description of the 'ages' that may elapse before the Parousia, while καιρῶν draws attention to the critical 'periods' (*articuli*) by which these 'ages' will be marked" (*St. Paul's Epistles to the Thessalonians* [London, 1908], p. 63).

were now to be similarly anointed and enabled to carry on His work.[29] This work would be a work of witness-bearing—a theme which is prominent in the apostolic preaching throughout Acts (cf. Chs. 2:32; 3:15; 5:32; 10:39; 13:31; 22:15, etc.). An OT prophet had called Israel to be God's witnesses in the world (Isa. 43:10; 44:8); the task which Israel as a nation had not fulfilled was taken up by Jesus, as the perfect Servant of the Lord, and passed on by Him to His disciples. The close relation between God's call to Israel in those Isaianic passages, "Ye are my witnesses," and Christ's words to His apostles, "ye shall be my witnesses," will be appreciated the more if we consider the implications of Paul's quotation of Isa. 49:6 in Acts 13:47 (see p. 283). There the heralds of the gospel are described as being a light to the Gentiles, bearing God's salvation "unto the uttermost part of the earth"; here "the uttermost part of the earth" and nothing short of that is to be the limit of the apostolic witness.

It has often been pointed out that the geographical terms of v. 8 provide a sort of "Index of Contents" for Acts. "Ye shall be my witnesses" might be regarded as the theme of the book; "in Jerusalem" covers the first seven chapters; "in all Judaea and Samaria" Chs. 8:1 to 11:18; and the remainder of the book deals with the progress of the gospel outside the frontiers of the Holy Land until at last it reaches Rome.[30]

9 This, then, was their commission. And when the risen Lord had made it sufficiently plain to them, He disappeared from their sight, and no further resurrection appearances were granted to them, of the kind which they had experienced on several occasions during the past forty days.

It is Luke's mention of this period of forty days that is responsible for the arrangement in the Christian calendar by which As-

---

[29] The apostles had already received the baptism of John; the promised baptism with the Holy Spirit was to complete for them, in their measure, the anointing with the Holy Spirit and power which Jesus Himself experienced on the occasion of His baptism in Jordan (cf. Ch. 10:38). He had been anointed then as God's King and Servant (the combination of Ps. 2:7 and Isa. 42:1 in the voice from heaven [Mark 1:11] is highly significant); they were soon to be anointed to proclaim His kingship and to continue His work as the faithful Servant, carrying His salvation throughout the world.

[30] It has been suggested that "the uttermost part of the earth" here is a direct reference to Rome, as in *Psalms of Solomon* 8:16, where Pompey is sent by God against the disobedient people of Jerusalem "from the uttermost part of the earth" (Gk. ἀπ' ἐσχάτου τῆς γῆς), i.e. from Rome. But we need not limit the sense of the words in the present context.

cension Day falls on the fortieth day after Easter. In the apostolic preaching the resurrection and ascension of Christ seem to represent one continuous movement, and both together constitute His exaltation. But His exaltation to the right hand of God, which is what Ascension Day really commemorates, was not postponed to the fortieth day after His triumph over death. This was not the first occasion when He vanished from before His companions' eyes after His resurrection; He did so, we remember, after He made Himself known in the breaking of the bread to the two with whom He walked to Emmaus (Luke 24:31). Nor should we imagine that the intervals between His resurrection appearances during the forty days were spent by Him in some intermediate, earth-bound state. The resurrection appearances, in which He condescended to the disciples' temporal conditions of life, even going so far as to eat with them, were visitations from that exalted and eternal world to which His "body of glory" now belonged. What happened on the fortieth day was that this series of visitations came to an end, with a scene which impressed on the disciples their Master's heavenly glory.[31]

This was not the first occasion, either, on which some at least of them had had His heavenly glory brought home to them in a similar way. The words "a cloud received him out of their sight" are reminiscent of the words with which the Gospel incident of the transfiguration comes to an end: "there came a cloud overshadowing them: and there came a voice out of the cloud, This is my beloved Son: hear ye him" (Mark *1:11*; cf. Matt. 17:5; Luke 9:34 f.).[32] They are reminiscent, too, of our Lord's own words when He described His coming *parousia,* both in the Olivet discourse—"then shall they see the Son of man coming in clouds with great power and glory" (Mark 13:26; cf. Matt. 24:30; Luke 21:27)— and in His reply to the high priest at His trial—"ye shall see the Son of man ... coming with the clouds of heaven" (Mark 14:62; cf. Matt. 26:64).[33] The transfiguration, the ascension (as here described), and the *parousia* are three successive manifestations of

[31] Cf. J. Denney, art. "Ascension", DB i (Edinburgh, 1898), pp. 161 f.; J. H. Bernard, art. "Assumption and Ascension", ERE ii (Edinburgh, 1909), pp. 151 ff.

[32] Cf. G. H. Boobyer, *St. Mark and the Transfiguration Story* (Edinburgh, 1942); A. M. Ramsey, *The Glory of God and the Transfiguration of Christ* (London, 1949).

[33] See the discussion by N. B. Stonehouse in *The Witness of Matthew and Mark to Christ* (Philadelphia, 1944), pp. 238 ff.

Christ's divine glory to men.[34] The cloud in each case is probably to be interpreted as the cloud of the Shekhinah—the cloud which, resting above the tent of meeting in the days of Moses, was the visible token to Israel that the glory of the Lord dwelt within (Ex. 40:34). So, in the last moment that the apostles saw their Lord with outward vision, they were granted "a theophany: Jesus is enveloped in the cloud of the divine presence."[35]

10 We need not be alarmed by suggestions that the ascension story is bound up with a pre-Copernican conception of the universe, and that the former is therefore as obsolete as the latter. Anyone appearing to leave the earth's surface must appear to spectators to be ascending, and so, when the cloud enveloped the visible form of their Lord, His disciples stood "looking stedfastly into heaven as he went." Some of them, perhaps, remembering a previous experience, expected that the cloud would dissolve and Jesus be left with them, as on the mount of transfiguration. Instead, they suddenly became aware of two white-garbed men standing by. Luke plainly intends his readers to understand these men to be angelic messengers. White was the conventional garb of angels (cf. Matt. 28:3; John 20:12; probably also Mark 16:5). Luke describes the two men who appeared to the women at the empty tomb of Christ as clothed "in dazzling apparel" (Luke 24:4)— a description which reminds us of the appearance of Christ's own garments when He was transfigured: "white and dazzling" (Luke 9:29; cf. Mark 9:3).

11 They need not stand gazing up skywards, said the two visitants. "This same Jesus" would indeed come back in the way in which He went—but the implication is that He would not appear again immediately. They had seen Him go in cloud and glory; in cloud and glory He would return. But an interval was to elapse between His exaltation and *parousia*, and in that interval the possession of the Spirit was to be the pledge of the coming consummation of glory.[36]

Christ is ascended, but His abiding presence and energy fill the

---

[34] Cf. Rev. 1:7.

[35] A. M. Ramsey, "What was the Ascension?", *Studiorum Novi Testamenti Societas*, Bulletin II (Oxford, 1951), pp. 43 ff. (The words quoted appear on p. 49.)

[36] Cf. Paul's description of the Holy Spirit as the "earnest" or "guarantee" (Gk. ἀρραβών) of our inheritance "until we acquire possession of it, to the praise of his glory" (Eph. 1:14, RSV).

whole book of Acts, and the whole succeeding story of His people on earth. His presence at God's right hand means that He is more effectually present with His people on earth "all the days, even unto the consummation of the age" (Matt. 28:20). He "ascended far above all the heavens, that he might fill all things" (Eph. 4:10).

(c) In the Upper Room (Ch. 1:12-14)

12 Then returned they unto Jerusalem from the mount called Olivet,[37] which is nigh unto Jerusalem, a sabbath day's journey off.

13 And when they were come in, they went up into the upper chamber, where they were abiding; both Peter and John and James and Andrew, Philip and Thomas, Bartholomew and Matthew, James *the son* of Alphaeus, and Simon the Zealot, and Judas *the son* of James.

14 These all with one accord continued stedfastly in prayer, with the women, and Mary the mother of Jesus, and with his brethren.

12 The apostles' immediate duty was plain: it was to wait in Jerusalem until the heavenly power came upon them. So they returned to the city. The place where their Master was taken from their sight, Luke tells us, was the mount of Olives, to the east of Jerusalem, "a sabbath day's journey off." This was a distance of two thousand cubits or six furlongs, ingeniously reckoned by interpreting Ex. 16:29 in the light of Num. 35:5.[38] According to Luke 24:50, Jesus "led them out until they were over against Bethany"; but it is not certain that the same occasion is intended there as here. Bethany lies on the eastern slopes of Olivet, about fifteen furlongs from Jerusalem (*cf.* John 11:18).

13 Back in Jerusalem, the apostles went to the place where their company was lodging in Jerusalem—"the upper chamber." It is possible (although naturally it cannot be proved) that this was the room where Jesus and His disciples had kept the Passover on the eve of His execution;[39] it may also have been the room where He appeared to some of them in Jerusalem after He rose from the

---

[37] Gk. ἐλαιών, "oliveyard".

[38] *Cf.* Mishnah, *Sotah* v. 3; the general regulations for sabbath observance and the sabbath limits are contained in the Mishnah tractates *Shabbath* and *'Erubin*.

[39] So Zahn, *Die Apostelgeschichte des Lucas*, p. 44; he argues that the article τό before ὑπερῷον would certainly have indicated one special upper room to early Christian readers.

dead (*cf.* Luke 24:33, 36; John 20:19, 26). It is an attractive speculation that the house in which this upper room was was the house of Mary, the mother of John Mark (*cf.* Ch. 12:12); but this is even less demonstrable.[40]

Luke now gives a list of the apostles[41], identical with that given earlier in Luke 6:14 ff., save for a few variations in order and, of course, the deletion of Judas Iscariot. The lists of the twelve in Mark 3:16 ff. and Matt. 10:2 ff. differ from Luke's lists mainly by putting Thaddaeus where he has "Judas the son of James."[42] Otherwise, while the lists vary considerably in order, the same apostles come together in each of the three groups of four names into which the twelve are divided by all three writers; and Peter, Philip and James the son of Alphaeus are always first, fifth and ninth respectively. There is no sufficient reason for supposing that James the son of Alphaeus was a blood-relation of Jesus, or that the name Alphaeus should be identified with Clopas (John 19:25).[43] Simon the Zealot, as he is called here and in Luke 6:15, is called "Simon the Cananaean" in Matt. 10:4 and Mark 3:18. "Cananaean" represents the Hebrew and Aramaic words corresponding to "Zealot", which is of Greek origin.[44] The Zealots constituted the militant wing of Jewish nationalism in the earlier decades of the first century A.D.; it was they who took the lead in the rebellion against Rome in A.D. 66. Josephus appears to date their rise from the revolt of Judas in A.D. 6[45] (see p. 125,

---

[40] *Cf.* Zahn, *op. cit.*, pp. 387 ff.

[41] *Cf.* the discussion of "The Twelve and the Apostles" by V. Taylor in *The Gospel according to St. Mark* (London, 1952), pp. 619 ff.

[42] Thaddaeus (Thaddai) may have been a hypocoristic name of this Judas.

[43] Alphaeus is Aram. *Halphai*. Clopas is said by Hegesippus to have been the brother of Joseph (the husband of Mary) and father of Simeon, who succeeded James the Just as leader of the Jerusalem church (*cf.* Eusebius, *Ecclesiastical History* iii. 11).

[44] Gk. ζηλωτής, Heb. *qannai*, Aram. *qannaya* or *qan'ana* (Hellenized Καναναῖος). The Zealots regarded themselves as the spiritual heirs of the Hasmonean insurgents of the second century B.C., who rose in response to the call of Mattathias, "Whosoever is zealous for the law (Gk. πᾶς ὁ ζηλῶν τῷ νόμῳ), and maintaineth the covenant, let him come forth after me" (I Macc. 2:27). Mattathias in his turn acted in the spirit of Phinehas, who "was jealous (Heb. *qinne*, LXX ἐζήλωσεν) for his God" (Num. 25:13; *cf.* Ps. 106:30 f.). *Cf.* Ch. 21:20.

[45] This is probably Josephus's intention, although Foakes Jackson and Kirsopp Lake conclude from his evidence that "the use of the name Zealot to describe a Jewish sect or party cannot be earlier than A.D. 66" ("The Zealots", *Beginnings* i [London, 1920], pp. 421 ff.). He does not call Judas and his

exposition of Ch. 5:37), and describes them curiously enough, with an eye to his Graeco-Roman readers, as the "fourth philosophic party" among the Jews (*Jewish War* ii.8.1; *Antiquities* xviii.1.1). As for "Judas the son of James," we may reasonably identify him with "Judas not Iscariot" of John 14:22.[46]

14 These eleven apostles had in their company the women who had gone up to Jerusalem from Galilee with Jesus and His followers (*cf.* Luke 8:2 f.), including Mary, the Mother of Jesus. It is worth noting that the latest occasion on which Mary figures in NT history—or in any other narrative which can be regarded as in any sense historical—finds her joining in worship with the other followers of Jesus after His ascension. With these women the "brethren" of Jesus are also mentioned. It has been warmly disputed whether these were His uterine brothers or more remote blood-relations. The burden of proof lies on those who wish to understand the term in another than its usual sense. Believers in the dogma of the perpetual virginity of Mary are, of course, precluded from regarding these relations as uterine brothers of Jesus, and consequently see in them either sons of Joseph by an earlier marriage or (preferably) first cousins of Jesus.[47] But those who do

followers Zealots, indeed, but his "fourth philosophy" is almost certainly an indirect way of indicating the Zealot party. In the Jewish War of A.D. 66–70 the term is applied more particularly to the followers of John of Gischala (*Jewish War* iv. 3.9, etc.). Of course, some ambiguity arises at times because the word "zealot" can be used as a non-technical common noun as well as in the technical party sense.

[46] In the Curetonian Syriac Gospels he is called "Judas Thomas"—*i.e.* "Judas the Twin." This leads to further speculation about his relation to the apostle Thomas. We have no means of identifying his father James.

[47] The view that they were sons of Joseph by a hypothetical earlier marriage was propounded in the fourth century by Epiphanius (*Heresies* xxix. 4). Others had held this view before him, including Hegesippus, from whom Epiphanius probably borrowed the information (without acknowledgment). Helvidius of Rome (*c.* A.D. 383) replied to Epiphanius, maintaining that the brothers of the Lord were sons of Joseph and Mary. This view had been asserted earlier, he claimed, by Tertullian and Victorinus of Pettau; but Helvidius repeated it because he deprecated the now prevalent assumption that virginity was a superior state to matrimony. The doughtiest champion of the blessedness of virginity, Jerome, entered the fray with a treatise *Against Helvidius concerning the perpetual virginity of Mary*, in which he propounded the view which rapidly gained acceptance, that the brothers of the Lord were really His first cousins, the sons of Alphaeus by "Mary of Clopas", whom he inferred (wrongly, it seems) from John 19:25 to be the sister of the Virgin Mary. Of the sons of this other Mary we know two by name, "James the little" and Joses (Mark 15:40). But "James the little", far from being James the Lord's brother, was probably called "the little" in contrast to the latter's prominence. See J. B.

44

not consider themselves bound to accept this dogma may most reasonably conclude that they were younger sons of Mary (*cf.* Matt. 1:25; Mark 6:3; Luke 2:7). They did not acknowledge Jesus as Messiah before His death (*cf.* John 7:5), but after His resurrection they are found among His followers. The most prominent figure among these brothers, James (*cf.* Chs. 12:17; 15:13 ff.; 21:18 ff.), was one of the individuals to whom Christ appeared in resurrection (I Cor. 15:7). Three other brothers of Jesus are mentioned by name, Joses, Judas and Simon (Mark 6:3);[48] of these Judas may be the author of the Epistle of Jude.[49] The fact that the brothers of Jesus are mentioned here separately from the apostles indicates that the James and Judas who appear in the third quaternion of the list of twelve apostles were not identical with the James and Judas named as two of the brothers of Jesus.[50] Together with the other members of this considerable company of believers in Jesus, His brothers are now recorded as faithfully observing the appointed seasons of united prayer.[51]

(d) Matthias Replaces Judas Iscariot (Ch. 1:15–26)

15 And in these days Peter stood up in the midst of the brethren, and said (and there was a multitude of persons *gathered* together, about a hundred and twenty),

16 Brethren, it was needful[52] that the scripture should be fulfilled, which the Holy Spirit spake before by the

Lightfoot, *The Epistle to the Galatians* (London, 1892), pp. 252 ff. (dissertation on "The Brethren of the Lord"); J. B. Mayor, *The Epistle of St. James* (London, 1897), pp. v ff.; Th. Zahn, "Brüder und Vettern Jesu", *Forschungen zur Geschichte des NT Kanons* vi (Leipzig, 1900), pp. 225 ff.; J. Chapman, "The Brethren of the Lord," JThS vii (1906), pp. 412 ff.

[48] In the parallel passage in Matt. 13:55 "Joseph" appears instead of Mark's "Joses". In both places the sisters of Jesus are also mentioned; and the whole implication is that the people are referring to the members of one family in the ordinary limited sense of the word.

[49] *Cf.* Jude 1, "Jude, a servant of Jesus Christ, and brother of James"; see also J. B. Mayor, *The Epistle of St. Jude and the Second Epistle of St. Peter* (London, 1907), pp. cxlvi ff.

[50] The fact that the brothers of Jesus did not believe in Him till after His resurrection is a further argument against identifying any of them with any of the twelve apostles.

[51] G. W. H. Lampe, *The Seal of the Spirit* (London, 1951), p. 44, points out that, as Jesus is represented as praying before the descent of the Spirit on Him in Luke 3:21, so the apostles and their companions are here represented as praying before the descent of the Spirit on *them*; this, he says, illustrates Luke's "repeated doctrine that the grand object of prayer is the gift of the Spirit."

[52] The Western reading is "it is needful" (δεῖ, not ἔδει).

mouth of David concerning Judas, who was guide to
them that took Jesus.

17 For he was numbered among us, and received his portion in this ministry.

18 (Now this man obtained a field with the reward of his
iniquity; and falling headlong,[53] he burst asunder in
the midst, and all his bowels gushed out.

19 And it became known to all the dwellers at Jerusalem;
insomuch that in their language that field was called
Akeldama,[54] that is, The field of blood.)

20 For it is written in the book of Psalms,
Let his habitation be made desolate,
And let no man dwell therein;
and,
His office[55] let another take.

21 Of the men therefore that have companied with us all
the time that the Lord Jesus[56] went in and went out
among us,[57]

22 beginning from the baptism of John, unto the day that
he was received up from us, of these must one become
a witness with us of his resurrection.

23 And they[58] put forward two, Joseph called Barsabbas,[59]
who was surnamed Justus, and Matthias.

24 And they prayed, and said, Thou, Lord, who knowest
the hearts of all men, show of these two the one whom
thou hast chosen,

[53] Gk. πρηνὴς γενόμενος. But there are grounds for translating the expression
here by "swelling up" (so RSV margin), as though πρηνής were connected with
πρήθω or πίμπρημι (cf. Ch. 28:6, πίμπρασθαι). In Wisdom 4:19 πρηνεῖς is
rendered inflatos in Vulgate (contrast the Douay-Challoner rendering "he shall
burst them puffed up and speechless" with ERV "he shall dash them speechless
to the ground"). Cf. F. H. Chase, "On πρηνὴς γενόμενος in Acts 1:18,"
JThS xiii (1912), pp. 278 ff., 415.

[54] Better transliterated Hakeldama ('Ακελδαμάχ with a rough breathing,
as in Westcott and Hort's text). It is an Aramaic expression, haqal dema, "the
field of blood."

[55] Gk. τὴν ἐπισκοπὴν αὐτοῦ, lit. "his overseership", "his superintendency"
(AV "his bishopric"); the word has no technical sense either here or in the
LXX passage quoted.

[56] The Western text adds "Christ"; such amplification of our Lord's name
is a feature of this text.

[57] Or "over us" (ARV margin), suggesting the Lord's relationship to His
disciples.

[58] The Western text has "he put forward", as though Peter took the
initiative in nominating them.

[59] The Western text has "Barnabas", by confusion with the Joseph of
Ch. 4:36.

25 to take the place in this ministry and apostleship from which Judas fell away, that he might go to his own place.
26 And they gave lots for them; and the lot fell upon Matthias; and he was numbered with the eleven[60] apostles.

15–17 The number of these followers of Jesus who were together in Jerusalem was a hundred and twenty or thereby.[61] In addition, there were many more elsewhere, mainly in Galilee. According to I Cor. 15:6, there was one occasion after the resurrection of Jesus when He appeared to more than five hundred of His followers; this is probably to be regarded as a Galilaean appearance.[62] We should not forget the presence and influence of so many of Jesus' followers in Galilee, even if Luke is concerned to trace the expansion of the gospel along the road which begins at Jerusalem and leads to Rome.[63]

The whole company of a hundred and twenty is here referred to as "brethren"—a wider use of the word than that which we have considered in v. 14. Among them Peter takes the leading place, as to a large extent he did during the time covered by the Gospel narrative. He is here represented as taking the lead in filling the vacancy among the twelve apostles caused by the defection of Judas Iscariot. Both the defection of Judas and the necessity of replacing him by someone more worthy are viewed as subjects of OT prophecy.

[60] The Western text has "twelve" (the clause would then have to be rendered "he was numbered among the twelve apostles"); Augustine conflates both readings: "he was counted twelfth with the eleven apostles" (this is accepted by Zahn as the original text; cf. his *Urausgabe*, pp. 29, 244).

[61] Luke regularly qualifies his numerical data by the particle ὡς or ὡσεί ("about").

[62] This *may* be regarded as the same occasion as is described in Matt. 28:16 ff., but the suggested identification is quite inconclusive; it is more reasonable, however, than the view that Paul is referring to a variant account of what happened on the day of Pentecost.

[63] R. Schütz in *Apostel und Jünger* (Giessen, 1921) argued for a stream of Gentile Christianity flowing northward from Galilee. There is something to be said for such a hypothesis, but it cannot be established on Schütz's premises, which are bound up with an unacceptable analysis of Acts as derived from a Judaean "apostles" source and a Galilaean "disciples" source. One may wonder whether the imperfect acquaintance with apostolic Christianity shown by Apollos (Ch. 18:25) and the dozen disciples of Ephesus (Ch. 19:1 ff.) was not due to their acquiring their knowledge of the gospel along a line of transmission which stemmed from Galilee and had no direct contact with the events of Pentecost.

The use of messianic "testimonies" from the OT—passages which found their fulfilment in the story of Jesus and its sequel and had therefore great evidential value—was a prominent feature of primitive Christian publicity and apologetic.[64] It is reasonable to regard the instruction given by Jesus Himself to His disciples on the fulfilment of OT prophecy (cf. Luke 24:25 ff., 44 ff.) as the nucleus of the collections of such "testimonies" which appear to have been compiled and circulated at a fairly early date for ready reference. It is plain that even before the time of Christ much of the material in the Psalter (especially in the "royal psalms") was interpreted in a messianic sense.[65] For those who believed that Jesus was the Messiah, this meant that many of the experiences predicated of the Psalmist (David) were understood as prophetically applicable to Jesus (cf. Ch. 2:25 ff., 34 ff.). Then what was said of the Psalmist's enemies would be interpreted of the enemies of Jesus (cf. Ch. 4:25 ff.). Among these enemies Judas was unenviably prominent. And there are other places in NT where "testimonies" to the fate of Judas are quoted or alluded to. "We are familiar with Matthew's proof of it, by a combined *Testimony* from Zechariah and Jeremiah," says J. Rendel Harris (*Testimonies* ii [Cambridge, 1920], p. 82). We remember also Jesus's application of Ps. 41:9 to Judas in John 13:18 and the words in His prayer for His disciples in John 17:12, "not one of them perished, but the son of perdition; *that the scripture might be fulfilled.*" So Peter here adduces further "testimonies" from the Psalter to the same effect. Their real author, he avers, is the Holy Spirit, who spoke through the prophets. David, being a prophet (Ch. 2:30), was but a spokesman or mouthpiece (cf. Ch. 4:25, p. 105, with n. 29) of the inspiring Spirit.

18–19 But before Luke reports the actual passages from the Psalter which Peter quoted to establish his point, he inserts a parenthesis in order that his readers may understand the back-

---

[64] See on this subject E. C. Selwyn, *The Oracles in the NT* (London, 1911); J. R. Harris, *Testimonies* i and ii (Cambridge, 1916 and 1920); R. V. G. Tasker, *The OT in the NT* (London, 1946); P. B. W. S. Hunt, *Primitive Gospel Sources* (London, 1951); C. H. Dodd, *The Old Testament in the New* (London, 1952), and *According to the Scriptures* (London, 1952).

[65] That the person indicated by the title "my lord" in Ps. 110:1 is Messiah is common ground to Jesus and the Pharisees (Mark 12:35 ff.). The words addressed to the Lord's anointed in Ps. 2:9 are referred to the future Messiah in *Psalms of Solomon* 17:26 (about the middle of the first century B.C.).

ground of Peter's remarks. Peter did not need to tell his hearers in the upper room what had happened to Judas, nor can the words of v. 19, "in *their* language that field was called Hakeldama," be part of Peter's direct speech. But when Luke visited Jerusalem in A.D. 57, he was no doubt told the story of Judas's death, and he inserts it here. Judas, the story goes, bought a field with his ill-gotten gain. (According to Matt. 27:7, it was the chief priests who bought it with the reward of treachery, which Judas had flung back in their faces. The common harmonization of the two accounts at this point—suggested, for example, by E. Jacquier in *Les Actes des Apôtres* [Paris, 1926], *ad loc.*—is that the chief priests, considering the thirty shekels to be legally Judas' property, bought the field with them in his name.) He did not live, however, to enjoy the fruits of his shameful act, for he swelled up[66] and sustained a fatal rupture. (The Latin Vulgate harmonizes this account with Matthew's by saying that "having hanged himself he burst asunder in the midst"; Augustine [*Against Felix the Manichaean* i. 4] says: "he fastened a rope round his neck and, falling on his face, burst asunder in the midst.") It should be noted by the English reader that "in the midst" does not mean "in the midst of the field", but refers to Judas's body.[67] The field was accordingly called by an Aramaic name meaning "the field of blood." (According to Matt. 27:7, it was the potter's field, and was used thereafter to bury aliens in.)

20 After this parenthesis, Luke continues with his report of Peter's speech, and quotes the two passages from the Psalms to which Peter appealed. The former, from Ps. 69:25, is a prayer that the dwelling-place of certain foes of the psalmist may become a desolation; the latter, from Ps. 109:8, prays that a certain enemy may die before his time and be replaced in his responsible position by someone else. Here, then, is warrant for the appointment of a successor to Judas; for it would not be fitting to leave the apostolic total short by one, when that total was intentionally

---

[66] See n. 53 above. The tradition that Judas swelled up to monstrous proportions was elaborated in Christian antiquity; its best-known record is in a fragment of Papias quoted by Apollinarius (for which see J. B. Lightfoot, *The Apostolic Fathers* [London, 1891], pp. 523 f., 534 f.). E. J. Goodspeed (*New Chapters in NT Study* [New York, 1937], p. 42) concludes that Papias was acquainted with Acts because his account of Judas's death is based on this passage.

[67] Gk. ἐλάκησεν μέσος.

fixed by Jesus to correspond to the twelve tribes of Israel (cf. Luke 22:30; Matt. 19:28).[68]

21-22 The essential qualifications of a successor were then set forth: he must have been a companion of the Lord and His apostles from the time when John the Baptist was active to the day of the Lord's ascension; he must in particular be a witness of the resurrection, as the rest of the apostles were. It is noteworthy in the first place that the period indicated is just the period covered by the primitive apostolic preaching—the *kerygma*, to use the Greek term as present-day theologians like to do.[69] (*Cf.* Chs. 10:37 and 13:24 f.) In the second place, the statement that the apostles had been companions of Christ from the days when John was baptizing agrees with the evidence of the fourth gospel, according to which nearly half the apostolic group began to follow Jesus in the days immediately following His baptism by John (*cf.* John 1:35 ff.). The call of the apostles recorded in the synoptic gospels, which took place after the Baptist's imprisonment (Mark 1:14 ff.), will then have been the sequel to their earlier acquaintance with Jesus, formed by the banks of Jordan.

23 Their choice fell upon two disciples who possessed the necessary qualifications. Joseph's surname Barsabbas seems to mean "son of the sabbath" (presumably because he was born on the sabbath day).[70] Like many other Jews at that time, he bore a Gentile name as well as his Jewish one:[71] the Latin name Justus was a well-known cognomen in Roman circles (*cf.* Ch. 18:7), and may have been regarded in such a case as this as a rendering of the Hebrew epithet *ha-tzaddiq*, 'the righteous'. According to Eusebius (*Ecclesiastical History* iii.39) and the later writer Philip of Sidé (*Christian History*), Papias reported on the authority of Philip's daughters (*cf.* Ch. 21:9) that this Joseph, when challenged by unbelievers, drank snake's venom in the Lord's name and suffered no untoward consequences.[72] Matthias is said by Eusebius (*Eccle-*

---

[68] *Cf.* also Rev. 21:12, 14.

[69] The age of fulfilment began with John (*cf.* Luke 16:16); the baptism in the Spirit which he foretold began to be accomplished when Jesus was baptized by him in Jordan and was endued with the Spirit for His messianic work. (*Cf.* Lampe, *op. cit.*, p. 32.)

[70] Representing Aram. *Bar-Shabba*; less probably *Bar-Saba*, "son of the elder." *Cf.* Ch. 15:22 for another bearer of the same patronymic.

[71] *Cf.* Ch. 12:12; 13:9; also "Jesus called Justus" in Col. 4:11.

[72] *Cf.* Mark 16:18. Goodspeed (*loc. cit.*) describes this statement of Papias as "a strong contact" with Acts (*cf.* n. 66 above).

siastical History i.12; ii.1) to have been one of the seventy disciples of Luke 10:1. This is quite probable, but Eusebius may only be guessing. Later tradition represents him as a missionary to the Ethiopians.

24–26 It should be observed that they did not cast lots haphazardly; they first selected the two men whom they judged worthiest to fill the vacancy.[73] It may well be that there was nothing to choose between Joseph and Matthias; in that case the casting of lots, which had very respectable precedent in Hebrew sacred history, was a very reasonable way of deciding on one of the two, especially as they besought God to overrule the lot.

> "The lot is cast into the lap;
> But the whole disposing thereof is of Jehovah"
> (Prov. 16:33).

There is, to be sure, no NT example of this procedure after the descent of the Spirit on the day of Pentecost (Ch. 2); this may or may not be significant.

The apostles' prayer is couched in dignified language, with liturgical echoes.[74] Whether the "Lord" addressed is God the Father or the Lord Jesus is uncertain; however, as the verb used in "thou hast chosen" (end of v. 24) is the same as that used in "he had chosen" (end of v. 2), it is reasonable to conclude that Jesus is the subject here as in the former place. Even if the words "that he might go to his own place" (v. 25)[75] are euphemistic, we may well mark and emulate the reticence with which the apostles referred to Judas's fate after death. The circumstances of his death gave them little ground for hope in this regard, but they would not take it upon themselves to say definitely what "his own place" was to which he went.

The lots, then, were cast; Matthias was indicated as the man to

[73] We may compare the method by which magistrates were elected in ancient Athens under Solon's constitution—by κλήρωσις ἐκ προκρίτων, *i.e.* casting lots between candidates previously selected on more rational grounds.

[74] Note in particular the invocation "Thou, Lord, who knowest the hearts of all men" (Gk. σὺ κύριε καρδιογνῶστα πάντων); the same epithet "heart-knowing" (καρδιογνώστης) occurs in Ch. 15:8 and for the rest appears chiefly in liturgical forms.

[75] There seems to be an echo of this expression in Ignatius's *Epistle to the Magnesians* 5:1, "each man is to go to his own place." If we could be sure that Ignatius (*c.* A.D. 115) is quoting Acts here, this, along with the contacts with Papias (see notes 66 and 72 above), would provide good evidence for the circulation of Acts early in the second century.

51

fill the vacant place. The number of the apostles was restored to twelve. It was Judas's defection and not the mere fact of his death that created the vacancy; no steps were taken to appoint a successor to James the son of Zebedee when he died by the executioner's sword some years later. Unlike Judas, he was faithful unto death, and might hope to reign with Christ in resurrection, if not (as he had once expected)[76] in this present life.

It has sometimes been suggested that the apostles were wrong in co-opting Matthias to complete their number; that they should have waited until Paul was ready to fill the vacancy in God's good time.[77] This is a complete mistake. Paul did not possess the qualifications set out in vv. 21 f. Besides, his apostleship was unique in character, as he himself maintains; he would certainly have dismissed as preposterous the idea that he was rightfully the twelfth apostle on the same footing as the rest of the eleven.

[76] Cf. Mark 10:35 ff.
[77] Cf. R. Stier, *The Words of the Apostles* (Eng. tr., Edinburgh, 1869), pp. 12 ff.; G. Campbell Morgan, *The Acts of the Apostles* (New York, 1924), *ad loc.*

CHAPTER II

2. THE DAY OF PENTECOST

(Ch. 2:1–47)

(a) The Descent of the Spirit (Ch. 2:1–4)

1 And[1] when the day of Pentecost was now come, they were all together in one place.

2 And suddenly there came from heaven a sound as of the rushing of a mighty wind, and it filled all the house where they were sitting.

3 And there appeared unto them tongues parting asunder, like as of fire; and it sat upon each one of them.

4 And they were all filled with the Holy Spirit, and began to speak with other tongues, as the Spirit gave them utterance.

1 The day of Pentecost was so called because it was celebrated on the fiftieth (Gk. *pentekostos*)[2] day after the presentation of the first harvested sheaf of the barley harvest, *i.e.* the fiftieth day from the first Sunday[3] after Passover (*cf.* Lev. 23:15 f.). It was known

---

[1] The Western text adds "it came to pass in those days."

[2] The feminine form of the Greek ordinal numeral, $ἡ$ $πεντηκοστή$ (*sc.* $ἡμέρα$ r $ἑ$ $ὁρτή$), is first found as a name for this feast in Tobit 2:1 and 2 Maccabees 12:32.

[3] This was the reckoning of the Sadducean party in the first century A.D. In the phrase "the morrow after the sabbath" (Lev. 23:15) they interpreted the sabbath as the weekly sabbath. While the temple stood, their interpretation would be normative for the public celebration of the festival; Christian tradition is therefore right in fixing the anniversary of the descent of the Spirit on a Sunday. (The "fifty days" of Lev. 23:15 are to be reckoned inclusively.) The Pharisees, however, interpreted the "sabbath" of Lev. 23:15 as the festival day of unleavened bread itself (on which, according to Lev. 23:7, no servile work was to be done); in that case Pentecost would always fall on the same day of the month (an important matter in the eyes of those to whom it marked the anniversary of the law-giving), but not on the same day of the week. The Pharisees could appeal to Josh. 5:11 ("the morrow after the passover"), read in the light of Lev. 23:10–14. It was the Pharisaic reckoning that became normative in Judaism after A.D. 70; thus in A.D. 1953 the first day of unleavened bread falls on Tuesday, March 31 (Nisan 15, 5713), and the first day of the feast of weeks falls on Wednesday, May 20 (Siwan 6, 5713), on the fiftieth day by inclusive reckoning from the second day of unleavened bread. *Cf.* Mishnah *Menachoth* x. 3; Tosefta *Menachoth* x. 23. 528; TB *Menachoth* 65a; see also L. Finkelstein, *The Pharisees* (Philadelphia, 1946), pp. 115 ff.

among Hebrew-speaking people as the "feast of weeks"[4] (*cf.* Ex. 34:22a; Deut. 16:10) and also as "the day of the first-fruits" (Num. 28:26; *cf.* Ex. 23:16a) because it was the day when "the first-fruits of wheat harvest" (Ex. 34:22a) were presented to God. In later Judaism it was reckoned to be the anniversary of the giving of the law at Sinai[5]—a reasonable deduction from the chronological note in Ex. 19:1.

2 On the morning of the day of Pentecost in the year of our Lord's passion, the house where His disciples were sitting together was suddenly filled with what seemed like a gale of wind from heaven.[6] It is perhaps pointless to ask explicit questions about this wind, for there is no likelihood of their being satisfactorily answered. Did the disciples only hear it, or was it audible to others? We have no means of knowing. But we do know that the wind was held to symbolize the Spirit of God. When Ezekiel, by divine command, prophesied to the wind and called it to blow upon the dead bodies in the valley of his vision, it was the breath of God that breathed upon them and filled them with new life (Ezek. 37:9–14). And, probably with an allusion to Ezekiel's vision, Jesus said to Nicodemus, "The wind bloweth where it will, and thou hearest the voice thereof, but knowest not whence it cometh, and whither it goeth: so is every one that is born of the Spirit" (John 3:8). Whatever else we may say about the disciples' experience, this at least is certain, and this is what really matters: the Spirit of God came upon them in power.

3 But the outward manifestation of the Spirit's advent was visual as well as audible: "there appeared to them tongues as of fire, distributed and resting on each one of them" (RSV). Here again we find it difficult to translate this experience into terms which convey the true significance to us. As in the burning bush (Ex. 3:2 ff.), fire denotes the divine presence. Matthew and Luke report John the Baptist as foretelling the arrival of one who would baptize "in the Holy Spirit and in fire" (Matt. 3:11; Luke 3:16); and in the present context the fire as well as the wind is an emblem of the Spirit's power. Perhaps no one has expressed the

---

[4] Heb. *Shabu'oth,* by which name the day is commonly designated among Jews.

[5] *Cf.* Jubilees 1:1 with 6:17; TB *Pesachim* 68b; Midrash *Tanchuma* 26c.

[6] Ephrem the Syrian (4th cent. A.D.) says the house was filled with fragrance; this is probably a reminiscence of Isa. 6:4.

spiritual meaning of the heavenly fire so effectively as Charles Wesley:

O Thou who camest from above
The pure celestial fire to impart,
Kindle a flame of sacred love
On the mean altar of my heart!

There let it for Thy glory burn
With inextinguishable blaze;
And trembling to its source return
In humble prayer and fervent praise.

Jesus, confirm my heart's desire
To work, and speak, and think for Thee;
Still let me guard the holy fire,
And still stir up Thy gift in me.

Ready for all Thy perfect will,
My acts of faith and love repeat,
Till death Thy endless mercies seal,
And make the sacrifice complete.

When this has been grasped, the difficulty of determining what the disciples really *saw* appears very unimportant. It does not seem probable that there is any direct allusion in the "tongues ... as of fire" to the "other tongues" of v. 4. F. H. Chase suggests "that, at the moment when the illuminating Spirit was poured upon the Church, the sunlight of a new day smote upon the Apostles", and he goes on to ask: "was it unnatural that Christians should see a deeper meaning in the sun's rays streaming through the colonnades and the arches of the Temple and resting upon the Apostles, and connecting the sight with the wonders of Apostolic utterance which ensued, should play upon a not uncommon use of the word 'tongue' and speak of 'tongues like as of fire' resting on the Apostles?" *(The Credibility of the Book of the Acts of the Apostles* [London, 1902], p. 35).

This, of course, implies that the "one place" (v. 1) where the disciples were all together, the "house where they were sitting" (v. 2), was situated within the temple precincts. Certainly the temple courts would be a suitable place for the gathering of over three thousand people who heard the words of Peter (vv. 14 ff.), and if (as we might at first suppose) the house where they were sitting was the house of the upper room (Ch. 1:13), they must have left it for the streets, or else their sudden outburst of inspired utterance would not have made the public impression that it did. We may consider two alternatives. On the one hand, they may have been in the temple courts when the divine power came upon them; according to Luke 24:53, they "were continually in the temple, blessing God", and they were all the more likely to be there early on that festal day.[7] If so, Chase's explanation of the tongues of fire is relevant. On the other hand, the Spirit may have come upon them in power while they were still in the upper room; in that case we must conclude that they came down into the streets, speaking with tongues, that the crowds gathered at the sound, and followed them to the temple area, where Peter, standing up with the eleven, turned and addressed them. This second alternative involves reading more into the narrative than Luke actually tells us, but probably any attempt to represent the scene to ourselves involves that. On the whole, we are inclined to prefer the former alternative.[8]

4 However we understand the sensible phenomena, there is no doubt about the disciples' inward experience: "they were all filled with the Holy Spirit." The spiritual baptism foretold by John and promised afresh by the Lord was now an accomplished fact. The filling with the Spirit was an experience to be repeated on several occasions (cf. Ch. 4:8, 31; 13:9); but the Spirit-baptism took place once for all, so far as the believing community was concerned.

In OT times the regular consequences of a man's being possessed by the Spirit of God was that he prophesied. So it was with Eldad and Medad when the Spirit rested upon them in the camp of Israel (Num. 11:26 ff.), and so it was with many another. So now the descent of the Spirit on the disciples was manifested by prophetic speech, but prophetic speech of a peculiar kind. They "began to speak with other tongues, as the Spirit gave them utterance."

Speaking with tongues, or *glossolalia* (to give the phenomenon

[7] The word οἶκος ("house") can, of course, refer to the temple as well as to a private house; cf. Ch. 7:47; Isa. 6:4 and frequently in LXX.
[8] R. A. Cole (*The New Temple* [London, 1950], p. 38, n. 18) points out that if the disciples were assembled in the temple precincts on the day of Pentecost we have here a link with Ezek. 47:1 ff. (where the life-giving stream issues from under the threshold of the house—a passage probably underlying John 7:38).

its Greek name), is not an unparalleled manifestation.[9] Not only are the speaker's words partially or completely beyond his conscious control, but they are uttered in a language of which he has no command in normal circumstances. We need not go outside the NT to find another form of *glossolalia*—it was a "spiritual gift" highly valued by the Corinthian church. Paul, in dealing with this "gift" in 1 Cor. 12:3 ff.; 14:2 ff., does not deny that it is a manifestation of the Holy Spirit, but deprecates the undue importance which his Corinthian converts were attaching to it. As cultivated in the church at Corinth, *glossolalia* was uttered in a speech which no hearer could understand until someone present received the correlative spiritual gift of interpretation. The abuse to which this variety of the phenomenon could lend itself can easily be imagined. But on the day of Pentecost the words spoken by the disciples in their divine ecstasy were immediately recognized by the visitors from many lands who heard them. Possibly "what happened on that occasion was that the multitude of pilgrims heard the Christians praising God in ecstatic utterances; and were amazed to observe that many of the words which they uttered were not Jewish or Greek words at all, but belonged to the local languages of Egypt, Asia Minor and Italy" (P. Loyd, *The Holy Spirit in the Acts* [London, 1952], p. 32).[10]

The mere fact of *glossolalia* or any other ecstatic utterance is no evidence of the presence of the Holy Spirit. In apostolic times it was necessary to provide criteria for deciding whether such utterances were of God or not, just as it had been necessary in OT times.[11] "Believe not every spirit," says John, "but prove the

---

[9] See K. Lake, *Earlier Epistles of Paul* (London, 1911), pp. 241 ff.; A. L. Drummond, *Edward Irving and his Circle* (London, 1937), pp. 236 ff., 278 ff., and his bibliography on p. 300; G. H. Lang, *The History and Diaries of an Indian Christian* (London, 1939), pp. 193 ff.; C. S. Lewis, *Transposition* (London, 1949), pp. 9 ff.

[10] *Cf.* also R. B. Rackham, *The Acts of the Apostles* (London, 1901), pp. 15 f.: "Every new beginning in thought or life is inevitably accompanied by disturbance. There is the struggle with the old, and the re-adjustment to the new, environment. So the coming of the Spirit is followed by irregular and abnormal phenomena. Like Jordan, the full and plenteous flood of the Spirit 'overflows all its banks' (Josh. 3:15). At first the old worn-out vessels of humanity cannot contain it; and there is a flood of strange and novel spiritual experiences. But when it has worn for itself a deep channel in the church, when the laws of the new spiritual life are learnt and understood, then some of the irregular phenomena disappear, others become normal, and what was thought to be miraculous is found to be a natural endowment of the Christian life."

[11] *Cf.* Deut. 18:22 (if a man's predictions fail to come true, he is a false

spirits, whether they be of God" (1 John 4:1), and the test he indicates is the testimony which the spirit (or the ecstatic utterance) bears to Christ. Paul had already laid down a similar test in 1 Cor. 12:3. We should do well to pay heed to these apostolic injunctions to-day, in relation not only to ecstatic utterances but to other utterances as well. The content is more important than the manner. On the present occasion, the content of the ecstatic utterances was "the mighty works of God," and the range of the languages in which these were proclaimed suggests that Luke thought of the coming of the Spirit more particularly as a preparation for the world-wide proclamation of the Gospel. The church of Christ still speaks in many tongues, and if her speech is not now of the supernatural order that marked the day of Pentecost, the message is the same—the mighty works of God.

(b) The Crowd's Amazement (Ch. 2:5–13)

5 Now there were dwelling at Jerusalem Jews,[12] devout men, from every nation under heaven.

6 And when this sound was heard, the multitude came together, and were confounded, because that every man heard them speaking in his own language.

7 And they were all amazed and marvelled, saying, Behold, are not all these that speak Galilaeans?

8 And how hear we, every man in our own language wherein we were born?

9 Parthians and Medes and Elamites, and the dwellers in Mesopotamia, in Judaea[13] and Cappadocia, in Pontus and Asia,

---

prophet); 13:1 ff. (even if his predictions do come true, but he seduces his hearers from their allegiance to the true God, he is a false prophet). See also the more pedestrian tests prescribed for prophets in the *Didache*. Chs. 11–12.

[12] "Jews" is missing in ℵ. F. Blass, J. H. Ropes and K. Lake support the omission. See p. 60.

[13] The reading 'Ιουδαίαν has been generally suspected, because (a) the word is properly an adjective, and requires to be preceded by the definite article if it is to be used as a substantive, (b) as Bede saw over twelve centuries ago, even if it could be regarded as a substantive, it would refer most naturally to the province of Judaea, the most southerly of the three divisions of Palestine; and it would hardly be worth noting that Judaeans were present in Jerusalem. This last difficulty is not greatly reduced if we take the word to denote the whole of Palestine (*cf.* Luke 4:44, ARV margin). Even if we take it of the ideal extent of Jewish territory, "from the river of Egypt [Wadi el-Arish] unto . . . the river Euphrates" (Gen. 15:17), the grammatical difficulty remains: "the anarthrous 'Ιουδαίαν . . . is certainly corrupt" (F. Blass, *Grammar of NT Greek* [Eng. tr., London, 1911], p. 153, n. 1). A variety of emendations have

10 in Phrygia and Pamphylia, in Egypt and the parts of
Libya about Cyrene, and sojourners from Rome, both
Jews and proselytes,

11 Cretans and Arabians, we hear them speaking in our
tongues the mighty works of God.

12 And they were all amazed, and were perplexed, saying
one to another, What meaneth this?

13 But others mocking said, They are filled with new
wine.

5-8 From the far-flung lands where the Jews of the dispersion
lived, great numbers had come to Jerusalem to celebrate the Feast
of Weeks, for only at the Jerusalem temple could they attend the
special sacrificial services prescribed for that "holy convocation"
(Num. 28:26 ff.). Many of them were astonished as they heard
the loud praises of God uttered by the disciples in inspired
language—for this, rather than the rushing noise of wind, is what is
meant by "this sound"[14] in v. 6—because they recognized the indigenous languages and dialects of their native lands. The visitors
from the lands east of Palestine knew Aramaic, and those from
the lands west of Palestine knew Greek, but neither Aramaic nor
Greek was a foreign tongue to the apostles. The Galilaean accent
was easily recognized[15], as Peter knew to his sorrow on an earlier
occasion, but these Galilaeans appeared for the moment to share
between them a command of most of the tongues spoken throughout the known world.

When the law was given at Sinai, according to one rabbinic
tradition, "the ten commandments were promulgated with a single
sound, yet it says, 'All the people perceived the voices' (Ex.
20:18);[16] this shows that when the voice went forth it was divided
into seven voices and then went into seventy tongues,[17] and every

---

been offered, e.g. Armenia (Tertullian and Augustine), Galatia (M. Dibelius),
India (R. Bentley), Ionia (W. L. Knox), Kurdistan (F. C. Burkitt), Syria
(Jerome). See n. 23 below.

[14] Gk. τῆς φωνῆς ταύτης (the word translated "sound" in v. 2 is ἦχος).

[15] The Galilaean dialect was noted for its confusing of the various guttural
sounds. Cf. Matt. 26:73.

[16] The real sense of Ex. 20:18 is made clear in ARV, "all the people
perceived the thunderings."

[17] The languages of the world were reckoned to be seventy in all, corresponding to the nations enumerated in Gen. 10. With this the rabbis linked
Deut. 32:8,

When the Most High gave to the nations their inheritance,
When he separated the children of men,

59

people received the law in their own language" (Midrash *Tanchuma* 26c). So now, on the reputed anniversary of the law-giving, people "from every nation under heaven" heard the praises of God, "every man ... in his own language." The parallel in the narrator's mind is plain: it has been caught and expressed by John Keble in his Whitsuntide hymn:

When God of old came down from heaven,
    In power and wrath He came;
Before His feet the clouds were riven,
    Half darkness and half flame:

But when He came the second time,
    He came in power and love;
Softer than gale at morning prime
    Hovered His holy Dove.

The fires, that rushed on Sinai down
    In sudden torrents dread,
Now gently light, a glorious crown,
    On every sainted head.[18]

And as on Israel's awestruck ear
    The voice exceeding loud,
The trump that angels quake to hear,
    Thrilled from the deep, dark cloud;

So, when the Spirit of our God
    Came down His flock to find,
A voice from heaven was heard abroad,
    A rushing, mighty wind...

The people from these many lands who heard the disciples speaking with tongues were, however, Jews or proselytes; this seems to be clear even if, with Codex Sinaiticus and some modern scholars, we omit the word "Jews" from v. 5. Apart from the

He set the bounds of the peoples
    According to the number of the children of Israel—
the "children of Israel," according to this interpretation, being the seventy "souls of the house of Jacob, that came into Egypt" (Gen. 46:27). In the LXX of Deut. 32:8 the opening words are ὅτε διεμέριζεν ὁ ὕψιστος ἔθνη, but it is excessively far-fetched to trace a connection between διεμέριζεν there and διαμεριζόμεναι ("parting asunder") in Acts 2:3!

[18] Keble's words here, even more than the words of Acts, are strongly reminiscent of Virgil's description of the lambent flame, betokening the favour of heaven, which played around the head of Iulus, son of Aeneas, when Troy fell (*Aeneid* ii. 681–686).

intrinsic improbability that the evangelization of Gentiles should be in view at such an early stage in the narrative of Acts—long before this revolutionary act is introduced with a fanfare of trumpets in Chs. 10 and 11—there is the consideration that the Greek word translated "devout men"[19] in v. 5 appears in NT to be reserved as an epithet for Jews. But even if they were Jews, these "devout men" are considered here by Luke to be representatives of the lands from which they came, and of the local dialects of those lands.

9–11 Then follows an impressive roll-call of the nations so represented. Such geographical lists appear elsewhere in ancient literature.[20] But the present list is relevant to its context and has some features of particular interest. "Parthians and Medes[21] and Elamites, and the dwellers in Mesopotamia" lived to the east of Judaea; the Jews in those parts spoke Aramaic. These were the lands of the earliest dispersion, to which exiles from the ten northern tribes of Israel had been carried by the Assyrians. They did not lose their identity so completely as is commonly supposed. Their numbers were later augmented by the Judaean deportations

---

[19] Gk. εὐλαβεῖς (omitted by Augustine). In Ch. 8:2 εὐλαβής is used of the men who buried Stephen, in Ch. 22:12 of Ananias of Damascus, in Luke 2:25 of the aged Simeon. The word is quite different from that used for Gentile God-fearers (*cf.* pp. 215 f., on Ch. 10:2).

[20] Stefan Weinstock ("The Geographical Catalogue in Acts 2:9–11", *Journal of Roman Studies* xxxviii [1948], pp. 43 ff.) reports an interesting marginal note which he found in an offprint of F. Cumont, "La plus ancienne géographie astrologique", *Klio* ix (1909), pp. 263 ff.—an article which deals with the division of the countries of the earth among the signs of the zodiac. This marginal note, in F. C. Burkitt's hand, tabulated the catalogue of nations in these verses alongside the list of nations, arranged in relation to the signs of the zodiac, found in the *Apotelesmatica* of the fourth-century A.D. astrological writer Paul of Alexandria. Weinstock concludes that Burkitt must have regarded astrological geography as the key to the understanding of Luke's catalogue, and that Luke consequently, "however strange his list is, meant in fact to say 'the whole world' . . . all nations who live under the twelve signs of the zodiac received the gift to understand their preaching immediately." Whatever may be the literary affinities of Luke's catalogue, we take leave to doubt the presence of astrological considerations in his mind. In view of our reference to Deut. 32:8 in n. 17, however, it is not irrelevant to recall that the LXX (followed by RSV) renders the second part of that verse "He set the boundaries of the nations according to the number of the angels of God" (ἀγγέλων θεοῦ, apparently representing a Hebrew text *bnê 'El* as against MT *bnê Yisra'el*)—a reading which has sometimes been interpreted (or misinterpreted) astrologically.

[21] In I Enoch 56:5 "Parthians and Medes" play a leading part in the last war of the Gentiles against Israel.

in Nebuchadrezzar's time. In spite of the Persian royal decrees, many of those exiles preferred to remain where they were instead of returning to Palestine, and their settlements were increased by further immigration, so that the number of Jews in these eastern territories ran into millions. Artaxerxes III of Persia planted some Jewish captives in Hyrcania on the Caspian Sea (*c.* 353 B.C.).[22] Josephus has much to tell about Jewish settlements in Mesopotamia and the adjacent regions; it was for their benefit that he produced the first draft of his *Jewish War* in Aramaic.

The reference to "Judaea" here is commonly regarded as a scribal error, mainly for grammatical reasons.[23] It is, besides, unlikely that special mention would be made of Judaeans as being present in Jerusalem. If, however, the word be retained, we should probably think of Judaea in its widest possible sense, denoting the extent of the land controlled directly and indirectly by the Judaean kings David and Solomon, from the Egyptian frontier to the Euphrates. This might explain the absence of Syria from the list.

As for those living in "Cappadocia, in Pontus and Asia, in Phrygia and Pamphylia," there is ample evidence of the large Jewish communities in those provinces of Asia Minor. The middle chapters of Acts (Chs. 13–19) afford abundant proof of this; Philo declares that "the Jews are exceedingly numerous in each city of Asia and Syria" (*Embassy to Gaius*, 245). From the north coast of Asia Minor some crossed the Black Sea; Jewish inscriptions from that period are found in the Crimea.

Those visitors who came from "Egypt and the parts of Libya about Cyrene" belonged to another very populous sector of the Diaspora. Jews had lived in Egypt continuously from the earlier years of the 6th century B.C., and were always receiving fresh

---

[22] Jerome, *Chronicle* (on Olympiad 105); Syncellus (ed. Dindorf) i. 486.

[23] See n. 13 above. Burkitt's emendation Γορδυαίαν (Kurdistan) for 'Ιουδαίαν (*Encyclopaedia Biblica* iv [London, 1903], col. 4992) has recently acquired fresh interest; as E. F. F. Bishop points out ("Professor Burkitt and the Geographical Catalogue", *Journal of Roman Studies* xlii [1952], pp. 84 f.), this reading has the support of a few Arabic MSS. of NT. The Bodleian MS. Canon. Or. 129 (Acts and the Epistles in Arabic) opens the geographical list with *Akrād* (plural of *Kurdi*)—a reading supported by the Old Cairo MS. 99 and by an early eighteenth-century Aleppo MS. of the complete NT in Arabic (in the library of the Maronite bishop), chiefly translated from the Peshitta, but not entirely, since its text of the geographical list agrees with that of the Bodleian MS. already mentioned.

accessions, especially since the Greek conquest of Egypt and the foundation of Alexandria in 331 B.C. Philo, an Alexandrian Jew himself, estimated in A.D. 38 that there were about a million Jews in Egypt; two out of the five wards which made up the city of Alexandria were Jewish in population (*On Flaccus* 6, 8). Jews of Cyrenaica are mentioned elsewhere in Acts (*cf*. Chs. 6:9; 11:20; 13:1). Ptolemy I of Egypt (323–283 B.C.) settled a number of Jews in Cyrenaica to ensure its loyalty.

It is noteworthy that the "sojourners from Rome, both Jews and proselytes," are the only contingent from the European mainland included in Luke's list. No doubt visitors from Greece were present as well, but they are not mentioned.[24] Luke, of course, is interested in Rome, because it is the goal to which the narrative of Acts is leading. But it is at least a possibility that the Roman church, whose origins are so obscure, may go back to some of these visitors from Rome who heard the gospel in Jerusalem on the day of Pentecost and carried it home to the imperial city. "By the autumn following the Crucifixion it is quite as possible that Jesus was honoured in the Jewish community at Rome as that He was at Damascus" (F. J. Foakes Jackson, *Peter, Prince of Apostles* [London, 1927], p. 195).[25]

There was a Jewish colony at Rome in the second century B.C., and it was augmented by the Jews who were brought there from Palestine in 62 B.C., to grace Pompey's triumph, and later set free. We have references in Roman inscriptions to at least seven Jewish synagogues in Rome.[26] It was probably the spread of Christian teaching in some of these synagogues that led to the Jewish riots of A.D. 49, in consequence of which Claudius expelled the Jews from Rome (*cf*. Ch. 18:2, and p. 368, n. 9).

Nowhere was Jewish proselytizing activity carried on more energetically than in Rome,[27] and it is not surprising that the Roman contingent included proselytes as well as Jews by birth.

[24] This is an argument against the Burkitt-Weinstock thesis referred to in n. 20 above; Paul of Alexandria's list places "Greece and Ionia" (under the sign of the Virgin) between Asia (under the Lion) and Libya and Cyrene (under the Scales).

[25] I have discussed this question more discursively in *The Dawn of Christianity* (London, 1950), pp. 155 ff.

[26] The synagogues of the Campenses, Augustenses, Agrippenses, Suburenses, Volumnenses, the "Hebrews" and the "Olive Tree."

[27] Even as late as the beginning of the second century, the poet Juvenal satirizes the proselytizing activity of Jews at Rome (*cf*. *Satire* xiv. 96–106).

A proselyte was a Gentile who undertook to keep the Jewish law in its entirety and was admitted into full fellowship with the people of Israel by a threefold rite: (1) circumcision (for male proselytes), (2) a purificatory self-baptism in the presence of witnesses,[28] and (3) the offering of a sacrifice.[29] Because of the first of these three requirements, full proselytization was more common among women than men. Many men were content with that looser attachment to the Jewish religion usually indicated by the term "God-fearers" (cf. pp. 215 f., on Ch. 10:2).

The catalogue is concluded with the reference to "Cretans and Arabians" (v. 11). Arabia in NT is the kingdom of the Nabataean Arabs, east of Syria and Palestine, stretching from the Red Sea to the Euphrates, with its capital at Petra. This kingdom was at the height of its power under Aretas IV (9 B.C.–A.D. 40).[30] This monarch's relations with Palestine may be illustrated by the fact that a daughter of his was the first wife of Herod Antipas, tetrarch of Galilee (4 B.C.–A.D. 39)—the wife whom he divorced in order to marry Herodias.[31]

All these visitors, then, heard the ecstatic exclamations of the apostles and their companions. The Jewish authorities in Palestine appear to have sanctioned the use of any language in reciting certain religious formularies—the Shema' ("Hear, O Israel ...", Deut. 6:4), the "Eighteen Benedictions,"[32] and the blessing invoked upon meals. The praises of God in various tongues were thus heard frequently in Jerusalem during the great festivals, when so many pilgrims from the Diaspora were present in the city. Now, to their surprise, these pilgrims heard the praises of God in all the tongues of the Diaspora being uttered by Galilaeans of all people! The event was surely nothing less than a reversal of the curse of Babel.[33]

[28] Cf. H. H. Rowley, "Jewish Proselyte Baptism and the Baptism of John", Hebrew Union College Annual xv (Cincinnati, 1940), pp. 313 ff.

[29] According to G. W. H. Lampe, The Seal of the Spirit (London, 1951), p. 83, this sacrifice "was not indispensable, and it was in any case probably a merely ideal or theoretical regulation, since there is no real evidence that this complex of ceremonies dates back to the days of the Temple."

[30] See II Cor. 11:32, and cf. pp. 203 ff. (on Ch. 9:23–25).

[31] Josephus, Antiquities xviii. 5.1–3.

[32] These eighteen ascriptions of blessing to God form the main element in the Jewish service of prayer. Cf. S. Singer, The Authorised Daily Prayer Book (London, 1939), pp. 44 ff.; B. F. Westcott, The Epistle to the Hebrews (London, 1892), pp. 208 ff.

[33] See J. G. Davies, "Pentecost and Glossolalia", JThS, NS iii (1952), pp.

12–13 The public amazement and perplexity spread. One kind of ecstasy is superficially very like another, and even the apostle Paul, who had the gift of *glossolalia* himself,[34] had to warn the Corinthian Christians that a stranger entering one of their meetings when they were all "speaking with tongues" would certainly conclude that they were mad (1 Cor. 14:23). So on this occasion there were some in the crowd who dismissed the strange event with a jibe: "They are filled with new wine"[35]—or rather, with sweet wine,[36] for though the vintage of the current year was still some months off, there were ways and means of keeping wine sweet all the year round.[37]

(c) Peter's Proclamation (Ch. 2:14–36)

14 But Peter, standing up with the eleven, lifted up his voice, and spake forth unto them, *saying*, Ye men of Judaea, and all ye that dwell at Jerusalem, be this known unto you, and give ear unto my words.

15 For these are not drunken, as ye suppose; seeing it is *but* the third hour of the day;

16 but this is that which hath been spoken through the prophet Joel:[38]

17 And it shall be in the last days, saith God,
I will pour forth of my Spirit upon all flesh:
And your sons and your daughters shall prophesy,
And your young men shall see visions,
And your old men shall dream dreams:

18 Yea and on my servants and on my handmaidens in those days
Will I pour forth of my Spirit; and they shall prophesy.[39]

228 ff., for an argument that "the account of Pentecost is dependent upon the account of Babel."

[34] *Cf.* 1 Cor. 14:18.

[35] *Cf.* the contrast in Eph. 5:18 between being "drunken with wine" and being "filled with the Spirit" (ARV margin: "filled in spirit").

[36] Gk. γλεῦκος. The words of Elihu in Job 32:19a, spoken under the constraint of the spirit within him, appear in LXX in a form which may be rendered: "My belly is like a bound wineskin fermenting with new (or 'sweet') wine" (Gk. γλεύκους ζέων).

[37] "If you wish to keep new wine sweet the whole year round," says the Roman writer Cato in his treatise *On Agriculture* (120), "put new wine in a jar, cover the stopper with pitch, place the jar in a fish-pond, take it out after the thirtieth day; you will have sweet wine all the year round."

[38] Cod. D and some other Western authorities omit "Joel."

[39] The Western text omits "and they shall prophesy" (probably by harmonization with OT text).

65

19 And I will show wonders in the heaven above,
   And signs on the earth beneath;
   Blood, and fire, and vapor of smoke:[40]
20 The sun shall be turned into darkness,
   And the moon into blood,
   Before the day of the Lord come,
   That great and notable *day*:
21 And it shall be, that whosoever shall call on the name
   of the Lord shall be saved.
22 Ye men of Israel, hear these words: Jesus of Nazareth, a man approved of God unto you by mighty
   works and wonders and signs which God did by him
   in the midst of you,[41] even as ye yourselves know;
23 him, being delivered up by the determinate counsel
   and foreknowledge of God, ye by the hand of lawless
   men did crucify[42] and slay:
24 whom God raised up, having loosed the pangs of death:
   because it was not possible that he should be holden
   of it.
25 For David saith concerning him,
   I beheld the Lord always before my face;
   For he is on my right hand, that I should not be moved:
26 Therefore my heart was glad, and my tongue rejoiced;
   Moreover my flesh also shall dwell in hope:
27 Because thou wilt not leave my soul unto Hades,
   Neither wilt thou give thy Holy One to see corruption.
28 Thou madest known unto me the ways of life;
   Thou shalt make me full of gladness with thy countenance.
29 Brethren, I may say unto you freely of the patriarch
   David, that he both died and was buried, and his tomb
   is with us unto this day.
30 Being therefore a prophet, and knowing that God had
   sworn with an oath to him, that of the fruit of his
   loins he would set *one* upon his throne;[43]
31 he foreseeing *this* spake of the resurrection of the
   Christ, that neither was he left unto Hades, nor did
   his flesh see corruption.

40 The Western text omits "Blood, and fire, and vapor of smoke."
41 The Western text has "us" (Gk. ἡμᾶς) for "you" (Gk. ὑμᾶς).
42 Gk. προσπήγνυμι (lit. "nail to . . .") and not the more usual σταυρόω (lit. "fasten to a stake").
43 The AV expansion, "that of the fruit of his loins, according to the flesh, he would raise up Christ to sit on his throne," goes back through the Byzantine text to a Western reading.

32 This Jesus did God raise up, whereof we all are witnesses.

33 Being therefore by the right hand of God exalted, and having received of the Father the promise of the Holy Spirit, he hath poured forth this,[44] which ye see and hear.

34 For David ascended not into the heavens: but he saith himself,

The Lord said unto my Lord, Sit thou on my right hand,

35 Till I make thine enemies the footstool of thy feet.

36 Let all the house of Israel therefore know assuredly, that God hath made him both Lord and Christ, this Jesus whom ye crucified.

The "speaking with tongues" had thus achieved a valuable purpose in gathering a large crowd around the disciples. Now Peter stood up, supported by his eleven fellow-apostles, and began to address those who had gathered round. Whatever account we may give of the geography of the first four verses of this chapter, it is difficult to think of a more appropriate setting for Peter's address than the outer court of the temple.

There is no suggestion that Peter's address was spoken in a tongue unknown to himself, although the verb translated "spake forth"[45] may be intended to indicate divine inspiration. The address is divided into two main sections: (i) an explanation of the phenomenon that had drawn the wondering multitude together (vv. 14-21); (ii) an outline of the *kerygma*,[46] the apostolic proclamation (vv. 22-36).

i. "This Is That" (vv. 14-21)

14-21 This part of the address opens with a brief rebuttal of the charge of drunkenness. If the charge itself was made in jest, there is good humour in Peter's dismissal of it: it is only the third hour since sunrise, he says, and therefore too early for them to have had any opportunity to drink to excess.

Then come words of tremendous import: "This is that which hath been spoken through the prophet Joel." Joel, like the other prophets, had spoken of what was going to take place "in the last

---

[44] Some Western authorities add "gift" after "this"; though probably not the authentic reading, it indicates the true meaning.

[45] Gk. ἀποφθέγγομαι, the same word as is translated "utterance" in v. 4.

[46] Gk. κήρυγμα, from κηρύσσω, "proclaim" as a herald (κῆρυξ).

days. (47) Peter's use of his prophecy announces that these days—the days of fulfilment—have arrived. In another place Peter himself tells how the prophets who foretold the coming manifestation of the grace of God "searched and inquired about this salvation; they inquired what person or time was indicated by the Spirit of Christ within them when predicting the sufferings of Christ and the subsequent glory" (1 Pet. 1:10 f., RSV). But now that Christ has been "manifested at the end of the times"[48] (1 Pet. 1:20), His apostles have no further need to search and inquire (as the prophets did) what person or time the prophetic Spirit pointed forward to; they *know* that the person is Jesus of Nazareth and that the time is that upon which they themselves have entered. The "last days" began with Christ's first advent and will end with His second advent; they are the days during which the age to come overlaps the present age (*cf.* p. 35). Hence the assurance with which Peter could quote the words of Joel and declare "This is that."

The quotation in vv. 17–21 is from Joel 2:28–32. Joel announces the coming of the day of the Lord, the day when He will act in righteousness and mercy. It is noteworthy that the context of Joel's prophecy contains a call to repentance in hope of divine forgiveness (Joel 2:12-14)—a call which is echoed by Peter later on (v. 38). But the prominent feature of the passage which Peter actually quotes is the prediction of the outpouring of God's Spirit "upon all flesh." Luke probably sees in these words an adumbration of the worldwide Gentile mission, even if Peter himself did not realize their full import when he quoted them on the day of Pentecost. Certainly the outpouring of the Spirit on a hundred and twenty Jews could not in itself fulfil the prediction of such outpouring "upon all flesh"; but it was the beginning of the fulfilment. The words as used by Joel may have harked back to Moses' exclamation, "Would that all Jehovah's people were prophets, that Jehovah would put his Spirit upon them!" (Num. 11:29). The effect

[47] The words "in the last days" are not found in the OT text of Joel 2:28, either MT or LXX; but no doubt they give the sense of Joel's expression "afterward" (for the phrase "in the last days" *cf.* Isa. 2:2; Mic. 4:1). There are other variations from the OT text in this citation: in OT "And your young men shall see visions" follows and does not precede the parallel prophecy about the old men; the words "and they shall prophesy" (v. 18) are absent from OT, as also are the words "above," "signs" and "beneath" (v. 19). In v. 20 "notable" (Gk. ἐπιφανής) follows LXX; MT has *nora*, "terrible" (LXX may imply a variant Hebrew reading *nir'eh*, "conspicuous").

[48] *Cf.* also 1 Cor. 10:11; Heb. 1:2; 9:26.

of the Spirit's outpouring is the prophetic gift, exercised in visions and dreams and by word of mouth.

The wonders and signs to be revealed in the world of nature, as described in vv. 19 and 20,[49] may have more relevance in the present context than is sometimes realized: it was little more than seven weeks since the people in Jerusalem had indeed seen the sun turned into darkness, during the early afternoon of the day of our Lord's crucifixion. And on the same afternoon the paschal full moon may well have appeared blood-red in the sky in consequence of that preternatural gloom.[50] These were to be understood as tokens of the advent of the day of the Lord, "that great and notable day," a day of judgment, to be sure, but more immediately the day of God's salvation to all who invoked His name.

ii. The Apostolic Preaching (vv. 22–36)

22–24   Peter now went on to his main theme: the proclamation of Jesus as Lord and Messiah. The early apostolic *kerygma* regularly falls into four parts, which may be summarized thus: (1) the announcement that the age of fulfilment has arrived; (2) a rehearsal of the ministry, death and triumph of Jesus: (3) citation of OT scriptures whose fulfilment in these events prove Jesus to be the Messiah; (4) a call to repentance. These four elements are present in Peter's proclamation here. He has already announced that the age of fulfilment has come (vv. 16ff.); now he rehearses the story of Jesus.

The "mighty works and wonders and signs" which God accomplished through Jesus of Nazareth[51] in the midst of the "men of Israel" needed no elaboration; they were fresh in the minds of all. That these acts were indeed performed by divine power had been

---

[49] *Cf.* the description of the Day of Wrath in Rev. 6:12, based on this same prophecy of Joel.

[50] It could not have been a solar eclipse, because the moon was full at the Passover festival. (On the text of Luke 23:44 f., see N. Geldenhuys's *Commentary on Luke* [London and Grand Rapids, 1950], p. 616, n. 19.)

[51] More strictly, "Jesus the Nazoraean" (Gk. Ἰησοῦν τὸν Ναζωραῖον, v. 22). In spite of a variety of other explanations of the title Ναζωραῖος as used of Jesus, it seems clear that the NT writers took it as synonymous with Ναζαρηνός ("belonging to Nazareth"). There is no difference in intention between Ἰησοῦν τὸν Ναζωραῖον here and Ἰησοῦν τὸν ἀπὸ Ναζαρέθ in Ch. 10:38. The form Ναζωραῖος is equivalent to Heb. *Notzri* ("Nazarene"), being derived more immediately from an Aramaic form *Netzorai*, which has undergone a vowel-shift. The anomalous ζ in the Greek word as the equivalent of Semitic צ may be simply accounted for by a false analogy with Ναζιραῖος, "Nazirite." See G. F. Moore, "Nazarene and Nazareth" in *Beginnings* ii (London, 1920), pp. 426 ff.; W. O. E. Oesterley, "Nazarene and Nazareth", ExT lii (1940–1),

generally acknowledged except by those who saw that such an acknowledgment would involve undesirable theological implications.[52] The miracles of Jesus were not mere "wonders"; they were "mighty works," evidences of the power of God operating among them; they were "signs" of the kingdom of God, "the powers of the age to come" (Heb. 6:5).[53] "If I by the finger of God cast out demons," said Jesus, "then is the kingdom of God come upon you" (Luke 11:20). And the generality of those who saw His mighty works agreed: "God hath visited his people" (Luke 7:16).[54]

Yet this Jesus had been put to death by crucifixion. While the hands that carried out the grisly work of crucifixion were the hands of "lawless men"—that is to say, the Romans, who were outside the range of the law received by Israel[55]—yet the instigators of the act were Jews. It was the chief-priestly leaders of the people who engineered His death; it was the Jerusalem mob, egged on by those leaders, who yelled "Crucify him!" But all who took part, directly or indirectly, in putting Him to death were unconsciously fulfilling "the determinate counsel and foreknowledge of God." For the purpose of God, revealed through His prophets, was that the Messiah should suffer (cf. Luke 24:25, 46; Acts 17:3; 26:23). This carries with it no diminution of the guilt of those who handed Him over to death and carried the sentence out; but it does point the way to the removal of their guilt and the assurance of divine pardon. Peter, however, says nothing about this until his audience are truly convicted of their sin.

The sentence which Jesus' human judges passed upon Him and

pp. 410 ff.; W. F. Albright, "The Names 'Nazareth' and 'Nazoraean'," JBL lxv (1946), pp. 397 ff.; M. Black, *An Aramaic Approach to the Gospels and Acts* (Oxford, 1946), pp. 143 ff. *Cf.* also the use of the plural Ναζωραῖοι for the followers of Jesus in Ch. 24:5 (p. 465, n. 7).

[52] *Cf.* Luke 11:15 for the charge that He cast out demons by the power of Beelzebul.

[53] *Cf.* D. S. Cairns, *The Faith that Rebels* (London, 1929); A. Richardson, *The Miracle-Stories of the Gospels* (London, 1941); F. F. Bruce, *Are the NT Documents Reliable?* (London, 1943), pp. 60 ff.

[54] The Greek word for "miracles" (τέρατα) is never used in NT except in conjunction with the word for "signs" (Gk. σημεῖα). Here a third word, "mighty works" (Gk. δυνάμεις) is added to make the significance of these miracles even plainer; *cf.* Heb. 2:4.

[55] Gk. ἄνομοι. As for the more general sense of the word (*cf.* AV "wicked"), it is relevant that the Romans are frequently referred to in Jewish literature as *ha-resha'im*, "the wicked"; the Roman Empire is described as Jewish as *malkuth ha-resha'im*, "the kingdom of the wicked."

70

His human executioners carried out has been reversed, Peter asserts, by a higher court. They put Him to death, but God raised Him up and loosed the bonds of death[56] which bound Him; it was not possible that God's Messiah should remain in the grip of death. If Messiah's suffering was ordained by the determinate counsel of God, so was His resurrection and glory.

25–28   Now comes an OT "testimony" in confirmation of Peter's claim. This quotation is from Ps. 16:8–11, in the LXX version.[57] From the earliest days, the Christian church maintained that the exaltation of Jesus took place in direct fulfilment of God's promises to David (*cf.* the quotation from Isa. 55:3 in Acts 13:34). In the psalm here quoted (Peter's argument runs), the words cannot refer to David, for his soul did go to the abode of the dead and his flesh did undergo corruption; no one would claim that David had been rescued from the grave. The words "thou wilt not abandon my soul to Hades, nor let thy Holy One see corruption (RSV) refer therefore to King Messiah, "great David's greater Son," whom David himself prefigured and in whose name he spoke these words by the Spirit of prophecy. (That a messianic interpretation of the words was current in Jewish tradition is suggested by the gloss on Ps. 16:9 in *Midrash Tehillim,* "my glory rejoices over King Messiah.") These prophetic words, Peter goes on to argue, were fulfilled in Jesus of Nazareth and in no one else; Jesus of Nazareth is therefore the promised Messiah.

29–32   It is needless to demonstrate that the words of Ps. 16 were not literally fulfilled in "the patriarch[58] David," said Peter;

---

[56] Gk. λύσας τὰς ὠδῖνας τοῦ θανάτου, "having loosed the pangs (lit. birth-pangs) of death" (v. 24). The Hebrew phrases *heble maweth,* "the cords of death" (Pss. 18:4 and 116:3), and *heble she'ol,* "the cords of Sheol" (Ps. 18:5), are rendered in LXX ὠδῖνες θανάτου and ὠδῖνες ᾅδου respectively, because of the similarity between Heb. *hebel* ("cord") and *hēbel* ("pang"). The rabbis spoke of the *heblo shel Mashiach,* "the birth-pangs of Messiah," in reference to the sorrows which would precede the messianic age (*cf.* Mark 13:8); here the pangs are endured by Messiah Himself in His death. Polycarp appears to echo this passage of Acts in his *Epistle to the Philippians* 1:2, written *c.* A.D. 120 (λύσας τὰς ὠδῖνας τοῦ ᾅδου, "having loosed the pangs of Hades").

[57] LXX has "I beheld" (Gk. προορώμην) for MT "I have set" (Heb. *shiwwithi*), and "my tongue" for MT "my glory" (Heb. *kebodi*); it renders Heb. *la-betach* ("in safety", "secure") by ἐπ᾽ ἐλπίδι ("in hope"), and Heb. *shachath* ("pit"; *cf.* ARV margin and RSV text of Ps. 16:10) by διαφθορά, "destruction" or "corruption."

[58] The Gk. word πατριάρχης (v. 29) properly denotes the founder or ancestor of a family, and is thus used of Abraham (Heb. 7:4) and of the twelve

71

everyone knows that he died and was buried in a tomb which could still be pointed out—to the south of the city, near Siloam. But David had already received a solemn promise from God, as Ps. 132:11 declares:

> Jehovah hath sworn unto David in truth;
> He will not turn from it:
> Of the fruit of thy body will I set upon thy throne.[59]

It was with regard to that descendant of his of whom the promise spoke that David, as an inspired prophet, uttered words betokening deliverance from the corruption of the grave and resurrection from the dead. And in asserting that Jesus of Nazareth had been so delivered and raised by God, Peter and his colleagues were making a claim which they could confirm by their personal ocular testimony: "This Jesus did God raise up, *whereof we all are witnesses.*"

33–35 But where was He now, if He was risen from the dead? He was set on high, exalted by God's right hand,[60] and having received from His Father the promised gift of the Holy Spirit, He had now poured out that Spirit upon His followers on earth, and all Peter's hearers had just witnessed the external tokens of this outpouring. The triumph of Jesus was attested by the testimony of His disciples and the testimony of OT prophecy, as it was also to be attested by His own enduring activity (Chs. 3:6; 4:10, etc.) and by the witness of the Holy Spirit (Ch. 5:32).

He who had earlier received the Spirit for the public discharge of His own messianic ministry had now received the same Spirit to impart to His representatives on earth, in order that they might continue the ministry which He began. His present impartation of the Spirit to them, attended as it was by sensible signs, was a further open vindication of the claim that He was the exalted Messiah. And the claim was clinched by another Scripture proof, this time from Ps. 110:1. The general belief that this too was a Davidic psalm, and that the "lord" to whom the words "Sit thou on my right hand" were spoken by God was the Messiah, is attested in the well-known Gospel incident recorded in Mark 12 : 35 ff (*cf.*

---

sons of Jacob (Ch. 7:8 f. below; *cf.* p. 148, n. 35). It is used of David here because he was the founder of a royal dynasty.

[59] *Cf.* Ch. 7:46 f. (p. 157 below) for another allusion to this psalm.

[60] There may be a reference here to Ps. 118:16 in the LXX version: "The right hand of the Lord has exalted me" (δεξιὰ κυρίου ὕψωσέν με). (MT reads differently: "The right hand of Jehovah is exalted.")

Matt. 22:41 ff.; Luke 20:41 ff.).[61] The argument here is similar to that already based on Ps. 16; David did not ascend to heaven in person, to take his seat at God's right hand;[62] the words point to Messiah, and have found their fulfilment in Jesus of Nazareth. He has been exalted not only *by* God's right hand (as v. 33 says), but *to* God's right hand, to the place of supremacy over the universe, in fulfilment of His own assurance to His judges: "From henceforth shall the Son of man be seated at the right hand of the power of God" (Luke 22:69). This exaltation of Jesus, in accordance with Ps. 110:1, is an integral part of the primitive apostolic message, as it has remained an integral element in the historic Christian creeds.

36 The gospel message has been proclaimed: the witness of the apostles and the testimony of prophecy have combined to give assurance of the truth of the proclamation. The attested facts point to one conclusion. "Let all the house of Israel[63] therefore know assuredly that God has made him both Lord and Christ, this Jesus whom you crucified" (RSV). Again the contrast is pointed between their treatment of Jesus, and God's. He claimed to be the Messiah, the Son of the Blessed (Mark 14 : 61). The Sanhedrin rejected His claim as blasphemous, and condemned Him to death. But God vindicated His claim as true, and brought Him back from death, exalting Him at His own right hand as Lord and Messiah.[64] His Messiahship was acclaimed at His baptism, and confirmed by His resurrection: He was "declared to be the Son of God with power ... by the resurrection from the dead" (Rom. 1:4). But He was exalted not only as Messiah, but as Lord. The first apostolic sermon leads up to the first apostolic creed: "Jesus is Lord" (*cf.* Rom. 10:9; I Cor. 12:3; Phil. 2:11)—"Lord" not only as the bearer of a courte-

---

[61] *Cf.* the use made of Ps. 110 in I Cor. 15:25; Heb. 1:13; 5:6 ff.

[62] David's body remained in his tomb, mentioned in v. 29 (where there may be an implied contrast between the still occupied tomb of David and the vacated tomb of Christ). Plainly, therefore, it was not David who sat enthroned at the right hand of the majesty on high.

[63] For the phrase "all the house of Israel" *cf.* Ezek. 37:11. It appears also in the Jewish liturgy in a well-known Aramaic prayer, the *Qaddish*:
"Magnified and sanctified be His great name
In the world which He created according to His will:
May He establish His kingdom during your life and during your days,
And during the life of *all the house of Israel*, speedily and
at a near time.
And say ye, Amen."

[64] *Cf.* the conjunction of the two titles, χριστὸς κύριος ("Christ the Lord"), in Luke 2:11 and also in the *Psalms of Solomon* 17:36.

sy title, but as bearer of "the name which is above every name" (Phil. 2:9). To a Jew, there was only one name "above every name"—the Ineffable Name of the God of Israel, represented in synagogue reading and in the LXX text by the title "Lord."[65] And that the apostles meant to give Jesus the title "Lord" in this highest sense of all is indicated by the way in which they do not hesitate on occasion to apply to Him passages of OT scripture referring to Jehovah.[66] Indeed, in this very context it may well be that the promise "that whosoever shall call on the name of Jehovah shall be delivered" (Joel 2:32) is viewed as being fulfilled in those members of Peter's audience who repentantly invoke Jesus as Lord.

(d) The Call to Repentance (Ch. 2:37–42)

37 Now when they heard *this*, they were pricked in their heart, and said unto Peter and the rest of the apostles, Brethren, what shall we do?[67]

38 And Peter *said* unto them, Repent ye, and be baptized every one of you in the name of[68] Jesus Christ unto the remission of your sins; and ye shall receive the gift of the Holy Spirit.

39 For to you is the promise, and to your children,[69] and to all that afar off, *even* as many as the Lord our God shall call unto him.

40 And with many other words he testified, and exhorted them, saying, Save yourselves from this crooked generation.

[65] The name whose consonantal skeleton is YHWH came to be regarded as so sacred among the Jews that it might not be pronounced. In MT it is usually supplied with the vowel points of *'Adonai*, "Lord", that the reader may know to pronounce that title in place of the Ineffable Name. Similarly, in LXX it is regularly represented by κύριος ("Lord") without the definite article. In Ps. 110:1 (LXX), quoted in v. 34 (εἶπεν κύριος τῷ κυρίῳ μου ...), the first κύριος represents YHWH; the second occurrence of the word, this time preceded by the definite article, represents Heb. *'adon*, a common noun meaning "lord." But when Peter says that God has made Jesus "Lord," he gives that title a fullness of meaning far beyond that of a mere courtesy title. Cf. V. Taylor, *The Names of Jesus* (London, 1953), pp. 38 ff.

[66] See, *e.g.*, the application of Isa. 45:23 in Phil. 2:10 ("that in the name of *Jesus* every knee should bow"), and of Isa. 8:13 in 1 Pet. 3:15 ("sanctify in your hearts *Christ* as Lord").

[67] Various Western authorities omit "the rest of" before "the apostles"; and frame the following question thus: "What shall we do then, brethren? Show us."

[68] The Western text inserts "the Lord" before "Jesus Christ."

[69] The Western text reads "to us . . . and to our children" (*cf.* n. 41).

41 They then that received his word were baptized: and there were added *unto them* in that day about three thousand souls.

42 And they continued stedfastly in the apostles' teaching[70] and fellowship, in the breaking of bread and the prayers.

37–38 Peter's preaching had been effective, not only convincing his hearer's minds but convicting their consciences. If Jesus of Nazareth was indeed the appointed Messiah, then no guilt could be greater than of treating Him as He had been treated. They had refused Him in whom all their hope of salvation rested; what hope of salvation was left to them now? Well might they cry out in anguish of heart, "Brethren, what shall we do?" Peter's reply was unspeakably reassuring. Incredible as it must appear, he told them that there was hope for them even now. Let them repent of their sin and turn to God; let them submit to baptism in the name of Jesus, confessed as Messiah; and their sins would be forgiven—nay more; they too would receive the gift of the Holy Spirit which had been bestowed upon the apostles themselves but an hour or two before.

"Acts 2 : 38 assuredly confronts the interpreter with weighty problems," says Professor Stonehouse (WThJ xiii [1950–1], p. 5).[71] The extent and diversity of the theological exegesis of the verse show how right he is. The call to repentance, which is "Peter's basic and primary demand"[72] here, raises little difficulty. Plainly a complete change of heart, a spiritual right-about-turn, was essential in those who had so lately rejected their Messiah, not recognizing Him in Jesus of Nazareth, if they were to enjoy the salvation which He came to earth to procure for them and which He was now offering them from His place of exaltation. The call to repentance, already sounded by John the Baptist and by Jesus in the years preceding the crucifixion (*cf.* Matt. 3:2; 4:17, etc.), remained an essential element in the proclamation of the Christian message (*cf.* Chs. 3:19; 8:22; 17:30; 20:21; 26:20).

But with the call to repentance a call to baptism is conjoined. And apparently the command to be baptized occasioned no surprise. The practice of baptism was tolerably familiar to Peter's

---

[70] The Western text adds "in Jerusalem."

[71] In his article on "Repentance, Baptism and the Gift of the Holy Spirit" (*op. cit.*, pp. 1 ff.), a valuable contribution to the exegesis of this and certain other passages in Acts (Chs. 8:16; 10:44 ff. with 11:15 ff.; 19:1 ff.).

[72] Stonehouse, *op. cit.*, p. 15.

audience; in particular, John the Baptist had proclaimed "the baptism of repentance unto remission of sins" (Mark 1:4; *cf.* Acts 13:24; 18:25; 19:3 f.). As John's converts were required to receive baptism in water as the outward and visible sign of their repentance, so Peter's convicted hearers were now required to submit to it. But there are now two new features in the rite of water-baptism: it is administered "in the name of Jesus Christ" and it is associated with "the gift of the Holy Spirit." Christian baptism "is still an eschatological rite, for it looks forward to the final redemption which is still to come at the Lord's return in glory; but, considered in relation to John's baptism, it represents a realization and fulfilment of Israel's hope" (G. W. H. Lampe, *The Seal of the Spirit* [London, 1951], p. 33).

It is administered "in the name of Jesus Christ"[73]—probably in the sense that the person being baptized confessed or invoked Jesus as Messiah (*cf.* Ch. 22:16). In addition, the person who baptized the convert appears to have named the name of Christ over him as he was being baptized (*cf.* Ch. 15:17; Jas. 2:7). And it is associated with the gift of the Holy Spirit. Here a number of interpreters have been conscious of a discrepancy with Ch. 1:5.[74] There the coming baptism "in the Holy Spirit" appears to supersede John's baptism "with water" (and *cf.* John's own words in Luke 3:6 and parallels). But here there is no suggestion that water-baptism is to be superseded by Spirit-baptism; the Spirit-baptism has been conferred indeed, but water-baptism remains in force, although it is now given a richer significance in consequence of the saving work of Christ and the descent of the Spirit. The baptism of the Spirit which it was our Lord's prerogative to bestow was, strictly speaking, something that took place once for all on the day of Pentecost when He poured forth "the promise of the Father" on His disciples and thus constituted them the new people of God;[75] baptism in

---

[73] The preposition ἐν ("in") is probably used here in an instrumental sense; "the name of Jesus Christ" (to use grammarians' jargon) was an "accompanying circumstance" of the baptism. We need not think of a precise formula here. The expression recurs in Ch. 10:48. For the similar, but not identical εἰς τὸ ὄνομα τοῦ κυρίου Ἰησοῦ (Chs. 8:16; 19:5), see p. 181, n. 32.

[74] *Cf.* Jackson and Lake in *Beginnings* i (London, 1920), pp. 338 ff.

[75] This is not a denial of the vital unity of the people of God under the New Covenant with the people of God in earlier days; it means that the new beginning to which OT believers had looked forward was now an accomplished fact in the experience of those upon whom the Spirit came on the day of Pentecost.

water continued to be the external sign by which individuals who believed the gospel message, repented of their sins, and acknowledged Jesus as Lord, were publicly incorporated into the Spirit-baptized fellowship of the new people of God.[76] When the matter is viewed thus, the discrepancy disappears.[77]

It would, of course, be a mistake to link the words "unto the remission of your sins" with the command "be baptized" to the exclusion of the prior command "Repent ye." It is against the whole genius of Biblical religion to suppose that the outward rite had any value except in so far as it was accompanied by true repentance within. In a similar passage in the following chapter, the blotting out of the people's sins is a direct consequence of their repenting and turning to God (Ch. 3:19);[78] nothing is said there about baptism, although it is no doubt implied (the idea of an unbaptized Christian is simply not entertained in NT). So too the reception of the Spirit here is associated not with baptism in itself but with baptism as the visible token of repentance.

We must distinguish the *gift* of the Spirit from the *gifts* of the Spirit. The *gift* of the Spirit is the Spirit Himself, bestowed by the Father through the Messiah; the *gifts* of the Spirit are those spiritual faculties which the Spirit imparts, "dividing to each one severally even as he will" (I Cor. 12:11). Now it is true, as has frequently been pointed out, that Luke thinks of the receiving of the Spirit in particular relation to the impressive outward manifestations which so commonly accompanied that inward experience in the apostolic age;[79] but the free gift which is promised in v. 38 to those who repent and are baptized is the Holy Spirit Himself. This gift of the Spirit may comprehend a variety of gifts of the Spirit, but first and foremost "the saving benefits of Christ's work as applied to the believer by the Spirit."[80] The relation between

[76] Cf. 1 Cor. 12:13, "in one Spirit were we all baptized into one body, whether Jews or Greeks . . ."

[77] Among recent works see H. G. Marsh, *The Origin and Significance of NT Baptism* (Manchester, 1941); F. J. Leenhardt, *Le baptême chrétien* (Paris, 1944); K. Barth, *The Teaching of the Church regarding Baptism* (Eng. tr., London, 1948); W. F. Flemington, *The NT Doctrine of Baptism* (London, 1948); O. Cullmann, *Baptism in the NT* (Eng. tr., London, 1950); G. W. H. Lampe, *The Seal of the Spirit* (London, 1951); J. Murray, *Christian Baptism* (Philadelphia, 1952); H. H. Rowley, *The Unity of the Bible* (London, 1953), pp. 149 ff.

[78] "Repentance will bring refreshing from on high, evidently through the work of the Spirit" (Stonehouse, *op. cit.*, p. 15).

[79] Cf. Lampe, *op. cit.*, pp. 47 f.

[80] Stonehouse, *op. cit.*, p. 16.

these saving benefits and the work of Christ by which they are made available to men is not explicitly set out by Luke in the present context, but it is implicit here and stated more expressly elsewhere in his record.

There is no suggestion here that the reception of the Spirit by those who believed[81] was conditional upon their having apostolic hands laid upon them. To be sure, in such a brief summary various details would inevitably be left out; but if Luke did believe that the laying on of hands was an indispensable prerequisite for the bestowal of the Spirit (as some have precariously inferred from Ch. 8:16), it is remarkable that he has nothing to say about it in this Pentecostal narrative.[82]

39 The promise of the gospel was extended not only to those present on that occasion, not only to the contemporary generation, but to their descendants as well;[83] not only to the people of Jerusalem, but to those of distant lands (and, as soon appeared, not only to Jews, but to Gentiles as well). Here two OT passages are brought together—Isa. 57:19 ("Peace, peace, to him that is far off and to him that is near, saith Jehovah") and Joel 2:32, where the words quoted by Peter in vv. 17–21 above are continued thus: "for in mount Zion and in Jerusalem there shall be those that escape, as Jehovah hath said, and among the remnant those whom Jehovah doth call." Those who call upon the name of the Lord are those whom the Lord Himself has called—and called effectually.

40 In this way, then, Peter bore his reasoned witness to the gospel facts and to the promise of salvation. The generation to which his hearers belonged had been upbraided by Jesus Himself as a "faithless and perverse generation" (Luke 9:41), as an "evil generation" because of its repudiation of Him whom God sent as Israel's anointed Saviour (Luke 11:29; 17:25). But there was a way of deliverance from the judgment which such faithlessness inevitably incurred. The salvation of which Joel had spoken was to

---

[81] Believing is not explicitly mentioned in v. 38, but it is certainly implied, as is confirmed by the opening words of v. 44.

[82] See Lampe, *op. cit.*, pp. 64 ff., with the literature to which he refers. Note his answer to the view that "be baptized" in v. 38 is used by synecdoche to cover the whole initiatory rite, including the imposition of apostolic hands: "there is absolutely no evidence to support it, so far as the New Testament is concerned . . ." (p. 68). *Cf.* pp. 181 ff. (on Ch. 8:16).

[83] *Cf.* the promises to Noah (Gen. 9:9), Abraham (Gen. 13:15; 17:7 ff.; Gal. 3:16); and David (Ps. 18:50; 89:34 ff.; 132:11 f.).

be enjoyed by a "remnant" of the whole people; so now Peter urged his hearers to make sure by repentant calling upon the Lord that they would belong to this remnant and so save themselves from that "crooked generation." The new believing community was, in fact, the faithful remnant of the old Israel and at the same time the nucleus of the new Israel, the Christian church.

41-42 Those of Peter's hearers, accordingly, who believed his message were baptized in token of their repentance, for the remission of their sins. We are certainly intended to understand that they also received the Holy Spirit, although this is not said in so many words. Their numbers amounted to three thousand—a much larger company won in a single day than Jesus had secured to His allegiance in two or three years of public ministry. No wonder that He told His disciples that, as a result of His returning to His Father, they would perform greater works than they had ever seen Him do (John 14:12).

The three thousand converts were then formed into a distinct community, the apostolic fellowship, constituted on the basis of the apostolic teaching. The apostolic teaching was authoritative because it was the teaching of the Lord communicated *through* the apostles.[84] In due course this apostolic teaching took written shape in the NT scriptures. To this day the apostolic succession, on which many ecclesiologists lay such emphasis, is most readily recognizable in those Christian churches which continue stedfastly in the apostles' teaching.

The fellowship which this new community enjoyed was expressed in a number of practical ways, of which two are mentioned in v. 42—"the breaking of bread and the prayers." The "breaking of bread" here denotes something more than the ordinary partaking of food together: the regular observance of the Lord's Supper is no doubt indicated. While this observance appears to have formed part of an ordinary meal, the emphasis on the act of breaking the bread, "a circumstance wholly trivial in itself," suggests that this was "the significant element of the celebration. ... But it could only be significant when it was a 'signum', viz. of Christ's being broken in death" (R. Otto, *The Kingdom of God and the Son of Man* [Eng.tr., London, 1943], p. 315). As for "the prayers" in

[84] For the authority of the apostles' teaching *cf.* 1 Cor. 12:28; 14:37; Eph. 2:20; 3:5. On the wider implications of v. 42 see P. H. Menoud, *La Vie de l'Eglise Naissante* (Neuchatel and Paris, 1952).

which they took part together, the primary reference is probably to their own appointed seasons for united prayer within the new community, although we know that they attended the public Jewish prayers as well (cf. Ch. 3:1).

(e) The First Christian Church (Ch. 2:43–47)

43 And fear came upon every soul: and many wonders and signs were done through the apostles.[85]

44 And all that believed were together, and had all things common;

45 and they sold their possessions and goods, and parted them[86] to all, according as any man had need.

46 And day by day, continuing stedfastly with one accord in the temple, and breaking bread at home, they took their food with gladness and singleness of heart,

47 praising God, and having favor with all the people.[87] And the Lord added to them[88] day by day those that were saved.

43 The conviction of sin that followed Peter's preaching was no momentary panic, but filled the people with a long-lasting sense of awe. This impression was intensified by the wonders and signs which the apostles performed. The words of Joel which Peter had quoted at the outset of his address declared that the "great and notable day" would be heralded not only by "wonders in the heaven above" but also by "signs on the earth beneath" (vv. 19 f.). Among the signs on the earth may surely be reckoned the "mighty works and wonders and signs" (v. 22) which God performed through Jesus of Nazareth, thus accrediting His messianic office. And just as the miracles of Jesus when He was on earth were "signs" of the kingdom of God, the miracles performed by His apostles partook of the same character (cf. Ch. 3:6).

44–45 In addition to the expressions of fellowship mentioned in v. 42, the members of the new community, living together[89] thus

---

[85] Codd. ℵ A C and some other authorities add: "in Jerusalem; and great fear was upon all."

[86] The Western text reads: "And as many as had possessions and goods sold them, and parted them daily . . ."

[87] The Western text reads "all the world"—perhaps a Semitic idiom meaning "everybody" (like French *tout le monde*).

[88] The Western text adds a gloss, "in the church."

[89] The Greek phrase ἐπὶ τὸ αὐτό, translated "together" in v. 44 and "to them" (ARV margin, "together") in v. 47, seems to have acquired a semi-technical sense, "in church fellowship." Cf. J. H. Moulton and W. F. Howard, *Grammar of NT Greek* ii (Edinburgh, 1929), p. 473.

with a deep sense of their unity in the Messiah, gave up the idea of private property and "had all things common." Those who had landed property, as well as those whose belongings were of a more portable character, began to sell their assets and divide the proceeds among the members of the community, according to individual need.[90] This pooling of property could be maintained only when their sense of the unity of the Spirit was exceptionally active; as soon as the flame began to burn a little lower, the attempt to maintain the communal life was beset with serious difficulties (*cf.* Chs. 4:32–5:11).

46–47 Day by day, then, in the weeks that followed the first Christian Pentecost, the believers met regularly in the temple precincts for public worship and public witness, while they took their fellowship meals in each other's homes and "broke the bread" in accordance with their Master's ordinance. The place in the temple where they seem habitually to have gathered was Solomon's colonnade, running along the east side of the outer court (*cf.* Chs. 3:11; 5:12). The community was organized along the lines of the voluntary type of association called a *haburah*, a central feature of which was the communal meal. The communal meal could not conveniently be eaten in the temple precincts, so they ate "by households", as we may translate the Greek phrase (AV "from house to house" gives the sense fairly well).[91] Within the community there was a spirit of rejoicing and generosity;[92] outside, they enjoyed great popular good-will. They ascribed all glory to God, and their numbers were constantly increased as more and more believers in Jesus were added by Him to the faithful remnant.[93] It is the Lord whose prerogative it is to add new members to His own community; it is the joyful duty of the community to welcome to their ranks those whom Christ has accepted (*cf.* Rom. 15:7).

[90] It is unnecessary to restrict this action to those Jews who had come to Jerusalem from their homes in the Diaspora and bought burial-plots in the Holy Land so as to enjoy certain advantages on the day of resurrection, as is suggested by K. Bornhäuser, *Studien zur Apostelgeschichte* (Gütersloh, 1934).

[91] Gk. κατ' οἶκον. The papyri illustrate the rendering "by households."

[92] Gk. ἀφελότης καρδίας may be rendered "generosity of heart"; *cf.* ἐν ἁπλότητι (τῆς) καρδίας in much the same sense in Eph. 6:5; Col. 3:22.

[93] In view of the way in which σώζω is used in vv. 21 and 40 we might almost translate τοὺς σωζομένους here as "the remnant."

81

3. A MIRACLE AND ITS CONSEQUENCES
(Ch. 3:1–4:31)

(a) A Lame Man Healed (Ch. 3:1–10)

1 Now Peter and John were going up into the temple[1] at the hour of prayer, *being* the ninth *hour*.

2 And a certain man that was lame from his mother's womb was carried, whom they laid daily at the door of the temple which is called Beautiful, to ask alms of them that entered into the temple;

3 who seeing Peter and John about to go into the temple. asked to receive an alms.

4 And Peter, fastening his eyes upon him, with John. said, Look on us.

5 And he gave heed unto them, expecting to receive something from them.

6 But Peter said, Silver and gold have I none; but what I have, that give I thee. In the name of Jesus Christ of Nazareth, walk.[2]

7 And he took him by the right hand, and raised him up: and immediately[3] his feet and his ankle-bones received strength.

8 And leaping up, he stood, and began to walk;[4] and he entered with them into the temple, walking, and leaping, and praising God.

9 And all the people saw him walking and praising God:

10 and they took knowledge of him, that it was he that sat for alms at the Beautiful Gate of the temple; and they were filled with wonder and amazement at that which had happened unto him.

1–3 "Many wonders and signs were done through the apostles," we were told in Ch. 2:43; Luke now gives us a fuller account of one of these, selecting one which received considerable publicity.

[1] After "temple" there is a Western addition, "for the evening (oblation)."

[2] The Byzantine text, with the Latin Vulgate and Syriac versions, reads "rise and walk."

[3] The Western text inserts "he stood up and."

[4] The Western text adds "rejoicing and exulting."

The apostles continued to live as observant Jews, attending the set seasons of worship in the temple at Jerusalem. One afternoon, as two of them, Peter and John,[5] were going up to the Court of Israel[6] for the service of prayer which accompanied the evening oblation (about 3 p.m.),[7] they were arrested by the sight of a lame man who lay begging on the steps which led up to the Beautiful Gate, as it was called. This was probably the gate, elsewhere called the Nicanor Gate,[8] through which one passed from the Court of the Gentiles into the Court of the Women. The name here given to it may be the more easily understood if it is further identified with a gate of Corinthian bronze described by Josephus, of such exquisite workmanship that it "far exceeded in value those gates that were plated with silver and set in gold" (*Jewish War*, v. 5.3).

4–6 Fixing his eyes on the lame man, Peter attracted his attention. When he looked up expectantly, he received something far more wonderful and valuable than the largest gift of alms that a charitable passer-by had ever bestowed upon him. "I have no silver or gold," said Peter, "but I give you what I have to give: in

---

[5] We may be sure that this John was Peter's fellow-apostle, the son of Zebedee.

[6] The Court of Israel was that part of the temple area to which Jewish laymen were admitted. The outer court of the temple as rebuilt and extended by Herod did not form part of the sacred area; Gentiles might walk about in it, and it was therefore called the Court of the Gentiles (*cf.* p. 158, with n. 72, on Ch. 7:46 f.). From the Court of the Gentiles, after ascending some steps, one might pass through the barrier which separated the outer court from the inner courts. Notices in Greek and Latin were fixed to this barrier, warning Gentiles not to penetrate farther, on pain of death (*cf.* pp. 433 f., with nn. 42–45, on Ch. 21:28 f.). Nine gates led through the barrier, of which the Beautiful Gate was probably one (see n. 8). The first of the inner courts was the Court of the Women, containing the treasury (*cf.* Mark 12:41 ff.): it was so called because Jewish women might enter thus far, but no farther. Jewish laymen might go farther, into the Court of Israel. Beyond this was the Court of the Priests, reserved for priests and Levites in the discharge of their respective duties; within this court stood the sanctuary building itself, with its two compartments, the Holy Place and the Holy of Holies.

[7] For the evening oblation *cf.* Ex. 29:39 ff. Josephus says that public sacrifices were offered in the temple "twice daily, in the early morning and about the ninth hour" (*Antiquities* xiv. 4.3). A service of public prayer accompanied these two sacrifices and there was a further service at sunset (*cf.* E. Schürer, *History of the Jewish People in the Time of Jesus Christ* [Eng. tr., Edinburgh, 1892–1901], II. i, pp. 290 f.).

[8] Mishnah, *Middoth* ii. 3. The Mishnaic tractate *Middoth* (lit. "Measurements") and the fifth chapter of Book V of Josephus's *Jewish War* are our two principal authorities for the details of the temple structure before its destruction in A.D. 70. *Cf.* E. Stauffer, "Das Tor des Nikanor," ZNW xliv (1952–3), pp. 44 ff.

the name of the Messiah Jesus of Nazareth, (get up and) walk!"[9]

Cornelius a Lapide tells us how Thomas Aquinas called upon Pope Innocent II once when the latter was counting a large sum of money. "You see, Thomas," said the Pope, "the Church can no longer say, 'Silver and gold have I none'." "True, holy father," said Thomas, "and neither can she now say, 'Arise and walk'." The moral of this tale may be pondered by any Christian communion that enjoys a fair degree of temporal prosperity!

7–8 Suiting his action to his word, Peter held out his hand and, taking the lame man's right hand, raised him to his feet. And in that very moment, this man who had never been able to stand or walk felt a strange strength in his legs and feet; they actually supported him instead of collapsing beneath him.[10] First he practised standing, and when he found he could do that, he put one foot forward and tried to walk; when he found that he could walk as well, ordinary walking seemed too humdrum a means of progress. His exultation must find more vigorous expression, and so, leaping in the air and bounding along, trying to find out all that his new limbs were capable of doing, he accompanied the two apostles through the gate which led from the outer court into the sacred precincts themselves.[11] Nor was it with his limbs alone that he rejoiced in God's goodness, but the temple courts echoed his shouts of grateful praise.

9–10 Naturally such indecorous behaviour collected a curious crowd. They recognized the man as the lame beggar who was such a familiar sight at the Beautiful Gate; they knew that there was nothing fraudulent about his lameness, for he had been born lame; naturally, then, they were "filled with wonder and amazement" at the spectacle. It was marvellous enough, to be sure, but it was more

[9] For a practical exposition and application of this incident it would be difficult to improve upon the chapter entitled "The Lamiter" in a Scottish vernacular work, *Sandy Scott's Bible Class* (reprinted from the *Northern Evangelist*, London, 1897), pp. 14 ff.

[10] "That which the physician observes during the months of the ordinary *gradual* cure of a lame man is here compressed into a moment" (A. Harnack, *Luke the Physician* [Eng. tr., London, 1907], p. 191). On the medical nature of Luke's vocabulary here *cf.* W. K. Hobart, *The Medical Language of St. Luke* (Dublin, 1882), pp. 34 ff.; but Hobart's lexical data must be carefully checked.

[11] In other words, "into the temple" (εἰς τὸ ἱερόν) in the sense in which this expression occurs in vv. 2, 3 and 8. The outer court did not form part of the ἱερόν in this stricter sense. The ἱερόν includes all the sacred precincts; the ναός is the sanctuary building itself (ναός is not used of the Jerusalem sanctuary in Acts, but it is frequently so used in the Gospels).

than a marvel: it was a sign. For the two apostles had not cured him by any power of their own; it was when they invoked the name and authority of Jesus Christ of Nazareth that he sprang up and found his feet for the first time in his life. Plainly, then, the power by which Jesus had healed cripples during His public ministry was still in their midst, exercised no longer directly, but through His disciples. But that power was not confined to bodily healing alone. On a memorable occasion in Capernaum, Jesus cured a paralysed man by commanding him to rise and walk; in language very similar to that which Peter had used just now;[12] and His word which enabled the paralytic to walk was intended to supply public confirmation of His authority to forgive sins as well as to heal the sick (Mark 2:10 f.). So, too, His disciples not only healed the sick in His name but also received from Him "power and commandment ... to declare and pronounce to His people, being penitent, the absolution and remission of their sins."[13] But again: the very behaviour of the former cripple was itself a token, to those who had eyes to see, of the advent of the messianic age. For that was the age of which it had been said long before, "Then shall the lame man leap as a hart" (Isa. 35:6).[14] That which Jesus' personal mighty works had signified was corroborated by this mighty work performed through His disciples: He was indeed Lord and Messiah.

(b) Peter's Address in Solomon's Colonnade (Ch. 3:11–26)

11 And as he held Peter and John, all the people ran together unto them in the porch that is called Solomon's, greatly wondering.[15]

12 And when Peter saw it, he answered unto the people, Ye men of Israel, why marvel ye at this man? or why fasten ye your eyes on us, as though by our own power or godliness[16] we had made him to walk?

---

[12] ἔγειρε καὶ περιπάτει (Luke 5:23; cf. Matt. 9:5; Mark 2:9); the Byzantine reading of v. 6 (see n. 2 above) is probably due to the influence of these Gospel passages.

[13] From the General Absolution in the Anglican *Book of Common Prayer*.

[14] Compare the terms in which Jesus reassured John the Baptist that He was indeed the "Coming One" (Luke 7:22; Matt. 11:4 f.); "the lame walk" was one of the signs which John's messengers were to report to him.

[15] There is a Western expansion of this verse: "And as Peter and John came out he came out with them, holding on to them; and the others, struck with wonder, took up their position in the colonnade that is called Solomon's."

[16] Chrysostom and several of the versions (Old Latin, Syriac and Armenian) read "authority" (ἐξουσία) for "godliness" (εὐσεβεία). The Latin version of Irenaeus omits "or godliness."

13 The God of Abraham, and of Isaac, and of Jacob,[17] the God of our fathers, hath glorified his Servant Jesus;[18] whom ye delivered up, and denied before the face of Pilate, when he had determined to release him.[19]

14 But ye denied[20] the Holy and Righteous One, and asked for a murderer to be granted unto you,

15 and killed the Prince of life; whom God raised from the dead; whereof we are witnesses.

16 And by faith in his name hath his name made this man strong,[21] whom ye behold and know: yea, the faith which is through him hath given him this perfect soundness in the presence of you all.

17 And now, brethren, I know[22] that in ignorance ye did it,[23] as did also your rulers.

18 But the things which God foreshowed by the mouth of all the prophets, that his Christ should suffer, he thus fulfilled.

19 Repent ye therefore, and turn again, that your sins may be blotted out, that so there may come seasons of refreshing from the presence of the Lord;

20 and that he may send the Christ who hath been appointed for you, *even* Jesus:

21 whom the heavens must receive until the times of restoration of all things, whereof God spake by the mouth of his holy prophets that have been from of old.[24]

[17] The Western text here, as in Ch. 7:32, repeats "the God" before "of Isaac" and "of Jacob" (in conformity with Ex. 3:6).

[18] After "Jesus" the Western text adds "Christ."

[19] After "Pilate" the Western text reads: "who judged him, when he was willing to release him."

[20] There is a Western reading "oppressed" (ἐβαρύνατε) instead of "denied" (ἠρνήσασθε), probably an effort to improve the style by avoiding the repetition of ἠρνήσασθε in two consecutive clauses. Attempts to explain the two readings as translation-variants have not been generally convincing.

[21] The awkwardness of the repetition of "his name" has caused many commentators to suspect textual corruption, and others to change the punctuation. C. C. Torrey (*Composition and Date of Acts* [Cambridge, Mass., 1916], pp. 14 ff.) discerns behind "hath his name made strong" an Aramaic phrase *taqqeph shemeh* which he believes should have been vocalized *taqqiph sameh*, "he has made him whole"; the passage would then run: "And by faith in his name he has healed this man whom you see and know."

[22] The Western text reads "we know" (ἐπιστάμεθα) for "I know" (οἶδα).

[23] The Western text, more explicitly, reads "ye did the evil thing."

[24] The Western text omits "from of old" (ἀπ' αἰῶνος), but cf. Luke 1:70.

22 Moses indeed said,[25] A prophet shall the Lord God raise up unto you from among your brethren, like unto me; to him shall ye hearken in all things whatsoever he shall speak unto you.

23 And it shall be, that every soul that shall not hearken to that prophet, shall be utterly destroyed from among the people.

24 Yea and all the prophets from Samuel and them that followed after, as many as have spoken, they also told of these days.

25 Ye are the sons of the prophets, and of the covenant which God made with your fathers, saying unto Abraham, And in thy seed shall all the families of the earth be blessed.

26 Unto you first God, having raised up his Servant, sent him to bless you, in turning away every one of you from your iniquities.

11 After the service of prayer and sacrifice was over, Peter and John, accompanied by the man who had been cured of his lameness, came out from the inner courts to the outer court, probably through the Beautiful Gate, and made their way to the east of the outer court, to the colonnade called after Solomon. The crowd of wondering spectators thronged them, and when they reached Solomon's colonnade, Peter had a large audience ready to listen to anything he might say. If the spiritual significance of the miracle escaped many of the crowd (as no doubt it did), Peter had an excellent opportunity of making it plain to them, and the man himself, who stuck fast by his two benefactors, provided visible confirmation of Peter's words.

12–15 Do not imagine, said Peter, addressing the multitude, that it was by any special power or piety of our own that we made this man walk. Do not stare at us, as though there were anything wonderful about us; and do not marvel so at what has happened to this man: this is God's doing. "The God of Abraham and of Isaac and of Jacob, the God of our fathers," he went on (using the time-honoured language of the Jewish liturgy),[26] "has glorified His Servant Jesus." In order to explain how the cripple had been

---

[25] The Western text adds "to your fathers."

[26] E.g., the Eighteen Benedictions (see p. 64, n. 32) begin with the words: "Blessed art thou, O Lord our God and God of our fathers, God of Abraham, God of Isaac, and God of Jacob . . ."

healed, Peter found it necessary to relate the act of God which had so lately been accomplished in their midst. The cripple had been healed because Jesus had been glorified. From His place of exaltation He had endowed His disciples with power to act in His name, and to perform mighty works such as He had performed in the days of His bodily presence among them.

In speaking of the exaltation of Jesus, following His humiliation and death, Peter used language taken from the prophecy of the obedient and suffering Servant of the Lord in Isa. 52:13–53:12, a prophecy which opens with the words "Behold, my servant shall ... be exalted and lifted up, and shall be very high." [27] The voice from heaven which came to Jesus at His baptism addressed Him in the language of Isa. 42:1, where this figure of the Servant makes its first appearance.[28] No passage of OT prophecy has made so deep and plain a mark on NT thought and language as this.[29]

Like the prophet, Peter began by speaking of the Servant's being glorified by God, and then went back to tell of His suffering. And he told his Jerusalemite audience quite outspokenly what their part in this shameful business had been. God has glorified His Servant, he said, but when He was in your power you handed Him over to be executed by the Romans; and when the Roman governor was disposed to discharge Him, you spoke against Him—spoke against the Holy and Righteous One, refusing to acknowledge Him as your divinely appointed King and Saviour, and you asked that a condemned murderer might be released when Pilate offered to release Jesus.[30] (The twofold title here given to Jesus as the Messiah, "the Holy and Righteous One," has its roots in OT language.)[31] Yes, Peter continued, you asked that

---

[27] This last verb appears in LXX as δοξασθήσεται ("shall be glorified"), whence ἐδόξασεν ("hath glorified") in this passage. In the Targum of Jonathan on the Prophets, "my Servant" in Isa. 52:13 (as in Isa. 42:1) is explained by the additional word "Messiah." On Peter's use of the "Servant" concept here, see O. Cullmann, *Peter: Disciple, Apostle, Martyr* (Eng. tr., London, 1953), pp. 66 ff.

[28] The implied identification of the Isaianic Servant ("my beloved, in thee I am well pleased") with the Davidic Messiah of Ps. 2:7 ("Thou art my Son") in the heavenly voice at the baptism is the earliest known instance of the messianic interpretation of the Servant.

[29] See Ch. 8:32 ff., with exposition and notes (pp. 187 ff.). *Cf.* J. Jeremias, *s.v.* παῖς θεοῦ, in TWNT v (Stuttgart, 1952), pp. 676 ff.

[30] For the detailed account see Luke 23:1 ff.

[31] The title "The Holy One" (ἅγιος, not ὅσιος as in Ch. 2:27) is paralleled

a murderer's life might be spared, but you put the very Author of life[32] to death—an amazing paradox! *You* killed Him, but *God* restored Him to life again, and we are here to bear witness to the fact of His resurrection. Note again how the apostles loved to emphasize the contrast between men's treatment of Christ and God's.

16 It is through His name—the name of the once humbled and now glorified Servant of God—that this man has been cured, said Peter; and it is by faith in that same name that he has appropriated the blessing and strength which he now exhibits. The complete cure that had been accomplished was plain for all to see; Peter impressed upon them that the power that wrought the cure resided in Jesus' name, and that the man had availed himself of this power by the exercise of faith. There was no merely magical efficacy in the sounds which Peter pronounced when he commanded the cripple to walk in Jesus' name; the cripple would have known no benefit had he not responded in faith to what Peter said; but once this response was made, the power of the risen Christ filled his body with health and strength. Here is a further principle which gives the healing miracles of Acts the same evangelical quality as those recorded in the Gospels.

in NT in Mark 1:24; Luke 4:34; 1 John 2:20; Rev. 3:7. In the first of these passages "it is probable . . . that the demoniac uses ὁ ἅγιος τοῦ θεοῦ with Messianic significance, as expressing a sense of the presence of a supernatural person" (V. Taylor, *The Gospel according to St. Mark* [London, 1952], p. 174). Similar titles are given in OT to Aaron the priest (Ps. 106:16) and Elisha the prophet (2 Kings 4:9). (Note that in LXX ἅγιος regularly represents Heb. *qadosh* while ὅσιος represents Heb. *hasid*; in the two places just mentioned we have *qadosh*, ἅγιος.) The title "The Righteous One" (δίκαιος) is paralleled in NT in Acts 7:52; 22:14; Jas. 5:6; 1 John 2:1. For OT insistence on the righteousness of the Lord's Anointed *cf.* 2 Sam. 23:3; Isa. 32:1; Zech. 9:9 (*cf.* also "my righteous Servant" in Isa. 53:11). Messiah is called "The Righteous One" in 1 Enoch 38:2 (*cf.* 1 Enoch 46:3; 53:6; *Psalms of Solomon* 17:35); the plural style, "righteous and holy ones", is used of the messianic people in 1 Enoch 38:5; 48:1, 7; 51:2. *Cf.* V. Taylor, *The Names of Jesus* (London, 1953), pp. 80 ff.

[32] Gk. τὸν . . . ἀρχηγὸν τῆς ζωῆς. The word ἀρχηγός is used four times of Christ in NT. Here and in Heb. 2:10 it denotes Christ as the Source of life or salvation (as "life" and "salvation" are both represented by Aramaic *hayye*, the phrase used here is practically synonymous with τὸν ἀρχηγὸν τῆς σωτηρίας in Heb. 2:10; *cf.* A. F. J. Klijn, "The Term 'Life' in Syriac Theology", *Scottish Journal of Theology* v [1952], pp. 390 ff.). In Ch. 5:31 ἀρχηγός is used rather in the sense of "prince" or "leader"; in Heb. 12:2 it is applied to Christ as the "pioneer" or "exemplar" of faith (τὸν τῆς πίστεως ἀρχηγόν).

17-18 Peter conceded that the treatment meted out by the people of Jerusalem to their Messiah was the result of ignorance.[33] They did not know that Jesus of Nazareth was indeed their Messiah. Even their rulers did not believe it, although He solemnly and explicitly assured them of the fact. We may think that Peter's words were surprisingly lenient to people like Caiaphas and his fellow-members of the chief-priestly families, who were so determined to have Jesus put to death. But however that may be, here is a proclamation of divine generosity, offering a free pardon to all who took part in the death of Christ, if only they realize their error, confess their sin, and turn to God in repentance. For all those things that happened to Jesus in His suffering and death happened in fulfilment of the words of the prophets, who foretold that the Messiah must suffer.[34] True, they did not foretell in so many words that it was the Messiah who was to suffer; they spoke of the obedient Servant of God as suffering for the sins of others; but Jesus Himself accepted and fulfilled His messianic mission in the terms of the prophecy of the suffering Servant, and the apostles' interpretation followed His own. The sufferings of the Servant were endured in order that through them salvation might be brought to many. God had foretold this through His servants the prophets, and Peter and his hearers had seen the prophetic oracles fulfilled and the salvation of God brought near in these last days.

cf. Ladd 356

19-21 All that they had to do to avail themselves of this salvation was to change their former attitude to Jesus and bring it into line with God's attitude. God had clearly shown His verdict by raising Him from the dead. Let them therefore repent, let them repudiate with abhorrence their acquiescence in the murder of their true Messiah, let them turn back in heart to God, and the salvation and blessing procured by their Messiah's death would be theirs. Their sins would be wiped out, even that sin of sins which they had unwittingly committed in clamouring for the death of the Author of life. Here, surely, is the heart of the gospel of grace; each responsive member of Peter's audience might have echoed in advance the wondering words of John Newton:

Amazing Grace!

---

[33] *Cf.* Luke 23:34 (with remarks on the text and interpretation in Geldenhuys's commentary, pp. 613 f., nn. 2-5); 1 Cor. 2:8; 1 Tim. 1:13.

[34] *Cf.* E. J. Young, *My Servants the Prophets* (Grand Rapids, 1952), pp. 191 f.

Alas! I knew not what I did,
But now my tears are vain;
Where shall my trembling soul be hid?
For I my Lord have slain.

A second look He gave, which said:
"I freely all forgive;
This blood is for thy ransom shed;
I die, that thou mayest live."

Thus, while His death my sin displays
In all its blackest hue;
Such is the mystery of grace,
It seals my pardon too.

With pleasing grief and mournful joy
My spirit now is filled,
That I should such a life destroy,
Yet live through Him I killed.

And not only would their sins be blotted out; those times of refreshment[35] and blessing which the prophets had described as features of the new age would be sent to them by God. Jesus, their Messiah, invested with this holy office by God Himself, had been received up into the divine presence, and would remain there until the consummation of all that the prophets, from earliest days, had foretold.[36] The gospel blessings that were to flow from His death and resurrection must spread abroad throughout the world, and then He would return from the right hand of power.

The exact meaning of these words of Peter has been debated

---

[35] The Gk. word rendered "refreshing" is ἀνάψυξις , "respite" (cf. Ex. 8:15, the only LXX occurrence of the word). Repentance would bring the people of Jerusalem a respite from the judgment pronounced by Jesus, as it brought the Ninevites a respite from the judgment pronounced by Jonah. But while Nineveh's doom was deferred, Jerusalem's fell within the time-limit announced: "this generation shall not pass away, until all these things be accomplished" (Mark 13:30).

[36] The Gk. word rendered "restoration" (v. 21), ἀποκατάστασις, should perhaps be rendered "fulfilment" or "establishment": the sense will then be: "until the times for the establishment of all that God has spoken by the mouth of His holy prophets." Cf. the verb ἀποκαθιστάνω in Ch. 1:6 (but the fulfilment here is much wider in scope than the restoration of the kingdom to Israel in the sense meant by the apostles) and in Mark 9:12 // Matt. 17:11, where Elijah is spoken of as coming to "restore" all things ("before the great and terrible day of Jehovah," Mal. 4:5). The ἀποκατάστασις here appears to be identical with the παλιγγενεσία ("regeneration") of Matt. 19:28. But the idea of restoration is not excluded; the final inauguration of the new age is accompanied by a renovation of all nature (cf. Rom. 8:18–23).

91

from various points of view. This at least may be said with assurance: the whole house of Israel, now as on the day of Pentecost, received a call to reverse the verdict of Passover Eve and to accord Jesus united acknowledgment as Messiah. Had Israel as a whole done this during these Pentecostal days, how different the course of world history and world evangelization would have been! How much more swiftly (we may imagine) would the consummation of Christ's kingdom have come! But it is pointless to pursue the "might-have-beens" of history. Israel as a whole declined the renewed offer of grace and refused to recognize Jesus as Messiah: this is one of the prominent themes of Luke throughout Acts, where the progressive acceptance of Jesus by Gentiles proceeds *pari passu* with His refusal by Jews. The grand consummation and the *parousia* of Jesus lie still in the future: "we see not yet all things subjected to him" (Heb. 2:8).

22-23 Did all the prophets, from earliest days, indeed speak of these days, as Peter maintained? Yes, even Moses, the first and greatest of Israel's prophets, had looked forward to the day of Christ. There follow words from Deut. 18:15 ff., in which Moses warns the Israelites that, when they wish to ascertain the divine will, they must not have recourse to magic arts for this purpose, after the manner of the Canaanites. When the Lord has a communication to make to them, he says, He "will raise up for you a prophet like me from among you, from your brethren—him you shall heed— ... and whoever will not give heed to my words which he shall speak in my name, I myself will require it of him" (vv. 15, 19, RSV).[37] The primary reference of these words of Moses is to the institution of prophets in Israel, as a way appointed by God for making His will known to His people.[38] But even before apostolic times this prophecy seems to have been interpreted as pointing to one particular prophet,[39] a second Moses, who would exercise the prophet's full mediatorial function as Moses had done. Among the Samaritans,[40] as later among the

---

[37] The concluding part of the quotation here bears a greater resemblance to Lev. 23:29 ("For whatsoever soul . . . he shall be cut off from his people") than to Deut. 18:19.

[38] *Cf.* G. E. Wright, *God Who Acts* (London, 1952), pp. 62, 68; E. J. Young, *op. cit.*, pp. 13, 20 ff., 34.

[39] *Cf.* the expectation reflected in John 1:21b, 25; 7:40.

[40] *Cf.* John 4:19, 25, 29. The Samaritans referred to this messianic prophet as the *ta'eb* or "restorer."

Ebionites,[41] the Messiah was envisaged in terms of this prophet like unto Moses, and the same may have been true of some orthodox Jewish circles as well; at any rate, we have clear evidence in the gospels, especially in the fourth, of people who found this form of messianic expectation fulfilled in Jesus.[42]   Here we see that from the earliest days of the apostolic preaching this passage from Deuteronomy was invoked as a Mosaic prediction of Jesus, and it appears to have been regularly included in the "testimony" compilations which circulated in the early church.[43]

24 The prophetic testimony to Christ which Moses had begun was carried on by Samuel and all the subsequent prophets.[44] Samuel may be specially mentioned as the next named prophet after the days of Moses. It might be difficult to find a recorded prophecy of Samuel which could be applied to Jesus so explicitly as the words of Moses just quoted; but Samuel was the prophet who anointed David as king and spoke of the establishment of his kingdom (1 Sam. 13:14; 15:28; 16:13; 28:17), and the promises made to David found their highest fulfilment in Jesus (*cf.* Ch. 13:34).   And all that the prophets spoke similarly found their highest fulfilment in Him. "This is that" which was spoken by them all.

25–26   These men of Israel who stood listening to Peter were "sons of the prophets"—not in the OT sense of the words which denoted the professional prophetic guild, but in the sense that they were heirs of the promises made by God through the prophets—promises which had found their fulfilment before their very eyes. So, too, they were "sons of the covenant" made by God with Abraham, and that in a special sense, for they had lived to see

[41] *Cf.* H. J. Schoeps, *Theologie und Geschichte des Judenchristentums* (Tübingen, 1949), pp. 87 ff.
[42] *Cf.* John 6:14 ("This is of a truth the prophet that cometh into the world"); the comparison of Jesus with Moses is pointed in the later part of the chapter. In the transfiguration narrative the heavenly voice adds the words "hear ye him" from Deut. 18:15 to "This is my Son [*i.e.* the Messiah], my chosen [*i.e.* the Servant]," thus identifying the Moses-like prophet with the Messiah and the Servant, and pointing to Jesus as the fulfiller of all three rôles (Luke 9:35). *Cf.* C. H. Dodd, *According to the Scriptures* (London, 1952), pp. 53 ff.
[43] The quotation in its present form (conflated with Lev. 23:29; *cf.* n. 37) recurs in the *Clementine Recognitions* i. 36; this suggests dependence on a testimony book. *Cf.* also the use made of the same prophecy in Stephen's speech (Ch. 7:37). *Cf.* V. Taylor, *The Names of Jesus*, pp. 15 ff.
[44] *Cf.* E. J. Young, *op. cit.*, pp. 79, 155, 162 f.

the day when that covenant came true in Christ: "In thy seed shall all the families of the earth be blessed."[45] For Christ was the descendant of Abraham in whom this blessing became a reality; and while the blessing was for all the families of the earth, the first opportunity of enjoying the blessing was naturally extended to the seed of Abraham according to the flesh.[46] It was in their midst that God had raised up His Servant Jesus—raised Him up to be their leader and deliverer, to be His mediatorial spokesman among them, even as centuries before He had raised up His servant Moses. (It is not so much the resurrection of Jesus from the dead that is meant in this verse.)[47] He came to them, as Abraham's promised seed, to bestow God's best blessing upon them, turning them away from their wickedness. They had not paid heed to Him at first when God sent Him; let them pay heed now, when God in His pardoning grace gave them a fresh opportunity; else they would forfeit the covenanted blessing.

[45] This quotation conflates Gen. 12:3 ("in thee shall all the families of the earth be blessed") and 22:18 ("in thy seed shall all the nations of the earth be blessed"). For the NT application of these promises cf. Gal. 3:6 ff., 16 ff.
[46] For the principle "to the Jew first" cf. Ch. 13:46; Rom. 1:16; 2:9 f.
[47] Cf. also Chs. 5:30; 13:33.

CHAPTER IV

(c) Arrest of Peter and John (Ch. 4:1–4)

1 And as they spake[1] unto the people, the priests[2] and the captain of the temple and the Sadducees came upon them,

2 being sore troubled because they taught the people, and proclaimed in Jesus the resurrection from the dead.[3]

3 And they laid hands on them, and put them in ward unto the morrow: for it was now eventide.

4 But many of them that heard the word believed; and the number of the men came to be about five thousand.

1–2 Such a crowd gathered round Peter and John while they spoke thus in Solomon's colonnade that the temple authorities intervened. The "captain of the temple",[4] the chief of the temple police, was responsible for maintaining order in the temple courts, and he may have had misgivings lest the obstruction caused by so large a crowd might lead to a riot. But some of the other temple authorities had strong religious objections to the content of the apostolic preaching, in particular to the announcement that Jesus had been raised from the dead. It is noteworthy that the Sadducees[5]—the party to which the chief-priestly families belonged—are specially mentioned in this regard; they objected on principle to the doctrine of resurrection in itself, and were greatly annoyed because the two apostles, by their insistence on the fact of Jesus'

[1] The Western text adds "these words."

[2] Cod. B and a few other authorities read "chief priests" (ἀρχιερεῖς) instead of "priests" (ἱερεῖς). Aside from the textual question, it was the chief priests rather than the rank and file of ordinary priests who led the opposition to the early Jerusalem church.

[3] Cod. D reverses the construction and reads ". . . announced Jesus in the resurrection of the dead."

[4] This is the official referred to in rabbinical literature as the chief *sagan* (or *segen*), and sometimes as *'ish har ha-bayith* ("the man of the mountain of the house"). He belonged to one of the chief-priestly families, and in the temple he ranked next to the high priest. The temple guard which he commanded was a picked body of Levites. (It was from this body, presumably, that sentries were detailed to guard the tomb of Jesus, Matt. 27:65 ff.). *Cf.* Ch. 5:24, 26.

[5] The origin of the name Sadducees is obscure; there is little evidence for the common belief that it is intended to proclaim the party's loyalty to the traditions of the high-priestly family of Zadok (see further p. 454, n. 18). The Sadducean party was closely associated with the old patrician families of

resurrection, were so publicly and cogently maintaining that doctrine.

3-4 It was now evening (an hour or two at least must have gone by since the afternoon prayers for which Peter and John had gone up to the temple in the first instance), and there was no time to hold an inquiry into the apostles' conduct before sundown. They were therefore locked up for the night. But the temple authorities could not undo the harm (as they considered it) which Peter and John had done; the healing of the lame man and the preaching which followed it had the effect of adding a large number to the three thousand believers of the day of Pentecost; the number of men alone[6] now totalled some five thousand.

(d) Peter and John before the Sanhedrin (Ch. 4:5-12)

5 And it came to pass on the morrow, that their rulers and elders and scribes were gathered together in Jerusalem;

6 and Annas the high priest *was there,* and Caiaphas, and John,[7] and Alexander, and as many as were of the kindred of the high priest.

7 And when they had set them in the midst, they inquired, By what power, or in what name, have ye done this?

8 Then Peter, filled with the Holy Spirit, said unto them, Ye rulers of the people, and elders,

Jerusalem, including those from which in NT times the high priests were regularly appointed. They tried to collaborate as far as possible with the Roman occupying power; as the peace of the land and the political survival of the people (not to mention the maintenance of their own influence) depended on Roman good-will, they sternly opposed all religious or nationalist movements which might incur the suspicion and reprisals of the Romans. (The policy of Caiaphas expressed in John 11:49 f. illustrates the Sadducean point of view very well.) At this time they were the dominant party in the Sanhedrin. In theology and morals they claimed to be conservatives, in contrast to the Pharisees (see p. 123, n. 42); they refused to accept what they regarded as the doctrinal innovations of bodily resurrection and the belief in a hierarchy of good and evil spirits. (*Cf.* Ch. 23:8, with exposition and notes, pp. 453 f.) They appear to have viewed the "Prophets" and "Writings" in the Hebrew Bible as less authoritative than the Pentateuch; it may have been for this reason that, when Jesus disputed with them concerning the principle of resurrection (Mark 12:18 ff. // Matt. 22:23 ff. // Luke 20:27 ff.), He appealed to Ex. 3:6 and not to what might have been looked upon as more obvious proof-texts in the "Prophets" (*e.g.* Isa. 26:19; Ezek. 37:1 ff.) or the "Writings" (*e.g.* Dan. 12:2).

[6] Gk. τῶν ἀνδρῶν, "of the men" as distinct from women and children (not τῶν ἀνθρώπων, "of the men" in the sense of human beings).

[7] For "John" the Western text reads "Jonathan" (*cf.* n. 14 below).

9 if we this day are examined concerning a good deed done to an impotent man, by what means this man is made whole;

10 be it known unto you all, and to all the people of Israel, that in the name of Jesus Christ of Nazareth, whom ye crucified, whom God raised from the dead, *even* in him doth this man stand here before you whole.[8]

11 He is the stone which was set at nought of you the builders, which was made the head of the corner.

12 And in none other is there salvation: for neither is there any other name under heaven, that is given among men, wherein we must be saved.

5–6 Next morning the Sanhedrin[9] met (probably in a building immediately to the west of the temple precincts),[10] and the chief-

---

[8] Some Western authorities add "and in no other" (*cf.* v. 12).

[9] The Sanhedrin (a Hebrew and Aramaic borrowing from Gk. συνέδριον, the word translated "council" in v. 15) was the senate and supreme court of the Jewish nation. In NT it is also called the πρεσβυτέριον ("body of elders", Ch. 22:5; Luke 22:66) and γερουσία ("senate," Ch. 5:21); Josephus also refers to it as the βουλή ("council," *Jewish War* ii. 15.6; 16:2; v. 13.1; *Antiquities* xx. 1.2). The Mishnah calls it the Sanhedrin, the Great Sanhedrin, the Sanhedrin of the Seventy-One, the Great Law-Court. It consisted of the high priest, who was president by virtue of his office, and seventy other members. It first appears in history in the Hellenistic period (*c.* 200 B.C.) as the body which regulated the internal affairs of the Jewish nation—a rôle which it maintained until the outbreak of war with the Romans in A.D. 66. After the fall of Jerusalem in A.D. 70, a new Sanhedrin of scholars was established at Jabneh in western Palestine, with Yochanan ben Zakkai as its first president. The Mishnah and later Jewish tradition project the constitution of this later Sanhedrin back into the period when the temple was still standing, and represent noted rabbis like Hillel and Gamaliel (see Ch. 5:34, p. 124) as presidents of the Sanhedrin. Some Jewish scholars of recent and modern times have argued for the existence of two Sanhedrins in NT times—the political body presided over by the high priest and the religious body presided over by a leading scholar. This view is upheld by A. Büchler, *Das Synhedrion in Jerusalem* (Vienna, 1902), and S. Zeitlin, *Who Crucified Jesus?* (New York and London, 1942). (See the critique of the latter book by N. B. Stonehouse in WThJ v [1943], pp. 137 ff.) These arguments for the co-existence of two Sanhedrins in the time of the Second Temple do not appear convincing.

The Sanhedrin at this time included a majority of members from the Sadducean party, supporting the chief-priestly interests, and a powerful minority from the Pharisaic party, to whom most of the scribes or professional exponents of the Law belonged. The body is frequently referred to in NT by some or all of its component groups: so here in v. 5, "their rulers and elders and scribes" (*cf.* v. 23, "the chief priests and the elders").

[10] The council-chamber, according to Josephus (*Jewish War* v. 4.2; *cf.* ii. 16.3; vi. 6.3), was situated at the eastern end of a bridge across the Tyropoeon valley, at the western end of which lay the open-air gathering-place called the

priestly, Sadducean, element in its membership was specially well represented. Annas,[11] the senior ex-high priest, was present, and so was his son-in-law Caiaphas,[12] the reigning high priest, who by virtue of his office was president of the Sanhedrin. Only a few weeks had passed since they had both taken a hand in the condemnation of Jesus.[13] Their hope that they had got rid of Him was but short-lived; it looked as if they were going to have even more trouble on His account than they had had before His crucifixion. With them were several of their kinsmen, two of whom are mentioned by name, although one of these cannot be identified with certainty, and the other cannot be identified at all.[14]

Xystos (i.e. "polished [floor]"). It may be for this reason that the council-chamber was called (as the name is preserved in the Mishnah) the lishkath ha-gazith ("the hall beside the Xystos" rather than the common rendering "the hall of hewn stones"). It stood therefore on the western side of the temple hill. See Schürer, op. cit., II. i, pp. 190 ff.; G. H. Dalman, Jerusalem und sein Gelände (Gütersloh, 1930), pp. 193 f.; J. Simons, Jerusalem in the OT (Leiden, 1952), pp. 252 f.

[11] Annas (better Hannas, from Ἅννας, as in Westcott and Hort), son of Seth, was appointed high priest by Quirinius, legate of Syria, in A.D. 6, and held the office for nine years. Even after his deposition he continued to exercise great influence; five of his sons, one grandson, and one son-in-law (Caiaphas) occupied the high priesthood at various times during the half-century preceding the revolt of A.D. 66. His real authority as the power behind the throne may be reflected in the pride of place which Luke gives him here; cf. Luke 3:2. (Both here and in Luke 3:2 Annas is called ἀρχιερεύς, a word which, in addition to its special sense of "high priest" was also applied more generally to the "chief priests"—the members of the families from which the high priests were drawn.)

[12] Caiaphas was appointed high priest by Valerius Gratus, procurator of Judaea, in A.D. 18, and held the office for the remarkably long term of eighteen years, including the ten years of Pilate's procuratorship, A.D. 26–36. He was deposed from the high priesthood by Vitellius (who as legate of Syria visited Judaea at the time of Pilate's recall in A.D. 36) and was replaced by Jonathan, son of Annas.

[13] For the part played by Annas cf. John 18:13–24.

[14] If we prefer the Western reading Jonathan for John (cf. n. 7 above), then the reference may be to Jonathan, son of Annas, who succeeded Caiaphas as high priest in A.D. 36. R. Eisler (The Enigma of the Fourth Gospel [London, 1938], pp. 44 f.) retains the reading "John" and supposes that the reference is to the son of Annas otherwise known as Theophilus, who was high priest from 37 to 41. (This identification might have commanded respectful attention had its author not gone on to identify the same person with Theophilus to whom Luke dedicated his twofold history—and with John the Evangelist! Cf. p. 31, n. 8.) The suggestion that this chief-priestly John was the rabbi Yochanan ben Zakkai, as the seventeenth-century John Lightfoot, F. W. Farrar (Life and Work of St. Paul, i [London, 1879], pp. 106 f.) and W. M. Christie (Palestine Calling [London, 1939], pp. 114, 167) have proposed, is quite unten-

7–10   When the members of the supreme court had taken their seats, Peter and John were fetched from the lock-up and set before them. They were then asked (presumably by the president) by what authority men like them[15] had presumed to act as they had done. For such an occasion as this the apostles had already received instructions from their Master: "Settle it therefore in your hearts, not to meditate beforehand how to answer: for I will give you a mouth and wisdom, which all your adversaries shall not be able to withstand or to gainsay" (Luke 21:14 f.). They now proved the truth of this assurance. In words inspired by the Holy Spirit,[16] Peter made his reply. If he and John were being examined with regard to a good deed performed on a cripple, he said—if the court wished to know how the man had been healed—then let them know, and let all the nation know, that the deed had been done in the name of Jesus of Nazareth, the Messiah. The former cripple was present in the court with them; either he had been locked up with them overnight, as being partly responsible for the commotion in Solomon's colonnade, or else he had been summoned as a witness. "This man stands here in your presence, completely healed," said Peter, "by the name of Jesus the Messiah —Jesus of Nazareth, whom you sent to the cross, whom God raised from the dead." Again we mark the pointed contrast between their treatment of Him and God's.

11   The apostles are technically on their defence, but actually they have gone over to the attack; Peter proceeds to preach the gospel to his judges, and he does so by citing a well-known OT scripture. "The stone which the builders rejected is become the head of the corner" (Ps. 118:22) is one of the earliest messianic testimonies. It was so used (by implication) by Jesus Himself, as the conclusion of the Parable of the Vineyard (Mark 12:10 f.).[17]

able; so is Farrar's further suggestion (*ibid.*), made earlier by Bishop John Pearson, that the Alexander here mentioned was Alexander of Alexandria, the brother of Philo. It is obvious from the context that both John and Alexander were members of the chief-priestly families. There is no information elsewhere about this Alexander.

[15] There is scornful emphasis in the position of the pronoun ὑμεῖς at the end of v. 7: "people like you."

[16] Gk. πλησθεὶς πνεύματος ἁγίου ("filled with [the] Holy Spirit"). We should distinguish between this use of the aorist passive, denoting a special moment of inspiration, and the use of the adjective πλήρης ("full") to denote the abiding character of a Spirit-filled man (*cf.* Stephen in Ch. 6:5).

[17] In the two parallel passages (Matt. 21:42 ff.; Luke 20:17 ff.), the stone

In the original OT context the rejected stone is perhaps Israel, despised by the nations but chosen by God for the accomplishment of His purpose. But, as in so many other instances, the purpose of God for Israel finds its fulfilment in the single-handed work of Christ.[18] So Jesus regards this passage from the Psalter "as reaching its true fulfilment in Himself, and as prophetic of His own triumph, which will follow His rejection. This verse from Ps. 118 became ... one of the passages most frequently quoted by the early Christian teachers to describe the temporary humiliation and subsequent rejection of Jesus the crucified and risen Messiah, but this does not mean that Jesus cannot have used it. On the contrary, it was a very natural form of expression for Him to use at this particular moment of His life, when the necessity for His rejection at the hands of His people was so great a reality to Him" (R. V. G. Tasker, *The OT in the NT* [Philadelphia, 1947], p. 36). In the NT and later Christian use of this "testimony," the builders are the leaders of the Jewish nation, who refused to acknowledge Jesus as their Messiah; but the Stone which they had thought nothing of had now received from God the place of honour as head-stone of the corner: Jesus now sat enthroned at God's right hand.

12 And from the once despised but now glorified Jesus, and

which the builders rejected is linked with the stone of stumbling on which "many shall . . . fall, and be broken" (Isa. 8:14 f.) and with the stone in Nebuchadnezzar's dream which struck the image so that the wind carried its dust away "like the chaff of the summer threshing-floors" (Dan. 2:35). In 1 Pet. 2:6 the rejected stone is further linked with the "precious corner stone of sure foundation" laid in Zion (Isa. 28:16), which is also interpreted of Christ by Paul in Rom. 9:33, and possibly in Eph. 2:20. The interdependent messianic exegesis of these passages in NT and early Christian literature in general is almost certainly a mark of that primitive collection of OT "testimonies" which goes back, in its earliest form, to Christ Himself. In later Christian writers other OT stones are brought into the interpretation, *e.g.* those of Gen. 28:11; Ex. 17:12, etc. (*cf.* Cyprian, *Testimonies* ii. 16). See J. A. Robinson, *The Epistle to the Ephesians* (London, 1904), pp. 163 f.; J. R. Harris, *Testimonies* i (Cambridge, 1916), pp. 30 f.; E. G. Selwyn, *The First Epistle of St. Peter* (London, 1946), pp. 268 ff.; P. B. W. Stather Hunt, *Primitive Gospel Sources* (London, 1951), pp. 126 ff.; C. H. Dodd, *According to the Scriptures* (London, 1952), pp. 35 f., 69, 99 f. Selwyn describes Ps. 118:22 as "one of the sheet-anchors of early Christian teaching" (*op. cit.*, p. 269); Stather Hunt concludes that "here we have something older than any extant Christian literature, and that St. Luke is right when he carries the idea back to the very beginning of things (Acts 4:11), and makes St. Peter use Ps. 118:22 as a proof-text concerning the sufferings of Christ and His future glory" (*op. cit.*, p. 127).

18 Consider the OT background of Christ as Abraham's seed (*cf.* Gen. 22:17 f.), as Son of man (*cf.* Dan. 7:13 f., 27), as Servant of the Lord (*cf.* Isa. 49:3, 6).

from Him alone, could true salvation come—not merely healing from a physical affliction, such as the cripple at the Beautiful Gate had received, but healing from the spiritual disease of sin and deliverance from coming judgment as well.[19] If the rulers persisted in their repudiation of Jesus, no such deliverance could be hoped for from any other quarter or by the power of any other name: the name of Jesus, by which the cripple had been enabled to spring to his feet and walk, was the name with which Israel's salvation was inextricably bound up. The course of duty and wisdom for the rulers was therefore clear; if they refused it and persisted in their present attitude, they would involve their nation as well as themselves in destruction.

(e) Peter and John Dismissed with a Caution (Ch. 4:13–22)

13 Now when they beheld the boldness of Peter and John, and had perceived that they were unlearned and ignorant men, they marvelled; and they took knowledge of them, that they had been with Jesus.

14 And seeing the man that was healed standing with them, they could say[20] nothing against it.

15 But when they had commanded them to go aside[21] out of the council, they conferred among themselves,

16 saying, What shall we do to these men? for that indeed a notable miracle hath been wrought through them, is manifest[22] to all that dwell in Jerusalem; and we cannot deny it.

17 But that it[23] spread no further among the people, let us threaten[24] them, that they speak henceforth to no man in this name.

18 And they called them, and charged them not to speak at all nor teach in the name of Jesus.

19 But Peter and John answered and said unto them,

---

[19] For the twofold sense of salvation (Gk. σωτηρία) cf. Ch. 14:9.

[20] The Western text reads "do or say."

[21] The Western text reads "to be led off" (ἀπαχθῆναι) for "to go aside" (ἀπελθεῖν).

[22] Cod. D has the comparative φανερώτερον (in the elative sense "very clear," "all too clear") for the positive φανερόν.

[23] Several Western authorities read "these words" (τὰ ῥήματα ταῦτα, perhaps to be rendered "these matters").

[24] The Byzantine text has the more emphatic ἀπειλῇ ἀπειλησώμεθα, rendered "let us straitly threaten" in AV (lit. "let us threaten with threatening") for the simple ἀπειλησώμεθα of our other authorities. Moulton and Milligan, following Blass, prefer the Byzantine reading here.

101

Whether it is right in the sight of God to hearken unto
you rather than unto God, judge ye:

20 for we cannot but speak the things which we saw and
heard.

21 And they, when they had further threatened them, let
them go, finding nothing how they might punish them,
because of the people; for all men glorified God for
that which was done.

22 For the man was more than forty years old, on whom
this miracle of healing was wrought.

13–14 Peter and John were obviously unversed in the formal
learning of the rabbinical schools, and yet they spoke with a freedom and forthrightness which impressed their judges. How could
untrained laymen[25] like these so ably sustain a theological disputation with the supreme court of the nation? The answer was
not far to seek: the judges took cognizance[26] of the fact that they
had been companions of Jesus. He too had sat at the feet of no
eminent rabbi, and yet He taught with an authority which they
could well remember. People expressed the same surprise about
Him: "How knoweth this man letters, having never learned?"
(John 7:15). None could equal Him in His sure handling of OT
scripture, His constant ability to go back to first principles for the
confirming of His own teaching and the discomfiture of His opponents. And plainly He had imparted the same gift to His
disciples. Not only so, but He had supported His teaching by the
mighty works which He performed; and now Peter and John had
done the same. That the cripple had been cured was evident; he
stood before them as a witness to the fact. Peter and John claimed
that the cure had been effected by the name of Jesus; their judges
were in no position to deny the claim.

[25] The text, "unlearned and ignorant men" (v. 13), represents Gk. ἀγράμματοι
. . . καὶ ἰδιῶται. The former word appears in the papyri in the sense "illiterate";
but the sense here is rather "uneducated" as regards a rabbinical training (cf.
John 7:15, πῶς οὗτος γράμματα οἶδεν μὴ μεμαθηκώς;). As for ἰδιώτης, which
means "private person" in ordinary Gk., it is interesting to note that it appears
as a loanword in later Hebrew and Aramaic, in the form *hedyot*, with the
sense of "commoner," "layman," "unskilled person." Peter and John were in
fact *'amme ha-'aretz*—"people of the land" in the rabbinical sense of the
phrase to denote the rank and file of the population who could not be expected
to know or practise the minutiae of the oral law (cf. John 7:49). The wonder
then was that they showed such mastery of Biblical argument.

[26] Gk. ἐπεγίνωσκον —they directed special attention to this fact as an
important piece of relevant evidence. It is this "directive" force that
distinguishes ἐπιγινώσκω in sense from γινώσκω.

15-17 Peter and John were accordingly sent outside the council-chamber while the council conferred.[27] It was difficult to know what action to take. They had broken no law in curing the cripple; besides, their action in doing so had made them popular heroes, and it would be impolitic to punish them. On the other hand, it would be equally impolitic to set them at liberty to go on teaching and healing in the name of Jesus; they would then be confronted once more with the problem they imagined they had solved when they procured Jesus' execution, and that in a more intractable form than previously. The action which they decided upon was a confession of their weakness: they would dismiss them, but threaten them with more serious consequences if they did the like again.

It is particularly striking that neither on this nor on any subsequent occasion (so far as our information goes) did the Sanhedrin take any serious action to disprove the apostles' central affirmation—the resurrection of Jesus. Had it seemed possible to refute them on this point, how readily would the Sanhedrin have seized the opportunity! Had they succeeded, how quickly and completely the new movement would have collapsed! It is plain that the apostles meant a physical resurrection when they said that Jesus was risen; it is equally plain that the rulers understood them in this sense. The body of Jesus had vanished so completely that all the authority they had at their command could not produce it; the apostles' claim that Jesus was alive again received public confirmation by the miracle of healing performed in His name. It was, for the Sanhedrin, a disturbing situation.

18-20 They recalled Peter and John and acquainted them with their decision. A complete ban was imposed on any further public mention of the name of Jesus. If they thought that any heed would be paid to this ban, they were quickly disillusioned. Peter and John had probably never heard of Socrates, and had

[27] The question arises whether Luke had any source of direct or indirect information about the conversation that took place when the apostles were sent out of the room. Moulton and Milligan (*Vocabulary of the Greek Testament* [Edinburgh, 1930], p. 55) wonder whether Paul was an eyewitness. Of course Paul may have heard of the proceedings through Gamaliel even if he was not an eyewitness. But no doubt the apostles commanded some secret sympathy in the Sanhedrin as Jesus had done. In any case, the decision taken by the Sanhedrin in the absence of Peter and John would be readily inferred from what they said when Peter and John were brought back.

certainly never read Plato's *Apology*, but they gave the same sort of answer as Socrates gave when he was offered his release on condition that he gave up the pursuit of truth and wisdom: "I shall obey God rather than you."[28] It is, of course, the sort of answer that any man of principle will give if he is offered his freedom provided that he desists from what his conscience knows to be right. But what weighed most of all with the apostles was their personal commitment to God as witnesses to Christ and the gospel. If the point were put to these judges in the abstract, whether the command of God or a human commandment should be obeyed in the event of a clash between the two, they would have had no hesitation in affirming that the divine command must be obeyed at all costs. Right, said Peter and John; "we cannot stop telling what we have seen and heard."

21-22 Despite this open defiance, the Sanhedrin did nothing but repeat their threats. The popular enthusiasm was too great for them to do anything more. Luke points out here, by way of explaining the extent of the public amazement, that the cripple who had been cured was over forty years old: he had reached an age when such cures simply do not occur. Peter and John were released.

"This," says a Jewish scholar, "was the first mistake which the Jewish leaders made with regard to the new sect. And this mistake was fatal. There was probably no need to arrest the Nazarenes, thus calling attention to them and making them 'martyrs.' But once arrested, they should not have been freed so quickly. The arrest and release increased the number of believers; for these events showed on the one hand that the new sect was a power which the authorities feared enough to persecute, and on the other hand they proved that there was no danger in being a disciple of Jesus (he, of course, being the one who had saved them from the hand of their persecutors!)" (J. Klausner, *From Jesus to Paul* [Eng.tr., London, 1944], pp. 282 f.).

(f) Peter and John Rejoin their Friends (Ch. 4:23-31)

23 And being let go, they came to their own company, and reported all that the chief priests and the elders had said unto them.

24 And they, when they heard it, lifted up their voice to

---

[28] Plato, *Apology of Socrates*, 29 D.

God with one accord, and said, O Lord, thou that didst
make the heaven and the earth and the sea, and all
that in them is:

25 who by the Holy Spirit, *by* the mouth of our father
David thy servant,[29] didst say,
Why did the Gentiles rage,
And the peoples imagine vain things?

26 The kings of the earth set themselves in array,
And the rulers were gathered together,
Against the Lord, and against his Anointed:

27 for of a truth in this city against thy holy Servant
Jesus, whom thou didst anoint, both Herod and Pontius Pilate, with the Gentiles and the peoples of Israel,
were gathered together,

28 to do whatsoever thy hand and thy counsel foreordained
to come to pass.

29 And now, Lord, look upon their threatenings: and
grant unto thy servants to speak thy word with all
boldness,

30 while thou stretchest forth thy hand to heal; and that
signs and wonders may be done through the name of
thy holy Servant Jesus.

31 And when they had prayed, the place was shaken
wherein they were gathered together; and they were
all filled with the Holy Spirit, and they spake the
word of God with boldness.[30]

23–28   The two apostles, on their release, returned to the place
where the other apostles were, and when they reported their experience before the Sanhedrin, the whole company resorted to
prayer. They addressed God as Sovereign Lord,[31] the Creator of

---

[29] The Gk. is very awkward here; Westcott and Hort refer to "the extreme
difficulty of text, which doubtless contains a primitive error." The only way to
translate the text as it stands (ὁ τοῦ πατρὸς ἡμῶν διὰ πνεύματος ἁγίου στόματος
Δαυεὶδ παιδός σου εἰπών) is to take David as the mouth (i.e. mouthpiece) of
the Holy Spirit: "who didst say through thy servant David our father, the
mouthpiece of the Holy Spirit." The Western text reads "who through the
Holy Spirit didst speak through the mouth of David thy servant." C. C. Torrey
(*Composition and Date of Acts* [Cambridge, Mass., 1916], pp. 16 ff.) envisages
an underlying Aramaic text which might be rendered: "as our father David,
thy servant, said by the mouth of the Holy Spirit." H. W. Moule (ExT li
[1939–40], p. 396) suggested that the writer put down a first draft and then
made corrections, and that a copyist, misunderstanding the signs for deletion
or addition, combined words which were intended to be alternatives.

[30] The Western text adds "to everyone who was willing to believe."

[31] Gk. δέσποτα, vocative of δεσπότης (*cf.* Luke 2:29; Rev. 6:10).

all, in time-honoured language derived from Hebrew scripture.[32] Then they quoted the opening words of the second Psalm, and found proof of their divine origin in the fulfilment which they themselves had experienced in recent days. This psalm, with its explicit reference to the Anointed (Messiah) of Jehovah, had been interpreted of the coming deliverer of David's line at least as early as the middle of the first century B.C.;[33] the words "Thou art my Son" (Ps. 2:7), spoken to Jesus at His baptism by the heavenly voice, actually hailed Him as this Messiah.[34] In conformity with this interpretation is the way in which the apostles now found the opening verses of the psalm fulfilled. The Gentiles raged against Jesus in the person of the Romans who sentenced Him to the cross and executed the sentence; the "peoples" who imagined vain things were His Jewish adversaries; the kings who set themselves in array were represented by Herod Antipas, tetrarch of Galilee and Peraea (cf. Luke 23:7 ff.), while the rulers were represented by Pontius Pilate.[35] But the prophetic language of the psalm showed that all these, in uniting against Jesus, were simply carrying out the foreordained counsel of God, that His Messiah must suffer (cf. Chs. 2:23a; 3:18). In these words of the apostles we have an explicit identification of God's "holy Servant Jesus" with the royal Son of God addressed in Ps. 2:7.[36] Jesus is both the obedient Servant and the one whom God anointed or made Messiah—at His baptism.[37]

29–30 The Sanhedrin might threaten, but their threats called

---

[32] Cf. Ex. 20:11; Neh. 9:6; Ps. 146:6; Isa. 42:5; Wisdom 13:3, 4, 9 (and see also Chs. 14:15; 17:24 below).

[33] In the *Psalms of Solomon* 17:26, where Ps. 2:9 is quoted of the expected "Christ the Lord." (Cf. p. 73, n. 64.)

[34] Cf. p. 88, n. 28.

[35] Tertullian (*On the Resurrection of the Flesh*, 20) gives a slightly different interpretation: "In the person of Pilate the heathen raged, and in the person of Israel the people imagined vain things; the kings of the earth in Herod and the rulers in Annas and Caiaphas were gathered together." The application to Israel of the plural λαοί instead of the singular λαός is unusual; it was no doubt dictated by the fact that the plural is the form actually used in Ps. 2:1 (Heb. *le'ummim*, in parallelism with *goyim*, ἔθνη).

[36] There may be some ambiguity in παῖς here; this word may mean either "servant" or "son," and therefore makes the oscillation in thought between the Isaianic Servant and the Davidic Son more natural than in English—or indeed than in the Aramaic which the apostles were presumably speaking.

[37] "Thou didst anoint" is Gk. ἔχρισας, from χρίω, the verb whose verbal adjective χριστός gives us the title "Christ." Similarly Messiah represents Heb. *mashiach*, a passive participle from the verb *mashach* ("anoint").

not for fear and silence but for increased boldness of speech. The apostles therefore prayed that they themselves might have courage to proclaim their message without fear or favour, and that God would place the seal of His public approval on their witness by granting further mighty works of healing and similar signs and wonders through the same name which had cured the lame man—the name of His "holy Servant Jesus."

31 The assurance of divine favour and help came even as they prayed. The place shook as with an earthquake—whether there was an objective shaking or whether this was the way in which God's presence and power were manifested in their consciousness we cannot say—and the Holy Spirit filled them all and sent them forth to proclaim the good news with renewed confidence. The description here is reminiscent of the description of what happened on the day of Pentecost, both in the external signs of the Spirit's advent and in the prayerful attitude of the disciples when He comes (cf. p. 45, n. 51); but while this was a fresh filling of the Spirit, it could not be called a fresh baptism.[38]

[38] *Cf.* the exposition of Ch. 2:38 (pp. 75 ff.).

4. ALL THINGS IN COMMON
(Chs. 4:32–5:11)

(a) The Community of Goods (Ch. 4:32–35)

32 And the multitude of them that believed were of one heart and soul:[39] and not one *of them* said that aught of the things which he possessed was his own; but they had all things common.

33 And with great power gave the apostles their witness of the resurrection of the Lord Jesus:[40] and great grace was upon them all.

34 For neither was there among them any that lacked: for as many as were possessors of lands or houses sold them, and brought the prices of the things that were sold,

35 and laid them at the apostles' feet: and distribution was made unto each, according as any one had need.

32–35 The summary contained in these verses is similar to that in Ch. 2:43–47 which concludes the narrative of the day of Pentecost. This, however, is not an adequate reason for believing that the narrative of Chs. 3:1–4:31 is a duplicate of the narrative of Pentecost. The account of the community of goods is repeated here in order to introduce the contrasted episodes of Barnabas and Ananias.

The Spirit-filled community[41] exhibited a remarkable unanimity, which expressed itself even in the attitude to private property. Each member regarded his private estate as being at the community's disposal: those who possessed houses and lands sold these in order that they might be more conveniently available to the community in the form of money. The richer members thus made provision for the poorer, and for a time no one had any room to

---

[39] The Western text adds: "and there was no division among them."

[40] Cod. D adds "Christ"; ℵ and A read "Jesus Christ the Lord."

[41] The Gk. word πλῆθος, rendered "multitude" in v. 32, in addition to its ordinary sense of "multitude" acquired the sense of a civic community (in Athens) and of a religious community (among Jews and Christians). In LXX it twice renders Heb. *qahal* (Ex. 12:6; 2 Chr. 31:18), more usually rendered ἐκκλησία (*cf.* Ch. 5:11 with n. 18 on p. 116). *Cf.* Chs. 6:2, 5; 15:12, 30.

complain of hunger or want.[42]   The apostles, as the community leaders, received the free-will offerings that were brought, but they apparently delegated the details of distribution to others, for they themselves had to devote their time and energy to their public testimony to the risen Christ.   As they did so, the power of God, shown in mighty works, attended their preaching—the very thing for which they had prayed (v. 30).   And they continued to enjoy the grace of God and the favour of the Jerusalem populace.

(b)   The Generosity of Barnabas (Ch. 4:36–37)

36 And Joseph, who by the apostles was surnamed Barnabas (which is, being interpreted, Son of exhortation),
   a Levite, a man of Cyprus by race,
37 having a field, sold it, and brought the money and laid
   it at the apostles' feet.

36–37   The exact etymology of Joseph's additional name Bar-nabas is a matter of debate,[43] but in all that we know about him he proved himself a true "son of encouragement."   He was a Cypriote Jew, but he had relatives in Jerusalem[44] and a piece of land as well.   The Pentateuchal regulations prohibiting Levites from holding landed property seem to have been regarded as a dead letter by the first century A.D.   We do not know whether Barnabas's property was a farm or merely a burial-ground;[45] whatever it was, he sold it and gave the purchase-price to the apostles for the use of the community.

[42] Later on, especially after the famine mentioned in Ch. 11:28, the Jerusalem church appears to have suffered from chronic poverty.

[43] Gk. παράκλησις may mean either "consolation" or "exhortation." If the former is the sense here, Barnabas may represent Aramaic *Bar-nawcha* or *Bar-newacha* ("son of refreshment"); if the latter, it may represent *Bar-nebiyya* ("son of the prophet" or "son of prophecy"; *cf.* Palmyrene *Bar-Nebo*). In either case, this use of the term "son" to indicate a man's character is a familiar Semitic idiom.

[44] *Cf.* Ch. 12:12 with Col. 4:10.

[45] The word used here is ἀγρός, which appears nowhere else in Acts; elsewhere in Acts the word used of a piece of land is χωρίον (*cf.* Chs. 1:18; 5:3, 8).

109

CHAPTER V

(c) Deceit and Death of Ananias (Ch. 5:1–6)

1 But a certain man named Ananias, with Sapphira his
wife, sold a possession,[1]

2 and kept back *part* of the price, his wife also being
privy to it, and brought a certain part, and laid it at
the apostles' feet.

3 But Peter said, Ananias, why hath Satan filled[2] thy
heart to lie to the Holy Spirit, and to keep back *part*
of the price of the land?

4 While it remained, did it not remain thine own? and
after it was sold, was it not in thy power? How is it
that thou hast conceived this thing[3] in thy heart? thou
hast not lied unto men, but unto God.

5 And Ananias hearing these words[4] fell down and gave
up the ghost: and great fear came upon all that
heard it.

6 And the young men arose and wrapped him round,
and they carried him out and buried him.

The story of Ananias is to the book of Acts what the story of
Achan is to the book of Joshua. In both narratives an act of
deceit interrupts the victorious progress of the people of God. It
may be that the author of Acts himself wished to point this comparison; at any rate, when he says that Ananias "kept back" part
of the price (v. 2), he uses the same Greek word as is used in the
Septuagint of Josh. 7:1 where it is said that the children of Israel
(in the person of Achan) "committed a trespass" by retaining for
private use property that had been devoted to God.[5]

The incident of Ananias and Sapphira is felt by many readers

---

[1] Gk. κτῆμα, referring here to landed property, as is clear from the use of
χωρίον ("land") in v. 3.

[2] Gk. ἐπλήρωσεν. By accidental omission of λ, Cod. ℵ reads ἐπήρωσεν
("maimed"); this inappropriate verb appears in some citations emended to the
more suitable ἐπείρασεν ("tempted"); hence Vulgate *temtauit*.

[3] The Western text reads "this evil thing."

[4] Cod. D inserts "immediately" (*cf.* v. 10).

[5] The verb is νοσφίζομαι (translated "purloin" in Tit. 2:10); with ἐνοσφίσατο
ἀπὸ τῆς τιμῆς here *cf.* ἐνοσφίσατο ἀπὸ τοῦ ἀναθέματος in Josh. 7:1, LXX.

to present a stumblingblock partly ethical and partly intellectual. The intellectual difficulty is not really so great as is commonly supposed. We know very little about the private beliefs of Ananias and his wife, but at a certain stage of religious awareness sudden death is a well-known sequel to the realization that one has unwittingly infringed a taboo. (This does not necessarily mean that Ananias's death must be accounted for in this way, but it does show how little substance there is in the idea that the story is essentially improbable.) As for the following death of Sapphira, if it is thought that this "adds such improbability as lies in a coincidence" (A. W. F. Blunt),[6] we must consider that she sustained the added shock of learning of her husband's sudden death.

It is really unnecessary to argue that the double death was not quite so sudden as the narrative suggests, as is done, for example, by Dr. Klausner, who says that when the couple's deceit was detected "Peter became angry at them and rebuked them; and when they died shortly thereafter, of course their death was attributed to this rebuke by the chief and first apostle" (*From Jesus to Paul* [Eng.tr., London, 1944], p. 289). Even more improbable is the suggestion made by P. H. Menoud in the recent Goguel *Festschrift*, that Ananias and Sapphira were the first members of the believing community to die, and that their natural death was such a shock to the others (who thought that Christ by His resurrection had abolished physical death for His people) that they felt obliged to account for it by the supposition that some previously undetected sin had thus found them out.[7]

A much more serious matter is the impression which the narrative gives us of the personality of Peter. It is absurd to try to make him directly responsible for the death of the couple, but his language to them, or more particularly to Sapphira, has seemed to many readers to reflect the spirit of Elijah calling down fire from heaven on the soldiers who came to arrest him, or Elisha pronouncing sentence of perpetual leprosy on Gehazi, than the spirit of their Master. "It could not of course be laid as a charge against St. Peter that after his stern rebuke of Ananias the offender fell down dead suddenly, though one would have expected St. Peter

---

[6] A. W. F. Blunt, *The Acts of the Apostles* (Oxford, 1923), p. 153.

[7] P. H. Menoud, "La Mort d'Ananias et de Saphira (Actes 5:1–11)," *Aux Sources de la Tradition Chrétienne: Mélanges offerts à M. Maurice Goguel* (Paris and Neuchâtel, 1950), pp. 146 ff.

in future to be more careful in rebuking the sinful members of the congregation. But the story goes on to relate that Ananias was buried without a word being said to his wife, although she must have been in the neighbourhood. When she came into the house three hours later, St. Peter instead of telling her of the dreadful fall of her husband so as to give her a chance of repentance cross-examined her in such a way that the sin in her heart was brought to light as a downright lie; and then he told her that her husband was dead and she would die too. ... Try how we may, we cannot imagine Christ acting towards sinners as St. Peter is here represented as doing" (L. E. Browne, *ad loc.*).

But to pass judgment on Peter, we should require to know much more than we are told here. Sapphira, for aught we know, may have suggested the deceit to her husband. It is no part of a commentator's work to pass moral judgments on Peter; in any case, it is not Peter's character or even Ananias and Sapphira's deserts that Luke is primarily interested in. What this narrative does emphasize is the reality of the Holy Spirit's indwelling presence in the church, and the solemn practical implications of that fact. So early was it necessary to enforce the lesson later formulated by Paul: "Know ye not that ye are a temple of God, and that the Spirit of God dwelleth in you? If any man destroyeth the temple of God, him shall God destroy; for the temple of God is holy, and such are ye" (1 Cor. 3:16 f.).

The incident shows us, too, that even in the earliest days the church was not a society of perfect people. The narrator refuses to idealize his picture of the primitive community, and lest his readers should over-estimate the unity and sanctity of the Christian body in those early days, he has put on record here one of those accounts which not only illustrate the honest realism of the Bible but serve as salutary warnings to its readers.[8]

1-2 Two members of the community, Ananias[9] and his wife Sapphira,[10] like many other members, sold a piece of land which

[8] H. A. W. Meyer's emphasis on the principle of church discipline is important for our assessment of the whole incident (*The Acts of the Apostles* i [Eng. tr., Edinburgh, 1877], p. 142). *Cf.* O. Cullmann, *Peter: Disciple, Apostle, Martyr* (Eng. tr., London, 1953), p. 34.

[9] Ananias (better Hananias, 'Ανανίας) is the OT Hananiah, "Jehovah has graciously given."

[10] Sapphira represents Aramaic *shappira*, "beautiful." J. Klausner suggests that this may be the Sapphira whose name appears in Aramaic and Greek on

they possessed. They retained part of the price for their private use (as they had every right to do), and Ananias brought the balance to the apostles to be used for community purposes, but represented this balance as being the total purchase-price that they had received.

3-4 Peter, perceiving the truth of the situation, broke out upon Ananias in words which conveyed to the wretched man the enormity of his sin. Sharp practice in the ordinary commerce of life was as common then as now, but a higher ethical standard must prevail among the followers of Christ. Ananias, in the effort to gain a reputation for greater generosity than he actually deserved, tried to deceive the believing community, but in trying to deceive the community he was really trying to deceive the Holy Spirit, whose life-giving power had created the community and maintained it in being. So real was the apostles' appreciation of the presence and authority of the Spirit in their midst. A lie told to Peter as a private man would have been relatively venial, but this—whether Ananias knew it or not—was a lie told to God,[11] something suggested by none other than the great adversary[12] of God and man.

No compulsion had been laid on Ananias to sell his property; the virtue of such an act as Barnabas's lay in its spontaneous generosity. The communalism of the primitive Jerusalem community was clearly quite voluntary. The piece of land belonged to Ananias; he could keep it or sell it as he pleased, and when he had sold it, the money he got for it was his to use as he chose. The voluntariness of the whole procedure forms an evident contrast to much that has claimed this early Christian practice as a precedent. But the voluntariness of the whole procedure made Ananias's deceitful behaviour all the more gratuitous. If it is no part of a commentator's business to pass moral judgments on Peter, perhaps he may permit himself to pass them on Ananias. But let him be careful: the temptation to seek a higher reputation than is our due for generosity or some other virtue is not so un-

an ossuary found in Jerusalem in 1923 (*From Jesus to Paul* [Eng. tr., London, 1944], pp. 289 f.). The identification cannot be other than speculative.

[11] A comparison of the language of v. 3 with that of v. 4 shows that the Holy Spirit is not only regarded as personal, but as God Himself present with His people.

[12] "Adversary" is the proper sense of Satan (Gk. Σατανᾶς); it is so used as a common noun in Hebrew. *Cf.* p. 265, n. 15.

common that we can afford to adopt a self-righteous attitude towards poor Ananias. Let us rather take warning from his example.

5–6 As Peter spoke, Ananias's sin came home to him, and he fell down dead. It was an evident act of judgment—the judgment that begins first at the house of God—and it is no wonder that great fear came on all who heard about it. But it may have been an act of mercy as well, if we think of the incident in the light of Paul's words about another offender against the Christian community: "deliver such a one unto Satan for the destruction of the flesh, that the spirit may be saved in the day of the Lord Jesus" (1 Cor. 5:5).[13] Some expositors have cited as a parallel to Ananias's sudden death the story of the Dean of St. Paul's who fell dead with fright because of an angry look which King Edward I of England darted at him. But it is no real parallel; it was not Peter's personality that stopped Ananias's heart from beating, but the sudden realization of the sacrilege that he had committed.

Immediately his dead body was carried out and buried by "the young men"—probably the younger members of the community rather than professional buriers. Burial in such a climate necessarily followed quickly after death, and such legal formalities as medical certification were not required. Apparently his wife was not told of his death: whether any attempt was made to communicate with her we have no means of knowing. The introduction of such details would have detracted from the impressiveness of the narrative, the first act of which is now to be followed by the second.

(d) The Death of Sapphira (Ch. 5:7–11)

7 And it was about the space of three hours after, when his wife, not knowing what was done, came in.

8 And Peter answered[14] unto her, Tell me whether ye sold the land for so much. And she said, Yea, for so much.

9 But Peter *said* unto her, How is it that ye have agreed together to try the Spirit of the Lord? behold, the feet

---

[13] It is not certain that the incestuous man in the Corinthian church was to die; the words of Paul may indicate some other form of physical affliction which would follow his excommunication. In either case, his ultimate spiritual welfare was the end in view. For the belief that Christians might die prematurely for grievous sin *cf.* 1 Cor. 11:30; Jas. 5:20; 1 John 5:16 f.

[14] Gk. ἀπεκρίθη. But Sapphira, so far as the record goes, had not spoken: here, as in some other places in NT and LXX, ἀποκρίνομαι means simply "address". Translate with RSV, "And Peter said to her."

of them that have buried thy husband are at the door,
and they shall carry thee out.

10 And she fell down immediately at his feet, and gave
up the ghost: and the young men came in and found
her dead, and they[15] carried her out and buried her
by her husband.

11 And great fear came upon the whole church, and upon
all that heard these things.

7-11 It may be that the death of Ananias came as a shock to
Peter, but the following three hours gave him time to consider the
tragedy and recognize in the sudden death the divine judgment for
an attempt to deceive the church, and the Spirit in the church.
When Sapphira came in, he asked her plainly if she and her husband had sold the land for the sum which had actually been
handed over. She had thus an opportunity to tell the truth, but
when she brazened it out and repeated her husband's falsehood,
Peter had no doubt that she would share her husband's fate, and
he told her so bluntly. They had been detected in a deliberately
conceived plan to see how far they could go in presuming upon
the forbearance of the Spirit of God (for that is what is meant
by "trying" Him);[16] and they had gone too far. The conviction
of complicity in this guilt, together with the rough and ready
announcement of her husband's death, proved too much for Sapphira: she in her turn fell down dead and was carried out and buried.

It is idle to ask if Ananias and Sapphira were genuine believers
or not. Certainly they did not behave as if they were. But we
cannot be sure that they were not, unless we are prepared to say
that no one who is guilty of an act of deliberate deceit can be a
true Christian. The fear which fell upon the whole community
suggests that many a member of it had reason to tremble and say
to himself, "There, but for the grace of God, go I." No better
answer can be found to such questions than the apostolic declaration: "Howbeit the firm foundation of God standeth, having this
seal, The Lord knoweth them that are his: and, Let every one
that nameth the name of the Lord depart from unrighteousness"
(2 Tim 2:19).

---

[15] Cod. D and the Syriac Peshitta (possibly preserving a Western reading)
have "wrapped her round and carried her out" (cf. v. 6).

[16] For the idea cf. Ex. 17:2, "wherefore do ye tempt Jehovah?" and Deut.
6:16, "Ye shall not tempt Jehovah your God" (quoted by our Lord in His
temptation, Matt. 4:7 // Luke 4:12).

The occurrence of the word "church" (Gk. *ekklesia*) in v. 11 is its first occurrence in the original text of Acts.[17] The Greek word has both a Gentile and a Jewish background. In its Gentile sense it denotes chiefly the citizen-assembly of a Greek city (*cf.* Ch. 19:32, 39, 41), but it is its Jewish usage that underlies its use to denote the community of believers in Jesus. In the Septuagint it is one of the words used to denote the nation of Israel in its religious character as the "congregation of Jehovah"; it is a pity that in the ordinary versions of the English Bible it should be rendered in NT by a term which does not appear in OT.[18] Readers of the Greek Bible could draw their own conclusions from the use of the word *ekklesia* in OT and NT alike. So could readers of William Tyndale's English translation when they came upon the word "congregacion" in both Testaments.

[17] See p. 80, n. 88, for its occurrence in the Western text of Ch. 2:47.

[18] In Deuteronomy and the following OT books, except Jeremiah and Ezekiel, ἐκκλησία is the regular LXX equivalent of Heb. *qahal* ("assembly" in ERV and ARV); in the first four books of the OT, and in Jeremiah and Ezekiel, *qahal* is regularly represented in LXX by συναγωγή, which is also used throughout LXX as the rendering of Heb. '*edah* ("congregation" in ERV and ARV). The Aramaic equivalent of '*edah*, and occasionally of *qahal*, was *kenishta*, which probably lies behind the Gk. ἐκκλησία in the sayings of Jesus in Matt. 16:18 and 18:17, and which may have been the term by which the Christian community was known in Jerusalem (the *kenishta* of the Nazarenes). Both ἐκκλησία and συναγωγή were Greek equivalents of Aram. *kenishta* (which denoted both the whole "congregation" of Israel and any individual Israelite congregation or synagogue). Of these two Greek terms the former was specialized for Christian meetings, the latter for Jewish meetings. The Christian ἐκκλησία was both new and old—new, because of its relation and witness to Jesus as the Messiah and to the epoch-making events of His death, exaltation, and sending of the Spirit; old, because it was the continuation and successor of the old "congregation of Jehovah" which had formerly been confined within the limits of one nation but was now to be thrown open to all believers without distinction. See F. J. A. Hort, *The Christian Ecclesia* (London, 1897); G. Johnston, *The Doctrine of the Church in the NT* (Cambridge, 1943); K. L. Schmidt, *The Church* (London, 1950; Eng. tr. of article ἐκκλησία in TWNT iii [Stuttgart, 1938], pp. 502 ff.).

5. ALL THE APOSTLES BEFORE
THE SANHEDRIN
(Ch. 5:12–42)

(a) Signs and Wonders (Ch. 5:12–16)

12 And by the hands of the apostles were many signs and
wonders wrought among the people: and they were all
with one accord in Solomon's porch.
13 But of the rest durst no man join himself to them:[19]
howbeit the people magnified them;[20]
14 and believers were the more added to the Lord, multitudes both of men and women:
15 insomuch that they even carried out the sick into the
streets,[21] and laid them on beds and couches, that, as
Peter came by, at the least his shadow might over-
shadow some one of them.[22]
16 And there also came together the multitude from the
cities round about Jerusalem, bringing sick folk, and
them that were vexed with unclean spirits: and they
were healed every one.

12–16 This paragraph is a further summary such as we have
seen already in Chs. 2:43–47 and 4:32–35. It provides a transition

[19] Because of a difficulty in reconciling v. 13a with v. 14a, attempts have
been made to emend "of the rest" (Gk. τῶν λοιπῶν) or "join himself"
(κολλᾶσθαι) or both. M. Dibelius emends τῶν δὲ λοιπῶν ("but of the rest") to
τῶν ἀρχόντων ("of the rulers"). A. Hilgenfeld emended λοιπῶν to Λευειτῶν
("Levites"); A. Pallis adopts this emendation and also emends κολλᾶσθαι αὐτοῖς
to κωλῦσαι αὐτούς, rendering the passage "And of the Levites none dared to
prevent them" (i.e. from holding meetings in the temple courts). Blass suggested
that κολλᾶσθαι αὐτοῖς might be translated "meddle with them"; unfortunately
no convincing evidence can be adduced for the use of κολλᾶσθαι in this sense.
C. C. Torrey's attempts to solve the problem by reference to an Aramaic
substratum are unconvincing (Composition and Date of Acts [Cambridge,
Mass., 1916], pp. 31 f.; Documents of the Primitive Church [New York, 1941],
p. 96); besides, it is unlikely that a summary paragraph like vv. 12–16 should
have been translated from an original Aramaic text. The difficulty may not
be so great as many feel, if the sense be something of the sort indicated in
our exposition.
[20] P45 omits "howbeit the people magnified them."
[21] Or "squares" (Gk. εἰς τὰς πλατείας, lit. "into the broadways").
[22] The Western text adds "for they were set free from every sickness which
each one of them had."

117

to the incident which opens in v. 17. Again we are told of the signs and wonders performed through the apostles, and the general atmosphere is like that of the earlier days of our Lord's Galilaean ministry (*cf.* Mark 1:32–34). Peter's shadow was as efficacious a medium of healing power as the hem of his Master's robe had been. No wonder that the people in general sounded the apostles' praises and that the number of believers increased. Of those who did not believe, however, none ventured to attach himself to the community; the fate of Ananias and Sapphira showed how perilous pretended or half-hearted adhesion might be.

(b) The Apostles Imprisoned and Examined (Ch. 5:17–32)

17 But the high priest rose up, and all they that were with him (which is the sect of the Sadducees), and they were filled with jealousy,

18 and laid hands on the apostles, and put them in public ward.[23]

19 But an angel of the Lord by night opened the prison doors, and brought them out, and said,

20 Go ye, and stand and speak in the temple to the people all the words of this Life.

21 And when they heard *this*, they entered into the temple about daybreak, and taught. But the high priest came, and they that were with him, and[24] called the council together, and all the senate of the children of Israel, and sent to the prison-house to have them brought.

22 But the officers that came[25] found them not in the prison; and they returned, and told,

23 saying, The prison-house we found shut in all safety, and the keepers standing at the doors: but when we had opened, we found no man within.

24 Now when the captain of the temple and the chief priests heard these words, they were much perplexed concerning them whereunto this would grow.

25 And there came one and told them, Behold, the men whom ye put in the prison are in the temple standing and teaching the people.

26 Then went the captain with the officers, and brought them, *but* without violence; for they feared the people, lest they should be stoned.

[23] The Western text adds "and each one went to his own home" (*cf.* John 7:53)

[24] The Western text adds "having risen early."

[25] The Western text adds "having opened the prison."

27 And when they had brought them, they set them before the council. And the high priest[26] asked them,

28 saying, We strictly charged you not to teach in this
name: and behold, ye have filled Jerusalem with your
teaching, and intend to bring this man's blood upon us.

29 But Peter and the apostles answered and said, We
must obey God rather than men.[27]

30 The God of our fathers raised up Jesus, whom ye slew,
hanging him on a tree.

31 Him did God exalt with his right hand *to be* a Prince
and a Saviour, to give repentance to Israel, and remission of sins.

32 And we are witnesses of these things; and *so is* the
Holy Spirit, whom God hath given to them that obey
him.

17–18 Not long before, Peter and John had been dismissed
after an examination before the Sanhedrin, and warned to give
up speaking and teaching in the name of Jesus (*cf.* Ch. 4:18–21).
But Peter and John assured the Sanhedrin that they would do no
such thing. Other works of healing, similar to that performed
upon the cripple at the Beautiful Gate, created even more excitement among the common people, and the Sadducean leaders of
the Sanhedrin, the partisans of the chief-priestly families, swooped
on the whole band of apostles—presumably while they were
preaching in Solomon's colonnade (v. 12)—and had them locked
up overnight. Next day they intended to take more drastic steps
than they had taken on the previous occasion.

19–25 But when next day dawned, and a meeting of the Sanhedrin was convened to deal with the apostles, the apostles could
not be found. The prison doors were locked, the members of the
temple police force who were guarding them were at their posts,
but the prisoners had gone. In classical literature we can trace
a special "form" in which it had become customary to describe
unaccountable escapes from prison, and elements of this "form"
have been detected here;[28] but "form criticism" of this kind tells

[26] Cod. D has ἱερεύς ("priest") for ἀρχιερεύς ("high priest"). The African
Latin codex h (which exhibits a Western text) has *praetor*, which probably
represents a Greek reading στρατηγός (*i.e.* captain of the temple).

[27] The Western text renders v. 29 more directly: "But Peter said to him in
reply, 'Who should be obeyed? God, or men?' And he said, 'God.' And Peter
said to him, 'The God of our fathers . . .'"

[28] *Cf.* R. Reitzenstein, *Die hellenistischen Wundererzählungen* (Leipzig,

us little about the real facts of the matter which is being narrated. In this instance, the leaders of the Sanhedrin were naturally perturbed by the news, and the captain of the temple and his officers were even more perturbed, for they were responsible for the prisoners' safe keeping. However, if the prisoners had escaped, they had not gone far away; while the Sanhedrin was in session, a messenger came in to tell them that the apostles were standing in the temple court again, teaching the people. The authorities drew the disquieting conclusion that the apostles had even more support than they had imagined; they had sympathizers, it appeared, in the ranks of the temple police—perhaps even in the Sanhedrin itself. How otherwise could they have been so unobtrusively released from prison? Where was all this going to end?

Luke, however, describes the escape in different terms. It was "an angel of the Lord by night," he says, that "opened the prison doors, and brought them out," and told them to go back and preach the gospel to the people in the temple court. The idiom is that of the OT; the expression used by Luke is the one which is employed in the Septuagint to denote "the angel of Jehovah"—Jehovah Himself in His manifestation to men (*cf.* p. 151, n. 49; on Ch. 7:30). This is hardly the sense in which Luke uses the expression here; yet he does mean that the doors were opened by divine agency, whether the agent was a supernatural being or a human "messenger" of God (for the Greek word translated "angel" in NT is the ordinary word for "messenger").[29] No such details of the release are given here as later in Ch. 12:6 ff. But whoever the "messenger" was, he had a voice, for when he brought the apostles out of prison, he told them to proclaim in the temple court "all the words of this Life"—an apt term for the message of salvation.[30]

26–27 The captain of the temple, hearing that the apostles were still within his jurisdiction, went with his lieutenants[31] and

1906), pp. 120 ff. In this as in all form-critical studies it must be remembered that the material is more important than the form; meat-pies and mud-pies may be made in pie-dishes of identical shape, but the identity of shape is the least important consideration in comparing the two kinds of pies.

[29] Gk. ἄγγελος, like Heb. *mal'akh*, means simply "messenger"; but in the Bible both words are most commonly used of the spiritual attendants of God.

[30] See p. 89, n. 32 (on Ch. 3:15) for the close relation between ζωή and σωτηρία. The present expression is almost identical with "the word of this salvation" in Ch. 13:26; in the Syriac Peshitta version the term *haye* ("life") is used in both places.

[31] Called "captains (of the temple)" in Luke 22:4, 52 (Gk. στρατηγοί).

persuaded the apostles to accompany him to the meeting of the Sanhedrin. No force was used, but no resistance was offered. Had the apostles been minded to resist, they could have relied upon the support of the crowd that was listening to them and the temple officials would have been faced with an akward situation; thanks to the apostles' restraint, there was no breach of the peace.

28 When they took their place before the Sanhedrin, the high priest, as president of the court, reminded them of the previous warning, and expostulated with them for the way in which they had ignored it, filling the whole city with their teaching, as if they were determined to fasten the responsibility for Jesus' death on the leaders of the Sanhedrin. Perhaps the way in which he referred to Jesus as "this man" (v. 28) is an early example of the curious reluctance to pronounce the name Jesus which has become so common in Jewish orthodoxy.[32]

29–31 The words "Peter and the apostles answered" no doubt imply that Peter answered on behalf of the whole group. His answer is simply a repetition of the apostolic proclamation, emphasizing once more the contrast between what the rulers of the people did to Jesus and what God did to Him. "The God of our fathers raised up Jesus" (v. 30) refers probably to the inauguration of Jesus' ministry: God raised Him up as Prophet and King to Israel (cf. Ch. 3:26). The rulers, however, compassed His death, and the manner of His death was one upon which the OT law pronounced a curse: "he that is hanged (on a tree) is accursed of God" (Deut. 21 : 23).[33] In other words, they had inflicted the utmost disgrace upon Him. But God's right hand exalted Him (cf. Ch. 2:33); God bestowed the utmost honour upon Him, investing Him with the authority of Prince[34] and Saviour, to bless His people with the grace of repentance and the gift of forgiveness. With such a proclamation to make, the apostles could do no other than insist as they had done before that they must obey God rather than men.[35] The authority of the Sanhedrin was great, but greater still was the authority of Him who had commissioned them to make this good news known.

---

[32] Cf. J. Jocz, *The Jewish People and Jesus Christ* (London, 1949), p. 111.
[33] Cf. Jewish references to Jesus as *Taluy* ("the hanged one", the very form used in Deut. 21:23). Cf. Gal. 3:13.
[34] Gk. ἀρχηγός, as in Ch. 3:15; cf. p. 89, n. 32.
[35] Cf. p. 104 (on Ch. 4:19 f.).

32 For they were not only heralds of the good news, but witnesses as well, and not simply witnesses on their individual initiative, but witnesses under the direction of the Divine Witness, the Holy Spirit, imparted by God to all who obeyed the gospel. In these words we mark again the apostolic community's consciousness of being possessed and indwelt by the Spirit to such a degree that they were His organ of expression; we also mark a noteworthy agreement with the words of Jesus reported in John 15:26 f., "But when the Comforter is come, whom I will send unto you from the Father, even the Spirit of truth, which proceedeth from the Father, he shall bear witness of me: and ye also bear witness, because ye have been with me from the beginning."

(c)   Gamaliel's Advice: the Apostles Dismissed (Ch. 5:33–42)

33 But they, when they heard this, were cut to the heart, and were minded to slay them.

34 But there stood up one in the council, a Pharisee, named Gamaliel, a doctor of the law, had in honor of all the people, and commanded to put the men forth a little while.

35 And he said unto them,[36] Ye men of Israel, take heed to yourselves as touching these men, what ye are about to do.

36 For before these days rose up Theudas, giving himself out to be somebody;[37] to whom a number of men, about four hundred, joined themselves, who was slain;[38] and all, as many as obeyed him, were dispersed, and came to nought.

37 After this man rose up Judas of Galilee in the days of the enrolment, and drew away *some of the* people after him: he also perished; and all,[39] as many as obeyed him, were scattered abroad.

38 And now I say unto you, Refrain from these men, and let them alone:[40] for if this counsel or this work be of men, it will be overthrown:

39 but if it is of God, ye will not be able to overthrow

---

[36] For "them" Cod. D has "the rulers and those who sat with them."

[37] The Western text has "some great one" (doubtless from Ch. 8:9).

[38] Cod. D reads "was destroyed through his own act" ($\kappa\alpha\tau\epsilon\lambda\acute{\upsilon}\theta\eta$ $\alpha\grave{\upsilon}\tau\grave{o}\varsigma$ $\delta\iota'$ $\alpha\grave{\upsilon}\tau o\tilde{\upsilon}$ for $\grave{\alpha}\nu\eta\varrho\acute{\epsilon}\theta\eta$).

[39] D and P^{45} omit "all."

[40] D adds "not defiling your hands."

them,[41] lest haply ye be found even to be fighting against God.

40 And to him they agreed: and when they had called the apostles unto them, they beat them and charged them not to speak in the name of Jesus, and let them go.

41 They therefore departed from the presence of the council, rejoicing that they were counted worthy to suffer dishonor for the Name.

42 And every day, in the temple and at home, they ceased not to teach and to preach Jesus *as* the Christ.

33-34 The Sadducean leaders of the Sanhedrin were so enraged at this defiance of their orders that they considered passing sentence of death (by stoning, no doubt) on the apostles. But they could take no such action without the support of the Pharisaic members of the court.[42] The Pharisees were in the minority, but they commanded much more popular respect than the Sadducees did, so much so that the Sadducean members of the Sanhedrin

[41] The Western text adds "neither you nor kings nor tyrants. Refrain therefore from these men."

[42] The word "Pharisees" (Gk. $\Phi\alpha\varrho\iota\sigma\alpha\tilde{\iota}o\iota$) is most commonly derived from Heb. *perushim*, Aram. *perishayya*, "separated ones" (but see p. 454). This name probably indicated both their general tendency to withdraw themselves from contact with those who were careless about ceremonial purity, and in particular their withdrawal from their alliance with the Hasmoneans after the success of the revolt against the Seleucids in the time of Antiochus IV (175–163 B.C.). For the Pharisees were descended from the *hasidim* (the "Hasidaeans," $^{\prime}A\sigma\iota\delta\alpha\tilde{\iota}o\iota$, of 1 Macc. 2:42; 7:13; 2 Macc. 14:6), the pious members of the community who in Hellenistic times gave themselves to the study and exposition of the written and oral law and opposed the popular Hellenizing tendencies. When Antiochus IV tried to abolish the Jewish religion, they gave their support to the Hasmoneans, the insurgent leaders, but withdrew their support when the Hasmoneans went on to establish civil as well as military supremacy for themselves and assumed the high priesthood. Thereafter they were in opposition to the ruling party except under Queen Salome Alexandra (76–67 B.C.), who gave them a position of great influence during her reign. In the first century A.D. they were about five or six thousand strong, organized in "brotherhoods" (*haburoth*). They had great religious influence with the people, the more so as most of the scribes, the public expositors of the law, belonged to their party. Their two chief schools in NT times were those of Hillel and Shammai, two leading rabbis who flourished in the later part of Herod's reign. After the fall of Jerusalem and the temple in A.D. 70 it was the Pharisaic party, and more particularly the school of Hillel, that proved best able to survive the collapse of the old temple-constitution and preserve the continuity of national life. For their distinctive beliefs see Ch. 23:6–8 (with exposition and notes). *Cf.* L. Finkelstein, *The Pharisees* (New York, 1938); J. Bowman, "The Pharisees", EQ xx (1948), pp. 125 ff.; H. L. Ellison, "Jesus and the Pharisees", *Journal of Transactions of Victoria Institute* lxxxv (1953), pp. 35 ff.; T. W. Manson, *The Servant-Messiah* (Cambridge, 1953), pp. 16 ff.

found it impolitic to oppose the Pharisees' demands.[43] This was particularly important in a case like the present, where the defendants enjoyed the people's good will.

There was present at this meeting of the Sanhedrin a Pharisaic leader of quite exceptional eminence, Rabban[44] Gamaliel the Elder, the greatest teacher of the day. He was a disciple of the gentle Hillel, and was now leader of the school of Hillel. He himself had many illustrious disciples, among them Saul of Tarsus (cf. Ch. 22:3). His prestige was such that in later days it could be said, "Since Rabban Gamaliel the Elder died there has been no more reverence for the Law, and purity and abstinence[45] died out at the same time" (Mishnah, Sota ix. 15). He now rose up in the Sanhedrin and directed that the apostles should be taken out of the council-chamber for a little, in order that he might speak his mind to his fellow-councillors.[46]

35–36 Gamaliel warned the others not to do anything rash. His advice consists of "sound Pharisaic teaching; God is over all, and needs no help from men for the fulfilment of His purposes; all men must do is to obey, and leave the issue to Him" (J. A. Findlay, *The Acts of the Apostles* [London, 1936], p. 85). We meet very similar sentiments in a dictum of a second-century rabbi, John the sandal-maker: "Every assembly which is in the name of heaven will finally be established, but that which is not in the name of heaven will not finally be established" (*Pirqe Aboth* iv. 14). This is exactly Gamaliel's point, and he illustrates it by reminding the Sanhedrin of other movements within their lifetime which for a time enjoyed considerable support but were not finally established, because (presumably) they were not "in the name of heaven."

First, he reminded them of an insurgent named Theudas, who made large claims for himself and secured a following of four hundred men, but he achieved nothing but his own destruction and the dispersal of his followers. We have no other certain infor-

---

[43] *Cf.* Josephus, *Antiquities* xviii. 1.4.

[44] *Rabban* (lit. "our teacher") was an Aramaic term applied as an honorific title to several successive leaders of the school of Hillel, marking them off from those who received the more ordinary title *Rabbi* (lit. "my teacher").

[45] The word translated "abstinence" is *perishuth*, from the same root as that from which "Pharisee" was popularly derived; it denotes therefore the sum-total of the true Pharisaic virtues.

[46] We need not stay long to inquire how Luke could know what Paul's teacher said in the Sanhedrin in the absence of the apostolic defendants.

mation about this Theudas, but we know that many insurgent leaders arose in Palestine when Herod the Great died in 4 B.C., and Theudas may have been one of them.[47]

37 We know more about the second occasion mentioned by Gamaliel. Judas of Galilee led a revolt in A.D. 6, when Judaea was reduced to the status of a Roman province and a census was held to assess the amount of tribute it should yield for the imperial exchequer. Judas, a man from Gamala in Gaulanitis (*cf.* the OT Golan), inaugurated a religious and nationalist revolt, contending that God alone was Israel's true King, and that it was therefore high treason against God to pay tribute to Caesar.[48] The revolt was crushed by Rome, but the movement lived on in the party of the Zealots.[49] It had not been so ineffective as Gamaliel's description suggests.

38-39 Therefore, said Gamaliel, take no direct action against these men. If their movement is not of God, it will come to nothing in any case; on the other hand, if after all it does prove to be of God, you would not wish to be found fighting against Him.[50]

[47] Josephus tells us (*Antiquities* xx. 5.1) about a magician called Theudas who led a large company to the Jordan, promising that at his word of command the river would be divided, that they might cross it dryshod. The procurator Cuspius Fadus (A.D. 44–46) sent a body of horsemen against them; they routed the multitude and brought the head of Theudas to Jerusalem. This event, however, took place several years after the incident now being described by Luke, and we cannot identify the two men called Theudas, which in any case was a sufficiently common name. They have, even so, been identified by some who are prepared to make Luke guilty of a double blunder—(*a*) making Gamaliel refer to a rising which did not take place until ten or more years later, (*b*) making an event of A.D. 44 or thereby take place before the rising of Judas in A.D. 6. The double blunder is accounted for by supposing that Luke misread Josephus (who goes on, after his account of the magician Theudas, to mention the *sons* of Judas). But the arguments for Luke's knowledge of Josephus's *Antiquities* are quite unconvincing, and involve us in the conclusion that Luke misread Josephus every time that he drew upon him. "Either Luke had not read Josephus, or else he forgot all that he had read" (E. Schürer, *Zeitschrift für wissenschaftliche Theologie* xix [1876], p. 582).

[48] *Cf.* Josephus, *Jewish War* ii. 8.1; *Antiquities* xviii. 1.1. The census was held by Publius Sulpicius Quirinius when he was imperial legate of Syria for the second time (A.D. 6–7). There has inevitably been some confusion between it and the earlier census held, according to Luke 2:2, on the first occasion "when Quirinius was governor of Syria." *Cf.* F. F. Bruce in *New Schaff-Herzog Relig. Encycl.*, Suppl. Vol. I, *s.v.* "Census."

[49] *Cf.* pp. 43 f., nn. 44, 45 (on Ch. 1:13).

[50] *Cf.* Nicodemus's plea to Pilate on Jesus' behalf in the apocryphal *Acts of Pilate* 5:1, "Let him alone and do not contrive any evil against him: if the signs which he performs are of God, they will stand, but if they are of men, they will come to nought." (In Nicodemus's argument the works of the

There is much common sense in this position, for certain kinds of men—and movements—can safely be relied upon to hang themselves if they are given enough rope; but Gamaliel's policy of "Wait and see" is not always the right one to adopt in religious life. His pupil Saul of Tarsus was of a very different mind.

40 However, Gamaliel's advice fortunately prevailed on this occasion. It probably represented the viewpoint of the other Pharisees in the Sanhedrin as well. The court was content to inflict the minor penalty of flogging (presumably with "forty stripes save one")[51] on the apostles for disobeying its previous order.

41-42 The apostles, having received their punishment, left the court in no way disheartened; they found cause for joy in the thought that God had counted them worthy to suffer this disgrace for the sake of Jesus' name.[52] It was insignificant, to be sure, when compared with the shame and anguish that He had endured; but, as far as it went, it was a participation in His sufferings, such as He had warned them to expect.[53] As for the Sanhedrin's repeated ban on speaking in the name of Jesus, they paid no more attention to it than they had done before, but continued daily, in the temple court and in their own homes, to proclaim Jesus as the Messiah.

Egyptian magicians Jannes and Jambres serve the purpose which the risings of Theudas and Judas serve in Gamaliel's argument. The apocryphal author is no doubt dependent on the present passage of Acts.)

[51] A limit based on Deut. 25:3 (cf. 2 Cor. 11:24).

[52] The text (v. 41) has simply "for the Name" (Gk. ὑπὲρ τοῦ ὀνόματος); to Christians there was one Name above every name, the Name of Jesus. This absolute use of τὸ ὄνομα recurs in 3 John 7 and is common in the Apostolic Fathers.

[53] Cf. Matt. 10:17 ff.; Mark 13:9 ff.; Luke 12:11 f.; 21:12 ff.; John 15:18 ff.; 16:2 ff.

CHAPTER VI

II. PERSECUTION LEADS TO EXPANSION
(Ch. 6:1–9:31)

1. STEPHEN
(Ch. 6:1–8:1a)

(a) The Appointing of the Seven (Ch. 6:1–6)

1 Now in these days, when the number of the disciples was multiplying, there arose a murmuring of the Grecian Jews against the Hebrews, because their widows were neglected in the daily ministration.[1]

2 And the twelve called the multitude of the disciples unto them, and said, It is not fit that we should forsake the word of God, and serve tables.

3 Look ye out therefore, brethren, from among you[2] seven men of good report, full of the Spirit and of wisdom, whom we may appoint over this business.

4 But we will continue stedfastly in prayer, and in the ministry of the word.

5 And the saying pleased the whole multitude: and they chose Stephen, a man full of faith and of the Holy Spirit, and Philip, and Prochorus, and Nicanor, and Timon, and Parmenas, and Nicolaus a proselyte of Antioch;

6 whom they set before the apostles; and when they had prayed, they laid their hands upon them.

The time has now come to record a new and momentous advance in the community of the followers of Jesus. This advance involved the large-scale evangelization of Gentiles. It was the Hellenistic group in the Jerusalem church who took the lead in this new work, and Luke therefore introduces his account of it by telling us something of this Hellenistic group and its leaders.

1 The church of Jerusalem comprised both "Hebrews" (Ara-

---

[1] The Western text adds a phrase which may be rendered "because it was being administered by Hebrews."

[2] The Western reading is "What is it then, brethren? Look out from among yourselves . . ."

maic-speaking Jews, most of them natives of Palestine) and Hellenists or "Grecian Jews" (Jews whose habitual language was Greek, many of whom were natives of the Greco-Roman lands of the dispersion or at least had affinities with those lands).[3] In the Jewish world as a whole there was some tension between "Hebrews" and Hellenists,[4] and this tension survived between members of the two groups who had acknowledged Jesus as the Messiah and been incorporated in the messianic community.

The tension came to a head (as tension often does) in what might appear a trifling matter. As daily allocations were made to the poorer members of the church from the common pool to which the wealthier members had contributed their estates, complaints began to arise that one group was being favoured at the expense of the other. Widows naturally formed a considerable proportion of the poorer members of the church, and the Hellenistic widows were said to be at a disadvantage in comparison with the "Hebrew" widows, perhaps because the distribution of charity was in the hands of "Hebrews."

2–4 The apostles wisely determined to put the trouble right at once. It was not their primary business to supervise the financial arrangements of the community or to take an active part in the "daylie handreachinge"[5] (as Coverdale's version of 1535 calls it). They therefore called the community together and bade them select seven men to be responsible for administering the charitable allocation. These seven must be men of honourable reputation, so that their probity might command complete confidence; they must be wise men, competent in administration and also qualified to deal wisely with a situation in which there were such delicate human susceptibilities to consider; above all, they must be men filled with the Holy Spirit. It would be well if this precedent were observed in all church appointments. If such men were ap-

---

[3] On the term "Hellenists," (Gk. *Ἑλληνισταί)* see H. J. Cadbury, "The Hellenists," in *Beginnings* v (London, 1933), pp. 59 ff.; H. Windisch in TWNT ii (Stuttgart, 1935), pp. 508 f., and W. Bauer, *Griechisch-deutsches Wörterbuch zum NT* (Berlin, 1952), s.v. *Ἑλληνιστής.* The word is derived from the verb *ἑλληνίζω* ("to speak Greek"), which was used of Greeks as well as of non-Greeks who affected Greek speech and ways.

[4] We find this tension in the early Hellenistic period (*cf.* 1 Macc. 1:11–15); for the later Hellenistic and early Roman period see the account by J. Klausner, *From Jesus to Paul* (Eng. tr., London, 1944), pp. 7 ff.

[5] This rendering plainly reflects Luther's "*in der täglichen Handreichung*."

pointed to take charge of the distribution and see that no further cause for complaint arose, the apostles would be free to devote their undistracted attention to the regular worship of the church and to the preaching of the gospel.

5 The apostolic suggestion met with approval, and seven men were duly selected. It is remarkable that all seven have Greek names, which may suggest that they all belonged to the Hellenistic group. Stephen heads the list: he is more particularly described as "a man full of faith and of the Holy Spirit"—a description whose relevance and significance appear very clearly as the story goes on. Philip also plays an important part in the later narrative of Acts.[6] About the other five we are less well informed. Later tradition represents Prochorus as amanuensis of John the Evangelist, as bishop of Nicomedia and as martyred at Antioch.[7] Luke himself gives us two interesting facts about the last-named of the seven: he was not even a Jew by birth, but a proselyte; and he belonged to Antioch—Syrian Antioch, of course. That the only member of the seven to have his place of origin named should belong to Antioch is a mark of Luke's special interest in that city which helps to confirm the tradition that he himself was an Antiochene.[8] As early as the time of Irenaeus[9] (c. A.D. 180) this Nicolaus was held to be the founder of the people called Nico-

[6] Cf. Chs. 8:5 ff.; 21:8 f. Luke may have been indebted to him for some of the material of this section of Acts (see p. 424 with nn. 11 and 12).

[7] Under his name there has come down to us an apocryphal fifth-century work called the *Acts of John* (an orthodox work, not to be confused with the earlier work of the same name by the Gnostic Lucius).

[8] James Smith points out, as a parallel to this passage, that out of eight accounts of Napoleon's Russian campaign—three by Frenchmen, three by Englishmen, and two by Scots—only the two Scots mention that the Russian general Barclay de Tolly was of Scots extraction (*Voyage and Shipwreck of St. Paul* [4th edn., London, 1880], p. 4). See p. 243, n. 32 (on Ch. 11:28).

[9] *Against Heresies* i. 26.3; cf. iii. 11.1. Victorinus of Pettau (c. A.D. 300), in the earliest extant Latin commentary on the Apocalypse, has this note on Rev. 2:6: "Before that time factious and pestilential men had made for themselves a heresy in the name of the deacon Nicolaus, teaching that meat offered to idols could be exorcized, so that it might be eaten, and that one who had committed fornication might receive absolution on the eighth day." Victorinus, who is more circumstantial in his account than Irenaeus, and appears to absolve Nicolaus from personal responsibility for Nicolaitanism, probably drew his information from Papias; and Papias must have known what he was talking about. The Nicolaitan teaching is represented in Rev. 2:14 f. as a breach of the decisions taken at the Council of Jerusalem (*cf.* exposition of Ch. 15:29, p. 316 below); it apparently aimed at making the Christian path in a pagan world a little smoother by permitting so much compromise with idolatry as would satisfy imperial and social requirements.

129

laitans in Rev. 2:6, 15. The word "Nicolaitans" is certainly derived from "Nicolaus"; but we cannot be sure whether they were actually called after this Nicolaus or some other of the same name.

6 It was the community as a whole that selected these seven men and presented them to the apostles for their approbation; it was the apostles who appointed them to their office. This they did by laying their hands on them after prayer. The ceremony of imposition of hands was used in the OT for the bestowal of a blessing (cf. Gen. 48:13 ff.), to express identification, as when the sacrificer laid his hands on the head of the sacrificial victim (cf. Lev. 1:4; 3:2; 4:4; 16:21, etc.), for commissioning a successor (cf. Num. 27:23) and the like. According to the Mishnah (Sanhedrin iv. 4) members of the Sanhedrin were admitted by the imposition of hands.[10] In the present instance the imposition of apostolic hands formally associated the seven with the twelve, as their deputies to discharge a special duty. It did not, of course, impart the gift of the Spirit; the seven were already "full of the Spirit" (v. 3).

The seven are traditionally called "deacons" and in many Christian circles this term has come to be used in a restricted sense of those who are responsible for the financial affairs of the church. While the Greek noun diakonos, from which "deacon" is derived, is not used in this passage,[11] the cognate noun diakonia is used (as is also the verb diakoneo, "to serve", in v. 2);[12] but diakonia is used impartially of "the daily ministration"[13] (v. 1) and "the ministry of the word"[14] (v. 4). With reference to their present function, it might be better to describe the seven as "almoners": and where Gk. diakonos appears elsewhere in NT to denote a class of service in the church distinct from that of the "bishop" (episkopos) or "elder" (presbyteros),[15] it might be better to render it by the more general term "minister" (cf. Phil. 1:1; 1 Tim. 3:8 ff.).

[10] The ceremony was called semikhah in Hebrew. Cf. Chs. 8:17; 9:12, 17; 19:6, with accompanying exposition and notes.

[11] The NT uses διάκονος in a wide variety of senses, e.g. of domestic servants, civil magistrates as servants of God, Christian preachers and teachers as servants of Christ, and even Christ Himself (cf. Rom. 15:8).

[12] Gk. διακονεῖν τραπέζαις, "to serve tables."

[13] Gk. τῇ διακονίᾳ τῇ καθημερινῇ.

[14] Gk. τῇ διακονίᾳ τοῦ λόγου.

[15] For πρεσβύτερος and ἐπίσκοπος see Ch. 20: 17, 28, with exposition and notes.

While the seven are here described as almoners, it is plain that their activity was by no means confined to this kind of service. They may in fact have been regarded as leaders of the Hellenistic group within the church. The activity of Stephen and Philip, at any rate, which Luke goes on to describe in detail, shows that these two members of the seven were well equipped for other forms of service—Stephen for the defence of the faith and Philip for the work of evangelism.

(b)   Fresh Progress (Ch. 6:7)

7 And the word of God increased; and the number of the disciples multiplied in Jerusalem exceedingly; and a great company of the priests[16] were obedient to the faith.[17]

7 At this point Luke interrupts his narrative with a brief report of progress. Six such brief reports appear at intervals throughout the book and serve to punctuate his history.[18] But here, immediately before the account of Stephen's activity, there is special relevance in Luke's emphasis on the church's increase in numbers and popularity. In particular, the fact that so many priests joined the community meant that the ties which attached so many of the believers to the temple-order would be strengthened.[19] It is not suggested that these priests relinquished their priestly office; the logic of such a step would not be generally appreciated at this stage. The ordinary priests were socially and in other ways far removed from the wealthy chief-priestly families from which the main opposition to the gospel came. Many of the

---

[16] There is a variant reading "Jews" instead of "priests" in Cod. ℵ and a few minuscules; there is also a Western variant "in the temple" (ἐν τῷ ἱερῷ for τῶν ἱερέων).

[17] This objective use of "faith" as that which is believed (practically equivalent to "gospel") is rare in Acts; possibly we should render "were obedient by faith" (cf. "obedience of faith" in Rom. 1:5; 16:26).

[18] Cf. Chs. 9:31; 12:24; 16:5; 19:20; 28:31. C. H. Turner points out that Acts is thus cut into six "panels" covering on an average five years each (Hastings' DB, i [Edinburgh, 1898], pp. 421 ff., in article "Chronology of the NT").

[19] "There is tremendous tension in the few words in Acts 6:7, 'a great company of the priests were obedient to the faith,' coming, as it does, just before the great cleavage" (R. A. Cole, *The New Temple* [London, 1950], p. 33). K. Bornhäuser interpreted the Epistle to the Hebrews on the improbable theory that it was written to these believing priests (*Empfänger und Verfasser des Briefes an die Hebräer*, Gütersloh, 1932). Cf. C. Spicq, *L'Epître aux Hébreux* (Paris, 1952–3), i, pp. 218, 226 ff.

ordinary priests were no doubt men holy and humble of heart, like Zacharias, the father of John the Baptist, men who would be readily convinced of the truth of the gospel. But it was not good that the new movement should be too closely attached to the old order.

(c) Stephen's Activity Arouses Opposition (Ch. 6:8-15)

8 And Stephen, full of grace and power, wrought great wonders and signs among the people.[20]

9 But there arose certain of them that were of the synagogue called *the synagogue* of the Libertines, and of the Cyrenians, and of the Alexandrians, and of them of Cilicia and Asia, disputing with Stephen.

10 And they were not able to withstand[21] the wisdom and the Spirit by which he spake.

11 Then they suborned men, who said, We have heard him speak blasphemous words against Moses, and *against* God.

12 And they stirred up the people, and the elders, and the scribes, and came upon him, and seized him, and brought him into the council,

13 and set up false witnesses, who said, This man ceaseth not to speak words against this holy place, and the law:

14 for we have heard him say, that this Jesus of Nazareth shall destroy this place, and shall change the customs which Moses delivered unto us.

15 And all that sat in the council, fastening their eyes on him, saw his face as it had been the face of an angel.[22]

8 Whether Stephen performed wonders and signs before he was appointed one of the seven is not apparent. According to one point of view, it is through the imposition of apostolic hands that "the Seven evidently receive (or rather, Stephen and Philip evidently receive) what Luke regards as the distinctive mode of the Spirit's activity in the missionary enterprise—the Spirit of God which confirms the word of God with signs and wonders" (G. W. H. Lampe, *The Seal of the Spirit* [London, 1951], p. 74). Stephen,

---

20 There is a Western addition, "by the name of the Lord (Jesus Christ)."

21 After "withstand" the Western text continues: ". . . the wisdom which was in him and the Holy Spirit by whom he spoke, for they were confuted before him with all boldness of speech. Being unable, therefore, to face up to him, they suborned men . . ."

22 The Western text adds "standing in their midst."

132

however, is described as "a man full of faith and of the Holy Spirit" at the time of his appointment (v. 5) and it seems reasonable to suppose that his fulness of the Spirit was manifested by these signs even before the apostles laid their hands on him for a special work. This aspect of his activity would naturally bring him into favour "among the people", as it brought the apostles (Ch. 5:12 f.). But another aspect of his activity incurred general and fierce hostility.

9–10 Stephen expounded his distinctive teaching about the implications of the gospel in one of the synagogues of Jerusalem which was frequented by Jews from a number of the lands of the dispersion, the synagogue "of the Libertines, that is to say of the Cyrenians, and of the Alexandrians, and of them of Cilicia and Asia."[23] (There is much difference of opinion about the exact meaning of these terms, but the synagogue in question was probably attended by freedmen and their descendants from the four areas mentioned.[24] The mention of Cilicia suggests that this may have been the synagogue which Saul of Tarsus attended in Jerusalem.) Stephen's reasoning provoked keen opposition, and a full-dress debate was probably arranged.[25] The exact subject of the debate is not stated; it no doubt concerned the Messiahship of Jesus, but Stephen expounded the implications of His Messiahship more radically than his fellow-believers had hitherto expounded it. The nature of his argument may be inferred from the charges which were brought against him (vv. 13 f.) and from his reply (Ch. 7). The strength of his case was such that his opponents in the debate found themselves worsted. They accepted his premises (which were based on their joint acknowledgment of the authority

---

[23] The synagogue was instituted, perhaps as early as the Babylonian exile, for the reading and exposition of the sacred scriptures. Especially in the lands of the dispersion, it served as the general community centre for the Jews in any locality. In a large town there would be several Jewish synagogues, although the Talmudic statement that there were four hundred and eighty in Jerusalem before its destruction (TJ *Megillah* 73 d) may be taken with a grain of salt!

[24] It is most likely that only one synagogue is indicated, although others have seen a reference to two, three, four or five synagogues in the text. The emendation of "Libertines" to "Libyans" (so Beza, Tischendorf, M. Dibelius) is tempting in the vicinity of "Cyrenians" and "Alexandrians"; but the temptation should be resisted. A *libertinus* (the Latin term here appearing as a loanword in Gk.) was either a freedman or the son of a freedman.

[25] *Cf.* R. A. Cole, *op. cit.*, p. 34.

of OT Scripture), but they refused to accept his conclusions, so scandalous and revolutionary did they appear.

11 Unable to silence Stephen in open debate, his opponents adopted another course. Informers were put up to represent his arguments in the most damaging light. "We have heard him speak blasphemous words against Moses, and against God." Against Moses, for his arguments appeared to challenge the abiding validity of the law. Against God, for they appeared to undermine the temple-order, the very foundation of national worship. According to the later formulation of rabbinical law, blasphemy involved the profane use of the Ineffable Name of the God of Israel (Mishnah, *Sanhedrin* vii. 5).[26] But, as the narrative of the trial of our Lord before the Sanhedrin shows, blasphemy was interpreted in a wider sense in the early decades of the first century A.D. (*cf.* Mark 14:61–64). Stephen, it appears, maintained and emphasized the claim which, on the lips of Jesus, had called forth a unanimous verdict that He was guilty of blasphemy. But it is interesting to note that, while Stephen is later reported as making a claim for Jesus very similar to that which He Himself had made before the Sanhedrin (Ch. 7:56), at this stage the charge of blasphemy was evidently based on the allegation that he had used language about the temple similar to the language which Jesus was unsuccessfully accused of using about it.

12–14 The charge brought against Stephen was all the deadlier because it was one which would infuriate the people of Jerusalem. Any threat to the temple—real or imagined—was a threat to their livelihood as well as to their religious interests. The chief-priestly party knew that they need have no fear of popular disapproval this time in prosecuting a leading member of the messianic community; on the contrary, the people would support and indeed demand the severest sanctions of the law against this man. Stephen was accordingly arrested and put on his trial before the Sanhedrin.

The witnesses gave their evidence. "This man never ceases speaking against this holy place and the law,[27] for we have heard him say that this Jesus the Nazarene will destroy this place and

---

[26] "The blasphemer is not guilty until he have expressly uttered the Name." The Jewish law of blasphemy is an amplification of the Third Commandment (Ex. 20:7; Deut. 5:11).

[27] *Cf.* the charge brought against Paul in Ch. 21:28.

change the customs which have been handed down to us by Moses."
The holy place is, of course, the temple. The words spoken by
Stephen against the temple turn out to be, according to these
witnesses, his statement that Jesus would destroy it. The words
spoken against the law, according to them, consisted in his claim
that Jesus would alter the Mosaic tradition.

They are called "false witnesses," as those who brought similar
testimony against Jesus are called (Matt. 26:59–61; Mark 14:55–
59). But in both cases the falseness of their testimony consisted
not in wholesale fabrication but in subtle and deadly misrepresen-
tation of words actually spoken. The charge brought against Jesus
was that He had said, "I will destroy this temple that is made
with hands, and in three days I will build another made without
hands" (Mark 14:58; cf. Matt. 26:61).[28] It is the fourth Evangelist
who supplies us with the words which Jesus really spoke, and
(what is equally important) with their true significance. "Destroy
this temple, and in three days I will raise it up." The bystanders
thought He meant that He could rebuild in three days the material
temple whose restoration, inaugurated by Herod the Great in 20–
19 B.C., had now been going on for forty-six years. "But," says
the Evangelist, "he spake of the temple of his body" (John 2:19–
21). And, as so often in the fourth Gospel, we may recognize a
double relevance in the words "the temple of his body." First of
all, there is a reference to our Lord's bodily resurrection. But is
there not also a reference to "the church which is his body" (cf.
Eph. 1:22 f.), that spiritual house of living stones where spiritual
sacrifices are offered up by a holy priesthood, acceptable to God
through Jesus Christ (cf. I Pet. 2:5)?

Whatever form of words Stephen used which gave rise to the
charge that he said Jesus the Nazarene would destroy the temple,
it seems plain that he had not only repeated the words which
Jesus Himself had spoken, but also grasped and expounded their
inner meaning. The apostles and many of the rank and file of
the Jerusalem church might continue to attend the temple services
and be looked upon as devout and observant Jews; Stephen saw
that the work of Christ logically involved the abrogation of the
whole temple order and its supersession by a new edifice not
made with hands, and yet within the main stream of OT reve-

[28] Cf. Ch. 7:48, with accompanying exposition and notes.

135

lation. Jesus Himself had said, "one greater than the temple is here" (Matt. 12:6); these and other sayings of His about the temple were apparently preserved by the early church in Jerusalem, but it was Stephen who appreciated their full force. The gospel meant the end of the sacrificial cultus and all the ceremonial law. These were the outward and visible signs of Jewish particularism, and could not be reconciled with the universal scope of the Christian message of salvation accomplished. This was the argument, pressed by Stephen in synagogue debate, which formed the real basis of the case for the prosecution.

15 But while his accusers pressed their charge against him, Stephen stood before the Sanhedrin with face aglow, as one who stood in the presence of God.[29]   This was "not the mild, gentle look that is often seen in paintings of angels; not the fierce look of an avenging angel, but a look that told of inspiration within, clear eyes burning with the inner light. We can hardly doubt that it was Saul who remembered that look, a look which burnt into his soul until he too was turned to accept Jesus as his master and learnt in his own life to experience the presence of the Holy Spirit" (L. E. Browne, *The Acts of the Apostles* (London, 1925], *ad loc.*).

---

[29] *Cf.* the description of Paul in the second-century *Acts of Paul* (see p. 288 with n. 7): "full of grace, for at times he looked like a man, and at times he had the face of an angel."

CHAPTER VII

(d)   Stephen's Defence (Ch. 7:1–50)

1 And the high priest said,[1] Are these things so?
2 And he said,
   Brethren and fathers, hearken: The God of glory appeared unto our father Abraham, when he was in Mesopotamia, before he dwelt in Haran,
3 and said unto him, Get thee out of thy land, and from thy kindred, and come into the land which I shall show thee.
4 Then came he out of the land of the Chaldaeans, and dwelt in Haran: and from thence, when his father was dead, *God* removed him into this land, wherein ye now dwell:[2]
5 and he gave him none inheritance in it, no, not so much as to set his foot on: and he promised that he would give it to him in possession, and to his seed after him, when *as yet* he had no child.
6 And God spake on this wise, that his seed should sojourn in a strange land, and that they should bring them into bondage, and treat them ill, four hundred years.
7 And the nation to which they shall be in bondage will I judge, said God: and after that shall they come forth, and serve me in this place.
8 And he gave him the covenant of circumcision: and so *Abraham* begat Isaac, and circumcised him the eighth day; and Isaac *begat* Jacob, and Jacob the twelve patriarchs.
9 And the patriarchs, moved with jealousy against Joseph, sold him into Egypt: and God was with him,
10 and delivered him out of all his afflictions, and gave him favor and wisdom before Pharaoh king of Egypt; and he made him governor over Egypt and all his house.
11 Now there came a famine over all Egypt and Canaan,

---

[1] The Western text adds "to Stephen."
[2] The Western text adds "and your fathers before you."

and great affliction: and our fathers found no sustenance.

12 But when Jacob heard that there was grain in Egypt, he sent forth our fathers the first time.

13 And at the second time Joseph was made known to his brethren; and Joseph's race became manifest unto Pharaoh.

14 And Joseph sent, and called to him Jacob his father, and all his kindred, three score and fifteen souls.

15 And Jacob went down into Egypt;[3] and he died, himself and our fathers;

16 and they were carried over unto Shechem, and laid in the tomb that Abraham bought for a price in silver of the sons of Hamor in Shechem.[4]

17 But as the time of the promise drew nigh which God vouchsafed[5] unto Abraham, the people grew and multiplied in Egypt.

18 till there arose another king over Egypt, who knew not[6] Joseph.

19 The same dealt craftily with our race, and ill-treated our fathers, that they should cast out their babes to the end they might not live.

20 At which season Moses was born, and was exceeding fair;[7] and he was nourished three months in his father's house:

21 and when he was cast out, Pharaoh's daughter took him up, and nourished him for her own son.

22 And Moses was instructed in all the wisdom of the Egyptians; and he was mighty in his words and works.

23 But when he was well-nigh forty years old, it came into his heart to visit his brethren the children of Israel.

[3] Cod. B omits "into Egypt."

[4] The Western and Byzantine texts have "of Shechem", whence AV "the father of Shechem."

[5] Gk. ὡμολόγησεν. The Western text and P45 have ἐπηγγείλατο ("promised"); the Byzantine text and the normally Alexandrian minuscule 81 have ὤμοσεν ("swore").

[6] The Western text has "did not remember."

[7] Literally "fair to God" (Gk. ἀστεῖος τῷ θεῷ.) Such expressions occur elsewhere with elative force; cf. Jonah 3:3, where "an exceeding great city" (ARV) represents the Hebrew idiom "a city great unto God" (ARV mg.); cf. LXX, πόλις μεγάλη τῷ θεῷ. Moses is described as ἀστεῖος in Ex. 2:2 (LXX); Heb. 11:23.

24 And seeing one *of them* suffer wrong, he defended
   him, and avenged him that was oppressed, smiting the
   Egyptian:[8]

25 and he supposed that his brethren understood that God
   by his hand was giving them deliverance; but they
   understood not.

26 And the day following he appeared unto them as they
   strove, and would have set them at one again, saying,
   Sirs, ye are brethren;[9] why do ye wrong one to another?

27 But he that did his neighbor wrong thrust him away,
   saying, Who made thee a ruler and a judge over us?

28 Wouldest thou kill me, as thou killedst the Egyptian
   yesterday?

29 And Moses fled at this saying, and became a sojourner
   in the land of Midian, where he begat two sons.

30 And when forty years were fulfilled, an angel appeared
   to him in the wilderness of Mount Sinai, in a flame
   of fire in a bush.

31 And when Moses saw it, he wondered at the sight:
   and as he drew near to behold, there came a voice of
   the Lord,[10]

32 I am the God of thy fathers, the God of Abraham,
   and of Isaac, and of Jacob.[11] And Moses trembled,
   and durst not behold.

33 And the Lord said unto him, Loose the shoes from thy
   feet, for the place whereon thou standest is holy ground.

34 I have surely seen the affliction of my people that is
   in Egypt, and have heard their groaning, and I am
   come down to deliver them: and now come, I will
   send thee into Egypt.

35 This Moses, whom they refused, saying, Who made
   thee a ruler and a judge?[12] him hath God sent *to be*
   both a ruler and a deliverer with the hand of the angel
   that appeared to him in the bush.

36 This man led them forth, having wrought wonders

[8] The Western text adds "of his race" after "suffer wrong" and "and buried
him in the sand" after "Egyptian" (following Ex. 2:12).

[9] The Western text has "What are you doing, brethren?"

[10] The Western text has "the Lord spoke to him, saying."

[11] The Western text follows the OT (Ex. 3:6) by repeating "the God" before
"of Isaac" and "of Jacob."

[12] The Western text and some Alexandrian authorities (א A C 81) add
"over us" from v. 27.

and signs in Egypt, and in the Red Sea, and in the wilderness forty years.

37 This is that Moses, who said unto the children of Israel, A prophet shall God raise up unto you from among your brethren, like unto me.[13]

38 This is he that was in the church in the wilderness with the angel that spake to him in the mount Sinai, and with our fathers: who received living oracles to give unto us:

39 to whom our fathers would not be obedient, but thrust him from them, and turned back in their hearts unto Egypt,

40 saying unto Aaron, Make us gods that shall go before us: for as for this Moses, who led us forth out of the land of Egypt, we know not what is become of him.

41 And they made a calf in those days, and brought a sacrifice unto the idol, and rejoiced in the works of their hands.

42 But God turned, and gave them up to serve the host of heaven; as it is written in the book of the prophets,
Did ye offer unto me slain beasts and sacrifices
Forty years in the wilderness, O house of Israel?

43 And ye took up the tabernacle of Moloch,
And the star of the god Rephan,
The figures which ye made to worship them:
And I will carry you away beyond Babylon.[14]

44 Our fathers had the tabernacle of the testimony in the wilderness, even as he appointed who spake unto Moses, that he should make it according to the figure that he had seen.

45 Which also our fathers, in their turn, brought in with Joshua when they entered on the possession of the nations, that God thrust out before the face of our fathers, unto the days of David;

46 who found favor in the sight of God, and asked to find a habitation for the God[15] of Jacob.

[13] The Western text, following OT (Deut. 18:15) adds "him shall ye hear."
[14] For "beyond Babylon" the Western reading is "to the parts of Babylon"; this was probably calculated to agree better with "beyond Damascus" in Amos 5:27.
[15] For "God" (Gk. $\theta \epsilon \tilde{\omega}$) there is a strongly attested variant "house" (Gk. οἴκῳ), found in א B D H S 429 and the Sahidic version. Those who prefer οἴκῳ —e.g. Lake–Cadbury, (*Beginnings* iv [London, 1933], *ad loc.*), H. J. Schoeps (*Theologie und Geschichte des Judenchristentums* [Tübingen, 1949], p. 238), F. C. Synge in *Theology* lv (1952), p. 25—suppose the reading $\theta \epsilon \tilde{\omega}$

47 But Solomon built him a house.
48 Howbeit the Most High dwelleth not in *houses* made
   with hands; as saith the prophet,
49 The heaven is my throne,
   And the earth the footstool of my feet:
   What manner of house will ye build me? saith the Lord:
   Or what is the place of my rest?
50 Did not my hand make all these things?

This speech is commonly called Stephen's defence, or apology,
but it is obviously not a speech for the defence in the forensic sense
of the term.[16] Such a speech as this was by no means calculated to
secure an acquittal before the Sanhedrin. It is rather a defence of
pure Christianity as God's appointed way of worship; Stephen
here shows himself to be the precursor of the later Christian
apologists, especially those who defended Christianity against
Judaism. The charges brought against Stephen by the witnesses
for the prosecution (Ch. 6:13 f.) were garbled; Stephen sets forth
here the arguments of which these charges were travesties.

The beginning and end of the speech, in particular, insist that
the presence of God is not restricted to any one land or any
material building. God revealed Himself to Abraham long
before Abraham settled in the holy land; He gave His law to the
people of Israel through Moses when they were wanderers in a
wilderness. The people of God similarly should not be restricted
to any one locality; a movable tent such as they had in the wilderness and in the earlier years of their settlement in Canaan was
a more fitting shrine for the Divine Presence in their midst than
the fixed structure of stone which King Solomon built. The period
which Israel spent as a pilgrim people, "the church in the wilderness," is viewed as setting forth the ideal order—in this respect
(as in others) Stephen echoes the teaching of the great OT prophets

to be a harmonization with the LXX of Ps. 132:5, of which the present passage
is a quotation. F. J. A. Hort (*cf.* Westcott and Hort, *ad loc.*) and J. H. Ropes
(*Beginnings* iii [London, 1926], *ad loc.*), agreeing that θεῷ may have been an
emendation of οἴκῳ, suggest that οἴκῳ itself may have been a corruption of
an original κυρίῳ ("Lord"). For a recent defence of θεῷ, cf. M. Simon in
Journal of Ecclesiastical History ii (1951), p. 128.

[16] On Stephen's speech see B. W. Bacon, "Stephen's Speech: its Argument
and Doctrinal Relationship", in *Biblical and Semitic Studies* (Yale Bicentennial
Publications, 1901), pp. 213 ff.; H. J. Schoeps, *op. cit.*, pp. 440 ff.; M. Simon,
"Saint Stephen and the Jerusalem Temple," in *Journal of Ecclesiastical
History* ii (1951), pp. 127 ff.; W. Manson, *The Epistle to the Hebrews* (London,
1951), pp. 25 ff.

(*cf.* Jer. 2:2; Hos. 11:1 ff.; Amos 2:9 ff.)—though even in the wilderness Israel fell short of the divine ideal.

Another feature of the speech becomes a regular element in later anti-Judaic apologetic writings—the insistence that the Jewish people's refusal to acknowledge Jesus as Messiah was all of a piece with their attitude to God's messengers throughout the OT period. Joseph's brothers hated him, although he was God's appointed deliverer for them; Moses, another divinely appointed deliverer, was repudiated by his people more than once. The prophets too were persecuted and killed by those to whom they ministered, and at last He of whom the prophets spoke had been handed over to death by those to whom His saving message was first brought near.

An attempt has recently been made to relate the viewpoint represented in Stephen's speech with that of the Ebionites, those Judaizing Christians who for several centuries maintained their distinctness from catholic Christianity.[17] They shared to some extent Stephen's attitude towards the temple order and ritual, and looked upon Jesus as the Deuteronomic "prophet like unto Moses" (*cf.* v. 37). But these resemblances are superficial. The Ebionite attitude to the temple and all that it stood for was largely the result of the catastrophe of A.D. 70, but Stephen appreciated the logic of the situation nearly forty years before that.

The Ebionites were far from sympathizing with the Gentile world-mission which Stephen's argument logically implied and which his death inaugurated. The Christians who embarked upon this world-mission were Hellenists, members of the group to which Stephen himself belonged, and in this speech of Stephen

---

[17] *Cf.* Schoeps, *loc. cit.* Schoeps pays special attention to similarities between the representation of Stephen in Acts and that of James the Just in the pseudo-Clementine literature which preserves much Ebionite material. There are indeed several striking parallels between these two representations, and they present us with an interesting problem in literary and historical criticism. But the true solution of the problem is certainly not that propounded by Schoeps, who concludes that Stephen, "far from being a historical character, is an *ersatz* figure brought forward by Luke for tendentious reasons, in order to unload on to him doctrines which the author found it inconvenient to acknowledge as his own" (*op. cit.*, p. 441). M. Simon (*op. cit.*, p. 140) suggests, on the contrary, that Stephen is the original and that the pseudo-Clementine James is the tendentious creation. We may also bear in mind that "the Essenes and the sect of Damascus declined to take part in the Temple sacrifice so long as it was controlled by defiled and irreligious priests" (L. Finkelstein, *The Pharisees* [Philadelphia, 1946], i, p. 291). But Stephen's arguments against the temple system are more fundamental.

we may well see the first manifesto of Hellenistic Christianity.[18] Stephen and his fellow-Hellenists, as has already been pointed out, were more far-sighted than their "Hebrew" brethren in appreciating the breach with the temple-order which the words of Jesus involved. But it looks as if they were also more far-sighted than the "Hebrews" in appreciating the supra-national and universal character of the Gospel, although the world-wide mission was plainly enjoined in the words of the risen Lord to His apostles recorded in Ch. 1:8, "ye shall be my witnesses ... unto the uttermost part of the earth." The opening words of Stephen's defence imply that the people of God must be on the march, must pull up their tent-stakes as Abraham did, leaving national particularism and ancestral ritual, and go out where God may lead. In this Stephen blazes a trail later followed by Paul, and more particularly by the author of the Epistle to the Hebrews.

Stephen is, in fact, the spiritual father of that unknown writer; a comparative study of Stephen's speech and the Epistle to the Hebrews reveals an impressive series of parallels,[19] suggesting a basic identity of outlook and approach in the two documents.[20]

The suggestion has been made that Stephen's attitude towards the temple-order, viewing it as a departure from the authentic tradition of Israel's worship, reflects a particular tendency within Hellenistic Judaism.[21] This is doubtful. There are, indeed, a

[18] This case is particularly well argued by W. Manson in *The Epistle to the Hebrews* (Chapter II, "Stephen and the World-Mission of Christianity").

[19] W. Manson (*op. cit.*, p. 36) enumerates eight important features of Stephen's speech which recur in Hebrews, and suggests accordingly that Stephen's outlook may provide us with the starting-point from which to seek an understanding of that epistle.

[20] Unlike Professor Manson, M. Simon contrasts Stephen's approach with that of Hebrews, particularly with regard to the temple. "To Stephen, the Temple means, from the very beginning, a falling away from the authentic tradition of Israel, as God inspired and directed it. ... the view most commonly held later on was, I think, that which is expressed in *Hebrews*: the Temple and its cult was, together with the whole ritual Law, 'a shadow of good things to come.' It is indeed imperfect, but by no means bad and perverse. For these things are, as *Hebrews* again puts it, 'figures of the true'. Stephen's view is almost unparalleled in early Christian ecclesiastical thought" (*op. cit.*, pp. 127 f.). But on the one hand, Stephen's attitude is not so extreme as is here suggested (see the exposition of vv. 46–47, pp. 157 ff.); and on the other hand, it is significant that the author of Hebrews uses the tabernacle, not the temple, as the Holy Spirit's "parable for the time now present" (Heb. 9:9, ERV).

[21] M. Simon (*op. cit.*, pp. 132 ff.) adduces some evidence, including the carefully chosen wording of the LXX in some significant passages, suggesting that a section of the Jewish dispersion "may well have directed against the Temple in Jerusalem, its ritual and its sacrifices, the same criticism which some

number of parallels with Hellenistic Jewish thought throughout his speech, but Stephen's attitude towards the temple-order is bound up with his acceptance and understanding of the early Christian teaching about the New Temple.[22]

1   The high priest was probably still Caiaphas,[23] as at the trial of Jesus: he remained in office until A.D. 36. If Caiaphas was indeed high priest, presiding over the Sanhedrin in virtue of his office, there may be a sinister implication in his question "Are these things so?" For Caiaphas had been president of the Sanhedrin on the occasion when Jesus was arraigned before that body on very similar charges to those now brought against Stephen. On the former occasion the witnesses who tried to reproduce in court Jesus' words about destroying and rebuilding the temple presented conflicting evidence, and when Jesus was asked to give His account of the matter, He refused to say anything in answer to this charge. Now, when similar charges are brought against Stephen, he in his turn is asked to reply. If the Master could not be convicted of disparaging the temple, it might be possible to convict the servant, and thus to discredit the whole new movement in the eyes of pious Jews.

2–3   Stephen has his reply ready. It takes the form of a historical retrospect—a form well established in Jewish tradition. "The protestation of faith is, in the Old Testament, often associated with a recital of the divine intervention in the life of Israel. 'God in history' was the underlying basis of Rabbinic optimism. The declaration at the bringing of the first-fruits (Deut. 26:5–10) is paralleled by Psalms 78 and 107. ... Stephen's address in Acts 7 is thus in the true form. It is in the *sequel* that he differs from

---

Greek philosophers used to utter against the traditional pagan religion, its temples and ritual." Certainly in their proselytizing propaganda many Jews of the dispersion emphasized the moral and spiritual character of their religion and soft-pedalled its ritual requirements. See in particular the material quoted by E. Schürer in his section on "Jewish Propaganda under a Heathen Mask" (*History of the Jewish People in the Time of Jesus Christ* [Eng. tr., Edinburgh, 1892–1901], II, iii, p. 270 ff.); *cf.* also J. Klausner, *From Jesus to Paul* (Eng. tr., London, 1944). Book 3, "Hellenistic Jewish Thought" (pp. 123 ff.). But the hostility which Stephen's thesis provoked in Jewish *Hellenistic* circles suggests that opposition on principle to the temple and its ritual was not generally acceptable in Hellenistic Judaism.

[22] See especially on this point R. A. Cole, *The New Temple* (London, 1950).
[23] See p. 98, n. 12 (on Ch. 4:6).

Hebrew models" (I. Abrahams, *Studies in Pharisaism and the Gospels,* Series II [Cambridge, 1924], p. 18).[24]

Stephen's historical survey reviews the history of the nation from the call of Abraham to the building of Solomon's temple. It concentrates on three main topics: (i) the patriarchal period (vv. 2–16), (ii) Moses and the law (vv. 17–43), (iii) the tabernacle and the temple (vv. 44–50). The first of the three sections of his speech is an introduction to the central themes, the second deals with the charge of blasphemy against Moses, the third with the charge of blasphemy against God.

i. The Patriarchal Period (vv. 2–16)

It was in Mesopotamia,[25] far from the promised land, that God first revealed Himself to Abraham. We might well ask what could have persuaded Abraham to uproot himself as he did from the land of his birth and set out upon a journey whose goal he did not know in advance. By all the prudential canons of ordinary life, it was a mad adventure; but as related in the Biblical narrative it was an act of true wisdom, for it was "the God of glory"—God all-glorious—who appeared to him and summoned him to the land of promise. Those who are obedient to the heavenly vision, Stephen seems to suggest, will always live loose to any one spot on earth, will always be ready to get out and go wherever God may guide.

A glance at any edition of the NT—Greek or English—in which OT quotations or allusions are set in distinctive type, will show clearly how far the very language of the OT enters into the texture of Stephen's speech. (He quotes it regularly in the LXX form.)[26] But the speech is no mere catena of quotations, studiously

---

[24] To the OT passages adduced by Abrahams we might add Pss. 105, 106, 135, 136; Neh. 9; and *cf.* Paul's speech at Pisidian Antioch (Acts 13:16 ff.).

[25] Mesopotamia represents the fuller Gk. expression Συρία Μεσοποταμία ("Syria between the rivers"), corresponding to Heb. *Aram-Naharaim* ("Aram of the two rivers"), the name of that part of north Syria which lies between the Orontes and Euphrates. Ancient Mesopotamia did not include the southern half of modern Iraq, and therefore did not include the Babylonian city of Ur, near the mouth of the Euphrates. The Biblical Ur of the Chaldees, which Abraham left to go to Haran, may have lain much farther north than Babylonian Ur. See p. 146, n. 29.

[26] In pre-Christian times the only part of the LXX to be authorized in a more or less stereotyped text was the Pentateuch. The Greek version of the prophets and other OT books was much more fluid. What we commonly refer to as the LXX version of these books is the more stereotyped form which they assumed as a result of the work of Christian scholars (notably Origen). There-

put together; the way in which they are introduced suggests that the author has the OT narrative at his finger-tips and is able to use it with a striking freshness and freedom.[27] Here, in v. 3, he quotes from Gen. 12:1 the words which God spoke to Abraham in Haran after his father's death, but gives them a setting before Abraham migrated to Haran on the first stage of his journey. Gen. 15:7 and Neh. 9:7 state that God brought Abraham from Ur, implying that he received a divine communication there as well as later when he had settled in Haran. Philo and Josephus concur.[28]

4-5 Abraham accordingly left "the land of the Chaldaeans"[29]— a term which is obviously synonymous with "Mesopotamia" of v. 2—and settled in Haran, in the upper Euphrates valley, which is known to have been a flourishing city early in the second millennium B.C.[30] There he stayed until his father Terah died;[31]

fore, when we say that NT writers quote from the LXX, this does not imply that we can check their quotations by reference to a contemporary LXX norm (except, to some degree, for quotations from the Pentateuch).

[27] Thus, in vv. 6 f., the words spoken to Abraham in Gen. 15:13 f. are rounded off with the clause "and [they shall] serve me in this place" (*i.e.* in Canaan), which is an echo of the words addressed to *Moses* in Ex. 3:12, "ye shall serve God upon this mountain" (*i.e.* on Sinai). With this telescoping of separate OT passages we may compare the telescoping of separate incidents in v. 16 (see n. 39 below).

[28] *Cf.* Philo, *On Abraham* 71; Josephus, *Antiquities* i. 7.

[29] In LXX "Ur of the Chaldees" is regularly represented by "the land (Gk. χώρα, not γῆ as here) of the Chaldaeans." Josephus places the Chaldaeans in Mesopotamia, i.e. in what we should nowadays call Upper Mesopotamia (*Antiquities* i. 7). These "Chaldaeans" may have been the people referred to in cuneiform records as the *Khaldu* of Urartu (north Mesopotamia and Armenia) and not the *Kaldu* of southern Babylonia. Both were known to the Greeks as Χαλδαῖοι. The name of Abraham's more remote ancestor Arpachshad (Gen. 11:10 ff.) is probably connected with the ancient place-name Arrapkha (modern Kirkuk), in the territory known to the Greeks as Arpachitis.

[30] *Cf.* J. Finegan, *Light from the Ancient Past* (Princeton, 1946), pp. 55 ff. In the same area there were in that period a number of cities bearing names of some members of Abraham's family, *e.g.* Nahor, Serug, Terah. (But the place-name Haran is not the same as the name of Abraham's brother Haran mentioned in Gen. 11:26 ff.: the place-name is Heb. חָרָן , the personal name is הָרָן .)

[31] The chronological data of Gen. 11:26, 32; 12:4, would suggest that Terah's death took place sixty years after Abraham's departure from Haran. The older chronologers harmonized the evidence of Genesis with this statement of Stephen's by supposing that Terah was seventy years old (Gen. 11:26) when his oldest son (Haran) was born, and that Abraham was not born until Terah was a hundred and thirty—an improbable expedient. That Abraham did not

after that, under divine direction, he continued his migration and arrived in Canaan. But even then Abraham was given no part of the land in actual possession; for the rest of his life he lived as a resident alien there. It was a promised land to him, indeed— promised to him and his posterity before he had any children— but to him and his immediate posterity it remained no more than a *promised* land. Abraham had no tangible object in which to trust; he believed the bare word of God, and acted upon it.

6–7 Not only did Abraham receive no portion of the land as a present possession; his faith was further tested by the revelation that his descendants would leave that land for one that was not their own, and that they would suffer oppression and servitude there for several generations.[32] Yet their exile would not be permanent; in due course God would avenge them of their adversaries and bring them back to worship Him in the land of Canaan.[33]

8 One sign was given to Abraham, the sign of circumcision, as the outward token of the covenant which God made with him.[34] Abraham's acceptance of this physical token for himself and his descendants was a further expression of his faith in God. And "thus, while there was still no holy place, all the essential conditions for the religion of Israel were fulfilled" (Lake-Cadbury, *ad loc.*); when Isaac was born, Abraham circumcised him on the eighth day, and the sign of the covenant was transmitted from

leave Haran until his father was dead is asserted also by Philo (*On the Migration of Abraham*, 177). It is implied by the Samaritan Pentateuch, which gives Terah's age at death as a hundred and forty-five, not two hundred and five, as MT and LXX do (Gen. 11:32). Possibly a Greek version of Gen. 11:32, agreeing with the Samaritan text on Terah's age at death, but no longer extant, underlies the statements of Stephen and Philo. P. E. Kahle says with even greater assurance: "Not a single MS. of the Christian 'Septuagint' has preserved in Gen. 11:32 a reading which Philo and Luke read in their Greek Tora in the first Christian century" (*The Cairo Geniza* [London, 1947], p. 144).

[32] The figure of "four hundred years" fixed for the oppression of the Israelites is taken from Gen. 15:13. According to Ex. 12:40 (MT) the sojourning of Israel in Egypt lasted four hundred and thirty years, for which the figure of four hundred might be taken as a round number. But rabbinical exegesis reckoned the four hundred years from the birth of Isaac to the Exodus; *cf.* Paul in Gal. 3:17, where the four hundred and thirty years run from Abraham's receiving the divine promise to the Exodus. This accords with the Samaritan and LXX reading of Ex. 12:40. The period spent in Egypt would then be considerably shorter; *cf.* Gen. 15:16, "in the fourth generation they shall come hither again."

[33] See n. 27 above.

[34] *Cf.* Gen. 17:9 ff. Circumcision, at puberty (*cf.* Gen. 17:25) if not in infancy, was practised by most of the nations with which Israel had dealings

generation to generation, from Isaac to Jacob and from Jacob to his twelve sons, the ancestors of the twelve tribes of Israel.[35]

9-10 As early as the patriarchal age, there was opposition to the purpose of God in calling Abraham and guiding the fortunes of his posterity. The sons of Jacob sold Joseph their brother into slavery in Egypt. But God was continuously superintending the accomplishment of that one increasing purpose which He inaugurated when He called the father of the faithful out of Mesopotamia, and which was to find its consummation with the coming of Christ. He so ordered the fortunes of Joseph in Egypt that he rose to high authority in that land as grand vizier to Pharaoh.[36]

11-16 This worked out to the advantage of Joseph's family, for when famine arose in Canaan the sons of Jacob went to buy food in Egypt, where the wisdom and authority of Joseph had prepared large stores of grain. On the second occasion when they went to Egypt to buy food, Joseph (whom they had not recognized the first time)[37] made himself known to them; is there a suggestion here that a greater than Joseph, who was not recognized by His brethren when they saw Him for the first time, will be acknowledged by them as their anointed deliverer when they see Him the second time? At any rate, the result of this recognition and reconciliation was that Jacob and all his family came down into Egypt— seventy-five persons in all, says Stephen, following the LXX reckoning.[38] There Jacob died; there too, in due course, his sons died, but they were buried, not in Egypt, but in the land which

in the patriarchal age, but only to Israel had it this special significance.

[35] The term "patriarchs" (Gk. πατριάρχαι) here used of the sons of Jacob as tribal ancestors, is so used of them in 4 Maccabees 16:25 and in the title of the Greek version of *The Testaments of the Twelve Patriarchs. Cf.* pp. 71 f., n. 58 (on Ch. 2:29).

[36] Stephen's language here reflects that of Ps. 105:16 ff. as well as that of Gen. 37—45.

[37] W. M. Ramsay argues that "the first time" (v. 12) must mean the first of three, the third time being the occasion when the whole family went down (*The Bearing of Recent Discovery on the Trustworthiness of the NT* [London, 1914], p. 254 n.). But Gk. πρῶτος cannot be pressed in this way in Hellenistic times; *cf.* p. 32, n. 12 (on Ch. 1:1). Here "the first time" is simply correlative to "the second time" of v. 13.

[38] In Gen. 46:27 and Ex. 1:5, LXX has "seventy-five" for MT "seventy." The MT total includes Jacob, Joseph, and Joseph's two sons; the LXX reckoning omits Jacob and Joseph, but includes *nine* sons of Joseph. Josephus follows the Hebrew text (*Antiquities* ii. 7.4; vi. 5.6); Philo knows both readings, and endeavours to harmonize them by a typical effort of allegorical exegesis (*On the Migration of Abraham*, 199 ff.).

God had promised to their children as their inheritance.[39] The presence of their tombs in the land of promise was the token that, even if they died down in Egypt, they died in faith.[40]

ii. Moses and the Law (vv. 17–43)

17–19 Their children and grandchildren, however, stayed in Egypt and multiplied there, until the appointed time came for God to redeem His promise to the patriarchs and give their descendants possession of the land of Canaan. The instrument in God's hand for bringing about their departure from Egypt was a new king (presumably one of the early kings of Dynasty XIX)[41] who tried to repress the increasing number of Israelites by forced labour and compulsory infanticide. But for his policy they might have found Egypt so comfortable that they would never have thought of leaving it!

20–22 The edict that every male child born to the Israelites was to be exposed was defied by the parents of Moses. They kept him for three months before exposing him, and when at last they did expose him, they did so in such a way that he was quickly rescued.[42] A daughter of the king[43] found him, adopted him, and brought him up as her son, in a style befitting a royal prince.

---

[39] Jacob was buried at Hebron, in the cave of Machpelah, which Abraham had bought from Ephron the Hittite for four hundred silver shekels (Gen. 23:16; 49:29 ff.; 50:13). Joseph was buried at Shechem, in the piece of ground which Jacob had bought for a hundred silver shekels from the sons of Hamor (Josh. 24:32). According to Josephus (*Antiquities* ii. 8.2), the other sons of Jacob were buried at Hebron. The two purchases of land are telescoped here in much the same way as two separate calls of Abraham are telescoped in v. 2 and two separate Pentateuchal quotations in v. 7. The reference to Shechem, the sacred place of the schismatic Samaritans, would not give pleasure to a Jerusalem audience.

[40] *Cf.* Heb. 11:13.

[41] It is evident from the early chapters of Exodus that the Egyptian court was not far distant from the place of the Hebrews' residence in Egypt; this fits the nineteenth rather than the eighteenth dynasty. The reference to the building of Rameses in Ex. 1:11 probably points to Per-Ramesese-Mry-Amun (later Tanis), built by Rameses II (*c.* 1301–1234 B.C.), chief king of the nineteenth dynasty (*c.* 1320–1200 B.C.). *Cf.* H. H. Rowley, *From Joseph to Joshua* (London, 1950), *passim*.

[42] *Cf.* Ex. 2:1 ff.

[43] It is probably a vain task to try to identify this princess with any known daughter of an Egyptian king. The Hellenistic Jewish writer Artabanus, in his work *Concerning the Jews* (quoted by Eusebius, *Preparation for the Gospel* ix. 27) calls her Merris, a name quite similar to that borne by a daughter of Rameses II by his Hittite wife—but this daughter of Rameses was probably younger than Moses.

149

Thus Moses received the best education that the Egyptian court could provide, "and he was mighty in his words and works."[44] Stephen expresses himself with more moderation than other Hellenistic Jews, who represent Moses as the father of all science and culture and as the founder of Egyptian civilization.[45]

23-28 That an Egyptian king should try to frustrate the divine purpose was intelligible, but some of the chosen people themselves set themselves unwittingly against it. If Pharaoh was God's instrument in weaning the Israelites from their attachment to Egypt, Moses was His agent in leading them out. Moses was aware of this, but his fellow-Israelites were slow to recognize him as their God-appointed deliverer. When he had grown to full manhood[46] he presented himself to them as their champion, but his intervention on their behalf was not appreciated. "He supposed that his brethren understood that God by his hand was giving them deliverance; but they understood not" (v. 25). Here again Stephen traces a pattern of Jewish behaviour which was to find its complete and final expression when Christ Himself appeared among them as the Saviour provided by God.

29-34 Moses had exposed himself to grave peril by his attempt to champion his oppressed people's cause; his action in killing an Egyptian bully was more widely known than he wished, and he had to leave Egypt in haste, and find refuge in north-west Arabia.[47]

---

[44] That he was mighty in his words may seem to conflict with his disclaimer of eloquence in Ex. 4:10, but the reference could be to his writings. The statement that he was mighty in action is illustrated by the legend preserved by Josephus (*Antiquities* ii. 10) of his leading an Egyptian campaign against the Ethiopians (a legend perhaps invented to account for the Cushite wife of Num. 12:1, called an Ethiopian in LXX).

[45] Artabanus (*loc. cit.*) says that the Egyptians owed all their civilization to Moses; he identifies him with the Musaeus of the Greeks and with the Egyptian Hermes (Thoth). An earlier Hellenistic Jew, Eupolemus (author of a work *On the Kings in Judaea*, quoted by Eusebius, *op. cit.*, ix. 26), describes Moses as the inventor of alphabetic writing (a suggestion repeated in our day by Sir Charles Marston, *The Bible Comes Alive* [London, 1937], p. 180). According to Philo (*Life of Moses* i, 20 ff.), Moses was proficient in arithmetic, geometry, poetry, music, philosophy, astrology, and all branches of learning. Josephus (*Antiquities* ii. 9.6) describes him as unique in wisdom, stature and beauty. After all this, Stephen's language comes to us almost as an understatement!

[46] "When Moses was grown up," says Ex. 2:11 (*cf.* Heb. 11:24); but Stephen gives his age at the time as forty. This is paralleled in rabbinical tradition, which divides Moses' life of a hundred and twenty years (Deut. 34:7) into three equal parts, the first ending at this point and the second at the Exodus (*cf.* Ex. 7:7).

[47] The land of Midian probably lay to the east of the Gulf of Akaba.

There he in turn, like his patriarchal ancestors, became "a sojourner in a foreign land" (Ex. 2:22)—a fact which he acknowledged when he called his first-born son Gershom ("a sojourner there").[48] But Moses' exile was part of the divine plan; it was there in north-west Arabia, "in the wilderness of Mount Sinai," that the angel of God appeared to him in the burning bush, and the voice of God addressed him.[49] As to Abraham, so to Moses the heavenly vision came far away from the frontiers of the holy land. That spot of Gentile territory was "holy ground," for the simple reason that God revealed Himself to Moses there.[50] Here, then, we have a central principle of the gospel: that no place on earth possesses an innate sanctity of its own. William Cowper expresses it excellently:

> Jesus, where'er Thy people meet,
> There they behold Thy mercy-seat;
> Where'er they seek Thee, Thou art found,
> And every place is hallowed ground.

The message which Moses received from God at that holy place was one of faithfulness to His promise. God had not forgotten His covenant with the patriarchs: He remained "the God of Abraham, and of Isaac, and of Jacob" (v. 32). Nor had He forgotten the distress of their children in Egypt: He was on the point of intervening for their deliverance, and Moses was to be His agent in this deliverance. "And now come, I will send thee into Egypt."

35–36 The very man whom they had refused was the man chosen by God as their ruler and redeemer. They had rejected him the first time (as Joseph's brothers repudiated Joseph), but the second time that he came to them they had no option but to accept him (as Joseph's brothers recognized him the second time). The parallel with their refusal of Christ is too plain to require elabo-

[48] Only one son is mentioned in Ex. 2:22; for the other see Ex. 18:3 f.

[49] *Cf.* Ex. 3:1 ff. The "mountain of God" is referred to there as Horeb; the identity of Horeb and Sinai is implied by a comparison of Ex. 3:12 and Deut. 1:6, etc., with Ex. 19:11 ff. The traditional location of Sinai in the Sinai Peninsula (Jebel Musa) does not appear to be earlier than the *Pilgrimage of Silvia* (A.D. 385–8). The "angel" whom Moses saw (v. 30) was the special "angel of Jehovah" (Ex. 3:2)—*i.e.* God Himself in His manifestation to men. In Ex. 3 the speaker is variously called "the angel of Jehovah" (v. 2), "God" (v. 4) and "Jehovah" (v. 7); so here the angel speaks with the voice of the Lord (v. 31), claims to be God (v. 32) and is called "the Lord" (v. 33). *Cf.* vv. 35, 38, 53 below (and notes 54, 84).

[50] *Cf.* Ex. 20:24b. The removal of the shoes was a mark of reverence in the Divine Presence, as it was a mark of respect to one's host when paying a visit.

ration. All the authority of the divine messenger whom he had seen at the burning bush lay behind Moses when he went back to Egypt to lead his people out, and lead them out he did, amid tokens of his heavenly commission that none could gainsay—"wonders and signs[51] in Egypt, and in the Red sea, and in the wilderness forty years."[52]

37-41 Was Moses in all this a fore-runner of the Messiah, as Stephen claimed? Moses' own words supply a sufficient answer—and here Stephen quoted the passage about the prophet like unto Moses from Deut. 18:15 which Peter had previously quoted in the temple court (Ch. 3:22; see p. 92 above).

There in the wilderness Moses was guide to the people; there they were constituted the *ekklesia*[53] of God; there they had the "Angel of the Presence"[54] in their midst; there they received through Moses the living oracles of God.[55] What more could the people of God want?—and it was all theirs in the wilderness, far

---

[51] So Jesus was divinely accredited to His contemporaries by "mighty works and wonders and signs which God did by him" in their midst (Ch. 2:22).

[52] The narrative of the Exodus well illustrates the two principal ways in which God revealed Himself in OT times—mighty works and prophetic communication. The mighty works attending the Exodus would not have been properly understood by the Hebrews had not Moses, as the prophet or spokesman of God, interpreted their significance to them both before and after they took place; but the mighty works were not caused by Moses or his words, being plainly beyond all human control. The mighty works and the prophetic words supported each other and both together made God known to His people. *Cf.* H. H. Rowley, *The Authority of the Bible* (Birmingham, 1949), pp. 12ff.

[53] In Deut. 18:16, immediately after Moses' reference to the prophet like himself, he reminds the people of their request to God "in Horeb in the day of assembly" that they might not hear His voice again speaking to them directly. The Hebrew word there translated "assembly" is *qahal*, appearing in LXX as ἐκκλησία. As Moses was with the old ἐκκλησία, Christ is with the new, and it is still a pilgrim ἐκκλησία, "the church in the wilderness." *Cf.* p. 116, n. 18 (on Ch. 5:11).

[54] The "angel of the presence" of God (lit. the messenger of His face, Heb. *mal'akh panaw*) is the angel who makes His presence real to men—in other words, the angel of Jehovah (referred to in n. 49 above). The narrative of Exodus makes no mention of this angel in the narrative of the giving of the law; we may compare, however, "the angel of God" in Ex. 14:19; also Ex. 33:14, "My presence shall go with thee," where "my presence" is lit. "my face" (Heb. *panai*, but LXX αὐτός, "I myself"). *Cf.* also Isa. 63:9, "In all their affliction he was afflicted, and the angel of his presence saved them" (where LXX, representing another Hebrew text than MT, reads: "Not an ambassador nor a messenger, but He Himself saved them"). According to Jubilees 1:27 and 2:1, an angel talked with Moses on Sinai. See further on this subject n. 84 below (on v. 53).

[55] *Cf.* Rom. 3:2; Heb. 4:12; 1 Pet. 1:23.

from the promised land and the holy city. But even so, they were not content; they disobeyed Moses and repudiated his leadership, although he was the spokesman and vicegerent of God among them. Was Stephen charged with speaking "blasphemous words against Moses"—with propagating doctrines which threatened the abiding validity of "the customs which Moses delivered unto us"? Such a charge came well from the descendants of those who had refused Moses' authority in his very lifetime, from people whose attitude to the greater Prophet than Moses had shown them to be such worthy children of their fathers! Why, those Israelites in the wilderness, for all their sacred privileges, longed to go back to Egypt, from which Moses had led them out. The invisible presence of God was not enough for them; they craved for something that they could see. When Moses was absent, communing with God on Mount Sinai, they persuaded Aaron to manufacture "gods that shall go before us."[56] Thus they showed how much they cared for the divine order of worship. The long history of Israel's idolatry, against which prophet after prophet inveighed and which brought them into exile, had its beginnings in the wilderness, when they paid sacrificial homage to the golden calf, "and rejoiced in the works of their hands."[57] But the climax of this attitude, in Stephen's eyes, did not lie in any such overt worship of golden calf or heavenly host, but in the repudiation of the Son of God Himself.

42–43 The course of their idolatry, as traced throughout the OT, from the wilderness wanderings to the Babylonian exile, Stephen finds summed up in the words of Amos 5:25–27. The full-blown worship of the host of heaven, the planetary powers, to which Jerusalem gave itself over in the later years of the monarchy, was the fruition of that earlier idolatry in the wilderness.[58] It was more than its fruition, in fact; it was the divinely-inflicted judgment for that rebellious attitude. "God turned, and gave them up to serve the host of heaven." These are terrible words, but the principle that God gives men up to the due consequences of their settled choice is well established in Scripture. While Stephen asserts it here in relation to the Jewish people,

[56] Ex. 32:1 ff.

[57] *Cf.* Ps. 115:4 and 135:15, where the idols of the nations are described as "silver and gold, the work of men's hands."

[58] For the host of heaven *cf.* Deut. 4:19; 17:3; 2 Kings 21:3, 5; 23:4 f.; Jer. 8:2; 19:13; Zeph. 1:5. See n. 64 below.

Paul asserts it in relation to the Gentile world in Rom. 1:24, 26, 28.

The Massoretic text of the words quoted from Amos differs considerably from the form reproduced here (the LXX rendering, with variations). In MT, Amos, prophesying on the eve of the Assyrian invasions which brought the northern kingdom of Israel to an end, warns the Israelites that they will be deported "beyond Damascus" and that they will carry with them into exile the very tokens of that idolatry for which God is about to bring this judgment upon them.[59] But both forms of the text begin with the question, "Did ye offer unto me slain beasts and sacrifices forty years in the wilderness, O house of Israel?" The form of the question implies the answer "No."

We must ask here (a) how Amos understood the implied answer "No," and (b) how Stephen understood it. As for the former question, it is unlikely that Amos meant that Israel's worship in the wilderness was entirely nonsacrificial, although this is the sense in which his words have commonly been interpreted. His question more probably meant, "Was it mere sacrifices and offerings, sacrifices and offerings that were an end in themselves and not the expression of your loyalty of spirit, that you offered in the wilderness days?" The expected answer will then be: "No; we offered something more than this; we brought true heart-worship and righteousness."[60]

But Stephen uses the prophetic words with a different emphasis. He has just emphasized the unfaithfulness of Israel in worshipping the golden calf, and his point is that the idolatry which the prophets condemned could be traced right back to the wilderness period. Even then the people had been rebellious in heart. The implied answer "No" in Stephen's context will then mean: "No; we offered sacrifices indeed, but we offered them to other gods."[61]

---

[59] A similar judgment is pronounced upon Babylon in Isa. 46:1 f.

[60] For this interpretation of the words of Amos cf. H. H. Rowley in BJRL xxix (1946), pp. 340 ff.; ExT lviii (1946–47), pp. 69 ff., 305 ff.; BJRL xxxiii (1950), pp. 79 f. He cites D. B. Macdonald as propounding the same view in *JBL* xviii (1899), pp. 214 f.

[61] On the other view, that the implied "No" meant to Stephen at any rate that Israel had not offered sacrifices in the wilderness, see Schoeps, *op. cit.*, pp. 221 ff., 238, 442 ff. This view, of course, would associate Stephen more closely with the Ebionites, according to whom the sacrificial legislation was a spurious interpolation in the Mosaic law; one of the tasks of Messiah, the prophet like Moses (cf. v. 37), when he came, was (they believed) to remove these accretions and restore the law to its original purity. It is just possible to suppose that Stephen believed that, while the sacrificial law was indeed

"In other words, what Amos meant, according to Stephen, was not that God had not commanded sacrifices and oblations, but that Israel had diverted its offerings and its sanctuary to idolatrous purposes" (W. Manson, *The Epistle to the Hebrews* [London, 1951], p. 30).

Does Stephen then, quoting the LXX form of the words which puts the taking up of the idolatrous objects in the past tense, mean that the worship of Moloch and Rephan dates back to the wilderness period? Does he mean that the tabernacle in the wilderness, far from being the place of Jehovah's worship, was actually "the tabernacle of Moloch," because of their perversion of the true order of worship?[62] This is unlikely, in view of the way in which he goes on to speak of the Mosaic tabernacle in the following verses. Moloch and Rephan are planetary divinities, members of the "host of heaven" referred to in the earlier part of v. 42.[63] What Stephen means is that the idolatry which began in the wilderness with the worship of the golden calf found its climax under

given through Moses in the wilderness, it was not to be carried into effect until after the settlement in Canaan (*cf.* Deut. 5:31b and more particularly Num. 15:2b). But the view adopted in the exposition above appears preferable.

[62] *Cf.* M. Simon, *op. cit.*, p. 138: "Sacrifices, even if offered to Jahveh, a temple, even if built in Jerusalem, remain what they were in the beginning—works of idolatry. They proceed in all cases from mere human initiative and vanity: they have never been approved or sanctified by God. They are not only a consequence, accepted by God to prevent the worship of the golden calf: they are on a level with the golden calf." This deduction from Stephen's words is on a par with the deduction drawn from the great OT prophets' attack on contemporary sacrificial practice, that they were opposed to the principle of sacrifice in itself and not simply to its misuse. The deduction in both cases results from an inadequate appreciation of prophetic diction—its tendency to say "not this, but that," where we should say "not only this, but also that," "not this without that," or "that more than this." Stephen speaks in the true prophetic tradition.

[63] "The tabernacle of Moloch" would represent Heb. *sukkath Molekh,* as against MT *Sikkuth malkekhem.* "Sakkuth your king" (RSV). *Sikkuth* is the Akkadian *Sakkut,* a name of the god of the planet Saturn, spelt with the vowels of Heb. *shiqqutz,* "abomination". (Similarly Moloch, better Molech, is probably Heb. *melekh,* "king", used as a divine title among various Canaanite groups, spelt with the vowels of *bosheth,* "shame"—although Otto Eissfeldt explains it as a technical term for human sacrifice, found in Carthaginian inscriptions in the form *molk.*) The MT reading which corresponds to "the star of the god Rephan, the figures . . ." is *Kiyyun tzalmeikhem kokhab 'eloheikhem,* which RSV renders "Kaiwan your star-god, your images . . ." *Kaiwan* is an Assyrian name for the planet Saturn, also spelt in MT (*Kiyyun*) with the vowels of *shiqqutz.* In LXX it is represented by Rephan (for which Remphan, Rompha, and a number of other variants are found); this may be a form of *Repa,* an Egyptian name for the god of the planet Saturn, substituted by the Alexandrian translators for the less intelligible *Kiyyun.*

the monarchy with the worship of the planetary powers,[64] for which the nation lost its freedom and suffered deportation. Amos, foretelling the Assyrian exile of the northern kingdom, described the place of their captivity as "beyond Damascus"; but the same disloyalty to the God of Israel brought a similar judgment on the southern kingdom more than a century later, in the Babylonian exile, and Stephen accordingly substitutes "beyond Babylon" for "beyond Damascus."[65] The idols which they had made for worship could give them no help in that terrible day.

iii. The Tabernacle and the Temple (vv. 44–50)

44–45 But had the people of Israel no sanctuary in the wilderness, no reminder of the presence of God in their midst, that they should so unaccountably and so quickly forget Him and lapse into idolatry? Yes indeed, says Stephen, "our fathers had the tabernacle of the testimony in the wilderness"–the "Trysting tent," to use Moffatt's OT rendering.[66] But just as they rebelled against Moses, so also they disregarded the shrine which told them that God was continually dwelling among them as they moved on from place to place. Stephen has just countered the charge of blasphemy against Moses with a *tu quoque*; he now proceeds to counter the charge of blasphemy against God (*i.e.* against His dwelling-place) in the same way. This tabernacle of testimony was no ordinary shrine; it was made by the direct command of God, and constructed in every detail according to the pattern which Moses had been shown on the holy mount.[67] When the people at last entered the land of Canaan under Joshua,[68] they took the tabernacle with them, together with the ark of the

---

[64] It was more particularly under the Assyrian influence in the eighth century B.C. that the worship of the planetary divinities became so popular in Israel, but the evidence of Canaanite place-names shows that they were worshipped as early as the period of the Tell el-Amarna correspondence (*c.* 1370 B.C.).

[65] The Western text harmonizes Stephen with Amos; *cf.* n. 14 above.

[66] The "testimony" consisted of the tables of the law kept in the sacred ark, which was thus known as "the ark of the testimony" (*e.g.* Ex. 25:22). LXX uses ἡ σκηνὴ τοῦ μαρτυρίου to render not only Heb. *'ohel 'eduth* (correctly) but also *'ohel mo'ed*, which properly means "the tent of meeting" (it is this latter expression which Moffatt translates as "Trysting tent").

[67] Ex. 25:9, 40; 26:30; 27:8; and *cf.* the elaboration of this theme in Heb. 8:5 ff.

[68] Gk. Ἰησοῦς, whence AV "Jesus", as in Heb. 4:8. There is perhaps a tacit suggestion that it is not by accident that the leader who brought them

covenant, containing the tablets of the law, which the tabernacle enshrined. And the tabernacle remained with them all through the early period of the settlement in Canaan and the dispossession of the Canaanites—a process not completed until the reign of David.[69] "In its mobile character—so we may here fill out the interstices of the argument—the tent was a type or figure of God's never-ceasing, never-halted appointments for His people's salvation" (W. Manson, *op. cit.*, pp. 33 f.).

46–47 King David, after putting down his enemies inside and outside the land, longed to provide a nobler dwelling-place for the ark than the new tent-shrine which he had erected for it on Mount Zion when he brought it out of the long obscurity in which it had remained since its capture and restoration by the Philistines.[70] Ps. 132, which underlies the words of Stephen here, describes

> How he sware unto Jehovah,
> And vowed unto the Mighty One of Jacob:
> Surely I will not come into the tabernacle of my house,
> Nor go up into my bed;
> I will not give sleep to mine eyes,
> Or slumber to mine eyelids;
> Until I find out a place for Jehovah,
> A tabernacle for the Mighty One of Jacob (vv. 2–5).[71]

The contrast between David's own palace, panelled in cedarwood, and the curtained tent within which the ark abode, weighed upon his mind. He confided in the prophet Nathan, and Nathan's first reaction was to bid the king act upon his inclination and build a palace for the ark of God. But Nathan soon ascertained the mind of God more clearly, and went back to David with the message that God desired no house of cedar at his hands, but would Himself establish David's house in perpetuity. Yet a son of David would arise, and build a house for God (2 Sam. 7).

into the earthly land of promise bore the same name as the One under whom they might inherit better promises.

[69] *Cf.* Ch. 13:19–22.

[70] *Cf.* 1 Sam. 4:1b–7:2; 2 Sam. 6:1–7:29.

[71] According to M. Simon (*op. cit.*, p. 129), the "place" (Gk. τόπος) in this quotation is Jerusalem, the "tabernacle" (Gk. σκήνωμα) is the tent-shrine on Mount Zion which David constructed for the ark (*cf.* 2 Sam. 6:17; 1 Chron. 15:1), by contrast with the "house" (Gk. οἶκος) which King Solomon built (v. 47; *cf.* 2 Sam. 7:6 with 1 Chron. 17:5).

Evidently Stephen does not consider that the building of Solomon's temple was an adequate fulfilment of God's promise that David's son would build Him a house. It is plain that the early Christians interpreted the parallel promise, that this son of David would have his throne established for ever, as fulfilled in Christ.

> He shall be great, and shall be called the Son of the Most High:
> And the Lord God shall give unto him the throne of his father
> David:
> And he shall reign over the house of Jacob for ever;
> And of his kingdom there shall be no end (Luke 1:32 f.).

It was in Christ, too, that the promise of a new house, built for the name of God, was truly fulfilled. It was directly after His entry into Jerusalem, hailed as the son of David, that He went into the temple and ejected from the court of the Gentiles the trespassers whose presence and activity there prevented it from fulfilling its proper purpose. "Is it not written," He asked, "My house shall be called a house of prayer *for all the nations*?" (Mark 11:17).[72] Here we may find some adumbration of that new temple in which those who were formerly "strangers and sojourners" now find themselves "fellow-citizens with the saints, and of the household of God, being built upon the foundation of the apostles and prophets, Christ Jesus himself being the chief corner stone" (Eph. 2:19 f.). The new temple is Christ Himself, but the corporate Christ, the Redeemer of God's elect along with His elect, of Gentile and Jewish derivation alike (*cf.* p. 310, on Ch. 15:16). And the work of building began with His resurrection: "he spake of the temple of his body" when He promised to raise up the new temple in three days (John 2:20 f.). If we are right in tracing some such intention in Stephen's language here, it underlines the relevance of this speech as a theological introduction to Luke's narrative of the Gentile mission.

---

[72] Was it our Lord's implied concern for those Gentiles who desired to draw as near as they could to worship the God of Israel that led to the Greeks' desire to see Him, as John 12:21 records? It is noteworthy that He went on immediately to speak of His imminent glorifying—His lifting up in a twofold sense—as the means by which He would draw to Himself not Jewish believers only, but all men without distinction. It is noteworthy, too, that while the description of the temple as a house of prayer for all the nations is taken directly from Isa. 56:7, it also echoes a passage in Solomon's prayer at the dedication of the temple, where provision is made for the foreigner to "pray toward this house" (1 Kings 8:41–43).

[73] Gk. σκήνωμα, as in the LXX translation of Ps. 132:5 (*cf.* n. 71 above).

David then, says Stephen, having found grace in the sight of God, desired to build Him a "habitation"—more accurately, a tabernacle, a bivouac.[73] But the habitation that his son Solomon built for God was a house, a static erection of stone, immobile and fixed to one spot.[74] The brevity with which Solomon's building is introduced and dismissed, and the contrast implied with David's intention, which was not to be fulfilled until the advent of a greater than Solomon, expresses plain disapproval. Yet it is not Solomon's own act that Stephen deprecates—Solomon himself confessed that no temple made with hands could house the God of heaven. "But will God in very deed dwell on the earth? behold, heaven and the heaven of heavens cannot contain thee; how much less this house that I have builded!" (1 Kings 8:27).[75] It was rather the state of mind to which the temple gave rise—a state of mind which the mobile tabernacle could not have engendered—that Stephen reprobates, as Jeremiah did in his day (cf. Jer. 7:1 ff.; 26:1 ff.).

48–50 The gods of the heathen might be accommodated in material shrines, but not so God Most High.[76] The contrast between the terms "made with hands" and "not made with hands" is a prominent feature of the primitive catechesis about the new temple which runs throughout the NT and early Christian apologetics.[77] It goes back most probably to our Lord Himself, for

[74] Cf. 1 Kings 6:2, "the house (Heb. *bayith*. Gk. οἶκος) which king Solomon built for Jehovah."

[75] It should also be observed that in the whole of Solomon's dedicatory prayer (1 Kings 8:23–53) there is not a word about the use of the temple for sacrifices; its prime function appears to be that of a house of prayer. Cf. the view ascribed to the Jew Trypho in Justin's *Dialogue* (117.2), that Mal. 1:10–12 means that "God did not accept the sacrifices of those who dwelt then in Jerusalem, and were called Israelites; but declares His pleasure with the prayers of the dispersed members of that nation, and calls their prayers sacrifices." But this belongs to a period long after the destruction of the temple.

[76] This was constantly emphasized in Jewish, and later also in Christian, propaganda against paganism. Cf. Ch. 17:24 f.; also *Sibylline Oracles* iv. 8 ff.: "He has not for His habitation a stone dragged into a temple, deaf and dumb, a bane and woe to mortals; but one which may not be seen from earth or measured by mortal eyes, nor was fashioned by mortal hand." (Some later lines of this poem, 25 ff., may be compared with the view of Trypho mentioned in the preceding note: "Happy among men shall they be upon earth who . . . shall turn away their eyes from every temple and all altars, vain structures of stones that cannot hear, defiled with the blood of living things and sacrifices of four-footed beasts; and will have an eye to the glory of the one God.") But the same truth was taught by the higher paganism five centuries before; cf. the quotation from Euripides on p. 357, n. 41.

[77] Cf. M. Simon, *op. cit.*, pp. 133 ff.; C. F. D. Moule, "Sanctuary and Sacrifice in the Church of the NT", JThS, NS i (1950), pp. 29 ff.

although the evidence given at His trial that He said, "I will destroy this temple that is made with hands, and in three days I will build another made without hands" (Mark 14:58), is described as "false witness", it is not likely to have been false on this point.

To emphasize the full agreement of his case with OT revelation, Stephen quotes the opening words of Isa. 66—words which clearly anticipate his own argument, whether their primary reference was to the building of the second temple or to some other occasion. There the prophet goes on to say, in the name of Jehovah, almost immediately after the passage quoted here, "but to this man will I look, even to him that is poor and of a contrite spirit, and that trembleth at my word" (Isa. 66:2b). This well describes the character of the people of God, who constitute His true temple (*cf.* Isa. 57:15). But to those who imagine that they can localize the Presence of God, His scornful question comes, "What is the place of my rest?" Do they think they can make God "stay put"— imprison Him in a golden cage?[78] "The point is that the Temple was not intended, any more than the Tabernacle, to become a *permanent* institution, halting the advance of the divine plan for the people of God" (W. Manson, *op. cit.*, p. 34).

Stephen's argument is thus concluded; all that remains is to drive it home to the consciences of his audience. He has answered the charges brought forward by the prosecution. As for the charge of subverting the Mosaic tradition, it is not he but the nation

---

[78] This is surely the *gravamen* of Stephen's argument. In many respects the tabernacle and the temple were comparable. Both were copies of divinely given patterns: the wilderness tabernacle was made according to the archetype which Moses was shown on Mount Sinai, and Solomon's temple, according to the Chronicler, was constructed according to a plan which David "had by the Spirit," which he was "made to understand in writing from the hand of Jehovah" (1 Chron. 28:12, 19). Both, according to the canonical OT writings, were associated with sacrificial ritual; and there is no suggestion that Stephen rejected any part of these canonical writings or had recourse to the curious expedients by which later Christian apologists contrived to disprove the divine origin of Jewish sacrifice—whether, like the author of the Epistle of Barnabas (7–10), they maintained that the sacrificial laws were meant to be understood allegorically and not literally, or, like Justin Martyr (*Dialogue* 18:2; 22:1 ff.) and the author of the *Didascalia* (ii. 5a), they regarded them as a punishment imposed upon the Jews for their worship of the golden calf and other acts of disobedience, or, like Chrysostom (*Homilies against the Jews* iv. 6), they explained them as a prophylactic against idolatry in view of the Jews' chronic tendency to this sin. (For a full discussion of these arguments *cf.* M. Simon, *Verus Israel* [Paris, 1948], pp. 111 ff.) The point on which Stephen concentrates is the one point which distinguished the tabernacle from the temple: the tabernacle was mobile, the temple was stationary.

before whose representatives he stands that should plead guilty to this; their guilt is amply attested by their own sacred scriptures, back to the very lifetime of Moses himself. As for the charge of blaspheming God by proclaiming the supersession of the temple by "this Jesus of Nazareth," he makes no attempt to deny it but justifies his position by the claim that it is the position held by the patriarchs and prophets, whereas the position of his opponents involves a point-blank denial of the consistent teaching of the OT scriptures. "Stephen's speech thus resolves itself into a great defence of the doctrine of the Church Invisible, based on a broad survey of the history of the people of God" (R. A. Cole, *The New Temple* [London, 1950], p. 38).

(e) Stephen Goes Over to the Attack (Ch. 7:51–53)

51 Ye stiffnecked and uncircumcised in heart and ears, ye do always resist the Holy Spirit: as your fathers did, so do ye.

52 Which of the prophets did not your fathers persecute? and they killed them that showed before of the coming[79] of the Righteous One; of whom ye have now become betrayers and murderers;

53 ye who received the law as it was ordained by angels, and kept it not.

51 Having defended his position thus, Stephen now applied the moral to the consciences of his hearers in the true prophetic vein. The suddenness of his invective has taken some of his commentators by surprise, as it perhaps took some of his hearers; and it is suggested that his immediately preceding words must have occasioned an angry outburst in the court, to which vv. 51–53 supply his answer. But there is no good reason to think that he was in fact interrupted at this point; there was really nothing to add after his quotation from Isa. 66:1 f.; that clinched his case. The words which now follow sum up in a pointed and personal way the indictment which he had been building up against the nation.

That the nation was "stiffnecked" was a complaint as old as the wilderness wanderings, a complaint made by God Himself (Ex. 33:5). The description of them as "uncircumcised in heart and

---

[79] Gk. ἔλευσις, not otherwise found in Biblical Greek. It appears to have been in use already as a technical term of Hellenistic Judaism, denoting the messianic advent (*cf.* G. D. Kilpatrick in JThS xlvi [1945], pp. 136 ff.).

ears" meant that, while they were circumcised in the literal sense, their disobedience and unresponsiveness to God's revelation were such as might have been expected from the Gentiles to whom He had not made known His will as He did to Israel (*cf.* Lev. 26:41; Deut. 10:16; Jer. 4:4; 6:10; 9:26; Ezek. 44:7). Moses and the prophets had described the fathers in these terms; they are equally true, says Stephen, of their children of the contemporary generation.

52 It was the regular lot of the true prophets of God in OT times to suffer persecution and sometimes death itself for their faithfulness to the divine commission. There is ample evidence of this in the canonical OT books, and Jewish tradition elaborated the theme,[80] describing, for example, the martyrdom of Isaiah by sawing asunder in the reign of Manasseh[81] and of Jeremiah by stoning at the hands of the people who had forced him to go down to Egypt with them.[82] But much of that opposition to the prophets was due to their attack on Israel's perverted notions of the true worship of God—an attack of which the prophetic passages quoted by Stephen are samples. Stephen placed himself in the prophetic succession by attacking the people at this very point; it is therefore especially relevant that Israel's traditional hostility to the prophets should be mentioned here.

But did not the Jews of later days reprobate their ancestors' behaviour towards the prophets? Yes indeed; "If we had been in the days of our fathers," they said, "we should not have been partakers with them in the blood of the prophets" (Matt. 23:30). They paid tribute to the prophets' memory and built monuments in their honour. But Jesus assured them that even so they were still true sons of their fathers, maintaining the same hostility to the messengers of God (Matt. 23:29–37); and Stephen now repeated the charge. Their fathers had killed the messengers in days gone by who foretold the advent of the Righteous One;[83] they themselves had gone still farther and handed over the Righteous One Himself to violent death.

[80] *Cf.* the legendary *Lives of the Prophets* (ed. C. C. Torrey, Philadelphia, 1946), and H. J. Schoeps, "Die jüdischen Prophetenmorde", *Aus frühchristlicher Zeit* (Tübingen, 1950), pp. 126 ff.

[81] *Cf.* TB *Yebamoth* 49b; *Sanhedrin* 103b; *Ascension of Isaiah* (2nd cent. A.D.); Justin, *Dialogue* 120; Tertullian, *On Patience* 14.

[82] *Cf.* Tertullian, *Remedy against Scorpions* 8; Jerome, *Against Jovinian* ii. 37. How far back this tradition goes is uncertain.

[83] For this title *cf.* Chs. 3:14 (with p. 89, n. 31) and 22:14.

53 By rejecting their Messiah, then, they had filled up the measure of their fathers. The nation which had all along resisted the plan of God, the very purpose for which He had made them a nation and brought them into covenant with Himself, was but running true to type when it resisted and repudiated the One through whom the divine plan and purpose was to be consummated. In its earliest days as a nation, it rejected the law of God, although it had received that law by angelic mediation.[84] And now in these last days, when God had spoken to them through no angel but by the promised Messiah Himself, it had with even greater decisiveness rejected *Him.*

(f) Stephen Stoned to Death (Ch. 7:54–8:1a)

54 Now when they heard these things, they were cut to the heart, and they gnashed on him with their teeth.
55 But he, being full of the Holy Spirit, looked up stedfastly into heaven, and saw the glory of God, and Jesus[85] standing on the right hand of God,
56 and said, Behold, I see the heavens opened, and the Son of man standing on the right hand of God.
57 But they[86] cried out with a loud voice, and stopped their ears, and rushed upon him with one accord;
58 and they cast him out of the city, and stoned him: and the witnesses laid down their garments at the feet of a young man named Saul.

[84] The angels through whose mediation the law is said to have been ordained are mentioned elsewhere in NT. In Gal. 3:19 the fact that the law "was ordained through angels by the hand of a mediator" is adduced by Paul to show its inferiority to the promise which God made to Abraham without any intermediary. In Heb. 2:2 the argument is that if even the law, "spoken through angels," imposed inexorable penalties on those who infringed it, much more inexorable will be the penalty of disregarding God's latest revelation which was communicated not by angels but by His Son, "so much better than the angels, as he hath inherited a more excellent name than they" (Heb. 1:4). These angels are not mentioned in the account of the law-giving in Exodus; but *cf.* Deut. 33:2, LXX, "The Lord has come from Sinai, and shone forth unto us in Seir; He came with haste from Mount Paran, with the myriads of Kadesh were angels with Him at His right hand" (contrast MT: ". . . he came from the ten thousands of holy ones: at his right hand was a fiery law unto them"). (For other references to this angelic mediation of the law *cf.* Jubilees 1:29; *Testament of Dan* 6:2; Philo, *On Dreams* i. 141 ff.; Josephus, *Antiquities* xv. 5.3.)
[85] The Western text has "the Lord Jesus."
[86] One Western authority (the African Latin) says it was "the populace" that cried out.

59 And they stoned Stephen, calling upon *the Lord,* and
saying, Lord Jesus, receive my spirit.

60 And he kneeled down, and cried with a loud voice,
Lord, lay not this sin to their charge. And when he
had said this he fell asleep.

1 And Saul was consenting unto his death.

54 To the earlier part of Stephen's defence his judges had no doubt
listened with considerable interest and a measure of agreement.[87]
But as the drift of his argument became clear, they must have
heard him with increasing anger and horror; this was blasphemy indeed, this was unabashed contempt of the Shekhinah.[88]
And when he flung the charge of blasphemy, persistent opposition to the ways of God, back upon themselves, their vexation
and rage could no longer be restrained.[89]

55–56 While his audience gave unchecked vent to their passion,
Stephen remained calm, fully controlled as before by the Spirit

[87] Bernard Shaw (*Androcles and the Lion* [London, 1928], p. lxxxv) sums
up the contents of Acts 7 thus: "A quite intolerable young speaker named
Stephen delivered an oration to the council, in which he first inflicted on them
a tedious sketch of the history of Israel, with which they were presumably
as well acquainted as he, and then reviled them in the most insulting terms as
'stiffnecked and uncircumcized.' Finally, after boring and annoying them to
the utmost bearable extremity, he looked up and declared that he saw the
heavens open, and Christ standing on the right hand of God. This was too
much: they threw him out of the city and stoned him to death. It was a
severe way of suppressing a tactless and conceited bore; but it was pardonable
and human in comparison to the slaughter of poor Ananias and Sapphira."
Our general reading of the situation and character of Stephen differs considerably from Shaw's, but in particular his suggestion that the Sanhedrin would
have found a sketch of the history of Israel boring or tedious betrays great
ignorance of their customs and interests.

[88] The rabbis debated whether the Shekhinah did or did not rest on the
second temple as it did on Solomon's (1 Chron. 5:13 f.; 7:1 f.). In TB *Zebachim*
118b it is asserted that the Shekhinah rested in Shiloh, Nob, Gibeon, and in
"the eternal house"—the "eternal house" being presumably the Jerusalem
temple as such, with no particular emphasis on Solomon's or Zerubbabel's.
In TB *Yoma* 9b, however, it is denied that the Shekhinah rested on the second
temple—because the second temple was built by the Persians, who were
descended from Japheth, and it is written: "God shall enlarge Japheth, *but
He shall dwell in the tents of Shem*" (Gen. 9:27). This, however, was theorizing
after the event; while the second temple stood, it was generally venerated as
the habitation of God (*cf.* Matt. 23:21, "he that sweareth by the temple,
sweareth by it, and by him that dwelleth therein").

[89] "They were cut (Gk. διεπρίοντο) to the heart": for this verb (literally
"they were sawn asunder") used of fierce annoyance *cf.* Ch. 5:33. For teeth-
gnashing as a sign of rage *cf.* Job 16:9; Ps. 35:14. Elsewhere it is used of the
fruitless anguish of despair; *cf.* Luke 13:28 (βρυγμός, from βρύχω, the verb
used here).

of God, when suddenly, as he kept his gaze fixed upward, a vision of the glory of God met his inward eye. Much more real to him in that moment than the angry gestures and cries of his enemies was the presence of Jesus at God's right hand. "Look!" he cried, "I see the heavens parted and the Son of man standing at God's right hand."[90]

Not many years before, another prisoner had stood at the bar before the same court, charged with almost the same offences. But when the hostile evidence broke down, the high priest put that prisoner on his oath to tell them plainly if He was indeed the Messiah, the Son of the Blessed One. "I am," said He: "and you will see the Son of man seated at the right hand of the Almighty, and coming with the clouds of heaven" (Mark 14:62).[91] No more was required; Jesus was found guilty of blasphemy and condemned to death. And now Stephen in the same place was making the same claim on Jesus' behalf as He had made for Himself: he was claiming, in fact, that the words of Jesus had not been blasphemous and false but words of sober truth which had received their vindication and fulfilment from God. Unless the judges were prepared to admit that their former decision was tragically mistaken, they had no logical option but to find Stephen guilty of blasphemy as well.

This final occurrence of the title "Son of man" in the NT narrative[92] is full of meaning. These words of Stephen "represent the only instance in the New Testament of the apocalyptic title

[90] Similarly James the Just, according to the account of Hegesippus preserved by Eusebius (*Ecclesiastical History* ii. 23), said to his judges, "Why do you ask me about the Son of man? He sits at the right hand of the Almighty in heaven, and He will come on the clouds of heaven."

[91] In these words Jesus claimed to combine in His own person the "one like unto a son of man" who in Dan. 7:13 f. approaches the throne of God to receive universal and everlasting dominion and the priest-king of Ps. 110 who is invited by God to sit at His right hand. This twofold claim was interpreted by His judges as a claim to be the peer of the Most High and accordingly condemned as blasphemy. See J. Bowman, "The Background of the Term 'Son of Man'," *ExT* lix (1947–8), pp. 283 ff.; A. E. Guilding, "The Son of Man and the Ancient of Days," *EQ* xxiii (1951), pp. 210 ff.; V. Taylor, *The Gospel according to St. Mark* (London, 1952), pp. 567 ff.; F. F. Bruce, *The Dawn of Christianity* (London, 1950), pp. 55 f.; *The Growing Day* (London, 1951), p. 151 f., for discussions on the supposedly blasphemous element in these words of Jesus. On the meaning and fulfilment of His words see also N. B. Stonehouse, *The Witness of Matthew and Mark to Christ* (Philadelphia, 1944), pp. 240 ff.

[92] The expression in Rev. 1:13 and 14:14 is not the title ὁ υἱὸς τοῦ ἀνθρώπου but ὅμοιον υἱὸν ἀνθρώπου ("one like unto a son of man" as in Dan. 7:13).

'Son of Man' being found on any lips but those of Jesus. This remarkable fact is not one to be undervalued or ignored. It is, on the face of it, a very distinct piece of evidence that, actually and historically, *Stephen grasped and asserted the more-than-Jewish-Messianic sense in which the office and significance of Jesus in religious history were to be understood* ... Whereas the Jewish nationalists were holding to the permanence of their national historical privilege, and even the 'Hebrew' Christians gathered round the Apostles were, with all their new Messianic faith, idealising the sacred institutions of the past, 'continuing stedfastly in the temple,' 'going up to the temple at the hour of prayer' which was also the hour of the sacrificial service, sheltering under the eaves of the Holy Place, Stephen saw that the Messiah was on the throne of the Universe" (W. Manson, *op. cit.*, pp. 31 f.).[93]

And the presence of Messiah at God's right hand meant that for His people there was now a way of access to God more immediate and heart-satisfying than the obsolete temple ritual had ever been able to provide. It meant that the hour of fulfilment had struck, and the age of particularism was finished. When in Daniel's vision "one like unto a son of man" was brought into the presence of the Ancient of Days, it was to receive at His hands "dominion, and glory, and a kingdom, that all the peoples, nations and languages should serve him: his dominion is an everlasting dominion, which shall not pass away, and his kingdom that which shall not be destroyed" (Dan. 7:13 f.).[94] Messiah's sovereignty is

---

[93] As Professor Manson goes on to say (p. 32), Stephen testified to the fact that the Son of Man had arrived in the presence of God and received unlimited dominion from Him, that the vision of Dan. 7:13 f. had thus found its fulfilment, that all the institutions of the past were accordingly antiquated and superseded, and that the call was now to go forward under the direction of the once crucified but now exalted Son of Man, "to whom the throne of the world and the Lordship of the Age to Come belonged."

[94] True, in the primary sense of Dan. 7, the "one like unto a son of man" represents "the people of the saints of the Most High" just as the wild beasts whom he supersedes represent pagan world-empires. But the figure of "one like unto a son of man" had in the meantime acquired individuality as "the Son of man"; and in the Christian fulfilment the Son of man of Dan. 7:13 is Jesus Himself, while "the people of the saints of the Most High" of v. 27 are His church, called to share His suffering and sovereignty. On the Son of man see, in addition to literature mentioned at the end of n. 91, T. W. Manson, *The Teaching of Jesus* (2nd edn., Cambridge, 1935), pp. 211 ff., and "The Son of Man in Daniel, Enoch and the Gospels," BJRL xxxii (1950), pp. 171 ff.; R. Otto, *The Kingdom of God and the Son of Man* (Eng. tr., 2nd edn., London, 1943), pp. 159 ff.; E. A. McDowell, *Son of Man and Suffering Servant* (Nashville, 1944); E. Sjöberg, *Der Menschensohn im äthiopischen Henochbuch* (Lund.

to embrace all nations without distinction; there is no place here for any institution which gives religious privileges to one nation in particular, such as the traditional temple worship gave to the Jews.

The words which Jesus spoke in reply to the high priest's adjuration combined with this passage from the book of Daniel the opening words of Ps. 110: "Jehovah saith unto my Lord, Sit thou at my right hand, Until I make thine enemies thy footstool." But these words, whose significance has already been discussed in this volume (see on Ch. 2:34 f., pp. 72 f.), speak of the Messiah as invited to *sit* at God's right hand, and every other allusion to them in the NT speaks of Messiah as *seated* there. Is there any significance in Stephen's unique reference to the Son of man as *standing* at God's right hand?

Perhaps not;[95] G. H. Dalman may be right when he says that this "is merely a verbal change" in the expression. But when he adds, "There is, of course, no thought of a 'rising up' after being seated" (*The Words of Jesus* [Eng.tr., Edinburgh, 1902], p. 311), may he not dismiss too cavalierly the suggestion that Jesus is here represented as rising momentarily from the throne of glory to greet His proto-martyr? We cannot so readily reject this view outright.

> For ah, the Master is so fair,
> His smile so sweet to banished men,
> That they who meet it unaware
> Can never rest on earth again;
> And they who see Him risen afar
> At God's right hand to welcome them,
> Forgetful stand of home and land,
> Desiring fair Jerusalem.

There is much less to be said for the view that Stephen saw the Son of man standing because He had not yet taken His seat on the right hand of the throne of God. For this "dispensational" inter-

1946); G. S. Duncan, *Jesus, Son of Man* (London, 1947); A. Bentzen, *Messias— Moses redivivus—Menschensohn* (Zürich, 1948); M. Black, "The 'Son of Man' in the Old Biblical Literature", ExT lx (1948–9), pp. 11 f.; "The 'Son of Man' in the Teaching of Jesus", *ib.*, pp. 32 ff.; M. Black, "Servant of the Lord and Son of Man," *Scottish Journal of Theology* vi (1953), pp. 1 ff.; V. Taylor, *The Names of Jesus* (London, 1953), pp. 25 ff.

[95] *Cf.* C. H. Dodd, *According to the Scriptures* (London, 1952), p. 35 n.: "It is hardly likely that the substitution of the verb ἑστάναι for the καθῆσθαι of the LXX is significant, for ἑστάναι, like 'stand' in English and עמד in Hebrew, has commonly the sense 'to be situated,' without any necessary implication of an upright attitude ('*se tenir debout*')."

pretation we may quote William Kelly: "It was as yet a transitional time and Jesus he saw 'standing' there: He had not taken definitely His seat, but was still giving the Jews a final opportunity. Would they reject the testimony to Him gone on high indeed, but as a sign waiting if peradventure they might repent and He might be sent to bring in the times of refreshing here below? Stephen in these last words accentuated the call" (*An Exposition of the Acts of the Apostles* [3rd edn., London, 1952], pp. 102 f.). But surely Stephen's appeal was no "final opportunity" to the Jewish people; throughout Acts we see them receiving further opportunity after opportunity, up to the closing verses of Ch. 28. The ultra-dispensationalist E. W. Bullinger saw this plainly, and so he made the "transitional time" stretch to the beginning of Paul's two years of house arrest in Rome (Ch. 28:30); then only, in his view, does the Christian dispensation proper begin, and therefore Paul's captivity epistles, written after that point of time, are more directly relevant to Christians to-day than his earlier epistles or other parts of the NT.[96] This thesis might well seem to be its own *reductio ad absurdum*; but the whole assumption, that the gospel has at any time ceased to be offered to Jews as freely as to Gentiles, is completely devoid of substance.[97]

It may be, however, that a standing posture is mentioned here because the Son of man at God's right hand is not only viewed as king and priest, but also—and this is most relevant to Stephen's special situation—as a witness. Stephen has been confessing Christ before men, and now he sees Christ confessing His servant before God. The proper posture for a witness is the standing posture. Stephen, condemned by an earthly court, appeals for vindication to a heavenly court, and his vindicator in that supreme court is Jesus, who stands at God's right hand as Stephen's advocate, his "paraclete."[98] When we are faced with words so wealthy in

[96] These views are set forth concisely in *The Companion Bible* (London, 1909–21), which serves this ultra-dispensationalism in much the same way as the *Scofield Reference Bible* (New York, 1909) serves common dispensationalism. *Cf.* also E. W. Bullinger, *The Gospel of the Kingdom* (London, 1905), and *The Foundations of Dispensational Truth* (London, 1930).

[97] *Cf.* P. Mauro, *The Gospel of the Kingdom* (Boston, Mass., 1928) and *The Hope of Israel* (Boston, Mass., 1929); G. H. Lang, *The Gospel of the Kingdom* (2nd edn., London, 1944); O. T. Allis, *Prophecy and the Church* (Philadelphia, 1945).

[98] *Cf.* for a deeply instructive discussion, C. F. D. Moule, "From Defendant to Judge—and Deliverer," *Studiorum Novi Testamenti Societas*, Bulletin III (Oxford, 1952), pp. 40 ff.

association as these words of Stephen, it is unwise to suppose that any single interpretation exhausts their significance.   All the meaning that had attached to Ps. 110:1 and Dan. 7:13 f. is present here, including especially the meaning that springs from their combination on the lips of Jesus when He appeared before the Sanhedrin; but the replacement of "sitting" by "standing" probably makes its own contribution to the total meaning of the words in this context—a contribution distinctively appropriate to Stephen's present rôle as martyr-witness.[99]   If Stephen had some foretaste of this beatific vision at the moment when he was about to begin to bear his witness before the court, no wonder that his face shone like an angel's (Ch. 6:15).

57–58 There is some doubt about what happened next. Did the crowd of bystanders take the law into their own hands and lynch Stephen? This is the view of Joseph Klausner, according to whom Stephen's stoning was the work of "some fanatical persons" among the bystanders "who decided the case for themselves. They saw in Stephen a 'blasphemer' worthy of stoning, although according to the Talmudic rule 'the blasphemer is not culpable unless he pronounces the Name itself'—which Stephen had not done. The fanatics did not trouble themselves about the judicial rule; they took Stephen outside the city and stoned him" (*From Jesus to Paul* [Eng.tr., London, 1944], p. 292). It may be true, as Klausner goes on to say, that "in the opinion of the Pharisees there was in his words no actual blasphemy, but only an offense requiring the forty stripes lacking one." But that does not justify the conclusion that "the Sanhedrin could not see fit to impose the death sentence on him." He concedes that Stephen "may have been deserving of that according to the rules of the Sadducees"; and in the trial of Stephen, as in the trial of Jesus, it was the Sadducean chief priests who played the leading part. We must beware of supposing that trials before the Sanhedrin in the early decades of the first century A. D. were invariably conducted in the atmosphere of severe impartiality and judicial calm prescribed in the following century in the Mishnah tractate *Sanhedrin.*[100]

The reference to the witnesses suggests that Stephen's stoning

[99] It is relevant to recall here that "martyr" is simply the Gk. word meaning "witness" ($\mu\acute{\alpha}\varrho\tau\upsilon\varsigma$). *Cf.* Ch. 22:20 (p. 443, n. 25).

[100] There is a brief discussion of this point, in relation to the trial of Jesus, in F. F. Bruce, *The Dawn of Christianity*, pp. 54 ff.

was carried out as a legal execution—the penalty for blasphemy (and blasphemy in a wider sense than that defined by the idealizing rabbis of a later day). For it was the duty of the witnesses to play the chief part in such an execution—a duty prescribed not only in the Mishnah but in the written Torah itself (*cf.* Lev. 24:14; Deut. 17:7). To throw the first stones the witnesses would naturally divest themselves of their outer garments, as they are here said to have done.

But if it was a legal execution, how are we to account for its being carried out on the spot, without the authorization from the Roman governor which was required in the case of Jesus? Some have answered this question by suggesting that the incident took place after Pilate's recall in A.D. 36 and before the arrival of his successor Marcellus. (A parallel excess of high-priestly jurisdiction in a procuratorial interregnum was the judicial murder of James the Just in A.D. 61.)[101] But Stephen's martyrdom was probably earlier than A.D. 36. If it took place while Pilate was still procurator, no doubt Pilate could be relied upon to turn a blind eye on occasion. He had good reason for conciliating the chief-priestly group, and had probably established a mutual understanding with Caiaphas. Besides, he normally lived in Caesarea, and when strong feelings were stirred up in Jerusalem, they were not easily held in check. Stephen's echoing of the claim that Jesus as Son of man was exalted at God's right hand was, to his hearers, the last word in his blasphemy; they would hear no more; he was hustled from the court-room to the place of execution and stoned to death.

59–60 "The hand of the witnesses shall be first upon him to put him to death, and afterward the hand of all the people": so ran the ancient law (Deut. 17:7). In the second century A.D. this was interpreted as follows in the Mishnah: "When the trial is finished, the man convicted is brought out to be stoned. The stoning place was outside the court ... When ten cubits from the stoning place they say to him, 'Confess: for it is the custom of all about to be put to death to make confession; and every one who confesses has a share in the world to come.'[102] ... Four cubits from the stoning place the criminal is stripped[103]... The drop from the

---

101 *Cf.* Josephus, *Antiquities* xx. 9.1; see also p. 253 (on Ch. 12:17).
102 *Cf.* the case of Achan, Josh. 7:19.
103 For this reason F. C. Conybeare suggested that "their garments" (v. 58)

stoning place was twice the height of a man. One of the witnesses pushes the criminal from behind, so that he falls face downward. He is then turned over on his back. If he die from this fall, that is sufficient.[104] If not, the second witness takes the stone and drops it on his heart. If this cause death that is sufficient; if not, he is stoned by all the congregation of Israel." (*Sanhedrin* vi. 1-4). In the Mishnah this (or any other) form of execution is regarded as an unwelcome necessity, to be avoided if the slightest legal loop-hole can be found; we do not gather that Stephen's executioners stoned him as a disagreeable but unavoidable duty.

Nor did Stephen make confession to his judges and executioners; instead, as they were stoning him he committed himself to his exalted Advocate with the words "Lord Jesus, receive my spirit." These words are reminiscent of our Lord's final utterance on the cross: "Father, into thy hands I commend my spirit" (Luke 23:46).[105] But there is a striking difference: whereas Jesus commended His spirit to the Father, Stephen commended his to Jesus. This is surely an early, if tacit, testimony to the Christian belief in our Lord's essential deity.

But there was yet another of our Lord's utterances upon the cross that Stephen echoed. For, on his knees amid the flying stones, he made his last appeal to the heavenly court—not this time for his own vindication but for mercy towards his executioners. Before he was finally battered into silence and death, they heard him call aloud, "Lord, do not put this sin to their account."

There is a story in the OT of another messenger of God who for his faithfulness was stoned to death—Zechariah the son of Jehoiada, prophet and priest, who was put to death thus in the very temple court itself—"between the altar and the sanctuary," as our Lord said (Luke 11:51; *cf*. Matt. 23:35). But as Zechariah breathed his last beneath the pile of stones, he prayed, "Jehovah look upon it, and require it" (2 Chron. 24:22). The martyr-deaths were similar; the dying prayers widely different. Stephen had learned his lesson in the school of Him who, as He was being

should be emended to "his [Stephen's] garments" (*Expositor* VIII. vi [1913], pp. 466 ff.). But the text as it stands is confirmed by Ch. 22:20.

[104] The account of the death of James the Just, as described by Hegesippus (*cf*. n. 90 above), resembles these Mishnaic prescriptions: "Then they seized him and threw him down and began to stone him, since he did not die from his fall."

[105] A quotation from Ps. 31:5, prefaced by the vocative "Father."

fixed to the cross, prayed, "Father, forgive them; for they know not what they do" (Luke 23:34).[106] And having prayed thus, says Luke, "he fell asleep"—an unexpectedly beautiful and peaceful description of so brutal a death, but one which fits the spirit in which Stephen accepted his martyrdom.

1a It is customary to regard Philip as Luke's chief informant for the narrative of Chs. 6–8.[107] But some at least of the features in his account of the trial and death of Stephen are due more probably to another informant. Who remembered the angelic glory of Stephen's countenance as he faced his judges? Who heard him commit his spirit to the Lord Jesus and pray for those who were stoning him? Who but the young man Saul who is introduced to us in Ch. 7:58 as the one who kept the clothes of the witnesses while they took the lead in the deed of death?[108]

Saul, a native of the Cilician city of Tarsus, as we learn later (Ch. 9:11), may have attended the synagogue in Jerusalem where Stephen engaged in disputation with the spokesmen for the old order (Ch. 6:9). He too was exceptionally far-sighted, and realized as clearly as Stephen did the fundamental incompatibility between the old order and the new. The temporizing policy of his master Gamaliel[109] (Ch. 5:34 ff.) was not for him; he saw that no compromise was possible, and if the old order was to be preserved intact, the new faith must be stamped out. Hence he expressed approval[110] of Stephen's execution in a public manner by keeping

---

106 For the textual problem presented by these words of Jesus *cf.* Norval Geldenhuys's *Commentary on the Gospel of Luke* in this series (London and Grand Rapids, 1950), pp. 613 f.; see also J. R. Harris, *Side-lights on NT Research* (London, 1908), pp. 96 ff.; B. H. Streeter, *The Four Gospels* (London, 1930), pp. 138 f. In Hegesippus's narrative, James the Just, while he was being stoned, prayed, "I beseech Thee, Lord God and Father, forgive them; for they know not what they do."

107 *Cf.* A. Harnack, *Luke the Physician* (Eng. tr., London, 1907), pp. 155 ff.; see also p. 424 (on Ch. 21:9).

108 Even here there is a parallel between the narratives of Stephen and James, for in the *Clementine Recognitions* i. 70 Simon Magus, who is a transparent disguise for Paul (the *bête noire* of the Ebionites), stirs up a tumult against James, and throws him down headlong from the top of a flight of steps in the temple courts. Schoeps (*Theologie und Geschichte des Judenchristentums*, pp. 381 ff.) is probably right in tracing this and much else in the pseudo-Clementine literature back to an Ebionite *Acts of the Apostles*, composed as a counterblast to the canonical Acts; but in that case the Ebionite picture of James is much more likely to be based upon the Lukan Stephen than *vice versa* (*cf.* n. 17 above).

109 *Cf.* also Ch. 22:3.

110 The expression "was consenting" (Ch. 8:1; it recurs in Ch. 22:20) need

the clothes of the executioners—an act which he did not readily forget (*cf.* Ch. 22:20). The same refusal to compromise in the issue between Judaism and Christianity which determined his present attitude continued to determine his policy in later days when, as the apostle to the Gentiles, he built up the work which at first he had endeavoured to destroy.

not be taken to mean that Saul was actually a member of the Sanhedrin. F. C. Conybeare (*loc. cit.*) argues that he acted as herald at Stephen's execution, proclaiming the name of the accused and the crime for which he was being punished. (*Cf.* Ch. 26:10, p. 490.)

CHAPTER VIII

2. PHILIP

(Ch. 8:1b–40)

(a) Persecution and Dispersion (Ch. 8:1b–3)

And there arose on that day a great persecution[1]
against the church which was in Jerusalem; and they
were all scattered abroad throughout the regions of
Judaea and Samaria, except the apostles.[2]

2 And devout men buried Stephen, and made great
lamentation over him.

3 But Saul laid waste the church, entering into every
house, and dragging men and women committed them
to prison.

1b–2 The law prescribed the duty of burying the bodies of
executed persons, but the Mishnah (*Sanhedrin* vi. 6) forbade public
lamentation for them. Stephen, at any rate, received the funeral
tribute due to him from devout[3] men who disapproved of the
Sanhedrin's condemnation of him.

His death, however, was the signal for an immediate campaign
of repression against the Jerusalem church. If we read the present
paragraph in its wider context, we may conclude that it was the
Hellenists in the church (the group in which Stephen had been a
leader) who formed the main target of attack, and that it was
they for the most part who were compelled to leave Jerusalem.[4]
From this time onward the Jerusalem church appears to have
consisted almost entirely of "Hebrews."[5] The twelve apostles

---

[1] The Western text adds "and tribulation" (the term used in Ch. 11:19).

[2] The Western text adds "who remained in Jerusalem" (expressing, after its
manner, what is in any case implied).

[3] Gk. εὐλαβεῖς, used regularly of devout Jews in NT (*cf.* p. 61, n. 19; on
Ch. 2:5); here, no doubt, of Jewish Christians.

[4] *Cf.* Ch. 11:19 f.

[5] That is to say, until A.D. 135. After the Emperor Hadrian refounded
Jerusalem as the Roman colony of Aelia Capitolina, the Church of Jerusalem
was a completely Gentile-Christian body, having no continuity with the
Jewish-Christian Church of Jerusalem of the first century.

remained in Jerusalem, partly no doubt because they conceived it to be their duty to stay at their posts, and partly, we may gather, because the popular resentment was directed not so much at them as at the leaders of the Hellenists in the church. The persecution and dispersion, however, brought about a beginning of the fulfilment of our Lord's commission to His disciples in Ch. 1:8, "ye shall be my witnesses both in Jerusalem, and in all Judaea and Samaria ..." "The churches of God which are in Judaea in Christ Jesus"[6] (to borrow Paul's language in 1 Thess. 2:14) were born in this time of persecution.

3 The prime mover in the repressive campaign was Saul of Tarsus, who now carried into more effective action the attitude to the new movement which he had displayed at the stoning of Stephen. Armed with the necessary authority from the Sanhedrin's chief-priestly leaders,[7] he harried[8] the church, arresting men and women in their own homes and sending them off to prison. A zealot for the ancestral traditions of his nation,[9] he saw that the new faith menaced these traditions. Drastic action was called for; these people, he thought, were not merely misguided enthusiasts whose sincerity in embracing error might merit a measure of pity; they were deliberate impostors, proclaiming that God had raised from the grave as Lord and Messiah one whose manner of death was sufficient to show that the divine curse rested on him.[10]

(b) Philip in Samaria (Ch. 8:4–8)

4 They therefore that were scattered abroad went about preaching the word.

5 And Philip went down to the[11] city of Samaria, and proclaimed unto them the Christ.

6 And the multitudes gave heed with one accord unto the things that were spoken by Philip, when they heard, and saw the signs which he did.

[6] For a different expression denoting the same people see Ch. 9:31.

[7] *Cf.* Ch. 26:10.

[8] Gk. $\dot{\epsilon}\lambda\nu\mu\alpha\dot{\iota}\nu\epsilon\tau o$ (v. 3); according to Lake-Cadbury (*ad loc.*), it refers especially to the ravaging of a body by a wild beast.

[9] *Cf.* Gal. 1:14.

[10] *Cf.* Gal. 3:13, and the exposition of Ch. 5:30 above.

[11] Some authorities (the codices C D 81, the Byzantine text, and the two main Coptic versions) read "a city" (omitting $\tau\dot{\eta}\nu$ before $\pi\dot{o}\lambda\iota\nu$). See p. 177.

7 For *from* many of those that had unclean spirits, they came out, crying with a loud voice: and many that were palsied, and that were lame, were healed.

8 And there was much joy in that city.

4 As the old Israel had its Diaspora among the Gentiles, so must the new people of God be dispersed.[12] The words of an apocalyptic writer have been adduced as a parallel to the present narrative: "I will scatter this people among the Gentiles, that they may do good to the Gentiles" (2 Baruch 1:4).[13] These dispersed Christians did the utmost good to the people among whom they went, by proclaiming the good news of the deliverance accomplished by Christ. Not only did they do this in Palestine, but later on they carried the message much farther afield, as we shall see in a later passage of Acts (Ch. 11:19 ff.).

5 For the present, however, the interest of the narrative is concentrated on Philip, another Hellenistic leader who, like Stephen, was one of the seven almoners. Driven from his work in Jerusalem, Philip went north to Samaria and preached the gospel there.

Between the populations of Judaea and Samaria there was a long-standing cleavage, going back to very early times.[14] In spite of attempts to effect a reconciliation in post-exilic times,[15] the cleavage was widened by the Samaritans' erection on their sacred hill Gerizim of a rival temple to the restored temple at Jerusalem.[16] The Judaeans regarded the Samaritans as racial and religious half-breeds because of the foreign settlers planted in Samaria by the Assyrians to take the place of the upper classes of the land who were deported at the time of the fall of the

[12] *Cf.* the epistolary superscriptions in Jas. 1:1 ("to the twelve tribes which are of the Dispersion") and 1 Pet. 1:1 ("to the elect who are sojourners of the Dispersion").

[13] This work, the Syriac *Apocalypse of Baruch*, probably belongs to the second half of the first century.

[14] Going back ultimately to the isolation of Judah from the northern tribes of Israel in the settlement period; it found its most notable expression of OT times in the disruption of the Hebrew monarchy after Solomon's death (*c.* 930 B.C.).

[15] And even in pre-exilic times, under Hezekiah (2 Chr. 30:1 ff.) and Josiah (2 Kings 23:15 ff.).

[16] Josephus, *Antiquities* xi. 8.2, 4. It was to the Gerizim shrine that the woman of Sychar referred when she said to our Lord, "Our fathers worshipped in this mountain" (John 4:20).

northern kingdom of Israel.[17] Before long, these settlers abandoned their former pagan worship and became indistinguishable from the Israelites among whom they dwelt, but their alien origin continued to be used by the Jews as a pretext for refusing to have any dealings with them.[18] The Hasmonean king John Hyrcanus I (135–104 B.C.) conquered the Samaritans and destroyed their schismatic temple. With the Roman conquest of Palestine, the Samaritans were liberated from Judaean domination, but the NT bears ample witness to the unfriendly relations which persisted between the two groups.

It was thus a bold action on Philip's part to proclaim the good news to the Samaritans. They did, however, share with the Jews the hope of the coming Messiah,[19] whom they envisaged in terms of the Moses-like prophet of Deut. 18:15 ff., describing him as the *ta'eb* or "restorer."[20]

It is uncertain if "the city of Samaria" was the city which in OT times actually bore the name Samaria. That city had been rebuilt by Herod the Great as a Greek city and given the new name Sebaste in honour of the Roman emperor.[21] If it were the city meant, we might have expected it to be called Sebaste here instead of Samaria. Some textual authorities omit the definite article before "city" (*cf.* p. 175, n. 11); if, accordingly, we read with RSV "a city of Samaria", the reference may be to Gitta, which we know from Justin Martyr[22] (*Apology* I, 26) to have been the birthplace of Simon the sorcerer (see v. 9 below).

6–8 Whichever city it was, Philip's visit there was marked by such exorcizing of demon spirits from those who were possessed by them and such acts of healing performed on people who were paralysed and lame that great numbers believed his message and were filled with rejoicing. As in the ministry of Christ Himself and of His apostles, so in the ministry of Philip these mighty works were external "signs" confirming the message that he announced.

---

[17] *Cf.* 2 Kings 17:24 ff.; Ezra 4:2, 9 f. The Assyrian king Sargon II (721–705 B.C.) claims to have deported 27,290 people from the city of Samaria itself.

[18] They sometimes described them in mockery as "proselytes of the lions" because of the incident mentioned in 2 Kings 17:25 ff.

[19] *Cf.* John 4:25.

[20] *Cf.* p. 92 f. (on Ch. 3:22 f.).

[21] Gk. Σεβαστός (*cf.* Ch. 25:21) was used as the equivalent of Lat. *Augustus.*

[22] Justin himself was a native of Samaria, having been born *c.* A.D. 100 at Flavia Neapolis (modern Nablus, near the ancient Shechem).

(c) Simon the Sorcerer Is Baptized (Ch. 8:9–13)

9 But there was a certain man, Simon by name, who
beforetime in the city used sorcery, and amazed the
people of Samaria, giving out that himself was some
great one:

10 to whom they all gave heed, from the least to the
greatest, saying, This man is that power of God which
is called Great.

11 And they gave heed to him, because that of long time
he had amazed them with his sorceries.

12 But when they believed Philip preaching good tidings
concerning the kingdom of God and the name of Jesus
Christ, they were baptized, both men and women.

13 And Simon also himself believed; and being baptized,
he continued with Philip; and beholding signs and
great miracles wrought, he was amazed.

9–11 Simon the sorcerer, or Simon Magus (as he is usually
called) plays an extraordinary rôle in early Christian literature.
In post-apostolic times he is depicted as the father of the Gnostic
heresies.[23] Justin Martyr tells how by his magic power he secured
a following of devotees not only in Samaria but in Rome, to which
he went in the reign of Claudius.[24] In the apocryphal *Acts of Peter*
we are told how he corrupted the Christians in Rome by his false
teaching and made the authorities ill-disposed towards them, and
how at last he was worsted in a magical contest with Peter. But it
is in the pseudo-Clementine *Recognitions* and *Homilies* that the

---

[23] Irenaeus (*Against Heresies* i. 23) avers that Simon was the founder of
Gnosticism—"of the knowledge which is falsely so called" (τῆς ψευδωνύμου
γνώσεως), he says, quoting 1 Tim. 6:20—and that the sect of the Simonians
was derived from him. He further tells how Simon went about with a woman
named Helena, whom he had redeemed from slavery at Tyre, and whom he
declared to be the current incarnation of Ἔννοια (the thought or conception
of the divine mind), from whom the angelic powers and the material universe
had proceeded. Hippolytus (*Refutation of All Heresies* vi. 2–15) gives a fuller
account of Simon's alleged system, based on a Gnostic work entitled *The Great
Disclosure*, and relates how he allowed himself to be buried alive in Rome,
promising to rise on the third day, but the miracle did not happen.

[24] At Rome, according to Justin (*Apology* I, 26), Simon was honoured with
a statue dedicated "To Simon the holy god"; either Justin or the Simonians
themselves were misled by an inscription beginning SEMONI SANCO DEO—
"To the god Semo Sancus" (an ancient Sabine deity)—which they read as
SIMONI SANCTO DEO. Tertullian also connects the statue and inscription
with Simon Magus.

Simon-legend is most curiously elaborated: in them he appears as the untiring adversary of Peter, and to some extent at least it is reasonably certain that Simon is intended as a camouflage for Paul and reflects anti-Pauline sentiments among some Ebionites and other exclusive Jewish-Christian groups.[25] What relation the Simon of legend bears to the Simon of Acts is not clear; it may be that the heresiarch Simon, the founder of the Gnostic sect of the Simonians,[26] was a different person from the Simon of Acts, but that they became confused in later tradition.

At any rate, the Samaritan Simon impressed his fellow-countrymen greatly by the exercise of his magic powers, so much so that they accepted his own account of himself and regarded him as the Grand Vizier of the supreme God, the channel both of divine power and of divine revelation.[27]

12–13 But Simon Magus himself was impressed by the actions and words of Philip. Like the magicians of Egypt, he recognized that the messenger of the true God had access to a source of power that outstripped his own. The proclamation heralded by such an envoy must be accepted with respect, and Simon "believed". The nature of his belief must remain uncertain. No doubt it was sincere as far as it went, but was very superficial and unsatisfactory. Jesus Himself, we are told in John 2:23 f., attached little value to the faith that rested on miracles alone. Yet, when the others who believed Philip's message of "good tidings concerning the kingdom of God and the name of Jesus Christ"[28] were baptized, Simon came to receive baptism too, and remained in Philip's company. Perhaps he reckoned that, if he did not, he would lose his former adherents more irretrievably than ever;

[25] See F. J. Foakes Jackson, *Peter: Prince of Apostles* (London, 1927), pp. 165 ff.; H. J. Schoeps, *Theologie und Geschichte des Judenchristentums* (Tübingen, 1949), pp. 127 ff.; *Aus frühchristlicher Zeit* (Tübingen, 1950), pp. 239 ff. ("Simon Magus in der Haggada?").

[26] The Simonians survived to the middle of the third century at least (Origen, *Against Celsus* i. 57).

[27] Many other explanations of Simon's grandiloquent title have been offered, and many real or fancied parallels from various quarters have been adduced, but J. de Zwaan's account, that Simon claimed to be Grand Vizier (*Ba'al Zebul*) of the Lord of heaven (*Ba'al Shamain*) is most probable (*Beginnings* ii [London, 1922], p. 58), certainly more probable than G H. Dalman's view that he claimed to be God Almighty (Heb. *ha-gebhurah*) Himself (*Words of Jesus* [Eng. tr., Edinburgh, 1902], p. 200). On the whole question of Simon Magus see also R. P. Casey in *Beginnings* v (London, 1933), pp. 151 ff.

[28] *Cf.* pp. 34 ff. (on Ch. 1:3).

and perhaps he also hoped to master the secret of Philip's deeds of divine power.

(d) Peter and John Visit Samaria (Ch. 8:14–24)

14 Now when the apostles that were at Jerusalem heard that Samaria had received the word of God, they sent unto them Peter and John:

15 who, when they were come down, prayed for them, that they might receive the Holy Spirit:

16 for as yet it was fallen upon none of them: only they had been baptized into the name of the Lord Jesus.

17 Then laid they their hands on them, and they received the Holy Spirit.

18 Now when Simon saw that through the laying on of the apostles' hands the Holy[29] Spirit was given, he offered them money,

19 saying, Give me also this power, that on whomsoever I lay my hands, he may receive the Holy Spirit.

20 But Peter said unto him, Thy silver perish with thee, because thou hast thought to obtain the gift of God with money.

21 Thou hast neither part nor lot in this matter: for thy heart is not right before God.

22 Repent therefore of this thy wickedness, and pray the Lord, if perhaps the thought of thy heart shall be forgiven thee.

23 For I see that thou art in the gall of bitterness and in the bond of iniquity.

24 And Simon answered and said, Pray ye for me to the Lord, that none of the things which ye have spoken come upon me.[30]

14 News of Philip's evangelistic progress in Samaria was brought to Jerusalem, and the apostles sent two of their number to Samaria to inspect this work. In the earlier years of the Christian mission, the apostles appear to have regarded it as their duty to exercise a general supervision over the progress of the gospel wherever it might be carried (cf. Ch. 11:22). Peter and John were the two who were sent to Samaria.[31] John, with his brother James,

---

[29] Codd. ℵ and B and the Sahidic (Coptic) version omit "Holy" (so do Westcott and Hort).

[30] The Western text adds (awkwardly, at the end of the sentence), "who never stopped weeping copiously."

[31] Cf. Ch. 3:1 ff. This is the last occasion on which John figures in the

had once suggested that they should, Elijah-like, bring down fire from heaven on a Samaritan community for its inhospitable behaviour to their Master (Luke 9:52 ff.). It was with a very different attitude that he now set out with Peter to visit Samaria. The earlier ban on the apostles' entering any city of the Samaritans (Matt. 10:5) had been rescinded by the unlimited commission of witness laid upon them by the risen Christ, in which Samaria was one of the areas explicitly mentioned (Acts 1:8).

15–17 The sequel to the apostles' visit has been the subject of much theological debate. Unlike the Jerusalem converts on the day of Pentecost, the Samaritan believers, although baptized by Philip "into the name of the Lord Jesus"[32] (v. 16), had not at the same time received the gift of the Holy Spirit. But when Peter and John came to their city, they prayed for them, asking God to grant them the Holy Spirit, and then, when they laid their hands upon the converts, the Holy Spirit came upon them.[33] The context leaves us in no doubt that their reception of the Spirit was attended by external manifestations such as had marked His descent on the earliest disciples at Pentecost.[34]

narrative of Acts, although his name is mentioned in Ch. 12:2 and he may have been one of "the apostles" of Ch. 15:2 ff.

[32] This expression (Gk. εἰς τὸ ὄνομα τοῦ κυρίου Ἰησοῦ), repeated in Ch. 19:5, differs somewhat from ἐν τῷ ὀνόματι Ἰησοῦ Χριστοῦ in Chs. 2:38; 10:48 (cf. p. 76, n. 73). The phrase εἰς τὸ ὄνομα is common in a commercial context, where some property is transferred or paid "into the name" of someone. So the person baptized "into the name of the Lord Jesus" bears public witness that he has become the property of Jesus and that Jesus is his Lord and Owner. The longer expression in Matt. 28:19 (cf. Didache 7:1), where baptism is to be "into the name of the Father and of the Son and of the Holy Spirit", is appropriate for "disciples of all the nations" (i.e. Gentiles), turning from paganism to serve the living God, whereas Jews and Samaritans, who already acknowledged the one true God, were required only to confess Jesus as Lord and Messiah. (Cf. G. F. Moore, Judaism i [Cambridge, Mass., 1927], pp. 188 f.)

[33] J. Behm, Die Handauflegung im Urchristentum (Leipzig, 1911), pp. 24 ff., envisages two sources in Acts 8:1–25, in the former of which the Samaritans are evangelized by Philip, in the latter by Peter and John; v. 14 being the editorial link between the two. This is altogether too easy a way out.

[34] Cf. N. B. Stonehouse, "The Gift of the Holy Spirit," WThJ xiii (1950–1), pp. 10 f. The prior operation of the Spirit in regeneration and faith is not in view here. "To us that may seem baffling because the theological questions are of paramount and perennial interest. But one may not insist that the writer of Acts had to reflect upon these questions in our terms, and one must recognize the peculiar appropriateness in a volume largely concerned with the external course of early Christian history of centering attention upon the extraordinary miraculous power of the Spirit in the accomplishment of the divine plan for the people of God" (Stonehouse, ib., p. 11).

It has frequently been held, by ancient and modern commentators alike, that what Peter and John did was to perform the rite of confirmation; it has further been inferred that confirmation can be administered only by an apostle or someone in the succession of the apostolic ministry (*i.e.* in episcopal orders). But it is laying too great a burden on the present passage to extract this meaning from it. If confirmation by an apostle were necessary for the reception of the Spirit,[35] we should have expected to find further references to so important a matter in the NT. But no such thing is suggested even in passages where it would certainly be introduced if there were any substance in it. It is not suggested by Paul when he speaks in 2 Cor. 1:21 f. of Christians' being anointed, sealed, and given the earnest of the Spirit in their hearts; he does not include the power of thus imparting the Spirit in the list of spiritual gifts in 1 Cor. 12:4 ff., and when he thanks God that he did not baptize more than a handful of his Corinthian converts (1 Cor. 1:14 ff.) the whole force of his statement would be gone if we had to suppose that, even so, he confirmed them all. In other places in Acts, too, there is no suggestion that apostolic hands were laid on converts before they received the Spirit. Nothing is said about this being done to the Pentecostal believers in Ch. 2, to the Ethiopian chamberlain towards the end of Ch. 8, to the household of Cornelius in Ch. 10 or to the Philippian jailor's household in Ch. 16. The only near parallel to the present passage in Acts is the exceptional case of the Ephesian disciples in Ch. 19:1 ff. In general, it seems to be assumed in NT that those who believe and are baptized have also the Spirit of God.[36]

In the present instance, some special evidence may have been necessary to assure these Samaritans, so accustomed to being despised as outsiders by the people of Jerusalem, that they were fully incorporated into the new community of the people of God. Not until they had been acknowledged and welcomed by the leaders of the Jerusalem church did they experience the signs which confirmed and attested their membership of the Spirit-

---

[35] See for this point of view A. J. Mason, *The Relation of Confirmation to Baptism* (London, 1891); G. Dix, *Confirmation or the Laying on of Hands?* (London, 1936); *The Theology of Confirmation in Relation to Baptism* (London, 1946); N. Adler, *Taufe und Handauflegung* (Münster, 1951). A masterly critique of their arguments is provided by G. W. H. Lampe, *The Seal of the Spirit* (London, 1951).

[36] *Cf.* Rom. 5:5; 8:9–11; 1 Cor. 6:19; 12:3–13; Eph. 1:13; 4:30.

possessed company. "The imposition of hands is then primarily a token of fellowship and solidarity; it is only secondarily an effective symbol of the gift of the Spirit; it becomes such a symbol solely in virtue of being a sign of incorporation into the Church of the Spirit" (G. W. H. Lampe, *The Seal of the Spirit* [London, 1951], p. 70).

But Professor Lampe is probably right in finding the central significance of the episode elsewhere. "The preaching of the Gospel in Samaria represented a crucial moment in the first advance of Christianity. Hence, after the Baptism of the first Samaritan converts, the leaders of the Church's mission come down from Jerusalem and, by the sign of fellowship and 'contact' incorporate them into the apostolic (*i.e.* missionary) Church, with the result that there occurs a Samaritan 'Pentecost', at least to the extent that visible signs are manifested of the outpouring of the Spirit. It may not be too much to assert that this event is meant to demonstrate that a new nucleus of the missionary Church has been established, and to suggest that Luke's readers are intended to infer that the Gospel proceeded to radiate outwards from this new centre of the Spirit's mission" (*op. cit.*, p. 72).

18–19 Whether the external signs which accompanied the gift of the Spirit on this occasion were identical with the Pentecostal signs or not, they were at any rate of so impressive a nature that Simon Magus craved the power to reproduce them at will. Now he felt he was getting near the heart of these mysteries; the latest phenomena were obviously associated with the imposition of hands. If only they could be associated with the imposition of *his* hands, what an access of authority and prestige would be his! So, obviously regarding Peter and John as extraordinarily gifted practitioners of religious magic, he offered to buy from them a share in their secret power. It is this act of Simon that has given the term "simony" to our ecclesiastical vocabulary.

20–23 Simon was quite unprepared for the stern words which his simple-minded request evoked. His idea that God's free gift could be bought showed that he had no appreciation at all of the inward character of the gospel and the operation of the Spirit. "Perdition take your silver," said Peter, "as it will take you too unless you repent and seek forgiveness for your wicked thought." Simon had believed Philip's message and been baptized, but he still manifested the signs of his old unregenerate nature: he was still attached to the "bitter gall-root" of superstition and magic, he was still fast held in the "bond of iniquity."[37]

24 Simon was terror-stricken. That he should have incurred the displeasure of men who seemed to have such power at their command was an awful thought; the Western text which tells us that he kept on weeping all the time that Peter was speaking (see p. 180, n. 30) may be true enough to the facts, if Simon was the emotionally unstable type of spiritualist medium who is not unknown in our own day; although the picture does not agree so well with the Simon Magus of later tradition. Canonical literature, however, bids farewell to Simon with the entreaty on his lips that by the prayer of the apostles he may escape the judgment which his crooked[38] heart deserves.

(e) The Preachers Return to Jerusalem (Ch. 8:25)

25 They therefore, when they had testified and spoken the word of the Lord, returned to Jerusalem, and preached the gospel to many villages of the Samaritans.

25 After this, Philip went back to Jerusalem with Peter and John, and as they went, they evangelized many other Samaritan communities. That Philip as well as the two apostles went back is not stated explicitly here, but may be implied by the wording at the outset of the following narrative.

(f) Philip and the Ethiopian (Ch. 8:26–40)

26 But an angel of the Lord spake unto Philip, saying, Arise, and go toward the south unto the way that goeth down from Jerusalem unto Gaza: the same is desert.
27 And he arose and went: and behold, a man of Ethiopia, a eunuch of great authority under Candace, queen of

---

[37] On the other hand, Peter may mean that Simon is heading for the bitter gall and the bonds which are the penalty of iniquity. The construction ($εἰς$ $γὰρ$ $χολὴν$ $πικρίας$ ... $ὁρῶ$ $σε$ $ὄντα$) is that of the verb "to be" followed by $εἰς$, which in the papyri denotes destination, and is so used in v. 20, $τὸ$ $ἀργύριόν$ $σου$ ... $εἴη$ $εἰς$ $ἀπώλειαν$ (literally, "May your silver be for perdition"). The language of Peter has an OT flavour: cf. Deut. 29:18 (reflected in Heb. 12:15) and Isa. 58:6, noting particularly $ἐν$ $χολῇ$ $καὶ$ $πικρίᾳ$ in the LXX of the former passage and $σύνδεσμον$ $ἀδικίας$ in the LXX of the latter passage.

[38] "Your heart is not straight ($εὐθεῖα$)," says Peter in v. 21 (similarly Ps. 78:37, LXX).

the Ethiopians, who was over all her treasure, who had
come to Jerusalem to worship;

28 and he was returning and sitting in his chariot, and
was reading the prophet Isaiah.

29 And the Spirit said unto Philip, Go near, and join
thyself to this chariot.

30 And Philip ran to him, and heard him reading Isaiah
the prophet, and said, Understandest thou what thou
readest?

31 And he said, How can I, except some one shall guide
me? And he besought Philip to come up and sit with
him.

32 Now the passage of the scripture which he was read-
ing was this,
He was led as a sheep to the slaughter;
And as a lamb before his shearer is dumb,
So he openeth not his mouth:

33 In his humiliation his judgment was taken away:
His generation, who shall declare?
For his life is taken from the earth.

34 And the eunuch answered Philip, and said, I pray
thee, of whom speaketh the prophet this? of himself,
or of some other?

35 And Philip opened his mouth, and beginning from this
scripture, preached unto him Jesus.

36 And as they went on the way, they came unto a certain
water; and the eunuch saith, Behold, *here is* water;[39]
what doth hinder me to be baptized?[40]

38 And he commanded the chariot to stand still: and
they both went down into the water, both Philip and
the eunuch; and he baptized him.

39 And when they came up out of the water, the Spirit
of the Lord caught away Philip;[41] and the eunuch saw
him no more, for he went on his way rejoicing.

---

[39] P45 omits "Behold, here is water."

[40] The Western text adds: "And Philip said, If thou believest with thy
whole heart, it is permitted. And he said in answer, I believe the Son of God
to be Jesus Christ." The grammatical construction of the Ethiopian's confession
(πιστεύω τὸν υἱὸν τοῦ θεοῦ εἶναι τὸν Ἰησοῦν Χριστόν) is un-Lukan. Although
this addition is absent from the Byzantine text, it made its way into the
Received Text (and thence into AV, etc.) from the editions of Erasmus, who
included it because he thought it had fallen out of the Greek MSS. known to
him through negligence.

[41] The Western text reads "the Spirit of the Lord fell upon the eunuch,
and the angel of the Lord snatched Philip away."

40 But Philip was found at Azotus: and passing through he preached the gospel to all the cities, till he came to Caesarea.

26 The next part of the story of Philip is told in a style which is in some respects reminiscent of the OT narratives of Elijah and Elisha. While here, as in Ch. 5:19, the expression rendered "an angel of the Lord" is the same as that used in LXX for the supernatural messenger who manifested the Divine Presence to men,[42] Luke's statement that "an angel of the Lord spake unto Philip, saying, Arise" is probably a vivid way of denoting Philip's divine guidance. In the following narrative it is difficult to see any real distinction between the "angel of the Lord" and "the Spirit of the Lord", although the Western text introduces a distinction in v. 39 (see p. 185, n. 41).

However that may be, Philip received a divine command to go southwards to join the Jerusalem-Gaza road (probably the road which ran by way of Eleutheropolis). It is not clear whether the words "the same is desert" refer to the road or to Gaza; grammatically either alternative is possible. The older city of Gaza was destroyed by the Hasmonean king Alexander Jannaeus in 93 B.C., and was known as Old Gaza or Desert Gaza after a new city of Gaza was built nearer the sea by Gabinius in 57 B.C.

27–28 Along this road Philip found a covered waggon making its way southwards; in it was seated the treasurer of the Ethiopian court, who had been making a pilgrimage to Jerusalem and was now on his way home. The ancient kingdom of Ethiopia corresponded to the modern Nubia rather than to Abyssinia; it stretched from the first cataract of the Nile at Aswan south to the neighbourhood of Khartoum. Its two chief cities were Meroe and Napata. The king of Ethiopia was venerated as the child of the sun and regarded as too sacred a personage to discharge the secular functions of royalty; these were performed on his behalf by the queen-mother, who regularly bore the dynastic title Candace.[43]

The chamberlain was probably a God-fearing Gentile. The

---

[42] *Cf.* p. 151, n. 49, and p. 152, n. 54 (on Ch. 7:35, 38).

[43] According to Bion of Soli (*Aethiopica* 1), "the Ethiopians do not declare the fathers of their kings, but hand down a tradition that they are sons of the sun. They call the mother of each king Candace." *Cf.* also Strabo, *Geography* xvii. 1.54; Pliny, *Natural History*, vi. 186; Dio Cassius, *History*, liv. 5.4; Eusebius, *Ecclesiastical History* ii. 1.13.

rendering "eunuch" is no doubt correct; eunuchs were commonly employed as court officials in eastern lands from antiquity until quite recent times. It is questionable whether a eunuch could have been admitted to the commonwealth of Israel as a full proselyte; at an earlier time eunuchs were excluded from religious privileges in Israel (Deut. 23:1), although Isa. 56:3 ff. foreshadows the removal of this ban. At any rate, this man had visited Jerusalem as a worshipper, perhaps at the time of one of the great pilgrimage-festivals, and was now beguiling his homeward journey by studying a scroll of the book of Isaiah in the Greek version.[44]

29–31 The divine monitor (called the Spirit this time) instructed Philip to approach the waggon; and as Philip did so, he heard the Ethiopian reading aloud from his copy of Isaiah. Reading in ancient times was almost invariably aloud.[45] Why this should be so will be apparent to anyone who tries to read a copy of ancient manuscript; the words require to be spelt out, and this is done more easily aloud than in silence. In addition, beginners regularly read aloud; it requires considerable experience (not to say sophistication) to read silently, though this stage is reached more quickly with modern print than with ancient manuscript. The actual passage of the prophecy which the Ethiopian was reading aloud gave Philip his cue immediately: "Do you understand what you are reading?",[46] he asked. The man frankly acknowledged that he did not—that he could not without a guide. And as Philip appeared to know what he was talking about, he invited him to come up on the waggon and sit beside him. Certainly he could not have found a more reliable guide to the meaning of what he read than the man who had thus strangely accosted him.

32–33 For the passage which he was reading was the great prophecy of the Suffering Servant, which had found its fulfilment so recently in the self-sacrificing death of Jesus of Nazareth. The prophet himself, as he gave utterance to these words, might well have wondered and "inquired what person or time was indicated by the Spirit of Christ within" him when thus "predicting the

---

[44] The quotation in vv. 42 f. follows LXX.

[45] In his *Confessions* (vi. 3) Augustine mentions as something worthy of note the fact that Ambrose of Milan read silently.

[46] There is a play on words here (ἆρά γε γινώσκεις ἃ ἀναγινώσκεις;), reproduced in the Latin Vulgate, *intellegis quae legis?*

sufferings of Christ and the subsequent glory" (1 Pet. 1:11, RSV);
for it must have been almost impossible to understand how they
would be fulfilled until Christ came and fulfilled them. Christ
Himself spoke of His sufferings in terms of this prophecy: "the
Son of man," He said, "did not come to be served by others but
to be a Servant, and to give his life a ranson for many" (Mark
10:45; *cf.* the "many" in Isa. 53:11 f.). He accepted, interpreted
and discharged His messianic mission in terms of this prophecy,
in a manner which was indeed foreshadowed in the words of the
heavenly voice spoken to Him at His baptism (Mark 1:11).[47] There
is no evidence that between the time of the prophet and the time
of Christ anyone had identified the Suffering Servant of Isa. 53
with the Davidic Messiah of Isa. 11 or with the "one like unto
a son of man" of Dan. 7:13.[48] But Jesus identified them and fulfils
them in His own person and by His own act, thus confirming the
identification. "How is it written of the Son of man, that he should
suffer many things and be set at nought?" (Mark 9:12)—how indeed, unless the Son of man be also the Servant of the Lord? How
difficult it was to understand the prophecy before it was fulfilled;
how easy, once the fulfilment is known!

The Septuagint translators themselves had difficulty with this
prophecy, and their rendering is even less easy to translate than
the Hebrew text itself is in places. Here, however, is the RSV
rendering of the Septuagint text of Isa. 53:7 f. (the lines which
the Ethiopian was actually reading when Philip drew near to his
waggon), quoted here by Luke:

> "As a sheep led to the slaughter
> or a lamb before its shearer is dumb,
> so he opens not his mouth.
> In his humiliation justice was denied him.
> Who can describe his generation?
> For his life is taken up from the earth."[49]

[47] See p. 88, nn. 27, 28 (on Ch. 3:13).
[48] See p. 165, n. 91 (on Ch. 7:56).
[49] The Hebrew text of the last three lines is translated thus by C. R. North
(*The Suffering Servant in Deutero-Isaiah* [Oxford, 1948], p. 122):

> "After arrest and sentence he was taken off,
> And on his fate who reflected?
> For he was cut off from the land of the living."

Though justice was denied the Servant on earth, his righteousness was
vindicated by God when He exalted him (*cf.* Ch. 3:13). On the interpretation of
the Servant Songs, with special reference to their Christian fulfilment, see (in

34–35 The Ethiopian's question, "About whom, pray, does the prophet say this, about himself or about someone else?" (RSV), has often served in more recent times as the text for an essay or an examination question, so numerous are the answers that have been offered.[50] But Philip found no difficulty, nor did he hesitate between a number of alternative answers. The prophet himself might not have known, but now that the prophecy had come true, Philip knew, "and beginning with this scripture he told him the good news of Jesus" (RSV). In a day when only the OT scriptures were available, with what scripture could any evangelist have begun more appropriately in order to preach Jesus to one who did not know Him? For it was Jesus, and no other, who offered up His life as an offering for sin, and justified many by bearing their iniquities, exactly as had been written of the obedient Servant. As the historic fact of Jesus' undeserved suffering and death is certain, equally certain is it that through His suffering and death men and women of all nations have experienced forgiveness and redemption, just as the prophet foretold.

36–38 Philip's persuasive exposition of the Servant's passion found its way home to the Ethiopian's heart; apparently he also told him, as Peter had told his Jerusalem audience on the day of Pentecost, that the appropriate response to such good news was repentance and baptism for the remission of sins and the reception of the Holy Spirit. At any rate, as they journeyed on, they came to running water—whether the Wadi el-Hesi north-east of Gaza, which is pointed out as the place, is rightly or wrongly identified with it cannot be known. "See, here is water!" said the Ethiopian. "What is to prevent my being baptized?" So the waggon was halted, they both went down into the water, and Philip baptized him. This is the account in the original text. But at quite an early date (per-

addition to North's book just cited) V. Taylor, *Jesus and His Sacrifice* (London, 1937), pp. 39 ff.; J. W. Bowman, *The Intention of Jesus* (London, 1945), pp. 40 ff., 128 ff.; H. W. Wolff, *Jesaja 53 im Urchristentum* (Berlin, 1950); J. Jeremias in TWNT v (Stuttgart, 1952), *s.v.* παῖς θεοῦ (pp. 676 ff.); E. J. Young, *Isaiah Fifty-Three* (Grand Rapids, 1952); H. H. Rowley, *The Servant of the Lord and Other Essays on the OT* (London, 1952), pp. 3–88; M. Black, "Servant of the Lord and Son of Man," *Scottish Journal of Theology* vi (1953, pp. 1 ff. See p. 191, n. 56.

[50] *Cf.* C. R. North, *op. cit.*, pp. 6–116, for a summary of the answers offered from pre-Christian times to our own day, and H. H. Rowley, *op. cit.*, pp. 3 ff., for a survey of answers given since 1921, when S. Mowinckel propounded the view that the prophet did say these things "of himself."

haps in the first decades of the second century) it was felt that this was not quite adequate. Philip surely must have satisfied himself first of the genuineness of the Ethiopian's faith. (No doubt he did so satisfy himself, but there are some minds that cannot be content to leave such things to be inferred.) So we find the Western addition which appears in AV as v. 37 ("And Philip said, If thou believest with all thine heart, thou mayest. And he answered and said, I believe that Jesus Christ is the Son of God"). (See p. 185, n. 40.) This addition certainly reflects primitive Christian practice. When a convert was formally admitted to Christian fellowship by baptism, he made a public confession of his new faith, probably in response to a definite question.[51]

39 The divine purpose in sending Philip to the Gaza road was accomplished; he was now sped northwards by the Spirit on another mission.[52] The Western text, however, makes the *angel* of the Lord snatch him up, while the *Spirit* of the Lord falls on the Ethiopian (*cf.* p. 185, n. 41). The purpose of this textual alteration may be partly to bring in the angel of the Lord at the end of the incident, since he was mentioned at its beginning (v. 26); but the much more important effect of the longer reading is to make it clear that the Ethiopian's baptism was followed by the gift of the Spirit. However, even with the shorter reading it is a safe inference that he did receive the Spirit (*cf.* Lampe, *op. cit.*, pp. 43 n., 65, 67)—though it would be an impermissible inference from the standpoint of those who take v. 16 to signify that the Spirit is bestowed only through the imposition of apostolic hands. When he disappears from our sight, going "on his way rejoicing", we need not doubt that the joy which filled his heart was the joy which is part of the "fruit of the Spirit" (Gal. 5:22). What became of him we do not know. Irenaeus tells us (*Against Heresies* iii.12.8) that he became a missionary among his people, which we should naturally expect, though Irenaeus may have had no more information on the matter than we ourselves have.[53] Whether he was a full proselyte or only a God-fearer, his conversion marks a further advance towards the evangelization of Gentiles.

[51] *Cf.* Ch. 22:16 (and exposition on p. 442); see also O. Cullmann, *The Earliest Christian Confessions* (Eng. tr., London, 1949), pp. 19 f. *Cf.* p. 231, n. 60.
[52] For the action of the Spirit in catching Philip away *cf.* the experiences of Elijah (1 Kings 18:12; 2 Kings 2:16) and Ezekiel (Ezek. 3:14; 8:3).
[53] We have no record of the Ethiopic church earlier than the fourth century A.D.

40   Philip next appeared at Azotus, the old Philistine city of Ashdod, some twenty miles north of Gaza. From there he headed north along the coastal road, preaching the gospel in all the cities through which he passed,[54] until at last he reached Caesarea. There he seems to have settled down; at least, it is there that we find him when he makes his next appearance in the narrative, twenty years later (Ch. 21:8).[55] By that time he had become a family man, with four daughters all old enough to be prophetesses—worthy daughters of such a father.[56]

[54] Including perhaps Lydda and Joppa, shortly afterwards visited by Peter (Ch. 9:32 ff.).

[55] See p. 423.

[56] To the bibliography on p. 189, n. 49, add: A. Bentzen, *Messias—Moses redivivus—Menschensohn* (Zürich, 1948), pp. 42 ff.; C. R. North, "The Suffering Servant: Current Scandinavian Discussion", *Scottish Journal of Theology* iii (1950), pp. 363 ff.; W. H. Brownlee, "The Servant of the Lord in the Qumran Scrolls", *Bulletin of American Schools of Oriental Research*, 132 (December 1953), pp. 8 ff.; J. Bright, *The Kingdom of God* (New York, 1953) pp. 146 ff., 208 ff. See also p. 227, n. 47; p. 231, n. 62.

CHAPTER IX

3. CONVERSION OF SAUL OF TARSUS

(Ch. 9:1-31)

(a) Saul's Vision on the Road to Damascus (Ch. 9:1-9)

1 But Saul, yet breathing threatening and slaughter against the disciples of the Lord, went unto the high priest,

2 and asked of him letters to Damascus unto the synagogues, that if he found any that were of the Way, whether men or women, he might bring them bound to Jerusalem.

3 And as he journeyed, it came to pass that he drew nigh unto Damascus: and suddenly there shone round about him a light out of heaven:

4 and he fell upon the earth, and heard a voice saying unto him, Saul, Saul, why persecutest thou me?[1]

5 And he said, Who art thou, Lord? And he *said*,[2] I am Jesus[3] whom thou persecutest:[4]

6 but arise, and enter into the city, and it shall be told thee what thou must do.

7 And the men that journeyed with him stood speechless, hearing the voice, but beholding no man.[5]

8 And Saul arose from the earth; and when his eyes were

---

[1] The Western addition "it is hard for thee to kick against the goad" is in two Greek MSS and some versions transferred here from v. 5 (see n. 4 below) in order to harmonize with Ch. 26:14.

[2] The Byzantine text reads "And the Lord said."

[3] A few authorities, mainly Western in character, add "the Nazarene" from Ch. 22:8.

[4] There is a Western addition here (drawn in part from Chs. 22:10 and 26:14): "it is hard for thee to kick against the goad. And he, trembling and astonished, said, Lord, what wilt thou have me to do? And the Lord said to him" (the word "but" at the beginning of v. 6 is consequentially omitted). This addition occurs in no extant Greek MS, but is found in some Old Latin and Vulgate MSS., and also in part as an asterisked reading in the Harclean Syriac. Erasmus, considering that they had been lost from the Greek text by accident, translated them back into Greek from the Latin Vulgate, and incorporated them in his edition of the Greek NT; they thus formed part of the Received Text and so of AV.

[5] There is a Western addition (preserved only in the Old Latin MS. h): "when he spoke. But he said to them, Raise me up from the earth." The opening words of v. 8 run accordingly "And when they had raised him up . . ."

192

opened, he saw nothing; and they led him by the hand, and brought him into Damascus.

9 And he was three days without sight, and did neither eat nor drink.

1–2 The narrative now returns to Saul of Tarsus and his campaign of repression against the Christians, which received brief mention in Ch. 8:3. He was not content with driving them from Jerusalem; they must be pursued and rooted out wherever they fled, not only within the frontiers of the land of Israel[6] but beyond them as well. "In raging fury against them"—to quote his own words at a later time—"I persecuted them even to foreign cities" (Ch. 26:11, RSV).

In pursuance of this policy, he procured from the high priest a commission to demand the extradition from Damascus of any Christians who had escaped to that ancient city.[7] It is probable that it was refugees from Jerusalem and Judaea that Saul was principally concerned to arrest, rather than native Damascenes who believed in Jesus.[8] The high priest, as president of the Sanhedrin, was head of the Jewish state so far as its internal affairs were concerned. His authority was upheld by the Roman power and a matter like the present one would have their decided approval, as it could so easily be represented as required by the interests of public order. The high priest's decrees, or the decrees of the Sanhedrin, were binding not only in the Jewish communities of Palestine but also to a great extent in those outside Palestine.[9]

[6] The land of Israel at this time consisted in the main of the Roman province of Judaea (which included Samaria) and Herod Antipas's tetrarchy of Galilee and Peraea.

[7] This was not the first occasion when religious refugees had fled from Judaea to Damascus. The "New Covenanters"—from whose midst came the treatise represented by the *Fragments of a Zadokite Work* found in the Old Cairo *genizah* and first published under that title by Solomon Schechter (Cambridge, 1910)—appear to have fled to Damascus shortly before 130 B.C. Fresh light has been thrown on them by the recently discovered Dead Sea Scrolls: see in particular H. H. Rowley, *The Zadokite Fragments and the Dead Sea Scrolls* (Oxford, 1952). But any attempt to trace a connection between them and the primitive Damascene believers in Jesus is idle.

[8] In v. 13 Ananias of Damascus appears to have only hearsay knowledge of Saul. The expression τοὺς ἐχεῖσε ὄντας in Ch. 22:5 (see p. 441, n. 13) tends to confirm the conclusion that Saul was pursuing those who had eluded his vengeance in Judaea.

[9] In particular, the Romans in 138 B.C., in accordance with their treaty with the Jews in early Hasmonean times, instructed Ptolemy Euergetes II of Egypt and their other allies in the Near East to hand over to the jurisdiction of Simon the high priest Palestinian lawbreakers who sought refuge in their

The history of Damascus goes back to remote antiquity. It was a city in the days of Abraham. In the days of the divided monarchy of Israel and Judah, Damascus was the capital of a powerful Aramaean kingdom, which was overthrown by the Assyrians in 732 B.C. Since 64 B.C. it had formed part of the Roman province of Syria,[10] though the king of the Nabataean Arabs, whose realm stretched from the Gulf of Akaba northward to the neighbourhood of Damascus, enjoyed certain rights in the city because of the large number of his nationals in its population.[11] There was also a large Jewish community in Damascus (as we know from the fact that between ten and twenty thousand Jews were massacred there in A.D. 66);[12] there would accordingly be several synagogues.

The name by which Christianity is here described, "The Way" (v. 2), recurs in Chs. 19:9, 23; 22:4; 24:14, 22 (*cf.* also Chs. 16:17; 18:25 f.). It was evidently a term used by the early Christians to denote their own movement, considered as the way of life or the way of salvation. Similar words are used in a religious sense elsewhere.[13]

3–6 Armed with the high priest's commission, Saul set out for Damascus, accompanied by a suitable escort, and had almost reached its walls when the momentous event took place. About midday[14] a light which outshone the sun flashed round him, and as he lay on the ground to which he had fallen, a voice sounded in his ears, addressing him in his Aramaic mother-tongue,[15] "Saul! Saul! why are you persecuting me?"[16]

---

territories (1 Macc. 15:15 ff.); this right of extradition was no doubt included among the high priest's privileges and concessions which were ratified anew by Julius Caesar in 47 B.C. (Josephus, *Antiquities* xiv. 10.2).

[10] But it enjoyed certain civic rights as one of the ten cities of Syria and Transjordan linked together as the Decapolis (*cf.* Mark 5:20; 7:31).

[11] See n. 44 below.

[12] Josephus says ten thousand in the *Jewish War* ii. 20.2; in vii. 8.7 he says eighteen thousand. He tends to exaggerate his numbers, but even so the Jewish population of Damascus must have been very large.

[13] *Cf.* Rabbinical Hebrew *halakhah* in the sense of "rule" or "regulation" (literally "going"); also Syriac *'urcha* ("religion"), Arabic *as-sabil* ("the way" —*i.e.* of Islam), Indian *pathin* and *marga*, Chinese *tao*, etc.

[14] *Cf.* Chs. 22:6; 26:13.

[15] "In the Hebrew language", says Paul in Ch. 26:14. Except in Revelation, the "Hebrew" tongue in NT regularly means Aramaic. G. H. Dalman (*Jesus-Jeshua* [Eng. tr., London, 1929], p. 18) reconstructs the Aramaic wording as *Sha'ul Sha'ul ma 'att radephinni*.

[16] As Augustine puts it, "it was the head in heaven crying out on behalf of the members who were still on earth" (*Sermon* 279.1).

The voice which he heard, so far as literary parallels are concerned, is no doubt to be identified with the phenomenon known to the rabbis as the *bath qol*, "the daughter of the voice [of God]", the heavenly echo. The solemn repetition of the name of the person addressed is common in divine allocutions.[17]   But the voice that Paul heard came to him as the personal voice of the exalted Christ; for when he answered in surprise, "Who are you, Lord?",[18] he received the reply, "I am Jesus, whom you are persecuting; rise up, and go into the city, and you will be told what to do."

What account are we to give of this strange experience?   To find the key to his vision, as Dr. Klausner does, in epilepsy, is completely inadequate.   No doubt, as he says, "some epileptics have been great and powerful personalities, who made a name for themselves in world history: Mohammed, Augustine, Saint Bernard, Savonarola, Jakob Boehme, and Swedenborg among great figures of religion and mysticism; Julius Caesar, Peter the Great, and Napoleon I in the political field; and Pascal, Rousseau, and Dostoevsky in the world of thought."[19]   But was it these men's epilepsy that made them what they were?   Saul of Tarsus—or Paul, to give him the Roman name by which we know him better—never doubted that he was what he was in consequence of what happened to him outside Damascus; and (even if it were proved that he was an epileptic, which is far from being the case) something more than epilepsy is required to account for all that Paul became and achieved. He himself gave one consistent account: in that illuminating flash he saw the glorified Christ[20] and in the voice that followed he heard Him speak.   As truly as Jesus the crucified,

[17] *Cf.* Dalman, *ibid.*

[18] Or "Who are you, sir?" At this point Saul did not know the identity of the speaker. That is why RSV renders "Who are you, Lord?" and not "Who art thou, Lord?" in accordance with its principle of addressing the ascended Christ as "thou" (but this may serve as an illustration of the practical impossibility of applying this principle in a completely satisfactory and consistent manner).

[19] J. Klausner, *From Jesus to Paul* (Eng. tr., London, 1944), pp. 326 ff. The examples he adduces from Dostoevsky's experiences are peculiarly interesting. But an increase of *illumination* in the epileptic moment is a very different thing from a total *conversion* such as Saul experienced—a conversion of intellect, will and emotions, which dictated the abiding purpose and direction of his subsequent life.

[20] That he *saw* the risen Christ is not expressly stated in the narrative itself, but is confirmed in vv. 17 and 27 below, in Chs. 22:14 and 26:16, and in 1 Cor. 9:1; 15:8.

risen from the dead, had appeared alive after His passion to Peter and James and the rest during the days that followed the first Christian Easter, so truly now, "as to one untimely born", He had appeared to Paul.[21] The men who were with him saw the light that flashed so suddenly round them, but for them it was not accompanied by that blinding illumination within that wrought the revolution in the persecuting zealot, and diverted his zeal to the propagation of the faith which he had until then endeavoured to destroy.

Paul's own account of his experience is not only adequate to the sequel; it is in character with it too. The more one studies the event, the more one agrees with the eighteenth-century English statesman George Lyttelton, that "the conversion and apostleship of St. Paul alone, duly considered, was of itself a demonstration sufficient to prove Christianity to be a divine revelation."[22]

Perhaps the most striking modern parallel to the narrative of Paul's conversion is Sundar Singh's story of his own conversion after a period of bitter hostility to the gospel. Praying in his room in the early morning, he saw a great light. "Then as I prayed and looked into the light, I saw the form of the Lord Jesus Christ. It had such an appearance of glory and love. If it had been some Hindu incarnation I would have prostrated myself before it. But it was the Lord Jesus Christ whom I had been insulting a few days before. I felt that a vision like this could not come out of my own imagination. I heard a voice saying in Hindustani. 'How long will you persecute me? I have come to save you; you were praying to know the right way. Why do you not take it?' The thought then came to me, 'Jesus Christ is not dead but living and it must be He Himself.' So I fell at His feet and got this wonderful Peace which I could not get anywhere else. This is the joy I was wishing to get. When I got up, the vision had all disappeared, but although the vision disappeared the Peace and Joy have

---

[21] Cf. 1 Cor. 15:5–8.

[22] Of Lyttelton, Samuel Johnson says in his *Lives of the Most Eminent English Poets* (London, 1779–81), "He had, in the pride of juvenile confidence, with the help of corrupt conversation, entertained doubts of the truth of Christianity; but he thought the time now come when it was no longer fit to doubt or believe by chance, and applied himself seriously to the great question. His studies being honest, ended in conviction. He found that religion was true; and what he had learned he endeavoured to teach (1747) by *Observations on the Conversion of St. Paul;* a treatise to which infidelity has never been able to fabricate a specious answer." The words quoted come from the first paragraph of Lyttelton's *Observations*.

remained with me ever since." There were several circumstances which make it difficult to set down Sundar Singh's experience as a dream or as the effect of self-hypnotism; it is also interesting to be told that, to the best of his remembrance, "at that time he did not know the story of St. Paul's conversion; though, of course, on a point of that kind the human memory cannot be implicitly relied on" (B. H. Streeter and A. J. Appasamy, *The Sadhu* [London, 1921], pp. 6–8). Here too we cannot properly evaluate the Sadhu's account of his experience without taking into consideration the remarkable life which was its sequel and the extraordinary signs which attended his ministry (see p. 250 below).[23]

7 The statement in v. 7 that Paul's companions "stood speechless, hearing the voice, but beholding no man," has sometimes been thought to conflict with his own statement in Ch. 26:14, "we were all fallen to the earth," and still more with his statement in Ch. 22:9, "they that were with me beheld indeed the light, but they heard not the voice of him that spake to me." The first discrepancy is immaterial; presumably the others were able to get up while Saul was still lying flat on the ground. As for the other discrepancy, it has commonly been suggested that while they heard a noise (like the crowd in John 12:29 who "said that it had thundered" when Jesus' prayer was answered by a heavenly voice), they did not distinguish an articulate voice. On the other hand, Luke may very well mean here that it was Paul's voice that his companions heard, although they could neither see nor hear the person whom he appeared to be addressing.[24]

8–9 At last Saul was able to rise from the ground, and when he did so, he was unable to see, "blinded by excess of light." His companions therefore led him by the hand through the gate of

---

[23] I do not overlook, of course, either here or in the other illustration adduced from the Sadhu's life in the exposition of Ch. 12:7—11, the special character of the Biblical miracle as part of the history of revelation and redemption.

[24] Here the genitive τῆς φωνῆς is used after ἀκούοντες, whereas in Ch. 22:9 the accusative is used (τὴν δὲ φωνὴν οὐκ ἤκουσαν). It is accordingly suggested by many that the genitive here refers to the mere sound, while the accusative in Ch. 22:9 implies the intelligible words (*cf.* J. H. Moulton, *Grammar of NT Greek* i [Edinburgh, 1906], p. 66). But this is not the normal distinction between the accusative and genitive cases after ἀκούω. The second and more probable suggestion was made in ExT vi (1894–5), pp. 238 f., by a contributor signing himself "T." This is apparently how the present passage was interpreted in the Western recension (*cf.* n. 5 above).

Damascus to the place where, presumably, arrangements had been made for him to stay. There he remained for three days, unable to take food or drink.

(b) Ananias is Sent to Saul (Ch. 9:10–19a)

10 Now there was a certain disciple at Damascus, named Ananias, and the Lord said unto him in a vision, Ananias. And he said, Behold, I *am here*, Lord.

11 And the Lord *said* unto him, Arise, and go to the street which is called Straight, and inquire in the house of Judas for one named Saul, a man of Tarsus: for behold, he prayeth;

12 and he hath seen[25] a man named Ananias coming in, and laying his hands on him, that he might receive his sight.

13 But Ananias answered, Lord, I have heard from many of this man, how much evil he did to thy saints at Jerusalem:

14 and here he hath authority from the chief priests to bind all that call upon thy name.

15 But the Lord said unto him, Go thy way: for he is a chosen vessel unto me, to bear my name before the Gentiles and kings, and the children of Israel:

16 for I will show him how many things he must suffer for my name's sake.

17 And Ananias departed, and entered into the house; and laying his hands on him said, Brother Saul, the Lord, *even* Jesus, who appeared unto thee in the way which thou camest, hath sent me, that thou mayest receive thy sight, and be filled with the Holy Spirit.

18 And straightway there fell from his eyes as it were scales, and he received his sight;[26] and he arose and was baptized;

19 and he took food and was strengthened.

10–12 Towards the end of these three days, Saul, as he was praying, received a further vision,[27] in which a man named Ananias came to him and laid his hands on him, with the result that his sight was restored. This Ananias turned out to be a real person, a man of Damascus who believed in Jesus as the Messiah, although

[25] The Greek codices B and C, with the Byzantine text, add "in a vision" (*cf.* AV).

[26] A few inferior Greek MSS add "immediately" (Gk. παραχρῆμα).

[27] Although the words "in a vision" are probably no part of the original text of v. 12 (*cf.* n. 25 above), they are exegetically true.

he was probably not one of the refugees from the persecution in Jerusalem.[28] It appears that the gospel had already made its way independently to Damascus—possibly from its northern base in Galilee. He knew, however, about the persecution in Jerusalem which had dispersed so many of the believers in that city, and he knew of the leading part that Saul had played in it. He knew, too, that Saul had arrived in Damascus with authority to prosecute there the grim work that he had begun in Jerusalem.

We may judge of Ananias's astonishment, then, when he in his turn received directions from the risen Christ[29] in a vision to go to the place where Saul was staying and lay his hands upon him for the restoration of his sight. The "street which is called Straight", where Saul's host lived, is still one of the chief thoroughfares of Damascus, the *Darb al-Mustaqim*. The house of Judas is traditionally located near its western end.

13–14 "Lord", said Ananias, as he received these instructions, "I have heard from many about this man, how much evil he has done to thy saints[30] at Jerusalem; and here he has authority from the chief priests to bind all who call upon thy name" (RSV). Ananias evidently had had no personal experience of Saul's harrying of the Christians, but he had received ample information from those who could speak from first-hand evidence. For the expression "all who call upon thy name" we may compare Ch. 2:21, 38; in practice it denotes Christians, as those who address Jesus as Lord.

15–16 But Ananias's protest was overruled; the risen Lord had His eye upon the man of Tarsus and had a great work for him to perform. In spite of his recent record as a persecutor, he was a chosen instrument[31] in the Lord's hand, a messenger who would proclaim the good news in Jesus' name more widely than anyone else. The Gentile nations and their rulers, as well as the people of Israel, would hear the message of salvation from his lips. And while he himself had inflicted suffering on others who

[28] This may be inferred from the fuller description of the character of Ananias given by Paul in Ch. 22:12.

[29] That "the Lord" in v. 10 is the risen Christ is evident from v. 17.

[30] A common designation of Christians in NT, especially in the Pauline epistles; it denotes them as the new people of God, set apart for Him and His service.

[31] For Paul's own sense of his election for special service *cf.* Rom. 1:1 ff.; Gal. 1:15 f.

199

believed in Jesus, he in his turn would endure many more suffer-ings for the same name.[32]

17 Ananias obediently made his way to the street called Straight, and entered the house of Judas. There, without delay, he fulfilled his commission, laying his hands on the blind man and addressing him in terms of brotherly friendship:[33] "Brother Saul, the Lord Jesus who appeared to you on the road by which you came, has sent me that you may regain your sight and be filled with the Holy Spirit" (RSV).

In Ch. 22:14–16 Paul gives a fuller account of what Ananias said to him; in Ch. 26:16–18 he includes Ananias's communication in what was said to him during the heavenly vision. But even in the present narrative it is plain that the vision received by Paul on the eve of Ananias's visit and the words spoken to him by Ananias when he came in were mutually confirmatory; by this twofold communication he received his apostolic commission from the exalted Lord.

In the Epistle to the Galatians Paul is at pains to deny in the most unqualified terms that he received his apostolic commission from any man, or even through any man; he received it, he asserts, immediately from Christ (Gal. 1:1, 11 ff.). How does this square with the part ascribed to Ananias in Acts?

In the first place, Paul in Galatians is answering the charge that he was dependent, for such missionary authority as he might possess, on the apostles and other Christian leaders at Jerusalem. The part played by Ananias could not have affected the argument. In the eyes of Paul's opponents and critics, a private Christian like Ananias could not in any case have had the power to commission him. But in the second place, Ananias for this special purpose occupied such an exalted status that his words to Saul were the very words of Christ. Having been sent by the Lord to lay his hands on Saul, he was on this particular occasion a duly com-missioned apostle.[34] But he was more: he was a duly authorized

---

[32] For the expression *cf.* Chs. 5:41; 21:13. For a catalogue of Paul's sufferings *cf.* 2 Cor. 11:23 ff. In the kingdom of Christ suffering for His sake is a sign of His favour and an earnest of His reward (*cf.* Ch. 14:22; Matt. 5:11 f.; Rom. 8:17; 2 Tim. 2:12).

[33] And in Aramaic, as is suggested by the vocative Σαούλ (as in v. 4), simply transliterating Heb. and Aram. *Sha'ul*, instead of the more Graecized form Σαῦλε.

[34] *Cf.* G. W. H. Lampe, *The Seal of the Spirit* (London, 1951, pp. 72 ff.).

prophet. It was as the spokesman of Christ—as His very mouth-piece—that he went to Saul; he had nothing to say beyond the words that the Lord put in his mouth. Ananias uttered the words, but as he did so it was Christ Himself who commissioned Saul to be His ambassador. Ananias laid his hands on Saul, but it was the power of Christ that in the same moment enlightened his eyes and filled him with the Holy Spirit. Such filling with the Spirit was the indispensable qualification for the prophetic and apostolic service mapped out for Saul in the Lord's words of v. 15; hence-forth Saul performed this service as one endowed with heavenly power (cf. v. 22). The apostolic commission of Saul, and the part played by Ananias in it, must now, as in NT times, remain a stumblingblock in the path of those whose conception of the apostolic ministry is too rigidly formal. If the risen Christ then commissioned His most illustrious apostle in such an "irregular" way, may He not have done so again, may He not yet do so again, when the occasion requires it?

Ananias enters and leaves the narrative thus, and we know nothing more of him. But as Saul's first friend after his conversion, the first Christian to greet him as a brother, as well as the one who faithfully bore the Lord's commission to him, he has an honoured place in sacred history, and a special claim upon the gratitude of all who in one way or another have entered into the blessing that stems from the life and work of the great apostle.

18–19a When Ananias had executed his commission and laid his hands on Saul, a flaky substance fell away from Saul's eyes.[35] His sight came back to him; he rose up and was baptized forthwith in the name of Jesus (receiving his baptism at the hands of Ananias,[36] we should naturally suppose); he ate food for the first time in three days and a return of bodily strength accompanied the influx of new spiritual power.

(c)   Saul Preaches in Damascus (Ch. 9:19b–22)

And he was certain days[37] with the disciples that were at Damascus.

---

[35] Cf. Tobit 3:17 ("to scale away the white films from Tobit's eyes"); 11:13 ("the white films scaled away from the corners of his eyes").

[36] See p. 442 with n. 20 (on Ch. 22:16). Saul's baptism may, like that of Cornelius and his household in Ch. 10:44 ff., have followed his reception of the Spirit though this cannot be determined with certainty from the narrative.

[37] P45 says "many days" (ἡμέρας ἱκανάς).

20 And straightway in the synagogues he proclaimed Jesus, that he is[38] the Son of God.

21 And all that heard him were amazed, and said, Is not this he that in Jerusalem made havoc of them that called on this name? and he had come hither for this intent, that he might bring them bound before the chief priests.

22 But Saul increased the more in strength,[39] and confounded the Jews that dwelt at Damascus, proving that this is the Christ.[40]

19b–20 According to the autobiographical outline supplied by Paul himself in Gal. 1:15 ff., he "did not confer with flesh and blood" after the revelation of Christ (including, no doubt, what was revealed to him in Damascus through Ananias as well as what was revealed to him on the Damascus road), but went away to Arabia. This need not exclude a short period of such witness as is described in v. 20. On the other hand, his preaching in the Damascus synagogues may have followed his return to Damascus (Gal. 1:17 c); we need not press the word "straightway" in v. 20 overmuch, the more so since Luke has nothing to say of the visit to Arabia. The Arabia in question was the Nabataean kingdom, whose north-western limit was in the neighbourhood of Damascus.

It is perhaps more significant than might be at first supposed that the first, and indeed the only, occurrence of the title "Son of God" in Acts should be in this report of Saul's early preaching. The title "Son of God" or its equivalent is used in OT (1) of the nation of Israel (*e.g.*, Ex. 4:22; Hos. 11:1), (2) of the anointed king of Israel (*e.g.*, 2 Sam. 7:14; Ps. 89:26 ff.), and (3) of the coming Messiah (the former use merges into this; see especially Ps. 2:7, quoted in Ch. 13:33, and *cf.* Ch. 2:25 f.). For the messianic use of the title in the pseudepigrapha *cf.* 1 Enoch 105:2; 4 Ezra 7 : 28 f.; 13 : 32, 37, 52; 14 : 9. That our Lord's contemporaries believed the Messiah to be the Son of God is evident from the high priest's question to Him as His trial: "Are you the Messiah, the Son of the Blessed?" (Mark 14:61; *cf.* Matt. 26:63; Luke

---

[38] Some Western authorities insert "the Christ."
[39] Some Western authorities read "was the more strengthened in the word."
[40] The Western reading appears to have been "the Christ, in whom God was well pleased."

22:67, 70). As applied to our Lord, then, the title "Son of God" marks Him out as the true representative of the Israel of God and as God's anointed king, the promised Messiah; but it is no merely official title.   As He Himself used it, it reflected His unique relationship and fellowship with the Father, and His function as the revealer of the Father;[41] and it is this essential character of His Divine Sonship that is so prominent in the Pauline epistles. The proclamation of Jesus as the Son of God may therefore represent some advance on the way in which His Messiahship has been proclaimed thus far in Acts.

21–22 It was to the synagogues of Damascus that Saul had been sent with his special commission, and to the synagogues of Damascus he went. But instead of presenting his letters of credence and demanding the extradition of the disciples of Jesus, he figured as the bearer of a very different commission, issued by a greater potentate than the Jewish high priest, and as a disciple of Jesus himself he announced his Master's claims. No wonder that his hearers were amazed by the change that had come over him. The news of his mission had not been kept secret; here was the man whose arrival they had expected, but instead of arresting Christians he was confounding the Jews of Damascus by his powerful demonstration[42] that the Christians' claim was true: that Jesus was the Christ.

(d) Saul Escapes from Damascus (Ch. 9:23–25)

23 And when many days were fulfilled, the Jews took counsel together to kill him:

24 but their plot became known to Saul. And they watched the gates also day and night that they might kill him:

25 but his disciples took him by night, and let him down through the wall, lowering him in a basket.

23–25 With the adventure thus recorded by Luke we must compare Paul's account in 2 Cor. 11:32 f.: "In Damascus the ethnarch under Aretas the king guarded the city of the Damascenes

---

[41] See especially the famous *logion* Matt. 11:25–27 // Luke 10:21 f. *Cf.* J. Bieneck, *Sohn Gottes als Christusbezeichnung der Synoptiker* (Zürich, 1951); V. Taylor, *The Names of Jesus* (London, 1953), pp. 52 ff.; G. Vos, *The Self-Disclosure of Jesus* (Grand Rapids, 1954). pp. 141 ff. and, for the presentation in St. John's Gospel, W. F. Lofthouse, *The Father and the Son* (London, 1934).

[42] The word rendered "proving" in v. 22 (Gk. συμβιβάζων) means literally

in order to take me: and through a window was I let down in a basket by the wall, and escaped his hands." By putting the two narratives together we may obtain a fuller impression of the course of events than from one or the other of them by itself. Aretas IV (9 B.C.–A.D. 40) reigned over the Nabataean kingdom in which Paul spent some time after his conversion (Gal. 1:17). It is commonly supposed that Paul's sojourn in Arabia was of the nature of a religious retreat: that he sought the solitude of the desert–perhaps even going to Mount Horeb as Moses and Elijah did–in order to think out all the implications of his new life without disturbance. There may be something in this supposition; but we could also envisage him as engaging in some form of Christian witness in Nabataean Arabia itself.[43] At any rate, it is plain that he annoyed not only the Damascene Jews by his activity but the Nabataean authorities as well. There were many Nabataeans in the city, and their colony there was governed by an ethnarch, a representative of Aretas.[44] When the time came to take drastic steps against Saul, the local Jewish authorities and the Nabataean ethnarch appear to have made a concerted attempt to lay hands on him. But one of his sympathizers[45] had a house built on to the city wall, and while Saul's enemies were guarding the city gates to arrest him, he was lowered in a large basket or net[46] through a window of this house which was actually cut in the city wall.

"putting together"; here it implies that the prophetic Scriptures were put alongside their fulfilment, in order to prove that Jesus was the Messiah of whom they spoke. (*Cf.* Chs. 17:2 f.; 18:28; 26:22 f.)

[43] *Cf.* K. Lake, *Earlier Epistles of St. Paul* (London, 1914), pp. 320 ff.

[44] Eduard Meyer, *Ursprung und Anfänge des Christentums* iii (Stuttgart and Berlin, 1923), p. 346, describes the ethnarch as "head of the Nabataean colony in Damascus." (We may compare the position of the Jewish ethnarch in Alexandria.) The ethnarch had no authority to arrest Saul openly, as he would have had if Damascus had at this time been part of Aretas's realm. For arguments against this last view—inferred by E. Schürer (*History of the Jewish People in the Time of Christ* [Eng. tr., Edinburgh, 1892–1901], II. i, p. 98) and others from the absence of Roman coins at Damascus between A.D. 34 and 62—Meyer (*ibid.*) refers with approval to E. Schwartz, "Die Aeren von Gerasa Eleutheropolis," *Nachrichten der königlichen Gesellschaft der Wissenschaften zu Göttingen*, 1906, pp. 367 f.

[45] The expression "his disciples" (v. 25) suggests that Saul's preaching in Damascus and the neighbourhood had not been unfruitful.

[46] The word rendered "basket" here is σφυρίς (used also in the narrative of the feeding of the four thousand [Mark 8:8]); 2 Cor. 11:33 has σαργάνη, "a large woven or network bag or basket suitable for hay, straw . . . or for bales of wool" (Lake-Cadbury, *ad loc.*).

Luke says that this incident took place "when many days were fulfilled"; Paul, more definitely, tells us in Gal. 1:18 that it was three years after his conversion (by inclusive reckoning, no doubt) that he returned to Jerusalem—and from the narrative in Acts he seems to have returned to Jerusalem immediately after his escape from Damascus.[47]

(e) Saul Returns to Jerusalem and Is Sent to Tarsus (Ch. 9:26-30)

26 And when he was come to Jerusalem, he assayed to join himself to the disciples: and they were all afraid of him, not believing that he was a disciple.
27 But Barnabas took him, and brought him to the apostles, and declared unto them how he had seen the Lord in the way, and that he had spoken to him, and how at Damascus he had preached boldly in the name of Jesus.
28 And he was with them going in and going out at Jerusalem,
29 preaching boldly in the name of the Lord: and he spake and disputed against the Grecian Jews;[48] but they were seeking to kill him.
30 And when the brethren knew it, they brought him down to Caesarea, and sent him forth to Tarsus.

26–27 When Saul returned to Jerusalem, he was in a difficult position. His old associates knew all about his defection, and he could expect no friendly welcome from them. On the other hand, the disciples of Jesus, with whom he now wished to associate, had not forgotten his campaign of persecution. We can scarcely feel surprise at their suspicion of his new overtures. The rôle of the *agent provocateur* was as familiar in antiquity as in more recent times; what assurance had they that this was not a scheme of Saul's to gain their confidence for their more effective undoing? It was Barnabas who, true to his name, proved himself a "son of encouragement" and acted as Saul's sponsor. It seems likely that Barnabas was already acquainted with Saul, knew his integrity of character and was convinced of the genuineness of his conversion.[49] When Saul desperately needed a true friend in Damascus, Ananias

---

[47] We may tentatively date Saul's conversion in A.D. 33, and his return to Jerusalem sometime in 35.

[48] Gk. πρὸς τοὺς Ἑλληνιστάς. Cod. A reads Ἕλληνας ("Greeks").

[49] For an imaginative reconstruction of Barnabas's earlier relations with Saul see J. A. Robertson, *The Hidden Romance of the NT* (London, 1920), pp. 46 ff.

205

played that part to him; now, when he stood in equal need of one in Jerusalem, he found a friend in Barnabas. And Barnabas's prestige with the apostles and other Jerusalem Christians was such that, when he gave them his guarantee that Saul was now a true disciple of Jesus, they were reassured.

When Luke says that Barnabas brought Saul "to the apostles" (v. 27), we should probably recognize what grammarians call a "generalizing plural", in view of Paul's own statement in Gal. 1:18 f., that the only leaders of the Jerusalem church whom he met on this occasion were Peter (Cephas) and James the brother of Jesus (whom he apparently regards as an apostle).

28-30 But the whole passage in Galatians (Ch. 1:18-24) must be compared with Luke's narrative here. "Then after three years [says Paul] I went up to Jerusalem to visit[50] Cephas, and tarried with him fifteen days. But other of the apostles saw I none, save James the Lord's brother. Now touching the things which I write unto you, behold, before God, I lie not. Then I came into the regions of Syria and Cilicia. And I was still unknown by face unto the churches of Judaea which were in Christ: but they only heard say, He that once persecuted us now preacheth the faith of which he once made havoc; and they glorified God in me."

Again, we must remember that Paul's chief concern here is to show that he was in no way indebted for his missionary commission to the Jerusalem apostles. Thus, while Luke may generalize and say that he saw the apostles, it is important for Paul to particularize and say which apostles he actually saw. It is not so easy to reconcile Luke's description of Saul's public activity at Jerusalem in association with the apostles with the statement in Galatians that, until the time of his departure for Syria and Cilicia, he remained "unknown by face unto the churches of Judaea", who knew of him only by hearsay. L. E. Browne (*The Acts of the Apostles* [London, 1925], pp. 162 ff.) removes "at Jerusalem" (v. 28) as a gloss, and takes vv. 28 and 29 as a continuation of Barnabas's description of Saul's activity *at Damascus*. V. 30 then goes on: "And the brethren recognized[51] him (that is, as a disciple) and

---

[50] Perhaps we should press the word rendered "visit" (ἱστορῆσαι) to yield its fuller force: "to make inquiry of Cephas." *Cf.* C. H. Dodd, *The Apostolic Preaching and its Developments* (London, 1936), p. 26.

[51] For this sense of ἐπιγινώσκω (the verb used here) *cf.* 1 Cor. 16:18, where ARV renders it "acknowledge" and RSV "give recognition to."

brought him down to Caesarea and sent him forth to Tarsus."
Thus, as Professor Browne says, "the whole difficulty vanishes."
It is certainly an attractive explanation, but one has some reser-
vations about a textual emendation introduced not because it has
manuscript attestation or the like but mainly because it eases the
removal of a discrepancy (*cf.* p. 257, n. 28).

We may, however, take vv. 28 and 29 to describe what happened
at Jerusalem, and regard "Judaea" in Gal. 1:22 as meaning "the
rest of Judaea" (outside Jerusalem). It appears then that Saul
took up the work which Stephen had laid down at his death, by
engaging in disputations with the Hellenists.[52]   Their reaction
was swift and violent. Saul was worse than Stephen; he was in
their eyes a traitor to the true cause, and by his *volte-face* he
had let down those who formerly followed him loyally as their
leader in suppressing the Christian movement. Later in Acts (Ch.
22:17 ff.) he tells how about this time Jesus appeared to him again
while he was praying in the temple and told him to leave Jerusalem, because his witness would not be listened to. He protested
that he was a particularly valuable witness, because the people of
Jerusalem knew his earlier record as a persecutor and his approval
of Stephen's death. But the Lord repeated His command to depart
from Jerusalem, adding that He would send him to the Gentiles.[53]

Jerusalem was too hot to hold Saul. His new friends saved his
life by getting him safely away to Caesarea, the Mediterranean
seaport of Palestine built by Herod the Great, now the govern-
mental headquarters of the Roman province of Judaea. From
there he took ship for his native Tarsus, and—as he says himself
in Gal. 1:21—"came into the regions of Syria and Cilicia." Syria
and Cilicia formed one imperial province at this time. Tarsus, the
chief city of Cilicia, was now about a thousand years old. It had

---

[52] "The newly converted Saul was not one to keep silence for a fortnight,
and very probably preached in the city. The words 'coming in and going out
at Jerusalem' do not mean that he visited places outside the city, but that he
moved about freely and fearlessly in and out of houses in the city" (A. H.
McNeile and C. S. C. Williams, INT [Oxford, 1953], p. 113). See also H. N.
Ridderbos, *Galatians* (Grand Rapids, 1953), pp. 72 f.

[53] W. M. Ramsay (*St. Paul the Traveller* [14th edn., London, 1920], pp.
60 ff.) holds that the vision described in Ch. 22:17 ff. must have taken place
on Paul's second visit to Jerusalem (the famine-visit of Ch. 11:30) because
(among other reasons) the cause of his departure from Jerusalem at the end
of his first visit, as related here by Luke, was "totally different" from the cause
assigned in the vision. L. E. Browne (*loc. cit.*) points out that this is another
discrepancy removed by his emendation.

been subject in turn to the Assyrians, Persians, and Greco-Macedonians. It received a civic constitution from Antiochus IV in 171 B.C., and ranked as a free city under the Romans from 64 B.C. onwards. It was one of the three leading centres of learning in the world of those days, being what we should call a university city.[54] Its schools were devoted to philosophy, rhetoric and law. We should not, however, exaggerate the influence which its educational system exercised upon its most illustrious son.[55]

There, then, we leave Saul for some years; we shall meet him again in Ch. 11:25.

(f) The Church Enjoys Peace and Prosperity (Ch. 9:31)

31 So the church throughout all Judaea and Galilee and Samaria had peace, being edified; and, walking in the fear of the Lord and in the comfort of the Holy Spirit, was multiplied.[56]

31 Luke uses the singular "church" here where Paul prefers to use the plural and speak of the "churches of Judaea" (Gal. 1:22; cf. 1 Thess. 2:14). It was, however, in the main the original Jerusalem church in dispersion. "The Ecclesia was still confined to Jewish or semi-Jewish populations and to ancient Jewish soil; but it was no longer the Ecclesia of a single city, and yet it was one: probably as corresponding, by these three modern representative districts of Judaea, Galilee and Samaria, to the ancient Ecclesia which had its home in the whole land of Israel" (F. J. A. Hort, The Christian Ecclesia [London, 1897], pp. 55 f.).

With this summary of progress Luke's narrative of the conversion of Saul of Tarsus comes to an end. The persecution that followed Stephen's death died out with the conversion and departure of the chief persecutor. But, so great is the importance that Luke attaches to this event that, in spite of his limited space, he records

---

[54] Cf. Strabo, Geography, xiv. 5.13.

[55] W. M. Ramsay is inclined to over-estimate the influence of Tarsian culture on Paul: see his admirable section on "Tarsus" in The Cities of St. Paul (London, 1907), pp. 83–244. On the other hand, W. L. Knox underestimates the extent of Tarsian influence on him: "his whole knowledge of Greek thought, literature and language is that of Judaism. . . . There is not a scrap of evidence that he had any knowledge of Greek apart from the common stock of hellenistic Judaism, and there is no reason to suppose that he could not have acquired this at Jerusalem" (Some Hellenistic Elements in Primitive Christianity [London, 1943], p. 31).

[56] The Western and Byzantine texts read "So the churches . . . were multiplied." (Cf. AV.)

it in some detail on two later occasions, on both of which the story is told by Paul himself—once in his address to the mob in the temple court (Ch. 22:1–21) and again in his *apologia* before the younger Agrippa (Ch. 26:2–29).

With Luke's estimate of the importance of Paul's conversion neither the historian nor the theologian can quarrel. We cannot imagine the spread of Christianity in the Roman Empire apart from the work of Paul. He was indeed a chosen instrument in Christ's hand, fitted for his life-work long before his conversion—set apart for it, indeed, from his very birth, as he confesses (Gal. 1:15; Rom. 1:1). Born a "Hebrew" son of "Hebrew" parents, and given the best education in his ancestral traditions that contemporary Judaism could provide, he also inherited a large measure of Hellenistic culture and the coveted privilege of Roman citizenship. When in due course God "revealed His Son" in Saul of Tarsus, he devoted all this wealthy inheritance, together with his rare natural qualities, to the work of Gentile evangelization; and, late-comer though he was among the apostles, he "labored more abundantly than they all: yet not I [he adds], but the grace of God which was with me" (1 Cor. 15:10).

III. THE ACTS OF PETER AND BEGINNINGS OF GENTILE CHRISTIANITY

(Chs. 9:32–12:25)

1. PETER IN WESTERN PALESTINE

(Ch. 9:32–43)

(a) *Peter at Lydda: the Healing of Aeneas (Ch. 9:32–35)*

32 And it came to pass, as Peter went throughout all parts, he came down also to the saints that dwelt at Lydda.

33 And there he found a certain man named Aeneas, who had kept his bed eight years; for he was palsied.

34 And Peter said unto him, Aeneas, Jesus Christ healeth thee: arise, and make thy bed. And straightway he arose.

35 And all that dwelt at Lydda and in Sharon saw him, and they turned to the Lord.

32 We left Peter in Ch. 8:25 when he returned with John from their visit to Samaria. It appears that he engaged about this time in an itinerant ministry of visitation among the dispersed Christian communities of Judaea. The disciples at Lydda (Lod in OT) may have had their nucleus in refugees from the recent persecution in Jerusalem; we remember also that Philip passed through these parts preaching the gospel on his way from Gaza to Caesarea (Ch. 8:40).

33–35 We should naturally suppose that Aeneas, the man whom Peter cured from his eight-year-old paralysis[57] at Lydda, was one of the local Christian group, though this is not expressly stated. The words "Jesus Christ healeth thee" involve a play on words in the Greek.[58] The following words, "arise, and make

---

[57] It is possible to understand ἐξ ἐτῶν ὀκτώ (v. 33) in the sense "since eight years old", but the usual interpretation is more probable.

[58] Gk. ἰᾶταί σε 'Ιησοῦς Χριστός. In a Greek ear 'Ιησοῦς might well seem to be cognate with ἰάομαι (see p. 351, n. 21, on Ch. 17:18). H. J. Cadbury ("A Possible Perfect in Acts 9:34", JThS xlix [1948], pp. 57 f.) suggests that the verb might be accented ἰᾶται ("has healed").

thy bed," might also be rendered "arise and set the table for yourself"[59]—*i.e.* "get yourself something to eat." This latter rendering would accord well with the interest shown by Luke and other NT writers in nourishment for convalescents.[60]

The news of Aeneas's cure spread throughout the neighbouring country and all over the coastal plain of Sharon. Many of the people in that area came to see him, and the result was a further access of believers. As much of this territory was semi-Gentile in population, we trace a further widening of the range of the saving message.

(b) Peter at Joppa: the Raising of Dorcas (Ch. 9:36–43)

36 Now there was at Joppa a certain disciple named Tabitha, which by interpretation is called Dorcas: this woman was full of good works and almsdeeds which she did.

37 And it came to pass in those days, that she fell sick, and died: and when they had washed her, they laid her in an upper chamber.

38 And as Lydda was nigh unto Joppa, the disciples, hearing that Peter was there, sent two men unto him, entreating him, Delay not to come on unto us.

39 And Peter arose and went with them. And when he was come, they brought him into the upper chamber: and all the widows stood by him weeping, and showing the coats and garments which Dorcas made,[61] while she was with them.

40 But Peter put them all forth, and kneeled down, and prayed; and turning to the body, he said, Tabitha, arise.[62] And she opened her eyes; and when she saw Peter, she sat up.

41 And he gave her his hand, and raised her up; and calling the saints and widows, he presented her alive.

42 And it became known throughout all Joppa: and many believed on the Lord.

43 And it came to pass, that he abode many days in Joppa with one Simon a tanner.

---

[59] Gk. στρῶσον σεαυτῷ. The object to στρῶσον has to be supplied; στρώννυμι κλίνην means either "make the bed" or "set the couch" (for reclining at table).

[60] *Cf.* Ch. 9:19a; Luke 8:55. But this is no necessary indication of medical authorship, as is evident from Mark 5:43 (the parallel to Luke 8:55).

[61] P45 reads "had made for them."

[62] The Western text adds "in the name of the Lord Jesus Christ."

36-38 Joppa (modern Jaffa) is on the Mediterranean coast, about ten miles north-west of Lydda. It is mentioned in Egyptian records of the fifteenth century B.C., and several times in OT. Here, too, there was a group of believers in Jesus; and while Peter was in Lydda, a member of this group fell sick and died. Her name, Tabitha, means "gazelle" (for which Dorcas is the Greek); the corresponding Hebrew form occurs in OT as a proper name, Zibiah (2 Kings 12:1). Her works of Christian charity had specially endeared her to her friends, and (having heard perhaps of the healing of Aeneas) they sent to Lydda and begged Peter to come on to Joppa.[63] (It is interesting to note in Acts how frequently, as here, a delegation consists of two men.)

39-43 Peter went with the two messengers and was brought without delay into the upper room where the body of Dorcas lay, after it had been washed in accordance with the Jewish custom of "purification of the dead."[64] Around her stood the widows who had been the principal recipients of her charity, displaying, as they wore them,[65] the garments that Dorcas had made for them. But Peter sent them and the other mourners out of the room, as he had seen his Master do before He raised Jairus's daughter from her death-bed; and then he uttered a short sentence differing only in one letter from the words of Jesus to Jairus' daughter. Whereas Jesus had said *Talitha qumi* (Mark 5:41),[66] Peter now said *Tabitha qumi*—"Tabitha, arise." She opened her eyes and sat up, and Peter raised her from the pallet on which she had been laid and presented her alive to her wondering friends.[67] "The circumstantial details of the gradual recovery of Tabitha ... are quite in the style of medical description" (W. K. Hobart, *The Medical Language of St. Luke* [Dublin, 1882], p. 41). Many other inhabitants of Joppa inevitably joined the followers of a Master by whose power

[63] Their words in v. 38 ("Do not fail to come to us") amount simply to a polite request ("Please come to us").

[64] Cf. Mishnah, *Shabbath*, xxiii. 5.

[65] The middle voice, ἐπιδεικνύμεναι, suggests this. Widows are mentioned here, as in Ch. 6:1, as the natural recipients of charity, not as members of a special order attached to the church, such as we find later in 1 Tim. 5:3-16.

[66] The Western text of Mark 5:41, by confusion with this passage of Acts, reads Ταβειθά for ταλειθά.

[67] To "the saints and widows", says Luke, not meaning that the widows could not be saints. But no doubt Dorcas's charity extended beyond the bounds of the local Christian group.

so marvellous an act of healing had been accomplished, and Peter stayed on there for a considerable time.[68]

[68] "If St. Peter enters into a house on the seashore and stays there a long time . . ., we may perhaps assume that his trade of fisherman influenced him. He was no tanner" (A. Harnack, *The Acts of the Apostles* [Eng. tr., London, 1909], p. 85. The tanner probably used sea-water in his work.) Moreover, as Harnack points out (*ibid.*), "tanning was an uncleanly trade", and Peter's lodging with such a man was a mark of his increasing emancipation from ceremonial traditions. Luke appears to be interested in the names of his characters' hosts (*cf.* Chs. 9:11; 21:16), and in people's occupations (*cf.* Chs. 16:14; 18:3; 19:24).

CHAPTER X

2. THE STORY OF CORNELIUS

(Chs. 10:1–11:18)

(a) Cornelius Sees a Vision (Ch. 10:1–8)

1 Now *there was* a certain man in Caesarea, Cornelius by name, a centurion of the band called the Italian *band,*

2 a devout man, and one that feared God with all his house, who gave much alms to the people, and prayed to God always.

3 He saw in a vision openly, as it were about the ninth hour of the day, an angel of God coming in unto him, and saying to him, Cornelius.

4 And he, fastening his eyes upon him, and being affrighted, said, What is it, Lord? And he said unto him, Thy prayers and thine alms are gone up for a memorial before God.

5 And now send men to Joppa, and fetch one Simon, who is surnamed Peter:

6 he lodgeth with one Simon a tanner, whose house is by the sea side.

7 And when the angel that spake unto him was departed, he called two of his household-servants, and a devout soldier of them that waited on him continually;

8 and having rehearsed all things unto them, he sent them to Joppa.

1 The range of the apostolic message has been steadily broadening, and now the time has come for it to cross the barrier which separated Jews from Gentiles and be presented unambiguously to Gentiles.

The barrier was crossed in the mainly Gentile city of Caesarea, and crossed by the leader of the apostles, Simon Peter. The Gentiles who first heard the gospel from his lips were the family and friends of Cornelius,[1] a centurion in the Roman army, belonging to one of the auxiliary cohorts in Judaea.[2]

---

[1] Cornelius was a specially common name in Rome ever since Publius Cornelius Sulla in 82 B.C. liberated 10,000 slaves, who were enrolled in the *gens Cornelia*, to which he belonged.

[2] The word translated "band" in v. 1 (Gk. σπεῖρα) is the equivalent of Lat.

The centurions who make their appearance in the NT record all make a favourable impression. It is to be noted that the first Gentile with whom Jesus had dealings during His public ministry (so far as we are informed) was a Roman centurion, and that it was with reference to this man's faith that He said, "many shall come from the east and the west, and shall sit down with Abraham, and Isaac, and Jacob, in the kingdom of heaven" (Matt. 8:11; *cf.* also Luke 7:2 ff.).[3] These words now begin to find their fulfilment in another centurion. A centurion was nominally in command of a hundred men; his responsibilities corresponded to those of a modern army captain, his status was that of a non-commissioned officer. Centurions were the backbone of the Roman army. Polybius (*History* vi. 24) sums up their necessary qualifications thus: "Centurions are required not to be bold and adventurous so much as good leaders, of steady and prudent mind, not prone to take the offensive or start fighting wantonly, but able when overwhelmed and hard-pressed to stand fast and die at their post."

Peter and Cornelius were each prepared by a vision for their interview. The whole story of this chapter, which "bears the stamp both of probability and truth"[4] (Foakes Jackson), is of great importance not only because it tells how the "door of faith" was opened to Gentiles, but also because it introduces the questions of the social intercourse of Jewish Christians with Gentiles and of the admission of Gentiles to the church without circumcision. These questions were later debated at the Council of Jerusalem (*cf.* pp. 298 ff.), and the Cornelius episode was there adduced as a test case (Ch. 15:7–9). Luke's appreciation of the importance of the Cornelius episode is shown by the space which he devotes to Peter's rehearsal of his experience in Ch. 11, as well as by the repetition of salient features of the incident within the narrative of Ch. 10.

2 It is further important to observe that Cornelius was one of those Gentiles who are commonly classed as "God-fearers"—

cohors ("cohort"). A regular cohort, the tenth part of a legion, had a paper strength of 600 men; an auxiliary cohort usually comprised 1,000 men. (*Cf.* Ch. 27:1.) We have inscriptional evidence of the presence in Syria *c.* A.D. 69 of the auxiliary *Cohors II Italica ciuium Romanorum* ("second Italian cohort of Roman citizens"); *cf.* H. Dessau, *Inscriptiones Latinae Selectae* (Berlin, 1892–1916), No. 9168.

[3] *Cf.* also the centurion on duty at our Lord's crucifixion (Luke 23:47 and parallels) and the centurion Julius in Acts 27:1 ff.

[4] F. J. Foakes Jackson, *The Acts of the Apostles* (MNT, London, 1931), p. 87.

"God-fearers", that is, from a Jewish point of view. Many Gentiles in those days, while not prepared to enter this Jewish community as full proselytes,[5] were attracted by the simple monotheism of Jewish synagogue worship and by the ethical standard of the Jewish way of life. Some of them attended synagogue and were tolerably conversant with the prayers and Scripture lessons, which they heard read in the Greek version; some observed with more or less scrupulosity such distinctive Jewish practices as sabbath observance and abstinence from certain kinds of food. Cornelius's attachment to the Jewish religion appeared particularly in his regular prayer to the God of Israel and acts of charity to the people of Israel. We may say, indeed, that he had every qualification, short of circumcision, which could satisfy Jewish requirements.

That the first Gentile to hear and accept the gospel should be a God-fearer is the more significant because, as we shall see later in Acts, it was such God-fearers who formed the nucleus of the Christian community in one city after another in the course of Paul's missionary activity.

3–6 To Cornelius, then, one afternoon about the time of the evening oblation,[6] a heavenly messenger appeared in a vision. His initial alarm at being addressed by the angel was overcome when he was assured that his faithfulness in prayer and almsgiving had not been overlooked by God but had been accepted by Him as a worthy oblation. The angel's language here is full of sacrificial terminology such as we find in the early chapters of Leviticus.[7] God would give him His gracious response, and the nature of that response he would learn if he sent to a certain house in Joppa and invited one Simon Peter, who was lodging there, to come and visit him.

---

[5] See p. 64 (on Ch. 2:10).
[6] *Cf.* Ch. 3:1 (p. 83, n. 7).
[7] "Thy prayers and thine alms are gone up for a memorial before God" (v. 4); "are gone up" or "have ascended" (Gk. ἀνέβησαν) like the smoke of a sacrifice. The Hebrew term for a burnt-offering is *'olah*, which literally means an "ascending". For the sacrificial reference of the word "memorial" (Gk. μνημόσυνον), *cf.* Lev. 2:2, where this term is used in LXX of the part of the meal-offering which was burnt, *i.e.* presented to God. For the sacrificial efficacy of such religious acts as those of Cornelius *cf.* Ps. 141:2 ("the lifting up of my hands as the evening sacrifice"); Tobit 12:12 ("when thou didst pray, . . . I did bring the memorial of your prayer before the Holy One"); and in NT Phil. 4:18; Heb. 13:15 f.

216

7–8 Immediately Cornelius carried out the instructions he had received in the vision. He despatched two of his domestic servants and one of his orderlies, a pious soldier like himself, to Joppa.

(b) Peter Sees a Vision (Ch. 10:9–16)

9 Now on the morrow, as they were on their journey, and drew nigh unto the city, Peter went up upon the housetop to pray, about the sixth hour:

10 and he became hungry, and desired to eat: but while they made ready, he fell into a trance;

11 and he beholdeth the heaven opened, and a certain vessel[8] descending, as it were a great sheet, let down by four corners upon the earth:

12 wherein were all manner of fourfooted beasts and creeping things of the earth[9] and birds of the heaven.

13 And there came a voice to him, Rise, Peter;[10] kill and eat.

14 But Peter said, Not so, Lord; for I have never eaten anything that is common and unclean.

15 And a voice *came* unto him again the second time, What God hath cleansed, make not thou common.

16 And this was done thrice: and straightway[11] the vessel was received up into heaven.

9–10 But Peter must be prepared for the interview as well as Cornelius, and there were scruples to be overcome on Peter's side as there were not on Cornelius's. A God-fearer had no objection to the society of Jews, but even a moderately orthodox Jew would not willingly enter the dwelling of a Gentile, God-fearer though he were. No doubt some of Peter's inherited prejudices were wearing thin by this time, but a special revelation was necessary to make him consent to visit a Gentile.

The revelation came on the day after Cornelius's vision, when the messengers from Caesarea were approaching Joppa. About noon Peter went up on the roof of the tanner's house for quiet and prayer. Noon was not one of the appointed times for public

---

[8] Gk. σκεῦος here requires to be rendered by a more indefinite word than "vessel"—say "object" or "thing". P45 reads "a certain object, tied by the four corners, let down upon the earth."

[9] The Byzantine text places the words "of the earth" after "fourfooted beasts", not after "creeping things"; and adds "and wild beasts" after "earth" (*cf.* AV).

[10] P45 omits "Peter."

[11] The Western and Byzantine texts have "again" in place of "straightway" (*cf.* AV).

217

prayer, but pious Jews who prayed three times a day (*cf.* Ps. 55:17; Dan. 6:10) probably prayed then. While he was on the roof, he began to feel hungry,[12] and probably called down for some food. It was while this was being prepared that the revelation came to him in a vision, and it was no doubt because of his hunger that the vision centred around food.

11-13 In this ecstatic vision Peter seemed to see a large sheet-like object coming down from heaven. Whether it was the awning over the roof, or a sail on the Mediterranean horizon, that assumed this form to his inward eye, need not concern us. The sheet, however, when it came down where Peter was, proved to be full of all sorts of quadrupeds, reptiles and birds,[13] clean and unclean.[14] The vision of these was accompanied by a heavenly voice, "Rise, Peter! kill and eat."

14-16 This was all wrong, as Peter's ancestral conscience told him; unclean animals must not be used for food at all, and even clean animals must be slaughtered with ritual propriety before their flesh could be eaten. His protest against the divine injunction took verbal shape much as the prophet Ezekiel's protest had once done when he was commanded to prepare and eat "abominable flesh" (Ezek. 4:14). "No, Lord," said Peter; "for I have never eaten anything that is common or unclean."[15] Back came the heavenly voice, "What God has cleansed, you must not continue to treat as common." Three times over this interchange took place; then the sheet went up with its contents and the vision dissolved.

The abolition of Jewish ceremonial barriers was pressed home in the vision with special reference to food-laws,[16] but Peter soon

---

[12] The word translated "hungry" in v. 10 (Gk. πρόσπεινος) occurs elsewhere, so far as is known, only in a first century eye-doctor named Demosthenes. F. W. Dillistone (ExT xlvi [1934-5], p. 380) suggests that Luke may have been a pupil of his.

[13] The animal world is divided into these three divisions in Gen. 6:20 ("birds . . . cattle . . . every creeping thing of the ground").

[14] The laws distinguishing clean from unclean animals are laid down in Lev. 11. Those quadrupeds were clean (and therefore fit for food) which both chewed the cud and had cloven hooves.

[15] It has been asked at times whether Peter could not have killed and eaten one of the clean animals. But he was scandalized by the unholy mixture of clean animals with unclean; this is particularly important when we recall the practical way in which he had immediately to apply the lesson of the vision.

[16] The fact that Peter's vision had to do with food-laws, whereas the narrative in which it is set is concerned with the propriety of a Jew's entering a Gentile

grasped that its range was much wider. And perhaps, as he thought about the vision, he remembered hearing similar words on an earlier occasion, though he did not then understand their import. No doubt he was present when his Master, disputing with the Pharisees and scribes, insisted that it is not what goes into a man's stomach that defiles him, but what comes out of his heart (Mark 7:14 ff.). This was in effect an abrogation of cere-monial food-laws and much else of the same character, but it was not until later, as a result of his experience on the roof at Joppa, that Peter appreciated this. It is to Peter, probably, that we owe the remark appended to the Gospel narrative of Jesus' dispute with the Pharisees on this subject: "This he said, making all meats clean" (Mark 7:19b).

(c) The Messengers of Cornelius Arrive at Joppa (Ch. 10:17-23a)

17 Now while Peter was much perplexed in himself what the vision which he had seen might mean, behold, the men that were sent by Cornelius, having made inquiry for Simon's house, stood before the gate,

18 and called and asked whether Simon, who was sur-named Peter, were lodging there.

19 And while Peter thought on the vision, the Spirit said unto him, Behold, three[17] men seek thee.

20 But arise, and get thee down, and go with them, nothing doubting: for I have sent them.

21 And Peter went down to the men,[18] and said, Behold, I am he whom ye seek: what is the cause wherefore ye are come?

22 And they said, Cornelius a centurion, a righteous man and one that feareth God, and well reported of by all the nation of the Jews, was warned of God by a holy angel to send for thee into his house, and to hear words from thee.

23 So he called them in and lodged them.

house, is taken by Martin Dibelius as an indication that vv. 9–16 are part of Luke's working over of an original narrative which had nothing of the special significance which it acquires in the scheme of Luke's history ("Die Bekehrung des Cornelius", in *Aufsätze zur Apostelgeschichte* [Göttingen, 1951], pp. 96 ff.).

[17] Cod. B reads "two." The Western and Byzantine texts omit the numeral. The reading of B, being the most difficult (because of the apparent discrepancy with v. 7 and Ch. 11:11), may be original; if so, it suggests that the two domestic servants were the actual messengers, the soldier acting as a guard.

[18] The Byzantine text adds "who had been sent by Cornelius to him" (*cf.* AV).

17–20 The trance was over, but Peter remained on the roof, deep in thought, pondering the import of what he had seen and heard. Suddenly the Spirit of God, by an inward monition, gave him to know that some men were looking for him, and that he was to go with them without any doubt or hesitation. For at that moment, the messengers from Caesarea, having made inquiry for Simon the tanner's house, were standing at the street door. We may ask if there is any distinction between the angelic communication to Cornelius (vv. 3 ff.) and Peter's prompting by the Spirit, just as we had to consider a very similar question in the narrative of Philip and the Ethiopian (*cf.* p. 186). Here the distinction fairly obviously is that the angelic communication was made "in a vision openly", whereas Peter was conscious of a voice within. But a further question arises, concerning the relation between one's experience of the Holy Spirit and of the risen Christ—an almost unanswerable question, the more so as the risen Christ manifests His presence and power through the Holy Spirit. But whom did Peter consider that he was addressing as "Lord" when he declined to "kill and eat"? On that occasion the voice seemed to come from without, we gather, and it may have been a voice that Peter well remembered, and immediately recognized.

21–23a At any rate, Peter went down (by an outside stairway of stone, no doubt) and found the messengers from Cornelius at the door asking for Simon, surnamed Peter. He told them that he was the man they were looking for, and asked the reason of their visit. So they told him how their master Cornelius had been divinely instructed to invite him to his house, in order to hear an important communication from him. By this time the meal which Peter had called for was ready, and he brought the men in to share it. Not only so, but he provided accommodation for them overnight, as it was too late to set out for Caesarea after he had entertained them.

(d) Peter Enters the House of Cornelius (Ch. 10:23b–33)

> And on the morrow he arose and went forth with them, and certain of the brethren from Joppa accompanied him.
>
> 24 And on the morrow they entered into Caesarea. And[19]

[19] From here to the end of v. 25 the Western text has the expanded reading: "And Cornelius was expecting them, and having called together his

Cornelius was waiting for them, having called together his kinsmen and his near friends.

25 And when it came to pass that Peter entered, Cornelius met him, and fell down at his feet, and worshipped him.

26 But Peter raised him up, saying, Stand up; I myself also am a man.

27 And as he talked with him, he went in, and findeth many come together:

28 and he said unto them, Ye yourselves know[20] how it is an unlawful thing for a man that is a Jew to join himself or come unto one of another nation; and *yet* unto me hath God showed that I should not call any man common or unclean:

29 wherefore also I came without gainsaying, when I was sent for. I ask therefore with what intent ye sent for me.

30 And Cornelius said, Four[21] days ago, until this hour, I was keeping the ninth hour of prayer[22] in my house; and behold, a man stood before me in bright apparel,

31 and saith, Cornelius, thy prayer is heard, and thine alms are had in remembrance in the sight of God.

32 Send therefore to Joppa, and call unto thee Simon, who is surnamed Peter; he lodgeth in the house of Simon a tanner, by the sea side.[23]

33 Forthwith therefore I sent to thee;[24] and thou hast well done that thou art come.[25] Now therefore we are all here present in the sight of God,[26] to hear all things that have been commanded thee of the Lord.

23b–24 Next day Peter set out for Caesarea with the messengers from Cornelius. In view of the novelty of his mission, he acted wisely in taking some Christians of Joppa with him—six in number,

kinsmen and his near friends was waiting for them. And as Peter drew near to Caesarea, one of the slaves ran on in advance and announced that he had arrived. Then Cornelius, leaping up and going to meet him, fell down at his feet and worshipped him."

[20] Cod. D adds "very well" (Gk. βέλτιον).

[21] Cod. D has "three days ago"; this shortens the time taken for the journey from Joppa to Caesarea.

[22] The Western text reads "fasting and prayer"; this pietistic amplification is a Western characteristic.

[23] The Western and Byzantine texts add "who, having arrived, will speak to thee" (*cf.* AV).

[24] The Western text adds "requesting thee to come to us."

[25] The Western text adds "speedily."

[26] P^{45} omits "all" and "in the sight of God."

as he himself reports in Ch. 11:12. The larger company seems to have taken longer to complete the thirty miles' journey to Caesarea than Cornelius's messengers had taken, for according to the natural sense of v. 24 ("on the morrow they entered into Caesarea") they did not arrive till the following day. (The Western text of v. 30, however, makes it appear that they reached Caesarea the same day as they left Joppa; see p. 221, n. 21.) Meanwhile Cornelius had gathered his relatives and close friends in his house, ready for Peter's arrival.

25-26 When Peter arrived, Cornelius hastened out and paid him the respect which he judged fitting for a messenger of God, prostrating himself at the apostle's feet in an attitude of homage and supplication.[27] It is unlikely that Peter had ever had such reverence paid him before; and no doubt it embarrassed him considerably: "Please get up", he said, helping his host to rise; "I am but a man myself."

27-29 Then, talking in a friendly manner to him, Peter went indoors with him, and there was the whole company of Cornelius's Gentile friends full of eager expectation. A couple of days previously, Peter would not have believed it possible that he should find himself in such company, beneath a Gentile roof; but much had happened since then. "You know very well," he said to Cornelius and his friends, "that to mix in Gentile society is taboo[28] for a pious Jew; but God has taught me to call nobody common or unclean." Actually, the terms of his vision on the housetop at Joppa taught him to call no *food* common or unclean if God pronounced it clean; but he was quick to grasp the analogy between ceremonial food-laws and the regulations affecting intercourse with non-Jews. It was largely because of their carelessness in food matters that Gentiles were ritually unsafe people for a pious Jew to meet socially. Intercourse with Gentiles was not categorically forbidden; but it did render a Jew ceremonially unclean, as did even the entering of a Gentile building or the handling of articles belonging to Gentiles. The most ordinary kinds of food,

[27] As the footnote in ARV points out, the Greek word προσκυνέω, translated "worshipped" (v. 25), is used of an act of reverence whether paid to God or (as here) to a creature (of either angelic or human nature).

[28] A suitable word to use here as the equivalent of Gk. ἀθέμιτος (ARV "unlawful"). The word used in v. 28 for "one of another nation" is ἀλλόφυλος, which (significantly enough) is frequently used in LXX to denote an "uncircumcised Philistine."

such as bread, milk or olive oil, coming from Gentiles, might not be eaten by strict Jews, not to mention flesh, which might have come from an unclean animal or from one sacrificed to a pagan deity, and which in any case contained blood. Hence, of all forms of intercourse with Gentiles, to accept their hospitality and sit at table with them was the most intolerable. However, Peter's lesson had so impressed itself upon his mind that he accompanied Cornelius's messengers without scruple or protest. And now that he had arrived, he asked them to state more fully their reason for inviting him.

30–33 Cornelius then described the vision[29] which he had seen three[30] days previously, at the very hour at which he was now speaking, the hour of afternoon prayer, and the words of encouragement and direction spoken to him by the celestial visitant who stood before him in shining robes.[31] It was in accordance with these directions, he explained, that he had sent for Peter, and he heartily thanked him for coming so promptly.[32] "Now then," he said, "we are all present here before God, ready to hear all that the Lord has commanded you to say." Did ever a preacher of the gospel have a more promising audience than this?

(e) Gentiles Hear the Good News (Ch. 10:34–43)

34 And Peter opened his mouth, and said,
Of a truth I perceive that God is no respecter of persons:

35 but in every nation he that feareth him, and worketh righteousness, is acceptable to him.

36 The word which[33] he sent unto the children of Israel, preaching good tidings of peace by Jesus Christ (he is Lord of all)—

[29] Cornelius's description of his vision affords an opportunity of repeating part of a narrative very important in Luke's history, as Peter's description of *his* vision in Ch. 11:5 ff. affords an opportunity of repeating another part.

[30] "Four days ago" (v. 30) must be regarded as inclusive reckoning (but *cf.* n. 21 above).

[31] *Cf.* p. 41 (on Ch. 1:10).

[32] "Thou hast well done that thou art come" might be more idiomatically rendered "You have been so kind as to come" or "Thank you for coming."

[33] Cod. B omits "which" (probably a haplographic omission of ὅν after λόγον). The Western text recasts the construction of vv. 36–38 to make it run more coherently: "For you know the message which He sent to the children of Israel, which was published through all Judaea, when He preached good tidings of peace through Jesus Christ (He is Lord of all). For beginning in Galilee, after the baptism which John proclaimed, Jesus of Nazareth, whom

37 that saying[34] ye yourselves know, which was published throughout all Judaea, beginning from Galilee, after the baptism[35] which John preached;

38 *even* Jesus of Nazareth, how God anointed him with the Holy Spirit and with power: who went about doing good, and healing all that were oppressed of the devil; for God was with him.

39 And we are witnesses of all things which he did both in the country of the Jews, and in Jerusalem; whom also they slew, hanging him on a tree.

40 Him God raised up the third day,[36] and gave him to be made manifest,

41 not to all the people, but unto witnesses that were chosen before of God, *even* to us, who ate and drank with him after he rose from the dead.[37]

42 And he charged us to preach unto the people, and to testify that this is he who is ordained of God *to be* the Judge of the living and the dead.

43 To him bear all the prophets witness, that through his name every one that believeth on him shall receive remission of sins.

34-35 The expression "Peter opened his mouth" is one that is used to introduce some weighty utterance, and the first words that Peter spoke were words of the weightiest import, sweeping away the racial prejudices of centuries. The words of Cornelius confirmed the lesson that he himself had learned in Joppa: it was plain, then, that God had no favourites[38] as between one nation and another, but any man who feared Him and acted rightly[39] was

God anointed with Holy Spirit and power, went about doing good . . ."

34 For "that saying . . . which was published" (Gk. τὸ γενόμενον ῥῆμα) we might render "the thing that took place"; for this sense of ῥῆμα cf. Ch. 5:32 (where ῥήματα is translated "things").

35 Cod. B reads "proclamation" (κήρυγμα) for "baptism" (βάπτισμα).

36 Cod. D reads "after the third day" (an attempted harmonization with Matt. 27:63 and other passages).

37 The Western text reads "who ate and drank and conversed with him forty days after the resurrection from the dead."

38 Gk. προσωπολήμπτης ("respector of persons") reflects the Hebrew idiom *nasa panim*, "to lift someone's face", hence "to show favor" and, in a pejorative sense, "to show favoritism." This idiom is rendered in LXX by πρόσωπον λαμβάνειν and other phrases (cf. Luke 20:21; Gal. 2:6); the present word προσωπολήμπτης (here appearing for the first time in Greek literature and for the only time in NT) and προσωπολημψία ("partiality") are nouns formed on the basis of this phrase. Cf. Rom. 2:11; Eph. 6:9; Col. 3:25; Jas. 2:1; 1 Pet. 1:17.

39 "He that . . . worketh righteousness" (v. 35), representing Gk. ὁ ἐργαζόμενος

acceptable to Him, no matter what nation he belonged to. This may be the veriest truism to us, but it was a revolutionary revelation to Peter. Yet it was implicit in the teaching of the early prophets. They insisted that God's choice of Israel was an act of grace, not of partiality, and that it called for a response of obedient service, not of careless complacency. If God brought Israel out of Egypt, He had also brought the Philistines from Crete and the Syrians from Kir (Amos 9:7). If, as Micah said, the Lord's primary requirements were that a man should do justly and love mercy and walk humbly with his God (Micah 6:8), then a Gentile might fulfil these requirements as well as an Israelite. Luke, who appears to have been of Gentile birth himself, had good reason to emphasize the narrative of the bringing in of the Gentiles, by the cumulative repetitions of this narrative and by other means.

36–37 Peter's speech, which Foakes Jackson pronounced "peculiarly appropriate to the occasion"[40] (although Martin Dibelius regarded it as an interpolation in the Cornelius story),[41] is devoted almost entirely to a summary of the apostolic preaching. Some acquaintance with the main outline of the story of Jesus is presumed (for Peter's hearers were far from being raw pagans), but more details are given than in the summaries of Peter's earlier speeches (*cf.* Chs. 2:14 ff.; 3:12 ff.; 4:8 ff.; 5:29 ff.). How far this reflects the actual amount of detail given by Peter in his respective addresses, and how far it is due to the way in which Luke summarizes them, is difficult to decide. But C. H. Dodd is no doubt right in suggesting "that the speech before Cornelius represents the form of *kerygma* used by the primitive Church in its earliest approaches to a wider preaching" (*The Apostolic Preaching and its Developments* [Lon-

---

δικαιοσύνην, no doubt refers to righteousness in the widest sense, but it is relevant here to recall the more restricted sense of the word (like *tzedaqah* in Mishnaic Hebrew) to denote almsgiving (*cf.* Matt. 6:1), in view of Cornelius's practice.

[40] *Op. cit.,* p. 93.

[41] "In a legend of the conversion of a centurion, related among the Christians, such a comparatively long speech can have had no place" (*op. cit.,* p. 97). The speech is a literary composition of the author's, says Dibelius, as are the other speeches in Acts; there is nothing in the present speech relevant to the special question of Gentile evangelization (except the introductory remarks of vv. 34 f.), and Peter's own account of the proceedings leaves no room for such a speech, for he tells how the Holy Spirit fell upon Cornelius and his household "as I began to speak" (Ch. 11:15). But as Dibelius regards Peter's defence of his action in Ch. 11:4–17 as equally Luke's overworking of the original "legend", there seems to be little force in this contention.

don, 1936], p. 56). The scope of the *kerygma*, as attested by this address of Peter's, is almost exactly the scope of Mark's gospel,[42] beginning with John's baptism, and going on to tell of Jesus' ministry in Galilee,[43] Judaea[44] and Jerusalem, of His crucifixion and resurrection, followed by the insistence on personal witness and on the coming judgment, with the offer of forgiveness through faith in Him here and now.

In the house of Cornelius Peter may have spoken Greek, but perhaps it is more probable that he spoke in Aramaic through an interpreter.[45] At any rate, this speech is even more strongly marked by Aramaisms than his speeches recorded in the earlier chapters of Acts. The presence of Aramaisms, of course, is a sign that the speech is not Luke's free invention, but a rather literal reproduction of what he found in his source (whether that source was written or oral). The Greek of vv. 36–38 in particular reads somewhat awkwardly as also do the fairly literal renderings in our common English versions, but it can be turned back word for word into grammatical and intelligible Aramaic.[46]

38 The statement that Jesus of Nazareth was "anointed" by God "with the Holy Spirit and with power" reminds us of the words of Isa. 61:1 f. which Jesus read in the synagogue at Nazareth (Luke 4:18 f.)—"The Spirit of the Lord Jehovah is upon me; because Jehovah hath anointed me ..."—and which He claimed as fulfilled that day in Himself. These opening words of Isa. 61

[42] *Cf.* C. H. Dodd, "The Framework of the Gospel Narrative", ExT xliii (1931–2), pp. 396 ff. As against K. L. Schmidt's view that Mark consists mainly of independent *pericopae* strung together by means of short generalizing summaries (*Sammelberichte*) which have no historical value of their own, Dodd shows that these summaries, when put together, prove to make up a coherent outline of the life and work of Jesus, comparable to the outlines of the apostolic preaching found elsewhere in NT, and in particular to the outline of Peter's address in the house of Cornelius.

[43] "This emphasis on the beginning in Galilee seems to have been integral to the pattern of the *kerygma* from the first" (C. H. Dodd, *According to the Scriptures* [London, 1952], pp. 80 f.).

[44] The expressions "throughout all Judaea" (v. 37) and "in the country of the Jews" (v. 39) probably denote the whole of Palestine and not the southern province of Judaea only.

[45] According to Papias's account of the origin of Mark's Gospel (preserved in Eusebius, *Ecclesiastical History* iii. 39 and apparently reflected in the anti-Marcionite prologue to this Gospel), Peter even at a later date used the services of an interpreter (ἑρμηνευτής).

[46] *Cf.* C. C. Torrey, *Composition and Date of Acts* (Cambridge, Mass., 1916), pp. 27, 35 f.; F. F. Bruce, *The Speeches in the Acts of the Apostles* (London, 1942), p. 9.

are not usually reckoned along with the "Servant Songs" of Isa. 42–53,[47] but they do express the same ideas and, in fact, speak of the same person. The Servant, when first introduced by God in Isa. 42:1, is described as God's chosen one upon whom He has put His Spirit: this brings him into relation with the predicted ruler of David's line in Isa. 11:1 ff., upon whom "the Spirit of Jehovah shall rest". If we ask when Jesus of Nazareth was thus anointed, the natural answer is "at His baptism", for then the Holy Spirit descended upon Him visibly, while the voice from heaven hailed Him as God's Son (the Messiah of David's line on whom the Spirit was to rest) and chosen one (the obedient Servant on whom the Spirit similarly rested). Part of the meaning of these words of Peter will come home to us more forcibly if for a moment we render "God made him Messiah" instead of "God anointed Him."[48]

When He had been thus anointed, He proceeded to fulfil the programme mapped out for Him in the opening words of Isa. 61 and elsewhere—healing the sick and delivering the demon-possessed, "doing good and healing all that were oppressed by the devil, for God was with him." We should remember that this is probably a brief summary of what Peter said: his actual address may have contained examples of his Master's works of healing and power— "paradigms" as the form critics call them—such as are recorded in the Gospels.[49]

39 Peter emphasizes that he and his colleagues are eyewitnesses of all these things, which took place all over the land of Israel. Yet Jesus' acts of mercy and deliverance, he goes on, did not prevent Him from being put to death—and put to death by that means upon which the OT scriptures pronounced a curse, for they

---

[47] They have been so reckoned in recent times by C. C. Torrey, *The Second Isaiah* (Edinburgh, 1928), pp. 137 ff.; W. W. Cannon, "Isaiah 61:1–3 an Ebed-Jahweh Poem", ZAW xlvii (1929), pp. 284 ff.; O. Procksch, "Jesus der Gottesknecht", in *In Piam Memoriam Alexander von Bulmerincq* (Riga, 1938), pp. 146 ff.; B. Balscheit, *Der Gottesbund* (Zürich, 1943), pp. 173 ff.; and others mentioned by C. R. North in *The Suffering Servant in Deutero-Isaiah* (Oxford, 1948), pp. 137 f. See p. 231, n. 62.

[48] *Cf.* Ch. 4:27 (p. 106, n. 37). See also C. H. Dodd, *According to the Scriptures*, pp. 52 f., 94 ff.

[49] These examples would not be mere illustrations; they would be proofs of the fulfilment of prophecy, as Jesus Himself implied when He sent John the Baptist's disciples back to their master with the command, "Go and tell John the things which ye have seen and heard" (Luke 7:22). John would recognize from their report that the prophetic programme was indeed being carried out, and that therefore Jesus was certainly the Coming One of whom the prophets spoke.

killed Him by "hanging Him on a tree." We have already noted the significance of this particular expression as a way to describe death by crucifixion (*cf.* Ch. 5:30 with exposition and note).

40-41 Again, as so often in the apostolic preaching, comes the pointed contrast between men's treatment of the Christ and God's treatment of Him: the very one whom men put to death is the one whom God raised to newness of life on the third day.[50] There could be no doubt about this: He appeared to many witnesses—not indeed to the people at large but to those selected by God to see the risen Saviour, Peter and his fellow-disciples. They could bear certain witness to His resurrection, for they had not only seen Him alive again after His passion but had even eaten and drunk with Him. This was decisive proof that it was no bodiless phantom[51] that appeared to them (see p. 36, on Ch. 1:4).

42 During these resurrection appearances, Christ had commanded His apostles to proclaim the message of the kingdom of God, the good news which He had brought, and also to announce that He was the one appointed by God to be the judge of all men, living and dead—the "one like unto a son of man" of Daniel's vision to whom was committed authority to execute judgment (Dan. 7:13 f.; John 5:27).

43 But His function was by no means limited to the execution of judgment, for He was also the one through whom, as all the prophets agreed, those who believed on Him would have their sins forgiven.[52] As Jesus said Himself when He cured the paralytic in Capernaum, "the Son of man hath authority on earth to forgive sins" (Mark 2:10). Peter's reference to "all the prophets" was

[50] The "third day" (v. 40) is mentioned not only for chronological accuracy, but in order to emphasize a further fulfilment of prophecy. The OT testimonies quoted in the apostolic preaching sometimes reflect the recognition that the pattern of Messiah's experiences resembled the pattern of Israel's experiences; hence such a statement as "After two days will he revive us: on the third day he will raise us up, and we shall live before him" (Hos. 6:2) could find its fulfilment in the resurrection of Jesus. Paul's reference to the risen Christ as the "firstfruits" (in 1 Cor. 15:20, 23) suggests that when he describes Him as being "raised on the third day according to the scriptures" (1 Cor. 15:4), he has also in mind the ordinance of Lev. 23:10 f. about the presentation of the firstfruits of barley harvest to God the day after the paschal sabbath.

[51] *Cf.* the words put into the mouth of the risen Christ by a lost work quoted by Ignatius (*Smyrnaeans* 3:2), "I am not a bodiless spirit" (οὐκ εἰμὶ δαιμόνιον ἀσώματον).

[52] *Cf.* Ch. 26:18 and Luke 24:47.

228

doubtless supported by relevant quotations from their writings, including the prophecy of the suffering Servant who was to "justify many" and "bear their iniquities" (Isa. 53:11).

(f) Gentiles Receive the Holy Spirit (Ch. 10:44–48)

44 While Peter yet spake these words, the Holy Spirit fell on all them that heard the word.

45 And they of the circumcision that believed were amazed, as many as came with Peter, because that on the Gentiles also was poured out the gift of the Holy Spirit.

46 For they heard them speak with[53] tongues, and magnify God. Then answered Peter,

47 Can any man forbid the water, that these should not be baptized, who have received the Holy Spirit as well as we?

48 And he commanded them to be baptized in the name of[54] Jesus Christ. Then prayed they him to tarry certain days.

44 Peter had not yet finished his address when the "Pentecost of the Gentile world"[55] took place. The Holy Spirit fell on all his listeners. But the order of events differed markedly from that which was seen on the day of Pentecost in Jerusalem, so far at least as the hearers of the apostolic message were concerned. The hearers in Jerusalem were exhorted to repent and be baptized in order to receive the remission of sins and the gift of the Spirit. But the experience of the hearers in Caesarea reproduced rather that of the original company of disciples at Jerusalem, on whom the Spirit descended suddenly.[56] Peter, indeed (v. 47), draws a parallel between the household of Cornelius and the original disciples rather than between the household of Cornelius and the three thousand who believed on the day of Pentecost (*cf.* Chs. 11:15; 15:8).

45–46 The descent of the Spirit on these Gentiles was outwardly manifested in much the same way as it had been when

---

[53] The Western text inserts "other".

[54] The Western text inserts "the Lord" (*cf.* Ch. 2:38).

[55] So this occasion is called by F. H. Chase, *The Credibility of the Acts of the Apostles* (London, 1902), p. 79. "Yet," as N. B. Stonehouse says, "in spite of certain parallels with Pentecost, the development in Caesarea is undoubtedly viewed as somewhat subordinate to it, and as actually intimating the significance of Pentecost for the salvation of the Gentiles" (WThJ xiii [1950–1], p. 8).

[56] *Cf.* G. W. H. Lampe, *The Seal of the Spirit* (London, 1951), p. 66.

the original disciples received the Spirit at Pentecost: they spoke with tongues and proclaimed the mighty works of God.[57] Apart from such external manifestations, none of the Jewish Christians present, perhaps not even Peter himself, would have been so ready to accept the fact that the Spirit had really come upon them. Peter's Jewish Christian companions who had come with him from Joppa were astounded by what they saw and heard: *Gentiles*—those "lesser breeds without the law"—had actually received the same Holy Spirit as Jewish believers in Jesus had already received. How right Peter had been in his new insight into the impartiality of God as between men of one race and another!

47-48 If we compare these Gentile believers with the Jerusalemites who were convicted by Peter's words on the day of Pentecost, we may mark a difference in the order of events. In Ch. 2:37 ff. the order was conviction of sin, repentance and faith, baptism in the name of Jesus Christ for the remission of sins, and the reception of the gift of the Holy Spirit. Here the reception of the Spirit comes first. There is no explicit mention of faith in the immediate context, but it is inevitably implied; it is suggested more definitely in Peter's report in Ch. 11:17 (where his words "when we believed on the Lord Jesus Christ" clearly mean that the Gentiles received the Spirit when *they* believed),[58] and in Ch. 15:7-9 he expressly links the Gentiles' reception of the Spirit with the fact that they believed and had their hearts cleansed[59] by faith. Only after the descent of the Spirit on the believing Gentiles were they baptized. And as for the laying on of apostolic hands, it is obvious that (whatever inference we may draw from the silence on this subject in Ch. 2) nothing of the kind took place before they received the Spirit, and nothing is said about its taking place subsequently.

Had Peter not been confronted with a divine *fait accompli* in the descent of the Spirit on Cornelius and his friends, he might not have taken the initiative in baptizing them as he did. But as it was, God had plainly accepted them, and Peter had no option

---

[57] "Magnify God" ($μεγαλυνόντων$ $τὸν$ $θεόν$) in v. 46 is synonymous with "speaking . . . the mighty works of God" ($λαλούντων$ $τὰ$ $μεγαλεῖα$ $τοῦ$ $θεοῦ$) in Ch. 2:11.

[58] The repentance of these Gentiles is mentioned in Ch. 11:18.

[59] The "cleansing" of the Gentiles' hearts by faith is, of course, closely linked with the words spoken to Peter in his vision, "What God hath cleansed, make not thou common." The verb $καθαρίζω$ is used in both places.

but to accept what God had done. In justifying his action a short time afterwards (Ch. 11:17), he asked, "Who was I to resist God?"[60] So he commanded that these new believers should be baptized in the name of Jesus Christ.[61] The reception of the Spirit, be it noted, was not looked upon as a substitute for baptism in water. This baptism was rather the due response to the divine act. But no one appears to have suggested that Cornelius should be circumcised. His case thus served as a precedent when the question of the circumcision of Gentile believers was later raised at the Jerusalem council (Ch. 15).[62]

[60] Gk. "ἐγὼ τίς ἤμην δυνατὸς κωλῦσαι τὸν θεόν; This verb κωλύω appear also in Ch. 10:47, "Can any man *forbid* the water . . .?" and in the Ethiopian's question in Ch. 8:36, "what doth *hinder* me to be baptized?" This may suggest that it was a primitive Christian custom, before baptizing a convert, to inquire if there was any "cause or just impediment" why he should not be baptized. See O. Cullmann, *Baptism in the NT* (Eng. tr., London, 1950), pp. 71 ff.

[61] The same phrase as is used in Ch. 2:38 (*cf.* p. 76, n. 73).

[62] To the bibliography on p. 227, n. 47, of places where Isa. 61:1 ff. is reckoned together with the Servant Songs of Isa. 42–53, add: A. Bentzen, *Introduction to OT* (Copenhagen, 1948), ii, p. 110; O. Procksch, *Theologie des AT* (Gütersloh, 1950), p. 284; J. Bright, *The Kingdom of God* (New York, 1953), pp. 147, 198. L. Köhler, in his *Theologie des AT* (3rd edn., Tübingen, 1953), p. 231, points out that if the speaker of Isa. 61:1 ff. is the Servant of Isa. 52:13 ff., then the Servant is a messianic figure—a Messiah who suffers vicariously and brings salvation.

CHAPTER XI

(g) Peter Defends his Action (Ch. 11:1–18)

1 Now the apostles and the brethren that were in Judaea heard that the Gentiles also had received the word of God.[1]

2 And when Peter was come up to Jerusalem, they that were of the circumcision contended with him,[2]

3 saying, Thou wentest in to men uncircumcised, and didst eat with them.

4 But Peter began, and expounded *the matter* unto them in order, saying,

5 I was in the city of Joppa praying: and in a trance I saw a vision, a certain vessel descending, as it were a great sheet let down from heaven by four corners; and it came even unto me:

6 upon which when I had fastened mine eyes, I considered, and saw the fourfooted beasts of the earth and wild beasts and creeping things and birds of the heaven.

7 And I heard also a voice saying unto me, Rise, Peter; kill and eat.

8 But I said, Not so, Lord: for nothing common or unclean hath ever entered into my mouth.

9 But a voice answered the second time out of heaven,[3] What God hath cleansed, make not thou common.

10 And this was done thrice; and all were drawn up again into heaven.

11 And behold, forthwith three men stood before the house in which we were,[4] having been sent from Caesarea unto me.

---

[1] Some forms of the Western text add (prematurely) "and they glorified God."

[2] The Western text expands v. 2 as follows: "Peter then after a considerable time wished to go to Jerusalem; and calling the brethren to him and establishing them, he took his departure, engaging in much preaching throughout the regions and teaching them. When he met them (at Jerusalem), he reported to them the grace of God, but they that were of the circumcision contended with him."

[3] Cod. D reads "there came a voice from heaven to me."

[4] "We were" (Gk. ἦμεν) is the reading of ℵ A B D; but P45 with Codd. 33 and 81, the Byzantine text and all the versions read "I was" (Gk. ἤμην).

12 And the Spirit bade me go with them, making no distinction. And these six brethren also accompanied me; and we entered into the man's house:

13 and he told us how he had seen the angel standing in his house, and saying, Send to Joppa, and fetch Simon, whose surname is Peter;

14 who shall speak unto thee words, whereby thou shalt be saved, thou and all thy house.

15 And as I began to speak, the Holy Spirit fell on them, even as on us at the beginning.

16 And I remembered the word of the Lord, how he said, John indeed baptized with water; but ye shall be baptized in the Holy Spirit.

17 If then God gave unto them the like gift as *he did* also unto us, when we believed on the Lord Jesus Christ, who was I, that I could withstand God?[5]

18 And when they heard these things, they held their peace, and glorified God, saying, Then to the Gentiles also hath God granted repentance unto life.

1-3 The news of Peter's revolutionary behaviour, in entering a Gentile house at Caesarea, reached Jerusalem before he himself did. The Western text makes him spend a fairly long time at Caesarea, and then engage in teaching in the district between Caesarea and Jerusalem.[6] There may be some truth in this, although the Western reviser's main concern may have been to avoid giving the impression that the outpouring of the Spirit at Caesarea was followed immediately by controversy within the Spirit-filled community at Jerusalem. But however long the interval was, Peter's action could not fail to arouse alarm at Jerusalem. Hitherto, while Stephen and the Hellenists might incur popular hostility, the apostles had been able to enjoy a measure of general good will; but if the news got about that the leader of the apostolic company himself had begun to fraternize with Gentiles, that good will would soon be lost. And in fact it may well have turned out so. It was not long after this that Herod Agrippa I, appointed king of Judaea by the Emperor Claudius in A.D. 41, executed the

[5] The Western text reads "who was I that I could hinder God from giving them the Holy Spirit when they believed on Him?"

[6] See n. 2 above. Some scholars, accepting the Western reading here, link it with the Western reading of Ch. 21:16 which makes Mnason the Cypriote live in one of the villages between Caesarea and Jerusalem, and suppose that this "early disciple" was converted during Peter's present visit to these parts. See p. 426, nn. 18, 22.

apostle James and then, "when he saw that it pleased the Jews", arrested Peter as well (Ch. 12:1 ff.). And about the same time James, the brother of Jesus, emerges as acknowledged leader of the Jerusalem church rather than any of the twelve apostles (*cf.* Ch. 12:17; 15:13).

When Peter arrived home, then, he was immediately taken to task by those "that were of the circumcision" (v. 2)—by which expression we are perhaps to understand more particularly those Jewish Christians who were specially zealous for the law and sticklers for the ban on social intercourse between circumcised and uncircumcised.[7] "Why did you go to uncircumcised men and eat with them?" they asked (RSV).

Martin Dibelius ascribes the first eighteen verses of Ch. 11 to the author's elaboration of the simple original form of the Cornelius story.[8] In the original story, he suggests, Peter had no more need to defend himself for preaching the gospel to Cornelius than Philip had for preaching it to the Ethiopian eunuch. In the original story the question of eating with Gentiles was not raised; it was introduced later because of the part which it came to play in the discussion of the terms which must be laid down for the admission of Gentile believers to church membership. There is, indeed, no express reference to eating with Gentiles in Ch. 10. But the problem is present in the narrative by implication; it was the thought of eating with Gentiles in particular that made the idea of entering a Gentile house so objectionable, for Gentile food was "common and unclean"; and it is the thought of eating with Gentiles that supplies the link between Peter's vision in which the ceremonial food-laws were abrogated and his practical application of that lesson in ignoring the ceremonial objections to entering a Gentile house. The whole narrative, from Ch. 10:1 to 11:18, is perfectly coherent.

4–10 Peter's best defence of his conduct was a straightforward narration of his experience. So he told them of his vision on the roof of the tanner's house at Joppa. In this repetition of the story we observe the narrator's masterly combination of variety in expression with similarity in construction. In vv. 5 and 6 there is a vividness in Peter's description of the great sheet which contrasts

---

[7] The phrase is the same as in Ch. 10:45 (οἱ ἐκ περιτομῆς), but there it simply denotes people of Jewish birth as distinct from Gentiles.

[8] See his study, "Die Bekehrung des Cornelius", in *Aufsätze zur Apostelgeschichte* (Göttingen, 1951), pp. 96 ff.

with the comparative colourlessness of the third-personal account in Ch. 10:11 f.[9] Whereas Ch. 10:12 distinguishes three types of animals, Ch. 11:6 distinguishes four, adding "wild beasts" to "fourfooted beasts of the earth" (cf. Gen. 1:24 f.).[10] The version of Peter's refusal in v. 8 is even closer than the version in Ch. 10:14 to Ezekiel's protest, when directed to eat unclean food: "Ah Lord Jehovah! behold, my soul hath not been polluted; ... neither came there abominable flesh into my mouth" (Ezek. 4:14).

11–14 Then he told how Cornelius's messengers came to invite him to Caesarea, and how he went with them at the Spirit's bidding, "making no distinction" (v. 12). The six Christians from Joppa who had accompanied him to Caesarea had come with him also to Jerusalem, and they were present as witnesses to his account. The reference to "the angel" in v. 13 with its assumption that the story of Cornelius's supernatural visitant is already known is directed to the readers of Acts rather than to Peter's Jerusalem audience; we realize, of course, that what we have here is a brief summary of the story that Peter told. According to this account, the angel informed Cornelius that Peter would speak words by which he and his household would receive salvation. We have already seen (Ch. 10:35) that Cornelius was accepted by God as a man who feared Him and practised righteousness. Throughout the Bible, divine judgment is regularly pronounced in accordance with a man's works;[11] but salvation is not of works but of grace, and salvation did not enter Cornelius's house until Peter came there with the gospel. The "house" (v. 14) included not only Cornelius's family in the modern sense, but all who were under his authority—slaves, attendants, and others.[12]

15–17 Then Peter reached the climax of his narration, telling how he had hardly begun to address Cornelius[13] and his house-

---

[9] Similarly the verb "were drawn up" (Gk. ἀνεσπάσθη) in v. 10 is more vigorous than "was received up" (Gk. ἀνελήμφθη) in Ch. 10:16.

[10] Cf. the fourfold division in Ps. 148:10, "Beasts and all cattle; creeping things and flying birds."

[11] Cf., e.g., Rom. 2:6; Rev. 20:12 f.; 22:12.

[12] All who came within the scope of the Latin familia. Cf. the similar language used to the jailor of Philippi in Ch. 16:31.

[13] Gk. ἐν δὲ τῷ ἄρξασθαί με λέγειν (cf. Ch. 10:44, ἔτι λαλοῦντος τοῦ Πέτρου). The idea of beginning need not be pressed unduly (cf. p. 225, n. 41). In several places in the narrative portions of NT, ἄρχομαι is little more than a Semitizing redundant auxiliary; cf. J. H. Moulton, Grammar of NT Greek i (Edinburgh, 1906), pp. 14 f.

hold when the Holy Spirit descended upon them, just as He had descended upon Peter and his fellow-disciples at Pentecost. The words of the risen Christ to His disciples, "John indeed baptized with water; but ye shall be baptized in the Holy Spirit not many days hence" (Ch. 1:5), had been quickly fulfilled on the day of Pentecost; but as Peter saw what took place in the house of Cornelius, and heard those Gentiles speak with tongues and magnify God, these words came afresh to his mind, and he recognized that now they were being fulfilled anew. God had made no difference between believing Gentiles and believing Jews; how could Peter maintain a barrier which God plainly did not recognize? To do so would be to oppose God. There is no express reference here to the baptism of the Gentiles, though it is perhaps implied in the language of v. 17.

18 Nothing could be said to counter Peter's argument. God had acted, and clearly shown His will. That He had bestowed His blessing on Gentiles, giving them the change of heart and mind which results in eternal life, was a matter for wonder and praise. Their criticism ceased; their worship began. The practical problems which were to become so acute when large-scale Gentile evangelization began did not arise at this stage. Even so, we may surmise that the approval of Peter's action was more whole-hearted on the part of his fellow-apostles than on the part of the zealous rank and file of the Jerusalem church. This may have been one reason why some of them appear to have recognized the ascetic James the Just as their leader henceforth rather than the apostles, although there were other reasons as well.[14] But Jerusalem had at least admitted the principle of evangelizing Gentiles, and done so in time for a new advance farther north, as a result of which Gentiles were evangelized and converted to the Christian way on a scale which no one in Jerusalem had dreamed of.

[14] See p. 253 (on Ch. 12:17).

3. ANTIOCH

(Ch. 11:19–30)

(a) The First Gentile Church (Ch. 11:19–26)

19 They therefore that were scattered abroad upon the
tribulation that arose about Stephen travelled as far
as Phoenicia, and Cyprus, and Antioch, speaking the
word to none save only to Jews.

20 But there were some of them, men of Cyprus and
Cyrene, who, when they were come to Antioch, spake
unto the Greeks[15] also, preaching the Lord Jesus.

21 And the hand of the Lord was with them: and a great
number that believed turned unto the Lord.

22 And the report concerning them came to the ears of
the church which was in Jerusalem: and they sent
forth Barnabas as far as Antioch:

23 who, when he was come, and had seen the grace of
God, was glad; and he exhorted them all, that with
purpose of heart they would cleave unto the Lord:

24 for he was a good man, and full of the Holy Spirit and
of faith: and much people was added unto the Lord.[16]

25 And he went forth to Tarsus to seek for Saul;

26 and when he had found him, he brought him unto
Antioch.[17] And it came to pass, that even for a whole
year they were gathered together with the church, and
taught much people; and that the disciples were called
Christians first in Antioch.

[15] Gk. πρὸς τοὺς Ἕλληνας (this is the reading of אᶜ A D* 1518, Eusebius
and Chrysostom, and at first sight of all the versions, although Ἕλλην and
Ἑλληνιστής tend to fall together in the versions). B D² E 33 81 and the
Byzantine text have πρὸς τοὺς Ἑλληνιστάς (hence also the aberrant reading
εὐαγγελιστάς in א*). The context plainly requires the sense "Greeks" (as
opposed to Jews) and not Grecians or Hellenists; therefore, if Ἑλληνιστάς,
the more difficult reading, is preferred here, it must be used in a wider sense
("Greek-speakers") which includes Greek-speaking Gentiles as well as Greek-
speaking Jews.

[16] The first hand in Cod. B omits "unto the Lord".

[17] The Western text recasts this sentence: "And hearing that Saul was in
Tarsus he went away looking for him, and when he had met in with him he
encouraged him to come to Antioch." It then continues: "And when they
arrived they mingled for a whole year with the church and taught much
people, and then the disciples were first popularly called Christians at Antioch."

19 Luke's narrative now goes back to the same point of departure as we found in Ch. 8:4, which opens with the same words. There he related how those who were "scattered abroad" as a result of the persecution that followed Stephen's death "went about preaching the word"; here he tells how some of these in due course made their way north along the Phoenician seaboard, from which some took ship for Cyprus, while others continued along the coastal road until they reached Antioch.[18]

Antioch, situated fifteen miles from the mouth of the Orontes, was founded by Seleucus Nicator in 300 B.C., and became the capital city of the Seleucid monarchy.[19] When Syria was incorporated in the Roman Empire in 64 B.C., Antioch was made a free city, enjoying its own municipal government, and became the seat of the provincial administration of Syria. It was the third largest city in the world at this time, coming next to Rome and Alexandria, and like them it had a large Jewish community. It is Antioch that the Roman satirist Juvenal has in mind when he complains of the way in which "the sewage of the Syrian Orontes has for long been discharged into the Tiber" (*Satire* iii. 62).[20] The city was proverbial for its lax sexual morals; this reputation was mainly due to the cult of Artemis and Apollo at Daphne,[21] five miles distant, where the ancient Syrian worship of Astarte, with its ritual prostitution, was carried on under Greek nomenclature. But a new chapter in the city's history was now to begin, for Antioch was about to become the metropolis of Gentile Christianity.

20 Thus far, the Christians who had fled from the Jerusalem persecution, Hellenists though they were, had restricted their evangelizing activity to the Jewish communities of the various places to which they came. No doubt the members of these Jewish communities were Hellenists like themselves. But in Antioch some daring spirits among the incoming Christians, men of Cyprus and

[18] From this point onwards we have a narrative with Syrian Antioch as its centre of interest (apart from the incident of Ch. 12:1–23): it contains three episodes: (*a*) the evangelization of Antioch (Ch. 11:19–26); (*b*) the famine-relief delegation to Judaea (Chs. 11:27–30 and 12:25) and (*c*) the first missionary tour of Barnabas and Saul, based on Antioch (Chs. 13:1—14:28).

[19] See G. W. Elderkin, R. Stillwell and F. O. Waage, *Antioch-on-the-Orontes* (Princeton, 1934–48).

[20] In this "sewage" Juvenal may include Gentile Christianity, which took its rise on the banks of the Orontes.

[21] *Daphnici mores* became a synonym for this kind of immorality. Antioch itself was called at times ἡ ἐπὶ Δάφνῃ to distinguish it from other cities of the same name.

Cyrene, took a momentous step forward. If the gospel message was so good for Jews, might it not be good for Gentiles also? At any rate they would make the experiment. So they began to make known to the Greek population of Antioch the claims of Jesus as Lord and Saviour. To present Him as Messiah to people who knew nothing of the hope of Israel would have been a meaningless procedure, but the Greek terms *Kyrios* ("Lord") and *Soter* ("Saviour") were widely current in the religious world of the eastern Mediterranean.[22] Many were attempting to find in various mystery cults a divine lord who could guarantee salvation and immortality to his devotees; now the pagans of Antioch were assured that what they vainly sought in those quarters could be secured through the Son of God who had lately become man, suffered death and conquered the grave in Palestine.

21 This enterprise met with instant success. The Gentiles took to the Christian message as the very thing that they had been waiting for, as something that exactly suited their case, and a large number of them believed the gospel and yielded their allegiance to Jesus as Lord. It may be that some of the Gentiles who believed belonged to the class of God-fearers who already knew something of the OT revelation by attendance at Jewish synagogues; it would be in accordance with the analogy of other places if such people formed the nucleus of the Gentile converts in Antioch. But Luke does not say so, and we cannot be sure. At any rate, the power of God was manifest in the conversion of the Gentiles in this place. An Ethiopian eunuch might have become a Christian some time previously while sitting in his covered waggon on the Gaza road, and a Roman centurion and his household might have believed the gospel in his home at Caesarea as an apostle unfolded it to them, but the scale of Gentile evangelization in Antioch was something entirely new.

22–24 The leaders of the Jerusalem church recognized the novelty of the situation at Antioch when news of it reached them, and just as Peter and John had earlier gone to Samaria to investigate Philip's missionary service there, so now Jerusalem sent a delegate to Antioch to look into the strange events that were

---

[22] This does not mean that the proclamation of Jesus as Lord and Saviour was something of Gentile origin, derived from the terminology and viewpoint of the mystery cults. See the exhaustive and conclusive discussion by J. G. Machen in *The Origin of Paul's Religion* (New York, 1921), pp. 211–317.

being enacted in that great city. It was a critical moment: much—far more than they could have realized—depended on the delegate whom they chose to send. In the providence of God, they chose the best man for this delicate and important work—Barnabas, the "son of encouragement". Barnabas himself was a Cypriote Jew by birth, like some of those who had begun to preach the gospel to the Antiochene Gentiles, and his sympathies would in any case be wider than those of Jewish Christians who had never set foot outside Judaea.

To Antioch, then, Barnabas was sent, as the representative of the mother church in Jerusalem. When he reached Antioch, his generous spirit was filled with joy at what he found. Here was the grace of God in action, bringing blessing to Jews and Gentiles alike as they heard and accepted the good news. True to his name, Barnabas gave all the encouragement he could to missionaries and converts alike. They had begun well; what they needed was the gift of perseverance, and he urged them to carry on and maintain their loyal service and obedience to the Lord in whom they had believed. The presence of a man of such sterling character and faith, a man full of the Holy Spirit,[23] gave them the stimulus they needed to prosecute their missionary work even more vigorously; the number of converts increased rapidly.

25–26 Soon the dimensions of the work were such that Barnabas could not hope to supervise it single-handed. He must find a colleague. But it was no easy matter to find the right kind of colleague for this kind of responsibility. Barnabas, however, decided that he knew the right man for the situation, if only he could locate him. Several years had gone by since Saul of Tarsus had been escorted to Caesarea by his new Christian friends in Jerusalem, and had taken ship there for his native Tarsus. Barnabas could think of no man so eminently suited for the work to be done in Antioch. He therefore went to Tarsus in person to seek him out—perhaps a task of some difficulty, since Saul appears to have been disinherited for his Christian confession and could no longer be found at his ancestral home.[24] He found him, however, and

---

[23] *Cf.* the description of Stephen in Ch. 6:5.

[24] The verb translated "to seek for" (ἀναζητῆσαι) is found in the papyri, where, according to J. H. Moulton and G. Milligan, *The Vocabulary of the Greek Testament* (Edinburgh, 1930), p. 32, it "is specially used of searching for human beings, with an implication of difficulty, as in the NT passages." For the likelihood that Saul was disinherited *cf.* his statement in Phil 3:8, that for

took him to Antioch, and there for a whole year the good work proceeded apace. More converts were added to the Christian community, and when they were added, they received systematic instruction in the principles of Christian faith and life. No difficulty seems to have been felt at this stage about the joining in Christian fellowship of Jewish converts and Gentile converts. The new life into which they had entered was wide enough to accommodate believers of the most diverse backgrounds. Antioch was a cosmopolitan city, where Jew and Gentile, Greek and barbarian rubbed shoulders, where Mediterranean civilization met the Syrian desert; racial and religious differences which loomed so large in Judaea seemed much less important here. The church of Antioch from the outset had an *ethos* quite distinct from that of the Jerusalem church. The pagans of Antioch, too, knew all about these people, for the Christians did not keep quiet about their faith, but proclaimed it wherever they went. *Christos*—the Greek form of the title Messiah—might be the name of an office to Greek-speaking Jews, but to the pagans of Antioch it was simply the name of a man of whom these people were always talking: a curious name, to be sure, unless it were the same as the common slave-name *Chrestos* ("useful").[25] "Who are these people?" one Antiochene would ask another, as two or three unofficial missionaries gathered a knot of more or less interested hearers and disputants around them in one of the city colonnades. "O, these are the people who are always talking about Christos, the Christ-people, the Christians." And so it was in Antioch, says Luke, that the followers of Jesus first came to be popularly known as Christians.[26]

Christ's sake he had "suffered the loss of all things." It was probably during these hidden years in Tarsus and its neighbourhood that he endured some of the sufferings listed in 2 Cor. 11:23 ff., and the mysterious experience described in 2 Cor. 12:2 ff. We may indeed go farther and infer from certain indications in NT that he had begun Gentile evangelization on his own initiative before Barnabas brought him to Antioch. He had already received his commission for this work (Acts 22:21; *cf.* p. 443), and his references in Gal. 2:2, 7, to the gospel which he had been charged to preach among the Gentiles may look back to an earlier time than his being fetched to Antioch by Barnabas. Barnabas indeed may have known something of Saul's evangelistic work in Cilicia; at any rate the fact that he went to Tarsus to find him strengthens the impression received from Ch. 9:27, that he had known Saul at an earlier period than our narrative explicitly indicates.

[25] Suetonius (*Life of Claudius* xxv. 4) speaks of the riots which broke out within the Jewish community at Rome "at the instigation of Chrestus" (*cf.* p. 368 with n. 10, on Ch. 18:2).

[26] The verb rendered "were called" is χρηματίσαι, literally meaning "to

THE BOOK OF THE ACTS

(b) Famine Relief (Ch. 11:27-30)

27 Now in these days there came down prophets from Jerusalem unto Antioch.[27]

28 And there stood up one of them named Agabus, and signified by the Spirit that there should be a great famine over all the world: which came to pass in the days of Claudius.[28]

29 And the disciples, every man according to his ability, determined to send relief unto the brethren that dwelt in Judaea:

30 which also they did, sending it to the elders by the hand of Barnabas and Saul.

27 The gift of prophecy in the apostolic church was like the gift of tongues in that it was exercised under the immediate inspiration of God; it differed from it in that it was expressed in the speaker's ordinary language. The place for this spiritual gift in the church is recognized in the Pauline epistles,[29] and here and there the narrative of Acts illustrates how it was exercised.

28 Among prophets who came to Antioch from Jerusalem in

transact business". To transact business under a particular name is in effect to be generally known by that name (so here). E. J. Bickerman, "The Name of Christians", in HThR xlii (1949), pp. 71 ff., maintains that χρηματίζω must mean "assume the name," "style oneself," and that it was therefore the disciples who first began to call themselves Christians, meaning thereby "servants of Christ", *ministri regis* (*cf. οἱ τοῦ χριστοῦ* in 1 Cor. 15:23), just as the *Caesariani* were emperor's servants (*οἱ τοῦ Καίσαρος*). This χρηματίζω must be distinguished from χρηματίζω meaning "give an oracular response" (the passive of which is translated "was warned of God" in Ch. 10:22). *Cf.* J. H. Moulton and W. F. Howard, *Grammar of NT Greek* ii (Edinburgh, 1929), p. 265. The term "Christians" (Gk. Χριστιανοί, spelt Χρηστιανοί, "Chrestians" as if from Chrestus, in the codices ℵ and 81) is a Latin formation. In NT it appears in two other places—in Ch. 26:28 on the lips of the younger Agrippa, and in 1 Peter 4:16 in the language of the indictment when one is made to suffer "as a Christian." The earliest occurrences of the term in non-Christian literature are in Josephus, *Ant.* xviii. 3.3 (where "the tribe of Christians" is said to take its name from "the so-called Christ"); Pliny, *Epistles* x. 96, 97 (correspondence with Trajan about Christians); Tacitus, *Annals* xv. 44 (where Nero's scapegoats in A.D. 64 are said to have been "a class of people loathed for their vices, who were commonly styled Christians after Christ, who was executed by the procurator Pontius Pilate when Tiberius was emperor"); and Suetonius, *Life of Nero* xvi. 2 ("Punishment was inflicted on the Christians, a class of men addicted to a mischievous and novel superstition").

[27] The Western text links vv. 27 and 28 thus: "and there was much rejoicing; and when we were gathered together, one of them, Agabus by name, spoke signifying . . ."

[28] The Byzantine text reads "Claudius Caesar" (*cf.* AV).

[29] *Cf.* 1 Cor. 12:28; 14:29 ff.; Eph. 4:11.

242

those days was one called Agabus,[30] who announced, when he was under the control of the Holy Spirit, that there would be great famine throughout the whole Roman world.[31] As a matter of fact, says Luke, this actually happened in the reign of Claudius; and we know from other sources that this emperor's reign (A.D. 41–54) was indeed marked by a succession of bad harvests and serious famines in various parts of the empire.

If a true tradition is represented by the Western reading of this passage, according to which Agabus uttered his prophecy "when we were gathered together", then Luke had personal cause to remember Agabus and his words, and the effect which they produced on the church at Antioch. Although the Western reading is probably not part of the original text, it does reflect knowledge of the tradition which has been preserved independently in the anti-Marcionite prologue to the third Gospel (c. A.D. 170),[32] that Luke was a native of Syrian Antioch. If Luke was one of the Antiochene Gentiles who were evangelized in those days, we can readily appreciate both his interest in Antioch and his enthusiasm for the Gentile mission of Christianity.

29–30 The Christians of Antioch took the prophet's announcement seriously. In time of famine Palestine was liable to suffer severely; they therefore bethought themselves of the mother-church in Jerusalem and set aside a sum of money to relieve the plight of their brethren there. The relief-fund was a matter of individual concern; the various members of the Antiochene church appear to have set aside a fixed sum out of their property or income as a

---

[30] Agabus reappears in Ch. 21:10, in a "we" section of Acts.

[31] The "world" here and in Luke 2:1 is the οἰκουμένη —the Latin *orbis terrarum*. Although there was no single famine affecting the whole empire simultaneously in the reign of Claudius, classical writers testify to the famine-conditions which were prevalent in his dominions at various times during his reign (cf. Suetonius, *Life of Claudius* xviii. 2; Tacitus, *Annals* xii. 43; Dio Cassius, *History* lx. 11; Eusebius, *Chronicle*, Year of Abraham 2065; Orosius, *History* vii. 6.17). It would be better to keep the more general expression "great dearth" (as in AV) than to follow the more particular expression "a great famine" (as in ARV, ERV, RSV). In any case, there is no need to follow C. C. Torrey in his supposition that "all the world" represents a Greek misunderstanding of the Aramaic phrase which here means "all the land" (i.e. of Israel). This is not one of the sections of Acts where an Aramaic substratum is probable.

[32] This prologue begins with the words "Luke was an Antiochian of Syria"; the statement is repeated by Eusebius (*Ecclesiastical History* iii. 4) and Jerome (*On Illustrious Men*, 7; *Preface to Commentary on Matthew*). Cf. p. 17, n. 6, and Ch. 6:5 with exposition and note (p. 129. n. 8).

contribution to it, much as Paul later advised the Corinthian Christians to do (1 Cor. 16:1 ff.). When all was ready to send the money to Jerusalem, they deputed Barnabas and Saul to take it as their representatives.[33]

This Jerusalem visit of Barnabas and Saul is probably to be dated about A.D. 46. In or about that year Judaea was hard hit by famine, and Josephus tells us how Helena, the Jewish queen-mother of Adiabene, east of the Tigris, bought corn in Egypt and figs in Cyprus at that time and distributed them in Jerusalem to relieve the hungry population.[34]

This is probably the visit to Jerusalem which Paul describes in Gal. 2:1 ff. (Reasons against identifying the latter visit with that of Acts 15 are suggested on pp. 298 ff. below.) If our identification is right, Barnabas and Saul took the opportunity afforded by this famine-relief visit to have an interview with the leaders of the Jerusalem church[35]—Peter, John, and James the Lord's brother in particular—and satisfied themselves that their status as apostles to the Gentiles was recognized by the Jerusalem apostles.[36] Paul's statement in Gal. 2:2, that he went up to Jerusalem on that occasion "by revelation", agrees well enough with Luke's account of the prophecy of Agabus; and there is probably a direct allusion to the primary object of the visit in Gal. 2:10, which may be rendered: "Only they asked us to go on remembering their poor, and in fact I had made a special point of doing this very thing."[37]

[33] Such an act of fellowship was calculated to strengthen the bond between the totally Jewish-Christian church of Jerusalem and the mainly Gentile-Christian church of Antioch. The Jerusalem church appears at an early time to have suffered from chronic poverty; this may partly explain the name Ebionites (Heb. ha'ebyonim, "the poor") assumed by one influential Jewish-Christian community. Cf. p. 394 with n. 33, p. 425, n. 15, p. 429 with n. 28, p. 470 with n. 19, and pp. 405 f. on Paul's collection for the Jerusalem church.

[34] Josephus, Antiquities iii. 15.3; xx. 2.5; xx. 5.2. Josephus dates this event in the procuratorships of Cuspius Fadus (c. 44–46) and Tiberius Julius Alexander (c. 46–48).

[35] The contribution for famine-relief was handed over to the elders (v. 30), not to the apostles. With the dispersal of the Hellenistic almoners of Ch. 6 in the persecution that followed Stephen's death, the charge of such financial matters may have been taken over by the elders (Gk. πρεσβύτεροι). The elders of the Jerusalem church, among whom James the brother of Jesus was primus inter pares, seem to have constituted a kind of Nazarene Sanhedrin, distinct from the twelve apostles.

[36] Not that their apostolic status required such recognition (Gal. 2:6).

[37] See J. N. Sanders, Foundations of the Christian Faith (London, 1950), p. 34.

CHAPTER XII

4. HEROD AGRIPPA I AND THE CHURCH
(Ch. 12:1-25)

(a)   Peter's Imprisonment and Escape (Ch. 12:1-19)

1 Now about that time Herod the king put forth his
hands to afflict certain of the church.

2 And he killed James the brother of John with the
sword.

3 And when he saw that it[1] pleased the Jews, he proceeded to seize Peter also.   And *those* were the days
of unleavened bread.

4 And when he had taken him, he put him in prison, and
delivered him to four quaternions of soldiers to guard
him; intending after the Passover to bring him forth
to the people.

5 Peter therefore was kept in the prison:[2] but prayer
was made earnestly of the church unto God for him.

6 And when Herod was about to bring him forth, the
same night Peter was sleeping between two soldiers,
bound with two chains: and guards before the door
kept the prison.

7 And behold, an angel of the Lord stood by him, and
a light shined in the cell: and he smote Peter on the
side, and awoke him, saying, Rise up quickly.   And
his chains fell off from his hands.

8 And the angel said unto him, Gird thyself, and bind
on thy sandals.   And he did so.   And he saith unto him,
Cast thy garment about thee, and follow me.

9 And he went out, and followed; and he knew not that
it was true which was done by the angel, but thought
he saw a vision.

10 And when they were past the first and the second
guard, they came unto the iron gate that leadeth into
the city; which opened to them of its own accord: and
they went out,[3] and passed on through one street; and
straightway the angel departed from him.

---

[1] For "it" the Western text reads "his proceeding against the faithful."
[2] Some forms of the Western text add "by the king's cohort."
[3] The Western text adds "and went down the seven steps."

245

11 And when Peter was come to himself, he said, Now I know of a truth, that the Lord hath sent forth his angel and delivered me out of the hand of Herod, and from all the expectation of the people of the Jews.

12 And when he had considered *the thing,* he came to the house of Mary the mother of John whose surname was Mark; where many were gathered together and were praying.

13 And when he knocked at the door of the gate, a maid came to answer, named Rhoda.

14 And when she knew Peter's voice, she opened not the gate for joy, but ran in, and told that Peter stood before the gate.

15 And they said unto her, Thou art mad. But she confidently affirmed that it was even so. And they said, It is his angel.

16 But Peter continued knocking: and when they had opened, they saw him, and were amazed.

17 But he, beckoning unto them with the hand to hold their peace. declared unto them how the Lord had brought him forth out of the prison. And he said, Tell these things unto James, and to the brethren. And he departed, and went to another place.

18 Now as soon as it was day, there was no small stir among the soldiers, what was become of Peter.

19 And when Herod had sought for him, and found him not, he examined the guards, and commanded that they should be put to death. And he went down from Judaea to Caesarea, and tarried there.

1 "Herod the king" of this chapter is Herod Agrippa I, a grandson of Herod the Great and the Hasmonean princess Mariamne. born in 11 B.C. and sent by his mother to be brought up at Rome after the execution of his father Aristobulus in 7 B.C. At Rome he grew up on terms of intimate friendship with some members of the imperial family, especially with Gaius, the grand-nephew of the Emperor Tiberius. When Gaius succeeded Tiberius as emperor in A.D. 37, he bestowed upon Agrippa the former tetrarchies of Philip and Lysanias in southern Syria (*cf.* Luke 3:1), together with the title "king". Two years later Agrippa's kingdom was augmented by the addition of Galilee and Peraea, the former territory of his uncle Antipas, whom Gaius deposed from his rule and sent into exile. When Claudius was made emperor in A.D. 41, after the

assassination of Gaius, he further increased Agrippa's realm by the addition of Judaea, which since A.D. 6 had been administered on the emperor's behalf by a procurator. Agrippa was more popular with the Jews than most members of the Herod dynasty were, largely owing to his descent from the Hasmonean royal family; and he set himself sedulously to win and retain their good will.[4] It is evidence of a change in the attitude of the people of Jerusalem towards the apostles, who had not been molested in the persecution that followed Stephen's death, that Agrippa should make them his principal target in his attack upon the church.[5]

2   The first of his victims was James the son of Zebedee, whom he had executed. He was the first of the apostles to meet a martyr's death, and thus he experienced the fulfilment of Jesus' promise to him and his brother John, that they would drink from His cup and be baptized with His baptism (Mark 10:39). His brother John, on the other hand, after suffering in his turn "for the word of God and the testimony of Jesus" (Rev. 1:9), was to outlive all the other apostles. The theory propounded by some, that in the original form of the present narrative James and John were both executed by Herod, is quite without warrant.[6]

3   If we ask why this attack on the apostles should have "pleased the Jews", the answer may be found in the wider phase of apostolic activity which had recently set in with Peter's visit to the Gentile Cornelius in Caesarea. Those Jewish Christians who, under the leadership of the elders, maintained a more rigorous attitude to any

[4] The Mishnah (*Sota* vii. 8) relates how he read "the law of the kingdom" (Deut. 17:14–20) publicly at the Feast of Tabernacles in a sabbatical year (presumably A.D. 40), and wept as he read the words "thou mayest not put a foreigner over thee, who is not thy brother" (v. 15), for he remembered the Edomite ancestry of the Herods. But the people, thinking rather of his Hasmonean descent, cried out repeatedly, "Be not dismayed; you are indeed our brother!"

[5] The words "about that time" (v. 1) refer to the period of the events of Ch. 11:27–30; actually the events of Ch. 12 fell between the prophecy of Agabus and the departure of Barnabas and Saul for Jerusalem.

[6] E. Schwartz (ZNW xi [1910], pp. 89 ff.), followed by A. Loisy (*Les Actes des Apôtres* [Paris, 1920], pp. 482 ff.) and R. Eisler (*The Enigma of the Fourth Gospel* [London, 1938], pp. 73 ff.), argued that the original text read "James and John his brother" or the like, instead of "James the brother of John". The theory that John the apostle suffered martyrdom at Jewish hands either on this occasion or at some later time before the fall of Jerusalem rests on the flimsiest foundation: see the discussion by H. P. V. Nunn in *The Son of Zebedee and the Fourth Gospel* (London, 1932), pp. 1 ff., and in *The Authorship of the Fourth Gospel* (Eton, 1952), pp. 87 ff.

weakening of the bonds of Jewish particularism, continued to enjoy general toleration for some two decades more. It is no accident that, after putting James to death[7] and testing the popular reaction, Agrippa should lay hands upon the leader of the apostles— the one, moreover, who had taken the initiative in fraternizing with Gentiles.

4 The seven days of "unleavened bread" were beginning when Peter was arrested; he was therefore kept in prison for the duration of the festal period.[8] Agrippa's intention was to bring him out for trial and public execution immediately after this period had expired. But, knowing how many sympathizers—secret as well as open—the apostles had in Jerusalem, he took special precautions against an attempt to free the prisoner. Four relays of soldiers took it in turn to guard him: four guards at a time, one on either side, and two at his cell-door.[9]

5-9 Meanwhile continuous prayer was being offered for Peter by the united church in Jerusalem—the supplication of righteous men which "availeth much in its working" (Jas. 5:16). And while the Christians were continuing in fervent prayer during what, in Agrippa's intention, was to be Peter's last night on earth, their prayer, unknown to themselves, was receiving an effective answer. For Peter was roused from sleep—the calm sleep that springs from a good conscience and quiet confidence in God—by a blow on his side and a voice which bade him get up quickly. The fetters by which he was handcuffed to the soldiers on either side fell away as he rose. The cell was lit up; an unknown visiter stood by him, and ordered him to fasten his girdle and tie on his sandals, wrap his cloak around him and follow. Peter did so, amazed at it all,

[7] Eusebius (*Ecclesiastical History* ii. 9) preserves the tradition from Clement of Alexandria's seventh book of *Hypotyposes*, telling how the officer who guarded James was so impressed by his demeanor that he confessed himself a Christian and was beheaded along with him.

[8] The days of unleavened bread lasted from Nisan 14 (Passover Eve) to Nisan 21 (Ex. 12:18). "Passover" in v. 4 is used in a broad sense of the whole festal period which began with the paschal celebrations. *Cf.* Luke 22:1, and the discussion by Norval Geldenhuys in his *Commentary on Luke* (London and Grand Rapids, 1950), p. 548, n. 2, and pp. 661 ff.

[9] This may refer particularly to night-time, in which case there would be one quaternion for each watch of the night. Vegetius, in his treatise *On Military Affairs* iii. 8, says: "The watches are divided into four according to the water-clock so that it is not necessary to keep watch for more than three hours of the night."

not realizing that it was really taking place, but suspecting that it was all a dream, and that he would soon wake up to find himself with the soldiers in the cell, compelled to face whatever the morning might bring. Through one gate and another they passed, both of them guarded: Peter, however, was probably "allowed to pass the first and the second, being taken presumably as a servant; but no servant would be expected to pass beyond the outermost ward at night, and a different course was needed there" (W. M. Ramsay, *St. Paul the Traveller* [London, 1920], p. 28). Wonderful to relate, however, the outmost gate opened automatically[10] as Peter and his mysterious guide came to it, and they found themselves in the open street, after descending "the seven steps", as the Western text informs us. (This addition has such a circumstantial appearance that we may regard it as a genuine piece of local colour, derived from an informant who knew Jerusalem before its fall in A.D. 70.) We are not told where Peter's prison was, but it may well have been in the fortress of Antonia, north-west of the temple area (*cf*. Ch. 21:31 ff.).

10-11 They traversed one street, and Peter suddenly found himself alone. Thus far he had followed his rescuer like a man in a trance or a dream; now he woke up to his strange situation and took stock of it. This was the finger of God; it was an angel of the Lord who had come to snatch him from his imminent fate.

What account are we to give of Peter's escape from prison? What kind of messenger was it that released him? Whether human or superhuman, he was no doubt a messenger of God. There are indeed some features of the narrative which would lead a police detective to conclude that it was a carefully planned and skilfully executed "inside job"; probably that was Agrippa's own conclusion. There are other features which are strongly reminiscent of the "form" in which other stories of miraculous escapes from prison are related in ancient literature. But Peter apparently recognized divine intervention of a supernatural kind in the event, and so evidently did Luke; the opening words of v. 7 are very similar

---

[10] Gk. αὐτομάτη. Compare the opening of prison doors by a divine messenger in Ch. 5:19, and by an earthquake in Ch. 16:26. Josephus tells in the *Jewish War* vi. 5.3 how, shortly before the rebellion of A.D. 66, the heavy eastern gate of the inner court of the temple opened by night "of its own accord" (αὐτομάτως). Several other examples of the automatic opening of doors occur in Greek literature from Homer onwards.

to the words at the beginning of Luke 2:9, where the angel appears to the shepherds to announce the birth of Christ.

A striking modern parallel has been quoted more than once from the experiences of Sundar Singh. By order of the chief lama of a certain Tibetan community he was thrown into a dry well, the lid of which was securely locked. Here he was left to die, like many others before him, whose bones and rotting flesh lay at the bottom of the well. On the third night, when he had been crying to God in prayer, he heard someone unlocking the lid of the well and removing it, and then a voice spoke, telling him to take hold of the rope that was being lowered. He did so, and was glad to find a loop at the bottom of the rope in which he could place his foot. for his right arm had been injured before he was thrown down. He was then drawn up, the lid was replaced and locked, but when he looked round to thank his rescuer, he could find no trace of him. The fresh air revived him, and his injured arm felt whole again. When morning came, he returned to the city where he had been arrested, and resumed preaching. News was brought to the lama that the man who had been thrown into the execution-well for preaching had been liberated and was preaching again. Sundar Singh was brought before him and questioned, and told the story of his release. The lama declared that someone must have got hold of the key and let him out, but when search was made for the key, it was found attached to the lama's own girdle! (See B. H. Streeter and A. J. Appasamy, *The Sadhu* [London. 1921], pp. 30 ff.)

"Now," says L. E. Browne, "although this story is in our own time, its interpretation is as difficult as the story of St. Peter's escape. It is possible that both events were non-miraculous, that some well-disposed person acted as rescuer. But the difficulty in the way of a rescue in either case suggests that both were actually miraculous interventions of God. One striking difference between the two accounts is the opinion of the prisoner at the time. St. Peter thought it was all a vision until he found himself safe and sound. The Sadhu thought the rescuer was a man until he disappeared" (*The Acts of the Apostles* [London, 1925], pp. 204 f.).

The fact that Christianity is a revelation from God communicated through supernatural events does not mean that wherever in the Bible we have a narrative which is explicable both in natural and in supernatural terms, we must always prefer the supernatural explanation. In every such case the actual terms of the narrative, together with its context and significance, will guide us in our interpretation. Here, however, direct divine intervention is strongly indicated. But in any case the narrative is a witness to the delivering grace of God and to the power of earnest prayer. That James should die while Peter should escape is a mystery of divine providence which has been repeated countless times in the course of Christian history, down to our own day.

12 The first thing to do was to acquaint the Christians of Jerusalem with his escape; the next was to go into hiding, lest Agrippa's police should find him again. So first Peter made his way to one of the chief meeting-places of Jerusalem, the house of Mary, the mother of Mark. Here we have our first certain introduction to one who was to play an important part in Christian history over the next thirty years. According to later writers, Mark acted as Peter's interpreter in Rome and reproduced Peter's preaching in the second Gospel;[11] afterwards he is said to have gone to Egypt and founded the church in Alexandria.[12] He may have been Luke's informant for this and other narratives in the earlier part of Acts. It is an attractive, but unverifiable, surmise that this was the house in which our Lord and His disciples kept the Last Supper; this possibility links itself suggestively with the very probable view that the young man mentioned as being a witness of Christ's arrest in Mark 14:51 f. was Mark himself.[13]

13–16 The scene that now unfolds itself at the street-door of this house and inside the house is full of vivid humour. Rhoda's excitement at hearing Peter's voice makes her forget to open the door and let him in; those within cannot believe that the answer to their prayers is standing outside the door; Rhoda must be mad,

---

[11] Cf. the statements of Papias, Irenaeus, Clement of Alexandria and others quoted by Eusebius, *Ecclesiastical History* ii. 15; iii. 39; v. 8; vi. 14.

[12] Cf. Eusebius, *Ecclesiastical History* ii. 16, 24. It is difficult to be sure what (if any) element of historical fact underlies the tradition connecting Mark with Alexandria. Cf. Ch. 18:24, with exposition and note (p. 381. n. 53). "Mark's connection with Alexandria is not mentioned by Clement or Origen, and in the second half of the 3rd century Dionysius, Bishop of Alexandria, could write of Mark without recording so notable a tradition about his own see" (S. G. F. Brandon, *The Fall of Jerusalem and the Christian Church* [London, 1951], p. 222, n. 1).

[13] See J. A. Robertson, *The Hidden Romance of the NT* [London, 1920], pp. 25 ff.

or else it is Peter's guardian angel, his spirit-counterpart,[14] that she has heard; meanwhile Peter stands insistently and anxiously knocking for admission—not too loudly, for the hue and cry may already have been raised, and Mary's house is one of the first places to which a search-party will come.

17 When at last he was admitted, he told them about his miraculous release, and directed them to give this news to "James, and to the brethren." Then he took his departure, and went underground so successfully that no one to this day has succeeded in discovering for certain where he went. Peter himself did not tell anybody, and no one knew.[15]

The description of Peter's anxious gesture, as he besought the surprised and excited company to make less noise, is surely the authentic touch of an eyewitness—whether Luke got the story from Mark or, as Ramsay argued, from Rhoda the slave-girl (*Bearing of Recent Discovery on the Trustworthiness of the NT* [London, 1915], pp. 209 ff.).

In addition to the company which met in Mary's house, there was evidently another associated with James the brother of Jesus. They too must be told of Peter's escape. The "brethren" associated with James may include the "elders" mentioned in Ch. 11:30. It appears that by this time (A.D. 44) James had attained a position of leadership in the Jerusalem church. When Barnabas and Paul had their interview with the "pillars" of that church, recorded in

---

[14] Apparently this angel was regarded as capable of assuming the bodily appearance of the human being whom he protected, like the *fravashi* in Zoroastrianism. The rôle of the angel Raphael in Tobit 5:4 ff. probably reflects this *fravashi* conception. *Cf.* J. H. Moulton in JThS iii (1902), pp. 516 f., and his *Early Zoroastrianism* (London, 1913), pp. 254 ff. For the general ministry of guardian angels see Gen. 48:16; Dan. 3:28; 6:22; Matt. 18:10 (a specially relevant passage) and Heb. 1:14.

[15] The tradition, recorded in Eusebius's *Chronicon*, under the year 42, that Peter went to Rome at this time, does not square with the evidence of NT, according to which he was still in Jerusalem at the time of Paul's visits mentioned in Gal. 2:1 ff. and Acts 15:2 ff. It probably belongs to the traditions underlying the Clementine corpus which brought him to Rome at that early date to contend with Simon Magus (see p. 178 above, with notes 23–25). Antioch has been suggested as the "other place" to which Peter now went, in the light of Gal. 2:11, but the incident of Gal. 2:11 ff. probably belongs to a later date than A.D. 44. See D. F. Robinson ("Where and when did Peter die?", JBL lxiv [1945], pp. 255 ff.) and W. M. Smaltz ("Did Peter die in Jerusalem?", JBL lxxi [1952], pp. 211 ff.), for suggestions that the "other place" was the heavenly abode of the faithful departed, the narrative of Ch. 12:1 ff. being a pictorial account of Peter's martyrdom. It is difficult to take such interpretations seriously.

Gal. 2:1 ff.–an interview which probably took place on the occasion of their famine-relief visit from Antioch (see p. 244 above)–James, Peter and John were the three "pillars" whom they met, and that is the order in which Paul names them. But James on that occasion concurred with Peter and John in giving Barnabas and Paul "the right hand of fellowship" on the understanding that the latter two should evangelize the Gentiles while the Jerusalem leaders concentrated on evangelizing Jews. James was a much more broad-minded man than many of his legalistic followers, as his attitude later at the Council of Jerusalem shows (*cf.* Ch. 15:13 ff.), but he was careful to retain their confidence (*cf.* Ch. 21:18 ff.).

From the middle forties onwards, Peter and the other apostles were increasingly absent from Jerusalem; James, on the other hand, stayed there, administering the large and growing church of the city with the aid of his fellow-elders. He commanded the respect of the common people of Jerusalem, largely because of his severely ascetic life and his regular attendance at the temple services of prayer, where he interceded for the people. When he was sentenced to death by stoning in A.D. 61, at the instance of the high priest Annas the younger, who took advantage of the interval between the death of the procurator Festus and the arrival of his successor to take proceedings against a number of people of whom he disapproved, many of the people were gravely shocked; and in later years some ascribed the calamity which overtook the city not long after to the cessation of James's intercession on its behalf.[16]

18–19 Search was made for Peter, but he was nowhere to be found. Agrippa examined the soldiers who were responsible for guarding him, and sent them off to be punished,[17] suspecting no

[16] See Josephus, *Antiquities* xx. 9.1, and the more legendary account of Hegesippus preserved by Eusebius, *Ecclesiastical History* ii. 23. *Cf.* pp. 165, 171 f., nn. 90, 104, 106.

[17] ARV "be put to death" corresponds to ἀποκτανθῆναι of Cod. D (the chief Western authority) rather than to ἀπαχθῆναι of our other authorities, which means literally "be led off". In Attic Greek ἀπάγω was used idiomatically of leading off to execution (*cf.* Luke 23:26), but there is LXX and papyrus evidence for the Hellenistic use of the verb in the sense of arresting or leading off to prison. Perhaps we should translate "that they should be led away to punishment", while bearing in mind that the punishment in this case would in all probability be death. In Roman law (which, however, was not binding upon Agrippa in the internal administration of his kingdom) a guard who had allowed a prisoner to escape became liable to the same penalty as the escaped prisoner would have suffered (*Code of Justinian*, ix. 4.4).

doubt that Peter's escape was the result of a plot, and that the guards had been bribed. Soon afterwards, Agrippa left Jerusalem and went down[18] to his other capital, Caesarea.

(b) The Death of Herod Agrippa I (Ch. 12:20–23)

20 Now he was highly displeased with them of Tyre and Sidon: and they came with one accord to him, and, having made Blastus the king's chamberlain their friend, they asked for peace, because their country was fed from the king's country.

21 And upon a set day Herod arrayed himself in royal apparel, and sat on the throne, and made an oration unto them.[19]

22 And the people shouted, *saying*, The voice of a god, and not of a man.

23 And immediately an angel of the Lord smote him, because he gave not God the glory:[20] and he was eaten of worms, and gave up the ghost.

20 It was shortly after Agrippa went down to Caesarea that he met his death, and Luke relates the circumstances. The cities of the Phoenician seaboard, Tyre and Sidon, depended on Galilee for their food supply, as they had done in the days of Hiram and Solomon (*cf.* 1 Kings 5:9 ff.). When, therefore, they found that they had given Agrippa great offence in some way that we do not now know, they realized that the wisest course was to regain his favour as soon as possible. They made use accordingly of the good offices of his chamberlain Blastus, and an opportunity was found for them to present themselves before the king and make their peace with him publicly.

21–23 Here we are indebted to Josephus for a parallel account of what followed. At Caesarea, says Josephus, Agrippa "exhibited shows in honour of Caesar, inaugurating this as a festival for the emperor's welfare. And there came together to it a large number

---

[18] In saying that the king "went down from Judaea to Caesarea" (v. 19), Luke uses Judaea in its narrowest sense, of the territory of the Jews (the old tribe or kingdom of Judah); Caesarea was included in the Roman province of Judaea, being in fact its capital under the procurators. *Cf.* Ch. 21:10.

[19] The Western text adds "having been reconciled to the Tyrians".

[20] The Western text amplifies after "glory" as follows: "and having come down from the tribunal, he was eaten by worms while still alive, and so gave up the ghost."

of the provincial officials and others of distinguished position. On the second day of the shows Agrippa put on a robe made of silver throughout, of altogether wonderful weaving, and entered the theatre at break of day. Then the silver shone and glittered wonderfully as the sun's first rays fell on it, and its resplendence inspired a sort of fear and trembling in those who gazed on it. Immediately his flatterers called out from various directions, using language which boded him no good, for they addressed him as a god, and invoked him with the cry, 'Be gracious unto us! Hitherto we have reverenced thee as a man, but henceforth we acknowledge thee to be of more than mortal nature.' He did not rebuke them, nor did he repudiate their impious flattery. But soon afterwards he looked up and saw an owl[21] sitting on a rope above his head, and immediately recognized it as a messenger[22] of evil as it had on a former occasion been a messenger of good; and a pang of grief pierced his heart. At the same time he was seized by a severe pain in his belly, which began with a most violent attack... He was carried quickly into the palace ... and when he had suffered continuously for five days from the pain in his belly, he died, in the fifty-fourth year of his age and the seventh[23] of his reign" (*Antiquities* xix.8.2).

"In outline, in the time-indication,[24] and in the general concep-

[21] When he had been thrown into chains some years before, by order of Tiberius, he leaned against a tree on which an owl sat; a German fellow-prisoner told him that the bird betokened an early release and great good fortune, but that if ever he saw it again he would have but five days longer to live (Josephus, *Antiquities* xviii. 6.7).

[22] The fact that the bird here is called a messenger (Gk. ἄγγελος), while Luke tells us in v.23 that "an angel (ἄγγελος) of the Lord smote him", is nothing more than a verbal coincidence.

[23] The seventh year of his kingship; but he had been king of *Judaea* for three years only.

[24] Meyer follows E. Schwartz (*Nachrichten der königlichen Gesellschaft der Wissenschaften zu Göttingen,* 1907, pp. 265 f.) in supposing that the festival was one held in honour of the emperor every five years on the anniversary of the foundation of the city. As the anniversary of Caesarea's founding fell on March 5 (*cf.* Eusebius, *Martyrs of Palestine* xi. 30), a month or more before Passover (which fell on the unusually late date of May 1 in A.D. 44, owing to intercalation), we are faced with a difficulty. Either Peter's arrest and escape took place several weeks before the feast of unleavened bread (which Meyer supposes), or it took place in A.D. 43, nearly eleven months before the death of Agrippa (which is not the impression that we receive from Luke's narrative). It may be, however, that the festival arranged in honour of Claudius was not on March 5, but on August 1, which Suetonius (*Life of Claudius* ii. 1) tells us was that emperor's birthday.

tion," says Eduard Meyer, "both accounts are in full agreement. By its very interesting details, which are by no means to be explained as due to a 'tendency' or a popular tradition, Luke's account affords a guarantee that it is at least just as reliable as that of Josephus" (*Ursprung und Anfänge des Christentums*, iii [Stuttgart and Berlin, 1923], pp. 167 f.). (In point of fact, Luke's standard of reliability is higher than that of Josephus.)

When we use Josephus's narrative as a commentary on Luke's, we find that the "set day" on which the Phoenicians were to be reconciled to Agrippa was a festival which he himself instituted at Caesarea—possibly on August 1, the emperor's birthday. The "royal apparel" of which Luke speaks is described in greater detail by Josephus; both writers agree in saying that the king was hailed as a god and not a mere mortal, and in deprecating his tacit acceptance of such blasphemous adulation. The sudden pain which seized him is interpreted by Luke as a stroke of divine judgment; a medical colleague suggests that it was caused by the rupture of a hydatid cyst. This is borne out by Luke's description of the king as "eaten of worms"; this sort of terminology is used by several ancient writers in relating the deaths of people who were considered to have specially deserved so unpleasant an end.[25]

On the death of Agrippa, Judaea reverted to government by procurators. Three of his children figure later in the narrative of Acts—Drusilla (Ch. 24 : 24), Agrippa the younger and Bernice (Ch. 25:13).

(c) The Gospel Makes Further Progress (Ch. 12:24)

24 But the word of God[26] grew and multiplied.

24 This is a further report of progress, similar to those which we have found already in Chs. 6:7; 9:31. In the present one the progress and prosperity of the cause of the gospel are emphasized by contrast with the miserable end of the royal persecutor.

---

[25] Similar language is used in describing the deaths of Antiochus IV (2 Macc. 9:5 ff.); Herod the Great (Josephus, *Antiquities* vii. 6.5); Judas Iscariot (Papias, quoted by Apollinarius); Alexander the impostor (Lucian, *Alexander* 59); Galerius (Eusebius, *Ecclesiastical History* viii. 16); the uncle and namesake of Julian the Apostate (Theodoretus, *Ecclesiastical History* iii. 9).

[26] Cod. B and the Latin Vulgate have "the word of the Lord."

(d) Return of the Famine-Relief Delegation (Ch. 12:25)

25 And Barnabas and Saul[27] returned from Jerusalem,[28] when they had fulfilled their ministration, taking with them John, whose surname was Mark.[29]

25 Why does this note follow the record of Agrippa's persecution, while the account of the despatch of the delegation precedes it (Ch. 11:27–30)? Barnabas and Paul probably did not set out for Jerusalem until some time after Agrippa's death. "We have no reason to suppose that Luke intends us to understand that Barnabas and Paul went up to Jerusalem immediately after the prophecy[30] (they would have had precious little to bring unless they had collected week by week for a considerable period of time), and remained in the city throughout the whole reign of Herod with every hellenistic Jew thirsting for Paul's blood. Luke is merely following the normal practice of the ancient compiler of history in carrying on one source to a suitable stopping point before going on to another source . . . to suppose that Luke can be charged with inaccuracy in his dating here is to show a complete ignorance of the methods of ancient historians" (W. L. Knox, *The Acts of the Apostles* [Cambridge, 1948], pp. 36 f.).

Whereas Agrippa died in A.D. 44, a probable date for the

---

[27] The Western text adds "who was surnamed Paul" (*cf*. Ch. 13:9).

[28] The best attested reading (that of the Alexandrian and Byzantine textual families), as given in ARV margin, is "to Jerusalem" ($εἰς$ $Ἰερουσαλήμ$), which however is the opposite of what the sense requires—unless we contrive, by a *tour de force*, to render "Barnabas and Saul returned [*i.e.* to Antioch], having fulfilled their ministry at Jerusalem"; this is at least not so improbable as Kirsopp Lake's suggestion: they "returned [from Antioch] to Jerusalem in fulfilment of their ministry" (*Earlier Epistles of St. Paul* [London, 1914], pp. 317 ff.). The difficulty of this reading led to various early attempts at correction, of which the replacement of $εἰς$ by $ἐξ$ or $ἀπό$ is the commonest (underlying the English and most other versions). W. L. Knox, very reasonably, "cannot help feeling that $ἐξ$ is right and that $εἰς$ is due to a stupid copyist who was trying to harmonise Acts with Galatians and at the same time supposed that with $ἐξ$ the text implies that Barnabas and Paul were in Jerusalem for the whole period covered by 12:1–24" (*The Acts of the Apostles* [Cambridge, 1948], p. 37, n. 1). But the complexity of the textual situation is such that some have suggested that the Gordian knot should be cut by excising $εἰς$ $Ἰερουσαλήμ$ as a scribal gloss (J. V. Bartlet, *The Acts of the Apostles* [London, 1902], *ad loc.*; *cf*. L. E. Browne, *op. cit.*, pp. 210 f.).

[29] Ephrem the Syrian adds "and Luke the Cyrenean", commenting: "And these were both evangelists, and wrote before the discipleship of Paul." This comment is interesting because it identifies Luke the evangelist with Lucius of Cyrene of Ch. 13:1 (*cf*. p. 259, n. 1).

[30] That is to say, the prophecy of Agabus (*cf*. Ch. 11:28).

257

famine-relief visit of Barnabas and Paul is A.D. 46.[31] Having discharged the task entrusted to them by the church at Antioch, they returned there, and took Mark along with them. Mark, as we learn from Col. 4:10, was the cousin of Barnabas.[32] It is natural to suppose, then, that Barnabas and Paul lodged with his mother Mary during their stay in Jerusalem.

[31] It was about this year that Tiberius Julius Alexander succeeded Cuspius Fadus as procurator of Judaea, and Josephus dates the Palestinian famine during their governorships (*Antiquities* xx. 5.2).

[32] "Cousin" rather than "nephew" is the sense of Gk. ἀνεψιός, the word used in Col. 4:10.

CHAPTER XIII

IV. PAUL'S FIRST MISSIONARY TOUR AND THE APOSTOLIC DECREE
(Chs. 13:1–16:5)

1. BARNABAS AND SAUL GO TO CYPRUS
(Ch. 13:1–12)

(a) Barnabas and Saul Set Out from Antioch (Ch. 13:1–3)

1 Now there were at Antioch, in the church that was *there*, prophets and teachers, Barnabas, and Symeon that was called Niger, and Lucius of Cyrene, and Manaen the foster-brother of Herod the tetrach, and Saul.

2 And as they ministered to the Lord, and fasted, the Holy Spirit said,[1] Separate me Barnabas and Saul for the work whereunto I have called them.

3 Then, when they had[2] fasted and prayed, and laid their hands on them, they sent them away.

1 The Antiochene church had among its leaders some very remarkable men. In addition to Barnabas and Saul, three receive special mention as "prophets and teachers." Who was "Symeon

---

[1] A remarkable reading of vv. 1 and 2 down to this point is found in a Latin work entitled *Prophecies collected from all the books*, originating in the African church early in the fourth century: "Now there were in the church prophets and teachers, Barnabas and Saul, on whom the following prophets laid their hands—Symeon who is called Niger and Lucius of Cyrene who remains to this day, and Titus his foster-brother, who had received a response from the Holy Spirit, by reason of which they said . . ." As this work is also a witness for the Western reading at Ch. 11:27 f., which introduces Luke at Antioch, it may be that here it takes Lucius of Cyrene to be Luke the evangelist and Titus to be his brother. (That Titus, an Antiochene as we might infer from Gal. 2:1 ff., was the brother of Luke has been suggested by others; *cf.* Ramsay, *St. Paul the Traveller*, p. 390; *Luke the Physician* [London, 1908], pp. 17 f.; A. Souter in ExT xviii [1906–7], pp. 285, 335 f.) Zahn, however, in reconstructing the Greek text assumed to underlie this Latin reading, expands "Titus his foster-brother" to "Titus (an Antiochene, and Manaen, Herod the tetrarch's) foster-brother" (*Urausgabe der Apostelgeschichte* [Leipzig, 1916], pp. 280 f.; *cf.* the Latin text on p. 80). He takes this reading to be the original Western text of the passage.

[2] Cod. D adds "all."

that was called Niger"? Why was he given a *Latin* nickname?[3] The reason for the nickname, apart from its Latinity, is at any rate hardly to be doubted; he was presumably of dark complexion. In that case one begins to wonder if he was that "Simon of Cyrene, ... the father of Alexander and Rufus" (Mark 15:21) who carried the cross of Jesus. Mark mentions Alexander and Rufus presumably because they were well known in the Roman church when he wrote his gospel. One may speculate further. Among the Roman Christians to whom Paul sends greetings in Rom. 16 is one "Rufus the chosen in the Lord" (v. 13). If this Rufus was the son of Simon of Cyrene, it is tempting to explain Paul's reference to the mother of Rufus—"his mother and mine"—by supposing that Paul lodged in their home while he was in Antioch, and that it was there that the mother of Rufus proved herself a mother to Paul as well. But our speculations take us only so far and no farther. If Symeon of this passage was Simon of Cyrene, it is curious that not he, but his fellow-prophet Lucius, is here called a Cyrenean by Luke.

There is no evidence to connect this Lucius with the Lucius (Paul's "kinsman") of Rom. 16:21, and his identification with Luke the evangelist is not only unproven but improbable, although the identification was made in early times, as variant readings here and in Ch. 12:25 suggest (see p. 257, n. 29, and p. 259, n. 1).[4] Lucius was a common name in the Roman world. This Lucius was no doubt one of the men of Cyrene who, along with men of Cyprus, first preached the gospel to Gentiles in Antioch. There seems no reason to believe that Kyrenia in Cyprus is indicated rather than the African Cyrene.

Manaen is the Greek form of Hebrew Menahem (meaning "comforter"). The title "foster-brother" was given to boys of the same age as royal princes, who were brought up with them at court. (The word is found in inscriptions with the looser meaning "courtier" or "intimate friend",[5] but it is unnecessary to give the word this meaning here.) "Herod the tetrarch", to whom Manaen

---

[3] Latin was spoken in the Roman province of Africa, but that lay much farther west along the North African coast than Cyrene. Do the evangelists use Κυρηναῖος in the more general sense of "African"?

[4] See H. J. Cadbury's excursus, "Lucius of Cyrene", in *Beginnings*, v (London, 1933), pp. 489 ff.

[5] *Cf.* J. H. Moulton and G. Milligan, *Vocabulary of the Greek Testament* (Edinburgh, 1930), *s.v.* σύντροφος (p. 615).

was foster-brother, was Herod Antipas, son of Herod the Great and Malthace, who ruled Galilee and Peraea as tetrarch from 4 B.C. to A.D. 39. (*Cf.* Ch. 4:27.)

Josephus (*Antiquities* xv. 10.5) mentions an earlier Manaen, an Essene, who was honoured by Herod the Great for having foretold his rise to royal estate; he could well have been the grandfather of this Manaen. It is natural to suppose that Luke's special knowledge of members of the Herod dynasty may have been derived from Manaen. But what a commentary on the mystery and sovereignty of divine grace that, of these two foster-brothers, one should attain honour as a Christian leader, while the other should be best known for his shameful behaviour in the killing of John the Baptist and in the trial of Jesus!

2 As these prophets and teachers were carrying out their appointed ministry in the church, the Holy Spirit made known His will to them—doubtless through the prophetic utterance of one of their number (as the variant reading quoted on p. 259, n. 1, states). There are indications that NT Christians were specially sensitive to the Spirit's communications during fasting. On this occasion, the divine message directed the leaders of the church to set Barnabas and Saul apart for a special work to which He had called them. It is perhaps worth noticing that the two men who were to be released for what we should nowadays call missionary service overseas were the two most eminent and gifted leaders in the church.

3 After further fasting and prayer, Barnabas and Saul were released and commissioned for their new service. Their colleagues laid their hands on them and sent them away with their blessing and good will. It evident that the laying on of hands in this instance imparted no qualification to Barnabas and Saul which they did not already possess. But by this means the church of Antioch, through its leaders, expressed its fellowship with Barnabas and Saul and recognized them as its delegates or "apostles". They were sent out by the whole church, and it was to the whole church that they made their report when they returned to Antioch (Ch. 14:26 f.). But they were already apostles of Christ; this was a status which the church could not bestow but only recognize.

(b) Barnabas and Saul in Cyprus (Ch. 13:4–12)

4 So they, being sent forth by the Holy Spirit, went

down to Seleucia; and from thence they sailed to Cyprus.

5 And when they were at Salamis, they proclaimed the word of God in the synagogues of the Jews: and they had also John as their attendant.

6 And when they had gone through the whole island unto Paphos, they found a certain sorcerer, a false prophet, a Jew, whose name was Bar-Jesus;

7 who was with the proconsul, Sergius Paulus, a man of understanding. The same called unto him Barnabas and Saul, and sought to hear the word of God.

8 But Elymas[6] the sorcerer (for so is his name by interpretation) withstood them, seeking to turn aside the proconsul from the faith.

9 But Saul, who is also *called* Paul, filled with the Holy Spirit, fastened his eyes on him,

10 and said, O full of all guile and all villany, thou son of the devil, thou enemy of all righteousness, wilt thou not cease to pervert the right ways of the Lord?

11 And now, behold, the hand of the Lord is upon thee, and thou shalt be blind, not seeing the sun for a season. And immediately there fell on him a mist and a darkness; and he went about seeking some to lead him by the hand.

12 Then the proconsul, when he saw what was done, believed, being astonished at the teaching of the Lord.

4 Barnabas and Saul, then, having been sped on their way by the Antiochene church, took ship from Seleucia,[7] the port of Antioch, five miles north of the mouth of the Orontes, and sailed for Cyprus. Cyprus, an island of great importance in the Near East from very early times,[8] was annexed by Rome in 57 B.C. In 55 B.C. it was incorporated in the province of Cilicia; in 27 B.C. it became a separate province, governed on behalf of Augustus by an imperial legate; in 22 B.C. Augustus handed it over to the control of the Roman senate, and from that year, like other sena-

6 The Western text seems to have read Etymas or Hetoimas (these spellings remind one of Atomos, the name of another Jewish magician who is mentioned by Josephus as living in Cyprus about this time [*Antiquities* xx.7.2; *cf.* pp. 472 f. below]). See also n. 13 below.

7 Seleucia was founded by Seleucus Nicator, first king of the Seleucid dynasty, in 301 B.C.

8 Its OT name is Kittim (Gen. 10:4, etc.); *cf.* its Phoenician town of Kition (modern Larnaka).

torial provinces, it was administered by a proconsul, as Luke accurately indicates in giving the title of its governor in v. 7.[9]

5–8 When they landed in Cyprus, they traversed the island from east to west. John Mark, the cousin of Barnabas, whom they had lately taken with them from Jerusalem to Antioch (Ch. 12:25), accompanied them on this mission, and acted as their "attendant"— which some scholars have taken to mean that he put at their disposal his special knowledge of certain important phases of the story of Jesus, in particular the passion narrative.[10]

The first place in Cyprus where they preached was Salamis, a Greek city on the east coast of the island and the seat of government of Eastern Cyprus. It was a flourishing commercial centre, and its Jewish community was apparently large enough to require more synagogues than one. The practice of announcing the Christian message first of all in the Jewish synagogue or synagogues of each city they visited was to be a regular feature of Barnabas and Paul's missionary procedure. It was a practical expression of the principle that Paul lays down in Rom. 1:16—that the gospel is to be presented "to the Jew first." Besides, Paul "was always sure of a good opening for his Gentile mission among the 'God-fearing', who formed part of his audience in every synagogue" (W. M. Ramsay, *St. Paul the Traveller and Roman Citizen* (14th edn., London, 1920], p. 72).

From Salamis they made their way westward, until they reached Paphos, the seat of the provincial government. This was the Greek settlement of New Paphos, so called to distinguish it from the Phoenician foundation of Old Paphos, which lay about seven miles to the south-east. Both cities were noted, among other things, for the cult of the goddess called "the Paphian", a deity of Syrian origin identified with the Greek Aphrodite. Here the two missionaries had an interview with the proconsul; here, too, they met the

---

[9] As ὕπατος is the conventional Greek equivalent of Latin *consul*, so ἀνθύπατος represents Latin *proconsul*.

[10] The word rendered "attendant" is ὑπηρέτης, used also in Luke 1:2, ὑπηρέται ... τοῦ λόγου ("ministers of the word"—among whom Mark is probably reckoned). A. Wright, in his *Composition of the Four Gospels* (London, 1890), pp. 15 f., argues that Mark attended Paul and Barnabas as a duly authorized catechist. *Cf.* G. Salmon, *Some Thoughts on the Textual Criticism of the NT* (London, 1897), p. 142; and for the catechetical interest in Mark's Gospel *cf.* V. Taylor, *The Gospel according to St. Mark* (London, 1952), p. 133; *Studiorum Novi Testamenti Societas*, Bulletin III (Oxford, 1952), pp. 33 ff.

sorcerer Bar-Jesus, who was attached to the proconsular entourage. The proconsul at this time was Sergius Paullus (if we spell his name in the normal Latin way), possibly identical with the Lucius Sergius Paullus who is known to have been one of the curators of the Tiber in the reign of Claudius.[11] If the identification is justified, then he must have gone to Cyprus as proconsul after his curatorship of the Tiber. The proconsul summoned Barnabas and Saul to his presence, listened to their message, and showed an interest in it. But the sorcerer did his best to distract the proconsul's attention from the apostolic preaching, opposing it for all he was worth; no doubt he suspected that if the proconsul paid too much attention to this new faith, his own services as "court magician" would probably become superfluous.

The Greek word translated "sorcerer" is *magos*. The magi were originally a Median priestly caste, but in later Greek and Roman times the word was used more generally of practitioners of all sorts of magic and quackery.[12] The latter sense is required here; a Jew, even a renegade Jew (as this man was), could not have been a member of the magian priesthood. Luke calls him a false prophet, not in the sense that he foretold things which did not come to pass, but in the sense that he claimed falsely to be a medium of divine revelations. When Luke says (v. 8) "Elymas the sorcerer (for so is his name by interpretation)," he cannot mean that Elymas is the interpretation of Bar-Jesus, but that "sorcerer" (Gk. *magos*) is the interpretation of Elymas; Elymas is probably a Semitic word[13] with a similar meaning to Gk. *magos*.

9-11 For his attempt to prejudice the proconsul against the gospel, the sorcerer was severely rebuked by Saul (who here for the first time in Acts is given his Roman cognomen Paul,[14] by

---

[11] *Corpus Inscriptionum Latinarum* vi (Berlin, 1902), No. 31545.

[12] *Cf.* Herodotus, *History* i. 101, 140; J. H. Moulton, *Early Zoroastrianism* (London, 1913), pp. 182 ff. In Ch. 8:9 ff. Simon, the sorcerer of Samaria, is not designated by the substantive μάγος, but the participle μαγεύων is used of him in v. 9. The wise men (Gk. μάγοι) of Matt. 2:1 ff. were probably astrologers.

[13] Perhaps akin to Arabic *'alim*, "sage". On the basis of the Western text, however, an attempt has been made to associate the two proper names of vv. 6 and 8. The Western form of Bar-Jesus (v. 6) is Βαρ-Ἰησοῦα, which is actually an attempt to reproduce the Semitic *Bar-Yeshua'* more accurately; Klostermann and Zahn, however, have tried to connect it with Heb. *shawah*, one meaning of which is "be ready"—and that is easily linked with the Western variant Ἑτοιμᾶς for Ἐλύμας in v. 8 (*cf.* Gk. ἕτοιμος, "ready").

[14] The apostle, as a Roman citizen, must have had three names—*praenomen, nomen gentile* and *cognomen*—of which Paullus was his *cognomen*. It is

which he is henceforth regularly called). By his opposition to the truth he had shown himself a son of the devil[15] rather than a son or follower of Jesus (as his name Bar-Jesus implied).[16] Divine judgment had been pronounced against him, and it would take the form of temporary blindness. "The apostle," says the Venerable Bede, "remembering his own case, knew that by the darkening of the eyes the mind's darkness might be restored to light."[17] And as Paul spoke the words, the man was smitten with blindness, and fumbled round for someone to guide his unseeing steps.

12 The proconsul was greatly impressed. What exactly the narrative means by saying that he "believed" is disputed. Ramsay, rather pedantically, suggests that for Luke belief is the first stage in the process of conversion, the second being "turning to the Lord" (*The Bearing of Recent Discovery on the Trustworthiness of the NT* [London, 1915], p. 165). Lake and Cadbury, on the other hand, suggest that the missionaries "may have mistaken courtesy for conversion" (Commentary in *Beginnings,* iv, *ad loc.*). But to a matter-of-fact Roman official the sudden blindness which had fallen on the magician would be strong confirmation of the message in which he was already interested. Ramsay points out, quite rightly, that there is no evidence or even likelihood that he was baptized, but adduces epigraphic reasons for believing that in the next two generations certain members of his family were known as Christians.[18]

probably a mere coincidence that Luke should first designate him by his Roman *cognomen* in a context where another bearer of the same *cognomen* appears. The apostle's *praenomen* and *nomen gentile,* unfortunately, have not been preserved. Had Luke been a Roman, he would no doubt have mentioned them; for him as a Greek, however, it sufficed to mention the *cognomen.*

[15] Gk. διάβολος ("slanderer") was used as a rendering of Heb. *satan* ("adversary"). (*Cf.* Ch. 10:38.) In his letters Paul prefers to use Gk. Σατανᾶς (*cf.* p. 113, n. 12, on Ch. 5:3); διάβολος occurs in Eph. 4:27; 6:11; 1 Tim. 3:6 f.; 2 Tim. 2:26.

[16] His father's name was probably Joshua (Jeshua).

[17] *Cf.* also Chrysostom, *Homily* 28.

[18] See *The Bearing of Recent Discovery,* etc., pp. 150 ff. (the chapter entitled "Sergius Paullus and his Relation to Christian Faith"). He argues that Sergia Paulla, the proconsul's daughter, was a Christian, as also her son Gaius Caristanius Fronto, member of a prominent family of Pisidian Antioch.

2. PISIDIAN ANTIOCH
(Ch. 13:13–52)

(a) Arrival at Pisidian Antioch (Ch. 13:13–15)

13 Now Paul and his company set sail from Paphos, and
came to Perga in Pamphylia: and John departed from
them and returned to Jerusalem.

14 But they, passing through from Perga, came to Antioch
of Pisidia; and they went into the synagogue on the
sabbath day, and sat down.

15 And after the reading of the law and the prophets the
rulers of the synagogue sent unto them, saying, Brethren, if ye have any word of exhortation for the people,
say on.

13 Having evangelized part of Barnabas's native island, the
missionary party now crossed from Paphos to the south coast of
Paul's native land, Asia Minor. Probably they landed at Attalia
(modern Antalya) and went by land to Perga, which was twelve
miles away, although it had a river-harbour of its own on the
Cestrus, five miles downstream. Pamphylia was a coastal district
of Asia Minor, bounded on the north by the Taurus range, on
the west by Lycia, on the east by Cilicia, and on the south by
the Mediterranean.

Why John Mark left Barnabas and Paul at Perga and returned
to Jerusalem is uncertain; Paul, at any rate, regarded his departure
as desertion.[19] Perhaps he did not care for the increasing rigours
which evangelization in Asia Minor would involve; perhaps he
resented the way in which his cousin Barnabas was falling into
the second place. (When the expedition sets out from Syria, the
order is "Barnabas and Saul"; by the time they leave Cyprus, it
is "Paul and his company"!) But Barnabas does not seem to have
resented this at all: his greatness of soul illustrates the old couplet—

> "It takes more grace than I can tell
> To play the second fiddle well."

14–15 Paul and Barnabas now struck up country, crossing
the Taurus range, and entered the southern part of the Roman

---
[19] See Ch. 15:38.

province of Galatia.[20]   Ramsay infers from Gal. 4:13 that Paul caught malaria in the low-lying territory around Perga, and went to recuperate in the higher altitudes of southern Galatia (*St. Paul the Traveller*, pp. 94 ff.); this, however, is highly speculative.

"Antioch of Pisidia" (or Pisidian Antioch), the first city to which they came when they entered Galatia, was so called because it was near the border of Pisidia[21] (one of the regions into which the province was divided). But it was not "in Pisidia", as AV has it; it actually lay in the region probably known as Galatic Phrygia, and was the chief civil and military centre of that part of Galatia. It lay 3600 feet above sea-level.   The Emperor Augustus made it a Roman colony, with the title Colonia Caesarea.   Paul attached great importance to the evangelization of Roman colonies, which were planted at strategic points along the imperial roads to safeguard the interests of Rome. (See p. 330 with n. 28, on Ch. 16:12.)

There was a Jewish colony in this city, and therefore a synagogue too, and on the first sabbath day after their arrival the two missionaries went to the synagogue and took their places among the congregation. After the appropriate prayers had been recited and the two Scripture lessons read—one from the Pentateuch and the other from some place in the prophetical books bearing some relation to the subject of the Pentateuchal reading[22]—an address was normally delivered by some suitable member of the congregation. It was part of the duties of the "rulers of the synagogue" to appoint someone to deliver the address.[23] On this occasion they sent a message to the two strangers who had come to their city and

[20] The Roman province of Galatia, formed in 25 B.C. after the death of Amyntas, the last Galatian king, was much more extensive than the inland territory called Galatia from the Gauls who settled there after their invasion of Asia Minor in the third century B.C.; in addition to ethnic Galatia the province of that name included parts of Pontus, Phrygia, Lycaonia, Pisidia, Paphlagonia and Isauria, with a number of Greek cities and Roman colonies.

[21] Strabo (*Geography* xii. 6.4) refers to it as "Antioch near (*or* towards) Pisidia." That it actually lay in Phrygia is confirmed by two inscriptions found in the neighbourhood. See W. M. Ramsay, *The Cities of St. Paul* (London, 1907), pp. 247 ff.

[22] At this time the Pentateuch was read in the synagogue according to a triennial lectionary, the 154 or 155 lessons being still marked in Hebrew Bibles as the *sedarim*. *Cf.* A. Büchler in *Jewish Quarterly Review*, OS v (1893), pp. 420 ff.; vi (1894), pp. 1 ff.

[23] Among their other duties were to take charge of the building, see that nothing unseemly took place in it, and make arrangements for public worship. Sometimes there was one ruler in a synagogue, sometimes more, as here. Sometimes the office was held for life and remained in the same family, as

synagogue, inviting them to speak a word of exhortation[24] to the gathering.

(b) Paul's Sermon in Pisidian Antioch (Ch. 13:16–41)

16 And Paul stood up, and beckoning with the hand said, Men of Israel, and ye that fear God, hearken:

17 The God of this people Israel chose our fathers, and exalted the people when they sojourned in the land of Egypt, and with a high arm led he them forth out of it.

18 And for about the time of forty years as a nursing-father bare he them[25] in the wilderness.

19 And when he had destroyed seven nations in the land of Canaan, he gave *them* their land for an inheritance, for about four hundred and fifty years:[26]

20 and after these things[27] he gave *them* judges until Samuel the prophet.

21 And afterward they asked for a king: and God gave unto them Saul the son of Kish, a man of the tribe of Benjamin, for the space of forty years.

22 And when he had removed him, he raised up David to be their king; to whom also he bare witness and said, I have found David, the son of Jesse, a man after my heart, who shall do all my will.

23 Of this man's seed hath God according to promise brought[28] unto Israel a Saviour, Jesus;

inscriptions testify; as inscriptions also testify, the title was sometimes honorary and might be held by women and children.

[24] The expression "a word of exhortation" (Gk. λόγος παρακλήσεως) was perhaps a synagogue term for the sermon which followed the Scripture readings (*cf.* Heb. 13:22).

[25] The textual evidence is fairly evenly balanced between "as a nursing-father bare he them" (Gk. ἐτροφοφόρησεν) and "suffered he their manners" (ERV, Gk. ἐτροποφόρησεν). The same two variants are found in the LXX text of Deut. 1:31 (to which Paul is here alluding); the Hebrew text has simply *nasa*, "bore".

[26] The Western and Byzantine texts read "for about four hundred and fifty years" immediately before "he gave them judges" (v. 20) instead of in the present position (that of the Alexandrian family, the Latin Vulgate and the Armenian version).

[27] The Western text omits "after these things."

[28] A number of texts (including Codd. C D 33, the Peshitta and Harclean Syriac, the Sahidic Coptic and the Armenian version) have "raised up" (ἤγειρεν) instead of "brought" (ἤγαγεν) of the Alexandrian and Byzantine texts; the former reading was adopted for the Received Text (hence AV "hath ... raised"): it may have been influenced by such OT passages as Judg. 3:9, "Jehovah raised up a saviour to the children of Israel."

24 when John had first preached before his coming the
  baptism of repentance to all the people of Israel.

25 And as John was fulfilling his course, he said, What[29]
  suppose ye that I am?[30] I am not *he*. But behold, there
  cometh one after me the shoes of whose feet I am not
  worthy to unloose.

26 Brethren, children of the stock of Abraham, and those
  among you[31] that fear God, to us[32] is the word of this
  salvation sent forth.

27 For they[33] that dwell in Jerusalem, and their rulers,
  because they knew him not, nor the voices of the prophets which are read every sabbath, fulfilled *them* by
  condemning *him*.[34]

28 And though they found no cause of death *in him*, yet
  asked they of Pilate that he should be slain.

29 And when they had fulfilled all things that were
  written of him, they took him down from the tree,
  and laid him in a tomb.

30 But God raised him from the dead:

31 and he was seen for many days of them that came up
  with him from Galilee to Jerusalem, who are now his
  witnesses unto the people.

32 And we bring you good tidings of the promise made
  unto the fathers,

33 that God hath fulfilled the same unto our children,[35]

[29] The Western and Byzantine texts have "whom" for "what".

[30] It is possible to punctuate differently by omitting the question mark and
continuing the sentence in such a way as to give the sense, "I am not what
(*or*, he whom) you suppose me to be." The punctuation in the text gives
preferable emphasis.

[31] Codd. A D 81 read "among us."

[32] For "us" of the Alexandrian and some other authorities P[45] and the
Byzantine text read "you."

[33] The Western text of vv. 27–29 has been reconstructed by J. H. Ropes
(*Beginnings*, iii, p. 261) in a form which may be translated thus: "For the
inhabitants and rulers of Jerusalem, not understanding the writings of the
prophets which are read publicly every sabbath day, have fulfilled them, and
although they found no cause of death in him, they judged him and handed
him over to Pilate to be put to death. And when they were completing all
the things that had been written concerning him, they requested of Pilate after
his crucifixion that he might be taken down from the tree, and having obtained
their request they took him down and laid him in a tomb."

[34] The expression "by condemning him" (Gk. κρίναντες) was transferred by
Lachmann to follow immediately on "because they knew him not" (Moffatt
accepts this emendation in his version, "by condemning him in their ignorance").
Blass emended κρίναντες to μὴ ἀνακρίναντες ("not discerning").

[35] The best authorities (especially ℵ A B C* D with the Latin Vulgate
and Ethiopic version) read "unto our children" (τοῖς τέκνοις ἡμῶν), which is

in that he raised up Jesus;[36] as also it is written in the
second psalm,[37] Thou art my Son, this day have I
begotten thee.[38]

34 And as concerning that he raised him up from the
dead, now no more to return to corruption, he hath
spoken on this wise, I will give you the holy and sure
blessings of David.

35 Because he saith also in another *psalm*, Thou wilt not
give thy Holy One to see corruption.

36 For David, after he had in his own generation served
the counsel of God, fell asleep, and was laid unto his
fathers, and saw corruption:

37 but he whom God raised up saw no corruption.

38 Be it known unto you therefore, brethren, that through
this man is proclaimed unto you remission of sins:[39]

39 and by him every one that believeth is justified from
all things, from which ye could not be justified by the
law of Moses.

40 Beware therefore, lest that come upon *you* which is
spoken in the prophets;

41 Behold, ye despisers, and wonder, and perish;
For I work a work in your days,
A work which ye shall in no wise believe, if one
declare it unto you.[40]

accepted by ERV and ARV. But it gives awkward sense. As the promise was
made to the fathers, we should expect to be told that it was fulfilled to *their*
children. And in fact most other authorities read "to their children" (so the
Old Latin codex *gigas* and the Sahidic Coptic) or "to us their children" (so
the Byzantine text). The Bohairic Coptic omits the phrase altogether. F. H.
Chase (*Credibility of Acts* [London, 1902], p. 187 n.) suggested the reading
ἡμῖν καὶ τοῖς τέκνοις ἡμῶν ("to us and to our children")—a very attractive
emendation, which would bring this passage into line with Ch. 2:39 (*cf.* Psalms
of Solomon 8:39, "to us and to our children is His good pleasure for ever").

36 The Western text has the reverential expansion "the Lord Jesus Christ."

37 The Western text reads "for thus it is written in the first psalm." Origen
and other early fathers knew of certain forms of the Hebrew text which
reckoned the first two psalms as one. *P45* reads simply "in the psalms."

38 The Western text continues the OT quotation by adding "Ask of me and
I will give thee nations as thy inheritance, and the ends of the earth as thy
possession."

39 After "remission of sins" (v. 38) the Western text recasts v. 39 thus:
". . . and repentance from all things from which you could not be justified by
Moses' law; in him therefore everyone who believes is justified in the sight
of God."

40 The Western text adds "and he held his peace" (so Cod. 614 and the
margin of the Harclean Syriac; the reading of Cod. D, "and they held their
peace", is probably a corruption of this).

16 When the invitation was received by the two missionaries, Paul responded to it by going to the *bima* or pulpit and addressing the congregation. He made a gesture inviting attention, and then spoke. His opening words indicate quite clearly the twofold composition of his audience. There were "men of Israel" (Jews by birth or by proselytization) and there were Gentile God-fearers ("ye that fear God"). In this as in many another synagogue where Paul preached, it was the latter group that proved readier to accept the good news which he proclaimed.

There are two places in NT where we have a fairly detailed account of a synagogue service: this is one; the other is in Luke 4:16 ff., where Jesus preaches in the synagogue in Nazareth early in His Galilaean ministry. In the Nazareth synagogue Jesus read the second lesson (from Isa. 61:1 f.) before He delivered the sermon; and the sermon was based directly on the words which He had just read in the lesson. It is more difficult to decide if Paul's address at Pisidian Antioch was similarly based on one or both of the Scripture lessons. Jesus delivered His address in a sitting position (He had read the lesson standing); Paul stood to preach. Israel Abrahams[41] has explained this by pointing out that our Lord's address was an exposition of the Scriptures,[42] whereas Paul's was rather an exhortation.

i. Preparation for Christ (vv. 17–22)

17–22 Paul's exhortation, says Abrahams, "follows Jewish lines in its structure"—chiefly in that it takes the form of a historical retrospect, as Stephen's defence did. The historical retrospect outlines the course of God's dealings with His people Israel from His choice of their fathers and deliverance of the people in the Exodus until the accession of David and establishment of his dynasty; Paul then moves directly from David to Christ, as the One in whom the promises made concerning David and his house were fulfilled. G. Ernest Wright has recently shown that these verses contain a confessional summary, since they narrate "precisely those redemptive acts of God to which the Israelite bore witness in his confessional recital of the works of God" (*God Who*

---

[41] In his *Studies in Pharisaism and the Gospels*, Series I (Cambridge, 1917), p. 8. The whole of the first chapter in this volume, "The Freedom of the Synagogue", is highly interesting and relevant to the present subject.

[42] For our Lord's exposition of the Scriptures on that occasion, see N. B. Stonehouse, *The Witness of Luke to Christ* (London and Grand Rapids, 1951), pp. 68 ff.

Acts [London, 1952], p. 76). In the earliest days of the settlement in Canaan the Israelite worshipper acknowledged that God had chosen the patriarchs, that He had redeemed their descendants, the children of Israel, for Himself in the events of the Exodus, and that He had given them the land of Canaan as their inheritance (*cf.* Deut. 26:5 ff.; Josh. 24:2–13, 17 f.). To these acts of God Israelites of later days added His choice of David to be their king (*cf.* Ps. 78:67 ff.; 89:3 ff.). These events, in fact, constitute an OT *kerygma* which Paul here summarizes as a prelude to the NT *kerygma*, showing how inevitably the events proclaimed in the apostolic preaching took place as the sequel to God's dealings with His people in ancient days.

The language in which Paul outlines the history of Israel from patriarchal times to the rise of David is strongly reminiscent of the very wording of the OT narration. The "high arm" with which God led His people out of Egypt is an allusion to Ex. 6:1, 6 and Ps. 136:11 f.; it expresses the mighty power manifested by God at the Exodus. God's carrying them as a nursing-father (or, as the ARV margin puts it, suffering their manners) through the wilderness is taken from Deut. 1:31. The seven nations destroyed in the land of Canaan are enumerated in Deut. 7:1, the wording of which is reflected here; they are there described as "the Hittite, and the Girgashite, and the Amorite, and the Canaanite, and the Perizzite, and the Hivite, and the Jebusite, seven nations greater and mightier than thou." The dispossession of these nations and occupation of their territory were spread over a long term of years; it was not until the seventh year of David's reign that the Jebusites, the last mentioned, were reduced. (They were the Canaanite occupants of Jerusalem.) The four hundred and fifty years of v. 19 may be intended to cover the period up to David's reign; more probably they cover the four hundred years of sojourning (v. 17; *cf.* Ch. 7:6), along with the forty years of wandering in the wilderness and the period that elapsed between the crossing of the Jordan and the distribution of the land in Josh. 14:1 ff. (The wording of Josh. 14:1 f. has also left its mark on Paul's language in v. 19.)

The age of the judges, terminating with Samuel the prophet, was followed by the reign of Saul[43]—"a man of the tribe of

---

[43] The figure of forty years given for Saul's reign here is paralleled in Josephus, *Antiquities* vi. 14.9. In *Antiquities* x. 8.4, however, Josephus gives

Benjamin", as Paul is careful to point out, for was not he himself
another Saul of the tribe of Benjamin?[44] But King Saul was not
the man after God's heart, and his dynasty did not endure; he
was removed from his kingship and replaced by another (cf.
1 Sam. 13:13 f.; 15:23, 26, 28). This other was David, to whom
God confirmed His promise of abiding sovereignty, because he
was "a man after His own heart" (1 Sam. 13:14), and God bore
witness to him thus, in the words of Ps. 89:19 ff.:

> I have laid help upon one that is mighty;
> I have exalted one chosen out of the people.
> I have found David my servant;
> With my holy oil have I anointed him:
> With whom my hand shall be established;
> Mine arm also shall strengthen him. . .
>
> I also will make him my firstborn,
> The highest of the kings of the earth.
> My lovingkindness will I keep for him for evermore;
> And my covenant shall stand fast with him.
> His seed also will I make to endure for ever,
> And his throne as the days of heaven.[45]

These words of Ps. 89, recording the promises made by God
to David, were written in a day when disaster had overtaken
David's house, and the psalmist was bewildered by the contrast
between the divine promises and the sorry sight that met his
eyes—the crown of David profaned and cast to the ground. No
wonder that he cried (v. 49):

> Lord, where are thy former lovingkindnesses,
> Which thou swarest unto David in thy faithfulness?

In later days, however, when the sovereignty of the house of
David seemed to have passed away for ever, so far as human
agency was concerned, it came to be recognized that the promises
made to David would be completely fulfilled in a ruler of David's
line whom God would Himself raise up. The Davidic kingship,
said God through Ezekiel in the days of the fall of the Judaean

Saul a reign of twenty years. J. A. Bengel (*Gnomon Novi Testamenti* [Tübin-
gen, 1742], *ad loc.*) thought that the forty years here cover the administration
of Samuel as well as the reign of Saul.

[44] *Cf.* Phil. 3:5. It may have been in memory of King Saul, the most illustrious Benjamite in Israel's history, that Paul's parents gave him Saul as his
Jewish name.

[45] These verses of Ps. 89 are based on the narrative of 2 Sam. 7, where

monarchy, was to lie in ruins: "there shall not be even a trace of it until he comes whose right it is; and to him I will give it" (Ezek. 21:27, RSV). This coming ruler would be a new and greater David, one who would be in the fullest sense the anointed one (the Messiah) of the God of Israel, and who would restore and surpass the vanished glories of earlier days (Ezek. 34:23 f.; 37:24 f.; *cf*. Jer. 23:5; 30:9). As the post-exilic centuries passed, and especially after the brief space of national independence under the Hasmoneans was followed by the Roman conquest, the longing for this messianic deliverer became more intense than ever.[46]

ii. Fulfilment in Christ (vv. 23–37)

23 What Paul announced, therefore, was that the messianic deliverer of David's house had now been raised up by God in accordance with His promise, and that his name was Jesus.[47]

24–25 The announcement of Jesus as the Messiah is made in the regular form of the apostolic *kerygma*, beginning with the baptismal ministry of John (*cf*. Ch. 10:37). John's baptism of repentance paved the way for the public appearance of Jesus, as John himself made clear; for as he was completing his course as Messiah's forerunner he told the people who imagined that he himself might be the object of their expectation, "I am not he."[48] So far did he reckon himself beneath the Coming One whose way he was preparing that he declared himself unfit even to untie the laces of His sandals.

26–29 "To us", said Paul, again addressing the two elements in his audience, the Jews and the God-fearers, "to us has the message of this salvation been sent." And he went on to tell of the death of the Messiah: the people of Jerusalem, in the person of their rulers, through ignorance of the true meaning of prophetic scripture and consequent failure to recognize the Saviour whom it foretold, passed sentence of death upon Him, and thus

God undertakes to maintain the house of David in perpetuity (*cf*. Ch. 7:46 with the accompanying exposition on p. 157 above).

[46] *Cf*. the *Psalms of Solomon*, written shortly after the Roman conquest of Judaea in 63 B.C., especially 17:23 ff., the passage beginning: "Behold, O Lord, and raise up unto them their king, the son of David, in the time which thou, O God, knowest, that he may reign over Israel thy servant . . ."

[47] When Paul says "a Saviour, Jesus," he may have in mind the etymology of Jesus (Heb. *Yehoshua'*, "Jehovah is salvation"; *cf*. Matt. 1:21).

[48] *Cf*. Luke 3:15 ff.; John 1:20 ("I am not the Christ").

unwittingly fulfilled the prophecies which told how He must suffer and die. Yet the death sentence was completely unjustified: He did no more than claim to be the person He actually was. Nevertheless, in spite of His innocence, they asked Pilate to have the death sentence carried out, and carried out it was—by crucifixion. (Once again the cross is described as "the tree", in order to emphasize the connection with Deut. 21:23.)[49] When all was over, and the prophecies of His passion had been fulfilled, His body was taken down and buried.[50] The explicit mention of the tomb in which they laid Him may be intended to emphasize the reality of His death, and consequently of His resurrection;[51] besides, the burial of one who has been hanged on a tree is specifically enjoined in Deut. 21:23, and Paul may wish to indicate that everything was carried out in accordance with OT scripture.

30-31 But God reversed the sentence of men: here the constant note of triumph which made the apostolic preaching so joyful a message is struck again. God raised Jesus from the dead, and over a period of many days He appeared to His disciples who had come up from Galilee to Jerusalem with Him; they were now personal and public witnesses to His resurrection and Messiahship. Luke does not, any more than in his gospel, mention our Lord's resurrection-appearances in Galilee; nor is there here any reference to Paul's own vision of the risen Lord.

32-33 Here then is good news—that the promise made to the fathers in days gone by has now been fulfilled by God to their children. After long ages of earnest expectation, God had at last raised up[52] to Israel their true Messiah, the Son of David, in accordance with the royal allocution of Ps. 2:7, "Thou art my

---

49 *Cf.* Chs. 5:30; 10:39.

50 The plural subject, "they took him down . . . and laid him in a tomb", may be generalizing; in the Gospels Joseph of Arimathaea and Nicodemus (members of the Sanhedrin) are specially mentioned in this connection (*cf.* Luke 23:50 ff.; John 19:38 ff.). But the leaders of the Sanhedrin appear in any case to have taken steps to ensure that His body should be removed from the cross before sunset (*cf.* John 19:31).

51 The mention of the burial of Christ here and in 1 Cor. 15:4, immediately before the mention of His resurrection, implies that the tomb was found empty, as the Gospel narrative explicitly affirms.

52 This, rather than resurrection from the dead, seems to be the sense of ἀναστήσας in v. 33 (our Lord's resurrection from the dead comes in the next verse). For this sense of ἀνίστημι *cf.* Chs. 3:22, 26; 7:37; the synonymous ἐγείρω is used in this sense in Chs. 5:20; 13:22. An interpretation of Ps. 2:7 in reference to Christ's resurrection has indeed been supported by a passage in

275

Son; this day have I begotten thee." The day of the king's anointing in Israel of old "was ideally the day in which he, the nation's representative, was born into a new relation of sonship towards Jehovah" (F. H. Chase, *The Credibility of Acts* [London, 1902], p. 126). Jesus entered into no *new* relation of sonship towards Jehovah; but on the day when God anointed Him with the Holy Spirit and power[53] and invested Him with His messianic dignity, it was in the words of Ps. 2:7 that the heavenly voice addressed Him: "Thou art my Son" (indeed, the Western text of Luke 3:22 gives the full quotation from Ps. 2:7, "Thou art my Son; this day have I begotten thee").[54]

34–37 And not only did God raise up Jesus as Israel's Messiah, but He raised Him up also in another sense when He brought Him back from the dead, and this too was a fulfilment of OT scripture. The promises made to David and his posterity could not have been fulfilled apart from the resurrection of the crucified Messiah. Centuries after the promises were made to David himself, God renewed them by assuring His people that He would yet give them the holy and sure blessings promised to David (Isa. 55:3, quoted here in a form similar to the LXX).[55] But not only did these blessings require the resurrection of Christ for their realization; the resurrection of Christ was actually one of these promised blessings, in accordance with the words of Ps. 16:10, previously quoted in the same sense by Peter on the day of Pentecost (*cf.* Ch. 2:27): "Thou wilt not give thy Holy One[56] to see corruption."

Midrash *Tehillim* (on Ps. 2:7) and Midrash *Samuel*, ch. 19 (with the readings of *Yalqut Shim'oni*, ii. 620): "Rabbi Huna says in the name of Rabbi Acha, The sufferings are divided into three parts: one for David and the fathers, one for our own generation, and one for King Messiah, as it is written, 'He was wounded for our transgressions', etc. And when the hour comes, the Holy One —blessed be He!—says to them, I must create him a new creation, even as it is said, 'This day have I begotten thee.' This is the hour when he is made a new creation." But there does not appear to be much in common between this interpretation and Paul's application of Ps. 2:7 here. On the use of Ps. 2 in the apostolic witness *cf.* Ch. 4:25 f., with exposition and notes (p. 106 above).

[53] *Cf.* Ch. 10:38 with accompanying exposition (p. 226).

[54] *Cf.* C. H. Dodd, *According to the Scriptures* (London, 1952), pp. 31 f.

[55] The "sure mercies of David" ("my steadfast, sure love for David," RSV) represents Heb. *hasde Dawid ha-ne'emanim*, but LXX takes *hasde* (construct plural of *hesed*, "lovingkindness", "steadfast love") as coming from *hasid* ("holy") and renders the phrase τὰ ὅσια Δαυείδ τὰ πιστά ("the holy and sure things of David").

[56] Gk. τὸν ὅσιόν σου (Heb. "thy *hasid*"); *cf.* the use of the same adjective in the LXX of Isa. 55:3 quoted in v. 34.

The argument used by Peter on that earlier occasion is here repeated by Paul: these words of Ps. 16:10 could not refer personally to David, for he died, was buried, and "saw corruption" after he had accomplished the will of God in his own lifetime: the one who, in the language of the psalm, was not permitted "to see corruption" was the one whom God raised from the dead—Jesus, thus demonstrated to be the Messiah.

The similarity between Peter's speech in Jerusalem on the day of Pentecost and Paul's speech in the synagogue of Pisidian Antioch has caused some readers of Acts to question the authenticity of one if not both of these speeches. B. W. Bacon held that the present speech could not "be more than the historian's attempt to tell what Paul might have said: for as a whole it simply rehearses the speech of Peter at Pentecost, with a few variations, some of which remind us of the speech of Stephen. At all events, it is quite un-Pauline, and contains not one trait of his characteristic gospel" (*The Story of St. Paul* [London, 1905], p. 103). Percy Gardner, on the other hand, thought that Peter's speech at Pentecost "so nearly resembles the speeches given to Paul that we can scarcely be mistaken in regarding it as a free composition," whereas the matter of the present speech "is eminently Pauline; and the manner, apart from the mere choice of words, is also Pauline... We may then fairly consider the speech at Antioch as an abridgement of the kind of address used by Paul towards his own countrymen" ("The Speeches of St. Paul in Acts", in *Cambridge Biblical Essays*, ed. H. B. Swete [Cambridge, 1909], pp. 397 f.). H. J. Cadbury argues for the Lukan authorship of Petrine and Pauline speeches alike on the ground of their common style and common interdependent exegesis ("The Speeches in Acts", in *Beginnings* v, pp. 407 ff.).[57] But we should bear in mind (*a*) Paul's own insistence that the gospel story which he proclaimed was the same as that proclaimed by the other apostles (1 Cor. 15:11), (*b*) the fact that the common outline of the apostolic *kerygma* may be traced throughout the whole NT, no matter who the writer or speaker may be, (*c*) the evidence for a "testimony" collection used by all the early preachers of the gospel, which goes far to account for the common interdependent exegesis of OT passages.

[57] See on the other hand the remarks of C. H. Dodd on this speech in *The Apostolic Preaching and its Developments* (London, 1936), pp. 59 f., 62: "the general scheme, and the emphasis, correspond with what we have found in the

THE BOOK OF THE ACTS

iii. Call to Faith in Christ (vv. 38–41)

38–39 The *kerygma* was regularly rounded off with a direct application to the hearers, calling for repentance and offering the forgiveness of sins to all who believed. So Paul now proclaims through Christ the remission of sins, and goes on to add a word about justification as well. Knowing Paul's gospel as it is unfolded in the Epistles to the Galatians and to the Romans, we are not surprised to find this reference to justification in the first address ascribed to him in Acts. But we may be warned not to be misled by purely verbal coincidences. "The language of 13:39", says B. W. Bacon, "is claimed as Pauline because of the single word 'justify'. The doctrine is exactly that which Paul fundamentally repudiates, and which in Gal. 2:15–21 he demonstrates against Peter to be untenable, namely, that a man may rest upon the works of the law for his general justification, and rely on the death of Christ to make up the deficiencies" (*op. cit.*, p. 103 n.).

Bacon's exegesis of the passage need not involve so radical a contradiction with the position taken up in Galatians as he supposes. One could conceivably understand Paul to be arguing thus: "Even if you expect to enjoy a right relationship with God on the basis of Moses' law, remember that Moses' law makes hardly any provision for the remission of sins committed 'with a high hand'. For these, by contrast with sins of ignorance, Moses' law almost invariably prescribes nothing but the full penalty. Why, then, go on hoping to establish a right relationship with God in this way, now that you have presented to you a Saviour who assures justification from all sins and complete acceptance before God to all who put their faith in Him?"

It is just possible to understand Paul thus because grammatically his words could be taken to mean that by Christ all those who believe receive justification from all those things from which the law of Moses provides no justification—namely, most deliberate sins. But quite certainly his words mean that believers in Christ are *completely* justified—"justified from all things"—which they

epistles . . . if we recall the close general similarity of the *kerygma* as derived from the Pauline epistles to the *kerygma* as derived from Acts, as well as Paul's emphatic assertion of the identity of his gospel with the general Christian tradition, we shall not find it altogether incredible that the speech at Pisidian Antioch may represent in a general way one form of Paul's preaching, that form, perhaps, which he adopted in synagogues when he had the opportunity of preaching there."

could never be by Moses' law. In other words, Moses' law does not justify; faith in Christ does.[58] Not only is this interpretation of Paul's words here supported by the not irrelevant consideration that this is how the doctrine of justification is presented in his epistles; it is the interpretation required by the natural emphasis of the passage itself. Paul is not making partial but total claims for the power of the gospel over against the law.

40-41 His address concludes with a note of warning. The prophet Habakkuk, on the eve of Nebuchadrezzar's rise to world-power, had called on the nations, in the name of God, to look with astonishment on the impending invasion:

> Behold ye among the nations, and look,
>   and wonder marvellously;
> for I am working a work in your days,
>   which ye will not believe though it be told you
>   (Hab. 1:5).

As these words of Habakkuk's were reminiscent of a warning uttered by Isaiah in the days of the Assyrian peril (*cf.* Isa. 28:21 f.; 29:14), so Paul now takes them up—in the LXX version, which lent itself better to his purpose[59]—and applies them to the new situation in which God is offering deliverance through the greatest of all His mighty works. Great as was the disaster that overtook those who ignored the warnings of the prophets, an even greater disaster will fall upon those who refuse the gospel.[60]

(c) Paul's Sermon arouses Interest (Ch. 13:42-43)

42 And as they went out, they besought that these words
    might be spoken to them the next sabbath.
43 Now when the synagogue broke up, many of the
    Jews and of the devout proselytes followed Paul and
    Barnabas; who, speaking to them, urged them to con-
    tinue in the grace of God.

42-43 Paul's words aroused intense interest in a large part of his audience. They had heard expositions of Scripture before, and moral exhortations, but nothing like this. They must learn more of this new message, and so they asked Paul to continue

---

[58] *Cf.* William Tyndale's marginal note here in his NT translation: "Fayth iustifieth and not the lawe."

[59] LXX "ye despisers" in place of MT "among the nations" might reflect a variant Hebrew text *ha-bozim* for *ba-goyim*; it might, on the other hand, be due to the influence of Isa. 28:22 ("be ye not scoffers").

[60] *Cf.* Dodd, *According to the Scriptures*, p. 87.

speaking on the same subject next sabbath. But the synagogue authorities had listened to his discourse with misgivings. They dismissed the congregation, perhaps, as Hort suggests, "for prudential reasons."[61] Many of the hearers, however, both Jews and "devout converts to Judaism" (RSV), followed Paul and Barnabas and showed themselves plainly disposed to accept the salvation which they had been offered through Jesus. Paul and Barnabas encouraged them to continue in this mind, to persevere in their joyful response to the grace which God had extended to them in the gospel.

A question arises about the "devout proselytes" mentioned in v. 43. It is natural to think of them as the "God-fearers" of vv. 16 and 26, and the word rendered "devout" is commonly used to denote such people, but in that case "proselytes" would be used in a looser sense than anywhere else in NT. Perhaps this is why RSV renders it here by "converts to Judaism" rather than "proselytes". But probably we ought to understand "proselytes" in its regular sense, and take the Greek to mean "many of the Jews and the proselytes who were worshipping."[62]

(d) Gentile Interest Arouses Jewish Envy (Ch. 13:44–52)

44 And the next sabbath almost the whole city was gathered together to hear the word of God.[63]

45 But when the Jews saw the multitudes, they were filled with jealousy, and contradicted the things which were spoken by Paul, and blasphemed.[64]

46 And Paul and Barnabas spake out boldly, and said, It was necessary that the word of God should first be spoken to you. Seeing[65] ye thrust it from you, and judge yourselves unworthy of eternal life, lo, we turn to the Gentiles.

47 For so hath the Lord commanded us, *saying,*
I have set thee for a light of the Gentiles,

---

[61] In *Notes to Select Readings* (Appendix I to Vol. II of Westcott and Hort's edition of *The NT in the Original Greek* [London, 1882]), pp. 95 f.

[62] K. Lake in *Beginnings,* v (London, 1933), p. 88.

[63] There is strong support for the variant reading "the word of the Lord." (*Cf.* n. 67 below.) The Western text expands "to hear the word of the Lord" thus: "to hear Paul; and when he had made a long speech concerning the Lord . . ."

[64] The Western text says "contradicting and blaspheming" (the addition "contradicting and" is tautological after "contradicted" in the principal clause).

[65] Read "But seeing" ($\dot{\epsilon}\pi\epsilon\dot{\iota}\ \delta\acute{\epsilon}$) for "Seeing" ($\dot{\epsilon}\pi\epsilon\iota\delta\acute{\eta}$), following the reading of P^{45} C 81, adopted in the margin of Westcott and Hort's text.

That thou shouldest be for salvation unto the uttermost part of the earth.

48 And as the Gentiles heard this, they were glad, and glorified[66] the word of God:[67] and as many as were ordained to eternal life believed.

49 And the word of the Lord was spread abroad throughout all the region.

50 But the Jews urged on the devout women of honourable estate, and the chief men of the city, and stirred up a persecution[68] against Paul and Barnabas, and cast them out of their borders.

51 But they shook off the dust of their feet against them, and came unto Iconium.

52 And the disciples were filled with joy and with the Holy Spirit.

44–45 During the following week, the Gentiles who had heard Paul's address spread the news through the city to such good purpose that on the next sabbath day almost the whole Gentile population turned up at the synagogue. Knowing (as we unfortunately do) how pious Christian pewholders can manifest quite un-Christian indignation when they arrive at church on a Sunday morning to find their places occupied by rank outsiders who have come to hear a popular visiting preacher, we can readily appreciate the annoyance of the Jewish community at finding their synagogue practically taken over by a Gentile congregation on this occasion. But there was a further reason for their annoyance: these Gentiles were plainly minded to give a favourable hearing to a message which they themselves, for the most part, found unacceptable. To be sure, many of the Jews did welcome the gospel as Paul had proclaimed it the previous sabbath, but the majority, including no doubt most of the leaders of the community, had no use for a salvation which was apparently open to Gentiles as much as to Jews. It was just this, indeed, which decided them against it. So they spoke out in an endeavour to refute Paul's arguments, and cast abusive aspersions on the two apostles, perhaps including the name of Jesus in their defamatory remarks.

---

[66] Cod. D reads "accepted" ($\dot{\epsilon}\delta\dot{\epsilon}\xi\alpha\nu\tau o$) for "glorified" ($\dot{\epsilon}\delta\dot{o}\xi\alpha\zeta o\nu$).

[67] As in v. 44, a number of weighty authorities (including here P^{45}) read "the word of the Lord."

[68] The Western text reads "great tribulation and persecution" (cf. p. 174, n. 1).

46 Paul and Barnabas gave a plain answer to their railing. It was right and proper, they affirmed, that Jews should have the first opportunity of hearing and believing the good news. (See p. 263). Had the Jews of Pisidian Antioch accepted it, they would have had the honour of evangelizing their Gentile neighbours, in fulfilment of Israel's world-mission outlined in Isa. 42:1 ff. and 49:1 ff. But if they would not receive the light themselves, they could not be allowed to pursue a dog-in-the-manger policy. The life of the age to come[69] had been brought near to them here and now as God's free gift in Christ; if they showed themselves unworthy[70] of it by refusing to accept it, there were others who would appreciate it: it would be offered direct to the Gentiles. And thus we are introduced to a pattern of events that was to reproduce itself in almost every place to which Paul brought the gospel: the local Jews, almost invariably, refused as a body to believe it (though in every place there were individuals among them who did believe), and it was accordingly preached to the Gentiles, who embraced it in large numbers. (*Cf.* Ch. 28:28, with exposition on pp. 533 f.) And it was regularly the Gentile God-fearers who attended the synagogue that formed the nucleus of Paul's "churches of the Gentiles." This was a special cause of Jewish hostility to Paul: the Jewish communities regarded him as one who poached on their preserves, a sheep-stealer who seduced from attendance at the synagogue many well-disposed Gentiles for whose complete conversion to Judaism they had hoped—and seduced them from the synagogue by offering them God's full blessing on what seemed to be easier terms than those imposed by the synagogue on would-be proselytes. Paul's reply to this complaint would have been that it was only the Jews' refusal to receive the gospel light that prevented them from being themselves light-bearers to the Gentiles. A synagogue which yielded its allegiance to Jesus as the Messiah would not be in danger of losing its God-fearing adherents, but would instead be able to incorporate them as full members.

47 This was in effect what Paul and Barnabas said on this

---

[69] "Eternal life" (Gk. $\zeta\omega\dot{\eta}$ $\alpha i\dot{\omega}\nu\iota o\varsigma$) reflects the Hebrew *hayye ha-'olam ha-ba*, "the life of the age to come"—*i.e.* the resurrection age. In Christ, however, this life may be possessed and enjoyed here and now as God's free gift; it is Christ's own resurrection-life shared by Him with those who have believed in Him.

[70] For the thought of unworthiness and worthiness in this connection *cf.* Matt. 22:8 and Luke 20:35.

occasion, quoting the words of Isa. 49:6. It is noteworthy that in the context of this prophecy (the second Servant Song) the nation of Israel is first addressed as the servant of Jehovah (v. 3):

> Thou art my servant;
> Israel,[71] in whom I will be glorified.

But Israel as a whole was a disobedient servant, and the prophecy found its particular fulfilment in the Messiah, in whom the ideally obedient Israel was realized. It was of the infant Christ that the aged Simeon, seeing the long-expected Lord's Anointed lie at last in his arms, quoted the language of Isa. 49:6:

> Now lettest thou thy servant depart, Lord,
> According to thy word, in peace;
> For mine eyes have seen thy salvation,
> Which thou hast prepared before the face of all peoples;
> A light for revelation to the Gentiles,
> And the glory of thy people Israel (Luke 2:29–32).

And it was Christ, by His obedience and suffering and consequent triumph, who received the fulfilment of the promise of God through the prophet (Isa. 49:6):

> It is too light a thing that thou shouldest be my servant,
> to raise up the tribes of Jacob,
> and to restore the preserved of Israel:
> I will also give thee for a light to the Gentiles,
> that thou mayest be my salvation unto the end of the earth.

And now the torch is taken up by the pioneers of the new Israel, as they undertake the mission of the Servant entrusted to them by their Master, and bear His saving light throughout the nations.

48–49 Distasteful as this announcement was to the Jews of Pisidian Antioch, it was joyful news to the Gentiles who heard it, and many of them believed the gospel—all, in fact, who had been enrolled for eternal life in the records of heaven[72] (for this appears

---

[71] For arguments against the view that "Israel" should be extruded from the text here see H. H. Rowley, *The Servant of the Lord* (London, 1952), pp. 8 f.

[72] We cannot agree with those who attempt to tone down the predestinarian note of this phrase by rendering "as many as were disposed to eternal life" (so Alford, *ad loc.*). The Greek participle is τεταγμένοι from τάσσω, and there is papyrus evidence for this verb in the sense of "inscribe" or "enroll" (*cf.* ὁρισμὸν ἔταξας, "thou hast signed a decree," in Theodotion's version of Dan. 6:12). The idea of being enrolled in the book of life or the like is found in several Biblical passages (*e.g.* Ex. 32:32 f.; Ps: 69:28; Isa. 4:3; Dan. 12:1; Luke 10:20; Phil. 4:3; Rev. 13:8; 20:12 ff.; 21:27). in the Jewish pseudepigrapha

to be the sense of the words here used). And not only in the city itself, but throughout the surrounding countryside as well, those who believed the good news carried it to others.

50 The Jewish community could not prevent the Gentiles from accepting the gospel, but they could make the place too hot to hold the missionaries. This they did by prejudicing the leading citizens of Pisidian Antioch against them. The wives of many of these leading citizens—like well-to-do women in many another city of the Roman world—were loosely attached to the synagogue as God-fearers, and it was probably through them that their husbands were influenced to the disadvantage of Paul and Barnabas. Luke is at pains to show that throughout Paul's travels in the Roman world it was generally the Jewish communities that were foremost in stirring up opposition to him,[73] rather than the civic and provincial authorities acting on their own initiative. This is an element in his apologetic emphasis. As for the leading part played by the women, that, says Ramsay, "is in perfect accord with the manners of the country. In Athens or in an Ionian city, it would have been impossible" (*St. Paul the Traveller*, p. 102).

51–52 Thus forced to leave Pisidian Antioch, Paul and Barnabas "shook off the dust of their feet" against those who had expelled them[74]—a gesture which Christ commended to His disciples when they left an inhospitable place—and took the eastward road to Iconium. Iconium (modern Konya) was then the easternmost city of the region of Galatic Phrygia (see p. 288 with nn. 9 and 10, on Ch. 14:6).[75] Since the third century B.C. it had been ruled successively by the Seleucid, Galatian and Pontic kings. It came into the Roman sphere of influence in 65 B.C., and was incorporated in the Empire in 25 B.C., when Galatia became a Roman province. From Claudius the city received the honorary imperial

---

(*e.g.* Jubilees 30:20, 22; 1 Enoch 47:3; 104:1; 108:3), and in rabbinical literature (*e.g.* TJ *Rosh-ha-Shanah* i.9.57a; TB *Rosh-ha-Shanah* 16b). The Targum of Jonathan on Isa. 4:3 ("written among the living") explains this as being "written for eternal life" (lit. "the life of the age [to come]").

[73] Exceptions are the incidents at Philippi (Ch. 16:19 ff.) and Ephesus (Ch. 19:23 ff.).

[74] Perhaps against the Jewish community rather than against the city as a whole. The gesture (*cf.* Luke 9:5; 10:11) signified the breaking off of all intercourse, and among Jews was tantamount to calling a man a heathen. The expression here may be figurative, as it is in modern speech.

[75] See W. M. Ramsay, *The Cities of St. Paul*, pp. 317 ff.

prefix and became known as Claudiconium. To this city, then, the two missionaries came, but the converts whom they left behind in Pisidian Antioch, far from being discouraged by the expulsion of the men who had brought them the gospel, were (in spite of that expulsion and no doubt of some persecution which they themselves had to endure) filled with the joy that the good news imparted and with the Holy Spirit.

CHAPTER XIV

3. ICONIUM, LYSTRA, DERBE

(Ch. 14:1–28)

(a) Adventures in Iconium (Ch. 14:1–7)

1 And it came to pass in Iconium that they entered together[1] into the synagogue of the Jews, and so spake that a great multitude both of Jews and of Greeks believed.

2 But the Jews[2] that were disobedient stirred up the souls of the Gentiles, and made them evil affected against the brethren.

3 Long time therefore they tarried *there* speaking boldly in the Lord, who bare witness unto the word of his grace, granting signs and wonders to be done by their hands.

4 But the multitude of the city was divided; and part held with the Jews, and part with the apostles.[3]

5 And when there was made an onset both of the Gentiles and of the Jews with their rulers, to treat them shamefully and to stone them,

6 they became aware of it, and fled unto the cities of Lycaonia, Lystra and Derbe, and the region round about:

7 and there they preached the gospel.[4]

[1] Instead of "together" we may render "in the same manner" (Gk. κατὰ τὸ αὐτό).

[2] The Western text recasts v. 2 as follows: "But the synagogue-chiefs of the Jews and their rulers stirred up persecution againt the righteous, and made the souls of the Gentiles evil affected against the brethren; but the Lord soon gave peace." This tries to explain why the two apostles spent a long time at Iconium (v. 3) in spite of the Jewish action of v. 2. Ramsay regarded v. 3 as an early gloss (*St. Paul the Traveller*, pp. 107 ff.); Moffatt transposes vv. 2 and 3. The Western text implies two separate attacks (a short one in v. 2, at the beginning of the apostles' visit, and a more violent one in v. 5, at the end); but we may leave the text as it stands, taking v. 2 to indicate the beginning of the Jewish leaders' opposition and v. 5 the success of their attempt to stir up the magistrates and populace.

[3] The Western text adds "cleaving to them because of the word of God."

[4] The Western text adds "and the whole populace was moved at the teaching. And Paul and Barnabas spent some time in Lystra."

1–2 When Paul and Barnabas came to Iconium they followed the same procedure as in Pisidian Antioch, visiting the Jewish synagogue and proclaiming the gospel there. Here, too, many of their hearers believed the good news, Jews and Gentiles alike. But here, too, the Jews who would not accept the gospel took active steps to expel the two missionaries, and did their best to prejudice the minds of the civic authorities and the citizen body against them.

3 It took a long time, however, for the opposition to become serious, and the missionaries continued to preach the gospel freely and boldly. The preaching was attended by miraculous signs, of a kind which confirmed the apostolic witness in the eyes of the people. Later, when writing to the converts of Iconium and the other cities evangelized at this time in South Galatia,[5] Paul appeals to the mighty works performed by the power of the Spirit in their midst, as evidence that the message of faith, and not the preaching of the law, was the gospel approved by God (Gal. 3:5). The gospel is here called "the word of his grace"—*i.e.* the message that proclaims the grace of God (*cf.* Ch. 20:24, 32).

4–5 The longer that this work of evangelization went on, the more decisively did the population take sides, either with the Jewish leaders or with the apostles.[6] At last a riot broke out, and the city mob was incited to assault and stone the apostles.

6–7 Fortunately, the two men got wind of the plan to manhandle them, and made their escape from Iconium before the mob could gain its objective. But they had made their mark in Iconium. Paul, in particular, left an impression there that was not soon

---

[5] The view taken throughout this commentary, on what is regarded as conclusive evidence, is that the churches addressed by Paul in his Epistle to the Galatians were the churches planted during this missionary journey, at Pisidian Antioch, Iconium, Lystra and Derbe. See W. M. Ramsay, *A Historical Commentary on St. Paul's Epistle to the Galatians* (London, 1899); K. Lake, *The Earlier Epistles of St. Paul* (London, 1911), pp. 253–316; H. N. Ridderbos, *The Epistle of Paul to the Churches of Galatia* (Grand Rapids, 1953), pp. 22 ff.

[6] In vv. 4 and 14 Barnabas and Paul are referred to as "the apostles"; this is a more general use of the term than that found elsewhere in Acts. Barnabas, although not one of the twelve, may have been one of the hundred and twenty believers of Ch. 1:15 and a witness of the resurrection of Christ. Here the word may have the sense "missionaries" or "commissioners"; apart from Paul's special and direct commissioning by Christ, he and Barnabas were commissioned by the church of Syrian Antioch to undertake their present work, at the direction of the Holy Spirit. But that Barnabas was an apostle like himself seems to be implied by Paul in 1 Cor. 9:6; Gal. 2:9 f.

forgotten; it is reflected in the description of him preserved in the second-century *Acts of Paul*—a description so vigorous and unconventional that it must surely rest upon a good local tradition of what Paul looked like.[7] One Onesiphorus, a resident in Iconium, sets out to meet Paul, who is on his way to the city. "And he saw Paul approaching, a man small in size, with meeting eyebrows, with a rather large nose, bald-headed, bow-legged, strongly built, full of grace, for at times he looked like a man, and at times he' had the face of an angel."

From Iconium, then, Paul and Barnabas made their way to "the cities of Lycaonia, Lystra and Derbe" (v. 6). The implication is that Iconium itself was not in Lycaonia. The region of the province of Galatia called (probably) Galatic Lycaonia lay east of the region called Galatic Phrygia; it was politically distinct from the district called Antiochian Lycaonia which lay farther east and belonged to the domain of Antiochus, king of Commagene, and not to the province of Galatia.

Sir William Ramsay has recorded how it was this geographical note in v. 6 that led to his "first change of judgment" with regard to the historical value of Acts.[8] Xenophon, to be sure, in 401 B.C., refers to Iconium as "the last city of Phrygia" (*Anabasis* i. 2. 19); but writers such as Cicero (*Letters to his Friends* xv. 4. 2) and Pliny the Elder (*Natural History* v. 25),[9] who lived much nearer to apostolic times, call it a Lycaonian city. Ramsay at first assumed, as others had done, that the author of Acts, wishing to add verisimilitude to an account of events in an area with which he was not personally acquainted, borrowed from Xenophon the information that Iconium was in Phrygia, not realizing that the regional frontier had shifted since Xenophon's day. But further acquaintance with both literary and epigraphic evidence convinced him that the statement in Acts was entirely correct, that Iconium was as Phrygian a city in the middle of the first century as it had been 450 years earlier.[10] Those writers who refer to it as Lycaonian

---

[7] *Cf.* W. M. Ramsay, *The Church in the Roman Empire* (London, 1893), pp. 31 f.; M. R. James, *The Aprocryphal NT* (Oxford, 1924), p. 273. *Cf.* Ch. 6:15.

[8] *The Bearing of Recent Discovery on the Trustworthiness of the NT* (London, 1915), pp. 35 ff.

[9] But in a later passage in the same book of his *Natural History* (v. 41), Pliny mentions "Conium" (*i.e.* Iconium) as a Phrygian city.

[10] In the *Acts of Justin*, ch. 3 (*c.* A.D. 165) a Christian slave named Hierax says he was taken from "Iconium of Phrygia." In fact, Iconium remained

do so loosely because it lay near the frontier of Lycaonia and commonly shared the fortunes of that region.

Lystra,[11] like Pisidian Antioch, was made a Roman colony by Augustus in A.D. 6. The two colonies, which were about a hundred miles apart, were directly connected by a military road, which did not pass through Iconium. The site of Lystra was identified by J. R. S. Sterrett in 1885 at Zoldera, near Hatin Sarai.

(b) The Miracle at Lystra (Ch. 14:8–18)

8 And at Lystra there sat a certain man, impotent in his feet, a cripple from his mother's womb, who never had walked.

9 The same heard Paul speaking:[12] who, fastening his eyes upon him, and seeing that he had faith to be made whole,

10 said with a loud voice,[13] Stand upright on thy feet.[14] And he leaped up and walked.

11 And when the multitude saw what Paul had done, they lifted up their voice, saying in the speech of Lycaonia, The gods are come down to us in the likeness of men.

12 And they called Barnabas, Jupiter; and Paul, Mercury, because he was the chief speaker.

13 And the priest of Jupiter whose *temple* was before the city,[15] brought oxen and garlands unto the gates, and would have done sacrifice with the multitudes.

14 But when the apostles, Barnabas and Paul, heard of it, they rent their garments, and sprang forth[16] among the multitude, crying out

Phrygian until A.D. 295, when a province of Pisidia was formed, including Pisidian Antioch and Iconium. For epigraphic evidence see also W. M. Calder in *Journal of Hellenic Studies* xxxi (1911), pp. 188 ff. (in an article "Corpus Inscriptionum Neo-Phrygiarum", pp. 161 ff.), and especially in *Journal of Roman Studies* ii (1912), pp. 80 ff. (in an article "Colonia Caesareia Antiocheia"). Paul and Barnabas probably knew when they crossed the regional frontier not only by the change in the local vernacular but also by noting a boundary stone on the road.

[11] See Ramsay, *The Cities of St. Paul* (London, 1907), pp. 407 ff.

[12] The Western text adds "being in fear."

[13] The Western text inserts "I say unto thee in the name of the Lord Jesus Christ"—an addition which is calculated to intensify the resemblance to Ch. 3:6.

[14] The Western text adds "and walk" (*cf.* Ch. 3:6) and continues "And immediately straightway he leaped up and walked."

[15] The Western text reads "And the priests of the local Zeus Propolis."

[16] The Byzantine text has "sprang in" ($\varepsilon i\sigma\varepsilon\pi\acute\eta\delta\eta\sigma\alpha\nu$) for "sprang out" ($\dot\varepsilon\xi\varepsilon\pi\acute\eta\delta\eta\sigma\alpha\nu$).

15 and saying, Sirs, why do ye these things? We also[17] are men of like passions with you, and bring you good tidings, that ye should turn from these vain things unto a living God,[18] who made the heaven and the earth and the sea, and all that in them is:

16 who in the generations gone by suffered all the nations to walk in their own ways.

17 And yet he left not himself without witness, in that he did good and gave you from heaven rains and fruitful seasons, filling your hearts with food and gladness.

18 And with these sayings scarce restrained they the multitudes from doing sacrifice unto them.[19]

8 The description of the lame man at Lystra, and of his being healed by the word of power spoken by Paul, is notably similar to the description of the lame man in the temple court at Jerusalem in Ch. 3, who was healed through his faith in the name of Jesus invoked by Peter. But the sequel to the healing is totally different, and is narrated in a form remarkably full of local colour. The genuine and apparently incurable nature of the man's lameness is emphasized by repetition: he had, we are told, no strength in his feet; he was a cripple from birth; he had never walked.

9-10 Yet, as Paul was preaching, he saw this man listening to him and realized that he "had faith to be made whole." While the expression refers here to the recovery of bodily health, yet even in a pagan context "there lies latent in it[20] some undefined and hardly conscious thought of the spiritual and the moral, which made it suit Paul's purpose admirably" (W. M. Ramsay, *The Teaching of Paul in Terms of the Present Day* [London, 1914], p. 95). And in Acts, as in the Gospels, we should note how regularly faith is emphasized as a condition of receiving both physical and spiritual healing. That this lame man had faith was made plain by his ready obedience to Paul's command to stand

---

[17] P45 omits "also."

[18] Codd. A B C with a corrector of א and the second hand in D have "*a* living God"; most other authorities have "*the* living God", but in a sufficient variety of forms to suggest that the original text lacked the definite article.

[19] Codd. C 33 81 431 614 2147 with the Old Latin codex h, the margin of the Harclean Syriac and the Armenian version, add "but that they should each go home"—an addition which may belong to the original Western text.

[20] That is to say, in the verb σωθῆναι (as used here) or in its cognate noun σωτηρία ("health," "salvation").

up; he leaped to his feet, found that they supported his weight, and began to walk for the first time in his life.

11-12 The miraculous cure struck amazement into the crowd of bystanders. These were not the Roman citizens of the colony, whose language (as appears from funerary inscriptions) was Latin, but the native Anatolian population, who still spoke their Lycaonian vernacular. The fact that the crowd cried out in Lycaonian is specially mentioned by Luke (who possibly got his information from Paul) for two probable reasons: in the first place, Paul and Barnabas recognized that this was a different language from the Phrygian which they had heard on the lips of the indigenous population of Pisidian Antioch and Iconium; in the second place, the crowd's use of Lycaonian explains why Paul and Barnabas did not grasp what was afoot until the preparations to pay them divine honours were well advanced.

For the Lystrans, seeing the instantaneous cure performed on the lame man, concluded that they were being favoured with a divine visitation. Local legend told of earlier occasions when the gods had come down to them in the likeness of men—in particular, the two gods whom the Greeks knew as Zeus and Hermes.[21] These are the two names mentioned by Luke here, but we cannot be sure whether the crowd used these two names or the names of two Anatolian deities identified with Zeus and Hermes.

Ovid tells the story of an aged and pious couple of that region, Philemon and Baucis by name, who entertained Jupiter and Mercury (the Roman equivalents of Zeus and Hermes) unawares, and were rewarded for their hospitality (*Metamorphoses* viii. 626 ff.).[22] But in more recent times the evidence of epigraphy has effectively supplemented that of classical legend. Of two inscriptions from Sedasa, near Lystra, dating from the middle of the third century, and discovered by Professor W. M. Calder, one records the dedication to Zeus of a statue of Hermes by men with Lycaonian names; the other mentions "priests of Zeus".[23] Another

---

[21] These Greek names are the names given by Luke; the Latin equivalents Jupiter and Mercury (Mercurius, AV) given in AV, ERV, ARV, are due to an old and foolish fashion of replacing Greek proper names by their Latin equivalents in English translations from the Greek. It is a pity that ERV and ARV did not revert to the Greek forms, as RSV has rightly done. *Cf.* p. 395, n. 38 (on Ch. 19:24).

[22] See W. M. Calder, "New Light on Ovid's Story of Philemon and Baucis," in *Discovery* iii (1922), pp. 207 ff.

[23] See W. M. Calder in *Classical Review* xxiv (1910), pp. 76 ff., xxxviii

indication of the joint worship of Zeus and Hermes in those parts is provided by a stone altar discovered near Lystra by Professor Calder and Professor W. H. Buckler in 1926, dedicated to the "Hearer of Prayer" (presumably Zeus) and Hermes.[24]

Zeus was the chief god in the Greek pantheon; Hermes, son of Zeus by Maia, was the herald of the gods. Barnabas may have been identified with Zeus because of his more dignified bearing; Paul, the more animated of the two, was called Hermes "because he was the chief speaker"—a very similar expression is used of Hermes by the early fourth-century Neoplatonist writer Iamblichus when describing the Egyptian mysteries.[25]

13 If the gods had condescended to pay the people of Lystra a visit, they must receive appropriate honours, and the Lystrans, led by the priest of Zeus Propolis[26] (*i.e.* Zeus whose temple lay in front of the city gates), prepared to sacrifice oxen to them—the oxen being duly decked with woollen garlands or fillets as befitted animals about to be offered to the gods.

14 It was some time before Paul and Barnabas recognized what the people had in mind, and when they did so, they rushed out from the place where they were,[27] with every mark of horror[28] at the idolatrous worship of which they were to be the unwitting recipients, and protested against it as vehemently as they could.

15–17 The summary which Luke gives of their expostulation provides us with one of the two examples found in Acts of the preaching of the gospel to purely pagan audiences.[29] The other, and fuller, example is the speech delivered by Paul before the

---

(1924), p. 29, n. 1, and in *Expositor*, Ser. vii, Vol. x (1910), pp. 1 ff., 148 ff.

[24] See W. M. Calder in *Discovery* vii (1926), p. 262, and in ExT xxxvii (1925–6), p. 528.

[25] Iamblichus (*On the Egyptian Mysteries*, i) calls Hermes θεὸς ὁ τῶν λόγων ἡγεμών (the "god who is the leader in speaking"); *cf.* Luke's expression ὁ ἡγούμενος τοῦ λόγου (v. 12).

[26] On the significance of this title see Ramsay, *The Church in the Roman Empire*, pp. 51 ff. He further argues that the Western reading "priests" is probably "more true to actual facts."

[27] Ephrem Syrus thinks the sacrificial ox was brought to the door of the house where the apostles were staying.

[28] The rending of garments among the Jews was a gesture of horror at blasphemy (*cf.* Mark 14:63).

[29] Although Cornelius and his household were still technically Gentiles when Peter visited Caesarea, they were not raw pagans but God-fearers, acquainted both with the OT scriptures and with the general facts about Jesus of Nazareth.

Athenian Areopagus (Ch. 17:22 ff.).[30] We should not expect such preaching to insist on the fulfilment of OT prophecy, as preaching to Jews and God-fearers did; instead, an appeal to the natural revelation of God the Creator is put in the forefront. Yet this appeal is couched in language largely drawn from the OT. Martin Dibelius points out that the speech at Lystra shows dependence on the LXX—even more (he thinks) than the later speech at Athens does. "The proclamation of God … is made in complete OT fashion (see Ex. 20:11); the gods are described as 'vain ones' or 'vanities' as in 3 Kingdoms 16:2, 13, 26; 4 Kingdoms 17:15; Esther 4:17 (LXX expansion); Jer. 2:5; 8:19; Matt. 6:11" (*Aufsätze zur Apostelgeschichte* [Göttingen, 1951], p. 65, n. 3).[31]

If it be asked whether Paul would have expressed himself in this way, even to a pagan audience, it may be pointed out that his description of the Thessalonians' conversion from paganism in 1 Thess. 1:9 f. presupposes preaching very similar to that given here at Lystra. To Jews, who already know that God is one, and that He is the living and true God, the gospel proclaims that Jesus is the Christ, but pagans must first be taught what Jews already confess regarding the unity and character of God. "God is one," they are told, "and has not left Himself without witness; His works of creation and providence show Him to be the living God who supplies the needs of men; therefore abandon those gods which are no gods but utter vanities, and turn to the true God."[32]

That God in former days permitted the nations to "walk in their own ways" is parallel to the statement in Ch. 17:30 that He "overlooked" the times of ignorance before the full revelation of His will appeared. Yet the ignorance should not have been so great as it actually was, for the way in which God ordered the seasons, so as to give food to all flesh, ought to have made men mindful of Him and of His claims upon their worship. In Rom. 1:19 ff. Paul also emphasizes that if men had paid heed to the works of God in creation, they might even in them have found

---

[30] See pp. 352 ff. below. M. Lackmann, *Vom Geheimnis der Schöpfung* (Stuttgart, 1952), reviews the exegesis of both speeches and of Rom. 1:18–23; 2:14–16.

[31] From his essay "Paulus auf dem Areopag" (pp. 29 ff.), originally published in 1939 at Heidelberg. Dibelius considers that the content and outlook of the Lystra speech and of the Areopagitica make it impossible to ascribe them to Paul. See p. 354, nn. 32 and 33.

[32] The point at which a transition could be made from this general argument to distinctively Christian preaching may be seen in Ch. 17:30 f.

tokens of His "everlasting power and divinity" (v. 20). There is, indeed, a difference in emphasis between what he says in this regard to the Roman Christians and what he says to pagan audiences in Lystra and Athens: in Acts 14 and 17 the point is that, until the full revelation of God came to the Gentiles, He overlooked their errors which arose through ignorance of His will; in Rom. 1 God's giving them up to their own devices is the penalty for their rejection of even the limited light which was available to them. But His "overlooking" their errors betokened not indifference but patience.

The providence of God in giving men rainfall and harvest is an OT theme (*cf.* Gen. 8:22), and the conjunction of "food and gladness" (v. 17; *cf.* Ch. 2:46) is a feature of OT language (*cf.* Ps. 4:7; Isa. 25:6; Eccl. 9:7); for the idea of the heart's being satisfied with food *cf.* Luke 21:34.

18 Thus Paul and Barnabas spoke, and succeeded—albeit with difficulty—in dissuading the Lystrans from paying divine honours to "men of like passions" with themselves.[33]

(c) Persecution at Lystra: They Visit Derbe and Return to Syrian Antioch (Ch. 14:19–28)

19 But[34] there came Jews thither from Antioch and Iconium: and having persuaded the multitudes, they stoned Paul, and dragged him out of the city, supposing that he was dead.

20 But as the[35] disciples stood round about him, he rose up,[36] and entered into the city: and on the morrow he went forth with Barnabas to Derbe.

21 And when they had preached the gospel to that city, and had made many disciples, they returned to Lystra, and to Iconium, and to Antioch,

---

[33] M. Dibelius, who considers that the speech of vv. 15–17 is an editorial insertion in an independent and dramatic narrative, thinks that the narrative must originally have ended in a less "insipid" way (*op. cit.*, pp. 66, 167, n. 4).

[34] The Western text expands this verse: "And as they spent some time there and taught, there came certain Jews from Iconium and Antioch, and while they [the apostles] were discoursing with boldness they persuaded the crowds to revolt against them, saying, 'Nothing that they say is true; it is all lies.' And having stirred up the crowds and having stoned Paul, they dragged him out of the city..."

[35] P45 with D and E have "his disciples."

[36] The Old Latin codex h (a Western authority) and the Sahidic Coptic add "at evening", which is also implied by the paraphrase of Ephrem Syrus.

22 confirming the souls of the disciples, exhorting them
to continue in the faith, and that[37] through many tribulations we must enter into the kingdom of God.

23 And when they had appointed for them elders in every
church, and had prayed with fasting, they commended
them to the Lord, on whom they had believed.

24 And they passed through Pisidia, and came to Pamphylia.

25 And when they had spoken the word in Perga, they
went down to Attalia;[38]

26 and thence they sailed to Antioch, from whence they
had been committed to the grace of God for the work
which they had fulfilled.

27 And when they were come, and had gathered the
church together, they rehearsed all things that God
had done with them,[39] and that he had opened a door
of faith unto the Gentiles.

28 And they tarried no little time with the disciples.

19 We are not told if there was a Jewish community and
synagogue at Lystra. Probably there was, however; this would
explain more easily how Jews from Pisidian Antioch and Iconium
were able to incite the Lystrans against Paul and Barnabas. This
would not have been so easy had these Jews been complete
strangers lacking any point of contact with the populace of Lystra,
but they could achieve their purpose more conveniently through
a Jewish community in Lystra. In any case, although more than
a hundred miles separated Lystra from Pisidian Antioch, the
degree of intercourse between the two places is evidenced by the
fact that the citizens of Lystra set up a statue in Pisidian Antioch
(*cf.* W. M. Ramsay, *The Church in the Roman Empire* [London,
1893], pp. 47 ff.).

Paul, so lately acclaimed as the messenger of the Immortals,
was the chief target for the violent assault that followed. When,
some years later, he sums up all that he has had to endure for
the gospel's sake and includes the item, "once was I stoned"
(2 Cor. 11:25), this was the occasion he had in mind. And when,
writing to these very places in South Galatia, he says "I bear

---

[37] From "through many tribulations" to "kingdom of God" is direct speech;
it should therefore be introduced by "saying" instead of "and that."

[38] The Western text adds "preaching the gospel to them."

[39] For "with them" the Western text has the Semitism "with their souls"
(*cf.* Ps. 66:16).

295

branded on my body the marks of Jesus" (Gal. 6:17), the indelible scars to which he refers are almost certainly those which were left by the rough handling and stoning he received at Lystra. There is grim irony in the quick reversal of the local attitude to the two apostles!

20 The way in which Luke describes how Paul, after being stoned, dragged out of the city, and left for dead, suddenly stood up and went back into the city has a flavour of miracle about it. The additional statement found in some texts, that it was in the evening that he re-entered Lystra, is very probably true.

Derbe, to which he went with Barnabas on the following day, lay in the vicinity of the modern village of Zosta. According to the lexicographer Stephen of Byzantium, the name is derived from Lycaonian *delbeia*, meaning "juniper." It was at this time a frontier-city of the province of Galatia, and like Iconium it had the imperial title conferred upon it by Claudius, being known as Claudioderbe.[40]

21 Having preached the gospel and founded a church in Derbe, Paul and Barnabas retraced their steps. They had reached the limits of the province. "New magistrates," Ramsay suggests, "had now come into office in all the cities whence they had been driven; and it was therefore possible to go back" (*St. Paul the Traveller*, p. 120). Even so, we must pay our tribute to the courage of the two apostles in returning so soon to Lystra, Iconium and Pisidian Antioch—cities from which they had so lately been expelled with shameful brutality.

22–23 In these cities they strengthened the young churches which they had so recently planted, putting their administration on a firm basis by appointing suitable members as elders,[41] who would be true spiritual guides to their brethren, and giving them further instruction and encouragement in face of the hardship and persecution which they would inevitably have to face as they maintained their Christian witness. It is almost taken for granted in the NT that tribulation is the normal lot of Christians: it is

[40] See Ramsay, *The Cities of St. Paul*, pp. 384 ff.

[41] On the model of the elders of the Jerusalem church, but necessarily fewer in numbers. Many modern missionaries would probably think it unwise to appoint as elders men who had so recently been converted to Christianity. Paul and Barnabas were more conscious of the presence and power of the Holy Spirit in the Christian communities. *Cf.* R. Allen, *Missionary Methods: St. Paul's or Ours?* (London, 1927), pp. 107 ff.

those who suffer with Christ who are to share His royal glory (*cf.* Rom. 8:17; 2 Thess. 1:4 ff.; 2 Tim. 2:12). "No cross, no crown." Then, with prayer and fasting, they commended the young churches with their newly-appointed elders to the Lord, and continued their journey.

24–26 From Pisidian Antioch they crossed the regional frontier into Pisidia, the southernmost region of the Galatian province, and crossing it from north to south they entered the province of Pamphylia. Here they preached in Perga, where they had called when they landed in Asia Minor from Cyprus (Ch. 13:13); and then went down to the port of Attalia (modern Antalya) at the mouth of the Cataractes (modern Ak Su). There they took ship for the mouth of the Orontes, and so completed a very eventful circular tour.

27–28 When they came back to Syrian Antioch, the church was naturally eager to hear how they had fared. The church of Antioch had more than a natural interest in the wonderful story which Paul and Barnabas had to tell; they shared in the responsibility and the glory of their missionary service, for it was with the blessing and fellowship of the whole church of Antioch that the two apostles had set forth upon their campaign of Gentile evangelization. The missionary tour had occupied the best part of a year, and now Paul and Barnabas spent another year or thereby in Antioch. But their activity in Cyprus and Asia Minor was a matter of interest not only in Syrian Antioch but in other places as well; in particular, Jerusalem was concerned about the implications of a forward movement which so decisively altered the balance of Jews and Gentiles in the Church.

CHAPTER XV

4. THE COUNCIL OF JERUSALEM

(Ch. 15:1-29)

The Council of Jerusalem is an event to which Luke plainly attaches the highest importance; it is as epoch-making, in his eyes, as the conversion of Paul or the preaching of the gospel to Cornelius and his household. His account of this occasion has been impugned by a number of scholars as tendentious and largely unhistorical,[1] mainly because of the difficulty of reconciling it with the evidence of the Pauline evidence—a difficulty that has been felt by more conservative scholars as well. If Paul and the Jerusalem apostles reached such an agreement as Luke suggests, how are we to account for the apparent tension between him and them reflected in his Galatian and Corinthian correspondence? Why, in that correspondence, does he make no reference to the terms of the letter which was sent to the Gentile churches after the Council?[2] And what is the relation of the Council of Acts 15 to the interview which Paul and Barnabas had with James, Peter and John, as recorded in Gal. 2:1-10?

The view taken here is that Galatians was written shortly before the Council of Jerusalem. This would adequately explain why

---

[1] Cf., e.g., H. Windisch in Beginnings ii (London, 1922), pp. 321 ff.; A. D. Nock, St. Paul (London, 1938), pp. 114 ff.

[2] The reason for the absence of any reference to the letter in Galatians is suggested in the exposition above; the situation at Corinth was different. Whereas the Judaizers in the Galatian churches, before the Council of Jerusalem, carried on in James's name direct propaganda for their legalist position, such direct methods were inappropriate after the council. The primary tactics of the Judaizers at Corinth, who appealed to the name and prestige of Peter, were directed towards the undermining of Paul's authority in the eyes of his converts. It would have been pointless to quote the apostolic letter in reply to these tactics; besides, Paul had to counter them in such a way as to afford no handle to the antinomian party in the Corinthian church. And Paul knew a more excellent way of dealing with the question of meat offered to idols— a live issue in the Corinthian church—than the way of simple prohibition found in the apostolic letter. See W. L. Knox, The Acts of the Apostles (Cambridge, 1948), pp. 48 f.

that epistle makes no allusion to the Council of Jerusalem. If Gal. 2:1–10 and Acts 15:6–29 purported to relate one and the same set of events, then one at least of the two accounts could not be acquitted of misrepresenting the facts. But might not Gal. 2:1–10 narrate a private interview which took place during the visit of Paul and Barnabas to Jerusalem which also saw the Council of Acts 15?[3] In that case, Paul can scarcely be acquitted of *suppressio veri* in his letter to the Galatians; the discussions and decision of the Council, as represented by Luke, were distinctly relevant to the Galatian controversy. To suppose that such an apostolic letter as Luke describes was drawn up, but that Paul had nothing to do with it,[4] is to make Luke a writer of historical fiction, in face of his own assurance about his methods. Nor is it much more satisfactory to suppose that the Council took place rather later than the occasion to which Luke refers it—for example, during Paul's brief Jerusalem visit recorded in Acts 18:22.[5]

According to Acts, the visit which Paul paid to Jerusalem at the time of the Council was his third visit after his conversion. The first visit is mentioned in Ch. 9:26 ff.; the second in Chs. 11:30; 12:25. In Galatians Paul tells of two visits which he paid to Jerusalem after his conversion. The first (Gal. 1:18 ff.) may be identified fairly certainly with that of Acts 9:26 ff. The second (Gal. 2:1 ff.) is usually identified with that of Acts 15, but good arguments exist (as we have seen) for identifying it with that of Acts 11:30 *(cf.* p. 244).[6] It is unsatisfactory to suppose that Paul

---

[3] For this view see J. B. Lightfoot, *Galatians* (London, 1890), pp. 125 f.; H. N. Ridderbos, *Galatians* (Grand Rapids, 1953), pp. 78 ff. "We have no reason", says Wilfred Knox, "for supposing that the Church had by this date reached that stage of democracy in which the public meeting registers its assent to a decision reached in advance by its leading members" (*op. cit.,* p. 42). See the careful discussion by J. G. Machen in *The Origin of Paul's Religion* (New York, 1921), pp. 78 ff.

[4] *Cf.* Windisch, *op. cit.,* p. 328; H. Lietzmann, *The Beginnings of the Christian Church* (Eng. tr., London, 1949), pp. 108 f. O. Cullmann (*Peter: Disciple, Apostle, Martyr* [Eng. tr., London, 1953], pp. 42 ff.) identifies the meeting of Gal. 2:1 ff. with that of Acts 15:6 ff., and supposes that Acts is right in its chronological placing of the meeting, but wrong in attaching the decree to it: the decree was drawn up later, without Paul's knowledge.

[5] *Cf.* John Knox, *Chapters in a Life of Paul* (Nashville, 1950), pp. 64 ff.; D. T. Rowlingson, "The Jerusalem Conference and Jesus' Nazareth Visit", JBL lxxi (1952), pp. 69 ff.

[6] Is Luke then guilty of a serious *suppressio veri* in omitting to state that during this famine-relief visit Paul and Barnabas had the interview with the James, Peter and John described in Gal. 2:1 ff.? Hardly, because however

entirely omits to mention the visit of Acts 11:30 in the autobiographical sketch which he gives to the Galatians;[7] he is concerned to mention each occasion on which he visited Jerusalem after his conversion in order to show that on none of them did he receive his apostolic commission from the Jerusalem authorities. Had he failed to include one visit (however innocently), this failure would under the circumstances have aroused keen suspicion.[8] It is even less satisfactory to identify the visits of Acts 11:30 and 15:2 ff. and suppose that Luke, drawing upon two sources, has made two visits out of one.[9]

A reasonable and satisfying sequence of events can be reconstructed if we accept the view that the Epistle to the Galatians was written to the churches in South Galatia founded by Paul and Barnabas during their first missionary tour of that area, and written from Antioch shortly before the Council of Jerusalem.[10]

important that interview was when Paul wrote to the Galatians, its importance was swallowed up by that of the Jerusalem conference which took place a little later; and Luke may have known little, if anything, of the earlier interview. See W. L. Knox, *op. cit.*, pp. 44 f.

[7] J. B. Lightfoot (*op. cit.*, p. 127) suggests that at the time of the famine-relief visit the apostles were absent from Jerusalem as a result of the persecution under Herod Agrippa I, and Paul and Barnabas saw the elders only, so that Paul felt at liberty to ignore this visit in writing to the Galatians. But even the elders, many of whom had been in Christ before Paul, could conceivably have "added" something to him.

[8] The same objection would apply to T. W. Manson's suggestion that the Jerusalem visit of Gal. 2:1 ff. is not mentioned in Acts, but was paid on the eve of Barnabas and Paul's departure for Cyprus and Asia Minor (Acts 13:2 ff.). See his article "The Problem of the Epistle to the Galatians", BJRL xxiv (1940), pp. 59 ff.

[9] For this view *cf.* J. Wellhausen in *Nachrichten d. kgl. Gesellschaft d. Wissenschaften zu Göttingen*, phil.-hist. Kl., 1907, pp. 1 ff.; E. Schwartz, *ib.*, pp. 263 ff.; K. Lake, *Beginnings* v (London, 1933), pp. 199 ff.; H. Windisch, *ib.*, ii, p. 322; H. W. Beyer, *Die Apostelgeschichte* (Das NT Deutsch, Göttingen, 1951), *ad loc.* R. Eisler combined acceptance of this thesis with vindication of Luke's accuracy by supposing that the text of Acts had become dislocated, the original arrangement having been: 11:25 f.; 13:1–15:2; 11:27–30; 15:3–33 (34); 12:25; 12:1–24; 15:35–41 (*The Enigma of the Fourth Gospel* [London, 1938], p. 80).

[10] This view was formerly held by K. Lake: see his *Earlier Epistles of Paul* (London, 1911), pp. 297 ff.; it has also been maintained by V. Weber, *Die Abfassung des Galaterbriefs vor dem Apostelkonzil* (Ravensburg, 1900); D. Round, *The Date of St. Paul's Epistle to the Galatians* (Cambridge, 1906); W. M. Ramsay, *Teaching of Paul* (London, 1913), pp. 372 ff. and *St. Paul the Traveller* (14th edn., London, 1920), pp. xxii, xxxi; C. W. Emmet, *Galatians* (Reader's Commentary, London, 1912), pp. xiv ff. and *Beginnings* ii, pp. 269 ff.; A. W. F. Blunt, *Acts* (Clarendon Bible, Oxford, 1922), pp. 182 ff. (*cf.* his commentary on Galatians in the same series [1925], pp. 22 ff., 77 ff.); F. C.

The rapid progress of Gentile evangelization in Antioch itself and in Cyprus and Asia Minor presented the more conservative Jewish Christians with a serious problem. The Jerusalem apostles had aquiesced in Peter's action in the house of Cornelius because it was attended by such evident marks of divine approval; but now a completely new situation confronted them. Before long there would be more Gentile Christians than Jewish Christians in the world. The Jewish Christians feared that the influx of so many Gentile believers would bring about a weakening of Christian moral standards, and the evidence of Paul's Corinthian correspondence shows that their misgivings were not unfounded. How was this new situation to be controlled?

Many members of the Jerusalem church had a simple answer. Since so many Jews had refused to recognize Jesus as the Messiah, it was necessary, they conceded, to admit Gentiles into the messianic community in order to make up the full complement. But these Gentiles should be admitted on terms similar to those required of proselytes to Judaism: they must be circumcised and assume the obligation to keep the Mosaic law.

But it seems clear that these conditions had not been insisted upon outside Jerusalem. Even Cornelius and his household do not appear to have had the duty of circumcision pressed upon them; and certainly the Gentile converts of Antioch and South Galatia had been admitted to church fellowship without being circumcised. There were, indeed, some Jews in those days who thought that the outward rite of circumcision might be omitted, provided that its spiritual significance was realized;[11] but these formed a negligible minority. The vast majority, including even such a hellenized Jew as Philo of Alexandria,[12] insisted on

Burkitt, *Christian Beginnings* (London, 1924), pp. 116 ff.; H. N. Bate, *A Guide to the Epistles of St. Paul* (London, 1926), pp. 45 ff.; G. S. Duncan, *Galatians* (MNT, London, 1934), pp. xxii ff.; W. L. Knox, *op. cit.*, pp. 40 ff.; R. Heard, INT (London, 1950), p. 183; H. F. D. Sparks, *The Formation of the NT* (London, 1952), pp. 60 f. But it has often been overlooked that John Calvin's commentary on Galatians, published in 1548, identifies the Jerusalem visit of Gal. 2:1 ff. with that of Acts 11:30, and dates Galatians before the Council of Jerusalem.

[11] According to Josephus (*Antiquities* xx. 2. 4), Ananias, the Jewish instructor of Izates, king of Adiabene, advised him to worship God after the Jewish religion without being circumcised (c. A.D. 40).

[12] Philo (*Migration of Abraham* 89–94) opposes those Jews who neglect the literal observance of ceremonial laws on the ground that it is sufficient to learn and practise the spiritual lessons which these laws teach; "nor, because

circumcision as indispensable for all males in the commonwealth of Israel, whether they entered it by birth or by proselytization. This was no doubt the attitude of the rank and file in the Jerusalem church—"zealots for the law", as they are called on a later occasion (Ch. 21:20). For many of them the church was little more than a new party within the frontiers of Judaism, even if it was the party which embodied the ancestral hope which all Israel ought to have welcomed. If Paul and Barnabas neglected to bring the requirements of the law to the attention of Gentile members of the church of Antioch and her daughter churches, there were those in the Jerusalem church who were ready to repair this omission. Thus they precipitated the state of affairs which the Council of Jerusalem was convened to deal with.

(a) Paul and Barnabas Go Up to Jerusalem (Ch. 15:1–5)

1 And certain men[13] came down from Judaea and taught the brethren, saying, Except ye be circumcised[14] after the custom of Moses, ye cannot be saved.
2 And when Paul and Barnabas had no small dissension and questioning with them,[15] *the brethren* appointed that Paul and Barnabas, and certain other of them, should go up to Jerusalem unto the apostles and elders about this question.
3 They therefore, being brought on their way by the church, passed through both Phoenicia and Samaria, declaring the conversion of the Gentiles: and they caused great joy unto all the brethren.
4 And when they were come to Jerusalem, they were received of the church and the apostles and the elders, and they rehearsed all things that God had done with them.
5 But there rose up certain of the sect of the Pharisees

circumcision signifies the cutting away of pleasure and all passions and the destruction of impious glory..., let us abolish the law of circumcision."

13 After "certain men" the Western text adds "of the sect of the Pharisees who believed" (from v. 5).

14 After "circumcised" the Western text adds "and walk".

15 After "with them" the Western text adds: "for Paul insisted that they should remain just as they were when they believed, those who had come from Jerusalem charged Paul and Barnabas and certain others to go up to the apostles and elders at Jerusalem that they might be judged before them concerning this question" (a form of words perhaps borrowed in part from Ch. 25:9).

who believed, saying,[16] It is needful to circumcise
them,[17] and to charge them to keep the law of Moses.

1 "Certain men came down from Judaea." We take these men
to be the same as the "certain" who "came from James" in Paul's
narrative in Gal. 2:12.[18] These men exceeded the terms of their
commission (whatever their commission was) and took matters
into their own hands by their insistence that circumcision and
submission to the Mosaic law were necessary for salvation. The
Epistle to the Galatians enables us to fill out the brief summary
here provided by Luke.

These visitors from Judaea would naturally refuse all social
intercourse with uncircumcised persons, and that included the
common participation in the Lord's Supper. They thus introduced
a controversial situation into the Antiochene church in regard
both to the fundamental question of the way of salvation and to
the practical question of fellowship between Jewish and Gentile
Christians. Some who would have refused to compromise on the
former were inclined to make a temporary concession in respect
of the latter.

Peter was in residence at Antioch when the Judaean emissaries
arrived. When he first came to Antioch, he ate freely with Gentile
Christians; his experience on the roof of Simon's house at Joppa
and in the house of Cornelius at Caesarea had taught him not to
"call any man common or unclean" (Acts 10:28). But when the
Judaeans arrived and expressed their viewpoint so dogmatically,
he withdrew from Gentile society and sat at table with circumcised
persons only. No doubt he believed he was doing so in order to
conciliate the consciences of his "weaker" Judaean brethren. But
his example was bound to have a disastrous effect on others; it

---

[16] "But there rose up . . . saying": the Western text does not repeat the
reference to believing Pharisees, already introduced by it in v. 1, but recasts
the beginning of v. 5 thus: "But those who charged them to go up to the elders
rose up and said".

[17] Gk. αὐτούς, i.e. the Gentile converts. The antecedent is not expressed,
except in the Byzantine addition at the end of v. 4: "and that he had opened
a door of faith unto the Gentiles" (taken over from Ch. 14:27).

[18] It must be noted, however, that instead of τινας ("certain people") in
Gal. 2:12a, P46 (supported by the Latin authorities d e g r and the Latin text of
Irenaeus) reads τινα ("someone"), while in Gal. 2:12b, instead of ἦλθον ("they
came"), the singular ἦλθεν ("he came") is supported by P46 אB D* G d e g. (See
T. W. Manson's discussion in BJRL 24 [1940], pp. 69 ff.) But if we read the
singular throughout the verse, the person referred to may simply have been the
spokesman of a group.

would, unless checked, endanger the whole principle of Christian unity. Even Barnabas, who had so recently returned with Paul from their mission in Asia Minor,[19] was inclined to follow Peter's example. Paul saw quite clearly that the concession in the matter of table fellowship was bound in the long run to compromise the basic gospel principle that salvation was the gift of God's grace in Christ, to be received by faith alone. Refusal to have table fellowship with Gentiles would soon be followed by refusal to admit them to church membership or indeed to recognize them as Christians at all. Peter's concession appeared in Paul's eyes to be the thin end of the wedge; no wonder, then, that Paul "resisted him to the face" (Gal. 2:11), for his action implied that circumcision and all that it involved, if not necessary in theory for salvation, were none the less necessary in practice. Peter himself knew that they were not necessary in either respect; that is why Paul describes his action as "dissimulation" (Gal. 2:13). Happily, Peter seems to have taken the rebuke in good part; we hear no more of such untimely appeasement on his side.

But the trouble was not confined to Antioch; it spread to the young churches of South Galatia. These churches were visited by Judaizers who urged upon them that their faith in Jesus as Lord required to be supplemented by circumcision and observance of the Jewish ceremonial law. In their innocence, the South Galatian Christians were disposed to accept this new teaching. When news of this came to Paul at Antioch, he wrote his Epistle to the Galatians in white-hot urgency, beseeching these recent converts not to be seduced from Christian simplicity by a totally different gospel which in reality was not a gospel at all.

2 It was not enough to indulge in "dissension and questioning" at Antioch; the whole issue had to be discussed and decided "at the highest level," for there was grave danger of a complete cleavage between the churches of Jerusalem and Judaea on the one hand and the church of Antioch and her daughter churches on the other hand. The church of Antioch therefore sent Paul, Barnabas and a number of other responsible members to discuss

---

[19] Other interpretations of the order of events are possible; thus W. L. Knox (*op. cit.*, p. 49) supposes that the incident of Gal. 2:11 ff. preceded the first missionary expedition of Paul and Barnabas: that it was, in fact, the controversy which was occasioned by Peter's withdrawal from Gentile fellowship that decided the Antiochene church "to launch a vigorous Gentile mission".

the question with the leaders of the Jerusalem church—"the apostles and elders".

3 The delegates from Antioch had to pass through Phoenicia and Samaria on their way to Jerusalem, and they took the opportunity of visiting the churches in these regions and telling them of the success of the Gentile mission. As the churches of Phoenicia and Samaria were themselves the fruit of the Hellenistic mission which followed the death of Stephen (Chs. 8:5 ff.; 11:19), their outlook was naturally more liberal than that which prevailed at Jerusalem, and they rejoiced at what they heard.

4 The leaders and other members of the church of Jerusalem also listened with great interest to Paul and Barnabas's account of all "that God had done with them", but this interest by no means involved wholehearted satisfaction.

5 Dissatisfaction was voiced in particular by those members of the Jerusalem church who were associated with the Pharisaic party. Pharisees, as believers in the doctrine of resurrection, could become Christians without relinquishing their distinctive beliefs; to what they already believed they added the belief that Jesus of Nazareth had been raised from the dead and thus divinely proclaimed to be Lord and Messiah. But if their Christianity did not amount to more than this, they remained legalists at heart—unlike their illustrious fellow-Pharisee Paul, whose whole outlook was radically reorientated by his revolutionary conversion. These Christian Pharisees, then, were the leaders in insisting that Gentile converts should be instructed to submit to circumcision and the general obligation to keep the Mosaic law which that rite carried with it.[20]

(b) The Council Meets: Peter's Speech (Ch. 15:6–11)

6 And the apostles and the elders were gathered together to consider of this matter.

7 And when there had been much questioning, Peter rose up,[21] and said unto them,[22]

---

[20] *Cf.* Gal. 5:3, "I testify again to every man that receiveth circumcision, that he is a debtor to do the whole law."

[21] After "rose up", the Western text adds "in spirit" (*cf.* similar characteristic amplifications in vv. 29, 32).

[22] For "them" P^{45} reads "the apostles".

Brethren, ye know that a good while ago[23] God made choice among you,[24] that by my mouth the Gentiles should hear the word of the gospel, and believe.

8 And God, who knoweth the heart, bare them witness, giving[25] them the Holy Spirit, even as he did unto us;

9 and he made no distinction between us and them, cleansing[25] their hearts by faith.

10 Now therefore why make ye trial of God, that ye should put a yoke upon the neck of the disciples which neither our fathers nor we were able to bear?

11 But we believe that we shall be saved through the grace of the Lord Jesus, in like manner as they.

6 While "the apostles and the elders were gathered together" as the responsible leaders of the Jerusalem church, to deliberate with the Antiochene representatives, it appears from vv. 12 ("all the multitude") and 22 ("the whole church") that other members of the Jerusalem church were present as well.

7–9 Peter, as leader of the Twelve, spoke out unambiguously in the interests of gospel liberty.[26] He reminded the company that the fundamental principle which they were discussing had already been decided, when nearly ten years before he had been led by God to the house of Cornelius and Gentiles had heard the gospel for the first time from his lips. On that occasion God had given an evident token of His acceptance of Gentiles, for the Holy Spirit came upon them as they listened to Peter, just as He had come upon the apostles themselves on the first Christian Pentecost. Cornelius and his household had not even made an oral confession of faith when the Holy Spirit came upon them, but God, who reads the hearts of men, saw the faith within them. And if God accepted these Gentiles and cleansed their hearts by His Holy

[23] Gk. ἀφ' ἡμερῶν ἀρχαίων, "in the early days" (*i.e.* of the Jerusalem church).

[24] Gk. ἐν ὑμῖν ἐξελέξατο, which might be a Semitic idiom for "chose you" (*cf.* Neh. 9:7 [2 Esdras 19:7 LXX], ἐξελέξω ἐν 'Αβραάμ, 'thou didst choose Abraham'), though it is rather awkward to take it thus in this sentence.

[25] "giving... cleansing...": Both these participles, aorist in Gk. (δοὺς ... καθαρίσας), are examples of the "simultaneous" aorist participle: God testified to the genuineness of these people's faith by giving them the Spirit and cleansing their hearts in one regenerative moment.

[26] He has completely recovered from his temporary lapse at Antioch, which in any case did not correspond to his true attitude. "The figure of a Judaizing St. Peter is a figment of the Tübingen critics with no basis in history" (K. Lake, *Earlier Epistles of Paul*, p. 116).

306

Spirit as soon as they believed the gospel, why should further conditions now be imposed on them which God Himself plainly did not require?

10–11 Besides, the yoke which some were now proposing to lay on the necks of Gentile Christians was one which they themselves and their forefathers had proved unable to shoulder. The term "yoke" was particularly appropriate in this connection; a proselyte, when he undertook to fulfil the law, was said to "take up the yoke of the kingdom of heaven".[27] But to ordinary Jews like Peter and his hearers the traditional law, especially as expounded by the severe school of Shammai which was dominant at the time, was a heavy burden under which they groaned.[28] Only a few could claim, like Paul, to have fulfilled all the detailed requirements of the written and oral law—and Paul at any rate found that when he had succeeded in this by infinite painstaking, it brought him no true peace of conscience. By contrast with those "heavy burdens and grievous to be borne" (Matt. 23:4), Peter and his companions had learned to rejoice in the easy yoke of Christ (Matt. 11:29 f.). They recognized that their own salvation was due to the free grace of Christ; were they to acknowledge another principle of salvation for Gentile believers?

[27] This expression was later used to denote the recitation of the *Shema'*, the Jewish confession of faith, "Hear, O Israel..." (Deut. 6:4 f.).

[28] It has often been maintained, especially by Jewish scholars, that the NT picture of the law as an intolerable burden is a caricature of the truth. But it is unsafe to draw inferences from the bulk of the rabbinical literature about the Pharisaic position before A.D. 70. Peter's words may very well sum up the attitude of the ordinary man (the *'am ha-'aretz*) of the mid-first century. At this time the extreme position which insisted on the exact fulfilment of every jot and tittle of the law was probably characteristic of the school of Shammai. But the school of Shammai lost its dominance after A.D. 70; the leading rabbis of the new sanhedrin were members of the milder school of Hillel. And a further easing of the burden was introduced under the influence of Aqiba about A.D. 100. For he seems to have laid down the principle that a 51 per cent. fulfilment of the law sufficed to open the way to Paradise. "A man is not half bad who does three-fourths of his duty": so Israel Zangwill puts it in *Children of the Ghetto* (London, 1892), ch. xii. This is obviously a vastly different viewpoint from that quoted elsewhere in the NT: "whosoever shall keep the whole law, and yet stumble in one point, he is become guilty of all" (Jas. 2:10). "As compared with the teaching of the Pharisaic scribes whom Jesus knew, the developed doctrine of the Talmud is a reformed religion" (B. S. Easton, *Christ in the Gospels* [New York, 1930], p. 107). See *Pirqe Aboth* iii. 19; TJ Qiddushin i. 10, 61d; TB *Rosh-ha-Shanah* 16b, 17a; L. Finkelstein, *Akiba* (New York, 1936), p. 185 *et passim*; H. Danby, *Studies in Judaism* (Jerusalem, 1922), pp. 5, 19, *et passim*; C. G. Montefiore and H. Loewe, *A Rabbinic Anthology* (London, 1938), pp. 595 ff.

(c) The Summing Up (Ch. 15:12-21)

12 And [29] all the multitude kept silence; and they hearkened unto Barnabas and Paul rehearsing what signs and wonders God had wrought among the Gentiles through them.

13 And after they had held their peace, James answered, saying,
Brethren, hearken unto me:

14 Symeon [30] hath rehearsed how first God visited the Gentiles, to take out of them a people for his name.

15 And to this agree the words of the prophets; as it is written,

16 After these things I will return,
And I will build again the tabernacle of David, which is fallen;
And I will build again the ruins thereof,
And I will set it up:

17 That the residue of men may seek after the Lord,
And all the Gentiles, upon whom my name is called,

18 Saith the Lord, who maketh these things known from of old. [31]

19 Wherefore my judgment is, that we trouble not [32] them that from among the Gentiles turn to God;

20 but that we write unto them, that they abstain from the pollutions of idols, and from fornication, and from what is strangled, and from blood. [33]

21 For Moses from generations of old hath in every city [34] them that preach him, being read in the synagogues every sabbath.

12 Peter's argument was difficult to answer, as it was an appea.

---

[29] After "And" the Western text inserts: "when the elders had consented to the words spoken by Peter".

[30] Gk. Συμεών (cf. 2 Peter 1:1, Συμεὼν Πέτρος), the LXX form of the name Simeon, approaches the Hebrew and Aramaic pronunciation of the name more closely than does the commoner NT Σίμων.

[31] The Western text recasts these words: "saith the Lord who doeth these things. Known from of old to the Lord is his work" (Byzantine text, "...are all his works"; cf. A.V.).

[32] Better, "that we stop troubling" (μὴ παρενοχλεῖν, present infinitive).

[33] Gk. τοῦ ἀπέχεσθαι τῶν ἀλισγημάτων τῶν εἰδώλων καὶ τῆς πορνείας καὶ πνικτοῦ καὶ τοῦ αἵματος. The Western text omits καὶ πνικτοῦ, and after αἵματος adds καὶ ὅσα μὴ θέλουσιν ἑαυτοῖς γίνεσθαι ἑτέροις μὴ ποιεῖν. P45 and the Ethiopic version omit καὶ τῆς πορνείας. (The evidence of P45 is not available for the repetitions of the decree in v. 29 and Ch. 21:25.) See note 46 below.

[34] P45 omits "in every city".

to the acknowledged action of God. During the silence which followed, Barnabas and Paul (the old order of the names is naturally resumed in a Jerusalem setting) added further evidence which supported Peter's argument. The mind of God in this matter, already shown in the house of Cornelius, had been abundantly displayed in the blessing He had bestowed upon the Gentiles in Antioch and during the recent mission in Cyprus and Asia Minor.

13-15 Then the eyes of the company turned to James the brother of the Lord, a man who enjoyed the respect and confidence of all.[35] By this time James appears to have occupied a position of leadership among the elders of the Jerusalem church; if the elders were organized as a kind of Nazarene Sanhedrin, James was their president, *primus inter pares*. The circumcision party may have relied on James for support, but if so, they were disappointed. He summed up the position in words which recognized the logic of the preceding arguments.

"Listen to me, brethren", he said (*cf.* Jas. 2:5, "Hearken, my beloved brethren").[36] Then he summarized Peter's speech, referring to the apostle by his old name Symeon. If he made no reference to what Paul and Barnabas had said, that may have been politic; James knew how to carry his difficult audience with him. It was the work of Paul and Barnabas that had roused such apprehension in the minds of the Jerusalem rank and file.

The terms in which James summarized Peter's speech—"how first God visited the Gentiles, to take out of them a people for his name"[37]—have been misused in the interests of modern dispensationalism. If it is true, as the *Scofield Reference Bible* says (*ad loc.*), that "dispensationally, this is the most important passage in the N.T.", it is strange that it should have come from the lips of James—"austere, legal, ceremonial", as the same work elsewhere calls him (p. 1306). James meant that God had clearly shown His

---

[35] See p. 253 (on Ch. 12:17).

[36] J. B. Mayor has enumerated what he calls "remarkable agreements" between this speech and the Epistle of James (*The Epistle of St. James* [London, 1897], pp. iii f.).

[37] The wording of the English version, "God visited the Gentiles, to take out of them a people" (v. 14), scarcely conveys the paradoxical emphasis of the Gk., ἐξ ἐθνῶν λαόν, for λαός is the word used in LXX of Israel, the people of God, separated from the Gentiles. That the frontiers of the people of God should be enlarged to embrace Gentiles (ἔθνη) was indeed a new departure. *Cf.* John 10:16; 11:52; Rom. 15:9 ff.; Eph. 3:6 ff.; 1 Pet. 2:10.

pleasure that the new community which was to display His glory in the world should be drawn from Gentiles as well as from Jews. And in this he found the fulfilment of the prophetic words of Amos 9:11 f.

16–18 The prophecy of Amos is quoted in the main from the LXX. The chief deviations from the LXX are "After these things I will return" (*cf.* Jer. 12:15) instead of "In that day", and "who maketh these things known from of old" (*cf.* Isa. 45:21) instead of "who does this". More striking are the deviations of the LXX from MT at the beginning of v. 17: "that the residue of men may seek after the Lord"[38] has a widely different meaning from MT, "that they [Israel] may possess the remnant of Edom, and all the nations that are called by my name". The primary sense of the MT is that the fallen fortunes of the royal house of David will be restored and it will rule over all the territory which had been included in David's empire. But James's application of the prophecy finds the fulfilment of its first part (the rebuilding of the tabernacle of David) in the resurrection and exaltation of Christ, the Son of David, and the reconstitution of His disciples as the new Israel, and the fulfilment of its second part in the presence of believing Gentiles as well as believing Jews in the Church (*cf.* p. 158, on Ch. 7:46). Certainly the LXX version of the second part lends itself to James's application more than MT would. But C. C. Torrey points out rightly that "the LXX rendering of Am. 9:11 f. certainly represented a varying *Hebrew* text"; and he adds—what is still more to the point—that "even our Massoretic Hebrew would have served the present purpose admirably, since it predicted that 'the tabernacle of David', *i.e.* the church of the Messiah, would gain possession of all the nations which are called by the name [of the God of Israel]" (*Composition and Date of Acts* [Cambridge, Mass., 1916], pp. 38 f.).

The conjunction "and" before "all the Gentiles" (v. 17) is epexegetic; a better translation would be "even" or "that is to say". The "residue of men" who are to "seek after the Lord" are identical with "all the Gentiles, upon whom my name is called"— *i.e.*, the elect from every nation. According to v. 18 as translated

---

[38] The LXX text presupposes Heb. *yidreshu* ("will seek") and *'adam* ("man") in place of MT *yireshu* ("will inherit") and *'edom* ("Edom"); it also treats Heb. *she'erith* ("remnant") as subject, whereas in MT it is plainly object, being preceded by the accusative particle *'eth*.

in ARV, the inclusion of Gentiles in the ranks of God's people was revealed in OT days (*cf.* Paul's argument in Rom. 15:8 ff.).

19 James's conclusion amounted to this: that all attempts to impose circumcision and its attendant legal obligations on Gentile converts must be refused. The way of salvation and the terms of church fellowship were to be the same for Jews and Gentiles alike: their basis was God's free grace in Christ, to be received by faith alone. The fundamental principle of the gospel was thus safe-guarded.

20 There remained, however, a practical problem. In most of the churches Gentile believers had to live alongside Jewish believers, who had been brought up to observe various food-laws and to avoid intercourse with Gentiles as far as possible. While there was no more question of requiring the Gentiles to submit to the ceremonial law, they would do well to behave considerately to their "weaker brethren" of Jewish birth, not all of whom could be expected immediately to acquire such an emancipated outlook on food-laws and the like as Peter and Paul. Therefore, without compromising the Gentiles' Christian liberty, James gave it as his considered opinion that they should be asked to respect their Jewish brethren's scruples by avoiding meat which had idolatrous associations or from which the blood had not been properly drained, and by conforming to the high Jewish code of relations between the sexes instead of remaining content with the lower pagan standards to which they had been accustomed. This would smooth the path of social and table fellowship between Christians of Jewish and Gentile birth.

The author of Acts has been suspected of confusing two separate debates[39]—one on the obligations of the law and the other on table fellowship—and bringing both together as one discussion. But it is surely quite natural that, when once the matter of principle had been settled, an effort should have been made to provide a practical *modus vivendi* for two groups of people drawn from such different ways of life. The *modus vivendi* was probably similar to the terms on which Jews of the dispersion found it possible to have some degree of intercourse with God-fearers. The

[39] *Cf.* H. Lietzmann, "Der Sinn des Aposteldekrets und seine Textwand-lung", in *Amicitiae Corolla* (London, 1933), pp. 203 ff.; T. W. Manson in BJRL xxiv (1940), p. 77; H. W. Beyer, *Die Apostelgeschichte* (Göttingen, 1951), *ad loc.*

prohibition against eating flesh with the blood still in it was based on Gen. 9:4. At a later time, when the issue was no longer a live one, the provisions proposed by James and adopted by the council were modified so as to become purely ethical injunctions: thus the Western text makes James suggest "that they abstain from idolatry, from fornication and from bloodshed, and from doing to others what they would not like done to themselves".[40]

21 This proposal, James urged, would not work to the detriment of Israel's mission in the Gentile world; there was still ample opportunity for Gentiles to learn the law of Moses, for it was read publicly every sabbath in synagogues throughout the civilized world. But with regard to these Gentile Christians, "Moses, so to speak, would suffer no loss, in failing to obtain the allegiance of those who never had been his" (R. B. Rackham, *ad loc.*). This observation was perhaps intended to calm the apprehensions of the Pharisaic party in the Jerusalem church, in whose eyes it was specially important that the whole Torah should be taught among the Gentiles; this, said James, was being attended to already by the synagogues.[41]

(d) The Letter to the Gentile Churches (Ch. 15:22–29)

22 Then it seemed good to the apostles and the elders, with the whole church, to choose men out of their company, and send them to Antioch with Paul and Barnabas; *namely,* Judas called Barsabbas, and Silas, chief men among the brethren:

23 and they wrote *thus* by them, The apostles and the elders, brethren, unto the brethren who are of the Gentiles in Antioch and Syria and Cilicia, greeting:

24 Forasmuch as we have heard that certain who went

[40] Idolatry, fornication and murder were the three cardinal sins in Jewish eyes: avoidance of these was held to be binding on the whole human race from the time of Noah. After the Bar-Kokhba rebellion was put down (A.D. 135), the rabbis of Lydda laid it down that a Jew, if his life were at stake, might break any commandment of the law except those which prohibited these three things. But the situation at the Council of Jerusalem was quite different. The negative form of the golden rule, appended to these prohibitions in the Western text, appears elsewhere in Jewish and Christian literature; *cf.* Tobit 4:15; *Didache* 1:2; TB *Shabbath* 31a; *Aboth de R. Nathan* ii. 26. The idea that the positive form of the golden rule (*cf.* Matt. 7:12) is peculiar to Christianity is wrong: it is used by Maimonides in *Hilekhoth Abel* xiv. 1 (*Mishneh Torah* ii).

[41] A variant interpretation of v. 21 makes James mean that, since Jewish communities are to be found in every city, their scruples are to be respected.

out from us have troubled you with words, subverting[42] your souls;[43] to whom we gave no commandment;

25 it seemed good to us, having come to one accord, to choose out men and send them unto you with our beloved Barnabas and Paul,

26 men that have hazarded their lives for the name of our Lord Jesus Christ.[44]

27 We have sent therefore Judas and Silas, who themselves also shall tell you the same things by word of mouth.

28 For it seemed good to the Holy Spirit, and to us, to lay upon you no greater burden than these necessary things:[45]

29 that ye abstain from things sacrificed to idols, and from blood, and from things strangled, and from fornication;[46] from which if ye keep yourselves, it shall be well with you.[47] Fare ye well.

22 James's proposal commended itself to the Jerusalem leaders, and won the acquiescence at least of the Jerusalem church as a whole. Did it commend itself equally to the Antiochenes, and to Paul in particular? It has frequently been contended that Paul could never have accepted these terms, but this contention seems quite unfounded. Where no compromise of principle was involved, Paul was the most conciliatory of men (cf. Acts 16:3; 21:26; 1 Cor. 9:19 ff.); and in his epistles he himself urges that

---

[42] Gk. ἀνασκευάζοντες, a military metaphor, of plundering a city.

[43] Many Western authorities add: "saying that you should be circumcised and keep the law."

[44] The Western text adds "in every trial."

[45] Gk. τούτων τῶν ἐπάναγκες (ℵᶜ B C 81) or τῶν ἐπάναγκες τούτων (Byzantine), for which we should probably read τούτων· ἐπάναγκες (ℵ* D 33), punctuating after τούτων and beginning a new clause with ἐπάναγκες.

[46] The Western text omits καὶ πνικτῶν and adds καὶ ὅσα μὴ θέλετε ἑαυτοῖς γίνεσθαι ἑτέρῳ μὴ ποιεῖν, as in v. 20. Tertullian omits καὶ πνικτῶν, but does not add the negative golden rule; Origen omits καὶ πορνείας. It is suggested by some that the highest common factor of the readings in vv. 20 and 29 represents the original text: that the decree was exclusively a food-law, prohibiting the eating of meat which had been sacrificed to pagan divinities and meat from which the blood had not been completely drained; and that this twofold prohibition was later expanded in the various ways to which our several textual authorities bear witness. Cf. P. H. Menoud in Studiorum Novi Testamenti Societas, Bulletin II (Oxford, 1951), pp. 22 ff.; C. S. C. Williams, Alterations to the Text of the Synoptic Gospels and Acts (Oxford, 1951), pp. 72 ff.

[47] The Western text characteristically adds "being carried along by the Holy Spirit" (for the wording cf. 2 Pet. 1:21).

those Christians who are strong in faith should voluntarily restrict their liberty in matters of food and the like, so as not to offend weaker consciences (cf. Rom. 14:1 ff.; 1 Cor. 8:1 ff.).[48]

The Jerusalem leaders then selected two of their number to go to Antioch with Paul and Barnabas and carry the findings of the council to the church of that city. Of this Judas—who had the same surname as the Joseph mentioned in Ch. 1:23—we hear nothing more, except that he exercised his gift of prophetic exhortation in the church of Antioch during his stay there. Silas—also referred to in the NT by his Roman cognomen Silvanus (2 Cor. 1:19; 1 Thess. 1:1; 2 Thess. 1:1; 1 Pet. 5:12)—makes a further appearance in the narrative of Acts as a travelling companion of Paul's. It is preposterous exegesis to identify Judas and Silas with the troublesome emissaries from James mentioned by Paul in Gal. 2:12.[49]

23 Judas and Silas were not only to communicate the council's findings at Antioch by word of mouth, but also to carry a letter from the apostles and elders at Jerusalem. The punctuation of ARV, "The apostles and the elders, brethren," where "brethren" refers to both "apostles" and "elders" (similarly RSV), is according to C. C. Torrey "faultless Aramaic idiom" (op. cit., p. 39). But ERV, "The apostles and the elder brethren", is a more natural rendering of the Greek.[50] The letter is addressed to the Gentile Christians of Antioch and of the province of Syro-Cilicia of which Antioch was the capital. The recently founded churches of South Galatia might be looked upon as an extension of the work in Antioch, Tarsus, and the rest of Syro-Cilicia and not as a separate "province".

24–27 Since trouble had been caused by the unauthorized activity of previous Jerusalem visitors to Antioch (v. 1), it was

---

[48] In these passages he deals particularly with the problem of the flesh of animals which have been sacrificed in pagan worship, but lays down general principles as well.

[49] This identification is made by H. Lietzmann, *The Beginnings of the Christian Church* (Eng. tr., London, 1949), pp. 108 f.

[50] W. L. Knox (*op. cit.*, p. 50) regards the unusual expression οἱ πρεσβύτεροι ἀδελφοί as one of a number of peculiarities in this letter "which suggest that we are dealing with an original document copied by Luke more or less verbatim"; "There seems no reason why Luke should use the curious phrase as against πρεσβύτεροι in 14:23; 15:4, 6, etc., unless he found it in the original, or unless he knew at least that it was a characteristic phrase of the early Church at Jerusalem."

necessary to emphasize that the present delegates, whose business it was to undo the work of those earlier visitors, were fully accredited by the Jerusalem church; and a conciliatory note was added by the pointedly friendly reference to Barnabas and Paul and the hazards they had undergone in their work of evangelization.

28–29 The words "it seemed good to the Holy Spirit, and to us", with which the terms of the council's decision are introduced, emphasize the church's rôle as the vehicle of the Spirit.[51] So conscious were they of being possessed and controlled by Him that He was given prior mention as chief Author of their decision.

Although NT Greek is well supplied with verbs of commanding, it is noteworthy, as F. J. A. Hort pointed out, that none of them is used here. "The independence of the Ecclesia of Antioch had to be respected, and yet not in such a way as to encourage disregard either of the great mother Ecclesia, or of the Lord's own Apostles, or of the unity of the whole Christian body" (*The Christian Ecclesia* [London, 1914], p. 82). The end of v. 28 and beginning of v. 29 should probably run: "... to lay no burden on you except these things: it is necessary for you to abstain..." Then the four things from which they are to abstain are repeated from v. 20; here again the Western text recasts them in the form of a threefold ethical prohibition and adds the negative Golden Rule. The prohibition of fornication, understood generally, is of course an ethical prohibition in both forms of the text, but the word may be used here in a more specialized sense, of marriage within degrees of blood-relationship or affinity forbidden by the legislation of Lev. 18.[52] As for the food-laws, they appear to have been observed as late as A.D. 177 by the churches of the Rhone valley in Gaul,[53] which were in close relation with the churches of the

---

[51] "There is no parallel for such a phrase to pronounce a corporate decision by a deliberative body" (W. L. Knox, *ib.*).

[52] *Cf.* W. K. L. Clarke, *New Testament Problems* (London, 1929), pp. 59 ff.; F. W. Grosheide, *De Handelingen der Apostelen* (Korte Verklaring), ii (Kampen, 1945), p. 22. For such an example of πορνεία see 1 Cor. 5:1; this may also be the sense of the term in the "excepting clauses" of Matt. 5:32; 19:9. See also H. L. Goudge, *The Church of England and Reunion* (London, 1938), p. 222 n.; B. F. C. Atkinson, *The Christian's Use of the Old Testament* (London, 1952), p. 71 n.

[53] Eusebius, *Ecclesiastical History* v.1.26, reports one of the martyrs of Vienne and Lyons as protesting, "How could Christians eat children, when they are not allowed even to drink the blood of brute beasts?" A similar

province of Asia. In the province of Asia we find the general terms of the apostolic decision upheld at the end of the 1st century in Rev. 2:14, 20. And towards the end of the 9th century they were included by King Alfred of England in the preamble to his law-code.

attitude is attested from North Africa: "We abstain from eating strangled animals and those that have died of themselves" (Tertullian, *Apology* 9).

5. THE APOSTOLIC LETTER RECEIVED IN
ANTIOCH AND ANATOLIA

(Ch. 15:30–16:5)

(a) The Church at Antioch Receives the Letter (Ch. 15:30–35)

30 So they, when they were dismissed, came down to Antioch; and having gathered the multitude together, they delivered the epistle.

31 And when they had read it, they rejoiced for the consolation.

32 And Judas and Silas, being themselves also prophets,[54] exhorted the brethren with many words, and confirmed them.

33 And after they had spent some time *there,* they were dismissed in peace[55] from the brethren unto those that had sent them forth.

35 But Paul and Barnabas tarried in Antioch, teaching and preaching the word of the Lord, with many others also.

30–35 The news from Jerusalem brought great relief to the Christians of Antioch. The contents and tone of the apostolic letter were themselves encouraging, and further encouragement was supplied by the ministry of Judas and Silas, who possessed a similar gift of prophecy to that exercised by the five chief teachers of the Antiochene church itself (Ch. 13:1). When the time came for Judas and Silas to go home to Jerusalem, Paul and Barnabas remained for some time in Antioch, serving the Lord in the church there together with their colleagues in the ministry.

The words which appear in AV as v. 34 ("Notwithstanding, it pleased Silas to abide there still") are a Western addition which was taken over by the Byzantine text. They are intended to pave the way for v. 40, where Paul takes Silas as his missionary colleague, but they plainly contradict v. 33.

---

[54] The Western text adds "full of the Holy Spirit."
[55] That is to say, with the greeting "Go in peace" or "Peace be with you" (Heb. *shalom 'aleikhem*).

(b) Paul's Second Missionary Tour Begins (Ch. 15:36–41)

36 And after some days[56] Paul said unto Barnabas, Let us return now and visit the brethren in every city wherein we proclaimed the word of the Lord, *and see how they fare.*

37 And Barnabas was minded to take[57] with them John also, who was called Mark.

38 But Paul thought not good to take[57] with them him who withdrew from them from Pamphylia, and went not with them to the work.

39 And there arose a sharp contention, so that they parted asunder one from the other, and Barnabas took Mark with him, and sailed away unto Cyprus:

40 but Paul chose Silas, and went forth, being commended by the brethren to the grace of the Lord.

41 And he went through Syria and Cilicia, confirming the churches.

36–39 The story of the disagreement between Paul and Barnabas is not one that makes pleasant reading, and the fact that he does not gloss it over may be taken as a token of Luke's honesty, the more so as he does not relate it in such a way as to put Paul in the right and Barnabas in the wrong. Especially in view of Luke's restraint, it is idle for us to try to apportion the blame for the dispute. It is frequently maintained, of course,[58] that Luke misrepresents the real cause of the quarrel: that it actually arose out of the incident at Antioch when Barnabas was inclined to follow Peter's example of "play-acting",[59] to Paul's great indignation. It may be that on the present occasion the friction between the two would not have been so sharp if it had not been for that earlier difference: we cannot say. But Luke's account here is perfectly straightforward and adequate.

[56] A quite indefinite time-note (*cf.* Ch. 9:19).

[57] In v. 37 "to take with them" represents Gk. aorist infinitive (συνπαραλαβεῖν); in v. 38 the present infinitive (συνπαραλαμβάνειν). On this "delicate *nuance*" J. H. Moulton remarks: "Barnabas, with easy forgetfulness of risk, wishes συνπαραλαβεῖν Mark—Paul refuses συνπαραλαμβάνειν, to have with them day to day one who had shown himself unreliable" (*Grammar of NT Gk.*, i [London, 1906], p. 130).

[58] So, *e.g.*, F. C. Baur, *Paul* (Eng. tr., London, 1876), pp. 129 f., and many others since. No doubt it is a natural supposition, if Acts 15 be supposed to be Luke's version of the events of Gal. 2:1 ff., and if the incident of Gal. 2:11 ff. be dated after the council. But we have already indicated our dissent from this view.

[59] The literal sense of Gk. ὑπόκρισις (Gal. 2:13).

When Paul proposed to Barnabas that they should pay a second visit to the churches which they had planted on their previous tour of Cyprus and Asia Minor, Barnabas agreed, and suggested that Mark should accompany them again as he had done on the former occasion. But Paul, believing that Mark's departure from Perga during their former journey was unjustified,[60] and probably inferring that it revealed some defect of character which made him unfit for such work, refused point-blank to take him again. We can well believe that it would indeed have been unwise for Mark at this stage to join another missionary expedition of which Paul was one of the leaders. On the other hand, it appears that Barnabas discerned promising qualities in his young cousin which could be developed under his care rather than under Paul's. It would do Mark good to spend more time in the company of such a "son of encouragement", and in the event his latent qualities came to full development and were appreciated in due course by Paul himself (*cf.* Col. 4:10; Philem. 23; 2 Tim. 4:11). It was a pity that the present dispute was allowed to generate such mutual provocation, but in the providence of God it was overruled for good, for in the upshot there were two missionary expeditions this time instead of one. Barnabas took Mark and went back to continue the evangelization of his native Cyprus, while Paul returned to his native Anatolia to prosecute the same work there.

40–41 Paul had now to find a new travel-companion, and he fetched Silas from Jerusalem, to which he had recently returned. No doubt he had learned to value Silas's qualities during the latter's visit to Antioch after the Jerusalem council, and concluded that he would make a congenial colleague. It was advantageous, too, to have a member of the Jerusalem church as his companion; and it appears from the story of their adventures in Philippi that Silas, like Paul himself, was a Roman citizen (Ch. 16:37 f.). It would obviously be embarrassing if a situation arose in which Paul could claim for himself as a Roman citizen privileges or exemptions which his colleague could not share. Commended afresh to the divine grace by the Antiochene church, as on the former occasion (Ch. 13:3), Paul went with Silas through the churches of Syro-Cilicia, encouraging the Christians and no doubt, as the

---

[60] See Ch. 13:13b (p. 266).

Western text adds, "handing over to them the commands of the elders". (This is an obvious inference from Chs. 15:23 and 16:4). As Silas was mentioned by name in the apostolic letter, it was fitting that he should share with Paul the responsibility of handing it over to the Gentile churches.

CHAPTER XVI

(c) *In the Province of Galatia: Timothy Joins the Apostles (Ch. 16:1–5)*

1 And he came also to Derbe and to Lystra: and behold, a certain disciple was there, named[1] Timothy, the son of a Jewess that believed; but his father was a Greek.

2 The same was well reported of by the brethren that were at Lystra and Iconium.

3 Him would Paul have to go forth with him; and he took and circumcised him because of the Jews that were in those parts: for they all knew that his father was a Greek.

4 And[2] as they went on their way through the cities, they delivered them the decrees to keep which had been ordained of the apostles and elders that were at Jerusalem.

5 So the churches were strengthened in the faith, and increased in number daily.

1–2 Having passed through Cilicia, Paul and Silas crossed the Taurus range by the pass called the Cilician Gates,[3] and after traversing part of the kingdom of Antiochus[4] entered the province of Galatia. There they visited the cities which had been evangelized by Paul and Barnabas two or three years previously—Derbe, Lystra, Iconium and Pisidian Antioch.

At Lystra[5] (the common term in Derbe and Lystra of v. 1 and Lystra and Iconium of v. 2) Paul decided to take as a second travel-companion a young man named Timothy who with his

---

[1] P45 omits "named."

[2] The Western text reads: "And going through the cities they proclaimed the Lord Jesus Christ with all boldness, at the same time also handing over the commandments of the apostles and elders at Jerusalem."

[3] See W. M. Ramsay, *Pauline and Other Studies* (London, 1906), pp. 273 ff., for a detailed examination of "St. Paul's Road from Cilicia to Iconium."

[4] Antiochus, king of Commagene, had eastern Lycaonia and most of "Rough Cilicia" added to his realm in A.D. 37. See also pp. 288 (on Ch 14:6) and 380 (on Ch. 18:23).

[5] The Latin translation of Origen's commentary on Romans (Ch. 16:21) calls Timothy "a citizen of Derbe" (*cf.* Valckenaer and Blass's emendation of Ch. 20:4, mentioned on p. 403, n. 5).

mother had been converted to Christianity during the previous missionary visit and who had made promising progress in the Christian life in the interval. That he should be commended by the brethren in Lystra and Iconium rather than by those in Lystra and Derbe is quite natural: Lystra was nearer to Iconium, which lay across the regional frontier in Galatic Phrygia, than it was to Derbe, which belonged to the same region of Galatic Lycaonia.

The statement that Timothy's Jewish mother (Eunice by name, according to 2 Tim. 1:5) had married a Gentile suggests that a less exclusive standard obtained in Asia Minor than in Palestine. In Phrygia, says Ramsay, "there can be little doubt that the Jews married into the dominant families" (*The Bearing of Recent Discovery on the Trustworthiness of the NT* [London, 1915], p. 357).

3 It was Timothy's mixed parentage that made Paul decide to circumcise him before taking him along as a travel-companion. In the eyes of Jews, Timothy was a Gentile because he was the uncircumcised son of a Greek. In Gentile eyes, however, he was practically a Jew, having been brought up in his mother's religion. Paul therefore regularized his status (and, in Jewish eyes, legitimized him) by circumcising him.[6] That he should have done so is remarkable enough, in view of his strong language on this subject in the Epistle to the Galatians; but Timothy's was an exceptional case. He insisted that the Gentile Christians of the Galatian churches must not submit to circumcision because it was being urged on them as something necessary for full salvation, and because for them such submission involved an obligation to keep the whole Jewish law (*cf.* Gal. 5:3).[7] But Timothy had been brought up to observe the Jewish law; it was simple expediency that suggested the circumcising of one who was already a half-Jew with a view to his greater usefulness in the ministry of the gospel. In such a case circumcision was merely a minor surgical operation performed for a practical purpose, and not a religious rite. Paul's readiness to conciliate Jewish susceptibilities is illustrated else-

[6] In Luke's statement (v. 3) that "they all knew that his father was (Gk. ὑπῆρχεν) a Greek", the imperfect tense suggests that his father was now dead; had he been still alive, the present ὑπάρχει would have been used.

[7] But even when writing to the Galatians Paul points out that circumcision *per se* is religiously indifferent; only when performed as a legal obligation does it involve the assumption of the "yoke of the kingdom of heaven"—as the proselyte's undertaking was called (*cf.* Gal. 5:6).

where in Acts (*cf.*, *e.g.*, Ch. 21:26), and the principle by which he justified such conciliation is stated in 1 Cor. 9:20: "to the Jews I became as a Jew, that I might gain Jews; to them that are under the law, as under the law, not being myself under the law, that I might gain them that are under the law." Both in his own days and in more recent days there have never been lacking critics ready to charge the apostle with inconsistency in this and similar matters; but the consistency which some expect from Paul is that "foolish consistency" which R. W. Emerson, in his *Essay on Self-Reliance*, describes as "the hobgoblin of little minds, adored by little statesmen and philosophers and divines." They will search in vain for this so-called consistency in the great mind of Paul, and they will miss the true, large-scale consistency which brought all the activities of his life and thought "into captivity to the obedience of Christ" (2 Cor. 10:5) and subordinated every other interest to the interests of the gospel (1 Cor. 9:23).[8]

4 Paul and Silas, then, took Timothy with them—he appears to have been commissioned and commended to the ministry of the gospel by the elders of the church at Lystra[9]—and so continued their journey. As they visited one church after another in South Galatia, they handed over copies of the apostolic letter. The letter was not explicitly addressed to the churches of Galatia, but they received copies as well as the churches of Syria and Cilicia because they were daughter-churches of Antioch. Besides, if we are right in supposing that the Epistle to the Galatians had been written to them before the Council of Jerusalem met, the Jerusalem decisions went far to confirm Paul's argument in that epistle. From the Letters to the Seven Churches of Asia (*cf.* especially Rev. 2:14, 20) we may infer that the terms of the apostolic decision made their way in due course to the province of Asia, and from there they were probably carried to the churches of the Rhone valley

---

[8] On the subject of Paul's fundamental consistency see also F. J. Foakes Jackson, *Life of St. Paul* (London, 1927), p. 15.

[9] This seems to be suggested by 1 Tim. 4:14, where reference is made to a spiritual gift which Timothy was given "by prophecy, with the laying on of the hands of the presbytery" (*cf.* 1 Tim. 1:18); it is not certain if the same occasion is intended in 2 Tim. 1:6, where "the gift of God" is said to be in Timothy through the imposition of Paul's hands. Probably it was the same occasion; we can well believe that Paul (who with Barnabas had appointed these elders some two years previously) joined the elders of Lystra in laying hands on Timothy's head.

(see p. 315, n. 53). But after Paul delivered these copies to the Galatian churches, he does not appear to have invoked the Jerusalem decision in his instruction to the churches which he founded after this time, nor in his letter to the Roman church; he does not refer to it, for example, when he discusses the food question in 1 Cor. 8 and Rom. 14.[10]

5 What is perhaps the most crucial phase of Luke's narrative is now brought to a conclusion with a characteristic report of progress: the churches were strengthened in faith and the number of believers multiplied daily.

[10] See p. 298, n. 2.

V. EVANGELIZATION ON THE AEGEAN SHORES

(Chs. 16:6–19:20)

1. PHILIPPI

(Ch. 16:6–40)

(a) The Call from Macedonia (Ch. 16:6–10)

6 And they went through[11] the region of Phrygia and
Galatia, having been forbidden of the Holy Spirit to
speak the word in Asia;

7 and when they were come over against Mysia, they
assayed to go into Bithynia and the Spirit of Jesus[12]
suffered them not;

8 and passing by Mysia, they came down to Troas.[13]

9 And a vision appeared to Paul in the night: There
was a man of Macedonia standing, beseeching him,
and saying, Come over into Macedonia, and help us.

10 And when[14] he had seen the vision, straightway we
sought to go forth into Macedonia, concluding that God
had called us to preach the gospel unto them.

6–8 The missionary journeys of Paul exhibit an extraordinary
combination of strategic planning and keen sensitiveness to the
guidance of the Spirit of God, whether that guidance took the
form of inward prompting or the overruling of external circumstances. This combination is specially noteworthy in the present
passage.

Leaving Lystra with Silas and Timothy, he crossed the regional
boundary between Galatic Lycaonia and Galatic Phrygia and
traversed the latter region ("the region of Phrygia and Galatia",

---

[11] The Byzantine text reads "having gone through" (Gk. διελθόντες), which
suggests that the prohibition to preach in Asia came after they had passed
through Galatic Phrygia, whereas actually it came while they were still in that
region.

[12] The Byzantine text omits "of Jesus" (cf. AV).

[13] The Western text reads: "and passing through Mysia, they arrived at
Troas."

[14] The Western text recasts this verse: "Having awaked, then, he related the
vision to us, and we recognized that the Lord had called us to evangelize those
in Macedonia."

as it is called here—*i.e.* the region which is Phrygian and Galatian),[15] visiting Iconium and Pisidian Antioch, the two cities of the region which had been evangelized on his previous visit. But where was he to go next? Before crossing the regional frontier the party had been forbidden by the Holy Spirit (speaking perhaps through a prophet in the church at Lystra) to preach the gospel in the province of Asia—from which we may infer that their original plan had been to do this very thing, making for Ephesus by the Maeander valley.[16] The Spirit, we may observe, gave them ample warning to change their plans. If the province of Asia was not to be the field of their evangelistic activity for the present, then it was natural for them to cast their eyes farther north, and think of the highly civilized province of Bithynia in North-West Asia Minor, with its Greek cities (of which Nicomedia and Nicaea were the most important) and Jewish colonies.[17] So, instead of taking the westward road to Ephesus, they turned north from Pisidian Antioch, crossed the Sultan Dag range, arrived at Philomelium and struck north-west from there, by one of two possible routes leading through Asian Phrygia.[18] We could plot the remainder of their journey more certainly if we knew where they received the second divine monition, warning them away from Bithynia. If we take "over against Mysia"[19] in v. 7 to mean something like "opposite the eastern border of Mysia" (the north-western region of the province of Asia), then presumably they arrived at one or other of the road-junctions Dorylaeum or

[15] The most up-to-date study of this subject is by W. M. Calder, "The Boundary of Galatic Phrygia", in *Proceedings of the Orientalist Congress*, Istanbul, 1951. By the kindness of Professor Calder, I have seen this paper before publication. The view expressed by K. Lake (*Beginnings*, v [London, 1933], pp. 231 ff.) that "the region of Phrygia and Galatia" means "territory in which sometimes Phrygian and sometimes Gaelic [he means Gaulish] was the language of the villagers" is shown to be impossible.

[16] *Cf.* F. J. A. Hort, *Prolegomena to Romans and Ephesians* (London, 1895), p. 82; W. M. Ramsay, *Pauline and Other Studies*, pp. 77 f. (in his chapter on "The Statesmanship of Paul").

[17] Philo (*Embassy to Gaius*, 281) refers to Jewish colonies in Bithynia. The province was thoroughly evangelized some time later; for the presence of Christians there *cf.* 1 Pet. 1:1 and Pliny the Younger, *Epistle* x. 96 (his famous letter to the Emperor Trajan on the growth of Christianity in Bithynia).

[18] Paul and his friends had, of course, to pass through part of the province of Asia to get either to Bithynia or Troas; they were forbidden to preach in the province, not to traverse it.

[19] Gk. κατὰ τὴν Μυσίαν, where κατά may mean something like "in the latitude of"; *cf.* Herodotus, *History* i. 76, where the city of Pteria is said to lie "roughly in the longitude of Sinope" (κατὰ Σινώπην . . . μάλιστά κη κειμένη).

Cotiaeum, and instead of continuing their northward journey into Bithynia turned west until they reached the sea at Troas.[20]

In saying that this second prohibition was imposed by "the Spirit of Jesus" (v. 7), whereas the former one is ascribed to "the Holy Spirit" (v. 6), Luke poses an interesting theological question. One and the same Spirit is intended, of course, but is there any significance in the change of phraseology? Possibly the methods used to communicate the Spirit's will on the two occasions were different; it may be that on the second occasion the communication took a form closely associated with the exalted Christ. Since His ascension it is by His Spirit that Jesus communicates with His people; we may recall Paul's description of Him as "the last Adam" who became "a life-giving spirit" (1 Cor. 15:45).

9 Troas (whose full name was Alexandria Troas) was founded at the end of the 4th century B.C. and remained a free Greek city until the Emperor Augustus gave it the status of a Roman colony. It was a regular port of call for vessels journeying between Asia and Macedonia (*cf.* Ch. 20:5). It was here that the series of divine prohibitions gave way to a positive direction; the direction this time took the form of a night vision seen by Paul. In this vision a Macedonian stood beseeching Paul to come over into Macedonia and help the people there. Macedonia, which became the dominant power in the Greek world under Philip and Alexander the Great in the fourth century B.C., had been a Roman province since 146 B.C. It is needless to inquire how Paul recognized the man to be a Macedonian. His request, "Come over into Macedonia, and help us," indicated his nationality clearly enough.

10 At this point the narrator shows unobtrusively that he himself had now joined the missionary party as a fourth member, by continuing the story in the first instead of the third person plural.[21] Here the first of the "we" sections of the book begins.

---

[20] They had to pass through Mysia to reach Troas. which lay on the Mysian seaboard. The expression "passing by (Gk. παρελθόντες) Mysia" (v. 8) means not that they by-passed this area in the geographical sense but that they did not stay to preach there.

[21] The appearance of Luke at this point in the narrative suggests to W. Barclay (*The Acts of the Apostles Designed for Daily Bible Study* [Edinburgh, 1952], p. 131) that "Luke met Paul then because Paul needed his professional services, because he was in ill-health which barred him from making the journeys he would like. If this is so it is a great thought to think that Paul took even his weakness and his pain as a messenger from God." Barclay goes on to make the further interesting suggestion that the "man of

No other account of the transition from "they" to "we" is so simple or convincing as this. A writer incorporating into his narrative the diary of a personal eyewitness other than himself would not have done so in such an unobtrusive way.[22] Whether Luke was practising as a physician in Troas at the time or was there for some other purpose we have no means of discovering; at any rate, he joined Paul, Silas and Timothy and went over to Macedonia with them, for, as he says, when Paul related the vision to his companions, "immediately *we* sought to go on into Macedonia, concluding that God had called us to preach the gospel to them."

Paul's original plan had probably been, after visiting the churches of South Galatia, to go on to Ephesus and begin to evangelize the eastern shore of the Aegean by planting Christianity "in that great metropolis in which the East looked out upon the West" (F. J. A. Hort, *Prolegomena to Romans and Ephesians* [London, 1895], p. 83). This plan was only postponed, not jettisoned altogether. But first he was directed to the western shore of the Aegean, and planted the faith in Philippi, Thessalonica and Corinth before he settled in Ephesus. Strategic points on the circumference of the circle of which Ephesus was the centre were evangelized first—in Macedonia and Greece as well as in South Galatia—and then he completed his work in that whole area by nearly three years' ministry at the centre. The supernatural monitions did not spoil Paul's strategy, but improved it.

(b) The First Convert in Philippi (Ch. 16:11-15)

11 Setting sail[23] therefore from Troas, we made a

Macedonia" may have been associated in Paul's mind with Alexander the Great, the Macedonian world-conqueror, and that this put Macedonia in his mind as the next stage in his programme of world-conquest for Christ.

[22] On the uniformity of the style and language of the "we" sections of Acts with those of the rest of the book see A. Harnack, *Luke the Physician* (Eng. tr., London, 1907), pp. 26 ff., and J. C. Hawkins, *Horae Synopticae* (2nd edn., Oxford, 1909), pp. 182 ff. If the narrator incorporated the diary of someone else, he must have worked over it very thoroughly; why then did he leave this abrupt transition from the third person to the first, with no hint of the identity of the diarist? If, on the other hand, the first-personal narrative style were a fictitious device to suggest the presence of an eye-witness and thus give an impression of greater authority to the narrative, why was the device used so sparingly? The most satisfactory conclusion in the light of the evidence is that the whole book was written by the author of the "we" sections, who uses the pronoun "we" in those sections to indicate that he himself was present at the events recorded in them. See p. 19, n. 13.

[23] The Western text adds "next day."

straight course to Samothrace, and the day following to Neapolis;

12 and from thence to Philippi, which is a city of Macedonia, the first of the district,[24] a *Roman* colony: and we were in this city tarrying certain days.

13 And on the sabbath day we went forth without the gate by a river side, where we supposed there was a place of prayer;[25] and we sat down, and spake unto the women that were come together.

14 And a certain woman named Lydia, a seller of purple, of the city of Thyatira, one that worshipped God, heard us: whose heart the Lord opened to give heed unto the things which were spoken by Paul.

15 And when she was baptized, and her household, she besought us, saying, If ye have judged me to be faithful to the Lord, come into my house, and abide *there*. And she constrained us.

11 The wind was favourable for the voyage across the north Aegean, and they finished it in two days. (The reverse journey from Neapolis to Troas, recorded in Ch. 20:6, took five days.) At the end of the first day they reached Samothrace, a mountainous island, rising to 5,000 feet, which forms a conspicuous landmark. In religious history the chief importance of Samothrace is the fact that it was the seat of a famous mystery cult, the worship of the Cabiri, which had been practised there from time immemorial. Paul and his three friends did not linger there, however; next day their ship took them to Neapolis on the Macedonian coast. Neapolis, the modern Kavalla, was the port of Philippi, which lay some ten miles away. Here the great Egnatian Way, a Roman road linking the Adriatic with the Aegean, reached its eastern

---

[24] The true text may be, as emended by F. Field (*Notes on Translation of the NT* [Cambridge, 1899], p. 124) and F. Blass (*Philology of the Gospels* [London, 1898], pp. 67 ff.), "which is a city of the first district of Macedonia" (reading πρώτης μερίδος τῆς Μακεδονίας πόλις for πρώτη . . . πόλις. This reading, though attested in no Greek MS., is supported by some codices of the Latin Vulgate, and by mediæval versions in Provençal and German (Codex Teplensis). The Western text calls Philippi "the capital of Macedonia" (but Thessalonica, not Philippi, was the provincial capital).

[25] Our best authorities for the Alexandrian text are corrupt here (א A and B all require emendation), and the true reading may be preserved in the Byzantine text, οὗ ἐνομίζετο προσευχὴ εἶναι, correctly rendered in AV, "where prayer was wont to be made" (the Western reading οὗ ἐδόκει προσευχή εἶναι is probably due to the misinterpretation of ἐνομίζετο as "it was thought").

terminus.[26] Luke likes to mention ports of arrival and departure, and is specially careful to note the daily progress when he makes journeys by sea (cf. Chs. 20:6–16; 21:1–8; 27:2–44; 28:11–14).

12 Disembarking at Neapolis, they went on to Philippi. This city received its name from Philip of Macedon, who seized the gold-mines in the vicinity and fortified what had formerly been the Thasian settlement of Crenides. With the rest of Macedonia, Philippi passed under Roman control in 168 B.C. Near Philippi was fought the battle in 42 B.C. which resulted in the victory of Antony and Octavian (the future Emperor Augustus) over Brutus and Cassius, the assassins of Julius Caesar. (It is from Shakespeare's references to this battle in *Julius Caesar* that the undying misquotation, "We shall meet at Philippi", is taken.) After the battle, the victors settled a number of their veterans at Philippi and made it a Roman colony; Octavian settled other colonists there after his victory over Antony and Cleopatra at Actium in 31 B.C.

Luke, who apparently spent some years in Philippi from this time, shows a special interest in the place. He describes it as a city of the first district of Macedonia—*i.e.* the first of the four administrative areas into which Macedonia was divided by the Romans.[27] While he refers to several other cities which we know to have been Roman colonies, Philippi is the only one which he actually describes as a Roman colony, and the details of its administration which he gives in the following narrative are those which were specially characteristic of such a colony. A Roman colony used Roman law, and its constitution was modelled on the municipal constitution of Rome.[28]

[26] This road, whose western termini were at Apollonia and Dyrrhachium (modern Valona and Durazzo in Albania), was built after the Roman annexation of Macedonia as a province in 146 B.C.

[27] This is more probable than Ramsay's suggestion, based on the standard text (see n. 24 above), that Luke's interest in Philippi led him to call it "the leading city of its division of Macedonia" (*St. Paul the Traveller* [14th edn., London, 1920], p. 205). "Of old Amphipolis had been the chief city of the division, to which both belonged. Afterwards Philippi quite outstripped its rival; but it was at that time in such a position, that Amphipolis was ranked first by general consent, Philippi first by its own consent" (*op. cit.*, pp. 206 f.). It was in 167 B.C., the year after the battle of Pydna, that the Roman senate decreed that Macedonia should be divided into four independent districts, each administered by an oligarchical council.

[28] The original purpose of Roman colonies was military; it was plainly a good thing to have settlements of Roman citizens at strategic points throughout the empire. Other Roman colonies which appear in Acts are Pisidian Antioch, Lystra, Troas, Corinth and Ptolemais.

13 When Paul visited a new city, it was his practice, as we have seen, to attend the local Jewish synagogue on the first sabbath after his arrival and seek an opportunity there for making the Christian message known "to the Jew first". At Philippi, however, there does not appear to have been a synagogue. That can only mean that there were very few Jews in the place; had there been ten Jewish men, they would have sufficed to constitute a synagogue.[29] No number of women could compensate for the absence of even one man necessary to complete the quorum of ten. There was, however, an unofficial meeting-place outside the city where a number of women—Jewesses and God-fearing Gentiles—came together to go through the appointed Jewish service of prayer for the sabbath day, even if they could not constitute a regular synagogue congregation. Paul and his companions found this place, by the bank of the river Gangites, and sat down with the women and told them the story of Jesus.

14–15 One of these women, a God-fearer, came from Thyatira in the province of Asia. Her name Lydia, "the Lydian woman," reminds us that Thyatira lay in what had once been the ancient kingdom of Lydia. The people of that area were famed for their skill in the manufacture and use of purple dye,[30] and Lydia had come to Philippi as a trader in that dye. It may have been in her native Thyatira that she became a God-fearer; there was a Jewish colony in that city.[31]

As Paul and his friends spoke, Lydia believed what they said and acknowledged Jesus as Lord. She thus became Paul's first convert in Europe. When she was baptized, together with her household (presumably her servants and other dependents), she gave practical proof of her conversion by pressing the four missionaries to become her guests. The fancy that one of them became more than her guest—that, as S. Baring-Gould urged,[32]

---

[29] For ten as the minimum number (Heb. *minyan*) for a synagogue congregation *cf. Pirqe Aboth* iii. 7: "Rabbi Halafta ben Dosa, of the village of Hananya, said, 'When ten people sit together and occupy themselves with the Torah, the *Shekhinah* abides among them. as it is said, God standeth in the congregation (Heb. *'edah*) of God' (Ps. 82:1)."

[30] Homer (*Iliad* iv. 141 f.) refers in a simile to the art of purple dyeing practised by the women of Maeonia (*i.e.* Lydia) and Caria.

[31] *Cf.* Rev. 2:18 ff., and W. M. Ramsay, *Letters to the Seven Churches of Asia* (London, 1909), pp. 316 ff.

[32] *A Study of St. Paul* (London, 1897), p. 213; so, earlier, E. Renan, *St. Paul* (Paris. 1869), p. 148. Both suppose her to be the "true yokefellow" of

"she and Paul were either married at Philippi or would have been so but for untoward circumstances"—may be dismissed as nothing but a fancy.

(c) The Pythoness (Ch. 16:16–18)

16 And it came to pass, as we were going to the place of prayer, that a certain maid having a spirit of divination met us, who brought her masters much gain by soothsaying.

17 The same following after Paul and us cried out, saying, These men are servants[33] of the Most High God, who proclaim unto you[34] the way of salvation.

18 And this she did for many days. But Paul, being sore troubled, turned and said to the spirit, I charge thee in the name of Jesus Christ to come out of her. And it came out that very hour.

16 Three individuals are singled out by Luke among Paul's converts at Philippi, and they differ so much one from another that he might be thought to have deliberately selected them in order to show how the saving name of Jesus proved its power in the lives of the most diverse types of men and women. The first is Lydia, the independent business-woman of reputable character and God-fearing mind; as she heard the gospel story, "the Lord opened her heart to give heed to what was said by Paul" (RSV). But the second is a person of a very different stamp: an unfortunate demon-possessed slave-girl, whose owners exploited her infirmity for their material profit. She is described by Luke as a "pythoness",[35] i.e. as a person inspired by Apollo, the god particularly associated with the giving of oracles, who was worshipped as the "Pythian" god at the oracular shrine of Delphi (otherwise called Pytho) in central Greece. Her involuntary utterances were regarded as the voice of the god, and she was thus much in demand by people who wished to have their fortunes told.

Phil. 4:3. Clement of Alexandria (*Miscellanies* iii. 6. 53. 1) similarly thought the "yokefellow" was Paul's wife, but did not apparently identify her with Lydia. For a more probable identification see n. 63 below.

[33] P45 omits "servants" (δοῦλοι), probably by accident.

[34] The evidence is fairly evenly balanced between "you" (ὑμῖν) and "us" (ἡμῖν), with a slight preponderance in favour of "you."

[35] Plutarch (*The Failure of the Oracles* ix. 414 e) calls these people "ventriloquists" (Gk. ἐγγαστρίμυθοι) —ventriloquists, that is to say, whose utterances were really and not only apparently beyond their conscious control. In LXX

17 Her deliverance demanded much more spectacular measures than did Lydia's quiet turning in heart to the Lord. Day by day, as the missionaries went to the place of prayer,[36] she followed them through the streets of Philippi, advertising them aloud as servants of the Most High God, who proclaimed the way of salvation.[37] The title "Most High God"[38] was one which provided Jews and Gentiles with a convenient common denominator for the Supreme Being, and "salvation" in the religious sense was as eagerly sought by Gentiles as by Jews.[39]

18 The missionaries, however, did not appreciate her "unsolicited testimonials", and at last Paul, vexed by her continual clamour, exorcized the spirit that possessed her, commanding it in the name of Jesus Christ to come out of her. The words had scarcely left his lips before she was released from her familiar spirit.

> "Jesus! the name high over all,
> In hell, or earth, or sky:
> Angels and men before it fall,
> And devils fear and fly."

The superior authority which such spirits had recognized when Jesus Himself commanded them to leave their victims was equally recognized when His name was invoked by one of His apostles, and proved as potent in exorcism as in other forms of healing (*cf.* Ch. 3:6).

(d) Paul and Silas in Jail at Philippi (Ch. 16:19–34)

19 But when her masters saw that the hope of their gain was gone, they laid hold on Paul and Silas, and dragged them into the market-place before the rulers,

20 and when they had brought them unto the magistrates,

the same Greek word is used of those who had a "familiar spirit" (Heb. *'obh*), such as the witch of Endor.

[36] The word προσευχή may mean either "prayer" or "a place of prayer"; in the latter sense it was used as a synonym for συναγωγή ("synagogue").

[37] See p. 290 (exposition of Ch. 14:9) with n. 20.

[38] Gk. θεὸς ὕψιστος. In Jewish circles this was the equivalent of Heb. *'El 'Elyon*, the divine title found in Gen. 14:18, etc. Among pagans it was a title of Zeus.

[39] *Cf.* A. Harnack, *Mission and Expansion of Christianity* (Eng. tr., London, 1908), i, pp. 101 ff.; W. M. Ramsay, *Bearing of Recent Discovery on the Trustworthiness of NT* (London, 1915) pp. 173 ff. Among pagans salvation was the object of many prayers and vows to the "most high God" and other "saviour gods", and was held out for the attainment of initiates in the mystery cults.

they said, These men, being Jews, do exceedingly trouble our city,

21 and set forth customs which it is not lawful for us to receive, or to observe, being Romans.

22 And the multitude rose up together against them: and the magistrates rent their garments off them, and commanded to beat them with rods.

23 And when they had laid many stripes upon them, they cast them into prison, charging the jailor to keep them safely:

24 who, having received such a charge, cast them into the inner prison, and made their feet fast in the stocks.

25 But about midnight Paul and Silas were praying and singing hymns unto God, and the prisoners were listening to them;

26 and suddenly there was a great earthquake, so that the foundations of the prison-house were shaken: and immediately[40] all the doors were opened; and everyone's bands were loosed.

27 And the jailor, being roused out of sleep and seeing the prison doors open, drew his sword and was about to kill himself, supposing that the prisoners had escaped.

28 But Paul cried with a loud voice, saying, Do thyself no harm: for we are all here.

29 And he called for lights and sprang in, and, trembling for fear, fell down before Paul and Silas,

30 and brought them out[41] and said, Sirs, what must I do to be saved?

31 And they said, Believe on the Lord Jesus,[42] and thou shalt be saved, thou and thy house.

32 And they spake the word of the Lord[43] unto him, with all that were in his house.

33 And he took them the same hour of the night, and washed their stripes; and was baptized, he and all his, immediately.

---

[40] Cod. B omits "immediately."

[41] The Western text adds "having secured the other (prisoners)"—an addition which Ramsay is inclined to accept as authentic as "suggestive of the orderly well-disciplined character of the jailor" (*St. Paul the Traveller*, p. 222), while W. L. Knox dismisses it as "an amusing insertion" (*St. Paul and the Church of Jerusalem* [Cambridge, 1925], p. xxiv). The Western recension is prone to envisage what must have taken place and to add a statement to that effect in the text.

[42] The Western and Byzantine texts add "Christ."

[43] Cod. B and the first hand in ℵ read "God."

34 And he brought them up into his house, and set food
before them, and rejoiced greatly, with all his house,
having believed in God.

19 But the good deed done to the fortune-telling slave-girl was
not to the liking of her owners, for when Paul exorcized the spirit
that possessed her he exorcized their source of income as well: she
could no longer tell fortunes. Their righteous indignation was
aroused at this wanton attack on the sacred rights of property[44]
(as they saw it). Moreover, the men who had infringed these
rights were not respectable Roman citizens like themselves (or so
they thought); they were not even Greeks, like the population
around them, but wandering Jews, engaged in propagating some
variety of their own perverse superstition. They therefore dragged
Paul and Silas before the civic magistrates and lodged a complaint
against them. The reason why they laid hands on Paul and Silas
and not on Luke and Timothy may have been partly because Paul
and Silas were the leaders of the missionary party; but we should
also remember that Paul and Silas would be the most Jewish in
appearance: Luke was a Gentile and Timothy was half-Gentile.
Anti-Jewish sentiment lay very near the surface in Gentile antiquity.

20–21 As Philippi was a Roman colony, its municipal administration, like that of the city of Rome itself, was in the hands of
two collegiate magistrates. The collegiate magistrates of a Roman
colony were commonly called duumvirs, but sometimes they
preferred the more dignified title of praetors,[45] and the two
Philippian magistrates appear to have been given this title.[46]
Before the two praetors, then, Paul and Silas were dragged, and
were represented as vagabond Jews who were causing disturbances
in the city and teaching customs which Roman citizens of all
people could never admit or practise. The magistrates took cognizance of such religious activity as might provoke a breach of the
peace, or encourage unlawful practices or organizations; besides,

---

[44] The only two occasions on which Luke records a Gentile attack on the
apostles rise from a threat by the gospel to property interests; cf. Ch. 19:23 ff.

[45] Cicero's remarks on the chief magistrates of Capua have been quoted
frequently on this point: "While they are called duumvirs in our other colonies,
these men wished to be called praetors" (*On the Agrarian Law* ii. 93).

[46] Gk. στρατηγός (translated "magistrate" here) was used as the equivalent
of Lat. *praetor*.

335

there were laws prohibiting foreign-religious propaganda among Roman citizens.[47]

22–24 There was great indignation that Roman citizens should be molested by strolling peddlers of an outlandish religion. Such people must be taught to know their proper place and not trouble their betters. There was no serious investigation of the charge; Paul and Silas were summarily stripped[48] and handed over to the lictors—the magistrates' police-attendants—to be soundly beaten and the city jailor was then ordered to lock them up in jail.

The lictors were the official attendants upon the chief magistrates in Rome and other Roman cities. They carried as symbols of office bundles of rods, with an ax inserted among them under certain circumstances—the *fasces*[49] *et secures*—denoting the magistrates' right to inflict corporal and capital punishment. It was with the lictors' rods that the two missionaries were beaten on this occasion. It was not the only time that Paul had this treatment meted out to him; some five years later he tells how he was beaten with rods three times (2 Cor. 11:25), although we have no information about the other two occasions.

When, after this severe beating, they were entrusted to the jailor's custody, he interpreted his instructions strictly and fastened their legs in the stocks, in the inmost part of the prison. These stocks had more than two holes for the legs, which could be forced wide apart in such a way as to cause the utmost discomfort and cramping pain.[50] It was not the jailor's business to take any thought for his prisoner's comfort, but to make sure that they did not escape. He was probably a retired soldier, and while the training of a Roman soldier developed many fine qualities of character, these did not include much of the milk of human kindness. Yet this man is the third person in Philippi whom Luke describes as influenced by the power of Christ. He was a totally different character from Lydia and the fortune-teller, and it took an earthquake and imminent danger of death to make him take

[47] On the status of non-Roman religions in Roman law see S. L. Guterman, *Religious Toleration and Persecution in Ancient Rome* (London, 1951).

[48] The interpretation of some, that it was their own clothes that the praetors tore off (*cf.* Ch. 14:14), is hardly to be entertained.

[49] It was from this "bundle" (Lat. *fascis*) of rods and axes, used as an emblem, that the name of Benito Mussolini's Fascist party was derived.

[50] *Cf.* Eusebius's account of how this form of torture was endured by the confessors of Vienne and Lyons (*Ecclesiastical History* v. 1.27) and by Origen (*ib.*, vi. 39).

thought for his salvation; yet it was the same gospel as had blessed these two women that now brought blessing to him.

25-26 The double discomfort of the lictors' rods and the stocks was not calculated to fill Paul and Silas with joy, but about midnight the other prisoners, as they listened, heard sounds coming from the inmost part of the jail—sounds, not of groaning and cursing, but of prayer and hymn-singing. "The legs feel nothing in the stocks when the heart is in heaven," says Tertullian.[51] What sort of men were these? It must have been the awed impression which the two missionaries' behaviour produced on the other prisoners that enabled them to dissuade these others from making their escape while the going was good when a sudden earthquake shook the prison foundations, threw open the doors and loosened the staples that attached the prisoners' fetters to the wall.[52]

27 The earthquake that rocked the prison foundations wakened the jailor out of his midnight sleep. Immediately he went to investigate his charge. The worst had happened: the prison doors were open; the prisoners, of course, had seized their opportunity and escaped. For a man brought up to a Roman soldier's ideas of duty and discipline there was only one course open—suicide.

[51] *To the Martyrs*, 2. *Cf.* Epictetus (*Enchiridium* ii.6.26): "Then we shall be emulators of Socrates, when we are able to compose paeans in prison." W. K. Lowther Clarke (in JThS xv [1914], p. 599) has pointed out some remarkable verbal parallels between this narrative and that of the imprisonment of Joseph in the *Testament of Joseph* 8:5 (recension A), where Joseph, after being scourged and thrown into prison in Egypt, was heard giving thanks to the Lord and singing praises in the abode of darkness, and rejoicing with glad voice, glorifying God.

[52] For the miraculous release from prison *cf.* Chs. 5:19 and 12:6 ff., with accompanying exposition and notes. Celsus suggested a parallel between the narrative of the earthquake and escape here and the description of the deliverance of the Bacchic devotees and their deity in the *Bacchanals* of Euripides (lines 443 ff., 586 ff.); *cf.* Origen, *Against Celsus* ii.34. These parallels provide material for the exercise of form criticism; the Christian reader will recognize in Luke's narrative the power of God in operation, as Paul and Silas—and the jailor—certainly recognized it in the actual incident. M. Dibelius (*Aufsätze zur Apostelgeschichte* [Göttingen, 1951], pp. 26 f.) argues that the earthquake-narrative of vv. 25—34 constitutes an "independent legend" inserted by Luke into the original form of the narrative; that 35 follows naturally upon v. 24 without any suggestion of miraculous interposition. It is noteworthy, indeed, that in the authentic text (as distinct from the Western revision) there is no reference to the earhquake in vv. 35 ff.; it is a precarious critical procedure, however, to conclude that, because one passage of a narrative follows naturally upon another separated from it by a self-contained pericope, the intervening pericope is a later insertion.

28 But as he stood there, by the outer door of the prison, about to drive his short sword into his throat or heart, his hand was arrested by a voice from the darkness within: "Do not harm yourself, for we are all here" (RSV). While he could see nothing as he looked into the darkness, those within could see his figure silhouetted in the doorway and could see what he was about to do. Not only were Paul and Silas still there, but they had apparently restrained the other prisoners also. There was something uncanny about these two men!

29-30 So, calling for light, he sprang into the prison and (having first secured the others again, says the Western reviser) brought Paul and Silas out. "Sirs," he asked them earnestly, "what must I do to be saved?"

How much he meant by his question it would be difficult to say. He may have heard the fortune-teller's announcement that these men had come to proclaim "the way of salvation." Just what this salvation involved may not have been clear to him, but he was thoroughly shaken, in soul as well as in body, and there was something about these two men that convinced him that they were the men who could show him the way to inward release and security.

31-32 There and then the two missionaries told him that faith in Jesus as Lord was the way of salvation for himself and his family. And what faith in Jesus as Lord meant they at once made plain to them, setting the whole gospel message before them, in terms which they could readily grasp.

33-34 This was the message they had lived for! With joy they embraced it at once. The jailor bathed the wounded backs of the two missionaries before he took them into his house, possibly at a well in the prison courtyard, and there too he and his household received baptism at their hands.[53] "He washed and was washed," says Chrysostom; "he washed them from their stripes, and he himself was washed from his sins" (*Homily* xxxvi. 2). Then Paul and Silas received hospitable treatment in his house; food was set before them, and hosts and guests rejoiced together, united in Christian faith and love. The jailor was guilty of no

---

[53] For the baptism of the jailor's household *cf.* Chs. 10:44—48 with 11:14, and 16:15; also 1 Cor. 1:16. Nothing is said here of their reception of the Holy Spirit, but it is certainly implied in the mention of their great rejoicing in v. 34 (*cf.* Ch. 8:39).

breach of duty in thus taking Paul and Silas into his house; his responsibility was to produce his prisoners when called upon to do so. He had now no reason to fear that they would run away! Luke's third example of the power of Christ at Philippi is the most wonderful of all. And Paul and Silas no doubt reckoned the rods and the stocks well worth enduring for the joy that was brought into the jailor's home.

(e) Paul and Silas Leave Philippi (Ch. 16:35-40)

35 But when it was day,[54] the magistrates sent the serjeants, saying, Let those men go.

36 And the jailor reported the words to Paul, *saying,* The magistrates have sent to let you go: now therefore come forth, and go in peace.[55]

37 But Paul said unto them, They have beaten us publicly, uncondemned,[56] men that are Romans, and have cast us into prison; and do they now cast us out privily? nay verily; but let them come themselves and bring us out.

38 And the serjeants reported[57] these words unto the magistrates: and they feared when they heard that they were Romans;

39 and they came[58] and besought them; and when they had brought them out, they asked them to go away from the city.

40 And they went out of the prison, and entered into *the house of* Lydia; and when they had seen the brethren,[59] they comforted them, and departed.

35 By next morning the excitement of the previous day had

---

[54] After "when it was day", the Western text continues "the praetors came together into the forum and, calling to mind the earthquake that had taken place, they were affrighted and sent the lictors . . ." An answer was thus supplied to the natural question, What effect did the earthquake have on those outside the prison precincts?

[55] Some Western authorities omit "in peace."

[56] Here, as in Ch. 22:25, a better rendering than "uncondemned" for Gk. ἀκατακρίτους would be "without hearing our case" (Lat. *re incognita*). The Western text reads ἀναιτίους ("not guilty").

[57] The original reading of the Western text was apparently "reported to the magistrates the things which had been said."

[58] The Western text reads: "And having arrived with many friends at the prison they besought them to go out, saying, We did not know the truth about you, that you were righteous men. And having led them out they besought them, saying, Depart from this city lest perchance they come together to us again, crying out against you."

[59] The Western text adds "they related all that the Lord had done to them."

died down and the praetors decided that the two vagabond Jews had been taught the lesson they needed by the lictors' rods and the night in the lock-up. All that was necessary now was to release them and send them out of town; they would not come back in a hurry. Imprisonment in itself was not a common penalty for breaches of civil law; by having Paul and Silas locked up for a night after their beating the praetors had simply exercised the police right of *coercitio—i.e.* summary correction or chastisement. They now sent the lictors[60] to the jail with orders to the jailor to set the two prisoners free.

36-37 But when the jailor reported the message to Paul and Silas and told them that they were at liberty to depart, Paul demurred. An act of injustice had been committed, and it must not be covered up in this way. Silas and he were Roman citizens—as good Roman citizens as the colonists and magistrates of Philippi—and their rights as Roman citizens had been grossly violated. The charge brought against them ought to have been properly investigated, but they had been beaten and imprisoned without any inquiry. By the Valerian and Porcian laws, passed at various times between 509 B.C. (the traditional date of the founding of the Roman Republic) and 195 B.C., Roman citizens were exempted from degrading forms of punishment and had certain valued rights established for them in relation to the law. Why, we may ask, did Paul not protest his Roman citizenship the day before?[61] The answer sometimes given, that it would have been embarrassing for him to claim privileges which Silas could not share, seems to be excluded by the plain implication of the present passage, that both Silas and he were Roman citizens. It may be that they did protest, but that no one paid any attention to them in the excitement of the moment. A Roman citizen claimed his legal rights by the statement *ciuis Romanus sum*—"I am a Roman citizen."[62] We are not informed if there was any documentary evidence which could be produced on the spot in confirmation of the claim. At any rate,

---

[60] The word rendered as "serjeants" (RSV "police") is Gk. ῥαβδοῦχοι (literally "rod-bearers"), used as the equivalent of Lat. *lictores*.

[61] In Ch. 22:25 Paul is careful to claim his citizen rights before being beaten, but there he was about to be lashed with the murderous scourge, a more frightful instrument than the lictors' rods. See p. 445.

[62] Cicero (*Uerrine Orations* ii. 5.161 f.) relates, as a most disgraceful and illegal proceeding, how a Roman citizen was publicly beaten in the market-place of Messina in Sicily despite his protest *ciuis Romanus sum*.

Paul's claim neatly turns the tables on the self-important complaint of his accusers, that Roman citizens ought not to be disturbed by mere Jews. If the praetors wished them to leave Philippi, they must come and show them the courtesy due to Roman citizens, and not expel them in this hole-and-corner manner.

38–39 The lictors brought Paul's message back to the praetors, and they were dismayed at being told what, in the excitement of yesterday, they had omitted to ascertain—that the two Jews were as good Roman citizens as themselves. If a complaint of their illegal treatment of these Roman citizens reached the authorities in Rome, they would be in an awkward position. Their self-importance was very healthily deflated, as they went to the jail and requested Paul and Silas to leave Philippi. Roman citizens who had been convicted of no crime could not be expelled from a Roman city, but the responsibility of protecting two unpopular Roman citizens was more than the praetors felt able to undertake. They therefore apologized to them and conducted them out of the prison precincts, asking them to be good enough not to remain in Philippi any longer.

40 Paul's insistence on an official apology may have served to some degree as a protection to the members of the church which had been planted in Philippi during the period of his stay there. The later history of the Philippian church makes pleasant reading; the same kindness as provided Paul and his friends with hospitality in Lydia's home was shown in their repeated gifts to Paul during his subsequent travels (*cf.* Phil. 4:10 ff.). When Paul and Silas had been released from prison, they went to Lydia's house and spoke words of encouragement to the Christians; then, with Timothy, they departed from Philippi in the westward direction along the Egnatian Way. Luke apparently stayed behind; he reappears in Philippi in Ch. 20:5 f., at the beginning of the second "we" section of Acts.[63]

[63] Luke is probably the "true yokefellow" addressed by Paul in Phil. 4:3. (In my judgment, Paul's Epistle to the Philippians was written before the events of Acts 20:5 ff.; *cf.* p. 395, n. 35.)

CHAPTER XVII

2. THESSALONICA TO ATHENS

(Ch. 17:1–34)

(a) Thessalonica (Ch. 17:1–9)

1 Now when they had passed through Amphipolis[1] and Apollonia, they came to Thessalonica, where was a synagogue of the Jews:

2 and Paul, as his custom was, went in unto them, and for three sabbath days reasoned with them from the scriptures,

3 opening and alleging that it behooved the Christ to suffer, and to rise again from the dead; and that this Jesus, whom, *said he,* I proclaim unto you, is the Christ.

4 And some of them were persuaded,[2] and consorted with Paul and Silas; and of the devout Greeks a great multitude, and of the chief women not a few.

5 But the Jews, being moved with jealousy, took unto them certain vile fellows of the rabble, and gathering a crowd, set the city on an uproar; and assaulting the house of Jason, they sought to bring them forth to the people.

6 And when they found them not, they dragged Jason and certain brethren before the rulers of the city, crying, These that have turned the world upside down are come hither also;

7 whom Jason hath received: and these all act contrary to the decrees of Caesar, saying that there is another king, *one* Jesus.

8 And they troubled the multitude and the rulers of the city, when they heard these things.

9 And when they had taken security from Jason and the rest, they let them go.

[1] After "Amphipolis" the Western text continues: "they came down to Apollonia and from there to Thessalonica."

[2] After "persuaded", the Western text continues: "and many of the God-fearers adhered to the teaching, and a large number of the Greeks, and not a few of the wives of the principal men."

1 From Philippi Paul, Silas and Timothy, took the Egnatian Way westward through Amphipolis on the Strymon (formerly an important strategic point on the Thraco-Macedonian frontier) and Apollonia, a day's journey farther on, and came to Thessalonica (modern Saloniki), the chief city of Macedonia then as now. It received its name from Cassander, who founded it in 315 B.C. on the site of the earlier settlement of Therme, after the name of his wife, a step-sister of Alexander the Great. The three travellers apparently halted only for a night at Amphipolis and again at Apollonia, but at Thessalonica they made a longer stay; it was the next place after Philippi selected for intensive evangelization.

2–3 In accordance with his regular practice, Paul visited the local synagogue, and (having probably been asked to speak, as previously at Pisidian Antioch) he expounded the OT scriptures on three successive sabbath days, bringing forward as evidence of their fulfilment the historic facts accomplished in the ministry, death and exaltation of Jesus, setting the fulfilment alongside the predictions[3] in order that the force of his argument might be readily grasped. According to these predictions, the Messiah was appointed to suffer and then rise from the dead;[4] both these experiences had been fulfilled in Jesus of Nazareth (and in nobody else); therefore, said he, "this is the Messiah, this Jesus whom I am proclaiming to you."

4 As had happened in the cities of South Galatia, so here too some of Paul's Jewish hearers were convinced by what he said, but the majority of his converts were Gentile God-fearers. Among these were a considerable number of women of high station in the city, wives of the principal citizens. Jason, who is mentioned as Paul's host in v. 5, was presumably one of the Jews who believed (the Greek name Jason was assumed by many Jews whose Jewish name was Joshua); Aristarchus and Secundus, described as Thessalonians in Ch. 20:4, were probably also converted to Christianity at this time.

5 But this was not the only way in which the pattern of events in the South Galatian cities was reproduced at Thessalonica. Here

---

[3] This is the sense of the word translated "alleging" (Gk. παρατιθέμενος, "setting alongside", and hence "bringing forward as evidence").

[4] For the insistance on Messiah's suffering and subsequent exaltation as the two basic facts of the gospel *cf.* Ch. 3:18; 23:6 ff : 26:23; Luke 24:26, 46; 1 Cor. 15:3 ff.; 1 Pet. 1:11.

too the Jews who did not believe the gospel, incensed at the way in which so many of the God-fearing Gentiles embraced Paul's message and adhered to him, incited the city rabble against him and his colleagues. (It is in the light of this conduct that the severe words of 1 Thess. 2:14 ff., which some commentators have felt must be an interpolation, ought to be read and understood.) By the time that the rabble assaulted the house where the missionaries had been staying, they had succeeded in making their escape; no doubt some of the new converts, getting wind of what was afoot, hid them where they were not likely to be found. The mob was thus unable to drag them before the popular assembly[5] of the city, as it had intended to do.

6–7 But if Paul and his companions were not there, Jason himself, the owner of the house, was at home, and they dragged him, together with some other Christians, before the magistrates, and lodged a serious complaint against them. (The magistrates of Thessalonica are here called "politarchs"—a title which we know from inscriptions to have been used for the chief magistrates of several Macedonian towns, although it does not appear elsewhere in Greek literature.)[6] Jason and the others were charged with harbouring political messianic agitators[7]—men who had been guilty of seditious and revolutionary activity in other provinces of the Roman Empire and had now come to Thessalonica with their propaganda, which was not only illegal in itself but actually proclaimed a rival emperor, one Jesus by name, to him who ruled in Rome. This was a subtle charge; even an unfounded suspicion of this kind was enough to ruin many a man. In the present instance there was just enough colour of truth in the charge to

[5] This is probably what is meant by "the people" (Gk. $\delta\tilde{\eta}\mu o\varsigma$).

[6] The title $\pi o\lambda\iota\tau\acute{a}\varrho\chi\eta\varsigma$ or $\pi o\lambda\acute{\iota}\tau a\varrho\chi o\varsigma$ is found in some nineteen inscriptions from the 2nd century B.C. to the 3rd century A.D., and in the majority of these the reference is to magistrates of Macedonian cities. Five of the inscriptions refer to Thessalonica, which appears to have had a board of five politarchs at the beginning of the 1st century A.D. and six in the following century. See E. D. Burton, "The Politarchs", in AJTh ii (1898), pp. 598 ff.

[7] This is apparently the sense of the expression, "these that have turned the world upside down" (Gk. $o\dot{\iota}$ $\tau\dot{\eta}\nu$ $o\dot{\iota}\kappa o\nu\mu\acute{e}\nu\eta\nu$ $\dot{a}\nu a\sigma\tau a\tau\acute{\omega}\sigma a\nu\tau\varepsilon\varsigma$); $\dot{a}\nu a\sigma\tau a\tau\acute{o}\omega$ is regularly used in a pejorative sense, as in Ch. 21:38 ("stirred up to sedition"); Gal. 5:12 ("they that unsettle you"), and—perhaps most famous example of all —in the bad boy Theon's letter to his father, where he quotes his harassed mother as saying, "He upsets me ($\dot{a}\nu a\sigma\tau a\tau o\tilde{\iota}$ $\mu\varepsilon$); away with him!" (*Oxyrhynchus Papyri* i. 119.10; cf. A. Deissmann, *Light from the Ancient East* [Eng. tr., London, 1927], pp. 201 ff.).

make it plausible and deadly. The apostles proclaimed the kingdom of God, a very different kingdom from any secular empire, and no doubt they gave Jesus the Greek title *basileus* ("king"), by which the Roman Emperor was described by his Greek-speaking subjects.[8] From the summary of the apostolic message which the Thessalonian Christians accepted in 1 Thess. 1:9 f., and from other passages in both 1 and 2 Thessalonians, it is plain that there was a strong eschatological emphasis in Paul's preaching and teaching at Thessalonica.[9] As we have seen in certain parts of the world in our own day, this could easily be given by ill-disposed people an interpretation smacking of sedition.[10]

8-9 Under these circumstances, the Thessalonian politarchs appear to have behaved very sanely. The charge naturally alarmed them; the provincial authorities would not be pleased if they seemed to treat such serious accusations lightly. But the evidence for the charge was scanty, and the men against whom it was really brought could not be found. Jason and his companions were made responsible for seeing that there was no repetition of the trouble; this probably meant that Paul had to leave the city and that his friends guaranteed that he would not come back—at least, during the present magistrates' term of office. It is probably with reference to this situation that Paul, some weeks later, wrote to assure the Thessalonian Christians that he greatly desired to go back and see them, but "Satan hindered us" (1 Thess. 2:18).[11] Paul's friends had no doubt gone bail for him without his consent, but once they had done so, his hands were tied. He might well discern satanic machinations behind the politarchs' decision, while they themselves would regard their decision as mild but effective. The immediate sequel in the newly-planted church of Thessalonica may be learned from 1 Thessalonians; though it was subjected to open persecution and more subtle discouragement, it maintained

---

[8] *Cf.* βασιλεύς used of the Roman Emperor in John 19:15; 1 Pet. 2:13, 17.

[9] *Cf.* especially 2 Thess. 2:5, where he reminds the Thessalonian Christians of what he had told them when he was with them; the vagueness of his allusions to the imperial power in that context may be due in part to care lest he should write anything which might seem to confirm the charge of sedition.

[10] *Cf.* the charge brought against Jesus in Luke 23:2, and Jesus' reply to Pilate in John 18:34 ff.

[11] *Cf.* Ramsay, *St. Paul the Traveller* (London, 1920), p. 231.

its faith and Christian witness in a manner that filled the heart of Paul with unbounded joy when he heard of it.

(b) Beroea (Ch. 17:10–15)

10 And the brethren immediately sent away Paul and Silas by night unto Beroea: who when they were come thither went into the synagogue of the Jews.

11 Now these were more noble than those in Thessalonica, in that they received the word with all readiness of mind, examining the scriptures daily, whether these things were so.[12]

12 Many of them[13] therefore believed; also of the Greek women of honorable estate, and of men, not a few.

13 But when the Jews of Thessalonica had knowledge that the word of God was proclaimed of Paul at Beroea also, they came thither likewise, stirring up and troubling[14] the multitudes.

14 And then immediately the brethren sent forth Paul to go as far as to the sea:[15] and Silas and Timothy abode there still.

15 But they that conducted Paul brought him as far as Athens:[16] and receiving a commandment unto Silas and Timothy that they should come to him with all speed, they departed.

10 Paul and Silas were got away from Thessalonica quietly by those who had given security for their departure, and they made their way to Beroea, some sixty miles away. They no longer followed the Egnatian Way, but took the road which led to the south, through Thessaly to the province of Achaia. At Beroea they were rejoined by Timothy. Here too there was a Jewish synagogue, but the Jewish community of Beroea gave the gospel

---

[12] The Western text adds "as Paul declared."

[13] The Western text reads "Some of them therefore believed, but some believed not" (cf. Ch. 28:24), and goes on: "and many of the Greeks and men and women of honourable estate believed" (the Western reviser does not approve of women's receiving precedence over men).

[14] P45 omits "and troubling"; the Western text expands: "and did not cease stirring up and troubling . . ."

[15] The Western text reads "to the sea" (ἐπὶ τὴν θάλασσαν), the Byzantine text reads "as (if) to the sea" (ὡς ἐπὶ τὴν θάλασσαν), as against the Alexandrian authorities' "as far as to the sea" (ἕως ἐπὶ τὴν θάλασσαν).

[16] After "Athens" the Western text continues: "but he passed by Thessaly, for he was prevented from preaching the word to them; and they departed, having received a command from Paul to Silas and Timothy to come to him speedily." For the additional clauses cf. Ch. 16:6–8.

a reception far different from that given by their co-religionists at Thessalonica.

11–12 For, with commendable open-mindedness, they brought the claims made by Paul to the touchstone of Holy Writ instead of giving way to prejudice. Their procedure, "examining the scriptures daily to see if these things were so" (RSV), is worthy of imitation by all who have some new form of religious teaching pressed upon their acceptance. These Beroean Jews could not have foreseen how many Christian groups of later days would call themselves "Beroeans" after their worthy example of Bible study. As we might expect from people who welcomed the apostolic message with such eagerness of mind, many of them believed. As at Thessalonica, the believers included many God-fearing Greeks, both men and women, and some of these—particularly the women—belonged to the leading families in the city. Among the Beroean converts one at least is known to us by name—Sopater son of Pyrrhus, mentioned in Ch. 20:4 (*cf.* Rom. 16:21).

13 But as, on the earlier missionary tour, the Jews of Pisidian Antioch and Iconium followed the apostles to Lystra and stirred up trouble there, so now the Jews of Thessalonica, hearing that the missionaries had arrived in Beroea, sent a deputation there to repeat the course of action that had been so effective in Thessalonica.

14–15 Once again Paul, the main target for the opposition, had to be got out the city quickly and quietly. Some of his Beroean friends made as though they were taking him to the coast[17]—to Methone or Dium—but actually, having thus thrown possible pursuers off the track, they escorted him southwards as far as Athens. (This is perhaps the most satisfactory interpretation of the text, which is not altogether clear at this point, although it is also possible to infer that Paul, escorted by his friends, took ship for Athens at one or other of these ports.) He then sent his friends back to Beroea with instructions to Silas and Timothy to rejoin him in Athens as soon as possible, and he waited for them there.[18]

---

[17] This exposition follows the Byzantine reading of v. 14 (n. 15 above), and is implied in the Western reading of v. 15 (n. 16).

[18] The movements of Silas and Timothy between Paul's departure from Beroea and their rejoining him at Corinth (Ch. 18:5) must be reconstructed from Luke's narrative along with Paul's narrative in 1 Thess. 3:1 ff. It appears that, as instructed, they rejoined Paul in Athens (1 Thess. 3:1), whence

(c) Athens (Ch. 17:16–21)

16 Now while Paul waited for them at Athens, his spirit was provoked within him as he beheld the city full of idols.

17 So he reasoned in the synagogue with the Jews and the devout persons, and in the marketplace every day with them that met him.

18 And certain also of the Epicurean and Stoic philosophers encountered him. And some said, What would this babbler say? others, He seemeth to be a setter forth of strange gods: because he preached Jesus and the resurrection.

19 And they took hold of him, and brought him unto the Areopagus, saying, May we know what this new teaching is, which is spoken by thee?

20 For thou bringest certain strange things to our ears: we would know therefore what these things mean.

21 (Now all the Athenians and the strangers sojourning there spent their time in nothing else, but either to tell or to hear some new thing.)

16 Athens was not exactly on Paul's missionary programme, and during the days that he waited there for his two friends to rejoin him, he had leisure to walk round the violet-crowned city and view its masterpieces of architecture and sculpture.

Athens, although she had long since lost her political eminence of an earlier day, continued to represent the highest level of culture attained in classical antiquity. The sculpture, literature and oratory of Athens in the fifth and fourth centuries B.C. have, indeed, never been surpassed. In philosophy, too, she occupied the leading place, being the native city of Socrates and Plato, and the adopted home of Aristotle, Epicurus and Zeno. In all these fields Athens retained unchallenged prestige, and her political glory as the cradle of democracy was not completely dimmed. In consideration of her splendid past, the Romans left Athens free

Timothy was sent back to Thessalonica (1 Thess. 3:2). (T. W. Manson suggests that on this occasion Timothy was the bearer of 2 Thessalonians, which he believes to have been written before 1 Thessalonians.) Silas was sent to some other place in Macedonia (Ch. 18:5), perhaps to Philippi, as Ramsay suggests (*St. Paul the Traveller*, p. 240): Paul then went on from Athens to Corinth (Ch. 18:1), and was rejoined there by Silas and Timothy on their return from Macedonia (Ch. 18:5; 1 Thess. 3:6). See K. Lake, *The Earlier Epistles of St. Paul* (London, 1911), p. 74; T. W. Manson, "St. Paul in Greece", BJRL xxxv (1953), pp. 428 ff.

to carry on her own institutions as a free and allied city within the Roman Empire.

To-day, when we visit Athens and view the workmanship of the great architects and sculptors of the age of Pericles, we are free to admire them as works of art: to no one nowadays are they anything more. But in the first century of our era they were not viewed simply as works of art: they were temples and images of pagan deities. Temples and images of pagan deities were no new thing to a native of Tarsus, but this native of Tarsus had been brought up in the spirit of the First and Second Commandments. Whatever Paul may have felt in the way of artistic appreciation, the feeling that was uppermost in his mind as he walked here and there in Athens was one of indignation: the beautiful city was "full of idols", dedicated to the worship of gods which were no gods—for "the things which the Gentiles sacrifice, they sacrifice to demons, and not to God" (1 Cor. 10:20).

17 Paul was not the man to take a complete holiday from the main business of his life, and in any case the spectacle of a city so entirely dedicated to false worship stirred him to the conviction that here, if anywhere, were men and women who sorely needed the gospel that he knew. Athens afforded him ample confirmation of what he had already learned, that "in the wisdom of God the world through its wisdom knew not God" (1 Cor. 1:21). He visited the Jewish synagogue in Athens, therefore, and held discourse there with the Jews and God-fearers; and in the Agora, the centre of Athenian life and activity, he reasoned day by day with those who happened to be about. It is to be noted how subtly and accurately Luke suggests the local colour and atmosphere of each city that he deals with. "In Ephesus Paul taught 'in the school of Tyrannus'; in the city of Socrates he discussed moral questions in the market-place. How incongruous it would seem if the methods were transposed!" (W. M. Ramsay, *St. Paul the Traveller* [14th edn., London, 1920], p. 238). The Agora lay west of the Acropolis, and south-west of the Areopagus.

18 Among those whom Paul met and conversed with in the Agora were philosophers of the rival Stoic and Epicurean schools. The Stoics, who claimed the Cypriote Zeno (340–265 B.C.) as their founder, took the name of their school from the "painted Stoa" (portico) where he habitually taught in Athens. Their system aimed at living consistently with nature, and in practice they laid great emphasis on the primacy of the rational faculty in man, and on individual self-sufficiency. In theology they were essentially pantheistic, God being regarded as the World-soul. Their belief in a *cosmopolis* or world-state, in which all truly free souls had equal citizen-rights, helped to break down national and class distinctions. While Stoicism at its best was marked by great moral earnestness and a high sense of duty, it was marked also by a spiritual pride quite foreign to the spirit of Christianity. The authentic voice of Stoicism may be heard in the lines of one of our own poets, W. E. Henley:

> Out of the night that covers me,
> Black as the pit from pole to pole,
> I thank whatever gods may be
> For my unconquerable soul.
>
> In the fell clutch of circumstance
> I have not winced nor cried aloud.
> Under the bludgeonings of chance
> My head is bloody, but unbowed.
>
> Beyond this place of wrath and tears
> Looms but the Horror of the shade,
> And yet the menace of the years
> Finds, and shall find, me unafraid.
>
> It matters not how strait the gate,
> How charged with punishments the scroll,
> I am the master of my fate:
> I am the captain of my soul. [19]

Curiously enough, another English poet uses the same phrase "whatever gods may be," but uses them in a setting as distinctively Epicurean as Henley's is essentially Stoic. This is A. C. Swinburne, in that stanza of *The Garden of Proserpine* which runs:

> From too much love of living,
> From hope and fear set free,
> We thank with brief thanksgiving
> Whatever gods may be
> That no life lives for ever;
> That dead men rise up never;
> That even the weariest river
> Winds somewhere safe to sea.

The Epicurean school, founded by Epicurus (341–270 B.C.), held

[19] Henley's *Invictus*.

350

an ethical theory based on the atomic physics of Democritus, presenting pleasure as the chief end of life, the pleasure most worth enjoying being a life of tranquillity, free from pain, disturbing passions, and superstitious fears (including in particular the fear of death). It did not deny the existence of gods, but maintained that they took no interest in the life of men.

Stoicism and Epicureanism represent alternative attempts in pre-Christian paganism to come to terms with life, especially in times of uncertainty and hardship, and post-Christian paganism down to our own day has not been able to devise anything appreciably better. But Stoics and Epicureans alike, much as they might differ from each other, agreed at least in this, that the new-fangled message brought by this Jew of Tarsus was not one that could appeal to reasonable men. They looked upon him as a retailer of second-hand scraps of philosophy, a type of itinerant peddler of religion not unknown in the Athenian market-place, and they used a term of characteristic Athenian slang to describe him.[20] Others preferred to class him as a herald of strange divinities—he spoke of Jesus and *Anastasis* (the Greek word for "resurrection"), and in the ears of some frequenters of the Agora these two words sounded as if they denoted the personified and deified powers of "healing" and "restoration."[21]

19–20 But there was in Athens a venerable institution, the Court of the Areopagus, which exercised some jurisdiction over visitors like Paul.[22] This aristocratic body, of the most venerable antiquity, received its name from the Areopagus, the "hill of

---

[20] The word rendered "babbler" is σπερμολόγος, literally "seed-picker" (applicable in this sense to a gutter-sparrow); it was then used of one who picked up scraps in the market-place, a worthless character, a "loafer" (in this sense Demosthenes applies it contemptuously to Aeschines in his speech *On the Crown*, 127); finally it was used, as here, of one who picked up scraps of learning here and there and purveyed them where he could.

[21] F. H. Chase (*The Credibility of Acts* [London, 1902], pp. 205 f.) suggests that they may have associated Ἰησοῦς with ἴασις ("healing") and Ἰησώ, the Ionic form of the name of the goddess of health. "This interpretation of the words Ἰησοῦς and ἀνάστασις would be confirmed in the minds of the Athenians, if they caught the words σωτηρία and σωτήρ in St. Paul's teaching." The suggestion that he was a herald of strange divinities recalls the charges brought at an earlier date in Athens against Protagoras, Anaxagoras and Socrates (*cf.* Plato, *Euthyphro* 3 B, *Apology* 24 B—C).

[22] Ramsay (*St. Paul the Traveller*, p. 247) reminds us in this connection how "Cicero induced the Areopagus to pass a decree inviting Cratippus, the Peripatetic philosopher, to become a lecturer in Athens," and infers "that some advantage was thereby secured to him" (*cf.* Plutarch, *Cicero* 24).

Ares", on which it met in early times, and it retained that name even when it transferred its meeting-place to the Royal Portico in the city market-place.[23] Its traditional power was curtailed with the growth of Athenian democracy in the fifth century B.C., but it retained authority in matters of religion and morals, and in Roman times it enjoyed enhanced power and commanded great respect. Before this august court, then, Paul was brought, not to be put on trial in any forensic sense, but to give an account of his "philosophy." "The scene described in vv. 18–34," says Ramsay, "seems to prove that the recognised lecturers could take a strange lecturer before the Areopagus, and require him to give an account of his teaching and pass a test as to its character" (*St. Paul the Traveller*, p. 247).[24]

21 Then, commenting on the Athenians' interest in Paul because of the newness of the teaching which he brought, Luke sums up their general attitude in a sentence which Eduard Norden described as the "most Attic thing in the NT" (*Agnostos Theos* [Leipzig, 1912], p. 333). "Now all the Athenians and the foreigners who lived there spent their time in nothing except telling or hearing something new" (RSV). The Athenians themselves admitted this; the orator Demosthenes, for example, four hundred years earlier, had reproached them for going about asking if there was any fresh news in a day when Philip of Macedon's rise to power presented a threat which called for deeds, not words.[25]

(d) Paul before the Areopagus (Ch. 17:22–31)

22 And Paul stood in the midst of the Areopagus, and said,
Ye men of Athens, in all things I perceive that ye are very religious.

---

[23] That the term "the council of the Areopagus" (ἡ ἐν Ἀρείῳ πάγῳ βουλή) was shortened in common parlance to "the Areopagus" is attested by Cicero (*Letters to Atticus* i. 14.5), Seneca (*On Tranquillity*, 5), Valerius Maximus (*Memorable Deeds and Words* ii. 64), and by an inscription at Epidaurus (*Inscriptiones Graecae* iv [Berlin, 1902], No. 937, l. 2). But the council (which consisted of ex-magistrates of Athens) continued to meet on the Areopagus proper to judge cases of homicide.

[24] But Ramsay's imagination outstrips the evidence when he thinks of the Areopagus examining Paul in terms of a University Court interviewing a professorial candidate (*ibid.*).

[25] Demosthenes, *Philippic* i. 10; *cf.* Cleon's reproach in Thucydides's *History* ii. 38.5: "you are the best people at being deceived by something new that is said."

23 For as I passed along, and observed the objects of your worship, I found also an altar with this inscription, TO AN UNKNOWN GOD. What therefore ye worship in ignorance, this I set forth unto you.

24 The God that made the world and all things therein, he, being Lord of heaven and earth, dwelleth not in temples made with hands;

25 neither is he served by men's hands, as though he needed anything, seeing he himself giveth to all life, breath, and all things;

26 and he made of one[26] every nation of men to dwell on all the face of the earth, having determined *their* appointed seasons, and the bounds of their habitation;

27 that they should seek God,[27] if haply they might feel after him and find him, though he is not far from each one of us:

28 for in him we live, and move, and have our being; as certain even of your[28] own poets[29] have said,
For we are also his offspring.

29 Being then the offspring of God, we ought not to think that the Godhead is like unto gold, or silver, or stone, graven by art and device of man.

30 The times of ignorance therefore God overlooked; but now he commandeth men that they should all everywhere repent:

31 inasmuch as he hath appointed a day in which he will judge[30] the world in righteousness by the man whom he hath ordained; whereof he hath given assurance unto all men, in that he hath raised him from the dead.

Probably no ten verses in the Acts of the Apostles have formed the text for such an abundance of commentary as has gathered round Paul's *Areopagitica*.[31] There have been diametrically op-

[26] The Western and Byzantine texts add "blood."

[27] The Western text reads "especially that they might seek the divine nature" ($\tau\grave{o}$ $\theta\epsilon\tilde{\iota}o\nu$, as in v. 29, where ARV renders "the Godhead").

[28] The Alexandrian codices B and 33, and the Western codex 614, have "our" for "your" (Aratus, like Paul, was a Cilician).

[29] The Western text, omitting "poets", may be rendered "your own men"; for "poets" the Peshitta Syriac has "wise men."

[30] The Western text reads "a day to judge."

[31] In addition to discussions in commentaries, see E. Curtius, *Paulus in Athen* (Berlin, 1893); W. M. Ramsay, *St. Paul the Traveller*, pp. 237 ff.; *The Bearing of Recent Discovery on the Trustworthiness of the NT*, pp. 100 ff.; E. Norden, *Agnostos Theos* (Leipzig, 1912); A. Harnack, *Ist die Rede des*

posing views expressed on the question whether Paul did deliver, or indeed, could have delivered, such a speech as is summarized in these verses.[32] If B. W. Bacon, for example, concludes that this speech, "in distinction from that attributed to Paul in Acts 13:16–41, is really of Pauline type" (*The Story of St. Paul* [London, 1905], p. 164); Percy Gardner, on the other hand, finds the viewpoint expressed in this speech so different from—and indeed contradictory to—that of the first chapter of Romans, that he describes it as "the least authentic of the Pauline discourses in *Acts*" (in *Cambridge Biblical Essays*, ed. H. B. Swete [Cambridge, 1909], p. 401). In general, it is true to say that those classical students who have studied this speech and its setting are prominent among the scholars who have defended its authenticity.[33] Here, if anywhere in Acts, classical students feel that they are on home ground, and the scene and the argument have all the appearance of authenticity.

If the address at Pisidian Antioch in Ch. 13:16 ff. is intended to be a sample of Paul's proclamation of the gospel to Jewish and God-fearing audiences, the present address may well be intended

---

Paulus in Athen ein ursprünglicher Bestandteil der Apostelgeschichte? (Leipzig, 1913); A. Wikenhauser, *Die Apostelgeschichte und ihr Geschichtswert* (Münster, 1921), pp. 369 ff.; E. Meyer, *Ursprung und Anfänge des Christentums* iii (Stuttgart and Berlin, 1923), pp. 89 ff.; A. Schweitzer, *The Mysticism of Paul the Apostle* (Eng. tr., London, 1931), pp. 6 f.; K. Lake, in *Beginnings* v (London, 1933), pp. 240 ff. (articles "The Unknown God" and "'Your Own Poets'"); W. L. Knox, *St. Paul and the Church of the Gentiles* (Cambridge, 1939), pp. 1 ff.; M. Dibelius, *Paulus auf dem Areopag* (Heidelberg, 1939), and *Paulus in Athen* (Berlin, 1939), both of which discussions are reprinted in his posthumously published *Aufsätze zur Apostelgeschichte* (Göttingen, 1951), pp. 29 ff., 71 ff.; W. Schmid, "Die Rede des Apostels Paulus vor den Philosophen und Areopagiten in Athen", *Philologus* xcv (1942), pp. 79 ff.; F. F. Bruce, *The Speeches in the Acts* (London, 1942), pp. 14 ff.; R. Liechtenhan, *Die urchristliche Mission* (Zürich, 1946), pp. 92 ff.; M. Pohlenz, "Paulus und die Stoa" ZNW xlii (1949), pp. 69 ff.; N. B. Stonehouse, *The Areopagus Address* (London, 1951); G. Schrenk, *Studien zu Paulus* (Zürich, 1954), pp. 131 ff.

[32] *Cf.* the dogmatic assertion of Dibelius (with more particular reference to vv. 28 f.), "Paul would never have written thus" (*Aufsätze*, p. 57). So also Norden (*op. cit.*) regarded it as out of the question that Paul could have delivered this speech; E. Meyer, however, tells us that later Norden did admit the possibility that Luke correctly reproduced the contents of a genuine speech of Paul (*op. cit.*, p. 92, n. 4). For a critical examination of some of Dibelius's chief arguments see N. B. Stonehouse, *op. cit.*, and Schrenk, *op. cit.*

[33] "The classicists are among the most inclined to plead for the historicity of the scene of Paul at Athens," says H. J. Cadbury (*Beginnings* v, p. 406, n. 1); he refers in particular to Curtius, Blass and E. Meyer, quoting the remark of Meyer (*op. cit.*, iii, p. 105): "How this scene could be explained as an invention is one of those things that I have never been able to understand."

as a sample of his approach to pagans. (We may compare the much briefer summary of the protest to the people of Lystra in Ch. 14:15 ff.) Here Paul does not quote Hebrew prophecies quite unknown to his hearers; the direct quotations in this speech are quotations from Greek poets. But he does not descend to the level of his hearers by arguing from "first principles" as one of their own philosophers might. His argument is firmly based upon the Biblical revelation of God, echoing throughout the thought, and at times the very language, of the OT scriptures. Like the Biblical revelation itself, his argument begins with God the Creator of all and ends with God the Judge of all.

22 He begins by mentioning that what he has seen in their city has impressed him with the extraordinarily religious nature of the Athenians (an impression made on many other people in antiquity, some of whom considered the Athenians to be the most religious of all men).[34] This characterization of the Athenians was not necessarily intended by Paul to be complimentary; the expression he used may also mean "rather superstitious"[35] (cf. AV, "too superstitious"). It was, in fact, as vague a term in Greek as "religious" is in English, and what was piety to the Greeks was superstition in the eyes of the apostle. In any case, Paul is stating a fact, not paying a compliment; we are told that it was forbidden to use complimentary exordia when addressing the Areopagus, in hope of securing its goodwill.[36]

23 He then tells them that among the religious installations which he saw while going about their city, there was one which particularly attracted his attention–an altar inscribed "TO AN UNKNOWN GOD." We are informed by other writers that altars to "unknown gods" were to be seen at Athens,[37] and Jerome (in his *Commentary on Titus*, at Ch. 1:12) probably has such statements in mind when he suggests that Paul in his address

---

[34] *Cf.* Sophocles, *Oedipus at Colonus* 260 ("they say that Athens is most pious towards the gods"); Josephus, *Against Apion* ii. 11 ("the Athenians . . . are affirmed by all men . . . to be the most religious of the Greeks"); Pausanias, *Description of Greece* i. 17.1 ("The Athenians . . . venerate the gods more than other men").

[35] Gk. δεισιδαιμονεστέρους. *Cf.* Ch. 25:19 for the corresponding substantive.

[36] *Cf.* Lucian, *Anacharsis* 19.

[37] *Cf.* Pausanias, *Description of Greece* i. 1.4 (at Athens there are "altars of gods called 'unknown'"); Philostratus, *Life of Apollonius* vi. 3.5 ("at Athens, where even unknown divinities have altars erected to them").

replaced the plural "gods" by the singular.[38] But there is no ground for disbelieving in the existence of just such an altar as Paul describes; after all, if there were two or more altars each bearing an inscription "TO AN UNKNOWN GOD," these could well be referred to comprehensively as "altars to unknown gods." Whatever the original intention of the dedication was,[39] it provided Paul with his point of contact, with a text for what he had to say. This God whom they worshipped, while confessing that they did not know Him, was the God whom he now proposed to make known to them. Only, he did not express himself quite so personally, as if unreservedly identifying the "unknown god" of the inscription with the God whom he proclaimed; rather he announced that since they acknowledged their ignorance of the divine nature, he would tell them the truth about it. "Paul makes the most of their public profession of lack of knowledge concerning the objects of worship by virtually reading it back to them as a characterization of their religion. He says in effect, 'That which ye worship *acknowledging openly your ignorance, I proclaim unto you.*' The ignorance rather than the worship is thus underscored, and Paul is indicating that he will inform them with regard to that concerning which they acknowledge ignorance" (N. B. Stonehouse, *The Areopagus Address* [London, 1949], p. 25).

24 Paul then begins to tell them about the true God: He it is who created the universe and everything in it; He is Lord of heaven and earth. Here is the God of Biblical revelation; Paul allows no distinction between a Supreme Being and a Demiurge who fashioned the material world. And this God who is Creator of all and universal Lord is introduced in language strongly reminiscent of the OT scriptures. Equally reminiscent of those scriptures is the language with which he goes on to describe Him

---

[38] A similar suggestion is made by Didymus of Alexandria (*Commentary on 2 Cor. 10:5*).

[39] Theodore of Mopsuestia and many commentators since his day (350–428) have found illumination on the altar-inscription from a story told by Diogenes Laertius (*Lives of Philosophers* i. 110). In a time of pestilence the Athenians once consulted Epimenides the Cretan, who advised them to release black and white sheep from the Areopagus, and on the spot where each sheep halted to offer it in sacrifice to the god of the locality; in consequence, "anonymous altars" could still be seen throughout Attica in Diogenes's day (early 3rd century A.D.). This story certainly implies dedications in the singular. On Epimenides see W. M. Ramsay, *Asianic Elements in Greek Civilisation* (London, 1927), pp. 20 ff.

as not inhabiting sanctuaries which human hands had built.[40] If even the shrine at Jerusalem, erected for the worship of the God of Israel, could not contain Him, how much less the splendid shrines of the Athenian Acropolis, dedicated as they were to gods that were no gods! True, even the higher paganism had realized that no material house could accommodate the divine nature,[41] but the affinities of the terms here used by Paul are Biblical rather than classical.

25 The God who created all could not be envisaged as requiring anything from His creatures. Here again parallels to Paul's argument can be adduced from Greek literature and philosophy,[42] but the false idea which he demolishes here, that God is somehow dependent on His creatures for their worship and service, was one which the prophets of Israel had also to oppose, when they saw how devoted many of their own people were to it. We may think of the words of God in Ps. 50:9–12:

> I will take no bullock out of thy house,
>> Nor he-goats out of thy folds.
> For every beast of the forest is mine,
>> And the cattle upon a thousand hills.
> I know all the birds of the mountains,
>> And the wild beasts of the field are mine.
> If I were hungry, I would not tell thee;
>> For the world is mine, and the fulness thereof.[43]

No: God needs nothing from His creatures; far from their supplying any need of His, it is He who supplies every need of theirs: to them all He gives "life and breath and all things."

26 The Creator of all things in general is the Creator of mankind in particular. The Athenians might pride themselves on being autochthonous—sprung from the soil of their native Attica[44]—

---

[40] *Cf.* 1 Kings 8:27; Isa. 66:1 f.; and see the discussion on the similar passage in Stephen's speech (pp. 158 ff. above, on Ch. 7:47 ff.).

[41] *Cf.* Euripides, *Fragment* 968: "What house built by craftsmen could enclose the form divine within enfolding walls?"

[42] *Cf.* Euripides, *Heracles* 1345 f. ("God, if he be truly God, has need of nothing"); Plato, *Euthyphro* 14 e ("What advantage accrues to the gods from what they get from us?").

[43] *Cf.* Micah 6:6 ff. Yet M. Dibelius says that "only twice is it emphasized in LXX that God has need of nothing, and precisely these two places prove the Greek source of the thought" (*op. cit.*, p. 44): he refers to 2 Macc. 14:35 and 3 Macc. 2:9.

[44] This belief reflects the historic fact that the Athenians were the only

357

but this pride was ill founded. All mankind was one in origin—all created by God and all descended from one common ancestor. This removed all imagined justification for the belief that Greeks were innately superior to barbarians, as it removes all imagined justification for parallel beliefs to-day. Neither in nature nor in grace—neither in the old creation nor in the new—is there any room for ideas of racial superiority.

And God, having made the whole human race, has given them the whole earth to dwell in—or at least the habitable zones of the earth.[45] (It is not so probable that Paul has in mind the "living space" allocated by God to each individual nation;[46] there are many factors which enter into the delimitation of national frontiers.) According to the Biblical narrative, the earth was formed and furnished to be man's home before man himself was brought into being to occupy it: the tenses of the Greek verbs here similarly suggest that "the determination of man's home *preceded* his creation, in the Divine plan" (J. H. Moulton, *Grammar of NT Greek* i [Edinburgh, 1906], p. 133). And part of the forming and furnishing of man's home on earth consisted in the regulation of the "appointed seasons"—by which, following the analogy of the Lystran speech in Ch. 14:17, we are probably to understand the seasons of the year by whose sequence annual provision is made for supplying men with food. (If we think, however, that Paul is referring in this sentence to nations as such, then we might consider their "appointed seasons" to be the divinely determined periods for the rise and fall of nations, as set forth in the book of Daniel;[47] but this is less likely.)

27 And what was God's purpose in thus arranging time and

Greeks on the European mainland who had no tradition of their ancestors' coming into Greece; they belonged to the earliest (Ionian) wave of Greek immigration.

[45] *Cf.* Dibelius, *op. cit.*, pp. 32 f.

[46] This is also a Biblical idea; *cf.* Deut. 32:8, noting the LXX reading adopted in RSV. But Dibelius (*ibid.*) is probably right here in taking πᾶν ἔθνος ἀνθρώπων to mean "the whole human race" (*das ganze menschliche Geschlecht*) rather than "every nation of men" in the distributive sense.

[47] In this case we might trace a connection between the προστεταγμένοι καιροί here and the καιροὶ ἐθνῶν of Luke 21:24; but the connection would be purely verbal, because the καιροὶ ἐθνῶν are the epochs of Gentile domination of Jerusalem.

[48] In Paul's use of the verb ψηλαφάω we may have the idea of man's "groping" after God in the darkness or semi-darkness, when the light of His full revelation is not available.

place so providentially for the well-being of man? It was, says
Paul, in order that men might seek God, "in the hope that they
might feel after[48] him and find him" (RSV). For indeed, as Paul
says elsewhere, "ever since the creation of the world his invisible
nature, namely, his eternal power and deity, has been clearly
perceived in the things that have been made. So they are without
excuse; for although they knew God they did not honor him as
God or give thanks to him, but they became futile in their thinking
and their senseless minds were darkened" (Rom. 1:20 f., RSV).
Is Paul's attitude in the Epistle to the Romans so very different
from that of the *Areopagitica*? There is, of course, a difference
of emphasis, for there he is writing to established Christians and
here he is trying to gain a hearing from pagans; but there is no
suggestion here that the Athenians' acknowledged ignorance of
the divine nature was venial. Even some of their own teachers
had realized the folly of trying to house the divine nature in
material temples, worship it with material altars, or represent it
by material images, and had perceived, albeit dimly, how near
God was to those who would seek Him.

28   And at this point Paul illustrated his argument by two
quotations from Greek poets in which the relation of men to the
Supreme Being was set forth. One of these was the fourth line
of a quatrain which has been preserved from a poem attributed
to Epimenides the Cretan:

> They fashioned a tomb for thee, O holy and high one —
> The Cretans, always liars, evil beasts, idle bellies!
> But thou art not dead; thou livest and abidest for ever;
> For in thee we live and move and have our being.[49]

[49] The quatrain is quoted in a Syriac version by the ninth-century commentator Isho'dad (*cf.* M. D. Gibson, *Horae Semiticae* x [Cambridge, 1913], p. 40). Isho'dad was probably dependent on Theodore of Mopsuestia. He describes these words as addressed by the Cretan Minos to his father Zeus in protest against the Cretans' claim that they could point out the tomb of Zeus. The second line of the quatrain is the hexameter quoted in Tit. 1:12, which according to Clement of Alexandria (*Miscellanies* i.14.59.1 f.) comes from a work by Epimenides (*cf.* n. 39 above). This work might be the poem on Minos and Rhadamanthys ascribed to Epimenides by Diogenes Laertius (*Lives of Philosophers* i.112). These lines of Epimenides were probably imitated by Callimachus in his *Hymn to Zeus*, where he says (lines 7 f.): "The Cretans are always liars: for the Cretans, O King, actually fashioned a tomb for thee. But thou hast not died; thou livest for ever." The line quoted by Paul can with little difficulty be given hexameter form; Cod. D spoils the rhythm by adding "day by day" after "have our being."

The other is part of the fifth line of the *Phainomena* of Paul's fellow-Cilician Aratus, which opens with the words, "Let us begin with Zeus"—Zeus, considered not as the ruling member of the traditional pantheon of Greek mythology but as the Supreme Being of Greek philosophy. "Never, O men, let us leave him unmentioned," Aratus continues; "all ways are full of Zeus and all meeting-places of men; the sea and the harbours are full of him. In every direction we all have to do with Zeus; for we are also his offspring."[50] But surely Paul did not intend to identify the Zeus of Greek philosophy *simpliciter* with the God and Father of our Lord Jesus Christ? Is he, then, simply detaching from their original contexts sentiments which, so far as their actual phraseology goes, lend themselves to incorporation into his revelational context? Surely, if that were all his intention, he laid himself open to the protest that their own poets whom he was quoting had meant by those words something quite different from what he made them mean. It is quite consistent with Paul's general theological position, however, to allow that these pagan writers, "as creatures of God confronted with the divine revelation were capable of responses which were valid so long as and to the extent that they stood in isolation from their pagan systems. Thus, thoughts which in their pagan contexts were quite un-Christian and anti-Christian, could be acknowledged as up to a point involving an actual apprehension of revealed truth" (N. B. Stonehouse, *op. cit.*, p. 37).[51]

29 We are, then, the offspring of God, says Paul: not, of course, in the pantheistic sense intended by the Stoic poets, but in the sense of the Biblical doctrine of man, as a being created by God in His image and after His likeness. There is, indeed, a mighty difference between this relation of men to God in the old creation and that redemptive relation which men of the new creation enjoy as sons of God "through faith, in Christ Jesus" (Gal. 3:26). But Paul is dealing here with the responsibility of all men as

[50] These last words quoted from Aratus (τοῦ γὰρ καὶ γένος ἐσμέν) may have been borrowed from a similar expression in line 4 of Cleanthes' *Hymn to Zeus*, ἐκ σοῦ γὰρ γένος ἐσμέν. K. Lake (*Beginnings* v, p. 247) points out that the immediately following lines of Aratus's poem have "a strong general resemblance" to v. 26 of the *Areopagitica*.

[51] *Cf.* also R. Stob, *Christianity and Classical Civilization* (Grand Rapids, 1950), pp. 58 ff. For Paul's own language on the subject we may compare Col. 1:15–17.

God's creatures to give Him the honour which is His due. And this honour is certainly not given if men envisage the divine nature in terms of plastic images. Here he echoes the perpetual Jewish polemic against image-worship which has its roots in such OT passages as Isa. 44:9 ff.[52] Even if pagan philosophers rationalize the images as mere symbols of the invisible divinity, the great bulk of the worshippers pay divine homage to the images themselves.

30 Truly, then, did they acknowledge their ignorance of God. But, culpable as their ignorance was, God in mercy had passed it over. There is a parallel here not only to the statement in the Lystran speech that God had hitherto "suffered all the nations to walk in their own ways" (Ch. 14:16), but also to the teaching in Rom. 3:25 about "the passing over of the sins done aforetime, in the forbearance of God." In all these places it is implied that the coming of Christ means a fresh start. In the present place it is suggested that God has overlooked men's earlier ignorance of Himself in view of the perfect revelation that has been given in the advent and work of Christ.[53] But if their ignorance was culpable before, it is far less excusable now. Let all men therefore repent[54] of their former ignorance (with all the disobedience to God which it involved), and submit to the true knowledge of God now made available in the gospel.

31 For God the Creator of all is also God the Judge of all. Already in His sovereign counsels He has fixed a day in which He will "judge the world in righteousness"—another Biblical expression.[55] Greek thought had no room for such an eschatological judgment as the Biblical revelation announces.[56] But the judgment

---

[52] Cf. also Pss. 115:4 ff. and 135:15 ff.; the argument is developed in Wisdom 13:5, 10; 15:4, 15 ff., in the *Epistle of Aristeas* 134 ff., and in the Christian *Apologies*.

[53] In Rom. 3:25, of course, the passing over of sins committed previously is based on the propitiatory death of Christ. This is neither denied nor logically excluded by Paul's present argument.

[54] For the association of repentance with the passing over of sins cf. Wisdom 11:23, "thou overlookest the sins of men, to the end they may repent."

[55] Cf. Ps. 9:8; 96:13; 98:9. For other Pauline references to the appointed day of judgment see Rom. 2:5, 16; 1 Cor. 1:8; Phil. 1:6, 10; 1 Thess. 5:2, 4; 2 Thess. 1:10; 2:2.

[56] There is nothing properly eschatological about the judgment exercised in the realm of the dead by Minos, Rhadamanthys and Aeacus, three mortals who for piety in this life were appointed judges over the shades, according to

day is fixed, and the agent of the judgment is already appointed: he is the man in whom God's eternal purpose finds its fulfilment.[57] Paul does not refer directly to the "one like unto a son of man" of Dan. 7:13,[58] but this is "the man" whom he has in mind—the one to whom God the Father has given "authority to execute judgment, because he is a son of man" (John 5:27).[59] Moreover, he assures his audience, God has furnished firm proof that this is the man by whom He is going to judge the world, because this is the man whom He has raised from the dead.

Thus, then, Paul concludes his *Areopagitica*. There is no ground for supposing that the ridicule with which some of his hearers received his reference to Jesus' rising from the dead seriously curtailed the speech he intended to make. True, what we have here is no doubt a greatly shortened summary of his actual speech, but even so the speech appears to have been admirably calculated as an introductory lesson in Christianity for cultured pagans. This first lesson starts with their own confessed ignorance of the divine nature, and after a statement of the truth about God, in creation, providence and judgment, ends by introducing the Man of God's appointment. The second lesson would begin with this Man: if, as Paul claimed, God had raised Him from the dead, those who were not put off by this claim would want to know more about Him and the reason for His resurrection.

The speech no doubt is, as Dibelius says, concerned with "the true knowledge of God" (*Aufsätze zur Apostelgeschichte* [Göttingen, 1951], p. 54). But the knowledge of God set forth here is no merely intellectual discipline: it involves moral and religious responsibilities, and for lack of this knowledge, in the measure in which it was available to them, men are called upon to repent. The knowledge of God is viewed in the OT scriptures as belonging

Greek legend—nor is there anything eschatological about Plato's reinterpretation of the legend (*Gorgias* 523 ff.).

[57] *Cf*. Ch. 10:42.

[58] *Cf*. Ch. 7:56, with exposition and note (pp. 165 ff.).

[59] In John 5:26 f. the Son's authority, received from the Father, "to have life in himself" is closely associated with His further authority, likewise received from the Father, "to execute judgment." W. L. Knox (*Some Hellenistic Elements in Primitive Christianity* [London, 1944], p. 28) considers the Christology of the *Areopagitica* to be simply that of Rom. 1:4, where the resurrection of Christ marks Him out as Son of God—this in answer to the doubts expressed about the Christology of this passage by J. de Zwaan in HThR xvii (1924), pp. 132 ff. (in an article with which Knox is otherwise in general agreement).

to the same moral order as truth, goodness and steadfast love (*cf.* Hos. 4:1; 6:6); the lack of this knowledge brings destruction in its train (*cf.* Hos. 4:6); the earth will be filled with this knowledge when God's will is perfectly done and His covenant established finally with His people (*cf.* Hab. 2:14; Jer. 31:34). And it is in such OT categories that this speech, and the thought behind it, move, even if the OT is not formally quoted; the "delicately suited allusions" to Stoic and Epicurean tenets which have been recognized in the speech,[60] and the direct quotations from pagan poets, have their place as points of contact with the hearers, and illustrate the argument in terms familiar to them, but in no way commit the speaker to acquiescence in the realm of ideas which formed their original context. We may agree with Dibelius in looking at the speaker before the Areopagus as "the forerunner of the apologists" (*op. cit.*, p. 59) without denying that Paul could have filled this rôle and without assuming that such an apology to the Gentiles involves a compromise of Biblical principles.

(e) The Athenian Reaction (Ch. 17:32–34)

32 Now when they heard of the resurrection of the dead, some mocked; but others said, We will hear thee concerning this yet again.
33 Thus Paul went out from among them.
34 But certain men clave unto him, and believed: among whom also was Dionysius the Areopagite, and a woman named Damaris,[61] and others with them.

32 The idea of a resurrection of dead men was uncongenial to the minds of most of Paul's hearers. All of them but the Epicureans would no doubt have agreed with him had he spoken of the immortality of the individual soul; but as for resurrection, most of them would endorse the sentiments of the god Apollo, expressed on the occasion when that very court of the Areopagus was founded by the city's patron goddess Athene: "Once a man

---

[60] *Cf.* J. H. Moulton and W. F. Howard, *Grammar of NT Greek* ii (Edinburgh, 1929). p. 8, n. 3. Such allusions have been traced in v. 25, where we have parallels both to the Epicurean doctrine that God needs nothing from men and to the Stoic doctrine that He is the source of all life.

[61] Cod. D reads "one Dionysius, an Areopagite of honourable station" and omits all reference to Damaris; this, however, probably does not represent the true Western text. The Latino-Greek Cod. e/E attaches the description "of honourable station" to "woman", not to Areopagite.

dies and the earth drinks up his blood, there is *no resurrection.*"[62] Some of them, therefore, openly ridiculed a statement which seemed so absurd. Others, more polite, suggested that there might be an opportunity later for a further exposition of his teaching.[63]

33-34 Paul thèn left the council meeting, and not long afterwards he left Athens. But before he left he had secured a few adherents, two of whom are mentioned by name. One of them was actually a member of the Areopagus, Dionysius by name. We cannot assess the truth of the tradition, reported by Eusebius on the authority of Dionysius, bishop of Corinth about A.D. 170, that he became first bishop of Athens; it is the kind of tradition which would arise in any case (*Ecclesiastical History* iii. 4. 11; iv. 23. 3).[64] As for Damaris,[65] Ramsay suggested that she must have been "a foreign woman, perhaps one of the class of educated Hetairai", in view of the unlikelihood of an ordinary Athenian woman being present at any public meeting addressed by Paul (*St. Paul the Traveller,* p. 252). But she may have been a God-fearer who heard him in the synagogue.[66]

At any rate, Paul had few converts in Athens; we are not told that he planted a church there, and although Athens was in the Roman province of Achaia it is a family resident in Corinth that he describes as "the firstfruits of Achaia" (1 Cor. 16:15).[67] But

---

[62] Aeschylus, *Eumenides* 647 f.; the word there rendered "resurrection" is ἀνάστασις, as here.

[63] "I used to think this was just polite evasion, the eternal refuge of the procrastinating spirit. I am not so sure of it now. I think they were really touched and moved by the dramatic *kerygma.* This Resurrection message— righteousness vindicated, captivity led captive, death and the demons defeated —they wanted to believe it. For that pagan world was in the grip of fear. Neither philosophy nor mythology, neither astrology nor mystery cult, had been able to roll back the dark shadow of irrevocable fate. The race was in bondage to a destiny decreed and fixed for ever in the unfriendly stars, and the terror of a hostile cosmos held the human spirit in thrall. So these men at Athens resolved to hear the apostle again; for wistfully they hoped his message might be true" (J. S. Stewart, *A Faith to Proclaim* [London, 1953], p. 117).

[64] He had, of course, nothing to do with the corpus of Neoplatonic literature which was fathered on him in the 5th and 6th centuries A.D.

[65] Her name is a variant of δάμαλις, "heifer" (the Latin codex h actually spells it *Damalis*). Chrysostom misinterprets the present passage when he makes her the wife of Dionysius (*On the Priesthood* iv. 7).

[66] The original form of the Western text probably described her as εὐσχήμων ("of honourable estate"), like the God-fearing women of Beroea (v. 12).

[67] It is unnecessary to suppose, with Zahn (INT [Eng. tr., Edinburgh, 1909], i. p. 266) and others, that Stephanas must have been converted in Athens. See

we should remember that Athens played no part in Paul's plan
of campaign, he probably did not spend more than three or four
weeks there; and, for the rest, if the response to his preaching
during these weeks was scanty, the fault may be sought in the
Athenians rather than in Paul's message. The popular idea that
his determination, when he arrived in Corinth, to know nothing
there "save Jesus Christ, and him crucified," was the result of
disillusionment with the line of approach he had attempted at
Athens, has little to commend it.[68]

Ramsay's chapter "The Firstfruits of Achaia" in *The Bearing of Recent Discovery on the Trustworthiness of the NT*, pp. 385 ff.

[68] An excellent reply to this common opinion is given by N. B. Stonehouse, *op. cit.*, pp. 39 ff.

CHAPTER XVIII

3. CORINTH

(Ch. 18:1–17)

(a) Paul Arrives in Corinth (Ch. 18:1–4)

1 After these things he departed from Athens, and came
to Corinth.

2 And he found[1] a certain Jew named Aquila, a man of
Pontus by race, lately come from Italy, with his wife
Priscilla, because Claudius had commanded all the
Jews to depart from Rome: and he came unto them;

3 and because he was of the same trade, he abode with
them, and they wrought; for by their trade they were
tentmakers.

4 And[2] he reasoned in the synagogue every sabbath,
and persuaded[3] Jews and Greeks.

1 From Athens, Paul continued his journey in a southwesterly
direction, until he reached Corinth.

Corinth, on the Isthmus of Corinth, the land-bridge connecting
the Peloponnese with Northern Greece, occupied a most favourable
position for commercial enterprise, at the junction of sea-routes
to the west and east and of land-routes to the north and south. It
had two ports—Lechaeum, on the Gulf of Corinth (leading to the
Ionian Sea and western Mediterranean), and Cenchreae, on the
Saronic Gulf (leading to the Aegean Sea and eastern Mediterranean and Black Sea). For long Corinth was a political,

[1] The Western text of vv. 2 and 3 appears to have run somewhat as follows:
"And he found Aquila, a man of Pontus by family, a Jew, who had lately
come from Italy with Priscilla his wife, and he joined them. Now these had
come out from Rome because Claudius Caesar had commanded all Jews to
depart from Rome, and they settled in Achaia. And Paul became known to
Aquila because he was of the same race and the same trade, and he stayed
with them and worked; for they were tentmakers by trade."

[2] The Western text of v. 4 runs: "And entering into the synagogue each
sabbath day he held discourse, inserting the name of the Lord Jesus, and
sought to persuade not only Jews but also Greeks."

[3] The marginal rendering "sought to persuade" is preferable to "persuaded"
as a translation of the imperfect tense ἔπειθεν.

commercial and naval rival of Athens. In 146 B.C., in savage vengeance for an anti-Roman revolt, Corinth was levelled to the ground by the Roman general L. Mummius, and the site lay derelict for exactly a century. In 46 B.C. the city was refounded by Julius Caesar and given the status of a Roman colony, with the title *Laus Iulia Corinthus* ("Corinth, the praise of Julius"), and in 27 B.C. it became the capital of the Roman province of Achaia. Corinth was not long in regaining her old commercial prosperity, and therewith she regained a reputation which she had had in earlier days for a degree of sexual licence remarkable even in classical antiquity.[4] The difficulty which even Christians had in resisting the influence of this particular Corinthian characteristic is plain to readers of Paul's Epistles to the Corinthians.[5]

2–3 Even so, Corinth was the kind of city which Paul's strategic eye recognized as an admirable centre for intensive evangelism, and there he settled for a considerable time. Not long after his arrival, he met a married couple, recently come to Corinth from Rome, with whom he quickly formed a firm and lifelong friendship. These were Aquila and Priscilla, "tentmakers" or rather, more generally, leather-workers[6] by trade. It was this that seems first to have brought Paul into contact with them, for he himself had been apprenticed to the same trade. This trade was closely connected with the principal manufacture of Paul's native province, a cloth of goat's hair called *cilicium,* used for making cloaks, curtains and so forth. It was not considered proper for a scribe or rabbi to receive payment for his teaching, and many of them therefore practised a trade in addition to their study and teaching of the law.[7] Paul regularly earned his living in this way during

---

[4] In classical Greek κορινθιάζω (literally "act the Corinthian") means to practise fornication; Κορίνθιαι ἑταῖραι or Κορίνθιαι κόραι ("Corinthian companions" or "Corinthian girls") are harlots. The temple of Aphrodite on the Corinthian acropolis gave religious sanction to licence of this kind.

[5] *Cf.* 1 Cor. 5:1 ff.; 6:15 ff.

[6] For this extended sense of σκηνοποιός *cf.* the extended sense of the English word "saddler," which means a dealer in leather and not only a saddle-maker.

[7] This course was recommended by Rabbi Gamaliel III: "An excellent thing is the study of the Torah combined with some secular occupation, for the labour demanded by them both puts sin out of one's mind. All study of the Torah which is not combined with work will ultimately be futile and lead to sin" (*Pirqe Aboth* ii. 2). Similarly Rabbi Zadok said: "Make not of the Torah a crown wherewith to aggrandize thyself, or a spade wherewith to dig. So also used Hillel to say, He who makes a profit from the crown of the Torah shall waste away. Hence thou mayest infer that he who derives gain for himself

his missionary journeys and residences: *cf*. Ch. 20:34; 1 Cor. 9:1 ff.;
2 Cor. 11:7 ff.; 1 Thess. 2:9; 2 Thess. 3:8.

Aquila and Priscilla, we are told, had come to Corinth because
the Emperor Claudius had ordered all Jews to leave Rome. This
was not the only occasion on which the authorities at Rome saw
fit to clean up the city by expelling Jewish and other oriental
incomers. (The expulsion edict would not affect those Jews who
were Roman citizens, but probably in Rome and the west a Jew
who was a Roman citizen did not rank as a Jew in the eyes of
Roman law.)[8] Claudius's edict is usually connected with a statement
by Suetonius, in his *Life of Claudius* xxv. 4: "As the Jews were
indulging in constant riots at the instigation of Chrestus, he
banished them from Rome."[9] This Chrestus may have been an
otherwise unknown trouble-maker who was active in Jewish circles
in Rome about the middle of the first century, but in that case
Suetonius would probably have referred to him as "a certain
Chrestus." It is more likely that he had the Founder of Christianity
in mind, but that, writing some seventy years after the event and
not being particularly interested in Christian origins, he consulted
some record of the riots and imagined wrongly that Chrestus,[10]
who was mentioned as the leader of one of the parties concerned,
was actually in Rome at the time, taking a prominent part in the
strife. What we have to do with, in fact, in this statement of
Suetonius, is dissension and disorder in the Jewish community at
Rome resulting from the introduction of Christianity into one or
more of the synagogues of the city.

Had Aquila and Priscilla any part in this dissension? We cannot
say, but the odds appear to be in favour of the view that they

from the words of the Torah is helping on his own destruction" (*Pirqe Aboth*
iv. 7).

[8] See S. L. Guterman, *Religious Toleration and Persecution in Ancient Rome*
(London, 1951), pp. 89 ff.

[9] *Cf*. Dio Cassius, *History* lx. 6: "As the Jews had again increased in
numbers, but could hardly be banished from the city without a tumult because
of their multitude, he did not actually expel them, but forbade them to meet
in accordance with their ancestral customs"—this, of course, would in practice
amount to their expulsion. Dio places this decree at the beginning of Claudius's
reign; but this has been felt to be inconsistent with Josephus's account of
pro-Jewish edicts given at that time (*Antiquities* xix. 5.2 f.). A more probable
date is Claudius's ninth year (A.D. 49–50), which is given by Orosius (*History*
vii. 6.15 f.).

[10] *Chrestus* (Gk. Χρηστός, "useful", "kindly") was a common slave-name in
the Graeco-Roman world, and appears as a spelling variant for the unfamiliar
Christus (Χριστός). (In Greek the two words were pronounced alike.)

were already Christians before they left Rome.[11] From the fact that Priscilla is usually mentioned before her husband, it has been inferred that she belonged to a higher social class than her husband; she many have been connected with the noble Roman family called the *gens Prisca*.[12] When Paul mentions her in his letters, he refers to her by her formal name Prisca; Luke calls her by her more familiar name Priscilla, following a practice which is evident in the names of other characters in his narrative.[13] Whatever their antecedents were, however, they came to Corinth to pursue their trade there, and were joined by Paul, their fellow-tradesman.

4 A commercial city like Corinth inevitably had a large Jewish colony, and Paul was able immediately to follow his usual procedure and proclaim the Christian message in the local synagogue.[14] Here, sabbath by sabbath, he held discourse with the Jews and God-fearers, showing how Jesus had fulfilled the OT prophecies by inserting His name as an interpretative expansion in those passages which—as the event proved—pointed forward to Him.[15] So at least we are informed by the Western text of this

[11] See A. Harnack, "Probabilia über die Adresse und den Verfasser des Hebräerbriefs", in ZNW i (1900), pp. 16 ff.

[12] "There is probably much to discover with regard to this interesting pair" —this is as true to-day as it was when Ramsay penned the words for his first edition of *St. Paul the Traveller* (London, 1895). There is no direct evidence to connect this Priscilla with the lady of the same name after whom the "Cemetery of Priscilla," one of the earliest Christian burying-grounds in Rome, was called. While this cemetery contains a crypt belonging to the noble Roman family of the Acilii Glabriones, we should probably resist the temptation to connect the name Acilius with Aquila (Gk. Ἀκύλας). When we read that Aquila came from Pontus (the Roman province on the Anatolian shore of the Black Sea), we note an interesting coincidence (but nothing more) in that this was also the native province of a later Aquila, the proselyte who made a very literal translation of the Hebrew Bible into Greek in the second century A.D.

[13] "Luke regularly uses the language of conversation, in which the diminutive forms were usual; and so he speaks of Priscilla, Sopatros and Silas always, though Paul speaks of Prisca, Sosipatros and Silvanus" (Ramsay, *op. cit.*, p. 268).

[14] A fragmentary door-inscription in Greek, found at Corinth, and dated between 100 B.C. and A.D. 200, is believed to have read when complete, "Synagogue of the Hebrews" (*cf.* A. Deissmann, *Light from the Ancient East* [Eng. tr., London, 1927], p. 16).

[15] We may compare the way in which the Targum of Jonathan on the Prophets inserts the word "Messiah" after "my servant" in Isa. 42:1 and 52:13. But Paul went farther, and identified the one to whom the prophets pointed forward with an actual person of recent history—Jesus of Nazareth.

verse, and even if the additional words are not part of the original text, they certainly give us a true picture of the sort of thing that Paul did.

(b) Paul Spends Eighteen Months in Corinth (Ch. 18:5–11)

5 But when Silas and Timothy came down from Macedonia, Paul was constrained by the word, testifying to the Jews that Jesus[16] was the Christ.

6 And when they opposed themselves and blasphemed, he shook out his raiment and said unto them, Your blood *be* upon your own heads; I am clean; from henceforth I will go unto the Gentiles.

7 And he departed thence,[17] and went into the house of a certain man named Titus[18] Justus, one that worshipped God, whose house joined hard to the synagogue.

8 And Crispus, the ruler of the synagogue, believed in the Lord with all his house; and many of the Corinthians hearing believed, and were baptized.

9 And the Lord said unto Paul in the night by a vision, Be not afraid, but speak and hold not thy peace:

10 for I am with thee, and no man shall set on thee to harm thee: for I have much people in this city.

11 And he dwelt *there* a year and six months, teaching the word of God among them.

5 After a few weeks, Paul was rejoined by his colleagues Silas and Timothy. The news that they brought from Macedonia (especially Timothy's news about the steadfastness of the sorely-tried converts of Thessalonica) was a great relief to Paul;[19] and a gift of money which they brought him from his friends in Philippi[20] relieved him for the time being of the necessity to

[16] The Western text characteristically reads "the Lord Jesus", and adds at the end of the verse, "And when much discussion took place and the scriptures were interpreted . . ."

[17] For "thence" the Western text reads "from Aquila": this reading reflects a misunderstanding of Luke's meaning; Paul did not remove his private lodgings from Aquila's house to that of Justus, but made Justus's house his preaching headquarters instead of the synagogue.

[18] For "Titus" we should probably read "Titius" with the first hand in Cod. B, the second hand in Cod. D, and the Harclean Syriac. "Titus" is the reading of ℵ E and some minuscules, together with the Peshitta, the Coptic versions, and the Armenian. Many other authorities, including the Byzantine text, have neither Titus nor Titius, but simply Justus.

[19] *Cf.* 1 Thess. 3:6 ff. It was in response to Timothy's news that Paul wrote 1 Thessalonians.

[20] *Cf.* 2 Cor. 11:8 f.; Phil. 4:15.

support himself by leather-working; he was able therefore to concentrate on the preaching of the gospel, as he sought to convince the Jewish community that Jesus was the true Messiah.

6–7 At last his witness in the synagogue stirred up such intense opposition there that he had to find some other place to carry on his evangelism. By a spectacular gesture—shaking out his cloak that not a speck of dust from the synagogue might adhere to it[21]—he expressed his resolve to have done with that building and his abhorrence of the slanders in which his opponents were indulging against the reputation of Him whom Paul proclaimed as Messiah. He had discharged his responsibility to them, he assured them; if they would not accept the news of salvation which he brought, he was now free from blame. As at Pisidian Antioch and elsewhere, so at Corinth too he would take his saving message to people who knew how to appreciate it. And he had not far to go. For adjoining the synagogue was the house of a God-fearer who had listened to Paul and been persuaded of the truth of what he proclaimed. This man now placed his house at Paul's disposal, and people who had been accustomed to attend the synagogue did not have to leave their habitual route if they wished to continue hearing Paul; they made their way towards the synagogue as usual, but turned in next door.

The most probable form of this God-fearer's name, as given by Luke, is Titius Justus—a Roman *nomen* and *cognomen* suggesting that he was a Roman citizen, perhaps a member of one of the Roman families settled in Corinth at the time when Julius Caesar made it a Roman colony. But what was his *praenomen*? There is much to be said in favour of Ramsay's view (*Pictures of the Apostolic Church* [London, 1910], p. 205, n. 2) that it was Gaius, and that he is to be identified with "Gaius mine host" of Rom. 16:23 and the Gaius whom Paul mentions in 1 Cor. 1:14 as one of the few Corinthian converts whom he baptized with his own hands.[22]

8 In that same passage Paul mentions another Corinthian convert who was similarly baptized by him, Crispus by name. Luke shows us who this Crispus was—no less than the ruler of the

---

[21] *Cf.* Ch. 13:51.

[22] So also E. J. Goodspeed, "Gaius Titius Justus", in JBL lxix (1950), pp. 382 f. *Cf.* the Latin names of other Corinthian Christians in Rom. 16:23; 1 Cor. 1:14; 16:17.

synagogue which Paul had just left. This man and his family followed Paul on his departure from the synagogue, and joined the new Christian community in Corinth. And many other Corinthians came to hear the good news, and believing it they were baptized and swelled the new community.

9-10 Shortly after Paul left the synagogue and made the house of Titius Justus his headquarters, he had an encouraging experience—he received one of the visions which came to him at critical periods in his life, heartening him for the work that lay ahead.[23] In this particular vision the risen Christ appeared to him by night and assured him that no harm would befall him in Corinth, for all the opposition that his preaching might stir up. He should therefore abandon any fear that he might have, and go on proclaiming the gospel boldly; he would reap an abundant harvest by so doing, for the Lord had many people[24] in Corinth whom He had marked out for His own.

11 Thus filled with fresh confidence, Paul stayed in Corinth and continued his work of proclamation and teaching for eighteen months. The next five years, in fact, were devoted not so much to missionary journeys as to inaugurating and consolidating Christian witness in two important centres west and east of the Aegean—first Corinth and then Ephesus. The eighteen months which he spent in Corinth probably stretched from the autumn of A.D. 50 to the spring of 52; we are able to date this period of Paul's life with considerably accuracy from the following mention of Gallio as proconsul of Achaia.

(c) Paul before Gallio (Ch. 18:12-17)

12 But when Gallio was proconsul of Achaia, the Jews[25] with one accord rose up against Paul and brought him before the judgment-seat,

13 saying,[26] This man persuadeth men to worship God contrary to the law.

14 But when Paul was about to open his mouth, Gallio

---

[23] *Cf.* Chs. 23:11; 27:23 f.

[24] The word translated "people" (Gk. λαός) is that used especially of Israel as the people of God; here it is used of the new "chosen people" (*cf.* Ch. 15:14; Tit. 2:14; 1 Pet. 2:9 f.).

[25] The Western text reads "the Jews with one accord, having taken counsel among themselves against Paul, laid hands on him and led him to the proconsul."

[26] The Western text reads "shouting against him and saying."

said unto the Jews, If indeed it were a matter of wrong or of wicked villany, O ye Jews,[27] reason would that I should bear with you:

15 but if they are questions about words and names and your own law, look to it yourselves; I am not minded to be a judge of these matters.

16 And he drove them from the judgment-seat.

17 And they all[28] laid hold on Sosthenes, the ruler of the synagogue, and beat him before the judgment-seat. And Gallio cared for none of these things.[29]

12 Paul had received a divine promise that no harm would come to him through any attack in Corinth, but he was not promised that no attack would be made. An attack was indeed made on him, and one which might have had serious consequences. On this occasion his Jewish opponents, instead of stirring up the city rabble against him or accusing him before the civic magistrates, approached the Roman administration of the province. Any decision that civic magistrates, such as the politarchs of Thessalonica, might take would be valid only within their civic jurisdiction, but the verdict of a Roman governor would not only be effective within his province but would be followed as a precedent by the governors of other provinces. Had the proconsul of Achaia[30] pronounced a verdict unfavourable to Paul, the story of the progress of Christianity during the next decade or so would have been very different from what it actually was.

Gallio was a son of the elder Seneca, the rhetorician (c. 50 B.C.–c. A.D. 40), and brother of the younger Seneca, the philosopher (c. 3 B.C.–A.D. 65). He was born in Cordova shortly before the beginning of the Christian era, and his name originally was Marcus Annaeus Novatus, but after he came to Rome with his father in the reign of Tiberius, he was adopted by the rhetorician Lucius Junius Gallio, and thereafter bore the same name as his adoptive father. He appears to have been a man of considerable personal

---

27 Gk. ὦ Ἰουδαῖοι (but the Western text has the fuller form ὦ ἄνδρες Ἰουδαῖοι).

28 The Western and Byzantine texts read "all the Greeks."

29 The Western text reads "Gallio pretended not to see."

30 "Achaia was governed by a proconsul from B.C. 27 to A.D. 15, and from A.D. 44 onwards. It was a province of the second rank, and was administered by Roman officials, after holding the praetorship, and generally before the consulship. Corinth had now become the chief city of Achaia, and the residence of its governors" (Ramsay, St. Paul the Traveller, p. 258).

charm—"no mortal," said his brother Seneca, "is so pleasant to any one person as Gallio is to everybody" (*Natural Questions* iv a; Preface, 11), and Dio Cassius refers to his wit (*History* lxi. 35). After holding the praetorship, he was appointed proconsul of Achaia; from an inscription at Delphi in Central Greece recording a proclamation made by the Emperor Claudius between the end of 51 and August of 52, it can be inferred that he entered upon this proconsulship in July, 51.[31] He left Achaia because of a fever and went on a cruise for his health (Seneca, *Moral Epistles* civ. 1). At a later date we read of a cruise which he took from Rome to Egypt after his consulship, because of threatened phthisis (Pliny, *Natural History* xxxi. 33). In 65, along with Seneca and other members of his family, he fell a victim to Nero's suspicions.

13 The charge which was preferred against Paul before Gallio was that of propagating a religion not authorized by Roman law. Judaism was a *religio licita*, but Paul's Jewish opponents refused to recognize the gospel that he preached as having anything to do with their ancestral faith. It was something new and un-Jewish, which they wholeheartedly repudiated; it was, they urged, a *religio illicita* which accordingly ought to be banned by Roman law; Paul should be inhibited from its further propagation, if not indeed punished for his activity in propagating it thus far.[32]

14–16 Paul appeared before the proconsular tribunal to conduct his own defence. From his later speeches before Felix (Ch. 24:10 ff.) and the younger Agrippa (Ch. 26:2 ff.) we may infer what his line of defence would have been; he would have argued that the gospel which he proclaimed was the true ancestral faith of Israel, the fulfilment of the promises made by the God of Israel to Abraham and his descendants over many generations. But on this occasion he had no opportunity to defend himself; Gallio judged this to be superfluous. He listened to the charges and

[31] The inscription, which mentions Gallio as proconsul of Achaia. is datable by its reference to Claudius as having been acclaimed *imperator* for the twenty-sixth time; the evidence of other inscriptions indicates that the period during which Claudius could be so described covers the first seven months of A.D. 52. As a proconsul entered on his term of office (nominally) on July 1, it is just possible that Gallio became proconsul on July 1, A.D. 52, but much more probable that he did so on that date in the year 51. See A. Deissmann, *Paul* (Eng. tr.. London, 1926), pp. 261 ff.; K. Lake in *Beginnings* v (London, 1933), pp. 460 ff.

[32] See S. L. Guterman, *op. cit.*, and A. N. Sherwin–White. "The Early Persecutions and Roman Law Again", JThS, NS iii (1952), pp. 199 ff.

quickly decided that the dispute was one completely within the Jewish community; it had to do with detailed interpretations of the Jewish law. What Paul was propagating, in his view, was simply a variety of Judaism which did not happen to commend itself to the leaders of the Jewish colony in Corinth; and he had no intention of adjudicating on a matter of this kind. Had the charge been concerned with a real breach of Roman law,[33] he told the accusers, he would naturally have taken it up;[34] but as it was plainly an internal disagreement about Jewish religious terminology, they must settle it themselves. So he bade them begone from his tribunal.

17 As they went away, an incident occurred which reveals how prone the populace of these Gentile cities was to anti-Jewish demonstrations. Taking advantage of the snub which the proconsul had administered to the leaders of the Jewish community, the crowd of bystanders suddenly seized one of these leaders, Sosthenes,[35] who had recently succeeded Crispus as ruler of the synagogue, and beat him up in the very presence of Gallio, who had not yet left the tribunal. (The tribunal was, of course, set up in the open air.) But Gallio judged it politic to turn a blind eye to this brutal ventilation of popular anti-Jewish sentiment.[36]

Gallio's ruling, that the gospel shared the protection which Roman law extended to the Jewish religion, must have served as a precedent for other Roman judges, especially as it proceeded from a man whose brother occupied so influential a position at the imperial court as did Seneca. It meant that for the next ten or twelve years, until imperial policy towards the Christians underwent a complete reversal "at the highest level",[37] the Christian

---

33 Gk. ἀδίκημά τι ἢ ῥᾳδιούργημα πονηρόν, ¶ "some crime or malicious fraud." Moulton and Milligan (*Vocabulary of the Greek Testament* [Edinburgh, 1930], p. 563) quote ῥᾳδιουργία in the sense "false pretences" (*cf.* Ch. 13:10).

34 Gk. κατὰ λόγον ἂν ἀνεσχόμην ὑμῶν. W. Bauer (*Griechisch-deutsches Wörterbuch zu den Schriften des NT* [Berlin, 1952], col. 120) quotes ἀνέχομαι as a technical term of legal speech in the sense of taking up a complaint.

35 If this is the Sosthenes of 1 Cor. 1:1, then he must later have followed the example of Crispus and become a Christian too. *Cf.* F. W. Grosheide, *Commentary on 1 Corinthians* (Grand Rapids, 1953), p. 22. But we cannot be sure if he is the same person.

36 This, and not the usual homiletic application, is the sense of the words "Gallio cared for none of these things."

37 Imperial policy probably began to take a definitely anti-Christian turn about the year 62, when Nero married Poppaea Sabina, an adherent to the

message could be proclaimed in the provinces of the empire without fear of coming into conflict with Roman law. Luke's account of Gallio's decision is of high relevance to the apologetic motive of his history. And it may be that the memory of this decision was one of the things which encouraged Paul some years later to appeal "from the petty outlying court of the procurator of Judaea, who was always much under the influence of the ruling party in Jerusalem, to the supreme tribunal of the Empire" (Ramsay, *St. Paul the Traveller* [London, 1920], p. 260).[38]

Jewish religion; this anti-Christian trend became overt in the sequel to the Great Fire of Rome in 64.

[38] See Ch. 25:11, with exposition and notes.

4. EPHESUS
(Chs. 18:18–19:20)

(a) Hasty Visit to Ephesus (Ch. 18:18–21)

18 And Paul, having tarried after this yet many days,
took his leave of the brethren, and sailed thence for
Syria, and with him Priscilla and Aquila: having shorn
his head[39] in Cenchreae: for he had a vow.

19 And they came to Ephesus, and [40] he left them there:
but he himself entered into the synagogue, and reasoned
with the Jews.

20 And when they asked him to abide a longer time, he
consented not;

21 but taking his leave of them, and saying,[41] I will
return again unto you if God will, he set sail from
Ephesus.

18 Paul was not likely to leave Corinth immediately after
Gallio had given his favourable decision. That decision was given
probably soon after Gallio's arrival as proconsul, and Paul spent
several more months in Corinth, taking full advantage of the
liberty thus officially confirmed to him. At last, however, he left
Corinth, for he wished to visit Syria and Palestine. Along with
Priscilla and Aquila, he set sail across the Aegean from Cenchreae,
the eastern port of Corinth. At Cenchreae, we are told, he cut
his hair, "for he had a vow"—that is to say, for some purpose
perhaps connected with his missionary work at Corinth he had
undertaken a temporary Nazirite vow, for the duration of which
he allowed his hair to grow long.[42] The cutting of his hair indicates that the period of his vow had come to an end.

[39] The African Latin codex h (Western text) reads "Aquila, who, since he
had made a vow, had shorn his head"; the Latin Vulgate reads "Priscilla and
Aquila, who had shorn their heads in Cenchreae, for they had a vow."

[40] The Western text inserts "on the following sabbath."

[41] The Western and Byzantine texts add: "I must by all means keep the
coming festival in Jerusalem, but . . ."

[42] On Nazirite vows see Num. 6:1–21 and the Mishnah tractate *Nazir*.
Paul's vow may have been one of thanksgiving for divine protection during
his long stay at Corinth. It is grammatically possible that it was Aquila whose
hair was shorn, but "the natural emphasis marks Paul as the subject here"
(Ramsay, *op. cit.*, p. 263). Perhaps a feeling that Paul could not have indulged
in so Jewish a practice lies behind the Latin readings which refer the action

19 The ship in which they set sail brought them to Ephesus. Here Priscilla and Aquila settled down for some years,[43] either transferring their business from Corinth to Ephesus, or leaving their Corinthian branch in care of a manager (as perhaps they had already left their Roman branch) and opening a new branch in Ephesus. Ephesus was at that time the greatest commercial city of Asia Minor, although its harbour required constant dredging because of the alluvium carried down by the Cayster, at whose mouth it stood. Standing on the main route from Rome to the east, it enjoyed political importance in addition to its geographical advantages; it was the capital of the province of Asia, and at the same time a free Greek city, with its own senate and civic assembly; it was an assize town, and prided itself especially on its title "Warden of the Temple of Artemis." On the cult of this goddess, whose temple at Ephesus was one of the seven wonders of the ancient world, more is said in Ch. 19:23 ff. There was a large colony of Jews at Ephesus, and the privileges granted them in 44 B.C. by Dolabella (a partisan of Julius Caesar, and Roman consul in that year) were subsequently confirmed by the city authorities and by the Emperor Augustus (*cf.* Josephus, *Antiquities* xiv. 10. 12, 25; xvi. 6.2, 4.7). The site of Ephesus is marked to-day by the village of Ayasaluk, which perpetuates by its name the Ephesian residence of "John the Divine."[44] See W. M. Ramsay, *Letters to the Seven Churches of Asia* (London, 1909), pp. 210 ff.

20–21 Paul, according to the Western reading of v. 21, was eager to reach Jerusalem in time for one of the Jewish festivals. If this festival was Passover, there was probably a good reason for his haste: the seas were closed to navigation until March 10 (according to Vegetius, *On Military Affairs* iv. 39), and in A.D. 52 Passover fell early in April. His brief stay in Ephesus gave him

explicitly to Aquila or to Aquila and Priscilla (see n. 39). See also Ch. 21:23 ff., with exposition and notes.

[43] The death of Claudius in A.D. 54 appears to have been the signal for the return to Rome of many of the Jews whom he had expelled; there is some ground for thinking that the Roman church was reconstituted about that time. Among those who returned were Priscilla and Aquila, who were in Rome early in A.D. 57, if (as I believe) Rom. 16 is an integral part of the letter sent by Paul to Rome. See F. F. Bruce, *The Dawn of Christianity* (London, 1950), pp. 160, 166.

[44] Ayasaluk is a corruption of Gk. ἅγιος θεολόγος, the "holy divine." Justinian in the sixth century built the Church of St. John Theologos on the hill now called Ayasaluk.

time to visit the synagogue and hold some preparatory discourse with the Jews who met there, but although they were interested in what he had to say and asked him to stay longer, he was unable to do so. A ship was about to leave the Ephesian harbour which might bring him to Palestine in time for the festival, so he bade them farewell and promised to come back and spend more time with them, if such were God's will.

(b) Visit to Palestine (Ch. 18:22–23)

22 And when he had landed at Caesarea, he went up and saluted the church, and went down to Antioch.

23 And having spent some time *there*, he departed, and went through the region of Galatia, and Phrygia, in order, establishing all the disciples.

22 Paul's ship from Ephesus brought him to Caesarea, the Mediterranean port of Palestine. When the wind is east of north it is easier to put in at Caesarea than at Seleucia. Having landed at Caesarea, he went up to Jerusalem and greeted the church there. (Jerusalem is not explicitly mentioned, but it is certainly implied here; the church which he greeted cannot have been the Caesarean church,[45] for it is from Jerusalem, and certainly not from Caesarea, that one would "go down" to Antioch.) Whether he had any special commission to discharge in Jerusalem in connection with the festival or otherwise, Luke does not tell us; but when he had completed what he had to do in Jerusalem, he went down to Syrian Antioch (*cf.* Ch. 11:27 for the same expression).

23 Antioch was the base from which he had set out on his second, as earlier on his first, missionary journey, and no doubt on this occasion too he gathered the church of that city together and told them of God's dealings with him and of other Gentiles who had entered in by the door of faith (*cf.* Ch. 14:27). But after some time spent in Antioch, he set out on his travels again. An impression of haste is given by the succession of participles in the Greek text of vv. 22 and 23; and in fact a journey of 1500 miles is covered in these two verses and Ch. 19:1. Luke can cover the ground with surprising speed when he is relating a journey on

---

[45] *Pace* B. H. Streeter in JThS xxxiv (1933), p. 237, who maintains that Caesarea is intended and that the Western text of Ch. 19:1 (see p. 384, n. 1) should be transferred to this point, as explaining why Paul did not carry out his intention of going to Jerusalem, expressed in the Western text of v. 21 above (see p. 377, n. 41).

which he was not a companion of Paul's. From Antioch Paul set out for Asia Minor by the same land route which he and Silas had followed at the beginning of the second missionary expedition. He passed through "the Galatic region" (*i.e.* Galatic Lycaonia, so called to distinguish it from eastern Lycaonia, which lay, not in the province of Galatia, but in the territory of King Antiochus)[46] "and Phrygia" (including probably both Galatic and Asian Phrygia), but on this occasion there was no divine monition barring the road to the west. So, after he had encouraged and strengthened his old friends in the churches of South Galatia, his way was open to Ephesus.

(c) Apollos (Ch. 18:24–28)

24 Now a certain Jew named Apollos,[47] an Alexandrian by race, an eloquent man,[48] came to Ephesus; and he was mighty in the scriptures.

25 This man had been instructed[49] in the way of the Lord; and being fervent in spirit, he spake and taught accurately the things concerning Jesus, knowing only the baptism of John:

26 and he began to speak boldly in the synagogue. But when Priscilla and Aquila[50] heard him, they took him unto them, and expounded unto him the way of God more accurately.

27 And[51] when he was minded to pass over into Achaia,

[46] This explanation, maintained by W. M. Ramsay (*Dictionary of the Bible*, ed. J. Hastings, ii [Edinburgh, 1899], p. 90) and W. M. Calder (*Commentary on the Bible*, ed. A. S. Peake, Supplement [London, 1936], p. 32), is preferable to the view that the ethnic sense is intended, as maintained latterly by K. Lake (*cf. Beginnings* v, pp. 239 f.). Lake agrees that Ramsay's view, which he himself accepted in 1911 when he wrote *The Earlier Epistles of St. Paul* (pp. 260 f.), "certainly fits the facts." *Cf.* Ch. 16:6, with exposition and notes.

[47] Cod. ℵ calls him Apelles; Cod. D gives him his full name Apollonius; the Latin Vulgate has "Apollo."

[48] Gk. ἀνὴρ λόγιος, perhaps meaning "a man of learning."

[49] The Western text adds "in his native place."

[50] The Western text says "Aquila and Priscilla," reducing Priscilla's prominence. See p. 346, n. 13 (on Ch. 17:12).

[51] The Western text reads: "And some Corinthians who were sojourning in Ephesus and had heard him besought him to cross over with them to their native place. And when he consented, the Ephesians wrote to the disciples in Corinth to receive the man; and when he took up residence in Achaia he was of great help in the churches"—an expansion which "has all the marks of truth, and yet is clearly not original, but a text remodelled according to a good tradition" (Ramsay, *St. Paul the Traveller*, p. 267).

the brethren encouraged him, and wrote to the disciples
to receive him: and when he was come, he helped them
much that had believed through grace;

28 for he powerfully confuted the Jews, *and that* publicly,
showing[52] by the scriptures that Jesus was the Christ.

24-25 Between Paul's departure from Ephesus after his hasty
visit to it, and his return there after he had been to Palestine and
Syria, another extremely interesting Christian arrived in that city.
This was a man named Apollos, who belonged to a Jewish family
of Alexandria in Egypt. It is not explicitly stated (except in the
Western text) that Apollos received his accurate instruction "in
the way of the Lord" in his native Alexandria, but hy may well
have done so. The origins of Alexandrian Christianity are lost in
obscurity, but the gospel certainly reached the Egyptian capital at
a very early date.[53] Some of the visitors from other parts who
were present in Jerusalem at the first Christian Pentecost came
from Egypt (Ch. 2:10). Yet it is doubtful if we should look to
them for the provenance of Apollos's information.[54] For his understanding of Christianity differed in at least one important respect
from the form of Christianity, based on Jerusalem, which is
depicted for us in Acts: the only baptism which Apollos knew
was that which was instituted by John the Baptist. Baptism in the
name of Jesus, as proclaimed by Peter on the day of Pentecost

---

[52] The Western text reads "discoursing and showing."

[53] Some (*e.g.* S. Reinach, "La première allusion au christianisme dans l'histoire", in *Revue de l'histoire des religions* lxxxix [1924], pp. 108 ff., and
Orpheus [Eng. tr., London, 1931], p. 244) have found a reference to early
Alexandrian Christianity in a letter sent by the Emperor to the Jews of
Alexandria in A.D. 41, forbidding them to "introduce or invite Jews who sail
down to Alexandria from Syria or Egypt, thus compelling me to conceive the
greater suspicion; otherwise I will by all means take vengeance on you as
fomenting a general plague for the whole world." This has been thought to
reflect a situation in Alexandria similar to that in Rome which led to the
expulsion order mentioned in v. 2 (and we may compare the language of
Ch. 24:5), but we can make so such inference with any degree of certainty.
See H. I. Bell, *Jews and Christians in Egypt* (London, 1924), pp. 25, 29; *Juden
und Griechen im römischen Alexandreia* (Leipzig, 1926), p. 27; "Evidences of
Christianity in Egypt during the Roman Period," HThR xxxvii (1944),
pp. 185 ff. (especially pp. 188–190); W. O. E. Oesterley, *History of Israel*, ii
(Oxford, 1932), pp. 408 f.; R. Eisler, *The Enigma of the Fourth Gospel*
(London, 1938), pp. 96 f.; M. Goguel, *La Naissance du Christianisme* (Paris,
1946). pp. 18 f. (n. 6); S. G. F. Brandon, *The Fall of Jerusalem and the
Christian Church* (London, 1951), pp. 222 f.

[54] Nor yet to the Alexandrians of Ch. 6:9; they were Hellenistic Jews, not
Christians.

(cf. Ch. 2:38), was evidently unknown to him.[55] His knowledge of Christianity may have come him along a line of transmission originating in Galilee, or, as Blass suggested, it may have been derived from a primitive gospel-writing (*Philology of the Gospels* [London, 1898], pp. 29 ff.). But he combined great Biblical learning and accurate knowledge of the story of Jesus with spiritual enthusiasm,[56] and proved himself specially gifted in demonstrating from the OT prophecies that Jesus was the Messiah.

26 Priscilla and Aquila heard him interpret the OT scriptures in this sense in the synagogue at Ephesus, and were greatly impressed by the learning and zeal which he devoted to the defence of the gospel. It was a pity, they thought, that so able a champion of Christianity should not know the fulness of the gospel as they themselves had learned it, and so they invited him to their home in Ephesus and there set forth "the way of God" to him more accurately, making good the gaps which had existed in his understanding of that way hitherto. How much better it is to give such private help to a preacher whose ministry is defective than to correct or denounce him publicly!

[55] Brandon (*op. cit.*, p. 25) says "the statements which the writer of the Acts makes about the Alexandrian Apollos are demonstrably preposterous both in their substance and in their mutual contradiction." He finds that "the account in Acts of Apollos reveals on analysis an antipathy to Alexandrian Christianity" (p. xiii), and ascribes this antipathy to the direct derivation of Alexandrian Christianity from that of Jerusalem and its consequent difference from Pauline Christianity. It would, accordingly, appear defective to a Paulinist. This interpretation is bound up with his unconvincing rehabilitation of the Tübingen theory in the light of modern knowledge. The remarkably small place given to Alexandrian Christianity in NT is due in the main to the fact that Paul concentrated on the road from Jerusalem to Rome, and that Luke is concerned to relate the progress of the gospel along this road, rather than to such a situation as Brandon reconstructs, or, as W. Bauer suggested (*Rechtgläubigkeit und Ketzerei im ältesten Christentum* [Tübingen. 1934], pp. 49 ff.), to the heretical character of early Alexandrian Christianity from the standpoint of later orthodoxy. See also R. B. Rackham. *The Acts of the Apostles* (London, 1902). pp. 341 f.; W. Manson, *Jesus the Messiah* (London, 1943), pp. 166 f.

[56] Taking the "spirit" in v. 25 (ζέων τῷ πνεύματι, cf. Rom. 12:11) as Apollos's own spirit. Would the writer of Acts have thought of Apollos at this stage as possessed of the Holy Spirit? He does not say; nor is there any suggestion that Apollos received re-baptism or a manifest endowment with the Spirit as did the twelve Ephesian disciples in Ch. 19:6. "Possibly a direct commission from the Lord was deemed to have conferred upon him the Spirit, for he ranked high among the apostles, being regarded by the Corinthians as standing approximately upon the same level as St. Peter or St. Paul" (G. W. H. Lampe, *The Seal of the Spirit* [London, 1951], p. 66).

27-28 After some time, Apollos wished to cross the Aegean and visit Greece: according to the Western text, he was invited to do so by some Corinthian Christians who made his acquaintance in Ephesus. At any rate, he went to Corinth, armed with a letter of introduction from his friends in Ephesus to the Corinthian church. He proved himself a tower of strength to that church, both by his teaching within the church and by his preaching to those outside, especially to the Jews of Corinth, as he refuted their counter-arguments by showing how Jesus of Nazareth had fulfilled the ancient scriptures in such a way that His Messiahship could not be denied. The influence that Apollos exercised in Corinth may be gathered from the references made to him in Paul's Corinthian correspondence, where Paul speaks of him as watering the seed which he himself had sown.[57] If some of the Corinthian Christians were disposed to claim Apollos as a party-leader to the detriment of Paul[58] (impressed perhaps by his Alexandrian methods of Biblical interpretation),[59] there is no evidence that Apollos himself encouraged this tendency, and Paul speaks of him in the warmest terms as a fellow-apostle.[60]

[57] 1 Cor. 3:6.
[58] 1 Cor. 1:12; 3:4.
[59] Luther's suggestion that Apollos was the author of the Epistle to the Hebrews has been propounded afresh and supported by new arguments by T. W. Manson, "The Problem of the Epistle to the Hebrews", *Rylands Library Bulletin* xxxii (Manchester, 1949), pp. 1 ff. and by W. F. Howard, "The Epistle to the Hebrews", in *Interpretation*, Jan. 1951, pp. 80 ff.; *cf.* C. Spicq, *L'Épitre aux Hébreux* (Paris, 1952–3) i, pp. 209 ff.
[60] *Cf.* 1 Cor. 4:9; 16:12.

CHAPTER XIX

(d) Paul Returns to Ephesus (Ch. 19:1–7)

1 And[1] it came to pass, that, while Apollos was at Corinth, Paul having passed through the upper country came to Ephesus, and found certain disciples:

2 and he said unto them, Did ye receive the Holy Spirit when ye believed? And they *said* unto him, Nay, we did not so much as hear whether the Holy Spirit was *given*.[2]

3 And he said, Into what then were ye baptized? And they said, Into John's baptism.

4 And Paul said, John baptized with the baptism of repentance, saying unto the people that they should believe on him that should come after him, that is, on Jesus.

5 And when they heard this, they were baptized into the name of the Lord Jesus.[3]

6 And when Paul had laid his hands upon them, the Holy Spirit came on them; and they spake with tongues, and prophesied.

7 And they were in all about twelve men.

1 Having visited the churches of South Galatia, Paul continued his westward way to Ephesus, "taking the higher-lying and more direct route, not the regular trade route on the lower level down the Lycus and Maeander valleys" (W. M. Ramsay, *St. Paul the Traveller* [London, 1920], p. 265). Part of Asian Phrygia, through which he passed, was popularly known as "Upper Phrygia." He would approach Ephesus from the north side of Mount Messogis.

By the time he reached Ephesus, Apollos had crossed the Aegean to Corinth, but shortly after his arrival in Ephesus, Paul met a dozen men whose knowledge of Christianity was in much the

---

[1] The Western text reads: "But when Paul wished, according to his own plan, to go to Jerusalem, the Spirit bade him return to Asia, and having passed through the upper country he came to Ephesus." See pp. 377, 379, nn. 41 and 45 (on Ch. 18:21 f.).

[2] The Western text reads "whether people are receiving the Holy Spirit."

[3] The Western text adds "Christ", and continues "for the remission of sins" —ineptly, because these disciples had already received John's baptism to this end.

same defective condition as Apollo's knowledge had been before he met Priscilla and Aquila. But that these men were Christians is certainly to be inferred from the way in which Luke describes them as "disciples";[4] this is a term which he commonly uses for Christians, and had he meant to indicate that they were disciples not of Christ but of John the Baptist[5] (as has sometimes been deduced from v. 3), he would have said so explicitly. They may have received their knowledge of Christianity from a source similar to that from which Apollos received his;[6] or they may have received it from Apollos and been baptized by him during his earlier days in Ephesus, when he knew only the baptism of John.[7]

2 At any rate, Paul's question, "Did ye receive the Holy Spirit when ye believed?"[8] suggests strongly that he regarded them as true believers in Christ. But they professed complete ignorance of the Holy Spirit—their answer, as translated literally in RSV, was "No, we have never even heard that there is a Holy Spirit", although the addition of the word "given", as in ARV, may give the real intention of their words.[9] Even if they had only been baptized with John's baptism, they conceivably knew that John had spoken of a coming baptism with the Holy Spirit; they did

[4] See N. B. Stonehouse in WThJ xiii (1950–51), pp. 11 ff.; G. W. H. Lampe, *The Seal of the Spirit* (London, 1951), p. 75.

[5] The idea that there was a group of disciples of John the Baptist at Ephesus (against whom, incidentally, the Fourth Evangelist is alleged to polemicize) has no substantial evidence to support it, certainly not in the Fourth Gospel.

[6] See p. 381.

[7] S. G. F. Brandon, *The Fall of Jerusalem and the Christian Church* (London, 1951), p. 25, speaks of them as "twelve disciples who had presumably been baptized by Apollos, apparently before the time of his fuller instruction at the hands of Priscilla and Aquila." N. B. Stonehouse (*op. cit.*, p. 13, n. 12) says they "could be early believers in Christ who were baptized by John or, more probably, with his baptism by another"; and refers to G. Vos, *Biblical Theology* (Grand Rapids, 1948), pp. 341 f., where the significance of John's baptism is discussed.

[8] The normal relation between receiving the Spirit and believing is indicated by ARV (with ERV and RSV) better than by AV ("Have ye received the Holy Ghost since ye believed?"), as also in the similar passage in Eph. 1:13. The clause "when ye believed" renders the Gk. aorist participle πιστεύσαντες, the "coincident aorist participle" which "is doctrinally important" (J. H. Moulton, *Grammar of NT Greek*, i [3rd edn., Edinburgh, 1908], p. 131 n.). *Cf.* Ch. 11:17.

[9] *Cf.* the Western reading, quoted in n. 2 above. In the same way the statement in John 7:39, literally rendered "for the Spirit was not yet." is amplified in the Western and Byzantine texts by the addition of the word "given" (*cf.* ARV and RSV).

not know, however, that this expected baptism was now an accomplished fact.

3–4 Paul then enquired about their baptism,[10] and learned that it was the pre-Pentecostal baptism as proclaimed and administered by John the Baptist—a baptism of expectation rather than one of fulfilment, as Christian baptism now was. Accordingly, he explained to them the anticipatory character of the Johannite rite; it was closely bound up with John's proclamation of Jesus as the Coming One.[11] But now that Jesus had come and accomplished His mission on earth, now that He was raised from the dead and exalted at God's right hand, whence He had sent the promised gift of the Holy Spirit, an anticipatory baptism was inappropriate and inadequate.

5–7 The twelve men then received baptism "into the name of the Lord Jesus". This is the only account of re-baptism that we find in the NT. The apostles themselves appear to have been baptized with John's baptism (some of them certainly were), but no question of re-baptism seems to have arisen for them; probably their Pentecostal endowment with the Spirit transformed the preparatory significance of the baptism which they had already received into the consummative significance of Christian baptism. But these Ephesian disciples had received no such Pentecostal endowment.[12] They were therefore baptized again in a Christian sense, and when Paul laid his hands on them, they received the Holy Spirit in Pentecostal fashion. There may be an intended parallel here between the imposition of Paul's hands on these men and the imposition of Peter's (and John's) on the Samaritan con-

[10] Paul's question "Into what then were ye baptized?" implies a connection between the receiving of the Spirit and baptism. He assumes that they have been baptized (an unbaptized believer is not contemplated in NT), but regards it as anomalous that baptized persons should not have received the Spirit. *Cf.* Ch. 2:38.

[11] The Synoptists do not expressly state that John directed his hearers to *believe* in the Coming One, as Paul here states; but Paul's statement is in thorough agreement with the Fourth Gospel (*cf.* John 1:26 ff.; 3:25 ff.). Again, in the Synoptic Gospels John does not explicitly identify the Coming One with Jesus (see, however, Matt. 11:3; Luke 7:19); but he makes the identification quite definitely in John 1:29 ff. Similarly Paul's account of John the Baptist's ministry in Ch. 13:24 f. has points of contact with the account in John 1:19 ff.

[12] There is the added consideration that these Ephesians probably received John's baptism *after* the death and exaltation of Jesus, whereas the apostles had received it before these events.

verts in Ch. 8:17.[13] Professor Lampe, in pursuance of his thesis, points out that Paul's arrival at Ephesus marks "another decisive moment in the missionary history" (*The Seal of the Spirit* [London, 1951], p. 76). Ephesus was to be a new centre of the Gentile mission—the next in importance after Syrian Antioch—and these twelve disciples were to be the nucleus of the Ephesian church. By this exceptional procedure, then, they were associated in the apostolic and missionary task of the Christian Church.

(e) Signs and Wonders at Ephesus (Ch. 19:8–20)

8 And he entered into the synagogue, and spake boldly[14] for the space of three months, reasoning and persuading *as to* the things concerning the kingdom of God.

9 But when some were hardened and disobedient, speaking evil of the Way before the multitude, he departed from them, and separated the disciples, reasoning daily in the school of Tyrannus.[15]

10 And this continued for the space of two years; so that all they that dwelt in Asia heard the word of the Lord, both Jews and Greeks.

11 And God wrought special miracles by the hands of Paul:

12 insomuch that unto the sick were carried away from his body handkerchiefs or aprons, and the diseases departed from them, and the evil spirits went out.

13 But certain also of the strolling Jews, exorcists, took upon them to name over them that had the evil spirits the name of the Lord Jesus, saying, I adjure you by Jesus whom Paul preacheth.

14 And[16] there were seven sons of one Sceva, a Jew, a chief priest, who did this.

---

[13] Luke appears deliberately but unobtrusively to trace quite a number of parallels between Peter's ministry and Paul's; *e.g.* both at an early point in their ministry heal lame men (Chs. 3:2 ff.; 14:8 ff.), both exorcize demons (Chs. 5:16; 16:18), both have triumphant encounters with sorcerers (Chs. 8:18 ff.; 13:6 ff.), both raise the dead (Chs. 9:36 ff.; 20:9 ff.), both have miraculous escapes from prison (Chs. 12:7 ff.; 16:25 ff.). *Cf.* the exposition of v. 12 below (p. 389).

[14] The Western text adds "with great power."

[15] The Western text adds "from the fifth to the tenth hour."

[16] Verse 14 is expanded thus in the Western text: "among whom also the sons of Sceva a priest wished to do the same (they were accustomed to exorcize such people), and entering in to the demon-possessed man they began to invoke the Name, saying, 'We charge you, by Jesus whom Paul proclaims, to come out'." The Latin codex *gigas* says "two sons" (*cf.* n. 17).

15 And the evil spirit answered and said unto them, Jesus I know, and Paul I know; but who are ye?

16 And the man in whom the evil spirit was leaped on them, and mastered both[17] of them, and prevailed against them, so that they fled out of that house naked and wounded.

17 And this became known to all, both Jews and Greeks, that dwelt at Ephesus; and fear fell upon them all, and the name of the Lord Jesus was magnified.

18 Many also of them that had believed came, confessing, and declaring their deeds.

19 And not a few of them that practised magical arts brought their books together and burned them in the sight of all; and they counted the price of them, and found it fifty thousand pieces of silver.

20 So mightily grew the word of the Lord and prevailed.

8–9 Paul had already established relations with the Jews who met in the synagogue of Ephesus, and they had pressed him to stay longer. Now, having completed his business in Palestine and Syria, he had come back to Ephesus and resumed his synagogue discourses in accordance with his promise. But the usual pattern of events began to reproduce itself. For three months he debated with them in the synagogue, proclaiming the kingdom of God which had drawn near in Jesus the Messiah; but at last the party that opposed him made the situation so difficult, publicly slandering "The Way" and invoking curses upon it, that he abandoned the synagogue and used the lecture-hall of a teacher named Tyrannus[18] as his headquarters. Here those who had accepted his message while he proclaimed it in the synagogue followed him, and others as well, and day by day he held discourse and discussion in his new headquarters, during the hours when Tyrannus himself did not require the building. The Western text indicates that Paul had the use of the building from 11 A.M. to 4 P.M. Tyrannus no doubt held his classes in the early morning.

---

[17] RSV renders ἀμφοτέρων by "all of them", probably correctly; there is papyrus evidence for this looser sense of ἀμφότεροι (cf. F. G. Kenyon quoted by Moulton and Milligan, *The Vocabulary of the Greek Testament* [Edinburgh, 1930], p. 28, s.v. ἀμφότεροι). The apparent discrepancy between ἀμφοτέρων here and ἑπτά in v. 14 led the Western revisers to omit ἑπτά and the editor of the *gigas* text to emend it to Lat. *duo* (cf. n. 16).

[18] One wonders idly if this was the name his parents gave him or the name his pupils gave him!

Public activity ceased in the cities of Ionia[19] for several hours at 11 A.M., and (as Lake and Cadbury point out) more people would be asleep at 1 P.M. than at 1 A.M. But Paul, after spending the early hours of the day at his tent-making (*cf.* Ch. 20:34), devoted the hours of burden and heat to his more important and more exhausting business, and must have infected his hearers with his own energy and zeal, so that they were willing to sacrifice their siesta for the sake of listening to Paul.

10 For two full years[20] this work went on. Paul stayed in Ephesus, but a number of his colleagues carried on missionary activity in the neighboring cities as well. It was during these years that the churches in the Lycus valley—those at Colossae, Hierapolis and Laodicea—were founded, although Paul does not appear to have visited these cities in person (*cf.* Col. 2:1; 4:13); perhaps all seven of the churches of Asia addressed in the Revelation of John were founded about this time. The province was intensively evangelized, and became one of the leading centres of Christianity for centuries afterwards.

11–12 Paul's ministry in Ephesus was marked by mighty works of divine power, particularly of healing and exorcism. The healing of the sick by means of pieces of material which had been in contact with Paul is reminiscent of the healing of those who touched the fringe of Jesus' cloak (*cf.* Mark 5:27 ff.; 6:56); there may also be an intended parallel here to the healing effect of Peter's shadow (Ch. 5:15).[21] The pieces of material which had been in contact with Paul were those which he used as sweat-rags and aprons[22] while engaged in his leather-working, the sweat-rags being used for tying round his head and the aprons for tying round his waist.

13 So potent did the name of Jesus, as used by Paul, prove in the exorcizing of demons from those who were possessed by them, that other exorcists began to use it too. Many of these

[19] And in Rome as well, if we are to believe the poet Martial: "Rome prolongs her varied tasks to the fifth hour" (*Epigrams* iv. 8).
[20] The period denoted in v. 10 was probably rather more than two years; if we add the three months of v. 8, we have something approaching the "three years" of Ch. 20:31—probably from the autumn of 52 to the summer of 55.
[21] See n. 13 above.
[22] Both the Greek words used here are words of Latin origin—σουδάρια from *sudaria*, "sweat-rags" (*cf.* Luke 19:20; John 11:44; 20:7), and σιμικίνθια from *semicinctia*, "aprons."

exorcists were wandering Jews. Among practitioners of magic in ancient times Jews enjoyed high respect, for they were believed to have specially effective spells at their command. In particular, the fact that the name of the God of Israel was not to be pronounced by vulgar lips was generally known among the pagans, and misinterpreted by them according to regular magical principles. Several magical papyri which have been preserved to our day contain attempts to reproduce the correct pronunciation of the Ineffable Name[23]—Iao, Iae, Iaoue, and so forth—as well as other Jewish expressions and names such as Sabaoth and Abraham, used as elements in magic spells. The closest parallel to the Ephesian exorcists' misuse of the name of Jesus[24] appears in the Paris magical papyrus, No. 574, where we find an adjuration beginning on line 3018, "I adjure thee by Jesus the God of the Hebrews."

14-16 Among these Jewish exorcists were the sons of one Sceva, a Jew, described here as a chief priest. It is possible that Sceva actually belonged to one of the Jewish chief-priestly families, but more probably "Jewish Chief Priest" was his own designation of himself, set out on a placard, and Luke would have placed the words within quotation marks had they been invented in his day. A Jewish chief priest would enjoy high prestige in magical circles, for he was the sort of person most likely to know the true pronunciation of the Ineffable Name. It was not the Ineffable Name, however, but the name of Jesus that his seven sons employed in an attempt to imitate Paul's exorcism. But when they tried to use it, like an unfamiliar weapon wrongly handled it exploded in their hands. "Jesus whom Paul preacheth" was a well-known name to the demon that they were trying to cast out,[25] but what right had they to use it? And the man possessed by the demon, energized with abnormal strength, assaulted the would-be

---

[23] On the magical use of this name cf. Deissmann, *Bible Studies* (Eng. tr., Edinburgh, 1909), pp. 322 ff.

[24] The tendency for Jews to invoke the name of Jesus in healing was sternly denounced in the rabbinical writings; cf. Tosefta *Hullin* ii. 22 f., TJ *Shabbath* xiv. 4. 14d and *Abodah Zarah* ii. 2. 40d–41a, TB *Abodah Zarah* 27b.

[25] It is doubtful if we should attach too much importance to the different words for "know" in "Jesus I know (Gk. γινώσκω) and Paul I know (Gk. ἐπίσταμαι)." There was a distinction in fact, in that he knew Jesus by name and Paul by sight; but that is not the normal distinction between γινώσκω and ἐπίσταμαι.

exorcists so violently that all seven ran for their lives from the building in which they were, naked and wounded.

17 The news of this incident spread quickly and filled those who heard it with awe; this name, invoked by Paul and his colleagues with such beneficial results, was no name to be trifled with.

18–20 The whole atmosphere of this passage, in fact, tallies admirably with the reputation which Ephesus had in antiquity as a centre of magical practice. Readers of Shakespeare may remember the description of Ephesus which he puts into the mouth of the Syracusan Antipholus in his *Comedy of Errors* (Act I, Scene ii, lines 97 ff.):

> They say this town is full of cozenage,
> As, nimble jugglers that deceive the eye,
> Dark-working sorcerers that change the mind,
> Soul-killing witches that deform the body,
> Disguised cheaters, prating mountebanks,
> And many such-like liberties of sin.

Yet even among the Ephesian practitioners of magic the gospel proved its power. Many of them believed, and came to Paul and his fellow-missionaries, making confession and revealing their spells.[26] According to magical theory, the potency of a spell is bound up with its secrecy; if it be divulged, it becomes ineffective. So these converted magicians renounced their imagined power by rendering their spells inoperative. Many of them also gathered their magical papyri and parchments together and made a bonfire of them. A number of such magical scrolls have survived to our day; there are specially famous examples in the London, Paris and Leyden collections.[27] The special connection of Ephesus with

---

[26] Gk. πράξεις (translated "deeds" in ARV and "practices" in RSV) is used here (v. 18) in a technical sense of magic spells (*cf.* Deissmann, *op. cit.*, p. 323, n. 5, where he further points out that περίεργα, rendered "magical arts" in v. 19, is also a technical term for "magic").

[27] *Cf.* Deissmann, *Light from the Ancient East* (Eng. tr., London, 1927), pp. 254 ff., 302 ff., 453 ff. A papyrus amulet in the library of Princeton University has been edited with translation and notes by B. M. Metzger in *Papyri in the Princeton University Collections* iii (1942), pp. 78 f.; he has also given a popular account of it in "St. Paul and the Magicians", *Princeton Seminary Bulletin* xxxviii (1944), pp. 27 ff., where he describes it as "a first-hand specimen of the same sort of magical craft which Paul encountered at Ephesus."

magic is reflected in the use of the term "Ephesian scripts"[28] for such magical scrolls. The spells which they contain are the merest gibberish, a rigmarole of words and names considered to be unusually potent, arranged sometimes in patterns which were part of the essence of the spell, but they fetched high prices. On this occasion fifty thousand drachmae's worth of such documents went up in smoke. (The public burning of literature as an open repudiation of its contents can be paralleled both from antiquity and from more modern times.) The powers of darkness were worsted, but the gospel spread and triumphed.

[28] Gk. Ἐφέσια γράμματα (Anaxilas, quoted by Athenaeus, *Deipnosophists* xii. 548c; Plutarch, *Convivial Questions* 706e; Clement of Alexandria, *Miscellanies* v. 8.45.2).

VI. PAUL PLANS TO VISIT ROME AND GETS THERE BY AN UNFORESEEN ROUTE

(Chs. 19:21–28:31)

1. HE LEAVES EPHESUS FOR MACEDONIA AND GREECE

(Chs. 19:21–20:6)

(a) Paul Makes Plans for the Future (Ch. 19:21–22)

21 Now after these things were ended, Paul purposed in the spirit, when he had passed through Macedonia and Achaia, to go to Jerusalem, saying, After I have been there, I must also see Rome.

22 And having sent into Macedonia two of them that ministered unto him, Timothy and Erastus, he himself stayed in Asia for a while.

21 The period of Paul's Ephesian ministry drew to an end. It had been a most fruitful and encouraging ministry, even if it was attended by personal dangers of which little is said in Acts, although there are several allusions to them in the letters which Paul wrote about this time.[29] Now some two and a half years had passed since he made Ephesus his headquarters. Christianity had now a secure foothold on both shores of the Aegean, and the

---

[29] *Cf.* Ch. 20:19; 1 Cor. 15:30 ff.; 2 Cor. 1:8–10. It has been argued that one or more of his frequent imprisonments to which he refers soon after the end of his Ephesian ministry (2 Cor. 11:23) may have been endured in Ephesus. This hypothesis was introduced by Deissmann when lecturing at Herborn in 1897 (*cf.* his *Light from the Ancient East* [Eng. tr., London, 1927], p. 237 n.); see also H. Lisco, *Vincula Sanctorum* (Berlin, 1900); A. Deissmann, "Zur ephesinischen Gefangenschaft des Apostels Paulus" in *Anatolian Studies presented to Sir W. M. Ramsay* (Manchester, 1923), pp. 121 ff., and *Paul* (Eng. tr., London, 1926), pp. 16 ff.; W. Michaelis, *Die Gefangenschaft des Paulus in Ephesus* (Gütersloh, 1925) and *Einleitung in das NT* (Bern, 1946), pp. 205 ff., 217 ff., 267 ff.; G. S. Duncan, *St. Paul's Ephesian Ministry* (London, 1929); M. Dibelius, *Paul* (Eng. tr., London, 1953), p. 81. Luke's reticence on the troubles which Paul had to undergo in Ephesus (apart from the riot described in vv. 23 ff.) has been attributed to his apologetic motive; if these troubles were at all connected with the proconsul Junius Silanus (see p. 401, n. 70), it would probably have been impolitic to mention matters with which he was concerned (so Duncan, *op. cit.*, pp. 103 f.). See further four papers entitled "St. Paul in Ephesus" by T. W. Manson, BJRL, xxiii (1939), pp. 182 ff.; xxiv (1940), pp. 59 ff.; xxvi (1941–2), pp. 101 ff., 327 ff. Manson argues against the hypothesis of an Ephesian imprisonment of Paul.

young churches could safely be left to continue their work of fellowship and witness under the direction of the Holy Spirit. Paul's activity could be transferred elsewhere, and he looked around for new worlds to conquer for Christ. His settled policy not to build on another man's foundation[30] forbade him to consider missionary enterprise in Egypt and Cyrene; in Rome, too, there was already a Christian community. He looked forward, however, to paying a visit to Rome, not with the intention of settling down there but of halting there for some time on his way to Spain.[31] For Spain, the most westerly outpost of Roman civilization in Europe, was his new Macedonia which called him to come over and plant the faith among its hitherto unevangelized inhabitants. But Rome is the goal of Luke's history, and he is more interested in Paul's intention to call at Rome than in his Spanish project. From this point on Rome is the goal towards which the narrative moves, until at last, in Ch. 28, Paul reaches the imperial city by an unforeseen route and preaches the gospel there.

Verse 21, then, reveals what Ramsay calls "the clear conception of a far-reaching plan" in Paul's mind (*St. Paul the Traveller,* p. 274).[32]

But before putting this plan into execution he intended to visit his friends in Macedonia and Achaia, and then go to Jerusalem. Luke does not tell us the chief reason for this visit to Jerusalem, but Paul's own writings make it clear that he wished to hand over to the leaders of the Jerusalem church the gift which the Gentile churches east and west of the Aegean had collected for them.[33]

22 So he sent two of his companions, Timothy and Erastus, across to Macedonia in advance of his own journey thither. Timothy has not been mentioned in the narrative of Acts since the record

[30] Rom. 15:20.

[31] Rom. 15:24, 28.

[32] The expression "Paul purposed in the spirit", whether the Holy Spirit or Paul's own spirit is meant (an extraordinarily difficult point to determine), "seems intended to describe a purpose formed with intense earnestness" (J. H. Kennedy, *The Second and Third Epistles of St. Paul to the Corinthians* [London, 1900], p. 20). *Cf.* Ch. 20:22, "I go bound in the spirit unto Jerusalem."

[33] The only hint which Luke gives of this collection appears in Paul's words to Felix in Ch. 24:17. For Paul's own sense of the importance of the collection *cf.* 1 Cor. 16:1 ff.; 2 Cor. 8:1 ff.; Rom. 15:25 ff. It appears that 1 Corinthians was written before Paul's plan to visit Jerusalem was firmly fixed (*cf.* 1 Cor. 16:3 f.); in Romans, which was written after he left Ephesus, he definitely intends to go to Jerusalem in person with the gift.

of his return from Macedonia to rejoin Paul in Corinth (Ch. 18:5). But he was with Paul for part at least of the period of the Ephesian ministry; at some point during that period Paul sent him to Corinth and expected him to return to Ephesus (1 Cor. 4:17; 16:10 f.). That was probably not the occasion referred to here;[34] Timothy's present visit to Macedonia may be that mentioned by Paul in Phil. 2:19 (in which case Phil. 2:24 refers to Paul's Macedonian visit of Acts 20:1).[35] Whether the Erastus mentioned here is identical with Erastus the city treasurer of Corinth, mentioned in Rom. 16:23, we cannot say certainly; but it is not very likely.[36]

(b) The Riot at Ephesus (Ch. 19:23–41)

23 And about that time there arose no small stir concerning the Way.

24 For a certain man named Demetrius, a silversmith, who made silver[37] shrines of Diana,[38] brought no little business unto the craftsmen;

25 whom he gathered together, with the workmen of like occupation, and said, Sirs,[39] ye know that by this business we have our wealth.

26 And ye see and hear, that not alone at Ephesus,[40] but

---

[34] Timothy's visit to Corinth announced in 1 Cor. 4:17 and 16:10 f. was probably followed by a personal visit by Paul to Corinth, of which Luke tells us nothing, but which is implied by the references to the "third time" in 2 Cor. 12:14 and 13:1. See Kennedy, op. cit., pp. 69 ff.

[35] This, of course (like the identification of the "true yokefellow" on p. 341, n. 63), assumes that the Epistle to the Philippians was sent from Ephesus. On this see the works by Deissmann, Michaelis, Duncan and Dibelius mentioned in n. 29; also J. H. Michael, The Epistle to the Philippians (MNT, London, 1928), pp. xii ff.; P. Feine and J. Behm, Einleitung in das NT (Heidelberg, 1936), pp. 174 ff.; P. Benoit, Aux Philippiens (Jerusalem, 1949), pp. 11 f., and T. W. Manson in BJRL xxiii (1939), pp. 182 ff. (Manson, though he does not accept an Ephesian imprisonment of Paul, believes in the Ephesian provenance of Philippians.)

[36] The Corinthian Erastus is probably mentioned in an inscription discovered in Corinth in 1929: "Erastus, procurator of public buildings, laid this pavement at his own expense" (cf. A. M. Woodward in Journal of Hellenic Studies xlix [1929], p. 221). Cf. 2 Tim. 4:20.

[37] Cod. B omits "silver."

[38] Render "Artemis", with ARV margin and RSV. Diana was the Roman goddess corresponding to the Greek virgin-goddess Artemis. "But the Artemis of Ephesus is a divinity entirely different in character from the ordinary Greek Artemis; and that such a goddess should come to be represented in English by the name Diana is almost ridiculous" (A. Souter in Dictionary of the Apostolic Church, ed. J. Hastings [Edinburgh, 1915], i, p. 295 [s.v. "Diana"]). Cf. p. 291, n. 21 (on Ch. 14:12).

[39] The Western text reads "Fellow-craftsmen."

[40] The Western text reads "as far as Ephesus."

almost throughout all Asia, this Paul[41] hath persuaded and turned away much people, saying that they are no gods, that are made with hands:

27 and not only is there danger that this our trade come into disrepute; but also[42] that the temple of the great goddess Diana be made of no account, and that she should even be deposed from her magnificence whom all Asia and the world worshippeth.

28 And when they heard this they were filled with wrath, and[43] cried out, saying, Great *is* Diana of the Ephesians.[44]

29 And the city was filled with the confusion: and they rushed with one accord into the theatre, having seized Gaius and Aristarchus, men of Macedonia,[45] Paul's companions in travel.

30 And when Paul was minded to enter in unto the people, the disciples suffered him not.

31 And certain also of the Asiarchs, being his friends, sent unto him and besought him not to adventure himself into the theatre.

32 Some therefore cried one thing, and some another: for the assembly was in confusion; and the more part knew not wherefore they were come together.

33 And they brought Alexander out[46] of the multitude, the Jews putting him forward. And Alexander beckoned with the hand, and would have made a defence unto the people.

34 But when they perceived that he was a Jew, all with one voice about the space of two hours cried out, Great *is* Diana of the Ephesians.[47]

[41] The Western text adds "whoever he be" (τίς ποτε).

[42] The Western text recasts the following two clauses: "but also the temple of the great goddess Artemis will be brought into disrepute and her majesty is likely to be destroyed."

[43] The Western text adds "running into the square."

[44] The Western text makes this not a statement but an invocation: "Great Artemis of the Ephesians!"

[45] We should perhaps read, with the minuscules 307 and 431, "a man of Macedonia" (Μακεδόνα instead of the plural Μακεδόνας), referring to Aristarchus alone, since Gaius, according to Ch. 20:4, came from Derbe in south Galatia. The final ς of the received reading Μακεδόνας may have been due to dittography of the initial σ of the following word συνεκδήμους ("fellow-travellers"). But see p. 403, n. 5.

[46] The Western text says "they pulled him down" (κατεβίβασαν, *detraxerunt*); *i.e.* the crowd dragged him down when the Jews put him up to speak.

[47] As in v. 28, the Western text makes this an invocation (see n. 44); here

35 And when the town-clerk had quieted the multitude, he saith, Ye men of Ephesus, what man is there who knoweth not that the city of the Ephesians is temple-keeper of the great Diana, and of the *image* which fell down from[48] Jupiter?

36 Seeing then that these things cannot be gainsaid, ye ought to be quiet, and to do nothing rash.

37 For ye have brought *hither* these men, who are neither robbers of temples nor blasphemers of our goddess.

38 If therefore Demetrius, and the craftsmen that are with him, have a matter against any man, the courts are open, and there are proconsuls: let them accuse one another.

39 But if ye seek anything about other matters, it shall be settled in the regular assembly.

40 For indeed we are in danger to be accused concerning this day's riot,[49] there being no cause *for it:* and as touching it we shall not be able to give account of this concourse.

41 And when he had thus spoken, he dismissed the assembly.

23 Before Paul himself took his departure, however, a serious incident took place in Ephesus, which might have led to very ugly consequences. It arose out of the threat which the gospel presented to the cult of the great goddess Artemis at Ephesus, and to those trades which were largely dependent on the cult. Ephesian Artemis was a very different goddess from the "queen and huntress, chaste and fair"[50] whom the Greeks venerated by this name; she was in origin the ancient mother goddess of Asia Minor, worshipped in that land from time immemorial as the mother of gods and men.[51] Her temple at Ephesus was one of the seven wonders of the ancient world;[52] her image, enshrined in that temple, was believed to be

Cod. B repeats the phrase "Great is Artemis of the Ephesians"—"picturesquely", say Lake and Cadbury, who reproduce the repetition in their version (*Beginnings* iv, *ad loc.*), adding, "It may be a dittography; if so, it is a happy one."

[48] Translate: "that fell down from the sky" (Gk. διοπετής).

[49] Better: "For indeed we are in danger of being charged with riot on account of this day's assembly."

[50] Ben Jonson, *Hymn to Diana*, line 1.

[51] Commonly known as Cybele, but by a variety of other names as well.

[52] It replaced an earlier one which was set on fire by a young man named Herostratus in 356 B.C. (on the night when Alexander the Great was born, it was said); Herostratus said that he did it to make a name for himself. The present temple, measuring some 400 by 200 feet, was destroyed by invading

of heavenly workmanship: it appears to have been a meteorite in which the semblance of a many-breasted female was discerned.[53] Her worship was marked by the traditional features of nature-worship; it was presided over by eunuch-priests and three grades of priestesses. She had a special festival about the time of the spring equinox, at the beginning of the month Artemision: it may have been at the time of this festival in A.D. 55 that the trouble now described by Luke broke out.[54]

(i) The Speech of Demetrius (vv. 24–28)

24 The silversmiths of Ephesus regarded their guild as being under the special patronage of Artemis, in whose honour so many of their wares were manufactured. Among these wares were miniature silver niches, containing an image of the goddess, which her votaries bought to dedicate in her temple.[55] The sale of these small shrines was a source of considerable profit to the silversmiths, and they were alarmed at the fall in the demand for them which the spread of Christianity was causing.[56] When religious devotion and economic interest were simultaneously offended, a quite exceptionally fervid anger was engendered.[57]

25–27 Calling together all the workmen engaged in this trade, Demetrius, a prominent member of the guild of silversmiths, persuaded them to stage a mass protest against the disturbing propaganda spread by Paul and his colleagues. These preachers, by denying the existence of deities "made with hands",[58] were threatening the livelihood of those who carried on such a profitable

Goths about A.D. 262; its foundations were discovered by J. T. Wood in 1863 and the following years.

[53] Other meteorites which became cult-objects were the Palladium of Troy, the image of the Great Mother of the Gods taken from Pessinus to Rome in 204 B.C., the image of Tauric Artemis, the image of Ceres at Enna, and the image of El Gabal at Emesa. The Ephesian goddess was portrayed as many-breasted (πολύμαστος, *multimammia*) as embodying the nourishing capacity of nature.

[54] See Duncan, *op. cit.*, p. 140.

[55] We know of such miniature shrines of terra-cotta. An inscription found in the Ephesian theatre records how a Roman official, Gaius Vibius Salutaris, presented a silver image of Artemis and other statues to be set up in the theatre (Deissmann, *Light from the Ancient East*, pp. 112 f.). See n. 61 below.

[56] We may compare the report in Pliny's Letter to Trajan about the Christians (*Epistle* x. 96), that the business of supplying fodder for sacrificial animals was falling off in Bithynia owing to the spread of Christianity.

[57] Compare the resentment at Philippi when the gospel interfered with property rights (Ch. 16:19; see p. 335, n. 44).

[58] For this epithet *cf.* Chs. 7:48; 17:24, with exposition and notes.

business in the manufacture of images of Artemis, but more than that, they were challenging the divine majesty of the great goddess herself—a goddess venerated not only in Ephesus and the province of Asia, but over the whole civilized world.[59] It was intolerable that they should idly stand by and allow such an affront to be offered to the goddess and her temple, the most magnificent temple on earth.

28 Fired by the words of Demetrius, his hearers ran into the open street[60] (as the Western text tells us), invoking their goddess aloud with the cry, "Great Artemis of the Ephesians!"

(ii) The Demonstration in the Theatre (vv. 29–34)

29 The enthusiastic resentment of the silversmiths infected the general populace of Ephesus; and a demonstration was hastily staged in the great open-air theatre of the city, which is estimated to have accommodated 25,000 people.[61] As the populace hastened to the theatre, they laid hands on two of Paul's fellow-travellers, Gaius of Derbe and Aristarchus of Thessalonica,[62] and dragged them along with them. It was probably from one or the other of these two men that Luke received his vivid impression of the proceedings in the theatre.

30–31 They had not been able to lay hands on Paul, but as soon as he knew what was afoot, he made up his mind to go and face the unruly assembly in person. (For in the Greek world it was no unprecedented thing for an irregular meeting like this to constitute itself a formal meeting of the civic assembly.[63]) But

---

[59] K. Wernicke, in Pauly–Wissowa's *Realencyclopädie*, ii (Stuttgart. 1896), cols. 1385 f., enumerates thirty-three places, all over the known world, where Ephesian Artemis was worshipped.

[60] Or the square (Gk. ἄμφοδον, as in Mark 11:4). Ramsay supposes that this was the long straight street running from the inner harbour of Ephesus up to "the left front of the Great Theatre and the beginning of the steep ascent of Pion" (*Letters to the Seven Churches* [London, 1909], p. 224).

[61] This theatre is still in quite a good state of preservation. It appears to have been used for regular meetings of the city assembly; in the inscription mentioned in n. 55 above, the statues are to be set up in the theatre at a meeting of the assembly (ἐκκλησία).

[62] Their home-towns are given in Ch. 20:4.

[63] "Even this excited mob still retained some idea of method in conducting business. It was quite in the old Greek style that they should at once constitute themselves into a meeting of the Ephesian People, and proceed to discuss business and pass resolutions. . . . But this meeting was not conducted by persons used to business and possessing authority with the crowd" (Ramsay, *Letters to the Seven Churches*, pp. 224 f.).

the Ephesian Christians, in alarm, forcibly prevented him from doing what seemed to them such a mad thing; and the chief citizens of the place also sent a message urging him not to run such a risk. These chief citizens are called Asiarchs; this was a title given to the foremost men in the cities of the province, from whose ranks, incidentally, were drawn the annually elected high priests of the provincial cult of "Rome and the Emperor."[64] That these men were friendly to Paul indicates that imperial policy at this time was not hostile to Christianity, and that the more educated classes did not share the antipathy to Paul which the more superstitious classes felt.

32-34 In the theatre, however, the popular indignation was enjoying uninhibited expression. There was complete disorder, for the majority of the crowd had no idea why they were there—a remark which reveals Luke's Greek sense of humour.[65] The resentment against those who paid no honour to the great goddess was as much anti-Jewish as anti-Christian; and this alarmed the Jews of Ephesus. They judged it necessary to dissociate themselves openly from Paul and the other missionaries, and put up Alexander,[66] one of their number, to make it plain to the mob that the Jewish colony had nothing to do with the present trouble. But when Alexander got up to speak, the people paid no attention to what he wished to say. All that they cared for was that he was a Jew, and therefore no worshipper of Artemis; some of them may even have thought that he was the cause of the trouble, seeing that he appeared so eager to make a speech for the defence. When he beckoned for silence and attention, therefore, they shouted him down, and for the next two hours they kept up the cry, "Great Artemis of the Ephesians!"

(iii) The Town-Clerk's Intervention (vv. 35–41)

35 There was one man who was specially alarmed by the people's riotous conduct. This was the "town-clerk" or secretary

---

[64] *Cf.* Lily Ross Taylor, "The Asiarchs", in *Beginnings* v, pp. 256 ff. The headquarters of the cult of "Rome and the Emperor" were at Pergamum, where the chief temple of the cult was erected *c.* 29 B.C.

[65] On Luke's sense of humour see H. McLachlan, *St. Luke: the Man and his Work* (Manchester, 1920), pp. 144 ff.

[66] Whether this Alexander has any connection with "Alexander the coppersmith" of 2 Tim. 4:14 we cannot say. The Alexander of the present narrative is introduced as if he were a well-known character. (There is another mention of Alexander—whether the same one or someone else—in 1 Tim. 1:20.)

400

of the city,[67] the executive officer who published the decrees of the civic assembly. As he was the most important Ephesian official, he acted as liaison officer between the civic administration and the Roman provincial administration, whose headquarters were also in Ephesus. The provincial administration would hold him responsible for the riotous assembly, and might impose a severe penalty on the city. He therefore did his best to calm the assembly, and when at last he succeeded, he addressed them.

They need not be alarmed for the honour of the great goddess, he said, for everyone knew her fame and majesty; everyone knew that her image was of no mortal workmanship but had fallen from the sky to be guarded by the people of Ephesus; everyone knew that in consequence the city bore the proud title "Warden of the Temple of Artemis."[68]

36–37 Since this was so, he went on, the divine power of the goddess was undeniable and unassailable. They ought therefore to keep calm and not be led by excitement into some rash course of behaviour which they would regret later. The men whom they had dragged into the theatre were guilty of no crime: they had committed no sacrilege; they had spoken no evil of Artemis.[69]

38–41 If Demetrius and his fellow-craftsmen had a serious complaint to make, said the town-clerk, let them make it in the appropriate manner. There were regular assize-days—the days when the convention of citizens met under the presidency of the provincial governor. The provincial government was functioning, even if at the moment there was an interregnum between two proconsulates.[70] The aggrieved parties should avail themselves

---

[67] Gk. γραμματεύς.

[68] Gk. νεωκόρος, a word which literally means "temple-sweeper" and acquired a more honourable status, being given as a title of dignity first to individuals and then to cities. Ephesus is described as "Temple-Warden of Artemis" in *Corpus Inscriptionum Graecarum* ii (Berlin, 1843), No. 2972; she also bore the title "Temple-Warden" in relation to the imperial cult.

[69] Jewish tradition interpreted Ex. 22:28a (*cf.* p. 451) as prohibiting scurrilous attacks on pagan deities (Josephus, *Antiquities* iv. 8.10; *Against Apion* ii. 33).

[70] This may explain the generalizing plural, "there are proconsuls." There was only one proconsul at a time. The proconsul of Asia, Marcus Junius Silanus, who was, like Nero, a great-grandson of Augustus, was poisoned soon after Nero's accession to the imperial throne in October, A.D. 54, at the instigation of Nero's mother Agrippina (Tacitus, *Annals* xiii. 1). Other members of the Silanus family also incurred the imperial disfavour; this may account in part for Luke's silence about any of them. It has been suggested that the proconsular functions were discharged until the arrival of Silanus's successor by

of these legal means of redress. If the matters which caused them concern were such as might more suitably be dealt with by the citizen body of Ephesus, they should wait for one of the regular meetings of the civic assembly (of which there were three in each month),[71] instead of convening an irregular and riotous assembly like this. The Roman authorities would not tolerate such disorderly proceedings; as it was, they might very well arraign the city on a charge of riot in consequence of what had happened, and the city could plead no justification for it. By this time the people were considerably subdued, as they listened to the town-clerk's sobering arguments, and when he dismissed them, they went quietly home. The town-clerk's reasoned rebuttal of vulgar charges brought against Christians, not only in Ephesus but in other places too, is an important element in the apologetic motive of Acts.

Helius and Celer, the officials in charge of the emperor's private affairs in the province (H. M. Luckock, *Footprints of the Apostles as traced by St. Luke in the Acts* [London, 1897], ii, p. 189; G. S. Duncan, *op. cit.*, pp. 102 ff.; for a critique of this view *cf.* W. M. Ramsay in *Expositor* VI. ii [1900], pp. 334 f.).

[71] So says Chrysostom, *Homily* xlii. 2.

CHAPTER XX

(c) Paul Visits Macedonia and Greece (Ch. 20:1–6)

1 And after the uproar ceased, Paul having sent for the
disciples and exhorted them, took leave of them, and
departed to go into Macedonia.

2 And when he had gone through those parts, and had
given them much exhortation, he came into Greece.

3 And when he had spent three months *there,* and a plot
was laid against him by the Jews as he was about[1] to
set sail for Syria, he[2] determined to return through
Macedonia.

4 And there accompanied him as far as Asia,[3] Sopater
of Beroea, *the son* of Pyrrhus;[4] and of the Thessalonians,
Aristarchus and Secundus; and Gaius of Derbe,[5] and
Timothy; and of Asia,[6] Tychicus[7] and Trophimus.

5 But these had gone before,[8] and were waiting for us
at Troas.

[1] After "Jews" the Western text reads "he decided to take ship for Syria,"
as if his decision to go to Syria was due to the plot; this was plainly not so.

[2] The Western text reads "the Spirit bade him return through Macedonia"
(*cf.* a similarly characteristic introduction of the Spirit in the Western text of
Ch. 19:1).

[3] The phrase "as far as Asia" should be omitted, with ℵ B 33, the Latin
Vulgate, the Palestinian Syriac, the Coptic and Ethiopic versions.

[4] "The son of Pyrrhus" is omitted by the Byzantine text, with the Peshitta
and Harclean Syriac.

[5] The Western text calls Gaius a "Doberian" (instead of "Derbean"); *i.e.*
it makes him a native of Doberus in Macedonia (26 miles from Philippi).
This, of course, harmonizes better with the statement that he was a Macedonian, in the common text of Ch. 19:29 (if one and the same Gaius be
intended). But it may be that Gaius is not called a Macedonian in the original
text of Ch. 19:29 (see p. 396, n. 45). L. C. Valckenaer, followed by F. Blass,
emends the text to make it read: "of the Thessalonians, Aristarchus and
Secundus and Gaius; and the Derbean Timothy"; there is no necessity for such
an emendation, and in any case Timothy was more probably a Lystran (see
Ch. 16:1 f. with exposition).

[6] The Western text, more explicitly, calls them "Ephesians" instead of
"Asians." *Cf.* Ch. 21:29.

[7] Cod. D. calls him Eutychus, by confusion with the youth of v. 9.

[8] For "had gone before" (Gk. προελθόντες), which appears to be the Western
reading, the Alexandrian text has "had come" (Gk. προσελθόντες). But the
former reading, which is supported by the second hand in Cod. B, is the more
natural in the context.

6 And we sailed away from Philippi after the days of unleavened bread, and came unto them to Troas in five days; where we tarried seven days.

1 The riot in the Ephesian theatre was one of the last—if also one of the most spectacular—incidents of Paul's ministry in Ephesus. Soon after, he took his leave of the Christians of that city and made his way towards Macedonia, in accordance with the plan mentioned in Ch. 19:21. Ramsay supposes that he took a coasting ship from Ephesus to Troas (*St. Paul the Traveller* [London, 1920], p. 283). At Troas he expected to meet Titus, whom he had sent to report on the disquieting situation in the Corinthian church; and although there was ample opportunity for gospel witness in Troas, he could not settle down to take full advantage of it because of his anxiety about Corinth.[9] When Titus did not arrive, Paul bade farewell to his friends at Troas, and continued his journey to Macedonia[10] (perhaps by the same route as that outlined in Ch. 16:11); there at last he met Titus and was immeasurably relieved by the reassuring news which he brought from Corinth (2 Cor. 2:12 f.; 7:5 ff.).[11]

2 How long Paul spent in Macedonia Luke does not say, but it seems to have been a fairly prolonged period. It must have been at this time that he went as far as Illyricum (Rom. 15:19); his earlier Macedonian journey through Philippi, Thessalonica and Beroea (Chs. 16:12–17:10) did not bring him anywhere near the Illyrian frontier. On this occasion we must understand that he travelled west along the Egnatian Road, perhaps as far as its terminus at Dyrrhachium on the Adriatic. This would bring him close to the Illyrian frontier. We need not infer from Rom. 15:19

---

[9] T. W. Manson suggests that the reference in 2 Cor. 2:12 (εἰς τὴν Τρῳάδα) is not simply to the port of Alexandria Troas but to the whole area in which it lay, the Troad. He argues also that Paul did not return to Ephesus after his "painful visit" to Corinth, but visited Macedonia again, and then "set out on a missionary expedition in the Troad", while Titus went back to Corinth with Paul's "severe letter" (BJRL xxvi [1942], pp. 327 ff.).

[10] W. L. Knox takes 2 Cor. 2:12 f. to mean "that Titus was too late to reach Troas by sea, and would necessarily travel overland, and that Paul on the other hand could not risk sailing to Athens to meet him. Paul must have left Troas, in spite of the 'open door', when he realized that Titus had missed the last boat and would have to come through Macedonia" (*St. Paul and the Church of the Gentiles* [Cambridge, 1939], p. 144, n.).

[11] On the movements of Titus see J. H. Kennedy, *The Second and Third Epistles of St. Paul to the Corinthians* (London, 1900), pp. 115 ff.

that he actually crossed into the province of Illyricum.[12] But we are probably not far wrong in concluding that the period from his departure from Ephesus to his arrival in Greece (*i.e.* the province of Achaia), including his stay at Troas and his missionary and pastoral activity in Macedonia, covered something over a year—say from the summer of A.D. 55 to the late part of A.D. 56.

3 The three months that he spent in Greece were the winter months of A.D. 56–57. Most of this time was actually spent in Corinth, where he enjoyed the hospitality of his friend Gaius (not improbably Gaius Titius Justus),[13] and wrote his Epistle to the Romans, preparing the church of the imperial capital for the visit which he hoped to pay to their city quite soon, on his way to Spain.[14] Among the other things that he did in Macedonia and Greece at this time must be included the completed arrangements for conveying the collected gifts from the churches of these provinces to Jerusalem.[15] It appears to have been his first intention to take a pilgrim ship from Cenchreae (*cf.* Ch. 18:18), which picked up at the principal ports those who wished to be in Jerusalem for the forthcoming festival. But, getting wind of a plot to kill him when once he was on board this ship, he changed his plan, and decided to go back to Macedonia and sail from there. Originally the plan probably was to be in Jerusalem for Passover, but when the delay caused by the news of the plot made that impossible, he determined at least to arrive there in time for Pentecost (*cf.* v. 16).

4–5 Paul was not going to make his journey to Jerusalem unaccompanied. A number of Gentile Christians went with him: these were no doubt representatives of the various churches which were contributing to the gift for the relief of the poverty of the Jerusalem Christians. The churches of Macedonia were represented by Sopater,[16] Aristarchus[17] and Secundus; those of Galatia

---

[12] G. S. Duncan, however, thinks that after Paul reached Dyrrhachium "there was a period of evangelistic work, which need not have been extensive or prolonged, in Illyricum; from there, as winter approached, he sailed south to Nicopolis [*cf.* Tit. 3:12], and in course of time he came to Corinth" (*St. Paul's Ephesian Ministry* [London, 1929] p. 221). He links Titus's visit to Dalmatia in 2 Tim. 4:10 with this Illyrian ministry.

[13] See Rom. 16:23, and *cf.* Ch. 18:7 with exposition.

[14] *Cf.* Rom. 1:9 ff.; 15:22 ff.

[15] See p. 394, n. 33 (on Ch. 19:21).

[16] Possibly the Sosipater of Rom. 16:21 (*cf.* p. 369, n. 13).

[17] *Cf.* Chs. 19:29; 27:2; Col. 4:10.

by Gaius of Derbe[18] and Timothy (of Lystra), and those of Asia by Tychicus[19] and Trophimus.[20] No mention is made of representatives from Corinth, but we may infer from 2 Cor. 8:6 ff. that the Corinthian contribution was entrusted to Titus and two other brethren, sent by Paul to Corinth to receive it. The question then arises why Titus is not mentioned here, and that is part of a larger question, why one who appears from the Pauline epistles to have been such a trusted colleague of the apostle is mentioned nowhere in Acts. It is difficult to find a more convincing answer than that suggested by Ramsay, that Titus was Luke's brother (*St. Paul the Traveller*, pp. xxxviii, 390).[21] At any rate, it may be that when the "we" narrative is resumed in v. 5, Titus as well as Luke himself is tacitly included. The others who are mentioned by name crossed the Aegean ahead of the apostle and waited for him at Troas.

6 He, however, waited at Philippi until the week of the Unleavened Bread was completed (in A.D. 57 it lasted from April 7 to 14). Then he set sail with Luke (presumably from Neapolis; *cf.* Ch. 16:11). It is noteworthy that the new "we" narrative begins at Philippi, where the former one ended. Luke may have been the bearer of the gift from Philippi. They joined the other members of the party in five days; the prevailing winds made the voyage from Neapolis to Troas considerably longer than that from Troas to Neapolis (*cf.* Ch. 16:11).

18 See n. 5 above.
19 *Cf.* Eph. 6:21 f.; Col. 4:7 f.; 2 Tim. 4:12; Tit. 3:12.
20 *Cf.* Ch. 21:29; 2 Tim. 4:20.
21 The further question arises whether Luke himself may not have been one of the two brethren sent with Titus to receive the Corinthian contribution—more particularly, "the brother whose praise (ἔπαινος) in the gospel is spread through all the churches" (2 Cor. 8:18). This is suggested in a passage from Origen quoted by Eusebius (*Ecclesiastical History* vi. 25), where Luke's Gospel is described as "the Gospel praised (ἐπαινούμενον) by Paul." (Possibly, however, to Eusebius at least, ἐπαινούμενον simply means "quoted", and Eusebius has in his mind here the mistaken notion which he expresses in *Eccl. Hist.* iii. 4. that Paul's phrase "according to my gospel" in Rom. 2:16; 16:25, and 2 Tim. 2:8, refers to the Gospel according to Luke.) We may compare the echo of 2 Cor. 8:18 ("whose praise is in the Gospel") in the Collect for St. Luke's Day (October 18) in the Anglican *Book of Common Prayer* (quoted on p. 27).

2. THE JOURNEY TO JERUSALEM

(Chs. 20:7–21:16)

(a) Paul at Troas (Ch. 20:7–12)

7 And upon the first day of the week, when we were gathered together to break bread, Paul discoursed with them, intending to depart on the morrow; and prolonged his speech until midnight.

8 And there were many lights[22] in the upper chamber where we were gathered together.

9 And there sat in the window a certain young man named Eutychus, borne down with deep sleep; and as Paul discoursed yet longer, being borne down by his sleep he fell down from the third story, and was taken up dead.

10 And Paul went down, and fell on him, and embracing him said, Make ye no ado; for his life is in him.

11 And when he was gone up, and had broken the bread, and eaten, and had talked with them a long while, even till break of day, so he departed.

12 And they[23] brought the lad alive, and were not a little comforted.

The description of this critical journey of Paul and his disciples to Jerusalem is given in considerable detail; some have compared the detailed description in the Third Gospel of Jesus' critical journey to Jerusalem with *His* disciples. But the kind of detail is different; the chronological exactitude of this second "we" narrative of Acts is due mainly to the fact that Luke was one of the party and kept a log-book.

7 The statement that at Troas the travellers and their fellow-Christians dwelling in that port met together for the breaking of the bread "upon the first day of the week" is the earliest unambiguous evidence we have for the Christian practice of gathering

---

22 Better "torches" (Gk. λαμπάδες). Cod. D has ὑπολαμπάδες ("windows"), but the Latin text of the same MS. (d) has *faculae* ("little torches").

23 The Western text reads "And as they were saying farewell, he [*i.e.* Paul] brought the lad alive . . ."

together for worship on that day.[24] The breaking of the bread probably denotes a fellowship meal in the course of which the Eucharist was celebrated (*cf.* Ch. 2:42). This Sunday fell almost at the end of the travellers' week at Troas; they intended to continue their journey next day. They met in the evening[25]—a convenient time for many members of the Gentile churches, who were not their own masters and were not free in the daytime—and Paul talked to them. Church meetings were not regulated by the clock in those days, and the opportunity of listening to Paul was not one to be cut short; what did it matter if he went on conversing with them until midnight?

8–10 But the air in that crowded upper room began to grow heavy with the smoke of torches which had been lit to dispel the evening darkness, and a young man named Eutychus, even though he sat at the window (a mere opening in the wall), where the air was freshest, found it impossible to keep awake. Perhaps he had put in a hard day's work from dawn to sunset, and now in the stuffy atmosphere not even the words of an apostle could keep him from falling fast asleep. Suddenly he overbalanced, and fell through the window to the ground beneath—and the room was three stories up. No wonder then that he was "taken up dead," as Luke says, "implying apparently that, as a physician, he had satisfied himself on the point" (Ramsay, *St. Paul the Traveller*, pp. 290 f.). The treatment which Paul gave the youth—similar to that given in similar circumstances by Elijah and Elisha in the OT (1 Kings 17:21, 2 Kings 4:34 f.).—suggests artificial respiration. But Paul's words, as he bade the people stop making a fuss, "for his life is in him" (v. 10), should not be pressed to mean that he was not actually dead for a brief space of time in the strict sense of the word. Luke probably intends us to understand that his life returned to him when Paul embraced him. But it may have been a few hours before Eutychus recovered consciousness.

11–12 After this untoward interruption, Paul resumed his

[24] See O. Cullmann, *Early Christian Worship* (Eng. tr., London, 1953), pp. 10 ff., 88 ff. In the still earlier mention of the "first day of the week" in 1 Cor. 16:2 there is no explicit reference to a Christian gathering, though it may well be implied. *Cf.* also the implications of John 20:19, 26.

[25] On Sunday evening, not Saturday evening; Luke is not using the Jewish reckoning from sunset to sunset but the Roman reckoning from midnight to midnight; although it was apparently after sunset that they met, "break of day" (v. 11) was "on the morrow" (v. 7).

discourse. It was probably past midnight (and therefore properly Monday morning) when they "broke the bread" and took their fellowship meal;[26] then Paul continued to talk to them until daybreak. At daybreak the ship on which they were to sail was due to leave, and the party went on board—all except Paul, who stayed till the last possible moment, probably to be assured of Eutychus's complete restoration to consciousness and health, and then took a short cut by land to join the ship at Assos.

(b) From Troas to Miletus (Ch. 20:13–16)

13 But we,[27] going before to the ship, set sail for Assos, there intending to take in Paul: for so had he appointed, intending himself to go by land.

14 And when he met us at Assos, we took him in, and came to Mitylene.

15 And sailing from thence, we came the following day over against Chios; and the next day[28] we touched at Samos; and[29] the day after we came to Miletus.

16 For Paul had determined to sail past Ephesus, that he might not have to spend time in Asia; for he was hastening, if it were possible for him, to be at Jerusalem the day of Pentecost.

13 The ship which they boarded at Troas was a coasting vessel, due to put in at the main ports along the coast of Asia Minor, although it was a quicker vessel than some which they might have taken, as is evident from the fact that it did not put in at Ephesus. In one of the harbours of south-west Asia Minor they expected to find another ship which would take them to Syria and Palestine; and so it turned out (cf. Ch. 21:1 f.).

When it left Troas, the ship had to round Cape Lectum to get to Assos. Paul waited at Troas a little longer, and then, taking the

---

[26] In v. 11 κλάσας τὸν ἄρτον (where the article points back to κλάσαι ἄρτον in v. 7) refers to the eucharistic breaking of the bread, while γευσάμενος refers to the fellowship meal.

[27] Ephrem the Syrian's commentary on Acts (preserved in an Armenian translation) presupposes an Old Syriac text which read here: "But I Luke, and those who were with me, went on board." If this reconstruction is right, it affords evidence of the Lukan authorship of Acts comparable in date to that of the anti-Marcionite Prologue to the Third Gospel. See F. C. Conybeare's translation of Ephrem in *Beginnings* iii (London, 1926), p. 442.

[28] Cod. B and some minuscules read "in the evening."

[29] The Western and Byzantine texts insert "having tarried at Trogyllia (or Trogyllium)"; cf. AV.

THE BOOK OF THE ACTS

direct road by land to Assos, was able to get there in time to join his companions on board their ship.

14-16 From Assos, the ship brought them to Mitylene, the chief city of the island of Lesbos; then, sailing by the islands of Chios and Samos, they came to Miletus. The additional words, "and tarried at Trogyllia", which the Western and Byzantine texts exhibit after "Samos", are not likely to have been interpolated and may have fallen out of the Alexandrian textual tradition. Trogyllia is a promontory jutting out from the mainland to the south-east of Samos so as to form a narrow passage less than a mile wide. "On Wednesday morning," says Ramsay, "they ran straight across to the west point of Samos, and thence kept in towards Miletus; but when the wind fell, they had not got beyond the promontory Trogyllia at the entrance to the gulf, and there, as the Bezan text mentions, they spent the evening" (*op. cit.,* pp. 293 f.). Next day they arrived at Miletus, on the south shore of the Latonian Gulf, at the mouth of the river Maeander;[30] here the ship was to lie in harbour for three or four days. In spite of his natural desire to see Ephesus again, Paul had decided that this was impossible if he was to be sure of reaching Jerusalem in time for Pentecost; therefore, instead of setting sail from Troas in a ship which called at Ephesus, he chose a quicker one which took the straight course from Chios to Samos, across the mouth of the Ephesian Gulf.

(c) Paul Addresses the Elders of Ephesus (Ch. 20:17–35)

17 And from Miletus he sent to Ephesus, and called to him the elders of the church.
18 And when they were come to him, he said unto them, Ye yourselves know, from the first day that I set foot in Asia, after what manner I was with you all the time,[31]
19 serving the Lord with all lowliness of mind, and with tears, and with trials which befell me by the plots of the Jews;
20 how I shrank not from declaring unto you anything

[30] Even at that date the Latonian Gulf was largely silted up by the Maeander. The presence of a Jewish colony at Miletus is attested by an inscription in the theatre, allocating a section of the seats to Jews and God-fearers.
[31] Cod. D "for three years or even more" (*cf.* v. 31).

that was profitable, and teaching you publicly, and from house to house,

21 testifying both to Jews and to Greeks repentance toward God, and faith toward our Lord Jesus Christ.[32]

22 And now, behold, I go bound in the spirit unto Jerusalem, not knowing the things that shall befall me there:

23 save that the Holy Spirit testifieth unto me in every city, saying that bonds and afflictions abide me.

24 But I hold not my life of any account as dear unto myself,[33] so that I may accomplish my course,[34] and the ministry which I received from the Lord Jesus, to testify[35] the gospel of the grace of God.

25 And now, behold, I know that ye all, among whom I went about preaching the kingdom,[36] shall see my face no more.

26 Wherefore I testify unto you this day, that I am pure from the blood of all men.

27 For I shrank not from declaring unto you the whole counsel of God.

28 Take heed unto yourselves, and to all the flock, in which the Holy Spirit hath made you bishops, to feed the church of the Lord[37] which he purchased with his own blood.

29 I know that after my departing grievous wolves shall enter in among you, not sparing the flock;

30 and from among your own selves[38] shall men arise, speaking perverse things, to draw away the disciples after them.

[32] "Christ" is omitted by Cod. B and a few other authorities; Cod. D reads "through our Lord Jesus Christ."

[33] The Western text expands: "But I make no reckoning of anything for myself nor do I value my own life as precious to me." The Byzantine text reads: "But I make no reckoning of anything nor do I hold my life precious to myself" (cf. AV).

[34] The Byzantine text adds "with joy" (cf. AV).

[35] The Western text adds "to Jews and Greeks."

[36] The Western text adds "of Jesus"; the Byzantine text adds "of God" (cf. AV).

[37] Read "God" (τοῦ θεοῦ) with ℵ B and several other authorities, rather than "the Lord" (τοῦ κυρίου) with A C and the Western text. The Byzantine text exhibits the conflate reading "the Lord and God" (κυρίου καὶ θεοῦ). The reading "the Lord" was apparently substituted for "God" as a result of understanding τοῦ αἵματος τοῦ ἰδίου as meaning "His own blood" (this is, in fact, the only possible sense of the Byzantine text τοῦ ἰδίου αἵματος). For the true rendering, "the blood of His own (one)", see n. 59 below.

[38] Cod. B reads "you" (ὑμῶν) for "your own selves" (ὑμῶν αὐτῶν).

411

31 Wherefore watch ye, remembering that by the space
of three years I ceased not to admonish every one night
and day with tears.

32 And now I commend you to God,[39] and to the word of
his grace, which is able to build *you* up, and to give
you the inheritance among all them that are sanctified.[40]

33 I coveted no man's silver, or gold, or apparel.

34 Ye yourselves know that these hands ministered unto
my necessities, and to them that were with me.

35 In all things I gave you an example, that so laboring
ye ought to help the weak, and to remember the words
of the Lord Jesus, that he himself said, It is more
blessed to give than to receive.

17 While the ship remained in harbour at Miletus, Paul sent
a message to Ephesus, which lay some thirty miles away, asking
the elders of the church in that city to come and see him. Ramsay
calculates that they arrived at Miletus on the third day of Paul's
stay there.[41] Paul's desire was to give them such encouragement
and exhortation as they needed, and the speech that follows (vv.
18–35) gives a summary of what he said.

This speech is quite distinctive among all the speeches reported
in Acts. It is the only Pauline speech delivered to Christians which
Luke has recorded, and we should not be surprised to discover
how rich it is in parallels to the Pauline Epistles. To explain these
parallels on the lines of literary criticism, by supposing that Luke
drew some suitable material for the composition of this speech
from the epistles, appears to be ruled out by the consideration
that, elsewhere throughout Acts, Luke betrays no knowledge of
them, even in places where they would have served him as first-
rate sources had they been accessible to him. Besides, even on
grounds of literary criticism, the report could not be described as
a mere cento of passages from Paul's letters. "The speech is altogether in the style of the writer of *Acts,* and yet offers phenomena
which seem to imply that he was guided by memory in the composition" (Percy Gardner, "The Speeches of St. Paul in Acts", in
Cambridge Biblical Essays, ed. H. B. Swete [Cambridge, 1909],

---

[39] For "God" Cod. B and a few minuscules, together with the Old Latin
codex *gigas* and the Coptic versions, read "the Lord."

[40] The Western text appears to have added here: "To him be the glory for
ever and ever. Amen."

[41] *St. Paul the Traveller,* p. 294.

p. 403).[42] Just as the sermon in the synagogue at Pisidian Antioch (Ch. 13:16 ff.) is a sample of Paul's approach to synagogue audiences, and his speeches at Lystra (Ch. 14 : 15 ff.) and Athens (Ch. 17 : 22 ff.) are samples of his approach to pagan audiences, so we may say that this Milesian speech is a sample of his ministry to Christian audiences. But it is more than the sort of thing that Paul was accustomed to say to Christian audiences; it is plain that Luke was present when this speech was delivered (cf. Ch. 21:1), and there is every reason to believe that Luke is here giving the gist of what he remembered hearing Paul say on this particular occasion.[43]

This speech is mainly hortatory, but also in some degree apologetic. It seems to be implied here and there that Paul's adversaries in the province of Asia had been prejudicing his converts against him in his absence; he therefore defends his teaching and general behaviour by appealing to his hearers' personal knowledge of him.[44] He perceives that the opposition to his teaching which has already developed in the Ephesian church will increase, and that heretical teachers may be expected to arise—"fierce wolves ... not sparing the flock" (v. 29, RSV). The elders must therefore act as true shepherds to the sheep which have been entrusted to their care by the Holy Spirit Himself.

i. Paul's Defence of his Conduct (vv. 18–21)

18–21 In the introductory part of his speech he reminds them of his manner of life all the time he spent in their province—his humble and faithful service,[45] his sorrows, the dangers to which he was exposed by reason of Jewish hostility and conspiracy, his incessant proclamation of the gospel to Jews and Gentiles alike,[46] the profitable, all-embracing Christian instruction which he gave

---

[42] Gardner says that among the Pauline discourses in Acts "that at Miletus has the best claim of all to be historic" (op. cit., p. 401).

[43] Cf. also F. H. Chase, The Credibility of the Book of the Acts of the Apostles (London, 1902), pp. 234 ff.; A. Harnack, The Acts of the Apostles (Eng. tr., London, 1909), p. 129.

[44] For similar appeals to personal knowledge cf. Gal. 4:13; Phil. 4:15; 1 Thess. 2:1 f., 5, 10 f.; 2 Thess. 3:7 ff.

[45] Cf. 1 Cor. 2:3; 2 Cor. 10:1, etc.; for the general inculcation of his personal example cf. 1 Cor. 11:1; Phil. 4:9.

[46] Cf. Rom. 1:14 ff. for the collocation of Jews and Greeks. His summing up of the attitude which the preaching of the gospel was calculated to produce in its hearers as "repentance toward God, and faith toward our Lord Jesus Christ", finds parallels in Ch. 26:20; Rom. 10:9 ff.; 2 Cor. 5:20 ff.

to his converts both publicly[47] and in private homes. In v. 19 we have a hint of trying experiences in Ephesus of which Luke gives us little idea elsewhere in Acts, but of which further hints are given in Paul's own correspondence.[48] In so far as these trying experiences rose out of the opposition of the provincial Jews, they brought him face to face once again, and perhaps in a specially intensified form, with the problem of the Jews' general refusal of the gospel—the problem with which he grapples in Rom. 9–11, written only a few months before this address at Miletus.

ii. P a u l ' s   P r o s p e c t s (vv. 22–27)

22–24 He then goes on to tell them of his present enterprise: he is bound for Jerusalem under a sense of spiritual constraint.[49] When, a short time previously, he wrote to the Roman Christians about his plan to visit Jerusalem, he plainly had misgivings about the reception which might await him there: he asked for their prayers that he might be "delivered from them that are disobedient in Judaea," as also that the Gentile churches' contributions might be acceptable to the Jerusalem church (Rom. 15:31). These misgivings found increasing confirmation as he went from port to port on his voyage to Palestine: in city after city the Holy Spirit, speaking presumably through the lips of prophets, as later at Tyre and Caesarea (Ch. 21:4, 11), showed him that imprisonment and tribulation would be his lot when he reached Jerusalem. But he was ready to surrender his liberty and, if need be, his life itself for the sake of Christ and His service.[50] Self-preservation was not a motive highly esteemed by Paul; his main concern was to fulfil the course[51] which Christ had marked out for him, bearing witness to the good news of God's free grace in Christ. Life or death was not the issue that really mattered: what mattered most was, as he said himself to another church, that "Christ shall be magnified in my body, whether by life, or by death" (Phil. 1:20).

25–27 And now he was speaking to the leaders of the Ephesian church as one who spoke to them for the last time. He was bidding

[47] First in the synagogue and later in the lecture-hall of Tyrannus.
[48] See p. 393 with n. 29.
[49] Cf. Ch. 19:21 (with p. 394, n. 32).
[50] For Paul's ready surrender of himself for the gospel's sake cf. 2 Cor. 4:7 ff.; 6:4 ff.; 12:9 f.; Phil. 1:20; 2:17; 3:8; Col. 1:24.
[51] For the comparison of Christian service to a race to be run cf. 1 Cor. 9:24 ff.; Gal. 2:2; Phil. 2:16; 2 Tim. 4:7; and also Paul's own words about John the Baptist in Ch. 13:25.

farewell to the Aegean shores: henceforth, if he got safely away from Jerusalem, the western Mediterranean was to be his field of action.[52] (Whether in fact the Ephesians ever did see him again is not of primary relevance to the exegesis of these words.)[53] He had lived in their city and gone in and out among them as a herald of the kingdom of God:[54] he had planted the gospel seed, and it was their business to water it. They could bear witness to his faithfulness in the proclamation of the divine message: he had made the whole of God's will plain to them.[55] Like the trustworthy watchman in Ezek. 33:1–6, he had sounded the trumpet aloud so that all the province of Asia had heard: if there were any who paid no heed, their blood would be upon their own heads; Paul was free of responsibility for their doom.

iii. Paul's Charge and Example (vv. 28–35)

28 Upon these elders, then, lay a solemn responsibility. The Holy Spirit had entrusted them with the charge of the people of God in Ephesus: they had to care for them as shepherds for their flock. There was in apostolic times no distinction between elders (presbyters) and bishops such as we find from the second century onwards: the leaders of the Ephesian church are indiscriminately described as elders, bishops (*i.e.* superintendents) and shepherds (or pastors).[56]

[52] *Cf.* Rom. 15:23 ff.

[53] We can make no certain inference about the date of Acts from v. 25; in fact, directly contrary inferences have been drawn from it. Harnack, concluding from 2 Tim. 4 that Paul did visit Asia again, takes the fact that Luke records this premonition (which was, he holds, falsified by the event) as evidence that Acts was written before the death of Paul and indeed before his release from his first Roman imprisonment (*Date of the Acts and of the Synoptic Gospels* [Eng. tr., London, 1911], p. 103). Others have regarded v. 25 as proof positive that Paul was dead before Luke wrote (*cf.*, *e.g.*, J. V. Bartlet, *The Acts of the Apostles* [Century Bible, London, 1902], *ad loc.*; E. J. Goodspeed, INT [Chicago, 1937], pp. 191 ff.; M. Dibelius, *Paul* [Eng. tr., London, 1953], p. 10).

[54] A comparison of vv. 24 and 25 suggests that "to testify the gospel of grace of God" is synonymous with "preaching the kingdom"; the dispensationalist school, however, regards them as distinct, and deplores the "confusion which, mingling both characters, never enjoys the simple and full truth of either" (W. Kelly, *The Acts of the Apostles* [3rd edn., London, 1952], p. 306). For the proclamation of the kingdom of God see the exposition of Ch. 1:3 (pp. 33 ff.).

[55] A comparison of v. 27 with v. 20 shows that to Paul "the whole counsel of God" was the measure of what was truly "profitable."

[56] *Cf.* Ch. 14:23, with exposition and note (pp. 296 f.). The verb "feed" in this verse represents ποιμαίνειν, literally "tend as a shepherd", from ποιμήν, "a

Probably the reference to the Holy Spirit here does not mean that their appointment to this sacred ministry had been commanded by prophetic utterance in the church, but rather that they were so appointed and recognized because they were manifestly men on whom the Holy Spirit had bestowed the requisite qualifications for the work.[57] Their responsibility was all the greater in that the flock which they were called upon to tend was no other than the congregation of God which He had purchased for Himself (an echo this of OT language)[58]—and the ransom-price was nothing less than the life-blood of His beloved Son.[59]

29-31 Paul now looks forward to the future, and the prospects for the Ephesian church are not wholly promising. The elders will have to guard the sheep with unceasing vigilance, for ferocious wolves will try to make their way among them and ravage them. As in the parable of the Good Shepherd in John

shepherd" (*cf.* Eph. 4:11; 1 Peter 5:1–4). For other designations by which such men were known in NT times *cf.* Rom. 12:8; 1 Thess. 5:12; 1 Tim. 5:17; Heb. 13:17. The term "elder" (Gk. $\pi\rho\epsilon\sigma\beta\acute{\nu}\tau\epsilon\rho\sigma\varsigma$) has mainly Jewish antecedents, while "bishop" (Gk. $\dot{\epsilon}\pi\acute{\iota}\sigma\varkappa\sigma\pi\sigma\varsigma$, "overseer") has mainly Greek antecedents. *Cf.* Phil. 1:1, where $\dot{\epsilon}\pi\acute{\iota}\sigma\varkappa\sigma\pi\sigma\iota$ in the plural (*i.e.* presbyter-bishops) are mentioned alongside $\delta\iota\acute{\alpha}\varkappa\sigma\nu\sigma\iota$ (*cf.* exposition and notes on Ch. 6:6). In the Pastoral Epistles the terms $\pi\rho\epsilon\sigma\beta\acute{\nu}\tau\epsilon\rho\sigma\varsigma$ and $\dot{\epsilon}\pi\acute{\iota}\sigma\varkappa\sigma\pi\sigma\varsigma$ appear still to be used interchangeably (*cf.* 1 Tim. 3:1 ff.; Titus 1:5 ff.). See J. B. Lightfoot, *Philippians* (London, 1868), pp. 95 ff., 181 ff. (dissertation on "The Christian Ministry"); E. Hatch, *The Organisation of the Early Christian Churches* (London, 1888), pp. 26 ff.; T. M. Lindsay, *The Church and the Ministry in the Early Centuries* (London, 1902); H. B. Swete (ed.), *Essays on the Early History of the Church and Ministry* (London, 1918); B. H. Streeter, *The Primitive Church* (London, 1929), pp. 27 ff.; K. E. Kirk (ed.), *The Apostolic Ministry* (London, 1946); T. W. Manson, *The Church's Ministry* (London, 1948), pp. 53 ff.; F. F. Bruce, *The Growing Day* (London, 1951), pp. 65 ff.

[57] *Cf.* 1 Cor. 12:4 ff.

[58] *Cf.* in particular Ps. 74:2 ("Remember thy congregation [Heb. *'edah*, LXX $\sigma\nu\nu\alpha\gamma\omega\gamma\acute{\eta}$], which thou hast gotten of old, which thou hast redeemed . . ."); Isa. 43:21 ("the people which I formed for myself" [LXX $\pi\epsilon\rho\iota\epsilon\pi\sigma\iota\eta\sigma\acute{\alpha}\mu\eta\nu$, the same verb as is translated "purchased" here]). For "church" (Gk. $\dot{\epsilon}\varkappa\varkappa\lambda\eta\sigma\acute{\iota}\alpha$) *cf.* exposition and notes on Ch. 5:11 (p. 116).

[59] Gk. $\delta\iota\grave{\alpha}$ $\tau\sigma\tilde{\nu}$ $\alpha\tilde{\iota}\mu\alpha\tau\sigma\varsigma$ $\tau\sigma\tilde{\nu}$ $\dot{\iota}\delta\acute{\iota}\sigma\nu$ should be translated here "by means of the blood of His own one"; this sense of $\tilde{\iota}\delta\iota\sigma\varsigma$ is well attested in the papyri, where it is "used thus as a term of endearment to near relations, *e.g.* $\acute{\sigma}$ $\delta\epsilon\tilde{\iota}\nu\alpha$ $\tau\tilde{\omega}$ $\dot{\iota}\delta\acute{\iota}\omega$ $\chi\alpha\acute{\iota}\rho\epsilon\iota\nu$ ['So-and-so to his own (friend), greeting']" (J. H. Moulton, *Grammar of NT Greek* i [Edinburgh, 1906], p. 90). As used here, it is the equivalent of Heb. *yachid* ("only"), elsewhere represented by Gk. $\dot{\alpha}\gamma\alpha\pi\eta\tau\acute{\sigma}\varsigma$ ("beloved"), $\dot{\epsilon}\varkappa\lambda\epsilon\varkappa\tau\acute{\sigma}\varsigma$ ("choice") and $\mu\sigma\nu\sigma\gamma\epsilon\nu\acute{\eta}\varsigma$ ("only begotten"). In view of this, it is unnecessary to suppose, as Hort did, that $\nu\acute{\iota}\sigma\tilde{\nu}$ ("son") may have dropped out of the text after $\dot{\iota}\delta\acute{\iota}\sigma\nu$.

10:1 ff., so here the true pastors of the flock are contrasted with false teachers, described as wolves because of the havoc they cause.[60] But it is not only from intruders such as these that false teaching will proceed; from the ranks of the leaders of the church itself some will arise to seduce their followers into heretical by-paths. That this development did in fact take place at Ephesus is evident from the Pastoral Epistles (cf. 1 Tim. 1:19 f.; 4:1 ff.; 2 Tim. 1:15; 2:17 f.; 3:1 ff.) and from the letter to the Ephesian church in Rev. 2:1 ff. The Pastoral Epistles tell of a general revolt against Paul's teaching throughout the province of Asia; and John is bidden to reproach the Christians of Ephesus for having abandoned their first love. Foreseeing these trends, then, Paul urges the Ephesian elders to be watchful,[61] and to follow his own example, remembering how he himself had shown such careful and tearful concern for his converts during his three years in Ephesus,[62] pointing out unceasingly, night and day, the right path for their feet.[63]

32 And now he was leaving them; they could no longer count upon his personal presence for such pastoral guidance and wise admonition. But, though Paul might go, God was ever with them, and so was God's word which they had received—the word that proclaimed His grace in redeeming them and His grace in sanctifying them. To God, then, and to this word of His, Paul solemnly committed them. By that word, as they accepted and obeyed it, they would be built up in faith and love together with their fellow-Christians;[64] by that word, too, they were assured of their inheritance among all the people of God, sanctified by His grace.[65] In

60 "False prophets" are described as wolves in sheep's clothing in Matt. 7:15; cf. also 4 Ezra 5:18 and 1 Enoch 89:13 ff. for similar use of the wolf figure.

61 "Watch ye" in v. 31 represents Gk. γρηγορεῖτε (literally "keep awake")— a "pastoral word", as Bengel calls it in his *Gnomon* (*ad loc.*). Cf. 1 Cor. 16:13; Col. 4:2; 1 Thess. 5:6, 10, and also the synonymus ἀγρυπνέω in a similar context in Heb. 13:17 ("they watch in behalf of your souls").

62 For the chronology of Paul's residence at Ephesus cf. p. 389, n. 20 (on Ch. 19:10).

63 For "admonish" (Gk. νουθετέω) cf. 1 Cor. 4:14; Col. 1:28.

64 "This message of the free bounty of God is the word which has the greatest effect on the heart of man, and so it is *able to build up* the church" (R. B. Rackham, *The Acts of the Apostles* [London, 1902], *ad loc.*).

65 For the inheritance among the saints cf. Ch. 26:18b, and Col. 1:12 ("the Father . . . hath made us meet to be partakers of the inheritance of the saints in light").

due course Paul and all the apostles passed from earthly life; but the apostolic teaching which they left behind as a sacred deposit to be guarded by their successors, preserved not merely in the memory of their hearers but in the scriptures of the NT canon, remains with us to this day as the word of God's grace. And those are most truly in the apostolic succession who receive this apostolic teaching, along with the rest of Holy Writ, as their rule of faith and practice.

33–35 Returning once more to the example which he had set them, he reminds them finally that those who take care of the people of God must do so without thought of material reward. As Samuel called all Israel to witness when he was about to lay down his office as judge (1 Sam. 12:3), so Paul calls the Ephesian elders to witness that all the time he spent with them he coveted nothing that was not his; on the contrary, he did not even avail himself of his right to be maintained by those for whose spiritual welfare he cared, but earned his living—and that of his colleagues—by his own labours: "these hands," he said (inevitably with the attendant gesticulation), "ministered unto my necessities, and to them that were with me" (v. 34).[66] Let those to whom he was speaking likewise labour and thus support not only themselves but others as well—the sick in particular.[67] Thus they would fulfil the saying of the Lord Jesus, which they ought ever to bear in mind: "It is more blessed to give than to receive" (v. 35). This dominical *logion* does not appear in any of the Gospels, but its spirit is manifested in many other sayings of Jesus which they record (*cf.* Luke 6:38; 11:9 ff.; John 13:34).[68] And on this appropriate note Paul concludes his exhortation to the Epesian elders.

[66] For parallels to this insistence on Paul's part *cf.* 1 Cor. 4:12; 9:3 ff.; 2 Cor. 4:5; 10:1 ff.; 11:7 ff.; 12:13; 1 Thess. 2:3 ff.; 2 Thess. 3:7 ff.

[67] *Cf.* the admonitions in Rom. 15:1; Gal. 6:2; Eph. 4:28; 1 Thess. 4:11 f.; 5:14; 2 Thess. 3:10 ff.

[68] No doubt collections of the sayings of Jesus were already in circulation by A.D. 57. For other references in the epistles to sayings of Jesus see Rom. 14:14; 1 Cor. 7:10; 9:14; 11:24 f.; 1 Thess. 4:15 ff.; 1 Tim. 5:18. H. Windisch (in *Beginnings* ii [London, 1922], p. 331) argues that the occurrence of this *logion* here shows that Luke the physician could not have been the author of Luke-Acts, because if he were, he would certainly have incorporated "so fine a saying" in his Gospel. This argument, says W. L. Knox, "betrays a complete failure to understand his methods" (*Some Hellenistic Elements in Primitive Christianity* [London, 1944], p. 29). *Cf.* also J. Jeremias, *Unbekannte Jesusworte* (Zürich, 1948), pp. 10 f., 57 n., 67 ff.

(d)   He Leaves Miletus (Ch. 20:36–38)

36 And when he had thus spoken, he kneeled down and prayed with them all.

37 And they all wept sore, and fell on Paul's neck and kissed him,

38 sorrowing most of all for the word which he had spoken, that they should behold his face no more. And they brought him on his way unto the ship.

36–38 When Paul had finished speaking to them, and had knelt in prayer with them, they bade him an affectionate but sorrowful farewell. In particular, what he had said about their not seeing him again filled their hearts with grief and their eyes with tears. But the ship was about to set sail from Miletus after its stay of several days, and the Ephesian elders escorted Paul to the quay before returning home.

CHAPTER XXI

(e) Arrival at Tyre (Ch. 21:1–6)

1 And when it came to pass that we were parted from them and had set sail, we came with a straight course unto Cos, and the next day unto Rhodes, and from thence unto Patara;[1]

2 and having found a ship crossing over unto Phoenicia, we went aboard, and set sail.

3 And when we had come in sight of Cyprus, leaving it on the left hand, we sailed unto Syria, and landed at Tyre: for there the ship was to unlade her burden.

4 And having found the disciples, we tarried there seven days: and these said to Paul through the Spirit, that he should not set foot in Jerusalem.

5 And when it came to pass that we had accomplished the days, we departed and went on our journey; and they all, with wives and children, brought us on our way till we were out of the city: and kneeling down on the beach, we prayed, and bade each other farewell;

6 and we went on board the ship, but they returned home again.

1–2 The Ephesian elders escorted Paul and his friends to the ship, and at last, as Luke says, "we tore ourselves away from them" (if we press the verb he uses to yield its full etymological sense).[2] From Miletus they sailed to Cos, one of the islands of the Dodecanese, and the following day they put in at the harbour of Rhodes. "Rhodes" here refers to the city rather than to the island of the same name (the chief island of the Dodecanese). The city of Rhodes, lying at the island's north-eastern extremity, was founded in 408 B.C. by the amalgamation of three earlier settlements. As the prevailing wind was from the north-east, they were able to accomplish this part of the voyage with a straight course. From Rhodes they sailed east along the south coast of Lycia,

---

1 The Western text adds "and Myra." See n. 3 below.
2 The Greek verb here used is the passive of ἀποσπάω.

putting in at Patara and, according to the Western text, at Myra. It was in one or the other of these two Lycian ports that they found, as they had hoped, a ship bound for Syria and Palestine.[3]

3   The first port at which the new ship was to put in was the Phoenician port of Tyre. This meant a cross-sea voyage instead of a coasting voyage, and the journey was thus considerably shortened.[4] This helped Paul to achieve his intention of being in Jerusalem in time for Pentecost (cf. Ch. 20:16). According to Chrysostom (Homily xlv. 2) the passage from Patara to Tyre took five days. On the way Luke records that they sighted Cyprus on the port side. So they arrived at Tyre, and there it was necessary to spend a week, as the ship's cargo had to be discharged; but the time saved on the voyage from Lycia meant that the party could afford to wait at Tyre until the ship was ready to sail again.

4   They knew that there was a Christian church in Tyre; it had been founded as a result of the Hellenistic dispersion that followed Stephen's death (Ch. 11:19). So Paul and his friends sought out the Tyrian Christians, and spent the week with them. Among these Christians were some who had the gift of prophetic inspiration, and as they foresaw by its means that grave danger awaited Paul at Jerusalem, they besought him not to continue his journey there. But Paul's mind had been made up, and he was not to be diverted from his intention by such predictions. Tyre was not the first place in which such indications had been given him of what lay before him at Jerusalem (cf. Ch. 20:23). We should not conclude that his determination to go on was disobedience to the guidance of the Spirit of God; this determination of his was the fruit of an inward spiritual constraint which would not be gainsaid.[5] It was natural that his friends who by the prophetic spirit were able to foretell his tribulation and imprisonment should try to dissuade him from going on, but with a complete lack of concern for his own safety, so long as he could fulfil his sacred service, Paul

---

[3] Myra was the great port for cross-sea traffic to Syria and Egypt. The Western text may be right in making it the port of trans-shipment (see n. 1 above) if so, it will have fallen out of the Alexandrian textual tradition by homoeoteleuton. On the other hand, Myra may have been interpolated here by an editor who noted that it was the port of trans-shipment on Paul's later voyage to Rome (cf. Ch. 27:5).

[4] The ship was probably a large merchant vessel; smaller vessels hugged the coast.

[5] Cf. Chs. 19:21; 20:22.

like his Master "stedfastly set his face to go to Jerusalem" (cf. Luke 9:51).

5-6 The disciples at Tyre were not old friends of Paul's, as the Ephesian elders were, but the love of Christ is the strongest of bonds, and at the end of a week he and they were as firm friends as if they had known each other all their lives. When the ship was due to set sail, all the Christians of Tyre, with their families, accompanied Paul and his companions to the shore. There they knelt and prayed, before taking an affectionate farewell of each other.[6] Then the Tyrian disciples went back home, while the ship continued its journey.

(f) Arrival at Caesarea (Ch. 21:7-14)

7 And when we had finished the voyage[7] from Tyre, we arrived at Ptolemais; and we saluted the brethren, and abode with them one day.

8 And on the morrow we departed, and came unto Caesarea: and entering into the house of Philip the evangelist, who was one of the seven, we abode with him.

9 Now this man had four virgin daughters, who prophesied.

10 And as we tarried there some days, there came down from Judaea a certain prophet, named Agabus.

11 And coming to us, and taking Paul's girdle, he bound his own feet and hands, and said, Thus saith the Holy Spirit, So shall the Jews at Jerusalem bind the man that owneth this girdle, and shall deliver him into the hands of the Gentiles.

12 And when we heard these things, both we and they of that place besought him not to go up to Jerusalem.

13 Then Paul answered, What do ye, weeping and breaking my heart? for I am ready not to be bound only, but also to die at Jerusalem for the name of the Lord Jesus.

14 And when he would not be persuaded, we ceased, saying, The will of the Lord be done.

---

[6] In the Roman period Tyre was a prosperous commercial city, noted for its purple dye-works. The mole which Alexander the Great had constructed to facilitate his siege of island Tyre in 332 B.C. was continuously widened by accumulations of sand, which formed two smooth beaches.

[7] Or possibly "when we had continued the voyage" (Gk. τὸν πλοῦν διανύσαντες). The Greek expression is attested with the meaning "continue a voyage" rather than "finish a voyage" (see F. Field, *Notes on Translation of the NT* [Cambridge, 1899], pp. 134 f.).

7 From Tyre they continued their voyage, and put in next at Ptolemais, the most southerly of the Phoenician ports. It appears in the OT under the name Acco (*cf.* Judg. 1:31), and although it was known in Greco-Roman times by the name Ptolemais (which it received apparently in honour of Ptolemy II, 285–246 B.C.), it later resumed its original name, by which it is known to the present day—'Akka, or, as it was Gallicized in the days of the Crusades, Acre.[8] At this time it was a Roman colony. It had been evangelized probably at the same time as Tyre, and Paul and his friends spent the day during which the ship remained in harbour there in the company of the Christians of the city.

8 Having set sail again next day, they landed at Caesarea,[9] and here they were entertained by an old friend, Philip. Philip was one of the seven Hellenistic officers appointed in the very early days of the Jerusalem church to supervise the distribution of largesse from the common fund to those who were in need (*cf.* Ch. 6:3 ff.). Later he engaged in missionary activity in Samaria and in the coastal plain of Palestine,[10] and we last heard of him

[8] More fully, St. Jean d'Acre, after the Knights of St. John. The tendency for the old Semitic names to reassert themselves after the Greco-Roman period can be copiously paralleled in Syria and Palestine.

[9] Our exposition assumes that they continued the journey from Ptolemais to Caesarea by sea. This is the most probable interpretation; it is possible, however, though unlikely, that Ptolemais was their ship's terminus, and that they went on to Caesarea by road.

[10] It is this missionary activity that gives him the title "Philip the evangelist." He may be given this title to distinguish him from Philip the apostle, but even so the two Philips were confused by later Christian writers. Polycrates, bishop of Ephesus, writing to Victor of Rome *c.* A.D. 190, includes among the "great luminaries" whose tombs could be pointed out in the province of Asia "Philip, one of the twelve apostles, who sleeps at Hierapolis, with his two daughters who grew old as virgins, and another daughter who lived in the Holy Spirit and now rests in Ephesus." But Eusebius (*Ecclesiastical History* iii. 31), to whom we are indebted for this quotation, obviously understands the reference to be to Philip the evangelist, for he goes on to quote from the Montanist Proclus's *Dialogue* with the Roman presbyter Gaius (*c.* A.D. 200) the claim that "the four daughters of Philip, who were prophetesses, were in Hierapolis in Asia; their tomb is there, and their father's also"—and cites Acts 21:8 as the Biblical reference to this family. Most probably it was Philip the evangelist who later migrated to Asia with his daughters: *cf.* Th. Zahn, *Apostel und Apostelschüler in der Provinz Asien* (Leipzig, 1900), pp. 158 ff.; A. Harnack, *Luke the Physician* (Eng. tr., London, 1907), p. 153. The view that it was Philip the apostle and not the evangelist who went to Asia is expressed by J. B. Lightfoot, *The Epistles to the Colossians and Philemon* (London, 1879), pp. 45 ff., and J. Chapman, *John the Presbyter and the Fourth Gospel* (Oxford, 1911), pp. 64 ff. J. A. Robertson, *The Hidden Romance of the NT*

when he reached Caesarea (Ch. 8:40). Now, after a lapse of twenty years and more, we find him at Caesarea still. It is noteworthy that we left him there in the regular third-personal narrative of Acts, whereas we find him again in the same city in the course of a "'we'" section. This is an incidental confirmation of the integrity of the "we" sections with the main narrative of Acts, as is also the reference to "the seven."

9 By this time, Philip had a flourishing family of four daughters, all of them a credit to their father, for they were prophetesses every one. Some years later Philip and his daughters, with other Palestinian Christians, migrated to the province of Asia and spent their remaining days there. The daughters—or some of them at least—lived to a great age, and were highly esteemed as informants on persons and events belonging to the early years of Judaean Christianity.[11] But even at the time with which we are dealing there is reason to believe that the information which Philip and his daughters were able to give about these things was highly prized by Luke, who made use of the information in the composition of his twofold work[12]—not only during the few days which he spent at Caesarea now, but also during the two years during which Paul was kept in custody there (cf. Ch. 24:27). But we are not given the substance of any of their prophecies. Had the writer of Acts been a romancer, he would certainly not have missed the opportunity of putting some specific prophecies into the young ladies' mouths.

10–11 At Caesarea a further link between the "we" narrative and the general narrative of Acts is provided in the person of the prophet Agabus. In Ch. 11:27 f. we were told how he came down from Jerusalem to Antioch with some other prophets and foretold the famine of A.D. 46. Now, in this "we" section, he comes down[13]

(London, 1920), pp. 71 f., argues that the apostle and the evangelist were one and the same person.

[11] This information we owe to Papias, bishop of Asian Hierapolis, quoted by Eusebius (ib., iii. 39). For the story which they told about Joseph Barsabbas, see the exposition of Ch. 1:23 (p. 50).

[12] Cf. Harnack, Luke the Physician, pp. 155 ff.; J. V. Bartlet, The Acts of the Apostles (London, 1902), p. 23; J. A. Findlay, The Acts of the Apostles (London, 1934), pp. 49 f.

[13] When Luke says that Agabus "came down from Judaea" (v. 10), he uses "Judaea" in the older sense of the territory of Judah, and not in the official sense of the Roman province; Caesarea was in the Roman province of Judaea as much as Jerusalem was. Cf. Ch. 12:19.

to Caesarea and foretells Paul's arrest and imprisonment. Agabus, however, unlike the Tyrian Christians who also spoke "through the Spirit" (v. 4), does not draw the corollary that Paul ought not to continue his journey. The mode of his prophecy is reminiscent of much OT prophecy; it is conveyed in deed as well as in word. As Ahijah the Shilonite rent his new cloak to show how Solomon's kingdom would be disrupted (1 Kings 11:29 ff.), as Isaiah walked naked and barefoot to show how the Egyptians would be led away captive by Assyria (Isa. 20:2 ff.), as Ezekiel mimicked the Babylonian siege of Jerusalem by laying siege himself to a replica of the city (Ezek. 4:1 ff.), so Agabus foretold the binding of Paul by tying himself up with Paul's girdle. The action was as much part of the prophecy as the spoken words; both together communicated the powerful and self-fulfilling word of God (*cf.* Isa. 55:11). The words of Agabus's prophecy resemble our Lord's words about His own arrest by the Jerusalem authorities and delivery to the Gentiles (*cf.* Mark 10:33); in the event, however, Paul was delivered *by* the Gentiles *from* the Jews, who were compelled against their will to give him up.

12–14 If Agabus did not interpret his prophecy to mean that Paul should not go on to Jerusalem, Paul's companions and the Caesarean Christians drew that conclusion, and entreated him with tears not to proceed. But all their entreaties failed to dissuade him. Not that he was unmoved by their weeping; he felt his determination weakening under it,[14] and entreated them in turn to desist. He could not turn aside from the path of obedience and sacrifice, and he was prepared, if necessary, not merely to be imprisoned but to give up his very life in Jerusalem for his Master's sake.[15] They saw that his mind was made up, and so they desisted from their entreaties, praying that the Lord's will might be done. (We may be intended to trace in this prayer an

[14] By "breaking my heart" (Gk. συνθϱύπτοντές μου τὴν καϱδίαν) he means "trying to soften my will," as though they were "pounding it like a washerwoman" (J. A. Findlay, *ad loc.*).

[15] Luke does not explain why Paul regarded his visit to Jerusalem as so solemnly imperative. No doubt his sense of obligation in the matter was bound up with the Gentile collection; *cf.* M. Dibelius, *Paul* (London, 1953), p. 95: "Paul made it one of his special concerns, judging it to be of great importance for the cohesion of the Church (Rom. 15:25–32)—in fact, he deliberately risked his life in taking it to its destination."

echo of the Lord's own prayer in Gethsemane [Luke 22:42].)[16]

(g) Caesarea to Jerusalem (Ch. 21:15–16)

15 And after these days we took up our baggage[17] and went up to Jerusalem.
16 And there went with us also *certain* of the disciples from Caesarea, bringing *with them* one Mnason of Cyprus,[18] an early disciple, with whom we should lodge.

15–16 So, after spending several days in Caesarea, they set forth on the last stage of their journey; making ready for the road[19] they began the sixty-four miles' journey to Jerusalem. They were accompanied by some of the Christian friends from Caesarea, who knew a place in Jerusalem where they could be conveniently entertained.[20] This was the house of Mnason, a Cypriote by family and a foundation-member[21] of the Jerusalem church. Not every member of the intensely Jewish-Christian church of Jerusalem would be prepared to have a party of Gentile Christians in his home; but they might be sure of a hospitable reception from Mnason, who belonged presumably to the Hellenistic and more liberal wing of the church. There is little probability in the Western reading, according to which Mnason acted as their host not at Jerusalem but at some village between Caesarea and Jerusalem where they spent a night.[22] Luke's special mention of the

[16] We may also compare Polycarp's reply in a similar situation: "Let the will of God be done" (*Martyrdom of Polycarp* 7:1).

[17] The Western text reads "we bade them farewell."

[18] Translate rather with ARV margin, "bringing us to one Mnason of Cyprus". The Western text expands thus: "and these brought us to those with whom we were to lodge. And when we arrived at a certain village, we put up with one Mnason of Cyprus, an early disciple." See n. 22.

[19] The Greek term (ἐπισκευασάμενοι) may mean that they packed their baggage or that they got horses ready.

[20] The Caesarean Christians may have arranged this hospitality in Jerusalem during the days that Paul and his party spent at Caesarea.

[21] "An early disciple" (ἀρχαίῳ μαθητῇ) means probably one who had been a disciple from the beginning (ἀρχή).

[22] See n. 18 above. The Western reading here has, however, been read in the light of the Western text of Ch. 11:2 (see pp. 232 f., nn. 2, 6). Thus G. Salmon, reviewing F. Blass's *Acta Apostolorum* (Göttingen, 1895) in *Hermathena* ix (1896), p. 239, finds here a further point of contact between the earlier part of Acts and the "we" narrative, and says it is "a natural combination" that Mnason was one of Peter's converts on his way home from Caesarea to Jerusalem.

fact that Mnason was an early disciple—one of the original Jerusalem disciples—suggests that he acquired some valuable information about earlier days from this man as well as from the household of Philip. Ramsay thought that Mnason was Luke's authority for the episodes of Aeneas and Dorcas (*The Bearing of Recent Discovery on the Trustworthiness of the NT* [London, 1915], p. 309 n.).

3. PAUL AT JERUSALEM

(Chs. 21:17–23:30)

(a) Meeting with James and the Elders (Ch. 21:17–26)

17 And when we were come to Jerusalem,[23] the brethren received us gladly.

18 And the day following Paul went in with us unto James; and all the elders were present.

19 And when he had saluted them, he rehearsed one by one the things which God had wrought among the Gentiles through his ministry.

20 And they, when they heard it, glorified God; and they said unto him. Thou seest, brother, how many thousands there are among the Jews[24] of them that have believed; and they are all zealous for the law:

21 and they have been informed concerning thee, that thou teachest all[25] the Jews who are among the Gentiles to forsake Moses, telling them not to circumcise their children, neither to walk after the customs.

22 What is it therefore? they will certainly hear[26] that thou art come.

23 Do therefore this that we say to thee: We have four men that have a vow on them;

24 these take, and purify thyself with them, and be at charges for them, that they may shave their heads: and all shall know that there is no truth in the things whereof they have been informed concerning thee; but that thou thyself also walkest orderly, keeping the law.

25 But as touching the Gentiles that have believed, we[27]

---

[23] The Western text reads "And when we departed thence [*i.e.* from the half-way village], we came to Jerusalem."

[24] Cod. ℵ omits "among the Jews"; the Western text reads "in Judaea"; the Byzantine text reads "of Jews."

[25] A few authorities, including the Greek codices A D E 33, the Latin Vulgate and the Bohairic Coptic version, omit "all."

[26] We should probably read, with Codd. ℵ A C D, the Byzantine text, the Latin manuscripts e and g and the Vulgate, "a crowd is certainly bound to gather, for they will hear . . ." (*cf.* AV).

[27] The Western text, as in Ch. 15:20, 29, reads "we sent a message decreeing that they should observe nothing of the sort save to guard themselves from what has been sacrificed to idols and blood and fornication" (but the addition

428

wrote, giving judgment that they should keep themselves from things sacrificed to idols, and from blood, and from what is strangled, and from fornication.

26 Then Paul took the men, and the next day purifying himself with them went into the temple, declaring the fulfilment of the days of purification, until the offering was offered for every one of them.

17 On their arrival at Jerusalem, Paul and his companions received a friendly welcome from the leaders of the church. No doubt the gift from the Gentile churches was appreciated, although Luke says nothing about this. Paul had obviously not forgotten the injunction he received from the "pillars" of the Jerusalem church many years before: "Go on remembering the poor" (Gal. 2:10).[28]

18 Of these three "pillars", however, only one was now resident in Jerusalem. Peter and John, and the other original apostles who were still alive, had undertaken more extended missionary responsibilities. But James remained in Jerusalem, exercising wise and judicious leadership over the Nazarene community there, greatly respected not only by the members of that community but by the ordinary Jews of Jerusalem as well.[29] In his administrative responsibilities he had a band of colleagues—the elders of the Jerusalem church. How many they were we are not told, but in view of the multitude of believers in Jerusalem—several thousands,[30] we are told in v. 20—there may well have been seventy of them, constituting a sort of Nazarene Sanhedrin, with James as their president. The whole body of elders was present when, the day after their arrival in the city, Paul and his fellow-travellers paid a visit to James.[31]

of the negative Golden Rule is not repeated here). See p. 308, n. 33, and p. 313, n. 46.

28 See p. 244. While it was a voluntary gift from the Gentile churches, the Jerusalem Christians may have regarded it as something which was due to them, especially in view of the undertaking recorded in Gal. 2:10. Did they look on the Gentile contribution as something analogous to the annual half-shekel which proselytes to Judaism (like other Jews) paid into the temple treasury at Jerusalem?

29 The Jerusalem populace called him "James the Just" (Hegesippus, quoted by Eusebius, *Ecclesiastical History* ii. 23). See Chs. 12:17 and 15:13, with exposition and notes.

30 Gk. πόσαι μυριάδες, literally "how many myriads (tens of thousands)"; but the corresponding English idiom is "how many thousands."

31 In v. 18 the "we" narrative is discontinued, to be resumed in Ch. 27:1;

429

19-21 Paul's narrative of all that God had accomplished through his ministry on both sides of the Aegean since last he visited Jerusalem gave his hearers much cause for joy: the representatives of so many of the Gentile churches which he had planted were with him as living witnesses to the truth of his report, and the gifts which they brought showed that the grace of God which they had received was a matter of deed as well as word. So James and the elders glorified God for His astounding grace manifested to Gentiles.[32]

But there was something that caused them serious anxiety, and now they had an opportunity of unburdening their minds to Paul about it. It was freely rumoured among the Jewish Christians of Jerusalem that Paul not only refused to impose the requirements of the Jewish law on his Gentile converts (that, in the eyes of many, was bad enough, despite the decision taken at the Council of Jerusalem); but he actually dissuaded *Jewish* believers, it was said, from continuing to practise their ancestral customs, handed down from Moses: he even encouraged them to give up circumcising their sons. James and the elders apparently regarded these rumours as false (and indeed there is no evidence for their truth); but it would take more than a verbal assurance to convince the myriad "zealots for the law"[33] in the Jerusalem church that they had been misinformed.

22-24 There was, however, a way in which Paul himself could give the lie effectively to these disturbing reports. If he were seen publicly taking part in one of the ancestral customs, it would be realized that he was, after all, a pious and observant Jew. Now there were four of their number who had undertaken a temporary Nazirite vow.[34] They had apparently contracted some ceremonial defilement and had to undergo a purificatory rite in the temple. Seven days had to elapse before a Nazirite who had contracted such defilement could be purified: such a man

but this does not necessarily mean that Luke was absent from all the intervening incidents, but only that he played no part in them.

[32] *Cf.* Ch. 11:18.

[33] Gk. ζηλωταὶ τοῦ νόμου. The term is not used here in its technical sense (for which see Ch. 1:13, with exposition and notes), but probably as a description of those "of the sect of the Pharisees who believed" (Ch. 15:5); we may compare Paul's description of himself in his former days as a "zealot" for the ancestral traditions (Gal. 1:14).

[34] *Cf.* p. 377 and n. 42 (on Ch. 18:18).

shaved his head on the seventh day and brought his offering on the eighth day: it consisted of one he-lamb, one ewe-lamb, one ram, and accompanying cereal and drink offerings (*cf.* Num. 6:14 f.; Mishnah, *Nazir* vi. 6 ff.). These four men's appointed week would soon be completed; Paul was advised to join with them in the purificatory rite and to pay the expenses of their offering.[35] By this, said the elders, the whole multitude of Jerusalem believers (not to mention the rest of the population of the city) will see for themselves that you conform to the law of Moses and the ancestral customs.

25 They assured him further that they had no wish to go back on the decision of the Apostolic Council and impose legal requirements on Gentile converts.[36] As far as *they* are concerned, they said, we have already enjoined (as you know) that they should abstain from eating flesh that has been sacrificed to idols or killed in such a way that the blood has not been properly drained from it, and from the practice of fornication.

There seems to be no good reason for the frequently expressed opinion that this was really the first time that Paul was told of the terms of the apostolic decree.[37] The repetition of these terms is perfectly natural in the present context. The leaders of the Jerusalem church wish to assure him that their misgivings concern his teaching given to Jewish converts only. We are glad to know, they say in effect, that you do not teach Jewish believers to abandon the law, and we should like you to make this quite clear to the Jewish believers here. As for the Gentile believers, of course, we have already agreed that nothing is to be imposed on them apart from the abstentions detailed in the apostolic letter.

26 Paul fell in with their suggestion, and accompanied the

---

[35] It was regarded as an act of piety on the part of Herod Agrippa I that he paid the expenses of many Nazirites, as Josephus implies in *Antiquities* xix. 6.1.

[36] *Cf.* Ch. 15:19 ff., with exposition and notes (pp. 311 ff.).

[37] Thus H. Lietzmann (*The Beginnings of the Christian Church* [Eng. tr., London, 1949], p. 109) holds that the apostolic decree was drawn up at Jerusalem after the Council, and behind Paul's back, and that "only towards the end of his life, when he again visited Jerusalem, was he given any direct official information." But, as C. W. Emmet says, "it is a *tour de force* of criticism to exclude the Apostle of the Gentiles from any share in the decision which was the charter of their liberty" (in *Beginnings* ii [London, 1922]. p. 277). While the decree formally applied only to Gentile Christians of the double province of Syro-Cilicia, the Jerusalem elders naturally regarded it as applicable in principle to all Gentile Christians throughout the world.

four Nazirites into the temple. Whether he was wise in doing so may well be doubted. There is no evidence that his action produced any such reassuring effect on the zealots for the law as James and his fellow-elders had hoped;[38] and it certainly brought Paul himself into trouble of the gravest kind. But he cannot fairly be charged with a compromise of his own gospel principles.[39] On the contrary, he was acting in strict accordance with his own stated policy: "to those under the law, I became as one under the law—though not being myself under the law—that I might win those under the law" (1 Cor. 9:20, RSV).

(b) Riot in the Temple (Ch. 21:27-36)

27 And when the seven days were almost completed, the Jews from Asia, when they saw him in the temple, stirred up all the multitude and laid hands on him,

28 crying out, Men of Israel, help: This is the man that teacheth all men everywhere against the people, and the law, and this place; and moreover he brought Greeks also into the temple, and hath defiled this holy place.

29 For they had before seen with him in the city Trophimus the Ephesian, whom they supposed that Paul had brought into the temple.

30 And all the city was moved, and the people ran together; and they laid hold on Paul, and dragged him

---

[38] We have no evidence that the Jerusalem Christians bestirred themselves in Paul's behalf after his arrest in the temple court or during his subsequent imprisonment; but we must not press such an argument from silence.

[39] He had on an earlier occasion undertaken a similar Nazirite vow apparently on his own account (cf. Ch. 18:18). The ancestral customs were probably to him personally matters of use and wont, which he normally observed, and especially when doing so helped on his main object in life. But they were to him *religiously* indifferent. The implication of 1 Cor. 7:18a is apparently that Christians of Jewish birth need not give up their national customs. We may compare Paul's own circumcision of Timothy (Ch. 16:3; see exposition and notes on p. 322). What advice, if any, he gave to Jewish Christians about circumcising their sons we cannot say. He was probably not greatly interested in the matter. "Circumcision is nothing, and uncircumcision is nothing; but the keeping of the commandments of God" (1 Cor. 7:19). It was only when it was undertaken as a religious obligation that circumcision carried with it the duty to keep the whole Jewish law (Gal. 5:3). The Tübingen theologians drew sweeping inferences from the Epistle to the Galatians without making sufficient allowance for the controversial occasion of the letter; cf. the difficulties thus made of the present narrative by F. C. Baur, *Paul* (Eng. tr., London, 1876), i. pp. 198 ff., and E. Zeller, *The Acts of the Apostles* (Eng. tr., London, 1875), ii. pp. 68 ff. A truly emancipated spirit such as Paul's is not in bondage to its own emancipation.

out of the temple: and straightway the doors were
shut.

31 And as they were seeking to kill him, tidings came up
to the chief captain of the band, that all Jerusalem was
in confusion.

32 And forthwith he took soldiers and centurions, and ran
down upon them: and they, when they saw the chief
captain and the soldiers, left off beating Paul.

33 Then the chief captain came near, and laid hold on
him, and commanded him to be bound with two chains;
and inquired who he was, and what he had done.

34 And some shouted one thing, some another, among the
crowd: and when he could not know the certainty for
the uproar, he commanded him to be brought into the
castle.

35 And when he came upon the stairs, so it was that he
was borne of the soldiers for the violence of the crowd;

36 for the multitude of the people followed after, crying
out, Away with him.

27–29 The week prescribed for the purification was nearly
completed when a riot broke out in the temple courts. Among
the provincial Jews those of the province of Asia were particularly hostile to Paul, who had incurred their enmity during his
three years' ministry in Ephesus.[40] Some of these Asian Jews had
come to Jerusalem for the festival of Pentecost, and finding Paul
there, they determined to take more effective measures against
him now than they had found possible in Ephesus. Among the
Gentile friends who came with Paul to Jerusalem was the Ephesian
Trophimus, whom these Asian Jews recognized when they saw
him in Paul's company in Jerusalem. When they later came upon
Paul in the temple, in the "Court of Israel,"[41] discharging the
ritual obligations which he had undertaken, they took it into their
heads that Trophimus was still with him. But this was a capital
offence: Gentiles might visit the outer court of the temple (which
for this reason was also known as the Court of the Gentiles), but
they might not penetrate into any of the inner courts on pain of
death. The Roman authorities were so conciliatory of Jewish
religious scruples in this regard that they ratified the death

---

[40] Cf. Ch. 20:19.
[41] The "Court of Israel" was the area of the inner precincts to which
Jewish men who were not priests or Levites were admitted. Cf. p. 83 (on
Ch. 3:1 ff.).

sentence for this trespass even when it was passed on Roman citizens.[42] That no Gentile might unwittingly enter into the forbidden areas, notices in Greek and Latin were fixed to the barrier at the foot of the steps leading up to the inner precincts, warning them that death was the penalty for further ingress.[43] Two of these notices (both in Greek) have been found—one in 1871 and one in 1935[44]—the text of which runs: "No foreigner may enter within the barricade which surrounds the temple and enclosure. Anyone who is caught doing so will have himself to blame for his ensuing death."[45]

If the Asian Jews' charge against Paul had been justified,[46] he would certainly have been guilty of abetting and participating in a most serious crime against Jewish law, and one which was bound immediately to inflame all the Jews of Jerusalem against him. The Asian Jews were well aware of this when they raised a hue and cry against him: this man, they shouted, not content with the attacks on the Jewish people, law and sanctuary which he made in his teaching all over the world (how strongly reminiscent this accusation is of the charge brought against Stephen!),[47] had actually profaned the holy place by bringing Greeks into it.

30 A tumult broke out at once; the crowd that was present in the Court of Israel set upon Paul, and dragged him out of the inner precincts down the steps into the outer court. The news

[42] Titus, the Roman commander-in-chief, reminds the defenders of the temple of this concession in a speech attributed to him by Josephus (*Jewish War*, vi. 2.4).

[43] *Cf.* Josephus, *Jewish War*, v. 5.2; *Antiquities* xv. 11.5: *Against Apion* ii. 8; Philo, *Embassy to Gaius* 212.

[44] See *Palestine Exploration Fund Quarterly*, 1871, p. 132; J. H. Iliffe, "The ΘΑΝΑΤΟΣ Inscription from Herod's Temple: Fragments of a Second Copy," in *Quarterly of Department of Antiquities in Palestine* vi (1938), pp. 1 ff. The former one, discovered by C. S. Clermont–Ganneau, is in the Turkish State Museum in Istanbul; the latter is in the Palestine Museum.

[45] The temple-barrier was thus a very real token of the religious barrier separating Jew and Gentile; it may have been in Paul's mind when he referred to "the middle wall of partition" between the two which was broken down in Christ (Eph. 2:14).

[46] J. Klausner (*From Jesus to Paul* [Eng. tr., London, 1943], p. 400) thinks it possible that their charge was justified, since Paul would have seen no harm in taking a Gentile into the prohibited area, now that all such distinctions had been abolished in Christ. But it is absurd to think that Paul, who on this very occasion was going out of his way to appease Jewish susceptibilities, should have thus wantonly flouted Jewish law and run his own head into danger.

[47] *Cf.* Ch. 6:13, with exposition (pp. 134 f.).

spread quickly throughout the city, and many others hastened to the scene of action. The "gates of the sanctuary" leading from the outer into the inner courts were closed by the temple police, who thus excluded the unseemly violence of the crowd from outraging the sanctity of the sacred precincts proper.

31–32 Meantime, in the outer court, Paul was being fiercely assaulted and beaten by the mob, and his life would not have been worth more than a few minutes' purchase had it not been for the timely intervention of the Roman garrison. North-west of the temple area stood the fortress of Antonia, built by Herod the Great, garrisoned by a cohort of Roman troops under the command of a military tribune.[48] The fortress was connected with the outer court of the temple by two flights of steps, so that the garrison might intervene as quickly as possible in the event of rioting. On this occasion, then, as soon as the military tribune received a report of the tumult that was spreading throughout the city, he summoned a detachment of soldiers—not less than two hundred[49]—with their centurions, and they, running down the steps into the court, forced Paul's assailants to stop manhandling him.

33–34 The military tribune then formally arrested Paul, and ordered him to be handcuffed to two soldiers. No doubt (he thought) the man was a criminal, but whatever he had done to infuriate the mob against himself so, he must be dealt with legally and not by riotous violence. But when he tried to find out what the man had done, or who he was, he could get no clear answer; so confused and conflicting were the denunciations which they hurled at Paul. He must find out the truth of the matter by other means, and so he commanded the soldiers to bring Paul into the fortress.

35–36 The disappointed crowd, thus peremptorily robbed of their quarry, pressed hard upon the soldiers who had custody of Paul, and when they reached the steps leading up to the fortress, Paul had to be carried by the soldiers lest the crowd should pull him down. And as another Jerusalem mob had cried twenty-

[48] Gk. χιλίαρχος (cf. p. 458, n. 32). Details of the fortress are given by Josephus, *Jewish War* v.5.8.
[49] As centurions are mentioned in the plural (v. 32), we may conclude that there were at least two of them, commanding a hundred men apiece. (*Cf.* Ch. 23:23.)

seven years before, so these now kept up the shout, "Away with him!"[50]

(c) Paul Permitted to Address the Rioters (Chs. 21:37–22:1)

37 And as Paul was about to be brought into the castle, he saith unto the chief captain, May I say something unto thee? And he said, Dost thou know Greek?
38 Art thou not then the Egyptian, who before these days stirred up to sedition and led out into the wilderness the four thousand men of the Assassins?
39 But Paul said, I am a Jew, of Tarsus in Cilicia, a citizen of no mean city: and I beseech thee, give me leave to speak unto the people.
40 And when he had given him leave, Paul, standing on the stairs, beckoned with the hand unto the people; and when there was made a great silence, he spake unto them in the Hebrew language, saying,
1 Brethren and fathers, hear ye the defence which I now make unto you.

37–38 The military tribune, trying to size up the situation, suddenly jumped to a conclusion. Some three years previously, an Egyptian adventurer appeared in Jerusalem, claiming to be a prophet, and he led a large band of followers to the Mount of Olives.[51] There he bade them wait until, at his word of command, the walls of the city would fall flat; they should then march in, overthrow the Roman garrison and take possession of the place. But the procurator Felix sent a body of troops against them, who killed several of them and took others prisoner. The Egyptian himself disappeared, wisely. The feelings of those who had been duped by him would not be friendly. Now, thought the tribune, this impostor had been detected and the people were venting their rage on him.

He was therefore surprised when Paul, having been carried to the top of the steps, addressed him in an educated Greek voice and asked permission to speak to the throng below. "Do you speak Greek?" he asked. "I thought you were the Egyptian who

---

[50] Gk. αἶρε αὐτόν. Cf. Luke 23:18; John 19:15.
[51] The story is told by Josephus in *Jewish War* ii. 13.5 and *Antiquities* xx. 8.6. Josephus estimates the Egyptian's followers at 30,000; Luke's figure of 4.000 is more probable.

led four thousand *sicarii*[52] into the wilderness[53] some time back."

39 Paul assured him that he was no Egyptian, but a citizen of the illustrious Cilician city of Tarsus, born of Jewish stock; and he repeated his request for permission to address the angry crowd of Jews. He did not yet reveal his Roman citizenship—or possibly he meant Rome when he described himself as "a citizen of no mean city," but the tribune understood him to refer to his birthplace, Tarsus, which he had just mentioned.[54]

40 The tribune gave Paul the permission which he sought, and the apostle, standing at the top of the steps, which were no doubt strongly guarded by soldiers to prevent any of the crowd from trying to mount them, began to speak to the Jews standing down in the outer court of the temple, addressing them in their Aramaic vernacular. This was a not wholly unsuccessful bid for their tolerance while he spoke. Aramaic was not only the vernacular of Palestinian Jews, but was the common speech of all non-Greek speakers in western Asia, as far east as (and including) the Parthian empire beyond the Euphrates.[55]

1 Speaking Aramaic, then, he asked them to listen to what he had to say for himself, beginning with the same words as Stephen had used many years before at the outset of *his* defence.[56]

---

[52] The rendering "Assassins" (v. 38) represents Gk. σικάριοι, which is a loan-word from Lat. *sicarii*. The *sicarii* or "dagger-men" (from Lat. *sica*, "dagger") made their appearance during the procuratorship of Felix (A.D. 52–59) as bitter enemies of the Romans and pro-Roman Jews. They mingled with crowds at festivals and the like with daggers hidden beneath their cloaks, and stabbed their opponents by stealth. One of their victims was the former high priest Jonathan, son of Annas. *Cf.* Josephus, *Jewish War* ii.13.3; *Antiquities* xx. 8.5, 10.

[53] Josephus tells us that many impostors about this time led their dupes into the wilderness, promising to perform miracles for them (as Moses had done); *cf. Jewish War* ii. 13.4.

[54] See Ramsay, *The Cities of St. Paul* (London, 1907), pp. 174 ff., for the view "that the Jews of Tarsus were, as a body, citizens with full burgess rights." He thinks that this situation must have dated from 171 B.C. when Tarsus received its charter as a Greek city. But the Roman officer paid much more attention to Paul's *Roman* citizenship when it was brought to his notice (*cf.* Ch. 22:27 ff.) than he did to the information that he was a citizen of Tarsus.

[55] Aramaic appears to be meant wherever the "Hebrew" language is mentioned in NT, except in Rev. 9:11; 16:16. See F. Rosenthal, *Die aramaistische Forschung* (Leiden, 1939).

[56] Gk. ἄνδρες ἀδελφοὶ καὶ πατέρες, ἀκούσατε (*cf.* Ch. 7:2).

CHAPTER XXII

(d) Paul Addresses the Rioters (Ch. 22:2-21)

2 And when they heard that he spake unto them in the Hebrew language, they were the more quiet: and he saith,

3 I am a Jew, born in Tarsus of Cilicia, but brought up in this city, at the feet of Gamaliel, instructed according to the strict manner of the law of our fathers, being zealous for God,[1] even as ye all are this day:

4 and I persecuted this Way unto the death, binding and delivering into prisons both men and women.

5 As also the high priest[2] doth bear me witness, and all the estate of the elders: from whom also I received letters unto the brethren, and journeyed to Damascus to bring them also that were there unto Jerusalem in bonds to be punished.

6 And it came to pass, that, as I made my journey, and drew nigh unto Damascus, about noon, suddenly there shone from heaven a great light round about me.

7 And I fell unto the ground, and heard a voice saying unto me,[3] Saul, Saul, why persecutest thou me?[4]

8 And I answered, Who art thou, Lord? And he said unto me, I am Jesus of Nazareth, whom thou persecutest.

9 And they that were with me beheld indeed the light, but they heard not the voice of him that spake to me.

10 And I said, What shall I do, Lord? And the Lord said unto me, Arise, and go into Damascus; and there it shall be told thee of all things which are appointed for thee to do.[5]

---

[1] For "God" the Latin Vulgate reads "the law" and the Harclean Syriac has the asterisked reading "my ancestral traditions" (borrowed, no doubt, from Gal. 1:14).

[2] Some Western authorities add "Ananias" (cf. Ch. 23:2).

[3] Two Western authorities (the Latin codex *gigas* and the marginal reading of the Harclean Syriac) add "in the Hebrew speech" (borrowed from Ch. 26:14).

[4] A number of authorities, mainly Western in character, add "it is hard for thee to kick against the goad" (from Ch. 26:14).

[5] For "of all things which are appointed for thee to do" some Byzantine authorities read "what thou must do" (from Ch. 9:6).

438

11 And[6] when I could not see[7] for the glory of that light, being led by the hand of them that were with me I came into Damascus.

12 And one Ananias, a devout man according to the law, well reported of by all the Jews that dwelt there,

13 came unto me, and standing by me said unto me, Brother Saul, receive thy sight. And in that very hour I looked up on him.

14 And he said, The God of our fathers hath appointed thee to know his will, and to see the Righteous One, and to hear a voice from his mouth.

15 For thou shalt be a witness for him unto all men of what thou hast seen and heard.

16 And now why tarriest thou? arise, and be baptized, and wash away thy sins, calling on his name.

17 And it came to pass, that, when I had returned to Jerusalem, and while I prayed in the temple, I fell into a trance,

18 and saw him saying unto me, Make haste, and get thee quickly out of Jerusalem; because they will not receive of thee testimony concerning me.

19 And I said, Lord, they themselves know that I imprisoned and beat in every synagogue them that believed on thee:

20 and when the blood of Stephen thy witness was shed, I also was standing by, and consenting, and keeping the garments of them that slew him.

21 And he said unto me, Depart: for I will send thee forth far hence unto the Gentiles.

2 If an audience of Welsh or Irish nationalists, about to be addressed by someone whom they regarded as a traitor to the national cause, suddenly realized that he was speaking to them not in the despised Saxon tongue but in the Celtic vernacular, the gesture would no doubt call forth at least a temporary measure of good will. So it was with this Jerusalem mob as they realized that the man whom they execrated as a renegade was addressing them in Aramaic. The silence which they had reluctantly granted to Paul's beckoning hand became deeper still, and they allowed him to go on.

---

[6] The Western text reads "And rising up I could not see. And when I could not see . . ."

[7] For "could not see" Cod. B reads "saw nothing" (so Westcott and Hort's margin).

439

i. Paul's Heritage and Upbringing (vv. 3–4)

3–4 Paul's speech in the temple court is autobiographical and apologetic, as he tells his hearers (i) of his heritage and upbringing as a strictly orthodox Jew (vv. 3–4),[8] (ii) of his conversion at Damascus (vv. 5–16), and (iii) of his commission to evangelize the Gentiles (vv. 17–21. This speech is closely parallel to the speech delivered before the younger Agrippa (Ch. 26:2–29), but along with the virtual identity of the subject-matter there are subtle divergences of style and presentation between the two speeches, each of which is specially adapted to its audience. Here he emphasizes his education in that very city of Jerusalem at the feet of Gamaliel the Elder,[9] his zeal for God such as his hearers were showing that same day,[10] a zeal which he had expressed by harrying the infant Christian community in Jerusalem and elsewhere.[11] He speaks here as a Jew to Jews; "the brethren" at Damascus to whom he went with letters from the high priest and Sanhedrin (v. 5) are Jews, not Christians; he emphasizes the part played in his conversion at Damascus by "Ananias, a devout man according to the law" (v. 12).

ii. Paul's Conversion (vv. 5–16)

5–9 This is the second place in Acts where Paul's conversion is narrated, and the first of two places where the account is given in the first person by Paul himself (the other being in Ch. 26:12–18). In Ch. 9 the story is told in the third person by Luke.

Here Paul tells his hearers how, in pursuance of his campaign of repression against those who belonged to "The Way",[12] he went to Damascus, armed with letters accrediting him as an emissary from the high priest and Sanhedrin at Jerusalem, in

---

[8] *Cf.* Gal. 1:13 f.; Phil. 3:5 f. for parallels to this self-description of Paul's.

[9] On Gamaliel see Ch. 5:34, with exposition and notes. The pupil's persecuting zeal forms a sharp contrast to the moderation and tolerance of the master's policy; but the pupil probably saw more clearly than the master how grave a threat the new way presented to the old. The unnamed pupil of Gamaliel mentioned in TB *Shabbath* 30b, who manifested "impudence in matters of learning," is identified with Paul by Professor Klausner (*From Jesus to Paul* [Eng. tr., London, 1944], pp. 310 f.).

[10] *Cf.* Rom. 10:2, "they have a zeal for God, but not according to knowledge."

[11] *Cf.* Chs. 8:3; 9:1; 26:9–11; Gal. 1:13; Phil. 3:6 ("as touching zeal, persecuting the church").

[12] *Cf.* Ch. 9:2, with exposition and note.

order to procure the arrest and extradition of Christians who had fled for refuge to the ancient Syrian city.[13] He describes the blinding light that flashed around himself and his fellow-travellers about noon on the day that they approached the walls of Damascus, and the voice that challenged him, "Saul, Saul, why do you persecute me?" as he lay prostrate on the ground. "Who are you, Lord?" was Paul's surprised question, and more astounding still was the swift reply: "I am Jesus of Nazareth[14] whom you are persecuting." But while this interchange was going on between Paul and the glorified Christ, his companions stood by amazed. They too had seen the lightning-flash and were momentarily stunned by it; now they heard Paul speaking, but neither heard nor saw the person to whom his words were addressed.[15]

10–11 That convicting word, "I am Jesus of Nazareth," imposed upon Paul a lifelong allegiance to the Saviour whom in ignorance and unbelief he had hitherto withstood. Now he awaited the commands of one whom he henceforth acknowledged as Lord, and was told to go into Damascus, where further instructions would be given him. So in his blindness he was led by hand into Damascus.

12–16 Then he describes the visit paid him by Ananias, who is portrayed as a pious and law-abiding Jew of Damascus, enjoying the respect of all his fellow-Jews in that city. The first thing that Ananias did when he came into the house where Saul was staying was to announce the restoration of his eyesight in the name of the risen Christ. The words "Brother Saul, receive your sight" (v. 13), are a summary of the fuller statement reported in Ch. 9:17. But the words of Ananias in vv. 14–16 are reported more fully than in Ch. 9.[16] It was important to emphasize on the present occasion that the commission which Paul received from the risen Christ

---

13 That it was refugees from Jerusalem, rather than native Damascene Christians, whom Paul was to hunt down in Damascus, may be indicated by the use of the adverb ἐκεῖσε ("thither") in place of ἐκεῖ ("there") in v. 5 (the sense being perhaps "those who had gone thither" rather than "them . . . that were there", as in ARV).

14 This is the only one of the three narratives of Paul's conversion in Acts where Jesus calls Himself "Jesus the Nazarene" (Gk. Ἰησοῦς ὁ Ναζωραῖος); in Chs. 9:5 and 26:15 He says "I am Jesus." G. H. Dalman renders the original Aramaic words as 'ana Yeshua' Naṣeraya de-'att radephinneh (Jesus-Jeshua [Eng. tr., London, 1929], p. 18).

15 Cf. Ch. 9:7, with exposition and notes.

16 Cf., however, the instruction given to Ananias by the Lord in Ch. 9:15 f.

was to a large extent communicated by the lips of this pious and believing Jew, Ananias of Damascus.[17] In the later speech before Agrippa there was no call for this particular emphasis, and so the substance of what Ananias said to him in the name of the Lord is there included in the words spoken by the heavenly voice on the Damascus road (Ch. 26:16–18). "The God of our fathers," said Ananias, using the characteristic language of Jewish piety, "has appointed you to learn His will, to see the Righteous One,[18] and to hear the voice from His mouth; because you are to be His witness to all men concerning the things that you have seen and heard. And now, why delay? Rise up, get yourself baptized, and have your sins washed away, calling on His name."

Thus Paul received his apostolic commission. He had seen[19] the risen Christ, he had heard His voice; henceforth he was to tell forth with confidence what he had seen and heard, with all that that implied—that Jesus of Nazareth, crucified by men, exalted by God, was Israel's Messiah, glorified Son of God, and the Saviour of mankind. But first he must be baptized—the idea that Ananias bade him baptize himself is not really tenable.[20] His baptism was to be the outward and visible sign of his inward and spiritual cleansing from sin by the grace of God. And in the act of being baptized his invocation of Jesus as Lord would declare his intention in submitting to the divine ordinance.[21]

iii. Paul's Commission to the Gentiles (vv. 17–21)

17–21 The commission which he received in Damascus was

[17] On the relation of Ananias's rôle to the claim of Paul in Gal. 1:1, 11 f., see exposition of Ch. 9:17 (pp. 200 f.).

[18] For this title cf. Chs. 3:14; 7:52 (and see pp. 88 f., n. 31).

[19] That Paul actually saw the risen Lord outside Damascus in addition to hearing His voice is emphasized more explicitly in the Pauline letters than in Acts. It is mentioned indeed in Acts (both here in v. 14 and in Ch. 26:16), but Paul himself makes it plain that to him the vision of Christ was the central and all-important feature of his conversion-experience; see 1 Cor. 9:1; 15:8.

[20] For the idea that Paul was bidden to baptize himself see B. S. Easton, "Self-Baptism", AJTh xxiv (1920), pp. 513 ff. In its favour there is the analogy of proselyte-baptism, which was self-administered; on the other hand, we have the passive voice "he was baptized" (Gk. ἐβαπτίσθη) in Ch. 9:18. The middle voice used here (Gk. βάπτισαι) probably means "get yourself baptized" (cf. the aorist middle ἐβαπτίσαντο, "they got themselves baptized", in 1 Cor. 10:2). (The imperative "wash away" is also in the middle voice ἀπόλουσαι.)

[21] By his invocation of the name of Jesus he was baptized "in the name" of Jesus in the sense of Chs. 2:38 and 10:48. Such an invocation or confession may be the "word" (Gk. ῥῆμα) referred to in Eph. 5:26.

reaffirmed and amplified after his return to Jerusalem. The risen Lord appeared to him again and made it plain that he was to be His apostle in the Gentile lands. It is most natural to infer that Paul had this experience during his first brief visit to Jerusalem after his conversion (*cf.* Ch. 9:26 ff.); Ramsay's argument that it must be dated during his second post-conversion stay in Jerusalem is not conclusive (see p. 207, n. 53). Paul had certainly begun to evangelize Gentiles before his second Jerusalem visit. How otherwise was he engaged after he "came into the regions of Syria and Cilicia" (Gal. 1:21)?[22]

This new appearance of Christ came to him in a moment of ecstasy[23] while he was worshipping in the temple at Jerusalem in the third year after his conversion. He had begun to engage in vigorous debate with the Hellenistic Jews of Jerusalem, and immediately aroused keen hostility, the more so because they remembered his former zeal against the Christian movement, and looked upon him as a traitor and turncoat.[24] Nevertheless, he was minded to remain in Jerusalem, but now he received a command from his divine Master to leave the place, because his testimony would not be listened to. Paul tried to remonstrate, pointing out that his former anti-Christian activity in that very city was fresh in people's minds, and that many would remember the responsible part he had played in the stoning of Stephen;[25] his point seems to have been that people who knew his former record would be more readily convinced that his change of attitude must be based on the strongest grounds. But as a matter of fact their knowledge of his former record made them the more unwilling to hear him at all; and now the Lord bade him leave Jerusalem; henceforth his mission field was to be the Gentile world.

According to Ch. 9:29 f., the leaders of the Jerusalem church, getting wind of a plot against Paul's life about this time, escorted him to Caesarea and put him on board a ship bound for Tarsus.

---

22 *Cf.* pp. 240 f., n. 24 (on Ch. 11:25); see also M. Dibelius, *Paul* (Eng. tr., London, 1953), pp. 69 f.

23 Gk. ἐν ἐκστάσει, used also of Peter's experience on the roof at Joppa (Ch. 10:10; 11:5).

24 *Cf.* Ch. 9:29, with exposition and notes.

25 *Cf.* Ch. 7:58; 8:1a, with exposition and notes. In Paul's words "Stephen thy witness" (Gk. μάρτυς) we see the beginning of the semantic development from "witness" to "martyr" (*cf.* Rev. 2:13).

This is not the only place in our narrative where divine revelation and human action coincide.

(e) Paul Reveals his Roman Citizenship (Ch. 22:22–29)

22 And they gave him audience unto this word; and they lifted up their voice, and said, Away with such a fellow from the earth: for it is not fit that he should live.

23 And as they cried out, and threw off their garments, and cast dust into the air,

24 the chief captain commanded him to be brought into the castle, bidding that he should be examined by scourging, that he might know for what cause they so shouted against him.

25 And when they had tied him up with the thongs,[26] Paul said unto the centurion that stood by, Is it lawful for you to scourge a man that is a Roman, and uncondemned?[27]

26 And when the centurion heard it, he went to the chief captain and told him, saying, What art thou about to do? for this man is a Roman.

27 And the chief captain came and said unto him, Tell me, art thou a Roman? And he said, Yea.[28]

28 And the chief captain answered, With a great sum obtained I this citizenship.[29] And Paul said, But I am *a Roman* born.

29 They then that were about to examine him straightway departed from him: and the chief captain also was afraid when he knew that he was a Roman, and because he had bound him.

22–23 The crowd in the outer court of the temple listened patiently enough to Paul until he spoke of his mission to the Gentiles. This word made all their resentment blaze up with redoubled fury. They yelled and gesticulated in a riot of abandoned rage, and while it was quite impossible for the military tribune to discover the exact nature of their grievance against Paul, it was plain that they were bitterly hostile to him and were out for his blood. In a few well-chosen words Luke paints the scene

---

[26] Perhaps we should render with ARV margin "for the thongs" (*i.e.* the thongs of which the scourge was composed).

[27] Or "without hearing my case" (Gk. ἀκατάκριτον); cf. p. 339, n. 56 (on Ch. 16:37).

[28] Gk. ναί. Cod. D reads εἰμί ("I am").

[29] The Western text reads "I know for how large a sum I acquired this citizenship." Cf. n. 36 below.

vividly: we see them waving[30] their clothes in the air and throwing dust about in their excitement.[31] "In England," as Lake and Cadbury remark (*Beginnings* iv, *ad loc.*), "mud is more frequently available"; it was as well for Paul and his captors that loose stones were not lying conveniently about the court.

24 The tribune despaired of getting any coherent explanation of all this sound and fury from the rioters themselves; he must find out the truth from Paul himself[32]—and find it out by torture. He therefore ordered him to be scourged. The scourge (Latin *flagellum*) was a fearful instrument of torture, consisting of leather thongs, weighted with rough pieces of metal or bone, and attached to a stout wooden handle. If a man did not actually die under the scourge (which frequently happened), he would certainly be crippled for life. Paul had been beaten with rods on three occasions (presumably at the hands of Roman lictors), and five times he had been sentenced to the disciplinary lash inflicted by Jewish authority,[33] but neither of these penalties had the murderous quality of the *flagellum*.

25 Fortunately, it was a penalty from which Roman citizens were legally exempt.[34] In earlier days this exemption was total, and although under the Empire it was sometimes inflicted on citizens after conviction, they were still exempt from it as a "third degree" method of inquiry before trial. So, as a few soldiers were tying Paul up[35] in readiness for the lash, he asked the centurion in command of them if it was legal to treat a Roman citizen so, before he had received a fair trial.

26–28 The centurion at once went and told the tribune what Paul had said. The tribune, alarmed at the news, came quickly to

---

[30] "Waving" or "shaking" seems to be the sense of ῥιπτούντων here; the verb ῥιπτέω is a variant form of ῥίπτω ("cast", "throw"). Chrysostom (*Homily* xlviii. 2) describing the scene, explains ῥιπτέω by ἐκτινάσσω ("shake out"); cf. F. Field, *Notes on the Translation of the NT* (Cambridge, 1899), p. 136.

[31] It may be that horror at Paul's imagined blasphemy was also expressed by these actions. See H. J. Cadbury, "Dust and Garments", *Beginnings* v, pp. 269 ff.

[32] He had not, of course, been able to understand Paul's Aramaic speech, though he saw at the end how it infuriated the audience.

[33] *Cf.* 2 Cor. 11:24 f. One of the three beatings with rods was received at Philippi; *cf.* Ch. 16:22, with exposition and notes.

[34] By the Valerian and Porcian Laws; *cf.* exposition of Ch. 16:37.

[35] The victim has commonly been depicted as tied to a pillar or post of convenient height for scourging, but it is more likely that he was suspended some little distance above the ground. See Field, *op. cit.*, pp. 136 f.

the place of scourging and asked Paul if it was true that he was a Roman citizen. "Yes," said Paul. Perhaps he did not look like a Roman citizen at that moment; after being set upon by the crowd and dragged out into the outer court of the temple, along with the other rough usage he had received, he must have presented a battered and undignified spectacle. Something of this sort may have been in the tribune's mind as he said, "It cost *me* a very large sum of money to obtain Roman citizenship"—the implication being that the privilege must have become cheap of late if such a sorry-looking figure as Paul could claim it.[36]

He was the more astonished by the calm dignity of Paul's reply. The tribune had *bought* his citizenship—presumably, since his gentile name was Claudius (Ch. 23:26), he had done so in the reign of Claudius, under whom Roman citizenship became increasingly available for cash down[37]—but the man whom he was interrogating rather contemptuously was a Roman *born*. This means that Paul's father had been a Roman citizen before him. How the citizenship was originally acquired by one of Paul's ancestors we are not told, but analogy would suggest that it was for valuable services rendered to a Roman general or administrator in the south-eastern area of Asia Minor, perhaps to Pompey in 64 B.C.[38]

---

[36] The Venerable Bede, in his exposition of Acts, says here: "Another edition indicates more clearly what he said: 'The tribune said, Do you claim so easily to be a Roman citizen? For I know at how great a price I obtained this citizenship.'" *Cf.* the Western reading (n. 29 above).

[37] *Cf.* Dio Cassius, *History* lx. 17.5 f. It was sold by Claudius's wife Messalina and her court favourites as a means of lining their own pockets. The tribune's personal name Lysias indicates that he was of Greek birth. Wealth or influence (probably both) had enabled him to become not only a Roman citizen but also a superior officer in the Roman army.

[38] Professor W. M. Calder remarks in a letter: "Had not his father (or possibly grandfather) been made a citizen by Antony or Pompey? Were they not a firm of σκηνοποιοί able to be very useful to a fighting proconsul?" Jerome's statement that Paul's family came from Gischala in Galilee and migrated to Tarsus at the time of the Roman conquest of Palestine (*On Illustrious Men* 5) has been treated seriously by a number of scholars, *e.g.* M. Dibelius (*Paul*, p. 16), who links it with Paul's claim to be "a Hebrew of Hebrews" (Phil. 3:5). Ramsay, however, argues that Paul's family must have received Tarsian citizenship in 171 B.C., when Tarsus received its constitution as a Greek city, and that Jerome's story—"in itself an impossible one"—must be rejected (*The Cities of St. Paul* [London, 1907], p. 185). In any case, Paul's family must, as Roman citizens, have been counted among the social élite of Tarsus and Cilicia, even if their manner of life as strictly observant Jews prevented them from exploiting this prestige to the full.

29 The revelation of Paul's Roman citizenship gave the whole business a different aspect. Rough and ready methods which might be all right for ordinary mortals must be abandoned when the party affected was a Roman citizen by birth. The tribune shuddered as he realized how near he had come to perpetrating a serious illegality: in fact, he had already begun to perpetrate it by giving the order for Paul to be scourged;[39] but at least the scourging itself had been arrested. He must now institute an inquiry in accordance with the formal requirements of the law in order to ascertain the true cause of the disturbance.

(f) Paul Brought before the Sanhedrin (Ch. 22:30)

30 But on the morrow, desiring to know the certainty wherefore he was accused of the Jews, he loosed him, and commanded the chief priests and all the council to come together, and brought Paul down and set him before them.

30 If the agitated Jewish crowd could give no coherent account of their grievance against Paul, the Sanhedrin would surely be able to throw light on the situation. So next day the tribune commanded the Sanhedrin to hold a meeting, and when they were in session, he brought Paul down from the fortress of Antonia to the council-chamber.[40] If Paul were seriously charged with a breach of Jewish law, it was the business of the Sanhedrin to try him. First of all, however, it must be determined that there was a *prima facie* case for trial by the Sanhedrin.

[39] The tribune was also afraid "because he had bound him" (v. 29). This may refer to his being tied up for scourging (v. 25) rather than to his being "bound with two chains" (Ch. 21:33), for he evidently remained bound with a chain throughout his custody in Palestine (*cf.* Ch. 26:29) and later in Rome (*cf.* Ch. 28:20). On the other hand, the verb for his being tied up for scourging is not the ordinary verb for binding ($\delta\acute{\epsilon}\omega$) but one which denotes stretching out ($\pi\varrho o\tau\epsilon\acute{\iota}\nu\omega$). It may be that the chains of Ch. 21:33 were heavier and more penal than that which he later wore, but the same word $\H{\alpha}\lambda\upsilon\sigma\iota\varsigma$, denoting a hand-chain, is used of both. Again, according to v. 30, the tribune "loosed him" before bringing him before the Sanhedrin. This would naturally mean that he loosed him from his chain. Did he perhaps remain unbound from then until Felix's departure from Judaea (Ch. 24:27)? The whole situation with regard to Paul's binding and loosing remains rather obscure.

[40] The council-chamber was situated on the western slope of the temple hill (see pp. 97 f., n. 10).

447

(g) Discord in the Sanhedrin (Ch. 23:1–10)

1 And Paul, looking stedfastly on the council, said, Brethren, I have lived before God in all good conscience until this day.

2 And the high priest Ananias commanded them that stood by him to smite him on the mouth.

3 Then said Paul unto him, God shall smite thee, thou whited wall; and sittest thou to judge me according to the law, and commandest me to be smitten contrary to the law?

4 And they that stood by said, Revilest thou God's high priest?

5 And Paul said, I knew not, brethren, that he was high priest: for it is written, Thou shalt not speak evil of a ruler of thy people.

6 But when Paul perceived that the one part were Sadducees and the other Pharisees, he cried out in the council, Brethren, I am a Pharisee, a son of Pharisees: touching the hope and resurrection of the dead I am called in question.

7 And when he had so said, there arose a dissension between the Pharisees and Sadducees; and the assembly was divided.

8 For the Sadducees say that there is no resurrection, neither angel, nor spirit; but the Pharisees confess both.

9 And there arose a great clamor: and some of the scribes of the Pharisees' part stood up, and strove, saying, We find no evil in this man: and what if a spirit hath spoken to him, or an angel?

10 And when there arose a great dissension, the chief captain, fearing lest Paul should be torn in pieces by them, commanded the soldiers to go down and take him by force from among them, and bring him unto the castle.

1 Brought thus before the Sanhedrin, Paul took the initiative by addressing that body in his own defence. "Brethren," he said, "I have passed my life up to this day in all good conscience[1] in

---

[1] "The conscience is a consciousness which bears testimony with, or to, our personality within; and the subject-matter of the testimony is the moral value

the sight of God." This was a bold claim, but not an unparalleled one from Paul. Not long afterwards he assured the procurator Felix that it was his constant care to maintain a clear conscience towards God and men (Ch. 24:16); and we may compare his review of his earlier life in Phil. 3:6: "as touching the righteousness which is in the law, found blameless."[2] This claim might well be voiced as he stood before the Sanhedrin; it was no righteousness of his own, however, that he relied upon for his justification in the heavenly court (Phil. 3:9). The purest conscience was an unsafe object of trust under the scrutiny of God: "for I know nothing against myself," he wrote to the Corinthians; "yet am I not hereby justified: but he that judgeth me is the Lord" (1 Cor. 4:4).

2 He was not allowed to proceed far with this line of defence. The high priest was so incensed by his claim that he told those who stood beside him to strike him across the mouth.

The high priest at this time was Ananias, son of Nedebaeus, who received the office from Herod of Chalcis (a brother of Herod Agrippa I) in A.D. 47 and retained it for eleven or twelve years. He was one of the most disgraceful profaners of the sacred office. Josephus tells how he seized for himself the tithes that ought to have gone to the common priests (*Antiquities* xx. 9. 2); his rapacity and greed became a by-word, so much so that he was lampooned in a parody of Ps. 24, preserved in TB *Pesachim* 57a: "The temple court cried out, 'Lift up your heads, O ye gates; and let Yochanan[3]

---

of actions, the testimony itself being a pronouncement whether they are right or wrong. A *good conscience* gives a good verdict, and this it can only do if the faculty of judgment is itself clear" (R. B. Rackham, *The Acts of the Apostles* [London, 1902], pp. 432 f.). The Greek word translated "conscience" (συνείδησις) did not attain full literary status until shortly before the Christian era, and then in the sense of "awareness" or "consciousness of right or wrong"; it seems "to have been 'baptized' by Paul into a new and deeper connotation" (Moulton and Milligan, *Vocabulary of the Greek Testament* [Edinburgh, 1930], p. 604).

[2] Even his persecution of the Church had been carried out with a good conscience; he believed this to be his duty (*cf*. Ch. 26:9). If we ask how his present claim to have lived in all good conscience before God squares with the revelation of an inner conflict at some time in his life in Rom. 7:7 ff., the answer may be indicated by his use of the verb πεπολίτευμαι ("I have lived") here, which refers rather to his public life, to his life before men, than to those spiritual experiences of which none but God and himself had any knowledge. In respect of his outward life of word and action, the righteous behaviour which the law demands, he had preserved a good conscience in the sight of God.

[3] Ananias (OT Hananiah) represents Heb. חֲנַנְיָהוּ ("Yahweh has dealt

the son of Narbai,[4] the disciple of Pinqai,[5] enter and fill his stomach with the divine sacrifices.'"

Some five years before this time he had been sent to Rome by the governor of Syria on suspicion of complicity in a sanguinary outbreak between the Jews and Samaritans, but was cleared and restored to his high priesthood by the Emperor Claudius, thanks to the advocacy of the younger Agrippa. His great wealth made him a man to be reckoned with even after his deposition from office; and he made free use of violence and assassination to further his interests. His pro-Roman policy, however, made him an object of intense hostility to the national party in Judaea, and when the war against Rome broke out in A.D. 66 he was dragged by the insurgents from an aqueduct in which he had tried to hide, and put to death along with his brother Hezekiah. (*Cf.* Josephus, *Jewish War* ii. 17. 9.)[6]

3 Such improper behaviour from a member of the Sanhedrin stung Paul into an indignant retort. "God shall strike you, you white-washed wall," he said: "you sit there to judge me in accordance with the law, and yet break the law yourself by ordering me to be struck!" The rights of defendants were carefully safeguarded by Jewish law, and they were presumed innocent until proved guilty. Paul had not yet been properly charged, let alone tried and found guilty.

Paul's reaction has been contrasted with that of Jesus, "who, when he was reviled, reviled not again" (1 Pet. 2:23).[7] But we are not disposed to join in the chorus of disapproval voiced by many commentators, who feel free to condemn the apostle for his righteous protest in a situation which they themselves have not been called upon to face. The warm, impetuous humanity of a man of like passions with ourselves is vividly portrayed in this trial scene, and there is no doubt who presents the more dignified

graciously"); Yochanan ("John") represents יוֹחָנָן, the same Hebrew words in the reverse order.

[4] Narbai is probably a textual corruption for Nadbai, owing to the similarity of Heb. ר (*r*) and ד (*d*).

[5] There is a satirical word-play here on the proper name Pinqai—itself perhaps a variation on Pinchas (Phinehas)—and the noun *pinka*, "a meat-dish" (alluding to Ananias's proverbial greed).

[6] See also *Jewish War* ii. 12.6; ii. 17.6; *Antiquities* xx. 5.2; 6.2; 9.2, 4.

[7] *Cf.* W. Kelly: "The apostle throughout scarcely seems to be breathing his ordinary spiritual atmosphere" (*Exposition of Acts* [3rd edn., London, 1952], p. 344).

bearing—Paul or the high priest. The metaphor of the "whited wall" suggests a tottering wall whose precarious condition has been disguised by a generous coat of whitewash:[8] in spite of appearances, a man who behaved as Ananias did was bound to came to grief; his was the haughty spirit of Prov. 16:18, that goes before a fall. Paul's words were more prophetic than he realized; had he known the man intimately, he could not have spoken more aptly.

4–5 But the bystanders were shocked; that was no way to speak to the high priest.[9] They do not appear to have been so shocked by Ananias's outburst, although that was no way for the high priest to speak. As soon, however, as they pointed out to Paul that the man to whom he spoke so freely was God's high priest, he apologized to the official, if not to the man. And in the act of apology, he displayed his ready submission to the law which he was accused of flouting. "I did not know he was the high priest," he said, meaning that, had he known, he would not have spoken as he did—"for it is written, Thou shalt not speak evil of a ruler of thy people" (Ex. 22:28b). But what did he mean by saying that he did not know that the speaker was the high priest? At a regular meeting of the Sanhedrin the high priest presided, and would surely have been identifiable for that reason. Or was Paul not looking in the direction from which the words came, so that he could not be sure who actually uttered them? Or was he speaking ironically, as if to say, "I did not think a man who spoke like that could possibly be the high priest"?[10] The context leaves the matter uncertain. We may bear in mind, however, that it was not a regular session of the Sanhedrin, but a meeting convened by the tribune, and in that case the high priest may not have occupied his usual place or worn his robes of office. Paul, whose visits to Jerusalem for the past twenty years and more had been infrequent and short, would certainly not have known Ananias by sight. We need not go so far as Ramsay, who argues that a meeting convened by a Roman officer must have

---

[8] *Cf.* the wall in Ezek. 13:10 ff., daubed with untempered mortar. The verb here rendered "whited" (κεκονιαμένος) is the same as that used in our Lord's reference to "whited sepulchres" (Matt. 23:27), but the point of the comparison is different.

[9] *Cf.* the remonstrance addressed to our Lord in John 18:22, "Answerest thou the high priest so?"—words which were actually accompanied by a blow.

[10] Rackham (*ad loc.*) takes Paul's words to mean that he had not sufficiently reflected that the man who uttered the objectionable words was the high priest, and that therefore he should not have made such a vigorous retort.

been run like a Roman assembly, with Paul on one side, the Sanhedrin on the other, and the tribune presiding between them, with Luke and others forming the "circle of bystanders" (*Bearing of Recent Discovery on the Trustworthiness of the NT* [London, 1915], pp. 90 ff.).

6 The high priest's interruption had the effect of changing Paul's tactics. Instead of resuming the defence which he had hardly begun, he took stock of the fact that the Sanhedrin consisted in the main of the Sadducean majority and the strong Pharisaic minority. As he had addressed the tribune as a Roman citizen, so he now addresses the Sanhedrin as a Pharisee. "I am a Pharisee; my forebears were Pharisees; and the charge on which I am now being examined concerns the national hope, which depends for its fulfilment on the resurrection of the dead."[11] So we may amplify his meaning.

Here again Paul has been criticized by commentators. "If we think him very little to blame for his stern rebuke of the High Priest," says F. W. Farrar; "if, referring his conduct to that final court of appeal, which consists in comparing it with the precepts and example of his Lord, we can quite conceive that He who called Herod 'a fox' would also have called Ananias 'a whited wall'; on the other hand, we cannot but think that this creating of a division among common enemies on the grounds of a very partial and limited agreement with certain other tenets held by some of them, was hardly worthy of St. Paul; and knowing, as we do know, what the Pharisees were, we cannot imagine his Divine Master ever saying, under any circumstances, 'I am a Pharisee'" (*The Life and Work of St. Paul* [London, 1879], pp. 327 f.).[12] No, indeed, Paul's divine Master could not have said "I am a Pharisee", because He was not a Pharisee; Paul was—indeed, his claim may imply that he was the most consistent Pharisee of them all. Moreover, Paul knew what the Pharisees were much better than Dean Farrar and his contemporaries thought they knew. And the belief in resurrection, which Paul shared with the Pharisaic members of the Sanhedrin, far from being "a very partial and

---

[11] "The hope and resurrection of the dead" is probably an example of hendiadys; the words might be rendered "the hope *of* the resurrection of the dead," for the hope *is* the resurrection.

[12] Farrar goes on to say that "the device, besides being questionable, was not even politic. It added violence to a yet more infuriated reaction in men who felt that they had been the victims of a successful stratagem."

452

limited agreement," was fundamental.[13] Paul and they agreed that the ancestral hope of Israel was bound up with the resurrection of the dead. Paul, and the other Pharisees who believed in Jesus (*cf.* Ch. 15:5), went farther, and maintained that the hope of Israel was fulfilled in Him who had, less than thirty years previously, been raised from the dead; but the belief in the particular resurrection of Christ was bound up, in Paul's mind, with the belief in the resurrection of the dead in general: "for if the dead are not raised, neither hath Christ been raised: and if Christ hath not been raised, your faith is vain" (1 Cor. 15:16 f.). A Sadducee could not become a Christian without abandoning the distinctive theological position of his party; a Pharisee could become a Christian and remain a Pharisee—in the early decades of Christianity, at least.[14]

7–8 Paul's announcement threw the apple of discord into the Sanhedrin. The Pharisees were immediately inclined to concede that a man who was so sound on central Pharisaic doctrine could not be so bad at heart after all; the Sadducees were more enraged than ever, at this public invocation of what was in their eyes a new-fangled heresy. For, as Luke explains to his readers (who would not be conversant with the theological distinctions between the two main Jewish parties), the Sadducees denied the doctrine of bodily resurrection,[15] and rejected the belief in a spirit-world of angels and demons,[16] whereas the Pharisees accepted both[17] as

[13] W. Kelly (*op. cit.*), who agrees with Farrar in regarding Paul's behaviour here as scarcely worthy of him (he suggests that the spiritual atmosphere of Jerusalem had an unfortunate effect on him!), is yet far from ascribing a "very partial and limited" significance to this common belief in resurrection: "Nevertheless there was truth and important truth before all here," he says (p. 344).

[14] It was not until A.D. 90 or thereby that steps were taken to exclude Jewish Christians from participation in synagogue worship by the addition of a prayer—the *birkath ha-minim*— that "the Nazarenes and the heretics might perish as in a moment and be blotted out of the book of life."

[15] *Cf.* p. 95, n. 5 (on Ch. 4:1). Josephus, who tries to represent the Jewish parties in the guise of Greek philosophical schools, says it was the immortality of the soul that the Sadducees denied (*Jewish War* ii. 8.14; *Antiquities* xviii. 1.4).

[16] "What they rejected was the developed doctrine of the two kingdoms with their hierarchies of good and evil spirits" (T. W. Manson, *The Servant-Messiah* [Cambridge, 1953], p. 17, n. 3).

[17] The word "both" in v. 8 probably embraces (*a*) the belief in resurrection, (*b*) the belief in angels and spirits. It is less likely that we should see here another instance of the loose use of ἀμφότεροι as in Ch. 19:16 (*cf.* p. 388, n. 17), in which case the reference would be to the belief in (*a*) resurrection, (*b*) angels, (*c*) spirits.

essential tenets of their creed. The Sadducees claimed in this respect to represent the old orthodoxy of Israel, and there is something to be said for the view that the term "Pharisees" originated in the Sadducees' taunting designation of their opponents as "Persianizers".[18] But the messianic hope in post-exilic times was closely bound up with the doctrine of resurrection,[19] which thus became a fundamental principle of "normative" Judaism. The orthodox view is stated in the Mishnah, where people who say that there is no resurrection of the dead are included among those who have no share in the age to come (*Sanhedrin* x. 1).

9–10 The dispute which broke out at once between the two parties in the council-chamber excluded all possibility of securing a serious examination of Paul or a clarification of the charges against him. Some of the Pharisaic scholars[20] present contended that he had done no wrong; if he spoke of receiving divine instructions in visions it might well be that some spirit or angel had communicated with him. The Sadducees, of course, repudiated the very possibility that such communication could be made. Ramsay, developing his thesis that this meeting was conducted according to the forms of a Roman assembly, supposes that, after Paul's claim to be a champion of the Pharisaic viewpoint as against the Sadducean, the Pharisaic scribes crossed the floor "and fought for him, asserting that he was right. Then Paul was like to be torn asunder between the two factions: his supporters were on one side of him, *i.e.* behind him, while the Sadducees, his opponents, were over against him as before; and he thus was in their midst. Accordingly the officer ordered the guard to snatch Paul out of the midst of them" (*Bearing of Recent Discovery*, p. 93). It may not have happened exactly as Ramsay

---

[18] *Cf.* T. W. Manson, "Sadducee and Pharisee," BJRL xxii (1938), pp. 144 ff. It was, in that case, the Pharisees themselves who reinterpreted this designation as *perushim*, "separatists" or "holy people" in a good sense. Professor Manson further suggests that "Sadducee" was originally derived from Gk. σύνδικος, one of the names for a member of the supreme council, and that the Sadducees reinterpreted it in such a way as to suggest a kinship with *tzaddiq*, "righteous." See also his recent book *The Servant-Messiah*, pp. 10 ff.

[19] *Cf.* Dan. 12:2.

[20] The "scribes" or experts in the law belonged mostly to the Pharisaic party (*cf.* Mark 2:16). We may compare the delight with which "certain of the scribes" listened to our Lord's confutation of the Sadducean argument, and their confession, "Teacher, thou hast well said" (Luke 20:39). But the Sadducees had their legal experts as well.

reconstructs it; but the tribune's attempt to arrange an inquiry by the Sanhedrin certainly proved unsuccessful.

(h) The Lord Appears to Paul by Night (Ch. 23:11)

11 And the night following the Lord stood by him, and said, Be of good cheer:[21] for as thou hast testified concerning me at Jerusalem, so must thou bear witness also at Rome.

11 Paul's worst apprehensions of what might happen to him at Jerusalem looked like being fulfilled.[22] Where now were his plans for carrying the gospel to the far west, and visiting Rome on the way? He might well have been dejected and despondent after the events of these two days. But on the night following the abortive appearance before the Sanhedrin, the risen Lord appeared to him as He had done at critical moments before,[23] and bade him cheer up: he had borne witness to Him in Jerusalem (a reference this, no doubt, to his speech at the top of the steps to the crowd in the temple court), and he would live to bear witness similarly in Rome. This assurance meant much to Paul during the delays and anxieties of the next two years, and goes far to account for the calm and dignified bearing which seemed to mark him out as a master of events rather than their victim.

(i) The Plot against Paul Revealed to the Tribune (Ch. 23:12-24)

12 And when it was day, the Jews[24] banded together, and bound themselves under a curse, saying that they would neither eat nor drink till they had killed Paul.

13 And they were more than forty that made this conspiracy.

14 And they came to the chief priests and the elders, and said, We have bound ourselves under a great curse, to taste nothing until we have killed Paul.

15 Now[25] therefore do ye with the council signify to the chief captain that he bring him down unto you, as

---

[21] The Western and Byzantine texts add "Paul" (cf. Ch. 27:24, "Fear not, Paul").

[22] Cf. Ch. 20:22 f.; Rom. 15:31.

[23] Cf. Chs. 18:9; 22:17.

[24] The Western and Byzantine texts read "some of the Jews."

[25] The Western text exhibits an expanded reading: "Now therefore we ask you to grant us this (opportunity). Gather the Sanhedrin together and give notice to the tribune to bring him down to you."

though ye would judge of his case more exactly: and
we, before he comes near, are ready to slay him.[26]

16 But Paul's sister's son heard of their lying in wait,
and he came and entered into the castle and told Paul.

17 And Paul called unto him one of the centurions, and
said, Bring this young man unto the chief captain; for
he hath something to tell him.

18 So he took him, and brought him to the chief captain,
and saith, Paul the prisoner called me unto him, and
asked me to bring this young man unto thee, who hath
something to say to thee.

19 And the chief captain took him by the hand, and
going aside asked him privately, What is it that thou
hast to tell me?

20 And he said, The Jews have agreed to ask thee to
bring down Paul to-morrow unto the council, as though
thou[27] wouldest inquire somewhat more exactly concerning him.

21 Do not thou therefore yield unto them: for there lie in
wait for him of them more than forty men, who have
bound themselves under a curse, neither to eat nor to
drink till they have slain him: and now are they ready,
looking for the promise from thee.

22 So the chief captain let the young man go, charging
him, Tell no man that thou hast signified these things
to me.

23 And he called unto him two of the centurions, and
said, Make[28] ready two hundred soldiers to go as far
as Caesarea, and horsemen threescore and ten, and
spearmen two hundred, at the third hour of the night:

24 and *he bade them* provide beasts, that they might set
Paul thereon, and bring him safe unto Felix the governor.

12–15 Disappointed at having let Paul slip through their fingers,

---

[26] The Western text adds "even if we must die for it."

[27] The AV reading, "as though they would enquire", represents μέλλοντες
of the Received Text (probably the original Western reading) as against μέλλων,
which underlies ARV "thou wouldest". The third person plural certainly
agrees better with the context in general and with v. 15 in particular, and is
preferred by RSV.

[28] The Western text reads: "'Make ready soldiers under arms to go to
Caesarea, a hundred horsemen and two hundred spearmen.' And they said,
'They are ready.' And he ordered the centurions also to provide beasts that
they might set Paul on them and bring him safely by night to Caesarea to
Felix the governor. For he was afraid that the Jews might seize and kill him,
and that he himself should be blamed meanwhile for having taken bribes."

one group of zealots determined that they would engineer a second opportunity of killing him, and that they would not fail this time. They covenanted together, in a band of forty or more, swearing a solemn oath which probably took some such form as this: "So may God do to us, and more also, if we eat or drink until we have killed Paul."[29] They then went to the chief priests and leaders of the Sanhedrin, telling them of the oath that they had sworn, and suggesting that they should request the tribune to bring Paul down to the Sanhedrin for a further inquiry: they would be ready to attack him and kill him before ever he reached the council-chamber. This plan bespeaks the fanatical devotion of the conspirators, for Paul would be guarded by Roman soldiers, and an attempt to assassinate him, whether it succeeded or not, would inevitably involve the assassins in heavy loss of life.

16 And now comes one of the most tantalizing incidents in Acts, for all who are interested in Paul's private life and family relationships. Who was Paul's nephew, who received such prompt news of the plot—who perhaps was even present when it was hatched?[30] We wish we knew more than we do about Paul's family; it would be illuminating to have a background against which we could appreciate better the action now taken by this nephew. When Paul says in Phil. 3:8 that for Christ's sake he has "suffered the loss of all things," it is usually inferred (and very reasonably so) that he was disinherited for his acceptance and proclamation of Jesus as Messiah. His father, a provincial Roman citizen, would certainly be a wealthy man. But it appears that the mother of this young man retained some sisterly affection for her brother, and something of that affection had been passed on to her son. We do not even know if Paul's sister lived in Jerusalem; if she did, Paul had no thought, apparently, of lodging with her during his stay in the city. Perhaps, however, she lived in Tarsus, and her young son had come to Jerusalem for his education, as his uncle Paul had done in years gone by. It may be that the plotters, or whoever the young man's informants were, did not suspect his relationship to Paul, or if they did, it may

---

[29] The Mishnah makes provision for relief from such vows as could not be fulfilled "by reason of constraint" (*Nedarim* iii. 1, 3).

[30] V. 16 might be rendered: "But Paul's sister's son heard the plotting, having been present (παραγενόμενος), and he entered into the fortress and reported it to Paul."

have been common knowledge that Paul's bitterest opponents were the members of his own family. We wish we knew more, but we do not.

17-22 Paul, as a Roman citizen, was kept in honorable custody in the fortress of Antonia; he was allowed to receive visitors, and centurions promptly carried out his commissions. So, when his nephew came to the fortress and reported the plot to Paul, Paul immediately told a centurion to take the young man to the tribune, that he might hear for himself what was afoot. The tribune received the young man kindly, and listened to what he had to tell him. He treated his report seriously,[31] made up his mind at once what ought to be done, and dismissed the young man with a warning to tell nobody that he had given him this information about the plot.

23-24 Paul's life plainly was not safe in Jerusalem. And the tribune could not afford to incur responsibility for the assassination of a Roman citizen, or to expose himself to any of the other risks that he must inevitably run so long as he had Paul in his custody. Paul must be sent at once, under a strong guard, to Caesarea. He would be safer there, and he would be under the responsibility of the procurator of Judaea himself. So he summoned two centurions and commanded them to get ready a strong escort of heavy infantry, cavalry, and light-armed troops,[32] to set out by night for Caesarea with Paul. Horses or mules were to be provided for Paul; the sixty miles from Jerusalem to Caesarea must be covered as quickly as possible. The tribune felt that he could not rest until he knew that Paul was safe in the procurator's custody.

(j) Letter from Lysias to Felix (Ch. 23:25–30)

25 And he wrote a letter after this form:

---

[31] Unlike Dr. Klausner, who represents this plot as a "probably groundless" suspicion on Paul's part (*From Jesus to Paul* [Eng. tr., London, 1944], p. 403).

[32] The light-armed troops appear to have been lancers or spearmen, as AV, ARV and RSV understand. Cod. A makes them slingers or javelin-throwers (reading δεξιοβόλοι for δεξιολάβοι). The escort consisted of two hundred soldiers commanded by two centurions. This did not excessively weaken the garrison in the fortress of Antonia, for it was an auxiliary cohort, and such a cohort regularly comprised a thousand men. It is for this reason that the commanding officer (whose rank was denoted in Latin by *tribunus militum*) is referred to in Acts by the Greek term χιλίαρχος, which literally means "commander of a thousand."

26 Claudius Lysias unto the most excellent governor Felix,
greeting.
27 This man was seized by the Jews, and was about to be
slain of them, when I came upon them with the soldiers
and rescued him, having learned that he was a Roman.
28 And desiring to know the cause wherefore they accused
him, I brought him down unto their council:[33]
29 whom I found to be accused about questions of their
law,[34] but to have nothing laid to his charge worthy
of death or of bonds.[35]
30 And when it was shown to me that there would be a
plot against the man, I sent him to thee forthwith,[36]
charging his accusers also to speak against him[37] before
thee.[38]

25 It is idle to speculate how Luke knew the terms of the
letter which the tribune wrote to Felix to explain why he was
sending Paul to Caesarea. In any case, he does not profess to
reproduce it *verbatim*; the phrase "after this form"[39] may imply
that only the general purport of the letter is given. But the expression of the general purport is very true to life, especially in
the emphasis laid upon the tribune's own part in the events, and
in the slight manipulation of the order of these events at the end
of v. 27.

26 The tribune's name is now mentioned for the first time in
the narrative. He was evidently of Greek birth, and his Greek
name Lysias became his *cognomen* when he purchased Roman
citizenship; at that time he probably assumed the *nomen* Claudius
because it was that of the emperor (*cf.* Ch. 22:28, with exposition
and notes). The title "most excellent" by which he addresses Felix

---

[33] The clause "I brought him down unto their council" is lacking in Codices
B and 81, but has been supplied in the margin of B.

[34] The Western text adds "concerning Moses and a certain Jesus" (*cf.*
Ch. 25:19).

[35] The Western text adds "I brought him out with difficulty, by force."

[36] For "forthwith" (Gk. ἐξαυτῆς) some Alexandrian authorities read "from
among them" (ἐξ αὐτῶν).

[37] For "against him" (Gk. πρὸς αὐτόν) we should perhaps read, with
Cod. 81, the Byzantine text, and the Sahidic Coptic, "the things concerning
him" (τὰ πρὸς αὐτόν).

[38] Codices ℵ and 81, and the Byzantine text, add "Farewell."

[39] Gk. ἔχουσαν τὸν τύπον τοῦτον. The Western reading is περιέχουσαν τάδε,
"containing these things."

belonged properly to the equestrian order[40] in Roman society (of which Felix was not a member) and was also given to the governors of subordinate provinces such as Judaea, who were normally drawn from the equestrian order (*cf.* p. 31, n. 6).

27-30 The letter then summarizes the events from the temple riot which arose about Paul to Lysias's discovery of the conspiracy against his life. Lysias learned that Paul was a Roman citizen not, as the letter says (v. 27), before he rescued him from the rioters in the temple court, but after he had ordered him to be scourged—this last episode is diplomatically omitted! An account is then given of the fruitless interview with the Sanhedrin, from which Lysias gathered only that the dispute was not one of which Roman law took cognizance, but one of Jewish theological interpretation.[41] Lastly, Lysias tells Felix of the plot against Paul's life and of his consequent decision to send him to Caesarea, that the case might be dealt with in the procurator's court.

[40] The order of *equites* or "knights", who ranked next after senators.

[41] We may compare Gallio's pronouncement in Ch. 18:15. Lysias thus adds his contribution to the testimonies to the Christians' law-abiding conduct unobtrusively presented by Luke.

4. PAUL AT CAESAREA

(a) Paul Taken to Caesarea (Ch. 23:31-35)

31 So the soldiers, as it was commanded them, took Paul
   and brought him by night to Antipatris.
32 But on the morrow they left the horsemen to go with
   him, and returned to the castle:
33 and they, when they came to Caesarea and delivered
   the letter to the governor, presented Paul also before
   him.
34 And[42] when he had read it, he asked of what province
   he was; and when he understood that he was of Cilicia,
35 I will hear thee fully, said he, when thine accusers also
   are come: and he commanded him to be kept in Herod's
   palace.

31-32 The military escort set off about 9 p.m., and reached
Antipatris the following morning. It must have been a forced
march for the infantry, for Antipatris was some 35 miles from
Jerusalem. Antipatris, at the foot of the Judaean hills, on the
site of the modern Ras el-'Ain, was built by Herod the Great in
the well-watered and well-wooded plain of Kaphar-Saba and
called after his father Antipater. The conspirators had now been
left far behind, so it was no longer necessary for Paul to have
such a strong escort. The infantry therefore turned back at
Antipatris and left the cavalry to accompany Paul the remaining
27 miles or so to Caesarea. The remaining part of the journey
was through open country where the population was largely
Gentile.

33-35 The cavalry, then, went on to Caesarea, and Paul was
handed over to the custody of Felix. When Felix had read the
tribune's letter, he asked which province Paul came from. Had
Paul come from one of the client kingdoms in the Syrian or
Anatolian area, it would have been proper to consult the ruler

---

[42] The Western text runs: "And when he had read the letter, he asked
Paul, From what province are you? He said, A Cilician. And when he understood this, he said . . ."

of the state in question.[43] But as he came in fact from a Roman province, it was competent for a Roman governor to go ahead and deal with his case without external consultation. Felix accordingly told Paul that he would hold a full hearing of his case when his accusers arrived; for the present, he ordered him to be detained in the palace built by Herod the Great for himself at Caesarea, which now served as the procurator's headquarters or *praetorium*.[44]

Antonius Felix, procurator of Judaea from A.D. 52 to 59, was a man of servile origin, who owed his unprecedented advancement to a post of honour usually reserved for the equestrian order to the influence which his brother Pallas exercised at the imperial court under Claudius. Pallas was a freedman of Claudius's mother Antonia, and so also (to judge by his gentile name Antonius) was his brother Felix. Before he succeeded Ventidius Cumanus as procurator in A.D. 52, he seems to have occupied a subordinate post in Samaria under Cumanus from A.D. 48.[45] His term of office as procurator was marked by increasing insurgent activity throughout the province, and by the emergence of the *sicarii*. The ruthlessness with which he put down these risings alienated many of the more moderate Jews, and led to further risings. Tacitus sums up his career in the biting epigram, "He exercised the power of a king with the mind of a slave" (*Histories* v. 9). Despite his low birth, he was remarkably successful in marriage; his three successive wives were all princesses, according to Suetonius (*Life of Claudius,* 28). The first of the three was a grand-daughter of Antony and Cleopatra, the third was Drusilla, daughter of the elder Agrippa (of Ch. 12:1; *cf.* Ch. 24:24).[46] See Tacitus, *Annals* xii. 54; Josephus, *Jewish War* ii. 12.8–13.7; *Antiquities* xx. 7.1–8.9.

[43] Thus Pontius Pilate, procurator of Judaea, hearing that Jesus came from Galilee, remitted His case to Herod Antipas, who was tetrarch of that region—a courtesy which Antipas appears to have appreciated, even if he did not take full advantage of it (Luke 23:6 ff.).

[44] In the NT this word (appearing as a Greek loanword from Latin, πραιτώριον) is used of the official residence of a Roman provincial governor (Mark 15:16; John 18:28; Phil. 1:13).

[45] This may be inferred from Tacitus, *Annals* xii. 54.

[46] *Cf.* pp. 472 f.

(b) Paul Accused before Felix (Ch. 24:1–9)

1 And after five days the high priest Ananias came down with certain elders, and *with* an orator, one Tertullus; and they informed the governor against Paul.

2 And when he was called, Tertullus began to accuse him, saying,
Seeing that by thee we enjoy much peace, and that by thy providence evils are corrected for this nation,

3 we accept it in all ways and in all places, most excellent Felix, with all thankfulness,

4 But, that I be not further tedious unto thee, I entreat thee to hear us of thy clemency a few words.

5 For we have found this man a pestilent fellow, and a mover of insurrections among all the Jews throughout the world, and a ringleader of the sect of the Nazarenes:

6 who moreover assayed to profane the temple: on whom also we laid hold:[1]

8 from whom thou wilt be able, by examining him thyself, to take knowledge of all these things whereof we accuse him.

9 And the Jews also joined in the charge, affirming that these things were so.

1 Five days later, a deputation from the Sanhedrin, led by the high priest, came down to Caesarea to state their case against Paul. They enlisted the services of an advocate named Tertullus to state it in the conventional terms of forensic rhetoric. The advocate was probably a Hellenistic Jew; his name was a common one throughout the Roman world.

2–4 No doubt what we have here is a bare summary of the speech which Tertullus made for the prosecution, but it may be an echo of the proportion of the actual speech that so large a place is devoted here to the lavish flattery of the exordium. This

---

[1] The Western text adds the words which appear in the margin of ARV: "and we would have judged him according to our law. 7 But the chief captain Lysias came, and with great violence took him away out of our hands, 8 commanding his accusers to come before thee" (this expansion was taken over by the Received Text, whence it forms part of the AV text).

463

was part of the rhetorical fashion of the time. Tertullus might speak of "much peace" enjoyed by the people of Judaea as a result of Felix's administration, but there were many Jews who, if they had known them in time, would have applied to this "peace" the words which Tacitus puts into the mouth of the Caledonian hero Calgacus: "they [the Romans] create a desolation and call it peace."[2] The reference to the governor's "providence" is reminiscent of what is said of the high priest Onias III in 2 Macc. 4:6, "he saw that without the king's providence it was impossible for the state to obtain peace any more." This kind of language was regarded as appropriate when addressing rulers, especially in the Near East. It was also customary to promise brevity, as Tertullus does here (v. 4); the promise was sometimes kept, sometimes not, but it was calculated to secure good will for the speaker at the outset of his speech. So was such flattery as the reference to Felix's clemency or moderation[3]—a reference singularly inappropriate to a governor whose ferocity is attested by Josephus and Tacitus alike.

5–6 After the excessive courtesy of his proem, Tertullus proceeds to the charges against Paul. They are three in number, proceeding from the more general to the more particular:[4] Paul, he maintained, was (a) a thorough pest, fomenting risings among the Jews all over the empire; (b) a ringleader of the Nazarene sect, and (c) a man who had been caught in an attempt to profane the temple.

The first of these charges would have been serious enough in itself, if it could be shown to have any substance. The same charge, in very similar language, continued for long to be levelled against the preachers of Christianity or against Christianity itself, and it is (as we have seen) one of the prime motives of Luke in writing his twofold history to demonstrate that there was no substance in it at all—that competent and impartial judges had repeatedly confirmed the innocence of the Christian movement and the Christian missionaries in respect of Roman law. There were, it seems, subversive elements operating like a ferment among

---

[2] Tacitus, *Agricola*, 30.

[3] Gk. ἐπιείκεια, a term which is used at this time almost as an honorific title: "Your Clemency."

[4] Compare the threefold charge brought against our Lord before Pilate (Luke 23:2).

the Jewish communities in those days, with political tendencies sometimes vaguely described as "messianic";[5] Christianity might be lumped together with these, but only by people who were ignorant of its real nature.

The second count in the indictment against Paul was that he was a ringleader of the Nazarenes.[6] Was Felix expected to have some idea of what this meant, and if so what sort of impression was this information intended to make on his mind? This is the only place in NT where the term "Nazarene"—or "Nazoraean," as the particular Greek word here used may be more exactly rendered—is used of the followers of Jesus; elsewhere it is used only of Jesus Himself. The normal view is that it was first applied to Jesus because His home-town was Nazareth, and that from Him it came to be used of His followers as well.[7] It was probably used of Jewish Christians from very early days, and remained their designation in Semitic speech; to this day Christians are known in Hebrew and Arabic as "Nazarenes."[8] But the word, or another word like it, may have been current among first-century Jews to denote a group or a tendency on which Felix might be expected to look with disfavour;[9] the evidence, however, is inadequate for a positive statement.

---

[5] *Cf.* the charges brought against Paul and his colleagues at Thessalonica (Ch. 17:6 f.). What is sometimes loosely called political messianism sought the establishment of Jewish independence (followed, it might be, by Jewish imperialism) by the use of armed force, but it did not necessarily carry with it the belief in an individual Messiah. Thus the anti-Roman revolt of A.D. 66 was not in the strict sense messianic, whereas that of A.D. 132 was.

[6] The Nazarenes are here called a "sect" or "party"—the Greek term αἵρεσις being applied to them as it is to the Sadducees in Ch. 5:17 and to the Pharisees in Ch. 15:5. In Judaea the Christians were still reckoned as a Jewish party, albeit a subversive and heretical party from the Sanhedrin's point of view.

[7] See pp. 69 f., n. 51 (on Ch. 2:22).

[8] Heb. *Notzrim,* Arab. *Naṣārā,* Aram. and Syriac *Nāṣrāye* (the name by which the Mandaeans also call themselves in their sacred scriptures). Jesus and the Christians are regularly called *Notzrim* in the Talmud; the earliest recorded use of the Hebrew word to denote Christians is in the "Blessing in regard to the Heretics" (*birkath ha-minim*) mentioned on p. 453, n. 14. It may be that Jews associated the word with the "branch (Heb. *notzer*) of violence" which, according to the Hebrew text of Ecclesiasticus 40:15, "has no tender twig" (*i.e.* no lasting posterity), just as Christians associated it with the messianic Branch (Heb. *netzer*) of Isa. 11:1 (probably the scripture referred to in Matt. 1:23).

[9] Epiphanius makes a distinction between Nasaraeans (Gk. Ναϲαραῖοι) and Nazoraeans (Gk. Ναζωραῖοι) in his collection of heresies, the former coming fifth in his list of Jewish heresies (*Heresies* i. 18), the latter coming ninth in

465

The third charge was more concrete: Paul, it was alleged, had attempted to profane the temple. Even so, it was not so concrete as the rumour that had led to his arrest, which was that he actually had profaned the temple by taking a Gentile within the sacred precincts. Evidently his accusers knew that it was useless to claim that he had in fact done this, as that could easily be disproved; a charge of attempted profanation was more difficult either to prove or to disprove. But the Sanhedrin's case was that by arresting him they had prevented him from carrying out his plan. To represent the riotous attack by the mob as an orderly arrest carried out by the officers of the Sanhedrin or the temple police was to twist the facts even more violently than Lysias had done in his letter, but by this account Tertullus tried to score a point against Lysias, who would have had no right to interfere with those who were maintaining law and order within the temple courts in accordance with their appointed duty.

7–9 The complaint against Lysias is made explicit in the expanded Western text, which has found its way into the Received Text, and appears in AV text and ARV margin as the last clause of v. 6 together with the whole of v. 7 and the beginning of v. 8 (*cf.* n. 1). If we recollect the narrative of events in Ch. 21:27 ff., it is amusing to read this complaint of the "great violence" with which Lysias snatched Paul from the custody of those who were about to give him a fair trial in accordance with Jewish law! The tone of the Western addition is so thoroughly in accord with the rest of Tertullus's speech that one is inclined to accept it as genuine. It makes one small difference to the sense: if the addition be accepted, then "from whom" at the beginning of v. 8 refers to Lysias; otherwise it refers to Paul. It may be regarded as a point in favour of the shorter reading that it is in fact Paul whom the governor asks to speak after Tertullus; but of course Lysias was

his list of Christian heresies (*ib.* i. 29). By the Nazoraeans he means those Jewish Christian groups which were not in communion with the Catholic Church, but the Nasaraeans he represents as an ascetic Jewish group, similar to but not identical with the Essenes, living east of the Jordan, and dating back to pre-Christian times. Their name might be derived from Heb. *nōtzrim*, "observants"—a word almost identical with that meaning Nazarene, apart from the length of the *o* in the first syllable. Whether any confusion with some such Jewish group is involved in the present passage is quite uncertain, the more so in view of the gross inaccuracy of which Epiphanius is capable. He may be as far astray in distinguishing the Nasaraeans and Nazoraeans as he is in distinguishing the Essenes (*ib.* i. 10) and Ossenes (*ib.* i. 19).

not present to give his version, and Felix does later postpone further inquiry until Lysias himself comes down (v. 22).

Tertullus' speech seems to tail away in a very lame and impotent conclusion that forms a striking contrast to the rhetorical flourish with which it starts. But J. H. Moulton is probably too hard on him when he says that he "arrives at the goal by way of anacoluthon—Luke cruelly reports the orator *verbatim*" (*Grammar of NT Greek* i [Edinburgh, 1906], pp. 224 f.). After all, this is only a summary of his speech, and even so Tertullus is by no means the only public speaker reported in Acts who falls into anacoluthon.[10] The deputation from the Sanhedrin appears at any rate to have been satisfied with his general presentation of the case, for they affirmed their agreement with his statement of affairs.

(c) Paul's Defence before Felix (Ch. 24:10–21)

10 And when the governor had beckoned unto him[11] to speak, Paul answered,
   Forasmuch as I know that thou hast been of many years a judge of this nation, I cheerfully make my defence:

11 seeing that thou canst take knowledge that it is not more than twelve days since I went up to worship at Jerusalem:

12 and neither in the temple did they find me disputing with any man or stirring up a crowd, nor in the synagogues, nor in the city.

13 Neither can they prove to thee the things whereof they now accuse me.

14 But this I confess unto thee, that after the Way[12] which they call a sect, so serve I the God of our fathers, believing all things which are according to the law, and which are written in the prophets;

15 having hope toward God, which these also themselves look for, that there shall be a resurrection both of the just and unjust.

---

[10] Paul himself is represented as committing a very obvious anacoluthon in vv. 19 f.—and his epistles make it clear how prone he was to this sort of thing, so swiftly did his thought outstrip his words when dictating.

[11] There is a Western expansion in the margin of the Harclean Syriac: ". . . to make his defence, he took up a godlike attitude, and said . . ."

[12] The Western text may have omitted "the Way", reading "after the sect, as they call it, so serve I . . ."

16 Herein I also exercise myself to have a conscience void of offence toward God and men always.

17 Now after some years I came to bring alms to my nation, and offerings:

18 amidst which they found me purified in the temple, with no crowd, nor yet with tumult: but *there were* certain Jews from Asia—

19 who ought to have been here before thee, and to make accusation, if they had aught against me.

20 Or else let these men themselves say what wrong-doing they found when I stood before the council,

21 except it be for this one voice, that I cried standing among them, Touching the resurrection of the dead I am called in question before you this day.

10 Paul, invited to state his case in reply to Tertullus's speech for the prosecution, opened likewise with a complimentary ex-ordium, but one which was briefer and less fulsome than his accuser's. He professed himself the readier to make his defence before Felix because Felix was no newcomer to the administration of Judaea; he had governed the province for several years, and the experience of the Jewish nation which he had thus gained would enable him to assess the charge against Paul more accurately.

11–13 He went on to explain that he had been absent from Jerusalem for several years until his recent arrival in the city as a worshipper at the festival of Pentecost, and that arrival was not more than twelve days[13] previously. During the days that followed his arrival he had committed nothing to which legal exception could be taken: he had engaged in no public disputation, nor had he gathered a crowd or done anything to provoke a riotous assembly, either in the city, the temple or the synagogues. His accusers might bring a variety of charges against him, but

---

[13] The notes of time from Paul's arrival in Jerusalem (Ch. 21:17 f.) are given in great detail. But the seven days of Ch. 21:27 and the five days of Ch. 24:1 would in themselves make up twelve days, without taking into consideration the time-notes of Chs. 21:18, 26; 22:30; 23:11 f., 23, 32. We have therefore to suppose (with Rackham, *ad. loc.*) that the five days of Ch. 24:1 are reckoned from Paul's arrest in the temple (which strikes one as most improbable), or that the week prescribed for the four Nazirites' purification was nearly completed when Paul joined them, or that he was arrested early in the week. The last alternative seems to accord with the wording of Ch. 21:27 less well than the second one does.

468

there was not one which they could substantiate. The categorical negatives of Paul's reply form a decided contrast to the generalities of Tertullus's accusations.

14–16 While he had done none of the things that his opponents alleged, Paul had no hesitation in declaring what he actually did: he worshipped the ancestral God of Israel (as he had every freedom to do under Roman law) according to the true Way—that Way which his accusers described as a sect or party, although in fact it most faithfully embraced and fulfilled Israel's national hope. Far from deviating in any particular from the basis of Israel's ancient faith, he believed wholeheartedly everything that the sacred scriptures contained—"everything laid down by the law or written by the prophets" (RSV)—and cherished the hope of resurrection, as the majority of his nation did.[14] He seems to imply that his accusers themselves shared this hope (v. 15); the high priest and other Sadducees, of course, did not share it, but by this time it was part of Jewish orthodoxy, and although the Sadducees might claim to be old-fashioned conservatives in this regard (as in a number of others), it was really they and not the Pharisees and others who were guilty of doctrinal deviation in the matter. There may have been some Pharisees among the elders who came down to Caesarea with the high priest (v. 1); possibly the Pharisaic councillors' sudden outburst of good will towards Paul when he declared himself a Pharisee and a believer in resurrection (Ch. 23:6 ff.) had been considerably dissipated on cooler reflection. It is interesting to note that this is the one place in NT where Paul expresses unambiguous belief in a resurrection of the unrighteous as well as of the righteous dead. There is no reason to doubt that, like all Pharisees, he inherited and continued to accept the belief in such a twofold resurrection,[15] but when he develops the doctrine in his epistles (especially in 1 Cor. 15), it is on the resurrection of believers, raised after the likeness of Christ's resurrection, that he concentrates. As it is, with this firm belief in a coming resurrection and the consequent appearance

---

[14] Again he emphasizes the centrality of the resurrection faith (cf. Chs. 23:6; 26:8).

[15] The references to the resurrection of the just in our Lord's teaching in Luke 14:14 and 20:35 f. (for it is the resurrection of the just that is the subject of the latter passage) no doubt imply a resurrection of the unjust as well; for the twofold resurrection cf. Dan. 12:2; John 5:28 f.; Rev. 20:12 ff.

before the divine tribunal, he constantly set himself[16] (he assured Felix as he had already assured the Sanhedrin) to maintain a clear conscience towards God and men alike.[17]

17 The reason for his coming to Jerusalem after a lapse of some years,[18] he averred, was to bring alms and offerings to his fellow-Jews in Jerusalem. This is the clearest reference in Acts—indeed, we may say the only reference—to the collection which Paul had organized in the Gentile churches as a gift to the Jewish Christians of Jerusalem. He obviously attached great importance to it: in his eyes it was a proper acknowledgment on the part of the Gentile Christians of the debt they owed to Jerusalem, from which the gospel had started on its progress to them, and he also hoped that it might arouse in the Jerusalem church—especially in its extreme Judaistic members—a sense of gratitude to the Gentile churches which would help to weld both into a spiritual unity.[19] In this last respect the collection achieved at best only partial success.

18–19 Shortly after his coming to Jerusalem he was set upon in the temple, when he had just completed a purificatory ceremony in an orderly manner. He had done nothing to occasion the public tumult that broke out; those who caused it were some Jews from the province of Asia, and it was these Jews who ought to have come before Felix as Paul's prosecutors if they had any serious charge to bring against him. This was a strong point in his defence; the people who had raised the hue and cry in the first instance, claiming to be eyewitnesses of his alleged temple-profanation, had not troubled to appear. It may be that the Sanhedrin thought it best that the Asian Jews should not appear, as cross-examination would soon have revealed the hollowness of their charges, and a Roman judge would not look lightly upon people who wasted his time with unfounded accusations.

20–21 But since the Asian Jews had not thought fit to put in

---

[16] Gk. ἀσκῶ, "I exercise myself"; there is an implication of moral severity about the word without the full force of the later sense of asceticism.

[17] See pp. 448 f., nn. 1 and 2 (on Ch. 23:1).

[18] Five years had gone by since his hasty visit mentioned in Ch. 18:22; eight years since his visit at the time of the Council of Jerusalem.

[19] He does not go into these details when addressing Felix; all that was necessary to say to him was that he had come with a charitable gift for his fellow-Jews in Jerusalem. The Jerusalem Christians, of course, were still an integral part of the Jewish nation.

an appearance, said Paul, let the members of the Sanhedrin who were present state more explicitly than Tertullus had done what crime he was discovered to have committed when the military tribune brought him before the Sanhedrin for examination in Jerusalem. The only crime that they could charge him with as a result of that examination was the crime of having declared that the real point at issue in his case was the question of the resurrection of the dead—in other words, no crime at all.[20]

(d) Felix Adjourns the Proceedings (Ch. 24:22–23)

22 But Felix, having more exact knowledge concerning the Way, deferred them, saying, When Lysias the chief captain shall come down, I will determine your matter.

23 And he gave order to the centurion that he should be kept in charge, and should have indulgence; and not to forbid any of his friends to minister unto him.

22 Felix appears to have summed up the situation fairly accurately. Where he obtained his special information about Christianity we are not told; it may have been through his present wife Drusilla, a member of the Herod family. At any rate he probably saw where the truth of the matter lay, but for the present he adjourned the proceedings. The evidence of Lysias would plainly be of first-rate value; he had given a brief account of what happened in his letter (Ch. 23:25 ff.), but in view of the conflicting statements made by Tertullus and Paul, it would be necessary to ascertain further details from Lysias.[21]

23 Meanwhile he gave orders that Paul was to be kept in custody but to enjoy a reasonable degree of consideration, as befitted a Roman citizen against whom no crime was proved. In particular, he was free to receive visits and any other kind of attention from his friends.

We are not told if Lysias came down to Caesarea and if Felix resumed the hearing. No doubt Lysias did come down and supply further information, but no decision was reached. Felix

---

[20] Some commentators read a confession of wrong into the words of v. 21. "In the remark of St. Paul before the tribunal of Felix I seem to see—though none have noticed it—a certain sense of compunction for the method in which he had extricated himself from a pressing danger" (F. W. Farrar, *The Life and Work of St. Paul* ii [London, 1879], p. 328).

[21] As Tertullus himself had suggested, according to the probably genuine Western text of v. 8.

probably saw that there was no case against Paul, but he did not wish to offend the Sanhedrin by acquitting him. He had given enough offence during his administration of Judaea, and he did not care to give more, especially as under the new imperial régime at Rome he could not count on the unchallenged court influence of his brother Pallas as he had been able to do while Claudius was still emperor.[22]

(e) Paul's Interviews with Felix (Ch. 24:24-27)

24 But after certain days, Felix came with Drusilla, his wife, who was a Jewess,[23] and sent for Paul, and heard him concerning the faith in Christ Jesus.

25 And as he reasoned of righteousness, and self-control, and the judgment to come, Felix was terrified, and answered, Go thy way for this time; and when I have a more convenient season, I will call thee unto me.

26 He hoped withal that money would be given him of Paul: wherefore also he sent for him the oftener, and communed with him.

27 But when two years were fulfilled, Felix was succeeded by Porcius Festus; and desiring to gain favor with the Jews, Felix left Paul in bonds.

24 Having this eminent Christian in custody in Caesarea, Felix thought it a suitable opportunity to improve his already fairly accurate knowledge of "the Way". According to the Western text, it was Drusilla who was specially anxious to have an interview with Paul. Drusilla was the youngest daughter of Herod Agrippa I, and at this time (A.D. 57) was not yet twenty years old. As a small girl she had been betrothed to the crown prince of Commagene, in eastern Asia Minor, but the marriage did not take place, because the prospective bridegroom refused to embrace Judaism. Then her brother Agrippa II gave her in marriage to the king of Emesa, a petty state in Syria (modern Homs). But when she was still only sixteen, Felix, with the help of a Cypriote magician called Atomos,[24] persuaded her to leave

---

[22] According to Tacitus (*Annals* xiii. 14), Pallas was deposed by Nero in A.D. 55 from his very influential post as head of the imperial treasury.

[23] The Western text (preserved in the margin of the Harclean Syriac) adds: "who asked to see Paul and hear him speak, so wishing to satisfy her he summoned Paul."

[24] Some inferior manuscripts of Josephus (*Antiquities* xx. 7.2) call him Simon. The name Atomos reminds us of the Western reading of the name of another Cypriote magician, Hetoimas or Etymas (Ch. 13:8). The resemblance may be

her husband and marry him. She thus became Felix's third wife, and bore him a son named Agrippa, who met his death in the eruption of Vesuvius in A.D. 79.[25]

25 Felix and Drusilla, then, sent for Paul and listened as he expounded the Christian faith. But he made it clear that the Christian faith had ethical implications, and as he talked about these, Felix and Drusilla felt that the interview had taken an uncomfortably personal turn. It was certainly not an "abstract discussion", as Dr. Klausner says;[26] on the contrary, Paul's distinguished hearers had probably never listened to such pointed and practical teaching in their lives as when he talked to them about "righteousness and self-control and the judgment to come"—three subjects which that couple specially needed to learn about! No wonder that Felix began to feel afraid, and decided that he had heard enough of this for the time being.

26 But he was sufficiently interested to call the apostle to his presence fairly frequently and engage him in conversation, although, as Luke suggests, there was a further motive for these repeated interviews. In spite of stern and reiterated edicts prohibiting bribery, the wheels of Roman law in those days ran more smoothly and rapidly if they were judiciously greased; and provincial governors were deplorably venal. Felix had the impression that Paul was in a position to pay a handsome bribe for his release. How he got that impression is a question which need not delay us; Ramsay's argument that Paul had considerable command of money around this time is well known.[27] But whether Felix's expectations were well founded or not, they were disappointed.

27 Two years went by,[28] and Felix was recalled from his

fortuitous, or the Western reading of Ch. 13:8 may be due to an attempt to identify Elymas with Atomos.

25 See Josephus, *Antiquities* xix. 9.1; xx. 7.1 f.

26 "It is difficult to believe that even Drusilla understood this abstract discussion, which was so remote from the Judaism current in her half-assimilated circle of acquaintance" (J. Klausner, *From Jesus to Paul* [Eng. tr., London, 1944], p. 406).

27 *St. Paul the Traveller* (London, 1920), pp. 310 ff. Ramsay finds himself forced to the conclusion that the expenses of Paul's trial and other expenses incurred during his two years in Caesarea and two years in Rome were met from his hereditary property, which may have "come to him as legal heir (whose right could not be interfered with by any will)." But the whole matter belongs to the realm of speculation—as money-matters so often do!

28 These years may have proved a tedious period for Paul, but Luke no doubt made full use of them, in Caesarea and elsewhere in Palestine, in

governorship. The occasion of his recall was an outbreak of civil strife between the Jewish and Gentile inhabitants of Caesarea, in which Felix intervened with troops in such a way as to cause much bloodshed among the leaders of the Jewish faction.[29] On his return to Rome, he would have had severe punishment inflicted upon him, Josephus informs us, had it not been for the advocacy of his brother Pallas—a statement which involves a chronological difficulty.[30] He was succeeded as procurator of Judaea by Porcius Festus, a governor whose brief administration, though troubled, was not accompanied by such excesses as marked that of his predecessor or of his successors.[31] But the change of administration brought no advantage to Paul. Felix left him in custody, hoping that this at least would be accepted by the Jewish authorities as a gesture of good will; and the arrival of a new and inexperienced governor meant the reopening of the case in circumstances less favourable to Paul.

tracing the course of events accurately from the very beginnings of the Christian story (cf. Luke 1:3). Whether the idea that he produced a preliminary draft of his Gospel ("Proto-Luke") can be maintained or not, it is highly probable that by the end of these two years he had collected and digested the non-Markan material in his Gospel, as well as part of the early narrative of Acts.

[29] Josephus, *Jewish War* ii. 13.7; *Antiquities* xx. 8.7, 9.

[30] The difficulty is that Pallas had been dismissed from his position of influence in A.D. 55. Eusebius, to be sure, gives 55 as the year of Felix's replacement by Festus, and in this he has been followed not only by Jerome but by some scholars of more recent date. But it is difficult, if not indeed impossible, to reconcile this date with the evidence for Gallio's proconsulship of Achaia (cf. p. 374, n. 31), even if the "two years" of v. 27 are interpreted as meaning not the duration of Paul's imprisonment in Caesarea but the duration of Felix's procuratorship of Judaea. (See K. Lake in *Beginnings* v, pp. 464 ff., 470 ff.) If Josephus is right in saying that Felix got off lightly through the interposition of Pallas, we may conclude that Pallas continued to exercise considerable influence even after his removal from the treasury. At the time of his removal, Tacitus records, he was in a position to stipulate that there should be no inquiry into his past actions, and that his accounts with the state should be taken as passed. This suggests that his deposition did not deprive him of all his sources of power.

[31] *Jewish War* ii. 14.1; *Antiquities* xx. 8.10 f. Festus governed from 59 until his death in 61.

CHAPTER XXV

(f) Festus Visits Jerusalem (Ch. 25:1–5)

1 Festus therefore, having come into the province, after three days went up to Jerusalem from Caesarea.

2 And the chief priests and the principal men of the Jews informed him against Paul; and they besought him,

3 asking a favor against him, that he would send for him to Jerusalem;[1] laying a plot to kill him on the way.

4 Howbeit Festus answered, that Paul was kept in charge at Caesarea, and that he himself was about to depart *thither* shortly.

5 Let them therefore, saith he, that are of power among you go down with me, and if there is anything amiss in the man, let them accuse him.

1–3 It was desirable that a new procurator should make the acquaintance as soon as possible of the leading native representatives of the population of his province. Accordingly, three days after his arrival in Caesarea, Festus went up to Jerusalem to meet the Sanhedrin and other leading Jews. After the preliminary salutations, they lost no time in exploiting the favour which Felix had done them in leaving Paul in prison at Caesarea. Counting upon the new governor's inexperience, they raised the question of Paul with him, and asked him to send orders to Caesarea to bring Paul up to Jerusalem. The zealous forty who had been frustrated in an earlier plot to assassinate Paul—or others who emulated their zeal—might find a better opportunity on the road from Caesarea to Jerusalem.

4–5 Festus, however, saw no need to accede to this particular request. He did not intend to make a long stay in Jerusalem; he was shortly to go back to Caesarea, and if a responsible deputation from the Jewish rulers went along with him, they could accuse Paul before him there.

---

[1] The margin of the Harclean Syriac adds "those who had made a vow to get him into their hands," ascribing the present plot to the conspirators of Ch. 23:12 ff. This may be a solitary witness to the Western text of this verse.

(g) Paul appeals to Caesar (Ch. 25:6-12)

6 And when he had tarried among them not more than eight or ten days, he went down unto Caesarea; and on the morrow he sat on the judgment-seat, and commanded Paul to be brought.

7 And when he was come, the Jews that had come down from Jerusalem stood round about him, bringing against him many and grievous charges which they could not prove;

8 while Paul said in his defence, Neither against the law of the Jews, nor against the temple, nor against Caesar, have I sinned at all.

9 But Festus, desiring to gain favor with the Jews, answered Paul and said, Wilt thou go up to Jerusalem, and there be judged of these things before me?

10 But Paul said,[2] I am standing before Caesar's judgment-seat, where I ought to be judged: to the Jews have I done no wrong, as thou also very well knowest.

11 If then I am a wrong-doer, and have committed anything worthy of death, I refuse not to die; but if none of those things is *true* whereof these accuse me, no man can give me up unto them. I appeal unto Caesar.

12 Then Festus, when he had conferred with the council, answered, Thou hast appealed unto Caesar: unto Caesar shalt thou go.

6-8 The whole case against Paul was now opened afresh, thanks to Felix's neglect to pronounce his acquittal and discharge him. Festus spent a little over a week in Jerusalem and returned to Caesarea, and a deputation from the Sanhedrin accompanied him. The day after their arrival in Caesarea, Festus took his seat as judge, ordered Paul to be brought into court, and gave his accusers an opportunity to restate their charges against him. This they proceeded to do, but although the many charges which they brought against him were serious in character and deadly in intention (being probably along the lines of those detailed by Tertullus before Felix), they were completely void of proof. No witnesses were forthcoming to substantiate them, and all that Paul needed to do when replying in his defence was to deny them categorically one by one. He had done nothing, he declared,

---

[2] Cod. B repeats ἑστώς, giving the sense, "Standing at Caesar's judgment-seat, I am standing where I ought to be judged"—an attractive reading, which Lake and Cadbury approve.

against Jewish law in general or against the sanctity of the temple in particular; nor yet had he in any way acted against the emperor's interests (this was probably in answer to a charge that he had fomented disorders in various Roman provinces).[3]

9 Between the Sanhedrin's charges and Paul's denials Festus was at a loss, the more so as he could not make out what the real point of the argument was. But he had newly entered upon his period of office as governor of Judaea, the Sanhedrin was the supreme national court of the people he had come to govern, and it would be politic to begin his administration by doing something to gain their good will, if this could be done without infringing Roman justice. It was a matter of indifference so far as Roman justice was concerned whether the reopened case was heard in Caesarea or in Jerusalem. The Sanhedrin plainly desired it to be heard in Jerusalem: he would at least concede this to them. So he proposed to Paul that he should go up to Jerusalem and have the matter dealt with there; Festus himself would be the judge. It seemed a reasonable enough proposal, the more so as the crime with which Paul was charged—or rather the most specific of the crimes with which he was charged, the violation of the temple sanctity—was alleged to have been committed at Jerusalem.[4]

10–11 But Paul did not regard the proposal as reasonable at all. To go back to Jerusalem meant placing himself in jeopardy all over again. If Festus began by making a concession to the Sanhedrin, he might be inclined to make further concessions even more prejudicial to Paul's safety. Felix had been an experienced administrator of Judaea when Paul's case was submitted to him, but Festus was a novice, and the Sanhedrin might well exploit his inexperience to Paul's disadvantage. There was one way open to Paul as a Roman citizen to escape from this precarious situation, even if it was a way attended by special risks of its own. It was not, he assured Festus, that he wished to circumvent the law of Rome or escape the due reward of anything he might have done.

---

[3] *Cf.* Chs. 17:6 f.; 24:5.

[4] If a *prima facie* case could have been made out against Paul on the score of sacrilege, he would have been handed over to the Sanhedrin's jurisdiction; by accusing him of action against the emperor's interests, however, they overreached themselves, for this was a matter to be dealt with by the procurator alone, and one on which Paul might very properly appeal to the emperor himself.

If he had in fact committed a capital crime, as his accusers alleged, he was prepared to suffer the supreme penalty for it; but if there was no substance in their charges, he must not be placed in their power. Let Roman justice decide. As Festus was the representative of Caesar, the tribunal before which he stood was Caesar's; but since he had not sufficient confidence in that subordinate tribunal, he appealed to the supreme tribunal. "I appeal to Caesar," he declared. "*Ad Caesarem prouoco.*"

The right of appeal to the emperor (*prouocatio ad Caesarem*) took the place of the earlier right of appeal to the sovereign people of Rome (*prouocatio ad populum*), which Roman citizens had enjoyed from time immemorial.[5] It was usually exercised by appealing against the verdict of a lower court, but might be exercised at any stage in the proceedings, the defendant claiming that the case be tried at Rome and the verdict pronounced by the emperor. Ordinary provincial subjects of the Roman Empire had no such privilege.[6]

Paul had had encouraging experience of the justice and impartiality of Roman courts already, notably when he was accused before Gallio in Corinth (*cf.* Ch. 18:12 ff.). If he was apprehensive about the result of a trial before Festus in Jerusalem, it was not because he had lost his confidence in Roman justice, but because he feared that in Jerusalem Roman justice might be overborne by powerful local influences. There would be no reason for such fear at Rome. There (it might well seem to a Roman citizen who had in fact never been in Rome) Roman justice would be administered most impartially.[7]

---

[5] In addition to the right of *prouocatio*, Roman citizens enjoyed another right of appeal called *appellatio*. This was originally the right of appeal to a magistrate to veto the action of his colleague, and more particularly the appeal to a tribune of the plebs to exercise his power of absolute veto (*i.e.* his power to veto the action of any other magistrate). As the tribunician power was now vested in the person of the emperor (just as the popular sovereignty was), *appellatio* as well as *prouocatio* was addressed to him, and the two originally distinct civic privileges were now practically merged; it therefore mattered little whether Paul framed his appeal in the words *Ad Caesarem prouoco* or *Caesarem appello.*

[6] When the younger Pliny was confronted by the alarming spread of Christianity in Bithynia in A.D. 112, he took summary action against ordinary provincials convicted as Christians, but those who were Roman citizens he sent to Rome for appropriate examination and sentence, not being quite sure of the legal procedure (*Epistle* x. 96).

[7] He may even have hoped to secure recognition for Christianity as a *religio licita* distinct from Judaism.

478

To us who know Nero's record in relation to Roman Christianity, it may seem strange that Paul should have appealed with such confidence to him. But, whatever Nero's personal character might be, the first five years of his reign (A.D. 54–59), when the imperial administration was carried on under the influence of his tutor Seneca, the Stoic philosopher, and Afranius Burrus, the honest prefect of the praetorian guard, were looked back upon as a miniature Golden Age. There was little in A.D. 59 that gave warning of the events of A.D. 64.

12 Festus heard Paul's words with much relief. By appealing to the supreme court, Paul had shown him a way of escape from a difficult and disagreeable duty.[8] He conferred with his council[9]—a body consisting of the higher officials of his administration and younger men who accompanied him in order to gain experience in provincial government—and willingly granted Paul permission to have his case referred to Rome.

[8] H. J. Cadbury suggests that Paul simply intended to appeal (from the Sanhedrin) to Caesar in the person of the procurator who sat on Caesar's tribunal, insisting on his right to be tried there and not handed over to the Sanhedrin's jurisdiction; and that Festus interpreted his plea as an appeal direct to the emperor from the provincial court (*Beginnings* v, p. 319). This is an improbable reading of the passage.

[9] The "council" of v. 12 is not, of course, the Sanhedrin but the procurator's *concilium*. Festus could, if he chose, seek the advice of his council, but the responsibility for any decision rested with himself alone.

5. PAUL AND AGRIPPA

(Chs. 25:13–26:32)

(a) Herod Agrippa II Visits Festus (Ch. 25:13–22)

13 Now when certain days were passed, Agrippa the king and Bernice arrived at Caesarea, and saluted Festus.

14 And as they tarried there many days, Festus laid Paul's case before the king, saying, There is a certain man left a prisoner by Felix;

15 about whom, when I was at Jerusalem, the chief priests and the elders of the Jews informed *me*, asking for sentence against him.

16 To whom I answered, that it is not the custom of the Romans to give up any man, before that the accused have the accusers face to face, and have had opportunity to make his defence concerning the matter laid against him.

17 When therefore they were come together here, I made no delay, but on the next day sat on the judgment-seat, and commanded the man to be brought.

18 Concerning whom, when the accusers stood up, they brought no charge of such evil things[10] as I supposed;

19 but had certain questions against him of their own religion, and of one Jesus, who was dead, whom Paul affirmed to be alive.

20 And I, being perplexed how to inquire concerning these things, asked whether he would go to Jerusalem and there be judged of these matters.

21 But when Paul had appealed to be kept for the decision of the emperor, I commanded him to be kept till I should send him to Caesar.

22 And Agrippa *said* unto Festus, I also could wish to hear the man myself. To-morrow, saith he, thou shalt hear him.

13 A fresh difficulty now presented itself to Festus. When he

_____

[10] Gk. οὐδεμίαν αἰτίαν ... πονηρῶν. Codd. A C 33 make "evil" agree with "charge" (reading πονηράν for πονηρῶν) ; the Byzantine text omits "evil" altogether (*cf.* AV).

sent Paul to Rome to have his case heard before the emperor, it would be necessary for him to send a report of the case as it had developed up to that time. This was by no means an easy thing to do, especially as Festus could not grasp how the trouble had really started. Listening to the speeches for the prosecution and the defence only added to his perplexity.

Fortunately for Festus, a way out of this minor difficulty soon appeared. To the north-east of his province lay the petty kingdom which was ruled by Herod Agrippa II. This man was the son of Herod Agrippa I, king of Judaea from A.D. 41 to 44 (*cf.* Ch. 12:1). At the time of his father's death he was only seventeen years old, and although the Emperor Claudius thought of appointing him to succeed his father, he was dissuaded by his advisers, who pointed out that the government of Judaea involved problems which called for qualities of wisdom and experience beyond the capacity of a youth. Judaea therefore reverted to procuratorial administration. But soon after the death of Herod, king of Chalcis (younger brother of Herod Agrippa I), in A.D. 48, the younger Agrippa received that small kingdom (between Lebanon and Antilebanon) in succession to his uncle, together with the right of appointing Jewish high priests and having custody of the ceremonial vestments which they wore year by year on the Great Day of Atonement.[11] In 53 he gave up this kingdom in exchange for a larger one consisting of the former tetrarchies of Philip and Lysanias;[12] this territory was augmented three years later by Nero, who added to it a number of cities and villages around the Lake of Galilee. In token of gratitude to Nero, Agrippa changed the name of Caesarea Philippi,[13]

[11] Between A.D. 6 and 37 the high priests were appointed by Roman governors. But the right of appointment was granted to Herod Agrippa I in A.D. 41, and when he died three years later a Jewish deputation visited Rome and protested to Claudius against the attempt made by the new procurator, Cuspius Fadus, to secure that right and the custody of the vestments for himself. Their protest was supported by the younger Agrippa, and Claudius conciliated them by giving the twofold right to Herod of Chalcis, who was (in theory at least) a Jew. (*Cf.* Josephus, *Antiquities* xx. 2.1–3.)

[12] This was the territory which the Emperor Gaius had given to Herod Agrippa I in A.D. 37. For the two tetrarchies *cf.* Luke 3:1, where Philip's tetrarchy is described as "the region of Ituraea and Trachonitis" and that of Lysanias as "Abilene." See Appendix I ("History of Chalcis. Iturea and Abilene") to E. Schürer's *History of the Jewish People in the Time of Jesus Christ* (Eng. tr., Edinburgh, 1892–1901), I. ii, pp. 325 ff.

[13] Caesarea Philippi—*i.e.* Philip's Caesarea—was usually so called to distinguish it from the city of the same name on the Mediterranean seaboard of Palestine. It was the capital of Philip's tetrarchy from 4 B.C. to A.D. 34.

481

the capital of his kingdom, to Neronias.[14] His sister Bernice, a year younger than himself, who had been the wife of Herod of Chalcis,[15] was living with him at Caesarea Philippi at this time, and accompanied him to Caesarea in Palestine on the present occasion when he went, as was proper, to pay his respects to the new imperial representative in the province adjoining his client kingdom.[16]

14 Agrippa the younger had the reputation of being an authority on the Jewish religion, and Festus decided that he was the man who could best help him to frame the report which he had to remit to Rome in connection with Paul's appeal to the emperor. So at a suitable opportunity during Agrippa's stay in the provincial capital, Festus broached the subject of Paul's case to him.

15-19 He told the king how Paul had been left in prison by Felix, how the Sanhedrin had asked him to pronounce a verdict of condemnation against him, and how he had given them an answer in strict accordance with the principles of Roman law. An accused person must have an opportunity in open court of hearing the charges against him and replying to them.[17] When

---

[14] Agrippa later did his best to prevent the outbreak of the Jewish war against Rome in 66, but failed. He remained loyal to the Flavian dynasty and was rewarded with a further increase of territory by Vespasian. Josephus had some correspondence with him when composing his *Jewish War*. He died in A.D. 100, leaving no children, and may thus be called "the last of the Herods." See Josephus, *Jewish War* ii. 12.1, 7 f.; 15.1; 16.4; vii. 5.1; *Antiquities* xix. 9.2; xx. 5.2; 6.3; 7.1; 8.4; 9.6; *Autobiography* 65; *Against Apion* i. 9; Justus of Tiberius, quoted by Photius, *Library* 33.

[15] A remarkable number of marriages between uncles and nieces took place within the Herod family. Thus Herodias was married successively to two of her uncles—Herod Philip and Herod Antipas. Her daughter Salome married her father's half-brother and namesake Philip the tetrarch.

[16] Bernice was the popular Hellenistic pronunciation of the Macedonian name Berenice (the form by which Josephus always refers to this princess). Like her brother, she tried hard to avert the war of A.D. 66; she undertook a Nazirite vow in that year and endeavoured, at considerable risk to her own life, to prevent a massacre of Jews by the procurator Florus, but in vain. The Jewish extremists, however, showed her no gratitude; they burnt down her palace at Jerusalem along with Agrippa's. Later she became an ardent pro-Flavian. In the final stages of the war she attracted the attention of the commander-in-chief Titus, Vespasian's son and heir; when she came to Rome with Agrippa in 75 she lived with Titus as his wife, and Titus would have contracted a formal marriage with her but for the strong disapproval of the Roman people. See Josephus, *Jewish War* ii. 11.6; 15.1; 17.6; *Antiquities* xix. 5.1; 9.1; xx. 7.3; Tacitus, *History* ii. 2; Suetonius, *Life of Titus* 7; Dio Cassius, *History* lxv. 15; lxvi. 18; Juvenal, *Satire* vi. 156 ff.

[17] F. Field (*Notes on Translation of the NT* [Cambridge, 1899], p. 140)

such a court was held at Caesarea, the accusers said their say, but to Festus's surprise and perplexity, the accusations appeared mainly to centre round disputed points of Jewish religion,[18] with particular reference to "one Jesus, who was dead, whom Paul affirmed to be alive" (v. 19). The real point at issue had evidently been made clear enough, though Festus did not realize its import! Agrippa no doubt knew enough about the Christian movement to have his interest whetted by these words of Festus.

20–22 Festus went on to tell him of his suggestion that Paul should go up to Jerusalem and have the case tried there, and of Paul's appeal to Caesar.[19] Paul was now being kept in custody at Caesarea until an opportunity arrived of sending him to Rome. "Well," said Agrippa, "I should like to hear the man for myself." Festus accordingly undertook to arrange an audience for the following day.

(b)   Paul Appears before Agrippa (Ch. 25:23–27)

23 So on the morrow, when Agrippa was come, and Bernice, with great pomp, and they were entered into the place of hearing with the chief captains and the principal men of the city,[20] at the command of Festus Paul was brought in.

24 And Festus saith, King Agrippa, and all men who are here present with us, ye behold this man, about whom all the multitude of the Jews made suit to me, both at Jerusalem and here, crying that[21] he ought not to live any longer.

---

quotes from Appian, *Civil War* iii. 54, "The law requires, members of the council, that a man who is on trial should hear the accusation and speak in his own defence before judgment is passed on him."

[18] The word translated "religion" in v. 19 is Gk. δεισιδαιμονία, which might be less politely rendered "superstition" (as in AV). The corresponding adjective appears with the same ambiguity in Ch. 17:22 (see p. 355 with n. 35). But as Festus was speaking on this occasion to the "secular head of the Jewish church" he no doubt intended the word to be understood in its more polite sense, whatever his private opinion might be.

[19] Here (v. 21) and in v. 25 Festus refers to Caesar by the Greek title Σεβαστός, the equivalent of the Latin *Augustus* (*cf.* AV), the best modern equivalent of which would probably be "His Majesty." ERV, ARV and RSV render "the emperor."

[20] The Harclean margin preserves a Western addition, "who had come down from the province."

[21] The Western text runs: "that I should hand him over to them for punishment without any defence. But I could not hand him over, on account of the commands which we have from His Majesty. But if anyone was going

25 But[22] I found that he had committed nothing worthy of death: and as he himself appealed to the emperor I determined to send him.

26 Of whom I have no certain thing to write unto my lord. Wherefore I have brought him forth before you, and specially before thee, King Agrippa, that, after examination had, I may have somewhat to write.

27 For it seemeth to me unreasonable, in sending a prisoner, not withal to signify the charges against him.

23 Next day, then, an audience was held, and it was attended not only by Agrippa and his sister and Festus, but by members of the procurator's staff[23] and leading citizens of Caesarea. There is probably quiet humour in Luke's description of the "great pomp" with which they assembled; Luke had a very true sense of values, and knew that in his friend and teacher Paul there was a native greatness which did not need to be decked with the trappings of grandeur that surrounded his distinguished hearers. History has vindicated Luke's perspective. Most people nowadays who know anything about Agrippa and Bernice and Festus know of them as people who for a brief space of their lives crossed the path of Paul and heard him speak words which might have brought much blessing to them had they been disposed to pay serious heed to them. All these Very Important People would have been greatly surprised and not a little scandalized had they been able to foresee the relative estimates that later generations would form of them and of the handcuffed Jew who stood before them to plead his cause.

24–27 Paul was then conducted into the audience-chamber, and Festus introduced him to Agrippa and the others, telling how he could find no substance in the capital charges which his Jewish opponents urged against him, and how Paul had appealed to Caesar. It is plain from these words of Festus that he was quite at a loss about the terms in which he should draw up his report

to accuse him, I said that he should accompany me to Caesarea, where he was in custody; and when they came, they clamoured for his death."

[22] The Western text goes on (according to the Harclean margin): "But when I had heard the one side and the other, I found that he was by no means worthy of death. But when I said, 'Are you willing to be judged before them in Jerusalem?' he appealed to Caesar."

[23] The "chief captains" (*i.e.* military tribunes, Gk. $\chi\iota\lambda\iota\alpha\rho\chi\iota$) would be five in number, as there were five auxiliary cohorts stationed at Caesarea (Josephus, *Antiquities* xix. 9.2).

on Paul's case—"I have nothing definite to write to my lord[24] about him," he said (RSV)—and that he was very glad of Agrippa's cooperation in the matter. He therefore handed over the conduct of the inquiry to his royal visitor.

[24] The title "lord" (κύριος) with a divine connotation was given to Roman emperors in the eastern provinces as it had been given to the Ptolemies and other dynasts; Deissmann notes that there is a remarkable rise in the frequency of such inscriptions in the time of Nero and his successors (*Light from the Ancient East* [Eng. tr., London, 1927], pp. 353 ff.).

CHAPTER XXVI

(c) Paul's "Apologia Pro Vita Sua" (Ch. 26:1–23)

1 And Agrippa said unto Paul, Thou art permitted to speak for thyself. Then Paul[1] stretched forth his hand, and made his defence:

2 I think myself happy, king Agrippa, that I am to make my defence before thee this day touching all the things whereof I am accused by the Jews:

3 especially because[2] thou art expert in all customs and questions which are among the Jews: wherefore I beseech thee to hear me patiently.

4 My manner of life then from my youth up, which was from the beginning among mine own nation and at Jerusalem, know all the Jews;

5 having knowledge of me from the first, if they be willing to testify, that after the straitest sect of our religion I lived a Pharisee.

6 And now I stand *here* to be judged for the hope of the promise made of God unto our fathers;

7 unto which *promise* our twelve tribes, earnestly serving God night and day, hope to attain. And concerning this hope I am accused by the Jews, O king!

8 Why is it judged incredible with you,[3] if God doth raise the dead?

9 I verily thought with myself that I ought to do many things contrary to the name of Jesus of Nazareth.

10 And this I also did in Jerusalem: and I both shut up many of the saints in prisons, having received authority from the chief priests, and when they were put to death I gave my vote against them.

11 And punishing them oftentimes in all the synagogues, I strove to make them blaspheme; and being exceedingly

---

[1] There is a Western insertion, preserved by the margin of the Harclean Syriac: "confident, and encouraged by the Holy Spirit."

[2] Some authorities (including Codd. ℵ C A C 33 614 and the Syriac Peshitta) improve the Greek by reading "especially knowing (Gk. ἐπιστάμενος, absent from the majority of texts) that thou art expert . . ."

[3] One Western authority, P29, seems to omit "Why is it judged incredible with you." See also n. 25 below.

mad against them, I persecuted them even unto foreign cities.

12 Whereupon as I journeyed to Damascus with the authority and commission of the chief priests,

13 at midday, O king, I saw on the way a light from heaven, above the brightness of the sun, shining round about me and them that journeyed with me.

14 And when we were all fallen to the earth,[4] I[5] heard a voice saying unto me in the Hebrew language, Saul, Saul, why persecutest thou me? it is hard for thee to kick against the goad.

15 And I said, Who art thou, Lord? And the Lord said, I am Jesus[6] whom thou persecutest.

16 But arise, and stand[7] upon thy feet: for to this end have I appeared unto thee, to appoint thee a minister and a witness both of the things wherein thou hast seen me, and of the things wherein I will appear unto thee;

17 delivering thee from the people, and from the Gentiles, unto whom I send thee,

18 to open their eyes, that they may turn from darkness to light and from the power of Satan unto God, that they may receive remission of sins and an inheritance among them that are sanctified by faith in me.

19 Wherefore, O king Agrippa, I was not disobedient unto the heavenly vision:

20 but declared both to them of Damascus first, and at Jerusalem, and throughout[8] all the country of Judaea, and also to the Gentiles, that they should repent and turn to God, doing works worthy of repentance.

21 For this cause the Jews seized me in the temple, and assayed to kill me.

22 Having therefore obtained the help that is from God, I stand unto this day testifying both to small and great, saying nothing but what the prophets and Moses did say should come;

23 how that the Christ must suffer, *and* how that he first

---

[4] The Western text adds "for fear."

[5] The Western text reads "I myself alone."

[6] The Western text adds "the Nazarene" (from Ch. 22:8).

[7] Cod. B omits "and stand" ($\varkappa\alpha\grave{\iota}\ \sigma\tau\tilde{\eta}\theta\iota$) by accident after "arise" ($\mathring{\alpha}\nu\acute{\alpha}\sigma\tau\eta\theta\iota$).

[8] Only in the Byzantine text is there a Greek preposition corresponding to "throughout" ($\varepsilon\mathring{\iota}\varsigma$); the text without any such word, though well attested, is "hardly tolerable" (J. H. Ropes). There may be an ancient corruption here; *cf.* n. 24 below.

by the resurrection of the dead should proclaim light
both to the people and to the Gentiles.

1 Agrippa, turning to Paul, told him that he might state his
case, and Paul, raising his hand in salutation[9] to the king, proceeded to do so.

To a considerable extent this speech covers the same ground
as that which Paul delivered from the top of the steps leading to
the fortress of Antonia to the riotous crowd in the temple court
below, but the general tone and atmosphere of the two speeches
are different, each being adapted to its very distinctive audience.
Here, in the calm and dignified setting of the governor's audience-
chamber at Caesarea, he delivered the speech which, above all
his other speeches recorded in Acts, may worthily claim to be his
Apologia Pro Vita Sua. In it he undertakes to show that neither
his manner of life nor his teaching should arouse hostility—
especially from Jews. The construction of the speech is more
careful than usual, and the style more literary,[10] as befitted such
a distinguished audience. The argument is calculated to appeal
particularly to the mind of Agrippa, even if Festus did find himself completely out of his depth after the first few sentences. After
(i) a complimentary exordium (vv. 2 f.), Paul goes on to speak
of (ii) his Pharisaic heritage (vv. 4–8), (iii) his former persecuting
zeal (vv. 9–11), (iv) his vision on the Damascus road (vv. 12–18),
(v) his lifelong obedience to the vision (vv. 19 f.), (vi) his arrest
(v. 21), and (vii) his teaching (vv. 22 f.).

i. Exordium (vv. 2–3)

2–3 Paul congratulates himself first of all on the opportunity
to state his case before a man of Agrippa's eminence, particularly
one so expert in the customs and problems of the Jewish religion.
He, at least, might appreciate the strength of Paul's argument
that the message which he proclaimed was the proper consummation of Israel's ancestral faith. For such a hearer and examiner
no perfunctory plea, but a reasoned narrative and exposition of
his whole case, was appropriate; and no doubt what we read in
this chapter is but a brief epitome of what Paul really said. Unlike

---

[9] Gk. ἐκτείνας τὴν χεῖρα. The expression is different from that in Chs.
13:16 and 21:40, where the verb κατασείω is used to denote a gesture inviting
silence and attention.

[10] *Cf.* F. Blass, *The Philology of the Gospels* (London, 1898), p. 9, and his
commentary *in loco*.

Tertullus before Felix, Paul did not undertake to be brief, but asked for a patient hearing: probably he expected that Agrippa would be interested enough to listen to a fairly lengthy statement.

ii. His Pharisaic Heritage (vv. 4–8)

4–8 He went on, then, to describe his early upbringing, first in Tarsus and then at Jerusalem. His contemporaries knew all about this, and could testify if necessary that he had been brought up a Pharisee and lived according to the strictest rules of the sect.[11] That a faithful Pharisee believed in the resurrection of the dead, and saw no fulfilment of Israel's ancient hope apart from the resurrection, went without saying. But the amazing and indeed absurd feature of the present dispute was that he was being prosecuted for his proclamation of this very hope—and prosecuted by Jews, of all people![12] But this hope was the hope that God would keep the promise which He made to the fathers of the nation long ago; it was the hope which gave life and meaning and purpose to the ordinances of divine worship, faithfully maintained by all twelve tribes of Israel[13] generation after generation—the hope that God would one day come down to deliver His people as He had done when they were slaves in Egypt, that He would raise up a horn of salvation for them "in the house of His servant David, as He spoke by the mouth of His holy prophets from of old" (*cf.* Luke 1:69f.). Why should they think it incredible that God should raise the dead?[14] The Pharisees would answer that they did not think it incredible; they ardently believed in God as the raiser of the dead. But Paul's point was that this belief had now been validated in that God had already raised up one man

---

11 *Cf.* Gal. 1:13 f.

12 The position of ὑπὸ ᾿Ιουδαίων at the end of v. 7 may be emphatic: "I am accused by *Jews*!"

13 Neither Paul nor any other NT writer knows anything of the fiction of the ten "lost" tribes. *Cf.* Matt. 19:28; Luke 22:30; Jas. 1:1; Rev. 7:4 ff.; 21:12. See also p. 61 (on Ch. 2:9).

14 There is no definite article in the Greek text here: the clause may be rendered "that God raises up dead people." The plural is generalizing, but the apostle has one particular instance in his mind—the resurrection of Christ. *Cf.* Rom. 1:4, where Jesus is "declared to be the Son of God . . . by the resurrection of the dead" (ARV margin)—lit. "by resurrection of dead people" —here too the generalizing plural points to the resurrection of Christ in particular. It was useless, thought Paul, to acknowledge the resurrection of the dead in theory but to refuse to believe in one well-authenticated instance of such resurrection.

from the dead, and had by that very fact demonstrated that man to be Israel's long-expected Messiah and Deliverer, the one in whom the age-old hope was realized. Why should those who believed in the resurrection of the dead refuse to believe that God had in fact raised up Jesus, and so declared Him to be the Son of God? If God did not raise up Jesus, why believe that He raises the dead at all?

iii. His Persecuting Zeal (vv. 9–11)

9–11 But Paul understood their frame of mind very well, for he had once shared it himself. Yes, he thought it his duty to oppose the name and cause of Jesus the Nazarene with all his might. Pharisee though he was, and thus in theory a believer in the resurrection of the dead, he judged it incredible in this particular instance, and denounced and persecuted as impostors those followers of Jesus who claimed that they had seen Him alive again after His passion. He took the lead in the campaign to uproot this subversive heresy, as he thought it; armed with authority from the chief priests he went from house to house and dragged the followers of Jesus off to jail; he went from synagogue to synagogue and enforced judicial proceedings against them there, and when they were put on trial he cast his vote for their condemnation, and demanded the death sentence against them.[15] Not that he wished to make martyrs of them if he could help it; if he could make apostates of them, that was much more satisfactory, and he did his best in synagogue after synagogue to force them to blaspheme,[16] to call Jesus accursed, and thus repudiate His claims[17]— but such attempts met with singularly little success: they preferred death to apostasy. Nor did he confine his efforts to Jerusalem and Judaea: when his victims fled across the provincial frontier, he pursued them into the synagogues of Gentile cities as well, where the writ of the Sanhedrin was respected.

[15] The ruling body of each synagogue constituted a minor law-court or *beth din*. For his acquiescence in the execution of Stephen, who was tried and condemned by the supreme Sanhedrin, see pp. 172 f., n. 110 (on Ch. 8:1).

[16] AV "I . . . compelled them to blaspheme" is misleading; the imperfect ἠνάγκαζον indicates that he tried to compel them, but did not succeed.

[17] *Cf.* Pliny the Younger's report to Trajan: if people suspected of Christianity blasphemed Christ he discharged them, as he was informed that this was one of the things which "people who are really Christians cannot possibly be made to do" (*Epistle* x. 96).

iv. The Heavenly Vision (vv. 12–18)

12–15 It was while he was engaged thus that the revolution in his life took place. Again he tells of his journey to Damascus, of the lightning-flash that blinded him, of the challenge from the risen Christ. In our best authorities for the text of Acts, this is the only place in the three accounts of Paul's conversion to report the words: "it is hard for thee to kick against the goad."[18] This homely proverb[19] from agricultural life suggests that there was already in the depths of Paul's mind a half-conscious conviction that the Christian case was true. Stephen's arguments were perhaps more cogent than Paul allowed himself to admit, and his demeanour at his trial and in his death made a deep impression on Paul. It was probably in large measure to stifle this conviction and impression that Paul threw himself so furiously into the campaign of repression. But the goad kept on pricking his conscience, until at last the truth that Jesus was risen indeed burst forth into full realization and acknowledgment as He appeared to Paul in person and spoke to him by name outside the walls of Damascus.

16–18 There was no need this time to enlarge on the part played by Ananias, the "devout man according to the law," as Paul had done when addressing the mob in the outer court of the temple. Here the words of Christ to Paul through Ananias are merged with the words spoken on the Damascus road and with those spoken to him in the temple when he returned to Jerusalem (*cf.* Ch. 22:14 ff., 18 ff.). Paul relates the terms in which the glorified Lord commissioned him to be His messenger—terms which recall those in which the prophets Jeremiah[20] and Ezekiel[21] received their commissions in earlier days. And the commission itself echoes the commission of the Servant of the Lord in Isa. 42:1 ff.

---

[18] This is also the only place in the three accounts where the risen Christ is said to have addressed him in Aramaic, but we should have inferred this in any case from the vocative Σαούλ Σαούλ Chs. 9:4; 22:7), not Σαῦλε Σαῦλε. *Cf.* p. 200, n. 33.

[19] Several parallels to this proverb are adduced from Greek and Latin literature; none seems to be quoted from a Semitic source, but it is the sort of saying that would be familiar in any peasant community.

[20] *Cf.* Jer. 1:7 f.: "to whomsoever I shall send thee thou shalt go, and whatsoever I shall command thee thou shalt speak . . . for I am with thee to deliver thee".

[21] *Cf.* Ezek. 2:1, 3: "stand upon thy feet . . . I send thee to the children of Israel."

(or at least words in the immediate context of that commission)[22]—and very properly so, for the commission of Paul and of all Christian witnesses is the perpetuation of the Servant's commission, as has been made very plain already in Acts (*cf.* Ch. 13:47 and exposition on p. 283). As the Servant was to open the eyes of the blind and turn their darkness into light, so Paul was summoned to continue this healing ministry. The terms of his commission remained in his mind ever after; they are echoed in the words in which he reminds the Christians of Colossae how God the Father "made us meet to be partakers of the inheritance of the saints in light; who delivered us out of the power of darkness, and translated us into the kingdom of the Son of his love; in whom we have our redemption, the forgiveness of our sins" (Col. 1:12–14). For these words sum up the blessing which, in the heavenly vision, he was charged to proclaim to all who placed their faith in Christ, not only Jews, but Gentiles as well. That believing Gentiles were to have an equal and rightful share in the heritage of the holy people of God was a feature of the gospel which it was Paul's peculiar mission first to understand and make known (*cf.* Eph. 2:19; 3:1 ff.).[23] But we may wonder if even Agrippa, expert as he was in Jewish religious questions, grasped the purport of all this.

v. His Obedience to the Vision (vv. 19–20)

19–20 From the time that he heard the words "I am Jesus whom thou persecutest", Paul knew but one Master. For him henceforth to receive a commandment from that Master was to set about obeying it. So, after his conversion, he immediately proclaimed Jesus as the Son of God in Damascus, then among the Jews of Jerusalem and elsewhere,[24] and especially to the Gentiles.

---

[22] *Cf.* Isa. 42:6 f., "a light of the Gentiles; to open the blind eyes, to bring out the prisoners from the dungeon, and them that sit in darkness out of the prison-house." Whether the first Servant Song should be held to end at Isa. 42:4, or at v. 7, or at v. 9, is of small relevance when we are considering the NT allusions to the Servant. We must not expect the apostles to confine themselves to Duhm's delimitation of the Songs. On Isa. 42:5–9 *cf.* C. R. North, *The Suffering Servant in Deutero-Isaiah* (Oxford, 1948), pp. 131 ff.

[23] *Cf.* I Pet. 2:9 f.

[24] For πᾶσάν τε τὴν χώραν τῆς ᾽Ιουδαίας καὶ τοῖς ἔθνεσιν —which, in addition to being exceptionally awkward Greek, conflicts with the evidence of Ch. 9 and Gal. 1:18–24 that Paul did *not* preach the gospel "throughout all the country of Judaea"—Blass's emendation εἰς πᾶσάν τε χώραν ᾽Ιουδαίοις καὶ τοῖς ἔθνεσιν ("in every land to both Jews and Gentiles") makes a strong bid for

With this proclamation went the call to repent, to turn to God, and to perform deeds which were the natural fruit of true repentance. "None more firmly than Paul rejected works, before or after conversion, as a ground of salvation; none more firmly demanded good works as a consequence of salvation" (G. H. Lang, *The Gospel of the Kingdom* [London, 1933], p. 23).

vi. His Arrest (v. 21)

21 And it was for *this*, he exclaimed, that his own fellow-Jews laid violent hands on him in the temple, and tried to kill him. Festus had found it extremely difficult to determine why Paul had been arrested in the first place, and why the Jews were so anxious to have his blood, and yet it was important that he should find out, in order to include it in his report to Rome. He counted on Agrippa's help in this matter, and now Agrippa learnt why the Jews were so bitterly hostile to Paul and why they mobbed him and nearly lynched him in the temple. Knowing the Jews as he did, perhaps Agrippa understood why they would cherish such animosity towards a former rabbi who offered Gentile believers spiritual privileges on the same footing as the chosen people.

vii. What Paul Taught (vv. 22–23)

22–23 Finally, Paul emphasized that the teaching which, by God's help, he had constantly given to all to whom he witnessed was thoroughly loyal to Israel's faith and in complete harmony with the divine revelation communicated through Moses and the prophets. And here we are probably to understand that he adduced passage after passage from the OT scriptures which found their fulfilment in the life, death and triumph of Jesus. At an early period in the course of Christian preaching these passages appear to have been grouped together under appropriate headings, which sometimes took the form of questions. Here Luke does not give us Paul's citations of messianic "testimonies" *in extenso*, but indicates them briefly by quoting the interrogative captions under which they were grouped.[25] "Must the Messiah suffer?" "Must

---

acceptance. It was approved by Ramsay (*St. Paul the Traveller* [London, 1920], p. 382).

[25] The captions are here introduced by the interrogative εἰ ("if" as used in indirect questions—EVV inaccurately render the clauses as indirect statements). Eb. Nestle, mistakenly taking εἰ as conditional, looked for an apodosis and found it in v. 8, which he accordingly transferred to a position between vv. 22

He rise from the dead?" "Must He bring the light of salvation
to the people of Israel and to the Gentile nations?"[26] (The "must"
in these questions is the "must" of God's determinate counsel
and foreknowledge, revealed through His servants the prophets.)

*(d) Interchange between Festus, Paul and Agrippa
(Ch. 26:24–29)*

24 And as he thus made his defence, Festus saith with a
loud voice, Paul, thou art mad;[27] thy much learning
is turning thee mad.

25 But Paul[28] saith, I am not mad, most excellent Festus;
but speak forth words of truth and soberness.

26 For the king knoweth of these things, unto whom also[29]
I speak freely: for I am persuaded that none of these
things is hidden from him; for this hath not been done
in a corner.

27 King Agrippa, believest thou the prophets? I know
that thou believest.

28 And Agrippa *said* unto Paul, With but little persuasion
thou wouldest fain make me a Christian.[30]

and 23. This emendation was approved by J. Moffatt, who renders: "Why
should you consider it incredible that God raises the dead, that the Christ is
capable of suffering, and that he should be the first to rise from the dead and
bring the message of light to the People and to the Gentiles?" (In accordance
with the demands of English idiom, Moffatt and RSV follow AV in rendering
εἰ of v. 8 by "that"; ERV and ARV more literally render it by "if".) In any
case, there is neither justification nor necessity for the Nestle–Moffatt transposition.

[26] *Cf.* J. R. Harris, *Testimonies* i (Cambridge, 1916), pp. 19 f.; C. H. Dodd,
According to the Scriptures (London, 1952), pp. 16 f. For these themes as
founded upon OT prophecy *cf.* Ch. 17:2 f. Here Paul adds that the light
brought by Christ is for the Gentiles as well as for the Jews; this, of course,
is based on such passages as Isa. 42:6; 49:6; 60:3. *Cf.* Paul's development in
Rom. 15:9 ff. of the thesis that the Gentile mission was a subject of OT
prophecy. With the expression "first by the resurrection of the dead" (πρῶτος
ἐξ ἀναστάσεως νεκρῶν) *cf.* Rom. 1:4 (ἐξ ἀναστάσεως νεκρῶν); this is a further
example of the generalizing use of the plural νεκροί in such a context when the
resurrection of Christ Himself is primarily in view (*cf.* Chs. 17:32; 26:8). But
the AV rendering "that he should be the first that should rise from the dead"
preserves an important phase of the meaning here; *cf.* the description of the
risen Christ in 1 Cor. 15:20, 23 as "the firstfruits of them that are asleep."

[27] The Western text, preserved in the Old Latin manuscript h, has "Thou
art mad, Paul, thou art mad."

[28] The Western and Byzantine texts have "he."

[29] Cod. B omits "also."

[30] Gk. ἐν ὀλίγῳ με πείθεις Χριστιανὸν ποιῆσαι, literally, "In brief you are
persuading me (*i.e.* trying to persuade me) to act the Christian." For this
construction with ποιέω *cf.* the LXX of 3 Kingdoms 20:7 (MT 1 Kings 21:7),

29 And Paul *said*, I would to God, that whether with little or with much, not thou only, but also all that hear me this day, might become such as I am, except these bonds.

24 Festus could endure it no longer. Paul was obviously a man of tremendous learning, but equally obviously his learning had driven him mad. Otherwise he could never talk so earnestly and at such length about things to which a sensible Roman could attach no meaning, and no man who retained his senses would have antagonized his whole nation for such insubstantial philosophizing. "You're mad, Paul, you're mad," he exclaimed; "all this study is driving you crazy."

25–27 But what was sheer madness to the governor's way of thinking was the merest truth and sober good sense to Paul's. So he told Festus, and appealed for confirmation to Agrippa. The events which fulfilled the ancient promises were well-known and public; this was no hole-and-corner concern, no secret society. The ministry and death of Christ were matters of common knowledge; His resurrection was amply attested; the gospel had been openly proclaimed in His name. Anyone who believed the prophets and compared their predictions with the historical facts concerning Jesus of Nazareth must acknowledge the truth of Christianity. "You believe the prophets, don't you, Your Majesty? I know you do!" Agrippa could supply corroborating testimony and assure Festus that Paul's arguments were sane and well founded, that the gospel which he preached contained "nothing but what the prophets and Moses did say should come."

28 But the king was embarrassed by Paul's appeal. He may have listened with interest enough, and possibly Paul hoped that the apparent interest might develop into something more. The logic of the situation was so plain to the apostle that he could hardly imagine that such an expert in the Jewish religion would not accept the obvious conclusion. But Agrippa was not minded even to appear to lend support to Paul's case. What would Festus

σὺ νῦν οὕτως ποιεῖς βασιλέα ἐπὶ Ἰσραήλ; "Is this the way that you act the king over Israel?" Failure to recognize this construction has led to several variant readings: thus Cod. A has πείθῃ for πείθεις ("you trust that you can make me a Christian"; cf. Hort's emendation πέποιθας for με πείθεις); the Byzantine text has γενέσθαι for ποιῆσαι (whence AV "almost thou persuadest me to be a Christian").

think if he expressed—or even seemed to express—agreement with the man whose great learning had turned his head? Therefore he could not admit that he did believe the prophets; on the other hand, he could not say that he did not believe them, for his reputation for orthodoxy and his influence with the Jews would be gone if he did. So he turned Paul's appeal aside with a smile: "In short," he said, "you are trying to make me play the Christian"—for so his words ought to be understood. He was not going to be manoeuvred into anything like that!

29 "In short or at length," said Paul, "I could pray that not only Your Majesty, but all who are here to-day listening to me were Christians like myself—except for these chains" (holding up his shackled wrist).

(e) Agreement on Paul's Innocence (Ch. 26:30–32)

30 And[31] the king rose up, and the governor, and Bernice, and they that sat with them:

31 and when they had withdrawn, they spake one to another, saying, This man doeth nothing worthy of death or of bonds.

32 And Agrippa said unto Festus, This man might have been set at liberty, if he had not appealed unto Caesar.

30–32 However, enough had been heard for the immediate purpose. The audience was over, and the governor, Agrippa and Bernice, together with their adjutants and other members of their entourages, discussed what Paul had said. One thing at least was clear: even if he was as mad as Festus thought, he had done nothing deserving death or even imprisonment: in fact, he was completely innocent in the eyes of Roman law, and, as the king said, might have been freed there and then, if he had not appealed to Caesar. That appeal, however, had taken the decision out of the governor's hands, and he must be sent to Rome; presumably Agrippa had no difficulty in telling Festus what to write in his report.

The present unanimous agreement on Paul's innocence is a further contribution to Luke's general apologetic motive. But J. V. Bartlet thought that the readers of Acts would detect a sinister note in Agrippa's last words—"if he had not appealed

---

[31] The Western text adds "when he had said this."

unto Caesar."[32] They would understand, he thought, that by appealing to Caesar Paul had forfeited any prospect of ever being set free, for they would be familiar with the record of that particular Caesar to whom he had appealed—Nero. This is reading too much into the text. Nero is not mentioned by name, and after a very few decades the average reader might not immediately realize that Nero was emperor when Paul lodged his appeal, or draw the conclusion that Bartlet supposed he was meant to draw. Besides, these words were not uttered later than A.D. 59, and it is very unlikely that they had any sinister significance then.[33] They simply meant that by appealing Paul had put himself into a new position in relation to the law, and the course prescribed by the law for citizens in that position—appellants to the emperor— must now be followed. Paul must be sent to Rome.

[32] *Expositor* VIII, v. (1913), pp. 464 ff. *Cf.* p. 535, n. 48 (on Ch. 28:30).
[33] *Cf.* exposition of Ch. 25:11 (p. 479). There seems to have been a complete change in official policy towards the Christians from about the year 62, not long after Paul's release from his first Roman captivity. This was also the year which marked a turning-point in Nero's career, the year of Burrus's death and replacement by Tigellinus, Seneca's retirement, Nero's divorce of Octavia and his marriage with Poppaea. As Poppaea was not only a warm friend of the Jews but, according to Josephus (*Antiquities* xx. 8.11) actually a "God-fearer", her influence may have been specially inimical to Christianity. About this time it became increasingly clear that Christianity was not simply a movement within Judaism, sharing the recognition which Judaism enjoyed as a *religio licita*. It might therefore at any time be the object of suppression by the imperial police, and an opportunity for such measures arose after the fire of Rome in 64. But the situation in 59 was still largely what it had been when Gallio gave his favourable verdict seven or eight years before.

CHAPTER XXVII

6. THE VOYAGE AND SHIPWRECK OF PAUL

(Ch. 27:1–44)

Luke's narrative of the voyage and shipwreck of Paul is a small classic in its own right, as graphic a piece of descriptive writing as anything in the Bible. It is, besides, "one of the most instructive documents for the knowledge of ancient seamanship" (H. J. Holtzmann, *Handcommentar zum NT* [Freiburg im Breisgau, 1889], p. 421). Luke, who accompanied Paul on the voyage, viewed the sea through Greek eyes, and tells us what he saw in unforgettable word-pictures. He could also draw upon a well-established literary tradition for the description of a storm and wreck at sea—not that this in any way depreciates the factual worth of his narrative. From Homer's *Odyssey* onwards, the account of a Mediterranean voyage in antiquity almost invariably included a storm or shipwreck. Homer, in fact, set the fashion in which such accounts continued to be related for many centuries. Luke himself has in this chapter one or two unmistakable Homeric reminiscences. In the OT we have one famous narrative of the same kind, the story of Jonah's Mediterranean voyage and the storm into which he and his shipmates ran; and Luke appears to have drawn on this narrative as well.

Human life has often been compared to a voyage across a stormy sea. It is not surprising, therefore, that many readers and expositors have found an allegory of the soul's experience in Acts 27. Some have even detected in it a figurative prediction of the course of church history! This particular allegorization becomes specially interesting at the end of the story, when the ship is broken up and the passengers and crew have to make their way ashore as best they can.[1] Those who care for this sort of exposition may work the correspondences out for themselves, but let them beware of supposing that Luke had any such interpretation in mind when he penned his narrative.

[1] The allegorist's own ecclesiastical bias usually appears when he comes to identify the swimmers and those who got to land on planks and broken pieces of the ship!

That does not mean that the narrative is devoid of moral and spiritual lessons. They are here in abundance for those who have eyes to see. In particular, we may learn much from Luke's portrayal of Paul's character and behaviour in circumstances in which the real man is most likely to be revealed. We have seen Paul in many rôles, but here he stands out as the practical man in a critical emergency. Not once or twice the world has had to thank the great saints and mystics for providing timely help in moments of crisis when realistic, practical men of affairs were unable to supply it.

An indispensable handbook to the study of this chapter is *The Voyage and Shipwreck of St. Paul*, by James Smith. Smith, an experienced yachtsman and a man of no mean scholarship withal, made a careful study of Luke's narrative in relation to the route which it maps out—a part of the Mediterranean with which he himself was well acquainted—and formed the most favourable estimate of the accuracy of Luke's account of each stage of the voyage. For the seafaring technicalities of this chapter we shall lean heavily on Smith's work, the more so as it has been out of print since the exhaustion of its fourth edition (published in London in 1880).[2]

(a) To Crete via Myra (Ch. 27:1–8)

1 And when it was determined[3] that we should sail for Italy, they delivered Paul and certain other prisoners to a centurion named Julius, of the Augustan band.

2 And embarking in a ship of Adramyttium, which was about to sail unto the places on the coast of Asia, we put to sea, Aristarchus,[4] a Macedonian of Thessalonica, being with us.

3 And the next day we touched at Sidon: and Julius treated Paul kindly, and gave him leave to go unto his friends and refresh himself.

---

[2] The first edition is dated 1848. Another valuable work on ancient seamanship is A. Breusing, *Die Nautik der Alten* (Bremen, 1886). See also H. Balmer, *Die Romfahrt des Apostels Paulus und die Seefahrtskunde im römischen Kaiseralter* (Bern, 1905).

[3] The Western text has an expanded reading here: "So then the governor decided to send him to Caesar; and next day he called a certain centurion named Julius, of the Augustan cohort, and handed over to him Paul and other prisoners as well."

[4] The Western text adds Secundus, who is mentioned along with Aristarchus as a fellow-townsman and travel-companion in Ch. 20:4.

4 And putting to sea from thence, we sailed under the lee of Cyprus, because the winds were contrary.

5 And when we had sailed across the sea[5] which is off Cilicia and Pamphylia, we came to Myra,[6] *a city* of Lycia.

6 And there the centurion found a ship of Alexandria sailing for Italy; and he put us therein.

7 And when we had sailed slowly many days, and were come with difficulty over against Cnidus, the wind not further suffering us, we sailed under the lee of Crete, over against Salmone;

8 and with difficulty coasting along it we came unto a certain place called Fair Havens; nigh whereunto was the city of Lasea.

1 The "we" narrative is now resumed, after being broken off at Ch. 21:18. We have no direct information about Luke's movements during the two intervening years, but probably he was not far from Caesarea, where Paul was kept in custody.

Once it was decided that Paul must be sent to Rome to have his case tried in the imperial court, the first opportunity was taken to send him there under escort. The centurion Julius, in whose custody he was sent, belonged to the "Augustan" (or imperial)[7] cohort. Mommsen and Ramsay[8] identified this cohort with the corps of officer-couriers (Lat. *frumentarii*) detailed for communication-service between the emperor and his provincial armies. The term "Augustan", however, was a title of honour quite frequently bestowed on auxiliary troops.[9] Julius, at any rate, appears from the duties assigned to him to have been a legionary centurion, possibly seconded for service at this time with the cohort of officer-couriers; he had a body of soldiers under his

[5] The Western text gives fifteen days as the time spent in sailing across the open sea from Cyprus to Myra—a very reasonable estimate if the ship had to hug the south coast of Asia Minor for a good part of the voyage.

[6] See the Western text of Ch. 21:1 f. (pp. 420 f., nn. 1, 3).

[7] Gk. σεβαστός (*cf.* p. 483, n. 19, on Ch. 25:21).

[8] Th. Mommsen, *Sitzungsbericht der Akademie der Wissenschaften zu Berlin*, 1895, pp. 495 ff.; W. M. Ramsay, *St. Paul the Traveller*, p. 315. *Cf.* also p. 528 with n. 30 (on Ch. 28:16).

[9] We have inscriptional references to the *Cohors Augusta I* in Syria in the reign of Augustus (H. Dessau, *Inscriptiones Latinae Selectae* [Berlin, 1892], 2683) and the σπεῖρα Αὐγούστη in the same area some decades later (W. Dittenberger, *Orientis Graeci Inscriptiones Selectae* [Leipzig, 1903], 421); *cf.* also the *Cohors III Augusta* at Rome (*Corpus Inscriptionum Latinarum* vi [Berlin, 1876], 3508).

command on the voyage to Rome. Who the other prisoners were whom they had in charge we cannot tell; in any case, a Roman citizen who had appealed to the emperor would occupy a much more favourable position than ordinary prisoners.

2 The port of embarkation is not specified; probably it was Caesarea. Had it been any other (such as Ptolemais), Luke, in accordance with his usual practice, would doubtless have mentioned it. The ship in which they embarked belonged to Adramyttium, a seaport of Mysia in north-west Asia Minor, opposite the island of Lesbos. It was a coasting vessel, which was to call at various ports of the province of Asia; at one of these Julius knew he would find a ship bound for Rome.[10] Aristarchus of Thessalonica[11] is not expressly named later in this narrative; it is possible, therefore, that he was travelling home and did not join the second ship which took the party Romewards. On the other hand, he was in Paul's company in Rome at some point during the next two years (Col. 4:10; Philem. 24), so he may have gone all the way with Paul and Luke on this occasion; in that case he is no doubt included in Luke's "we" throughout this narrative. Ramsay argues that Luke and Aristarchus must have travelled as Paul's slaves, "not merely performing the duties of slaves ... but actually passing as slaves. In this way not merely had Paul faithful friends always beside him; his importance in the eyes of the centurion was much enhanced, and that was of great importance. The narrative clearly implies that Paul enjoyed much respect during this voyage, such as a penniless traveller without a servant to attend on him would never receive either in the first century or the nineteenth" (*St. Paul the Traveller*, p. 316). Ramsay's argument merits the respect due to his great knowledge of social history in the Roman Empire of the first century A.D.

3 The day after they set sail, they put in at Sidon, the ancient Phoenician metropolis, which was about 69 miles north of Caesarea. It had a double harbour.[12]

Here Paul received the first of a number of recorded kindnesses at the hands of Julius. (It is remarkable how uniformly centurions

---

[10] But if they arrived late and found that the period of sailing was over for the winter, they would no doubt take the land-route to Rome along the Egnatian Way from the Aegean to the Adriatic.

[11] *Cf.* Ch. 19:29.

[12] *Cf.* Achilles Tatius, *Leucippe and Cleitophon* i. 1.

receive favourable notice in the NT.)[13] In Sidon there was a Christian church, founded probably during the persecution that followed the death of Stephen (Ch. 11:19). Paul was permitted to go ashore and visit these people, for that is certainly what we are to understand by "his friends",[14] and receive all the care that their Christian love could suggest while the ship was in harbour. We may assume that a soldier was detailed to accompany him.

4 Putting out to sea again, they sailed east and north of Cyprus, that is to say, on the lee side of the island, as the prevailing winds in the Levant throughout the summer months are westerly.[15] A ship doing the reverse journey, from south-west Asia Minor to Syria, fared directly over the sea, passing west of Cyprus (*cf.* Ch. 21:1–3). Luke no doubt remembered doing this when he sailed with Paul to Palestine two years previously, and noted the different procedure on this occasion.

5 A stretch of open sea had to be crossed now—the sea between Cyprus and the south coast of Asia Minor. They reached the coast of Asia Minor at a point well to the east, and then the ship worked slowly westward, helped by local land breezes and by a steady westward current which runs along that coast. "The Adramyttian ship crept on from point to point up the coast, taking advantage of every opportunity to make a few miles, and lying at anchor in the shelter of the winding coast, when the westerly wind made progress impossible" (Ramsay, *St. Paul the Traveller*, p. 317). In this way they reached Myra, a port of Lycia, the most southerly region of the province of Asia. (The city of Myra lay inland, some two miles from the harbour;[16] the ruins of the city theatre and some tombs are still visible.)

6 At Myra the first part of the journey came to an end. For Myra was one of the chief ports of the grain fleet that plied between Egypt and Rome, and a vessel belonging to that fleet was in port, on its way to Rome, when the ship of Adramyttium put in there. Egypt was the chief granary of Rome, and the corn trade between Alexandria and Rome was of the highest importance.

---

[13] *Cf.* p. 215 with n. 3 (on Ch. 10:1).

[14] In his *Mission and Expansion of Christianity* (Eng. tr., London, 1908), i, pp. 419 ff., Harnack suggests that πρὸς τοὺς φίλους should be translated "to the Friends", regarding this as possibly one of the current designations by which Christians referred to each other. *Cf.* 3 John 15.

[15] Smith, *Voyage*, p. 68.

[16] Strabo, *Geography* xiv. 3.7.

The service of ships devoted to this trade was organized as a department of state.[17] The corporation of owners of these ships received special recognition from the Roman state, for they were in practice its agents and concessionaires. That the Rome-bound vessel which was in harbour at Myra when the centurion and his party arrived there belonged to this fleet is confirmed later in the story (v. 38), where it is said to have had a cargo of wheat on board. "With the westerly winds which prevail in those seas, ships, particularly those of the ancients, unprovided with a compass and ill calculated to work to windward, would naturally stand to the north till they made the land of Asia Minor, which is peculiarly favourable for navigation by such vessels, because the coast is bold and safe, and the elevation of the mountains makes it visible at a great distance; it abounds in harbours, and the sinuosities of its shores and the westerly current would enable them, if the wind was at all off the land, to work to windward, at least as far as Cnidus, where these advantages ceased. Myra lies due north from Alexandria, and its bay is well calculated to shelter a windbound ship" (Smith, *Voyage*, pp. 72 f.). "The ship was on its regular and ordinary course, and had quite probably been making a specially good run, for in the autumn there was always risk of the wind shifting round towards the north, and with the wind N.W. the Alexandrian ships could only fetch the Syrian coast" (Ramsay, *St. Paul the Traveller*, p. 319). At Myra, then, Julius trans-shipped his party to this Alexandrian vessel.

7   From Myra the going was slow and difficult, because of the strong north-west wind that was blowing.[18] After several days they reached Cnidus, a port on the Carian promontory of Triopium, which was frequented by merchant-ships from Egypt.[19] Here they had a choice of two alternatives. They might put into port at Cnidus and wait for a fair wind; there was ample accommodation for ships there, for Cnidus had two harbours, the eastern one being particularly large. When a fair wind came, they might then sail due west for the island of Cythera. But if they preferred to continue the voyage without delay, their only course was to run for the eastern extremity of Crete (Salmone) and, after rounding

---

[17] Ramsay, *St. Paul the Traveller*, p. 318; M. Rostovtzeff, *Social and Economic History of the Roman Empire* (Oxford, 1926), p. 595.
[18] Smith, *Voyage*, pp. 75 f.
[19] *Cf.* Thucydides, *History*, viii. 35.

it, sail under the lee of that island (along its south coast). This is what they did. From the fact that they succeeded in fetching Cape Salmone, Smith deduces that the wind must have been a north-wester, which in any case is "precisely the wind which might have been expected in those seas towards the end of summer" (*Voyage*, p. 76).

8 Even coasting along the south of Crete was difficult with the wind blowing from the north-west, but at last they came to the small bay which still, in its modern Greek form (Limeônas Kalous), retains the name Fair Havens. After they rounded Cape Salmone, this was their first convenient shelter, and here they put in and waited for the wind to change. Two leagues farther west lies Cape Matala, and beyond Cape Matala the south coast of Crete trends suddenly to the north, and would afford no more protection against a north-west wind. In the neighbourhood of Fair Havens, Luke points out, lay the city of Lasea—the place mentioned by Pliny the Elder (*Natural History* iv. 59) by the name Lasos or Alos. It has been identified with ruins a little to the east of Fair Havens.

(b) The Wind Euraquilo (Ch. 27:9–26)

9 And when much time was spent, and the voyage was now dangerous, because the Fast was now already gone by, Paul admonished them,

10 and said unto them, Sirs, I perceive that the voyage will be with injury and much loss, not only of the lading and the ship, but also of our lives.

11 But the centurion gave more heed to the master and to the owner of the ship, than to those things which were spoken by Paul.

12 And because the haven was not commodious to winter in, the more part advised to put to sea from thence, if by any means they could reach Phoenix, and winter *there; which is* a haven of Crete, looking north-east and south-east.[20]

13 And when the south wind blew softly, supposing that they had obtained their purpose, they weighed anchor and sailed along Crete, close in shore.

14 But after no long time there beat down from it a tempestuous wind, which is called Euraquilo:[21]

---

[20] Translate "facing south-west and north-west"; *cf.* n. 31 below.

[21] The Byzantine text has the variant "Euroclydon."

15 and when the ship was caught, and could not face the wind, we gave way *to it*, and were driven.[22]

16 And running under the lee of a small island called Cauda,[23] we were able, with difficulty, to secure the boat:

17 and when they had hoisted it up, they used helps, under-girding the ship; and, fearing lest they should be cast upon the Syrtis, they lowered the gear,[24] and so were driven.

18 And as we labored exceedingly with the storm, the next day they began to throw *the freight* overboard;

19 and the third day they cast out with their own hands[25] the tackling of the ship.

20 And when neither sun nor stars shone upon *us* for many days, and no small tempest lay on *us*, all hope that we should be saved was now taken away.

21 And when they had been long without food, then Paul stood forth in the midst of them, and said, Sirs, ye should have hearkened unto me, and not have set sail from Crete, and have gotten this injury and loss.

22 And now I exhort you to be of good cheer; for there shall be no loss of life among you, but *only* of the ship.

23 For there stood by me this night an angel of the God whose I am, whom also I serve,

24 saying, Fear not, Paul: thou must stand before Caesar; and lo, God hath granted thee all them that sail with thee.

25 Wherefore, sirs, be of good cheer: for I believe God, that it shall be even so as it hath been spoken unto me.

26 But we must be cast upon a certain island.

9   The delay that had been occasioned already by the adverse wind began to make them anxious. And as they waited for a change of wind at Fair Havens, it soon became clear that they would not complete the voyage to Italy before the onset of winter.

22 There is an expanded Western reading: "we gave way to the wind that was blowing and shortened sail (καὶ συστείλαντες τὰ ἱστία) and, as happens in such cases, scudded before it."

23 Many manuscripts have the variant spelling "Clauda", found also in several ancient authors.

24 Gk. χαλάσαντες τὸ σκεῦος. Some Gk. minuscules, followed by the Syriac Peshitta, have χαλάσαντες τὰ ἱστία ("slackening sail"), which may be the original Western reading. See nn. 39–41 below.

25 The Byzantine text has "we cast out with our hands"; the Western text adds "into the sea".

The dangerous season for sailing began about September 14 and lasted until November 11; after the latter date all navigation on the open sea came to an end until winter was over.[26] "It was now the dangerous season for sailing", says Luke, "and even the Fast had by this time gone by." By the "Fast" he means, of course, the Great Day of Atonement, which falls on Tishri 10. Luke's remark has point only if that date fell rather late in the solar calendar that year. In A.D. 59 it fell on October 5, but in all the neighbouring years from A.D. 57 to 62 it fell earlier.[27] A late date for the Day of Atonement is required also by the subsequent time-notes of the journey to Italy. When they set sail from Fair Havens, fifty or sixty miles brought them under the lee of Cauda (v. 16); on the fourteenth night from Cauda (v. 27) they drew near land, and the following day (v. 39) they landed on Malta, where they spent three months (Ch. 28:11). The seas were closed to sailing until the beginning of February at the earliest;[28] the three months spent in Malta must therefore have corresponded roughly to November, December and January; they must have left Fair Havens not much earlier than mid-October.[29] The solar date of the Day of Atonement in A.D. 59 thus accords well with Luke's implication that the Fast took place while they were at Fair Havens.

Under these circumstances Ramsay's suggestion is entirely probable that a ship's council was held, and that Paul, perhaps because he was an experienced traveller, was invited to attend it (*St. Paul the Traveller*, pp. 322 ff.). It would be at this council that Paul "admonished them" (ARV) or rather "offered his advice".

10 The advice which Paul gave them, if we combine the language here with that of v. 21, was that they should remain at Fair Havens for the winter, as any attempt to continue the voyage now would involve great peril not only to the ship and cargo but to the passengers and crew.

---

[26] Vegetius, *On Military Affairs*, iv. 39.

[27] *Cf.* W. P. Workman, "A New Date-Indication in Acts," Ex T xi (1899–1900), pp. 316 ff.

[28] Vegetius, *loc. cit.*

[29] "We might be disposed to infer that the Feast of Tabernacles, Oct. 10, fell after they left Fair Havens, otherwise Luke would have mentioned it rather than the Fast, as making the danger more apparent" (Ramsay, *St. Paul the Traveller*, p. 322).

11 The pilot and shipowner,[30] however, thought that there was a chance of making a more commodious port farther west along the south coast of Crete, and the centurion, not unnaturally, accepted their view rather than Paul's. A merchant-shipowner normally acted as captain of his own ship. The owner of this particular ship would be a contractor for the state transport of grain. But the final decision was left to the centurion; as the highest official on board, he ranked as commanding officer, the more so as this ship belonged to a state service. He ruled that the advice of the experts should be followed. Smith observes "that Fair Havens is so well protected by islands, that though not equal to Lutro [a port farther west along the coast], it must be a very fair winter harbour; and that considering the suddenness, the frequency, and the violence with which gales of northerly wind spring up, and the certainty that, if such a gale sprang up in the passage from Fair Havens to Lutro, the ship must be driven off to sea, the prudence of the advice given by the master and owner was extremely questionable, and that the advice given by St. Paul may probably be supported even on nautical grounds" (*Voyage*, p. 85 n.).

12 The view of the pilot and shipowner, and of the majority of the crew, was that Fair Havens was not a convenient harbour to spend the winter in. It is, as has just appeared from the quotation from Smith, protected by small islands; but it labours under the disadvantage of standing open to nearly half the compass. They therefore decided to set sail in hope of reaching the more commodious harbour of Phoenix.

Phoenix is described in the ARV text as "a haven of Crete, looking north-east and south-east" (margin: "down the south-west wind and down the north-west wind").[31] But this is an unnatural rendering of the Greek text, which would normally be taken to mean "facing south-west and north-west" (*cf.* AV, "lieth toward the south west and north west"). The reason for the rendering in

---

[30] The Gk. word for "shipowner" is ναύκληρος (Latinized as *nauicularius*). Ramsay (*St. Paul the Traveller*, p. 324 n.) quotes from *Inscriptiones Graecae* xiv (Berlin, 1891), No. 918, the expression οἱ ναύκληροι τοῦ πορευτικοῦ ᾽Αλεξανδρείνου στόλου ("the shipowners of the Alexandrian fleet"). *Cf.* Rostovtzeff, *op. cit.*, p. 532.

[31] Gk. βλέποντα κατὰ λίβα καὶ κατὰ χῶρον. The λίψ was a south-west wind, explained by a popular etymology as meaning "Libyan"; χῶρος is a loan-word from Lat. *caurus*, the north-west wind.

ARV (similarly ERV and RSV) is no doubt the identification of Phoenix with Lutro, a port some 34 miles west of Cape Matala. This identification has the weighty advocacy of Smith, according to whom Lutro has been called "the only secure harbour in all winds on the south coast of Crete" (*Voyage*, p. 91 n.). Ramsay also favoured Lutro, but recognized that Luke's Greek wording cannot be interpreted of a harbour facing east, as Lutro does. "But it must be observed," he says, "that Luke never saw the harbour, and merely speaks on Paul's report of the professional opinion. It is possible that the sailors described the entrance as one in which inward-bound ships looked towards N.W. and S.W., and that in transmission from mouth to mouth, the wrong impression was given that the harbour looked N.W. and S.W." (*St. Paul the Traveller*, p. 326). But it is not necessary to suppose that any such mistake was made. A short distance west of Lutro, on the other side of the peninsula of Muros, lies Phineka, which evidently preserves the ancient name Phoenix. Phineka lies open to any westerly wind and may have had quite a good harbour in the first century; the two streams shown as entering the bay in its vicinity may have silted it up in the course of the centuries.[32]

13 Soon after they made this decision, the wind changed in their favour. A gentle south wind sprang up, which promised to bring them to Phoenix with little difficulty. So they set out from Fair Havens and coasted along towards the west, keeping close in to the shore, until they rounded Cape Matala. A few hours would now take them to their desired haven, with this favouring wind to waft them across the mouth of the wide Gulf of Messara.

14 Suddenly, however, the wind changed again: "the sudden

---

[32] Luke's Phoenix has been identified with Phineka by C. Wordsworth, T. E. Page, and C. H. Prichard (*cf.* Lake–Cadbury, *ad loc.*). Smith, however, animadverting upon Wordsworth's argument, insists that "in the first place the south coast of Crete is now so well known, that we can say with certainty that there is no other harbour than Lutro in which a ship could winter to the west of Fair Havens, and that Phineka Bay is not open to Caurus" (*Voyage*, p. 92 n.). But C. Lattey ("The Harbour Phoenix", *Scripture* iv [1949–51], pp. 144 ff.) argues from Galen (*Works*, ed. C. G. Kühn, xvi [Leipzig, 1829], p. 406) that *caurus* may denote a south-west wind, and that Phineka Bay therefore does meet the requirements; the wind would in that case be indicated here both by Gk. λίψ and by Lat. *caurus*. It is not clear that the Galen passage will bear the weight of Lattey's argument; but even so Phineka is open to Lips at any rate, whereas Lutro is open neither to Caurus nor to Lips, and therefore in this respect suits Luke's description of Phoenix still less well than Phineka does.

change from a south wind to a violent northerly wind is a common occurrence in these seas" (Smith, *Voyage*, p. 102). A furious north-easter[33] sprang up and rushed down upon them from Mount Ida—a typhonic wind,[34] says Luke, referring to the whirling motion of the clouds and sea caused by the meeting of contrary currents of air. The sailors recognized this wind as an old enemy, and had a name for it—Euraquilo.[35]

15-16   The ship was caught up in the gale, and being unable to head up to it, scudded before it. Twenty-three miles or so to leeward lay the small island of Cauda, the modern Gavdho,[36] under the lee of which they soon ran, and made speedy and timely use of the brief space of shelter which it afforded. First of all they hauled the dinghy on board. The dinghy was normally towed astern, but taken aboard in bad weather. On this occasion there had been no time to do so, so suddenly did Euraquilo burst upon them. By this time it must have been full of water, and this made it all the more difficult to secure it. "We were able, with difficulty, to secure the boat," says Luke, using the first person plural; there were certain jobs which only trained members of the crew could carry out, but any landlubber could haul on a rope, and some of the passengers were pressed into service. "With difficulty," says Luke, probably remembering his blisters![37]

17   The next thing to do was to undergird the ship, passing cables round it transversely underneath in order to hold the timbers together. The word translated "helps"[38] was a nautical term used in such contexts as this. The typhoon is described by Pliny the Elder as "the chief plague of sailors, not only breaking up the spars but the hull itself" (*Natural History* ii. 132). As a

---

33 More precisely, an east-by-north-east wind (Smith, *Voyage*, pp. 103, 161).

34 Gk. ἄνεμος τυφωνικός.

35 Gk. Εὐρακύλων. The word is a hybrid, being derived from Gk. Εὖρος ("east wind") and Lat. *Aquilo* ("north wind"—or, as an accurate nautical term, "north-one-third-east wind").

36 Also known by its Italian name Gozzo. In the vicinity of this island the Battle of Cape Matapan was fought between the Italian and British navies on March 28, 1941. There is, according to Smith, an anchorage at Cauda, but it lies on the side of the island open to the east-north-east, and could therefore have given no protection to the ship (*Voyage*, p. 113 n.).

37 Lake–Cadbury (*ad loc.*) suggest that the foremast, which sloped forward, was used as a derrick.

38 Gk. βοήθειαι. The nautical use of this word is attested by Aristotle (*Rhetoric* ii. 5.18) and Philo (*On Joseph*, 33). A more explicit term for the "helps" used on this occasion is ὑποζώματα, "undergirders", "frapping cables."

safety measure, ancient vessels were provided with cables ready fitted for bracing the hulls to enable them to resist the destructive force of such winds.

There was still time for a third precautionary measure while they enjoyed the shelter of Cauda, but what the nature of this third measure was is not quite clear. The fear which led them to take it, however, is clear enough: they were afraid of being driven on to the Greater Syrtis, the quicksands off the African coast, west of Cyrene. The Greater Syrtis was still a great distance away, but the wind might continue to blow for many days, and that was the direction in which it was driving them. What, then, did they do? "They lowered the gear", says our version.[39] But "gear" is an indefinite word. Some have suggested that they dropped a floating anchor, the dragging of which would serve as a brake.[40] Smith, however, pointing out that the word, "when applied to a ship, means appurtenances of every kind, such as spars, sails, rigging, anchors and cables, etc.," adds: "Now, every ship situated as this one was, when preparing for a storm, sends down upon deck the 'top-hamper,' or gear connected with the fair-weather sails, such as the *suppara*, or top-sails. A modern ship sends down top-gallant masts and yards; a cutter strikes her topmast, when preparing for a gale" (*Voyage*, p. 111). In this case, he approves the suggestion that what was lowered was "not the mast, but the yard with the sail attached to it" (*ib.*, p. 112).[41] Then, when everything had been done that could be done in those circumstances, the ship was laid-to on the starboard tack (with her right side to the wind), with storm sails set, and so she drifted slowly, at a mean rate of one and a half miles per hour, in a direction about eight degrees north of west.

18–19 Next day, as there was no abatement of the gale, they

---

[39] Gk. χαλάσαντες τὸ σκεῦος. "It is not easy to imagine a more erroneous translation than that of our authorised version: 'Fearing lest they should fall into the quicksands, strake sail, and so were driven' (ver. 17). It is in fact equivalent to saying that, fearing a certain danger, they deprived themselves of the only possible means of avoiding it. It is not by striking mast or sail that such dangers are to be avoided" (Smith, *Voyage*, pp. 109 f.). See n. 24 above.

[40] *Cf.* J. Renié, "Summisso Vase", *Recherches de Science Religieuse* xxxv (1948), pp. 272 ff. This interpretation is presupposed by the Old Latin text of Codex *gigas*, "They let down a certain instrument to drag."

[41] *Cf.* the Old Latin text of Codex *Bobiensis* (s), "letting down the sails."

began to jettison the cargo.[42] The following day, a more drastic measure was necessary: the spare gear had to go, if the ship was to have a chance of surviving. Smith suggests that "the main-yard is meant; an immense spar, probably as long as the ship, which would require the united efforts of passengers and crew to launch overboard" (*Voyage*, p. 116). The AV uses the first person plural here—"we cast out with our own hands..."—and while this reading is not nearly so well supported as the third person, there is no doubt that, as Ramsay says, it "greatly increases the effect" (*St. Paul the Traveller*, p. 332).

20 Eleven dreary nights and days followed. The storm blotted out the sun by day and stars by night, and thus they had no means of keeping a reckoning. The ship was no doubt leaking badly, and they "could not tell which way to make for the nearest land, in order to run their ship ashore, the only resource for a sinking ship; but unless they did make the land, they must founder at sea" (*Voyage*, p. 117). No wonder, then, that they began to lose all hope of ever reaching safety.

21-26 Things being as they were, they had little heart to take food; besides, it would have been difficult to prepare food, and a good part of their supplies must have been spoiled by the sea-water. Among several parallels quoted by Smith is one (*Voyage*, p. 118) from the autobiography of John Newton, the celebrated English clergyman and hymn-writer, relating to his earlier sea-faring days: "We found that the water having floated all our movables in the hold, all the casks of provisions had been beaten in pieces by the violent motion of the ship. On the other hand, our live stock, such as pigs, sheep, and poultry, had been washed overboard in the storm; in effect, all the provisions we saved ... would have subsisted us but a week, at a scanty allowance" (*Omicron's Letters* [London, 1774], Letter VII). And anyone who has suffered from seasickness on board a well-appointed passenger liner of the present day can imagine something of what its horrors must have been in that storm-tossed vessel, and how little appetite for eating its victims must have had.

In the midst of this general dejection and despair, Paul stood up one morning and addressed his companions in distress. It

---

[42] *Cf.* Jonah 1:5, where the mariners, in a Mediterranean storm, "cast forth the wares that were in the ship into the sea, to lighten it unto them."

warms our hearts to see, first of all, that in some very human respects he was so like ourselves; he could not resist the temptation to say "I told you so" to those who had despised his good advice at Fair Havens! But what he went on to tell them was exactly what the situation most needed, a message of encouragement and hope. Nor was this simply the product of wishful thinking; he spoke as one who had received divine assurance. Earlier, at Fair Havens, he had warned them that loss of life, as well as of the ship and cargo, would be the result of their setting sail from that port. But on that occasion he spoke simply as an experienced traveller of sound judgment. This was not the first time that he had known the destructive power of a storm at sea; he remembered another ship in which he had once sailed: it had come to grief, and he had spent twenty-four hours in the open sea, probably supported by a spar from the wreck, until he was picked up or washed ashore (2 Cor. 11:25).[43] There had been considerable loss of life on that occasion, we may suppose, and he feared that the same thing might happen again. But now he is confident that, while the ship is doomed, no life will be lost. No amount of experience or shrewd calculation could have given him this assurance; he ascribes his new confidence to a supernatural revelation made to him during the past night by an angel of God. Not only would he himself survive to stand before the emperor; the lives of his shipmates were also to be spared for his sake.[44] The world has no idea how much it owes, in the mercy of God, to the presence in it of righteous men.[45]

Having received this communication from heaven, Paul was completely assured that it would turn out just as he had been told. The ship would go down, but the men would be saved; they would be washed ashore on some island or other.

(c) The Shipwreck (Ch. 27:27–44)

27 But when the fourteenth night was come, as we were driven to and fro in the *sea of* Adria, about midnight the sailors surmised that they were drawing near to some country:

[43] He had suffered shipwreck on three previous occasions (2 Cor. 11:25).

[44] In a vision two years before he had received the assurance that he would survive to bear witness at Rome (Ch. 23:11); this assurance was now repeated and amplified.

[45] *Cf.* Gen. 18:26 ff.

512

28 and they sounded, and found twenty fathoms; and after
a little space, they sounded again, and found fifteen
fathoms.

29 And fearing lest haply we should be cast ashore on
rocky ground, they let go four anchors from the stern,
and wished for the day.

30 And as the sailors were seeking to flee out of the ship,
and had lowered the boat into the sea, under color as
though they would lay out anchors from the foreship,

31 Paul said to the centurion and to the soldiers, Except
these abide in the ship, ye cannot be saved.

32 Then the soldiers cut away the ropes of the boat, and
let her fall off.

33 And while the day was coming on, Paul besought them
all to take some food, saying, This day is the fourteenth
day that ye wait and continue fasting, having taken
nothing.

34 Wherefore I beseech you to take some food: for this
is for your safety: for there shall not a hair perish
from the head of any of you.

35 And when he had said this, and had taken bread, he
gave thanks to God in the presence of all; and he brake
it, and began to eat.[46]

36 Then were they all of good cheer, and themselves also
took food.

37 And we were in all in the ship two hundred threescore
and sixteen souls.[47]

38 And when they had eaten enough, they lightened the
ship, throwing out the wheat into the sea.

39 And when it was day, they knew not the land: but they
perceived a certain bay with a beach, and they took
counsel whether they could drive[48] the ship upon it.

40 And casting off the anchors, they left them in the sea,
at the same time loosing the bands of the rudders;[49]
and hoisting up the foresail to the wind, they made for
the beach.

41 But lighting upon a place where two seas met, they

[46] The Western text adds "giving also to us."

[47] For the variant Alexandrian reading, "about seventy-six" (Cod. B and the
Sahidic version), see n. 60 below.

[48] Gk. ἐξῶσαι. The variant ἐκσῶσαι, found in B, C, several minuscules, and
the Sahidic, Bohairic and Armenian versions, and translated "bring the ship
safe to shore" in ARV margin, is a less natural expression here.

[49] Translate "steering-paddles", not "rudders" (Gk. πηδάλια).

ran the vessel[50] aground;[51] and the foreship struck
and remained unmoveable, but the stern began to break
up by the violence *of the waves.*

42 And the soldiers' counsel was to kill the prisoners,
lest any *of them* should swim out, and escape.

43 But the centurion,[52] desiring to save Paul, stayed them
from their purpose; and commanded that they who
could swim should cast themselves overboard, and get
first to the land;

44 and the rest, some on planks, and some on *other* things
from the ship. And so it came to pass, that they all
escaped safe to the land.

27–28 Smith relates how he made careful enquiries of experienced Mediterranean navigators in order to ascertain the
mean rate of drift of a ship of this kind laid-to in such a gale.
The conclusion which he reached was a mean drift of about
thirty-six miles in twenty-four hours. The soundings recorded in
v. 28 indicate that the ship was passing Koura, a point on the east
coast of Malta, on her way into St. Paul's Bay. "But the distance
from Clauda to the point of Koura ... is 476.6 miles, which, at the
rate as deduced from the information ..., would take exactly
thirteen days, one hour, and twenty-one minutes." And not only
so: "The coincidence of the actual bearing of St. Paul's Bay from
Clauda, and the direction in which a ship must have driven in
order to avoid the Syrtis, is if possible still more striking than that
of the time actually consumed, and the calculated time." Then,
after carefully reckoning the direction of the ship's course from
the direction of the wind, from the angle of the ship's head with
the wind, and from the lee-way, he goes on:

"Hence according to these calculations, a ship starting late in
the evening from Clauda would, by midnight on the 14th, be less

---

[50] Gk. ναῦς. Elsewhere in this narrative (and indeed elsewhere in NT) πλοῖον
is the word used for "ship." This solitary occurrence of the classical ναῦς
has been very plausibly explained by F. Blass as a Homeric reminiscence:
"Must we not accept it for a certainty that Luke, the physician of Antioch, had
gone through his Homer?" (*Philology of the Gospels* [London, 1898], p. 186).
There are one or two other possible Homeric reminiscences in this chapter.

[51] There is a Western addition here: "on a place where there was a quick-
sand."

[52] The Old Latin text of *gigas*, probably representing the original Western
reading, runs as follows: "But the centurion forbade this to be done, principally on Paul's account, in order to save him. And he commanded those who
could swim to get to land first, and some of the rest to make their way to
safety on planks; and thus all the souls escaped safe to the land."

than three miles from the entrance of St. Paul's Bay. I admit that a coincidence so very close as this, is to a certain extent accidental, but it is an accident which could not have happened had there been any inaccuracy on the part of the author of the narrative with regard to the numerous incidents upon which the calculations are founded, or had the ship been wrecked anywhere but at Malta, for there is no other place agreeing, either in name or description, within the limits to which we are tied down by calculations founded upon the narrative" (*Voyage*, pp. 126–8).

The "sea of Adria" mentioned in v. 27 is the central Mediterranean; it is so called in several places in ancient literature. A better transliteration than "Adria" would be "Hadria".[53] In former days some astonishingly perverse interpretations of this narrative were suggested by expositors who supposed that the Adriatic Sea was intended—as if an east-north-east gale could possibly have blown them in that direction from the south coast of Crete! (The Adriatic Sea was then known as the "*gulf* of Hadria" in distinction from the *sea* of Hadria.) The translation "as we were driven to and fro"[54] is wrong; translate: "while we were drifting through (or across) the sea of Hadria." And what "the sailors surmised", if we translate the words strictly, was not "that they were drawing near to some country" but "that some land was approaching,"[55] or, if we adopt an alternative reading, "that some land was resounding",[56] *i.e.*, that the breakers could be heard. Had it been daylight, they would have seen the breakers as well as heard them. For, as Smith tells us (*Voyage*, p. 121), no ship can enter St. Paul's Bay from the east without passing within a quarter of a mile of the point of Koura, and when she comes within that distance (and only then), the breakers cannot fail to be seen, for they are specially violent there in a north-east wind. The tradition which has given St. Paul's Bay its name as the place of the shipwreck is confirmed by the soundings which Luke records: these agree with the direction of a ship passing

---

53 *E.g.*, Strabo (*c.* A.D. 19) says that "the Ionian Sea is part of what is now called the sea of Hadria" (*Geography* ii.5.20).

54 Gk. διαφερομένων ἡμῶν.

55 Gk. προσάγειν τινα αὐτοῖς χώραν.

56 For προσάγειν of our other authorities, the first hand in B reads προσαχεῖν, the Doric equivalent of Attic προσηχεῖν. It was a dialect form which perhaps survived with a special sense in nautical language. The Old Latin texts of *gigas* and *Bobiensis* (s) reflect this reading; they have here *resonare* ("resound").

Koura on her way into the bay. The twenty fathoms' depth is close to the spot where they would first have had indications that land was approaching, bearing east by south from the fifteen fathoms' depth, at a distance which would allow preparations for anchoring in the way mentioned in v. 29. Smith estimates the "little space" of time between the two soundings as about half an hour.

29 It was dangerous to go any farther; the breakers warned them of rocks ahead, so they dropped four anchors to serve as a brake until daylight showed them where they were.[57] The anchors were dropped from the stern—an unusual procedure, but advantageous under certain circumstances.[58] Had they anchored by the bow, the ship would have swung round from the wind, whereas now the prow kept pointing to the shore, so that the ship was ready to be beached when once day broke and the anchor cables were cut.

30–32 The sailors now attempted to make sure of their own safety at the expense of the others on board. They lowered the dinghy into the sea, pretending that they were going to lay out anchors from the bow as well as from the stern, but actually with the intention of making for the shore. Paul detected their aim, and prevented it. Perhaps his own nautical experience told him that there could be no possible advantage in anchoring the ship by the bow under the present circumstances. Why the sailors' presence aboard was necessary for the safety of all is not expressly said; but plainly it would have been disastrous had the ship been left as it was with no skilled hands to work it. By this time the centurion had learned that it was unwise to disregard Paul's advice, though it is not certain that his advice was correctly interpreted when the soldiers cut the hawsers and let the dinghy go adrift. The dinghy could have been very useful in getting the ship's company and passengers ashore had it proved impossible

---

[57] "In St. Paul's Bay the anchorage is thus described in the sailing directions: 'The harbour of St. Paul is open to easterly and north-east winds. It is, notwithstanding, safe for small ships, the ground, generally, being very good; and while the cables hold there is no danger, *as the anchors will never start*'" (Smith, *Voyage*, p. 132).

[58] Smith reproduces, from a picture at Herculaneum, the figure of a ship fitted with hawse-holes aft, through which anchor-cables could be passed if necessary. "We see, therefore, that ships of the ancients were fitted to anchor by the stern; and in the present instance that mode of anchoring was attended with most important advantages" (*Voyage*, p. 135).

to beach the ship, or when the ship stuck fast as it later did
(v. 41). However, the centurion may have decided that the
soldiers' action was necessary to prevent the sailors from abandoning
the ship.

33-38 Paul now imparted further encouragement to his shipmates. As dawn was breaking he advised them to take some food,
after the enforced abstinence of fourteen long days. The situation
was now easier, and food could be more conveniently prepared:
hard work lay ahead if they were all to come safe to land, and
it would do them all good and give them fresh energy and
enthusiasm for what had yet to be done if they had something
to eat. Again he assured them that no harm would befall any
of them. Then he encouraged them by example as well as by
what he said; he took some bread himself, gave thanks to God,[59]
and began to eat it. The rest followed his example; there was
no further need to stint themselves, and they took a full meal.
It is noteworthy that this is the point at which Luke tells us how
many were on board;[60] perhaps it was necessary to count them
in order to divide the available bread among them fairly. When
they had eaten their fill, they used their new strength to jettison
the remainder of the wheat-cargo. A good part of it had been
thrown overboard at the beginning of the storm (v. 18), but some
must have been kept as ballast and possibly also for food. Now,
however, it was desirable that the ship should draw as little water
as possible, and run aground well up the beach.

39 By this time it was light, but the sailors did not recognize

[59] Gk. εὐχαρίστησεν. But "there is no ground for the observation of
Olshausen that it was, for the Christians, the celebration of the Lord's Supper
or of an agape. For though the terms are just such as were so employed, they
are no less expressly applied to an ordinary meal in Luke 24:30, and elsewhere . . . It is the object of the Eucharist which gives it its character; and
this was quite out of place here. But the most ordinary food should be
sanctified by the word of God and prayer, and the apostle here acts on his own
instructions to Timothy (1 Tim. 4:5, 6). No wonder that all became cheerful
and took food (v. 36) after long dejection and disinclination with death before
their eyes!" (W. Kelly, *Exposition of Acts* [3rd edn., London, 1952], p. 387).
See, however, Bo Reicke, "Die Mahlzeit mit Paulus auf den Wellen des
Mittelmeers," *Theologische Zeitschrift* iv (1948), pp. 401 ff.

[60] Although there is some ancient evidence for the reading "about seventy-
six" (*cf.* n. 47 above), there is nothing improbable in the larger and better-
attested number, "two hundred and seventy-six." Josephus tells us how in
A.D. 63 he set sail for Rome in a ship which had six hundred on board—and
it too went down in the sea of Hadria (*Autobiography*, 3).

the land which they had approached; St. Paul's Bay is some distance away from the main harbour of Valletta, with which they were probably familiar. But they noticed a creek with a sandy beach, and decided to try to run the ship aground there. The combination of this creek with the "rocky ground" (v. 29) and the "place where two seas met" (v. 41) confirms the tradition which places this incident in St. Paul's Bay. Smith shows in detail "how perfectly these features still distinguish the coast" (*Voyage*, p. 141). The west side of the bay, to which the ship must have been driven, is rocky, but has two creeks, and Smith locates the scene of the wreck at the creek which was nearer to the "place where two seas met."

40 They had no further use for the four anchors, so they slipped them and left them in the sea. At the same time they unleashed the lashings of the steering-paddles (which in an ancient ship served the purpose which rudders serve nowadays), and hoisted a small sail on the foremast;[61] thus they had the ship under command to run her aground on the beach which they had noticed.

41 But there was something which they had not noticed, because it could not be seen until they had entered the bay. "From the entrance of the bay, where the ship must have been anchored, they could not possibly have suspected that at the bottom of it there should be a communication with the sea outside" (Smith, *Voyage*, p. 143). St. Paul's Bay is sheltered on the north-west by the island of Salmonetta, which is separated from the Maltese mainland by a narrow channel about a hundred yards wide. This channel is the "place where two seas met". Here the ship, in Smith's words, "would strike a bottom of mud graduating into tenacious clay, into which the fore part would fix itself and be held fast, whilst the stern was exposed to the force of the waves" (*ib.*, p. 144).

"Thus," says Ramsay, "the foreship was held together, until every passenger got safe to dry land. Only the rarest conjunction of favourable circumstances could have brought about such a fortunate ending to their apparently hopeless situation; and one of the completest services that has ever been rendered to New Testament scholarship is James Smith's proof that all these circumstances are united in St. Paul's Bay. The only difficulty

---

[61] This "foresail" (Gk. ἀρτέμων, by far the earliest occurrence of the word in Gk.; it occurs earlier in Latin) was intended not to increase the speed of the vessel, but to guide its course.

to which he has applied a rather violent solution is the sandy beach: at the traditional point where the ship was run ashore there is no sandy beach; but he considers that it is 'now worn away by the wasting action of the sea.' On this detail only local knowledge would justify an opinion" (*St. Paul the Traveller,* p. 341).[62]

42–44 According to the traditional Roman discipline, the soldiers were responsible for the safe keeping of the prisoners in their charge. But now it would be easy for the prisoners to escape in the general confusion of abandoning ship. The soldiers, therefore, decided to prevent any such attempt by slaughtering them. Their centurion, however, forbade them to do any such thing; he felt too grateful to Paul to expose him to this fate. Let the prisoners get safe to land along with the others, he said; those who could swim should dive overboard and swim ashore; the rest might float ashore on planks and spars; some non-swimmers might even be carried ashore by swimmers.[63] At any rate, one way or the other, they all reached land in safety. The supernatural promise made to Paul in their darkest hour had been fulfilled to the letter: the ship and cargo were lost, but every life on board was saved.

[62] Throughout the above exposition James Smith's account has been followed. Recently, however, W. Burridge in *Seeking the Site of St. Paul's Shipwreck* (Valletta, 1952) has argued, on the basis of local observation, that the shipwreck took place not in St. Paul's Bay but in Melliha Bay farther north. Only expert examination on the spot could enable one to evaluate properly his correction of Smith on this point.

[63] The words "and some on other things from the ship"—literally "and some on some of the (things) from the ship" (Gk. οὕς δὲ ἐπί τινων τῶν ἀπὸ τοῦ πλοίου) might conceivably mean "and some on some of the (people) from the ship," *i.e.* on the backs of the crew.

CHAPTER XXVIII

7. IN MALTA

(Ch. 28:1–10)

(a) Paul and the Viper (Ch. 28:1–6)

1 And when we were escaped, then we knew that the island was called Melita.[1]

2 And the barbarians showed us no common kindness: for they kindled a fire, and received[2] us all, because of the present rain, and because of the cold.

3 But when Paul had gathered a bundle of sticks and laid them on the fire, a viper came out by reason of the heat, and fastened on his hand.

4 And when the barbarians saw the *venomous* creature[3] hanging from his hand, they said one to another, No doubt this man is a murderer, whom, though he hath escaped from the sea, yet Justice hath not suffered to live.

5 Howbeit he shook off the creature into the fire, and took no harm.

6 But they expected that he would have swollen, or fallen down dead suddenly: but when they were long in expectation and beheld nothing amiss come to him, they changed their minds, and said that he was a god.

1   It was not until they had got ashore that they learned which island it was that they had landed on. No doubt many of the crew knew Malta, but were accustomed to put in at Valletta, and did not recognize this part of the coast. The idea that the island on which they landed was Meleda off the Dalmatian coast[4]

[1] The first hand in B and a few other authorities have "Melitene" (Gk. Μελιτήνη) instead of "Melita" (Gk. Μελίτη); the Latin Vulgate has *Militene*. These longer forms have arisen through dittography of some of the letters in Μελίτη ἡ νῆσος.

[2] Gk. προσελάβοντο, "they brought (us to the fire)"; we should perhaps read προσανελάμβανον (ℵΨ 614 1518 etc.) and translate "they refreshed (us)" (*cf.* Vulgate *reficiebant*).

[3] Gk. θηρίον, literally "wild beast"; in later Gk. the word came to be specialized in the sense of "snake." (From the word in this sense is derived θηριακή, whence our "treacle," originally a medicine prepared from the flesh of snakes to cure snake-bite.)

[4] This identification was made by a variety of writers from Constantine Porphyrogenitus (the tenth-century emperor) to Samuel Taylor Coleridge. See Dissertation II, "On the Island Melita," in Smith, *Voyage*, pp. 162 ff.

is bound up with the misinterpretation of the "sea of Adria" (Ch. 27:27) as the Adriatic Sea; both are impossible identifications. The name Melita was first given to Malta by Phoenician sailors; it is the Canaanite word for "refuge", and no doubt they found it a true refuge on more than one occasion. It has even been suggested that what Luke means by saying, "then we knew that the island was called Melita," is "we recognized that it was well-named."[5] Paul, at least, would realize the meaning of the name from his knowledge of Hebrew.

2 The natives of Malta were largely of Phoenician extraction, and their language was a Phoenician dialect.[6] They were thus regarded by both Greeks and Romans as "barbarians"—a slightly patronizing word, comparable to the vulgar use of the term "natives" nowadays. But on this occasion, if they were barbarians in name, they showed themselves truly civilized in behaviour; they received the two hundred and seventy-six shipwrecked people with warm hospitality. It was a cold, rainy morning, and the men from the wrecked ship were wet and shivering as they came ashore; how good it was to see the fire which the Maltese had lit for them to dry and warm themselves!

3 Paul, who had shown himself such a practical and helpful person on board ship, continued to make himself useful on land. A wood-fire out of doors is an excellent thing, but it will soon burn out if it is not fed with fresh wood. Paul therefore started to gather fuel to help to keep the fire going. But when he had gathered one bundle of brushwood and put it on the fire, a poisonous snake crept from the fire and bit his hand or at least fastened on it. He had probably mistaken it for a small twig as it lay on the ground stiff with cold, but the fire quickly brought it back to life. A close parallel has been quoted from T. E. Lawrence (of Arabia): "When the fire grew hot a long black snake wound slowly out into our group; we must have gathered it, torpid, with the twigs" (*Revolt in the Desert* [London, 1927], p. 107).

What kind of snake was it? The Greek word literally means "viper".[7] But we are told there are no vipers, or indeed poisonous snakes of any kind, in Malta today. That, however, is an unim-

---

[5] *Cf.* J. R. Harris, "Clauda or Cauda?", ExT xxi (1909–10), p. 18.
[6] Modern Maltese is an Arabic dialect.
[7] Gk ἔχιδνα (v. 3).

portant matter. "The objections which have been advanced, that there are now no vipers in the island, and only one place where any wood grows, are too trivial to deserve notice. Such changes are natural and probable in a small island, populous and long civilised" (W. M. Ramsay, *St. Paul the Traveller*, p. 343).[8] We may compare Ireland, which has been free from snakes for long centuries, although tradition asserts that they were once plentiful there until they were banished—whether by Finn MacCumhail (according to the pagan legend) or by St. Patrick (according to the Christian account). When we read that this snake "fastened on" Paul's hand, we must understand that it bit him, if it was indeed a viper, as vipers do not coil.[9]

4-6 The Maltese looked at the reptile hanging on to the apostle's hand by its fangs,[10] and drew their own conclusions. It was plainly the will of heaven that this man should lose his life— probably he was a murderer, and Nemesis was on his trail. He had escaped the sea, indeed, but Divine Justice was not so easily baffled; she had devised this new way of punishing him.[11] For

[8] On the other hand, Ramsay suggests in *Luke the Physician* (London, 1908), pp. 63 ff., that it may have been *Coronella leopardinus*, a snake found in Malta and "so closely resembling a viper as to be taken for one by a good naturalist until he had caught and examined a specimen. It clings, and yet it also bites without doing harm. That the Maltese rustics should mistake this harmless snake for a venomous one is not strange. . . . Every detail as related by Luke is natural, and in accordance with the facts of the country."

[9] Gk. καθῆψεν. Blass insists on the meaning "bit" (*Acta Apostolorum* [Göttingen, 1895], *ad loc.*); so also Lake–Cadbury, *ad loc.* "But it is a well-assured fact that the viper, a poisonous snake, only strikes, fixes the poison-fangs in the flesh for a moment, and withdraws its head instantly. Its action could never be what is attributed by Luke the eye-witness to this Maltese viper; that it hung from Paul's hand, and was shaken off into the fire by him. On the other hand, constrictors, which have no poison-fangs, cling in the way described, but as a rule do not bite" (Ramsay, *Luke the Physician*, p. 63).

[10] *Coronella austriaca*, a species of the same family as *leopardinus* (*cf.* n. 8 above), "is known to be rather irritable, and to fix its small teeth so firmly into the human skin as to hang on and need a little force to pull it off, though the teeth are too short to do any real injury to the skin" (Ramsay, *Luke the Physician*, p. 64). Evidently we must leave the accurate identification of the reptile to the few scholars who combine expert knowledge of this branch of natural history with expert knowledge of the Greek terms used here by Luke. But due weight must be given to a further remark of Ramsay's in the same context (pp. 63 f.): "A trained medical man in ancient times was usually a good authority about serpents, to which great respect was paid in ancient medicine and custom."

[11] A poem in the Greek *Palatine Anthology* (vii. 290) tells of a murderer who escaped from a storm at sea and was shipwrecked on the Libyan coast, only to be killed by a viper.

some time, then, they stood watching him, after he shook the snake into the fire, but nothing happened; he did not begin to swell up or suffer any discomfort. Clearly their original conclusion had been wrong; he was no murderer pursued by divine justice, but a divine person, immune to mischances which would prove fatal to mortal men. It is not difficult to detect Luke's quiet humour in his account of their remarkable change of mind.[12]

(b) Deeds of Healing in Malta (Ch. 28:7–10)

7 Now in the neighborhood of that place were lands belonging to the chief man of the island, named Publius; who received us, and entertained us three days courteously.

8 And it was so, that the father of Publius lay sick of fever and dysentery: unto whom Paul entered in, and prayed, and laying his hands on him healed him.

9 And when this was done, the rest also that had diseases in the island came, and were cured:[13]

10 who also honored us with many honors; and when we sailed, they put on board such things as we needed.

7–8 The expression "the chief man of the island"—literally "the first man of the island"—is probably an official title; it appears on two Maltese inscriptions, one in Greek[14] and the other in Latin.[15] The "first man" at this time, Publius by name, had an estate near the place where the shipwrecked party came ashore, and he treated them at his guests for three days. Ramsay suggests that "the peasantry around spoke familiarly of 'Publius' by his *praenomen* simply; and Luke (who has no sympathy for Roman nomenclature)[16] took the name that he heard in common use" (*op. cit.*, p. 343). Publius's father was suffering from intermittent attacks of gastric fever[17] and dysentery, of which Paul cured him by laying his hands on him and praying for him.

---

[12] Their change of mind took the reverse direction to that of the men of Lystra, who first acclaimed Paul as a god, and afterwards stoned him within an inch of his life (Ch. 14:11–19).

[13] Rather, "were treated" (Gk. ἐθεραπεύοντο).

[14] *Inscriptiones Graecae* xiv (Berlin, 1891), 601.

[15] *Corpus Inscriptionum Latinarum* x (Berlin, 1883), 7495.

[16] Similarly the Greek historian Polybius regularly refers to the Roman general Publius Cornelius Scipio by his bare praenomen Publius (Gk. Πόπλιος, as here).

[17] Malta has long had a peculiarly unpleasant fever of its own— "Malta fever," due to a microbe in goats' milk.

9–10 The news of this act of healing spread rapidly; in consequence, everyone in Malta who was suffering from any physical
ailment came to receive suitable treatment; no doubt Luke was
able to add his medical skill to Paul's gift of healing. At any rate,
says Luke, they "honored us with many honors"[18]—which, in this
context, might well include honoraria or professional fees. Harnack,
pointing out that the whole of the preceding section (verses 3–6)
"is tinged with medical colouring", adds: "and seeing that in
verses 7–10 both subject-matter and phraseology are medical,
therefore the whole story of the abode of the narrator in Malta
is displayed in a medical light" (*Luke the Physician* [Eng.tr.. London, 1907], p. 179).

When at last the time came for the party to leave Malta, the
Maltese showed their appreciation of Paul and his friends by
putting on board for them things that would supply their need
and minister to their comfort for the remainder of the voyage.

---

[18] Gk. τιμή ('honour') may also mean 'honorarium'; *cf.* Ecclus. 38:1, "Honour
a physician according to thy need of him with the honours due unto him"--a
passage remarkably similar to the present one. The word may have the same
sense in 1 Tim. 5:17, "Let the elders that rule well be counted worthy of
double honor."

8. ROME AT LAST!

(Ch. 28:11–31)

(a) The Last Lap: "And so We Came to Rome" (Ch. 28:11–15)

11 And after three months we set sail in a ship of Alexandria which had wintered in the island, whose sign was The Twin Brothers.[19]
12 And touching at Syracuse, we tarried there three days.
13 And from thence we made a circuit,[20] and arrived at Rhegium: and after one day a south wind sprang up, and on the second day we came to Puteoli;
14 where we found brethren, and were entreated to tarry with them seven days: and so we came to Rome.
15 And from thence the brethren, when they heard of us, came to meet us as far as The Market of Appius and The Three Taverns; whom when Paul saw, he thanked God, and took courage.

11 The three months which they spent in Malta were the three months of winter; they could not continue their journey to Italy until early spring, when the seas began to be opened again for navigation. Pliny the Elder (*Natural History* ii. 122) says that navigation begins to be resumed when the west winds start to blow on February 8;[21] it was probably about this date that the party set sail from Malta. The ship in which they embarked was another Alexandrian ship—possibly another ship of the grain fleet—which had spent the winter in Malta, presumably in harbour at Valletta. Ships, like inns, took their names from their figureheads. "The Twin Brothers" who formed the figurehead of this ship were Castor and Pollux, patrons of navigation and favourite objects of sailors' devotion. Their constellation, Gemini, was considered a sign of

---

19 Gk. Διόσκουροι (Latinized *Dioscuri*), lit. "sons of Zeus."
20 Gk. περιελθόντες. The codices ℵ and B, however, read περιελόντες, "weighing anchor," "casting loose."
21 Vegetius (*On Military Affairs* iv. 39) says the seas are closed till March 10; this might refer to voyages farther away from the shore. In actual practice, the state of the weather would determine the resumption of navigation in any particular year.

good fortune in a storm.[22] Ramsay suggests that Luke refers to this ship by name, as he does not refer to any other, because the name was the first thing he knew about it; he heard the news about this vessel before he saw it, whereas he became acquainted with the others by seeing them (*St. Paul the Traveller*, p. 346).

12 In this ship, then, they set sail from Malta, and (probably after one day's sailing) reached the great port of Syracuse, on the east coast of Sicily. Here they spent three days—possibly, as Ramsay suggests, because the southerly wind, which brought them from Malta, fell. Syracuse, with its double harbour, was the most important city of Sicily. It was founded as a Corinthian colony in 734 B.C., and passed under the control of Rome in 212 B.C.

13 From Syracuse they made their way by tacking (perhaps in a north-westerly wind) to Rhegium, in the toe of Italy (Reggio di Calabria), Rhegium was an important harbour on the Italian side of the Strait of Messina, some six or seven miles across from Messina in Sicily. They had to wait at Rhegium for a suitable wind to take them through the strait, but they had not to wait long, for a south wind arose after one day, and the following day brought them to Puteoli (Pozzuoli) in the Bay of Naples, "having accomplished a distance of about 180 nautical miles in less than two days" (Smith, *Voyage*, pp. 156 f.).

"Puteoli was then, as it is now," Smith continues, "the most sheltered part of the Bay of Naples. It was the principal port of southern Italy, and, in particular, it was the great emporium for the Alexandrian wheat-ships. Seneca, in one of his epistles,[23] gives an interesting and graphic account of the arrival of the Alexandrian fleet. All ships entering the bay were obliged to strike their topsails (*suppara*), except wheat-ships, which were allowed to carry theirs. They could therefore be distinguished whenever they hove in sight. It was the practice to send forward fast-sailing vessels (*tabellariae*), to announce the speedy arrival of the fleet; and the circumstance of their carrying topsails made them distinguishable in a crowd of vessels. The supparum, therefore, was the distinguishing signal of the Alexandrian ships" (*Voyage*, p. 157).

[22]
"Then through the wild Aegean roar,
The breezes and the Brethren Twain
Shall waft my little boat ashore"
(Horace, *Odes.* iii. 29.62–4).

[23] Seneca, *Epistle* 77.

14 It is not surprising that Christians were to be found in such an important seaport. There was an important Jewish community there too—apparently the oldest in Italy after that of Rome.[24] Ramsay finds a difficulty in the ordinary text here: Paul was not a free agent and could not have yielded to the entreaty of the Christians at Puteoli to spend a week with them without the centurion's consent. "However friendly Julius was to Paul, he was a Roman officer, with whom discipline and obedience to rule were natural" (*St. Paul the Traveller*, p. 344 n.). He therefore adopts an inferior reading, "we found brethren, and were cheered among them, remaining seven days."[25] Whichever reading we prefer, we may conclude that the centurion's official business involved a week's halt at Puteoli, and that during that week Paul was allowed to receive the hospitality of the local church. We may compare the similar permission given to him at Sidon at the beginning of the voyage (Ch. 27:3). "And so we came to Rome", Luke adds, but he goes back and relates one particularly encouraging feature of that last stage of the journey.

15 A few miles' journey from Puteoli brought them on to the Appian Way, one of the great Roman roads of south Italy, called after Appius Claudius, in whose censorship it was planned (312 B.C.). Along this road they made for Rome. But news of their approach had reached the capital already, and a number of Christians set out southwards along the Appian Way to meet the apostle and escort him back to Rome.[26] Some of them got as far as The Three Taverns (Latin *Tres Tabernae*), a halting-place on the Appian Way about thirty-three miles from Rome; others walked ten miles farther and met him at the market-town of Appii Forum—

> Next Appii Forum, filled, e'en nigh to choke,
> With knavish publicans and boatmen folk.[27]

[24] *Cf.* Josephus, *Jewish War* ii. 7.1; *Antiquities* xvii. 12.1.

[25] So the Greek uncial H and the Harclean Syriac. The difference in Greek is simply that between the infinitive ἐπιμεῖναι ("to remain") and the participle ἐπιμείναντες ("having remained").

[26] This is the sense of Gk. ἦλθαν εἰς ἀπάντησιν ἡμῖν ("they came to meet us"); ἀπάντησις was almost a technical term for the official welcome of a visiting dignitary by a deputation which went out from the city to greet him and escort him for the last part of his journey; *cf.* the same use in Matt. 25:6; 1 Thess. 4:17.

[27] Horace, *Satire*, i. 5.3 f.

527

Paul might well thank God and take courage at the sight of these friends. He had long had a desire to visit Rome;[28] it was three years since he wrote his letter to the church of the capital to prepare the way for his visit and expound to them the gospel which he preached; now his prayer was granted and, in circumstances which he had not foreseen when he wrote his letter, he saw Roman Christians face to face. He probably wondered from time to time what kind of reception he would have from them; now all his misgivings were removed by the heart-warming action of those members of the Roman church who tramped out so far to bid him welcome to their midst.

(b) Paul Handed Over to be Kept under Guard (Ch. 28:16)

16 And when we entered into Rome, Paul was suffered to abide by himself with the soldier that guarded him.

16 So at last they came to Rome, entering the city by the Porta Capena. And here the "we" narrative comes to an end. But Luke did not desert his friend and master; the letters to Philemon and to the church of Colossae, written during Paul's period of detention in Rome, supply decisive evidence that Luke remained in his company, for part at least of that time.[29]

The Western text, followed in part by the Byzantine text, gives us fuller information at this point: "when we entered into Rome, the centurion handed his prisoners over to the stratopedarch, but Paul was allowed to stay by himself outside the camp with the soldier who guarded him." The "stratopedarch" might be the commander of the emperor's praetorian guard (at this time Afranius Burrus); there would be a special appropriateness in committing to his charge a defendant who had appealed to Caesar. But the Western reading does not explicitly say that Paul was committed to the "stratopedarch" but that the prisoners in general were handed over to him by the centurion. If the suggestion is right that this centurion was a member of the corps of officer-couriers (see on Ch. 27:1, p. 500 with n. 8), then there is force in Mommsen and Ramsay's further suggestion that the "stratopedarch" was the commander of this corps, the *princeps peregrinorum*,[30]

---

[28] Rom. 1:9 ff.; 15:23 f.

[29] Philem. 24; Col. 4:14.

[30] This Latin expression is actually the reading of Codex *gigas* here. The Greek term is στρατοπέδαρχος.

whose headquarters were on the Caelian hill, where these officer-couriers resided when they were in Rome. In either case, Paul was allowed a degree of liberty until the time came for his case to be heard; he was permitted to live as a private resident, and a soldier was detailed to guard him. To this soldier he would be lightly chained by the wrist (with the chain which he mentions below in v. 20). (What must it have meant to a Roman soldier to be chained by the wrist to a man like Paul? One recalls the remark of Sir David Baird's mother, when news came to her in Scotland in 1780 that Haidar Ali's British prisoners, of whom her son was one, lay in his dungeons, chained together in pairs: "Lord help the man who is chained to our Davie!")

(c) Paul's First Interview with the Roman Jews (Ch. 28:17-22)

17 And it came to pass, that after three days he called together those that were the chief of the Jews: and when they were come together, he said unto them, I, brethren, though I had done nothing against the people, or the customs of our fathers, yet was delivered prisoner from Jerusalem into the hands of the Romans:

18 who, when they had examined me,[31] desired to set me at liberty, because there was no cause of death in me.

19 But when the Jews spake against it,[32] I was constrained to appeal unto Caesar; not that I had aught whereof to accuse my nation.[33]

20 For this cause therefore did I entreat you to see and to speak with *me*: for because of the hope of Israel I am bound with this chain.

21 And they said unto him, We neither received letters from Judaea concerning thee, nor did any of the brethren come hither and report or speak any harm of thee.

22 But we desire to hear of thee what thou thinkest: for as concerning this sect, it is known to us that everywhere it is spoken against.

17-20 True to his fixed procedure, Paul took steps as soon as was practicable to make contact with the Jewish community of this new city in which he found himself. It was not so convenient here to go the synagogue to find them;[34] had he been able to do

---

[31] The Western text adds "much."

[32] The Western text adds "and crying out, 'Away with our enemy'."

[33] The Western text adds "but that I might deliver my soul from death."

[34] "Paul was treated in Rome with the utmost leniency. He was allowed to

that, there were several synagogues in Rome which he might have visited. We find the names of several Roman synagogues mentioned in inscriptions, some called after their locality and some acquiring names in other ways (see p. 63, n. 26). Instead of going to any of these, however, Paul invited the leaders of the Jewish community in Rome to come and see him. He briefly introduced himself and summarized the course of events which had brought him to Rome, taking care not to say much about the responsibility of the Jerusalem authorities, but at the same time emphasizing his own innocence of any breach of the ancestral law or tradition of his people. He insisted that he was strictly on his defence; that he had no complaint to make against the Jewish nation or its leaders in Judaea. His appeal to Caesar had been made simply to have his innocence established. As it was, it was his devotion to the ancestral hope of Israel that had cost him his freedom and brought him as a prisoner to Rome. In Rome as in Jerusalem he emphasized that the Christian message which he proclaimed, far from undermining the religion of Israel, was its divinely appointed fulfilment.[35]

21–22 The answer of the Jewish leaders to Paul is a model of diplomacy. They denied all knowledge of his case; no visitor or letter had come from Jerusalem about him, they assured him. This might be thought surprising enough, but we cannot say confidently that it cannot be true. The leaders of the Sanhedrin may have realized that if they could not proceed successfully against Paul before provincial magistrates, there was still less chance of a successful prosecution in Rome. A year or two later they might have been more hopeful; Poppaea Sabina, whom Nero married in A.D. 62, was very friendly to Jews; Josephus, indeed, goes so far as to call her a God-fearer (*Autobiography*, 3). But, in view of the regular communication between Rome and the East, we should have expected the Roman Jews to have some inkling of the trouble that had arisen over Paul; we may bear in mind, however, that under the present circumstances they would be anxious not to be

hire a house or a lodging in the city, and live there at his own convenience under the surveillance of a soldier who was responsible for his presence when required. A light chain fastened Paul's wrist to that of the soldier. No hindrance was offered to his inviting friends into his house, or to his preaching to all who came in to him; but he was not allowed to go out freely" (Ramsay, *St. Paul the Traveller*, p. 349).

[35] *Cf.* Ch. 23:6; 24:14–15; 26:6 ff.

associated with the prosecution of a Roman citizen who had secured a favourable hearing from Festus and Agrippa and was now to be heard by the emperor. They wished, in fact, to have as little to do as possible either with Paul or with his Christianity.

This must almost certainly be the reason for their unwillingness to admit any direct knowledge of Christianity. They had some second-hand information about it, they agreed, and it was not favourable; all that they knew about this new party was that it enjoyed universal ill-repute. But we may be quite sure that they had quite an extensive experience of Christianity in Rome itself. When the Christian community in Rome came into being is a matter of conjecture,[36] but when Paul wrote his epistle to the Roman church early in A.D. 57 it was already a well-established church and its Christian faith and loyalty were renowned throughout all the churches.[37] It may well have been one of the earliest churches to be founded outside Palestine, and we have seen ground for believing that ten years before Paul's arrival the advance of the gospel in the Jewish community at Rome led to riots which brought imperial displeasure upon the community (see p. 368, on Ch. 18:2). But on this occasion the leaders of the community judged it politic not to commit themselves on the subject—at any rate not until they heard Paul's account of himself and the message to which he had dedicated his life.

(d) Paul's Second Interview with the Roman Jews (Ch. 28:23–28)

23 And when they had appointed him a day, they came to him into his lodging[38] in great number; to whom he expounded *the matter*, testifying the kingdom of God, and persuading them concerning Jesus, both from the law of Moses and from the prophets, from morning till evening.

24 And some believed[39] the things which were spoken, and some disbelieved.

25 And when they agreed not among themselves, they

---

36 See p. 63 above (on Ch. 2:10).

37 *Cf.* Rom. 1:8.

38 Or "to receive his hospitality." Gk. ξενία means primarily "hospitality," but here, as in Philem. 22, it means rather the place where a guest is entertained.

39 Or at least "gave heed"; the imperfect tense (ἐπείθοντο) need mean no more than this.

departed after that Paul had spoken one word,[40] Well
spake the Holy Spirit through Isaiah the prophet unto
your fathers,

26 saying,
Go thou unto this people, and say,
By hearing ye shall hear,[41] and shall in no wise under-
stand;
And seeing ye shall see, and shall in no wise perceive:

27 For this people's heart is waxed gross,
And their ears are dull of hearing,
And their eyes they have closed;
Lest haply they should perceive with their eyes,
And hear with their ears,
And understand with their heart,
And should turn again,
And I should heal them.

28 Be it known therefore unto you, that this salvation of
God is sent unto the Gentiles: they will also hear.[42]

23 A day was fixed for a thorough-going discussion, and on
the day appointed they came to the place where Paul stayed and
heard what he had to say. No considerable summary of what
he said is recorded, but from accounts of his regular line of
argument in earlier parts of this book,[43] as well as from the
relevant material supplied by some of his own epistles, we may
infer the general outline of the exposition which he gave them,
"bearing witness to the kingdom of God and seeking to persuade
them about Jesus, from the law of Moses and from the prophets,
from early morning till evening." He certainly laboured to prove
to them that the gospel of Christ was the true and necessary
fulfilment of Israel's religion, of Old Testament history and
prophecy. His text was the whole volume of Hebrew scripture,
interpreted by the events of the advent, passion and triumph of
Jesus of Nazareth, "declared to be the Son of God with power,
according to the spirit of holiness, by the resurrection from the

[40] "Paul always gets the last word—generally with devastating effect"
(Lake–Cadbury, *ad loc.*).
[41] The construction "By hearing ye shall hear . . . and seeing ye shall see",
taken over here from LXX, represents the Hebrew use of the absolute infinitive
preceding the finite verb to express emphasis. We may translate with RSV,
"You shall indeed hear but never understand, and you shall indeed see but
never perceive."
[42] Or "they indeed will hear."
[43] *Cf.* Chs. 13:17 ff.; 17:2 f.; 26:22 f.

dead" (Rom. 1:4). Most of the messianic "testimonies" from the OT which have already been quoted in Acts[44] were adduced, no doubt, and more as well. We can readily conceive how Paul on this occasion must have exerted all his powerful qualities of mind and heart as he endeavoured to persuade the leading Jews in Rome of the truth of Christianity. And it would be a great mistake to suppose that the exposition took the form of a monologue. The debate must have been keen and impassioned.

24-28 Some of Paul's hearers were convinced of the truth of what he maintained, but others—and these apparently the majority—remained unpersuaded. The bulk of the Jewish colony in Rome, leaders and led alike, continued to oppose the gospel. In Rome as in other cities Paul approached the Jews first, and the pattern of events which had become almost constant elsewhere was repeated in Rome. Since the Jewish people, who had the prescriptive right to receive the gospel first, would not accept it, it must be offered direct to the Gentiles, and in what numbers they welcomed it is a matter of history. Acts records the expansion of Christianity among the Gentiles, but it also records *pari passu* the rejection of the same message by the majority of the Jews. This is the last instance of such a rejection recorded in the book, and this instance is therefore brought to a fitting conclusion by the quotation of one of the oldest Christian 'testimonies' from the OT—the passage from Isa. 6:9 f. in which Isaiah, on his call to the prophetic ministry, was warned not to expect a favourable response from the people. The effect of his ministry, divinely ordained though it was, would be but to make the deaf still more deaf (there are none so deaf as those who will not hear), to make the blind still more blind (there are none so blind as those who will not see). The early Christian use of this passage as an OT adumbration of the general Jewish refusal to obey the gospel had the highest authority; the words were quoted in this sense by our Lord Himself, as the Synoptic Gospels (Matt. 13:14 f.; Mark 4:12; Luke 8:10) and the Fourth Gospel (John 12:39 f.) alike testify.[45] Their position here at the end of Acts is strikingly comparable to their position in John 12:40, where they appear at the end of the first section of the Fourth Gospel—the section which might bear

[44] *Cf.* Chs. 2:16 ff., 25 ff., 34 ff.; 3:22 ff.; 4:25 f.; 8:32 f.; 13:33 ff.
[45] *Cf.* J. R. Harris, *Testimonies* ii (Cambridge, 1920), pp. 65, 74, 137: C. H. Dodd, *According to the Scriptures* (London, 1952), pp. 36 ff.

as its title the words of John 1:11, "He came unto his own, and they that were his own received him not." Compare Paul's further allusion to the same Isaianic passage (among others) in Rom. 11:8, and, more generally, his treatment of the sore problem of Israel's unbelief in Rom. 9–11. As before in Pisidian Antioch (Ch. 13:46), Corinth (Ch. 18:6) and elsewhere, so here again, but with a note of solemn finality, he announces that henceforth the Gentiles will have priority in receiving the message of salvation, and that, unlike the majority of the Jews, they will accept it. "The narrative reaches a solemn climax—rejection on the one side, unchecked success and hope on the other" (F. H. Chase, *Credibility of the Acts* [London, 1902], p. 52).

The sentence which follows as v. 29 in AV is a Western and Byzantine reading which finds no place in the best authorities for the text: "And when he had said these words, the Jews departed, having much disputing among themselves."

(e) The Gospel Advances Unhindered in Rome (Ch. 28:30–31)

30 And he abode two whole years in his own hired dwelling,[46] and received all that went in unto him,

31 preaching the kingdom of God, and teaching the things concerning the Lord Jesus Christ with all boldness, none forbidding him.[47]

30 For two years, then, Paul stayed in Rome. The conditions of his custody apparently did not permit him to go anywhere he wished, but anyone who wished might come and visit him, as the leaders of the Jewish community had done. Some wish to translate the Greek words underlying "in his own hired dwelling" as "on his own earnings" or "at his own expense"; it is a point which makes little practical difference. Perhaps he was able to carry on his tent-making, although that would have been rather awkward if he was continually chained by the wrist to a soldier.

The "two years" may have more significance than meets the eye. Ramsay argues that they consisted of the statutory period within which the prosecution might state its case (probably eighteen months), together with such further time as was necessary for the

[46] Gk. ἐν ἰδίῳ μισθώματι. This is the only extant occurrence of μίσθωμα in the sense "hired dwelling"; elsewhere it means "hire", "rent."

[47] There is a Western addition, "saying that this is the Christ, Jesus the Son of God, by whom the whole world is to be judged." This weakens the very effective ending of the true text.

formalities attending Paul's release (*The Teaching of Paul* [London, 1913], pp. 346 ff.). The Sanhedrin's case against him was probably allowed to go by default, the prosecutors judging it neither practicable nor wise to pursue it farther.[48] Roman law was apt to deal hardly with unsuccessful prosecutors, especially if their charges appeared under examination to be merely vexatious.

31 During this period the gospel was proclaimed freely in Rome through the lips of its chief messenger. The apologetic value of this fact was considerable. It is unlikely, Luke means to suggest, that if the gospel were illegal and subversive propaganda, it could have been taught for two years in the heart of the empire without let or hindrance, and that by a Roman citizen who had appealed to Caesar and was waiting under guard for his case to be heard. The authorities must have known what he was doing all that time, and yet they put no obstacle in his way. On this triumphant note, then, Acts is brought to an end. The kingdom of God and the story of Jesus are openly proclaimed and taught in Rome itself, under the complacent eye of imperial authority.[49] "The victory

[48] This presumes that Paul was released after his two years' detention, and that a gap of some years separated his release from his execution. This, of course, has been denied. Moffatt bluntly asserts that "as a matter of fact, Paul was not released" (INT [Edinburgh, 1918], p. 313). According to J. V. Bartlet, the prosecutors gave notice within the eighteen months' time-limit of their intention to proceed with the case, they reached Rome early in 62 and successfully prosecuted Paul as a disturber of the peace of the provinces (*cf.* Ch. 24:5), and it was not necessary for Luke to make explicit mention of Paul's condemnation and execution, since the readers of Acts knew from Nero's record what the inevitable result of such a prosecution before him would be (*Expositor* VIII. v [1913], pp. 464 ff.). *Cf.* also p. 497 (with nn. 32, 33. on Ch. 26:32). If, however, we date Paul's traditional execution in the period following the Great Fire of Rome in A.D. 64 (although this at best can be no more than a matter of probability), we have a gap between the end of A.D. 61 (the probable end of the two years of v. 30) and Paul's death. This accords with the tradition quoted by Eusebius (*Ecclesiastical History* ii. 22), "that after defending himself the apostle was sent again on his ministry of preaching, and coming a second time to the same city [Rome], suffered martyrdom under Nero." For an interesting reopening of the question of "Paul's Life after the Close of Acts" see L. P. Pherigo in JBL lxx (1951), pp. 277 ff. On the legal implications of the "two years" see also H. J. Cadbury, "Roman Law and the Trial of Paul," *Beginnings* v (1933), pp. 297 ff.

[49] Luke has reached his objective by tracing the progress of the gospel from Jerusalem to Rome, and brings his narrative to an end with an impressive and artistic conclusion. It is absurd to say, as Ramsay does, "No one can accept the ending of *Acts* as the conclusion of a rationally conceived history" (*St. Paul the Traveller*, pp. 351 f.), and precarious to argue, as he and some others (including Zahn) have done, that Luke must have planned a third volume to complete his history of Christian origins. The chief argument for dating Acts

of the word of God: Paul at Rome, the culmination of the gospel, the conclusion of Acts. ... It began at Jerusalem; it finishes at Rome. Here, O church, thou hast thy pattern; it is thy duty to keep it, and to guard thy deposit" (J. A. Bengel, *Gnomon of NT, ad loc.*).

shortly after the expiration of the two years of Ch. 28:30 is not simply that it does not record the death of Paul, but that the optimistic note on which it ends is more likely to have been struck before the persecution of Christians at Rome' which broke out in A.D. 64. We need not go so far as to suppose that Luke compiled his narrative to supply the information required for Paul's defence before the imperial tribunal (*cf.* p. 31, n. 9). But we may indeed believe that Luke wrote in order to win sympathy for Christianity among the intelligent reading-public of Rome at a time when the government had not yet finally committed itself by taking up a hostile attitude to it.

The effective way in which the narrative of Acts is brought to an end is a sufficient answer to those who explain the absence of any account of Paul's death by the hypothesis that Luke died before finishing his work (*cf.* J. de Zwaan, "Was the Book of Acts a Posthumous Edition?" in HThR xvii [1924], pp. 95 ff.; H. Lietzmann, *The Founding of the Church Universal* [Eng. tr., London, 1950], p. 78). On the question whether Paul's death is presupposed elsewhere in Acts, see p. 415, n. 53 (on Ch. 20:25).

INDEX OF CHIEF PERSONS, PLACES, AND SUBJECTS

INDEX OF SCRIPTURE REFERENCES

OLD TESTAMENT

NEW TESTAMENT

23:29 - 37	162	13:26	40	10:1	51
23:35	171	13:30	91	10:11	284
24:30	40	13:32	37	10:20	283
25:6	527	14:51f	251	10:21f	203
26:59 - 61	135	14:55 - 59	135	11:9	418
26:63	202	14:58	160	11:15, 20	70
26:64	40	14:61	73, 202	11:29	78
26:73	59	14:61 - 64	134	11:51	171
27:7	49	14:62	40, 165	12:11f	126
27:63	224	14:63	292	13:28	164
27:65ff	95	15:16	462	14:14	469
28:3	41	15:40	44	16:16	50
28:16ff	47	16:5	41	17:25	78
28:19	181	16:18	50	19:20	389
28:20	42	**LUKE**		20:17ff	99
		1:1 - 4	18, 32	20:21	224
MARK		1:2	261	20:27ff	96
1:4	76	1:3	31f, 474	20:35	280, 469
1:8	37	1:32f	158	20:39	454
1:11	39, 188	1:69f	489	20:41ff	73
1:14ff	34, 50	1:70	86	21	22
1:24	89	2:1	243	21:12ff	126
1:32 - 34	118	2:2	125	21:14f	99
2:9	85	2:7	45	21:24	358
2:10	85, 228	2:9	250	21:27	40
2:11	85	2:11	73	21:34	294
2:16	454	2:25	61	22:1	248
3:6	76	2:29	105	22:24ff	38
3:16ff, 19	43	2:29ff	283	22:30	50, 489
4:12	533	3:1	246, 481	22:42	426
5:20	194	3:2	98	22:66	97
5:27ff	389	3:15ff	274	22:67, 70	202f
5:41	212	3:16	37, 54	22:69	73
5:43	211	4:12	115	23:1ff	88
6:3	45	4:16ff	271	23:2	343, 464
6:56	389	4:18f	226	23:6ff	462
7:2ff	215	4:34	89	23:7ff	106
7:14ff	219	4:44	58	23:13ff	20
7:31	194	5:23	85	23:18	436
8:8	204	6:14ff	43	23:26	253
9:3	41	6:38	418	23:34	90, 172
9:12	91, 188	7:16	70	23:44f	69
9:26	40	7:19	386	23:46	171
10:33	425	7:22	85, 227	23:47	215
10:35ff	38, 52	8:2f	44	24:4	41
10:39	247	8:10	533	24:25	70
10:45	188	8:55	211	24:25ff	48
11:4	399	9:5	284	24:26	343
11:17	158	9:29	41	24:30	517
12:10f	99	9:34f	40	24:31	40
12:18ff	96	9:35	93	24:33, 36	43
12:35ff	48, 72	9:41	78	24:42f	36
12:41ff	83	9:51	422	24:44ff	32, 48
13:8	71	9:52ff	181	24:45 - 47	35
13:9ff	126			24:46	70, 343

549

550